University of the
West of England

BRISTOL

**FRENCHAY CAMPUS
(BOLLAND) LIBRARY**

Please ensure that this book is returned by the end of
the loan period for which it is issued.

UWE, BRISTOL   F366A.02.06
Printing & Stationery Services

Telephone Renewals: 0117 32 82092 (24 hours)
Library Web Address: www.uwe.ac.uk/library

Three-Dimensional Computer Vision

Olivier Faugeras

Three-Dimensional Computer Vision

A Geometric Viewpoint

The MIT Press
Cambridge, Massachusetts
London, England

Second printing, 1996

This book was formatted in ZzTEX by Paul Anagnostopoulos and typeset by Joe Snowden. The typeface is Lucida Bright and Lucida New Math, created by Charles Bigelow and Kris Holmes specifically for scientific and electronic publishing. The Lucida letterforms have the large x-heights and open interiors that aid legibility in modern printing technology, but also echo some of the rhythms and calligraphic details of lively Renaissance handwriting. Developed in the 1980s and 1990s, the extensive Lucida typeface family includes a wide variety of mathematical and technical symbols designed to harmonize with the text faces.

Library of Congress Cataloging-in-Publication Data

Faugeras, Olivier, 1949–
   Three-dimensional computer vision : a geometric viewpoint /
   Olivier Faugeras.
     p. cm. — (Artificial intelligence)
   Include bibliographical references and index.
   ISBN 0-262-06158-9
   1. Computer vision. I. Title. II. Series: Artificial
intelligence (Cambridge, Mass.)
TA1632.F38   1993
006.3'7—dc20

93-9126
CIP

Contents

Series Foreword

Artificial intelligence is the study of intelligence using the ideas and methods of computation. Unfortunately a definition of intelligence seems impossible at the moment because intelligence appears to be an amalgam of so many information-processing and information-representation abilities.

Of course psychology, philosophy, linguistics, and related disciplines offer various perspectives and methodologies for studying intelligence. For the most part, however, the theories proposed in these fields are too incomplete and too vaguely stated to be realized in computational terms. Something more is needed, even though valuable ideas, relationships, and constraints can be gleaned from traditional studies of what are, after all, impressive existence proofs that intelligence is in fact possible.

Artificial intelligence offers a new perspective and a new methodology. Its central goal is to make computers intelligent, both to make them more useful and to understand the principles that make intelligence possible. That intelligent computers will be extremely useful is obvious. The more profound point is that artificial intelligence aims to understand intelligence using the ideas and methods of computation, thus offering a radically new and different basis for theory formation. Most of the people doing work in artificial intelligence believe that these theories will apply to any intelligent information processor, whether biological or solid state.

There are side effects that deserve attention, too. Any program that will successfully model even a small part of intelligence will be inherently massive and complex. Consequently artificial intelligence continually confronts the limits of computer-science technology. The problem encountered have been hard enough and interesting enough to seduce artificial intelligence people into working on them with enthusiasm. It is natural, then, that there has been a steady flow of ideas from artificial intelligence to computer science, and the flow shows no sign of abating.

The purpose of this series in artificial intelligence is to provide people in many areas, both professionals and students, with timely, detailed information about what is happening on the frontiers in research centers all over the world.

J. Michael Brady
Daniel G. Bobrow
Randall Davis

Figures

Tables

Preface

"Ils ont usé leurs vies au parfum des images
Et croient avoir rêvé"
—Louis Aragon, *Les Poètes*

This book has been written over the course of five years, and I have suffered from the frustration Eric Grimson described in the preface of his book [Gri90]: Because computer vision is a topic of current interest, a book on the subject is out of date before it is completed.

Of the two options available in such a situation — namely, constantly trying to refine the material and never getting the manuscript to the publisher, or settling for publishing something that cannot be definitive — I have for a long time chosen the first. But this attitude cannot last forever, and publishers are here, among other things, to remind an author of deadlines. Aside from this very practical reason for finishing the book, there is another related to its initial motivation.

Five years ago I sent a proposal to the European Esprit I program for studying machine visual perception in the context of a robot moving in an indoor environment. I submitted this proposal jointly with several European colleagues from academia and industry, including GEC and Cambridge University in England, Elsag and the University of Genoa in Italy, and ITMI and Matra MS2I in France. The goal of the proposal was to do basic research in three-dimensional computer vision, build hardware implementing some of the results of the basic research, and use the hardware to demonstrate a number of simple perception and navigation tasks with a mobile robot.

The proposal was accepted, and this was the beginning of Esprit P940. Surprisingly enough, we achieved most of the objectives we had outlined in the proposal, and the final review of the project was successfully held in January 1992. Since many of the ideas that are described in this book have matured and developed during the progress of this effort, it seems natural to publish the book now that the project has come to a successful end.

The book is mostly about my own work and that of my collaborators and students within my research group at INRIA, in particular Nicholas Ayache, Jean-Daniel Boissonnat, Rachid Deriche, Martial Hébert, Elizabeth Lebras-Mehlman, Francis Lustman, Théo Papadopoulo, Luc Robert, Michel Schmitt, Giorgio Toscani, Régis Vaillant, and Zhengyou Zhang. It also includes information on some work that was done jointly with Steve Maybank from GEC.

During the course of the writing, I have benefited from many stimulating discussions with Nassir Navab, Tuan Luong, Peter Sander, and Thierry Vieville from my group at INRIA, as well as with Vincent Torre and Alessandro Verri from the University of Genoa; Giovanni Garibotto; Stefano Masciangiello from Elsag, Thomas Skordas from ITMI; Philippe Isambert and Eric Théron from MSII; Gérard Gaillat, formally from Matra; and Bernard Buxton from GEC.

I would also like to acknowledge the help of Giorgio Musso and Giovanni Garibotto from Elsag and that of the INRIA administration for their role in keeping the administrative maze that is sometimes generated by European projects to a minimum. This effort has been essential in bringing P940 to a successful end and allowing me to spend most of my time on the research part of the project.

Finally, and most important, I am extremely grateful to my wife, Agnès, and our sons Blaise, Clément, Cyrille, and Quentin. Completing this book took much more time than I thought it would, and I very much appreciate their patience and support.

Sophia-Antipolis, June 1992

1   Introduction

The world in which robots move and act is three-dimensional and dynamic; it changes because of the ego-motion of the robots and/or because of the motions of other objects or actors that are busy carrying out their own tasks. To interact swiftly with their environment, robots must therefore have sensing capabilities. Among these capabilities, vision has long been recognized as the one with the highest potential because many biological systems use vision as their most prominent way of gathering information about their environment, and because of the availability, for quite some time now, of relatively cheap and high-quality visual sensors such as TV cameras. These sensors can easily be hooked up to computers, whose information processing capabilities have increased dramatically while their cost has decreased just as dramatically (and continues to do so).

Computer vision has thus emerged over the years as the discipline, which we hope will soon attain the status of a science, that focuses on the following problems:

- What information should be extracted from the outputs of visual sensors?
- How is this information extracted?
- How should this information be represented?
- How must the information be used to allow a robotics system to perform its tasks?

Solving these problems is a formidable endeavor for several reasons:

- The question of what information is needed for a given task, even though it sounds rather innocuous, is in fact quite difficult to answer. Even if we assume that we can instantaneously compute arbitrarily detailed and accurate models of the environment, we have only pushed the question one step further: Where in these wonderful models do we find what we need to achieve our task? As an example of the difficulty involved, let us assume that we have a sensor that delivers to us dense three-dimensional maps at video rate, and that our task is to find out where we are. It is far from clear that the difficulty of the problem has been significantly reduced if we assume only that we have a few black-and-white images of this environment (assuming some reasonable level of lighting, of course). The space in which tasks are performed is usually so different from the space of visual measurements that using the first to guide the gathering of information in the second is an area that is still in its infancy.

- The question of how to extract this information has been at the core of computer vision from the early days. One of the key problems has been the recovery of three-dimensional information about the shape of objects and their motion. There are at least two reasons why this is difficult. The first is due to the fact that this information is usually lost in the imaging process, which creates a two-dimensional representation (an image) of the three-dimensional world. This two-dimensional image is related in a complex way to the structure of the real world through the physics of image formation and its geometry. In this book we stress mostly the geometry of this issue. The reader who is interested in the physics of the issue is referred to the book by Horn [Hor86]. A dimension (at least) is lost in the imaging process; one of the main thrusts of computer vision and of this book is to analyze the problem of recovering this lost dimension from sequences of images and to propose and implement methods for doing so.

- The question of how the information should be represented is important and difficult for several reasons. First, the representations that are built from visual data are used by computer programs that execute *algorithms*. These algorithms are characterized by their complexity, both in terms of how much computer memory they need (*space complexity*) and in terms of how much time they take to run on given sets of inputs (*time complexity*). Thus it is difficult to separate the representations from the algorithms that operate on them and create them. These issues have been recognized by the researchers in computer science from the very early days as deep and difficult.

Second, the representations that are needed in computer vision are very heterogeneous, including purely iconic ones, the images themselves, two-dimensional edges and junctions, their approximations with spline functions, descriptions of their image motion, three-dimensional points, curves, surfaces and volumes, groupings of these geometric primitives into objects, models of objects, etc. It should be clear from this nonexhaustive enumeration that there many different representations are necessary for solving the same problem, and this presents an added complexity.

Third, since we insist on incarnating computer vision in the real world to use it to help robots act, the issue of time becomes important, and we stumble upon another difficulty. The time constants that are necessary to compute these various representations may on the one hand be quite different for a given machine architecture (think about that needed for edge detection and for computing volume representations of free space, for example). On the other hand, these time constants must satisfy some very stringent constraints if the robotics systems is to survive in its environment. What emerges here is the notion of a real-time system with strict requirements for response time and a very heterogeneous structure. These systems are notoriously difficult to analyze and build.

Fourth, since computer vision deals with real sensors, we are confronted with the problem of processing noisy measurements. This is a very serious problem since this initial uncertainty must be tracked through all the representations that are built up by the system in order to achieve its tasks.

- The question of how to use the visual information to perform the robotics task at hand hints that perhaps the requirements for perception may change during the execution of the task and that, on the other hand, perception may become a task in itself that requires *active* and *reactive planning* and execution of actions. This area of *active vision* is still in its infancy, but we believe that it will become extremely important in the future.

In this general framework, this book is an attempt to propose solutions to the problems arising from the following scenario: A mobile platform must move about in an unknown indoor environment with capabilities allowing it to do the following:

1. Avoid static and mobile obstacles.

2. Build models of objects and places in order to be able to recognize and locate them.

3. Characterize its own motion and that of moving objects by providing descriptions of the corresponding three-dimensional motions.

We think that these tasks are in many respects generic in the sense that a large number of robotics systems should be able to perform them in order to be able to interact with fairly unconstrained environments. This hypothesized genericity has the consequence that this book is not only a set of solutions to specific problems, but that many of the ideas in it are general and can be used in different settings. The book can therefore also be read as a general book on computer vision.

We have stressed the mathematical soundness of our ideas in all our our approaches at the risk of scaring some readers away. We strongly believe that detailing the mathematics is worth the effort, for it is only through their use that computer vision can be established as a science. But there is a great danger that computer vision will become yet another area of applied mathematics. We are convinced that this danger can be avoided if we keep in mind the original goal of designing and building robotics systems that perceive and act. We believe that the challenge is big enough that computer vision can become, perhaps like physics, a rich source of inspiration and problems for mathematicians.

Another key feature of this book is the importance of geometry, in particular three-dimensional geometry. This is because the world where robots move and act is, like ours, three-dimensional, that we have decided to expend so much effort on describing three-dimensional geometry and its fascinating relationship with the imaging process by which many key three-dimensional features are distorted in an intricate manner.

We have also devoted a great deal of attention to the problem of uncertain data. Even though we think that geometry must play a crucial role in computer vision systems, this geometry has to be built from noisy measurements. It looks as if we are quite far from the idealized geometric world of Euclid. But perhaps we are not quite so far from it as we seem, since we show that many of the techniques that can be used to estimate the uncertainty of geometric data are themselves deeply rooted in geometry.

These are the general ideas expressed in this book. How have they been organized as a set of chapters? The leading role played by geometry is emphasized in chapter 2, which gives the necessary background and tools for relating the geometric properties of the environment to what can be measured in an image. Because a camera can be modeled as a geometric engine that establishes a mapping between *projective* spaces of different dimensions, we start by formulating some simple results in projective geometry that are used many times in the later chapters.

As our first application of these ideas, in chapter 3 we use projective geometry to model cameras and show that what they measure can be related in a quantitative manner to the 3-D world through a process known as calibration. We then make a digression, in chapter 4, to firmly establish an understanding of our main source of geometric features in images, namely edges.

In Chapter 5 we make our first attempt at providing answers to two of the questions asked earlier. The question regarding the representation of simple geometric entities such as points, lines, planes, and displacements is placed in the framework of *differential manifolds*, which we believe to be essential. The question regarding the computation of uncertainty is then answered quite naturally by the *implicit function theorem*.

The next four chapters deal with the problem of recovering distance (depth) and three-dimensional motion from several images. Stereo vision is studied in chapter 6, and there is an emphasis on the geometric constraints that can be used to decrease the difficulty of obtaining image correspondences. We also show in some detail how these correspondences can be used to reconstruct 3-D geometric primitives and their uncertainty as a first application of the principles discussed in chapter 5.

The next three chapters describe different aspects of motion estimation. Chapter 7 investigates the problem of estimating the 3-D displacement of a camera given a number of correspondences between geometric primitives in two or three images. Even though we give some practical methods for doing this, the chapter is essentially a detailed analysis of the intrinsic mathematical difficulty of the problem, which we show to be in fact quite extreme.

Chapter 8 is perhaps more practical and is an attempt to answer some of the questions that have been left unanswered in chapter 7. In particular, until chapter 8 we assume that correspondences have been established between the different views. This is not an easy thing to do, and we introduce the natural tools for tracking geometric tokens in a sequence of images. These tools are variations on the theme of recursive least-squares estimation and Kalman filtering and are also used in chapter 11. We present two examples of the application of these tools: tracking line segments in a sequence of images (2-D) and in a sequence of stereo reconstructions (3-D).

In chapter 9 we return to the problem of estimating 3-D displacements from a monocular sequence of images. We abandon the approach that prevailed in chapter 7 of using a small set of images corresponding to large camera displacements, and instead study the "instantaneous" case where the time interval between images is infinitely small, as is therefore the camera displacement. In keeping with the geometric approach of the book, we study in detail the kinds of motion fields that arise from moving three-dimensional lines and curves, and we give an original interpretation and solution to the so-called *aperture problem*.

Chapter 10 returns to the question of representation at a higher level than that presented in chapter 5. In particular, we try to explicitly answer the question of which representations are useful for navigation, obstacle avoidance, and recognition. We introduce several ideas that we believe to be essential to shape representation: *shape topologies*, *stochastic geometry*, and *computational geometry*. Chapter 11 shows how to bring together many of the concepts introduced in the previous chapters to accomplish some of the perceptual tasks that we have set out to perform: recognize and locate objects and places.

After each chapter we give a series of problems and exercises of various levels of difficulty that are intended to help the reader understand the material in the chapter and to complement this material. Answers to these problems can be found in chapter 12.

2 Projective Geometry

It may appear to be a bit strange for a book on computer vision to start with a chapter on projective geometry. We are accustomed to thinking that the space around us is euclidean and that therefore euclidean geometry is the right tool to use to design systems for modeling this world. But euclidean geometry is complicated when compared to projective geometry. In projective geometry, the principle of duality ensures that points and lines are equivalent, and the existence of homogeneous coordinates either makes the algebra linear or can readily make it so. Euclidean geometry is a special case of projective geometry, and questions are often more easily answered in the more general context of projective geometry, in which irrelevant details can be ignored.

There is a further very important reason for devoting some time to the study of projective geometry, which is related to the sort of sensors that machines and humans use for vision. It is known from geometric optics that any system of lenses can be approximated by a system that realizes a *perspective projection* of the world onto a plane. The best way, i.e., the simplest way, to look at such a system, as we will see in the next chapter, is to look at it *projectively*.

Another reason for studying projective geometry is that projective spaces are extremely useful to understand the structure of the set of line directions and the set of three-dimensional rotations (see chapter 5). Finally, projective geometry is used as the basis of many techniques in robotics to study the geometry and the kinematics of manipulators, as well as in computer graphics to represent geometric transformations of objects. These ideas are beginning to spread in the computer vision community as shown by Kanatani and Mohr [Kan91, Moh92]. The reader who is interested in this subject may find it profitable to read the beautifully written book by Semple and Kneebone [SK52].

2.1   How to read this chapter

Section 2.2 is a general introduction to projective spaces and can be read quickly the first time to get an idea of the concepts involved. Propositions 2.1 and 2.2 are fundamental in the sense that they give a practical way of changing coordinate systems in a projective space, an operation that must be done more often than we may wish. Theorem 2.1 is absolutely essential for understanding chapter 5.

Section 2.3 should allow the reader to develop an intuition about projective spaces since we are studying the simplest of them, the projective line. We introduce two fundamental concepts: the point at infinity, which is the key to understanding the relationship between the projective spaces and the usual affine spaces with which we are more familiar, and the cross-ratio, which is one of the most useful invariants.

Section 2.4 takes us one dimension higher to the projective plane. Since we will often model an image as "living" in a projective plane, this section is important to read and understand. We introduce four fundamental concepts. First is the principle of duality by which points and lines are essentially equivalent. This duality affords a systematic way of transferring proofs that have been made for points to lines and vice versa. Second is the line at infinity, which plays the same role as the point at infinity of the projective line in helping us to understand the relationship between the projective plane and the more familiar affine plane. Third is the cross-ratio of four lines intersecting at a point, which, like the cross-ratio of four points on a line, is one of the most useful invariants. Fourth is the idea of a pencil of lines, which is essential to understanding the epipolar geometry we use in the stereo analysis that is done in chapter 6. The material on conics is used both in chapter 3 to interpret the intrinsic parameters of a camera and in chapter 7 to prove the correctness of the five-point algorithm; it can be skipped on the first reading.

The last part of section 2.4 shows that there are strikingly simple relationships between the usual affine and euclidean planes and the projective plane. They arise from the choice of a special line, called the *line at infinity*, for the affine case, and the choice of two special points on that line, called the *absolute points*, for the euclidean case. The last notion in this section, that of a quadratic transformation, is used primarily in chapter 7 in the proof of the five-point algorithm; this also can be skipped on the first reading.

Section 2.5 takes us to the projective space. Since we will often model the real world as embedded in a projective space, it is important to read and understand this section. Its plan is very similar to that of the previous one. We introduce four fundamental concepts. First is the principle of duality, which extends to this case and makes points and planes equivalent. Second is the concept of the plane at infinity, which plays the same role as the line at infinity of the projective plane and the point at infinity of the projective line in helping us to understand the relationship between the projective space and the more familiar affine space. Third is the cross-ratio of four planes intersecting along a line which, like those defined in the two previous sections, is a very useful invariant. Fourth is the idea of a pencil of planes, which also plays an important role in clarifying the epipolar geometry. The concept of the absolute conic, although essential for one to understand the relationship between the euclidean and projective space, is used only in chapter 3 to interpret the significance of the intrinsic parameters of a camera, and in chapter 7 in the proof of the five-point algorithm. It may therefore be skipped on the first reading.

2.2 Projective spaces

We will begin with a general study of projective spaces of any dimension. A point of an n dimensional projective space, $\mathcal{P}^n$, is represented by an $n + 1$ vector of coordinates $\mathbf{x} = [x_1, \ldots x_{n+1}]^T$, where at least one of the x_i is nonzero. The numbers x_i are sometimes called the *homogeneous* or *projective coordinates* of the point, and the vector $\mathbf{x}$ is called a *coordinate vector*. Two $n + 1$ vectors $[x_1, \ldots x_{n+1}]^T$ and $[y_1, \ldots y_{n+1}]^T$ represent the same point if and only if there exists a nonzero scalar λ such that $x_i = \lambda y_i$ for $1 \leq i \leq n + 1$. Therefore, the correspondence between points and coordinate vectors is not one to one, and this makes the application of linear algebra to projective geometry a little more complicated.

2.2.1 Collineations

We will now look at the linear transformations of a projective space. An $(n + 1) \times (n + 1)$ matrix $\mathbf{A}$ such that $det(\mathbf{A})$ is different from 0 defines a linear transformation or *collineation* from $\mathcal{P}^n$ into itself. It is easy to see that the set of collineations is a group. This group is also known as the *projective group*. The matrix associated with a given collineation is defined up to a nonzero scale factor, which we usually denote by

$$\rho \mathbf{y} = \mathbf{A}\mathbf{x} \quad \text{and also} \quad \mathbf{x} \,\overline{\wedge}\, \mathbf{y}$$

2.2.2 Projective basis

A *projective basis* is a set of $n + 2$ points of $\mathcal{P}^n$ such that no $n + 1$ of them are linearly dependent. For example, the set $\mathbf{e}_i = [0, \ldots, 1, \ldots, 0]^T$, $i = 1, \ldots, n + 1$, where 1 is in the ith position, and $\mathbf{e}_{n+2} = [1, 1, \ldots, 1]^T$, is a projective basis, called the *standard projective basis*. Any point $\mathbf{x}$ of $\mathcal{P}^n$ can be described as a linear combination of any $n + 1$ points of the standard basis. For example:

$$\mathbf{x} = \sum_{i=1}^{n+1} x_i \mathbf{e}_i$$

Let us now prove a very important proposition that we borrow from the book by Semple and Kneebone [SK52].

Proposition 2.1
Let $\mathbf{x}_1, \ldots, \mathbf{x}_{n+2}$ be $n + 2$ coordinate vectors of points in $\mathcal{P}^n$, no $n + 1$ of which are linearly dependent, i.e., a projective basis. If $\mathbf{e}_1, \ldots, \mathbf{e}_{n+1}, \mathbf{e}_{n+2}$ is the standard projective basis, there exist nonsingular matrices $\mathbf{A}$ such that $\mathbf{A}\mathbf{e}_i = \lambda_i \mathbf{x}_i, i = 1, \ldots, n + 2$, where the λ_i are nonzero scalars; any two matrices with this property differ at most by a scalar factor.

Proof The matrix $\mathbf{A}$ satisfies the $n + 1$ conditions

$$\mathbf{A}\mathbf{e}_i = \lambda_i \mathbf{x}_i \qquad i = 1, \ldots, n + 1$$

if and only if it can be written $\mathbf{A} = [\lambda_1 \mathbf{x}_1, \ldots, \lambda_{n+1} \mathbf{x}_{n+1}]$. We must show that we can choose the values of $\lambda_1, \ldots, \lambda_{n+1}$, and λ_{n+2} in such a way that the equation

$$\mathbf{A}\mathbf{e}_{n+2} = \lambda_{n+2}\mathbf{x}_{n+2}$$

is also satisfied. But this is equivalent to

$$[\mathbf{x}_1,\ldots,\mathbf{x}_{n+1}]\begin{bmatrix} \lambda_1 \\ \vdots \\ \lambda_{n+1} \end{bmatrix} = \lambda_{n+2}\mathbf{x}_{n+2}$$

By the hypothesis concerning the linear independence of the vectors $\mathbf{x}_i$, the matrix on the left-hand side of the previous equation is of rank $n+1$. Thus the ratios of the λ_i are uniquely determined and, furthermore, none of the λ_i is zero. The matrix $\mathbf{A}$ is thus uniquely determined up to a scalar factor and is clearly nonsingular. ∎

This proposition will help us characterize the set of collineations.

2.2.3   Change of projective basis

Let us consider two sets of $n+2$ points represented by the coordinate vectors $\mathbf{x}_1,\ldots,\mathbf{x}_{n+2}$ and $\mathbf{y}_1,\ldots,\mathbf{y}_{n+2}$. We will prove that if the points in these two sets are in general position, there exists a unique collineation that maps the first set of points onto the second.

Proposition 2.2
If $\mathbf{x}_1,\ldots,\mathbf{x}_{n+2}$ and $\mathbf{y}_1,\ldots,\mathbf{y}_{n+2}$ are two sets of $n+2$ coordinate vectors such that in either set no $n+1$ vectors are linearly dependent, i.e., form two projective bases, then there exists a nonsingular $(n+1) \times (n+1)$ matrix $\mathbf{P}$ such that $\mathbf{P}\mathbf{x}_i = \rho_i\mathbf{y}_i, i = 1,\ldots,n+2$, where the ρ_i are scalars, and the matrix $\mathbf{P}$ is uniquely determined apart from a scalar factor.

Proof By the previous proposition, we can choose a nonsingular matrix $\mathbf{A}$ and a set of nonzero scalars $\lambda_1,\ldots,\lambda_{n+2}$ such that

$$\mathbf{A}\mathbf{e}_i = \lambda_i\mathbf{x}_i \qquad i = 1,\ldots,n+2$$

Similarly, we can choose $\mathbf{B}$ and $\mu_1,\ldots,\mu_{n+2}$ so that

$$\mathbf{B}\mathbf{e}_i = \mu_i\mathbf{y}_i \qquad i = 1,\ldots,n+2$$

Then

$$\mathbf{B}\mathbf{A}^{-1}\mathbf{x}_i = \frac{\mu_i}{\lambda_i}\mathbf{y}_i \qquad i = 1,\ldots,n+2$$

and we can take $\mathbf{P} = \mathbf{BA}^{-1}$ and $\rho_i = \frac{\mu_i}{\lambda_i}$. Furthermore, if $\mathbf{Px}_i = \rho_i \mathbf{y}_i$ and $\mathbf{Qx}_i = \sigma_i \mathbf{y}_i$, then $\mathbf{PAe}_i = \lambda_i \rho_i \mathbf{y}_i$ and $\mathbf{QAe}_i = \mu_i \rho_i \mathbf{y}_i$ and hence, by the previous proposition, $\mathbf{PA} = \tau \mathbf{QA}$, i.e., $\mathbf{P} = \tau \mathbf{Q}$ for some scalar τ.   ∎

This proposition shows that a collineation is defined by $n + 2$ pairs of corresponding points. We will use this property many times in the next chapters.

2.2.4   The relationship between $\mathcal{P}^m$ and the unit sphere S^m of R^{m+1}

Here we state a theorem that will turn out to be extremely useful in chapter 5.

Theorem 2.1
The space $\mathcal{P}^m$ is topologically equivalent to the unit sphere S^m of R^{m+1} in which we have identified antipodal points.

Proof This proof can be found in all books on algebraic topology, for example in the book by Greenberg and Harper [GH81]. We can develop an intuition about what is going on as follows. A point x of S^m is represented by a vector $\mathbf{x} = [x_1, \ldots, x_{n+1}]^T$ such that $\sum_{i=1}^{n+1} x_i^2 = 1$. This also represents a point of $\mathcal{P}^m$. The vector $-\mathbf{x}$ represents the antipodal point of x, which is also on S^m but represents the *same* point of $\mathcal{P}^m$.   ∎

In particular, this theorem says that all projective spaces are compact spaces. This comes as a bit of a surprise since we all know, at least vaguely, that projective spaces are about points at infinity and that compact subsets of R^n are bounded. But we should not follow our intuition. Projective spaces are indeed compact, although the attentive reader will have no doubt realized that the kind of compact space we are talking about, a sphere that has been folded upon itself by identifying antipodal points, is by no means easy to picture in the mind's eye.

In chapter 5 we will also study the differential structure of the space $\mathcal{P}^n$ and find it very simple, almost as simple as that of R^{m+1}. The importance of this theorem is due to the fact that the folded unit spheres of R^2 and R^3 very naturally appear in the problems of representing directions; the folded unit sphere of R^4 appears in the problem of using quaternions for representing three-dimensional rotations. Since $\mathcal{P}^n$ is simpler to use than the folded sphere S^n, we will use this theorem to construct simple representations of directions, lines, and rotations.

We now turn to the more detailed study of the cases $n = 1, 2$, and 3, which are the cases encountered in practice in computer vision.

2.3   The projective line

The space $\mathcal{P}^1$ is known as the projective line. It is the simplest of all projective spaces, which is the first reason why we start with it. The second reason is that many structures embedded in higher-dimensional projective spaces have the same structure as $\mathcal{P}^1$.

The standard projective basis of the projective line is $\mathbf{e}_1 = [1, 0]^T$, $\mathbf{e}_2 = [0, 1]^T$, and $\mathbf{e}_3 = [1, 1]^T$. A point on the line can be written as

$$\mathbf{x} = x_1 \mathbf{e}_1 + x_2 \mathbf{e}_2 \tag{2.1}$$

with x_1 and x_2 not both equal to 0. Let us consider a subset of $\mathcal{P}^1$ of the points such that $x_2 \neq 0$. This is the same as excluding the point represented by $\mathbf{e}_1$. Now since the homogeneous coordinates are defined up to a scalar, these points are described by a parameter α, $-\infty \leq \alpha \leq +\infty$ so that

$$\mathbf{x} = \alpha \mathbf{e}_1 + \mathbf{e}_2$$

where $\alpha = \frac{x_1}{x_2}$. The parameter α is often called the *projective parameter* of the point. Note that the point represented by $\mathbf{e}_2$ has a projective parameter equal to 0.

2.3.1   The point at infinity

The point represented by $\mathbf{e}_1$ is called the *point at infinity* of the line $\mathcal{P}^1$. It is defined by the linear equation $x_2 = 0$. The reason for this terminology is that, if we think of the projective line as containing the usual affine line under the correspondence $\alpha \rightarrow \alpha \mathbf{e}_1 + \mathbf{e}_2$, then the projective parameter α of the point gives us a one-to-one correspondence between the projective and affine lines for all values of α that are different from ∞. The values $\alpha = \pm\infty$ correspond to the point $\mathbf{e}_1$, which is outside the affine line but is the limit of points of the affine line with large values of α. This is an extremely useful interpretation of the relationship between the affine and projective lines and, as we show later, can be generalized to higher dimensions.

2.3.2   Collineations of $\mathcal{P}^1$

A collineation of $\mathcal{P}^1$ is defined by a 2×2 matrix $\mathbf{P} = \begin{bmatrix} r & s \\ t & u \end{bmatrix}$ of rank 2. This matrix is defined up to a scale factor. If a point has projective parameter α, the transformed point has projective parameter β given by

$$\beta = \frac{r\alpha + s}{t\alpha + u}$$

Note that the condition that the rank of $\mathbf{P}$ equals 2 is equivalent to $ru - st \neq 0$. According to proposition 2.1, a collineation of $\mathcal{P}^1$ is defined by three pairs of corresponding points.

2.3.3   The cross-ratio of four points

We now define the important concept of the cross-ratio, which is a quantity that remains invariant under the group of collineations. Let $a, b, c,$ and d be four points of $\mathcal{P}^1$ with their respective projective parameters α_a, α_b, α_c, and α_d. Then the cross-ratio $\{a, b; c, d\}$ is defined to be

$$\{a, b; c, d\} = \frac{\alpha_a - \alpha_c}{\alpha_a - \alpha_d} : \frac{\alpha_b - \alpha_c}{\alpha_b - \alpha_d} \tag{2.2}$$

The significance of the cross-ratio is that it is invariant under collineations of $\mathcal{P}^1$. In particular, $\{a, b; c, d\}$ is independent of the choice of coordinates in $\mathcal{P}^1$ (see problem 1).

2.4   The projective plane

The space $\mathcal{P}^2$ is known as the *projective plane*. The main reason for its importance is the fact that it is useful to model the image plane as a projective plane (see chapters 3, 6, and 7).

2.4.1 Points and lines

A point in $\mathcal{P}^2$ is defined by three numbers, not all zero (x_1, x_2, and x_3). They form a coordinate vector $\mathbf{x}$ defined up to a scale factor. In $\mathcal{P}^2$ there are objects other than points, such as lines. A line is also defined by a triplet of numbers (u_1, u_2, and u_3), not all zero. They form a coordinate vector $\mathbf{u}$ defined up to a scale factor. The equation of the line is

$$\sum_{i=1}^{3} u_i x_i = 0 \qquad\qquad\qquad (2.3)$$

in the standard projective basis ($\mathbf{e}_1, \mathbf{e}_2, \mathbf{e}_3$, and $\mathbf{e}_4$) of $\mathcal{P}^2$.

   Formally, there is no difference between points and lines in $\mathcal{P}^2$. This is known as the *principle of duality*.[1] A point represented by $\mathbf{x}$ can be thought of as the set of lines through it. These lines are represented by the coordinate vector $\mathbf{u}$, satisfying $\mathbf{u}^T\mathbf{x} = 0$. This is sometimes referred to as the *line equation* of the point. Inversely, a line represented by $\mathbf{u}$ can be thought of as the set of points represented by $\mathbf{x}$ and satisfying the same equation, called the *point equation* of the line. We can now prove the following result, which will be useful later:

Proposition 2.3
A line going through two points m_1 and m_2, represented by $\mathbf{m}_1$ and $\mathbf{m}_2$, is represented by the cross-product $\mathbf{m}_1 \wedge \mathbf{m}_2$.

Proof A coordinate vector of a point on the line is given by

$$\mathbf{x} = \alpha\mathbf{m}_1 + \beta\mathbf{m}_2$$

for arbitrary values of the scalars α and β. This is equivalent to writing that the determinant $(\mathbf{x}, \mathbf{m}_1, \mathbf{m}_2) = 0$. But this determinant can also be written as

$$\mathbf{x}^T(\mathbf{m}_1 \wedge \mathbf{m}_2) = 0$$

from which the proposition follows. ∎

---

1. Note that this idea is at the origin of the so called Hough transform (see chapter 11), which has been patented [Hou62].

2.4.2   The line at infinity

Among all possible lines, the one whose equation is $x_3 = 0$ is called the
line at infinity of $\mathcal{P}^2$, denoted by l_∞. The reason for this terminology
is that we think of the projective plane as containing the usual affine
plane under the correspondence $[X_1, X_2]^T \to [X_1, X_2, 1]^T$ or $X_1 \mathbf{e}_1 + X_2 \mathbf{e}_2 +$
$\mathbf{e}_3$. This is a one-to-one correspondence between the affine plane and the
projective plane minus the line of equation $x_3 = 0$. For each projective
point of coordinates (x_1, x_2, x_3) that is not on that line, we have

$$X_1 = \tfrac{x_1}{x_3} \quad X_2 = \tfrac{x_2}{x_3} \tag{2.4}$$

If $X_1 \to \infty$ while X_2 does not, we obtain $\mathbf{e}_1$, which is on l_∞. Similarly, when
$X_2 \to \infty$ while X_1 does not, we obtain $\mathbf{e}_2$.

Each line in the projective plane of the form of equation (2.3) intersects l_∞ at the point $(-u_2, u_1, 0)$, which is that line's point at infinity.
Note that the vector $[-u_2, u_1]^T$ gives the direction of the affine line of
equation $u_1 X_1 + u_2 X_2 + u_3 = 0$. This gives us a neat interpretation of the
line at infinity: Each point on that line, with coordinates $(x_1, x_2, 0)$, can
be thought of as a direction in the underlying affine plane, the direction
parallel to the vector $[x_1, x_2]^T$. Indeed, it does not matter if x_1 and x_2 are
defined only up to a scale factor since the direction does not change. We
will use this observation in chapter 5 when we discuss the problem of
representing two-dimensional directions.

Another useful property is the following:

Proposition 2.4
The representation of the point of intersection of two distinct projective
lines is the cross-product of their representations.

Proof   To see this, simply apply the principle of duality. We have seen
that the representation of the line going through two points is the cross-
product of the representation of those points, and this implies that the
representation of the point of intersection of two lines is the cross-
product of their representations. For an alternate proof see problem 4.
∎

Note that this implies that, in projective geometry, two distinct lines
always intersect.

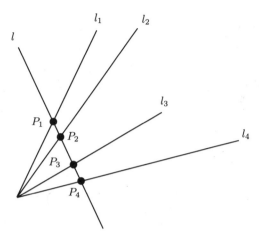

Figure 2.1   Cross-ratio of four lines: $\{l_1, l_2; l_3, l_4\} = \{P_1, P_2; P_3, P_4\}$.

2.4.3   The cross-ratio of four lines intersecting at a point

Let us now generalize the notion of cross-ratio, which was introduced in section 2.3.3 for four points of $\mathcal{P}^1$, to four lines of $\mathcal{P}^2$ intersecting at a point. Given four lines l_1, l_2, l_3, l_4 of $\mathcal{P}^2$ that intersect at a point, their cross-ratio $\{l_1, l_2; l_3, l_4\}$ is defined as the cross-ratio $\{P_1, P_2; P_3, P_4\}$ of their four points of intersection with any line l (see figure 2.1). This value is of course independent of the choice of l (see problem 5).

2.4.4   Pencils of lines

There is a structure of the projective plane that has numerous applications, especially in stereo and motion. The name of this structure is a *pencil of lines*. The set of lines in $\mathcal{P}^2$ passing through a fixed point is a one-dimensional projective space known as a pencil of lines. Let us consider two lines l_1 and l_2 of the pencil represented by their coordinate vectors $\mathbf{u}_1$ and $\mathbf{u}_2$. Any line l of the pencil goes through the point of intersection of l_1 and l_2 represented by $\mathbf{u}_1 \wedge \mathbf{u}_2$ (proposition 2.4). Thus, its coordinate vector $\mathbf{u}$ satisfies $\mathbf{u}^T(\mathbf{u}_1 \wedge \mathbf{u}_2) = 0$, or equivalently

$$\mathbf{u} = \alpha\mathbf{u}_1 + \beta\mathbf{u}_2$$

for two scalars α and β. This equation is formally equivalent to equation (2.1), and therefore the structure of a pencil of lines is the same as that of the projective line $\mathcal{P}^1$. Another, perhaps more elegant, way of proving this result is to apply the principle of duality: The set of lines going through a point is the dual of the set of points on a line, i.e., a projective line.

2.4.5 Collineations of $\mathcal{P}^2$

Collineations of $\mathcal{P}^2$ are defined by 3×3 invertible matrices, defined up to a scalar factor. According to proposition 2.1, such a collineation is defined by four pairs of corresponding points. Collineations transform points, lines, and pencils of lines into points, lines, and pencils of lines, and preserve cross-ratios.

2.4.6 Conics

Here we give some simple properties of conics that will be used in chapter 7.

2.4.6.1 *Definition of a conic*

A conic is a curve defined by the locus of points of the projective plane that satisfy the equation

$$S = \sum_{i,j=1}^{3} a_{ij} x_i x_j = 0$$

where the scalars a_{ij} satisfy $a_{ij} = a_{ji}$ for all i, j and form a 3×3 symmetric matrix $\mathbf{A}$. We can rewrite this equation in matrix form as

$$S(\mathbf{x}) = \mathbf{x}^T \mathbf{A} \mathbf{x} = 0$$

This defines the conic up to a scale factor, and thus the conic depends on five independent parameters.

2.4.6.2 *Intersection of a conic with a line*

Let Q and R be two points of the plane represented by $\mathbf{y}$ and $\mathbf{z}$, respectively. A variable point on the line $\langle Q, R \rangle$ with projective parameter θ is represented by $\mathbf{y} + \theta\mathbf{z}$, and this point lies on the conic S if and only if

$$S(\mathbf{y} + \theta\mathbf{z}) = 0$$

If we expand this and group terms of similar degrees in θ, we have

$$S(\mathbf{y}) + 2\theta S(\mathbf{y}, \mathbf{z}) + \theta^2 S(\mathbf{z}) = 0 \qquad (2.5)$$

where

$$S(\mathbf{y}, \mathbf{z}) = \mathbf{y}^T \mathbf{A} \mathbf{z}$$

This means that, in general, there are two points of intersection of the line $\langle Q, R \rangle$ with the conic S. These intersection points can be real or complex and are obtained by solving the quadratic equation (2.5).

2.4.6.3   *Tangents to a conic from a point*

The line $\langle Q, R \rangle$ is tangent to S when the discriminant of the quadratic equation (2.5) is equal to 0, i.e.,

$$S(\mathbf{y}, \mathbf{z})^2 - S(\mathbf{y})S(\mathbf{z}) = 0 \qquad (2.6)$$

This equation has an interesting interpretation. If we keep Q fixed and let R vary while keeping the line $\langle Q, R \rangle$ tangent to S, equation 2.6, when considered as an equation in $\mathbf{z}$, is the equation of the tangents to S drawn from Q. Since this equation is quadratic, we can conclude that in general there are two tangents, real or complex, distinct or identical, to a conic from any given point. The tangents are identical if and only if Q lies on S.

2.4.6.4   *Classification of conics*

The rank of matrix $\mathbf{A}$ is a projective invariant of the conic S, i.e., it does not change if we change the projective basis. In order to see this, assume that we apply a collineation of matrix $\mathbf{P}$ to the projective plane. Under the substitution $\mathbf{x} \to \mathbf{P}\mathbf{x}'$, it can be seen that the conic equation becomes

$$\mathbf{x}'^T \mathbf{P}^T \mathbf{A} \mathbf{P} \mathbf{x}' = 0$$

Since matrix $\mathbf{P}$ has full rank, the rank of $\mathbf{P}^T \mathbf{A} \mathbf{P}$ is the same as that of $\mathbf{A}$.

If the rank of $\mathbf{A}$ is equal to 3, the conic is said to be nondegenerate. When the rank of $\mathbf{A}$ is less than 3, the conic is said to be degenerate. If it is equal to 2, we can choose the matrix **P** in such a way that the conic equation becomes

$$d_1x_1^2 + d_2x_2^2 = 0$$

which can then be factored as

$$(\sqrt{d_1}x_1 + \sqrt{-d_2}x_2)(\sqrt{d_1}x_1 - \sqrt{-d_2}x_2) = 0$$

The conic is therefore a pair of lines (real or complex) intersecting at the point represented by $\mathbf{e}_3$.

If the rank is equal to 1, the same reasoning shows that the equation can be written

$$d_1x_1^2 = 0$$

The conic is therefore reduced to a single line taken twice.

2.4.7   Affine transformations of the plane

We have seen that there is a one-to-one correspondence between the usual affine plane and the projective plane minus the line at infinity. In the affine plane, we know that an affine transformation defines a correspondence $\mathbf{X} \to \mathbf{X}'$, which can be expressed in matrix form as

$$\mathbf{X}' = \mathbf{B}\mathbf{X} + \mathbf{b} \tag{2.7}$$

where **B** is a 2×2 matrix of rank 2, and **b** is a 2×1 vector. From this equation it is clear that these transformations form a group called the *affine group*, which is a subgroup of the projective group. This subgroup has the interesting property that it preserves the line at infinity.

Let **A** be the matrix of a collineation that leaves l_∞ invariant. The matrix **A** can be written as

$$\mathbf{A} = \begin{bmatrix} \mathbf{C} & \mathbf{c} \\ \mathbf{0}_2^T & a_{33} \end{bmatrix}$$

where **C** is a 2×2 matrix and **c** is a 2×1 vector. The condition that the rank of **A** is 3 implies that $a_{33} \neq 0$ and the rank of **C** is equal to 2. Using the equations (2.4) we can write equation (2.7) with $\mathbf{B} = \frac{1}{a_{33}}\mathbf{C}$ and $\mathbf{b} = \frac{1}{a_{33}}\mathbf{c}$.

2.4.8   Euclidean transformations of the plane: the absolute points

We can further specialize the set of affine transformations and require
that they preserve not only the line at infinity, but also two special points
on that line called the *absolute points* **i** and **j** with coordinates $(1, \pm i, 0)$,
where $i = \sqrt{-1}$. This imposes constraints on matrix **B** in equation (2.7).
Since we insist that **i** and **j** remain invariant, we have

$$\frac{1}{i} = \frac{b_{11}1 + b_{12}i + b_10}{b_{21}1 + b_{22}i + b_20}$$

$$\frac{1}{-i} = \frac{b_{11}1 - b_{12}i + b_10}{b_{21}1 - b_{22}i + b_20}$$

which yields

$$(b_{11} - b_{22})i - (b_{12} + b_{21}) = 0$$

and

$$-(b_{11} - b_{22})i - (b_{12} + b_{21}) = 0$$

Therefore $b_{11} - b_{22} = b_{12} + b_{21} = 0$, and we can write

$$\mathbf{X}' = c \begin{bmatrix} \cos \alpha & \sin \alpha \\ -\sin \alpha & \cos \alpha \end{bmatrix} \mathbf{X} + \mathbf{b} \tag{2.8}$$

with $c > 0$ and $0 \le \alpha < 2\pi$.

This class of transformations is sometimes called the class of *similarity
transformations*. It forms a subgroup of the projective group as shown
in problem 9. This group is called the *similitude group*. The affine point
represented by **X** is first rotated by α around the origin, then scaled by c
and translated by **b**. If we further specialize the class of transformations
by assuming that $c = 1$, we obtain another subgroup called the euclidean
group. If we require **i** and **j** to be recognizable only as a point pair and not
individually, we broaden the class of transformations (see problem 8).

As an application of the use of the absolute points, we will show how
they can be used to define the angle between two lines. The angle α
between two lines l_1 and l_2 can be defined by considering their point of
intersection **a** and the two lines i_a and j_a joining **a** to the absolute points
i and **j** (see figure 2.2). The angle is given by the Laguerre formula (see
problem 3):

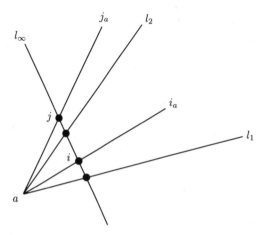

Figure 2.2   The angle α between l_1 and l_2 is given by the Laguerre formula: $\alpha = \frac{1}{2i}\log(\{l_1, l_2; i_a, j_a\})$.

$$\alpha = \frac{1}{2i}\log(\{l_1, l_2; i_a, j_a\}) \tag{2.9}$$

Because $e^{i\pi} = \cos\pi + i\sin\pi = -1$, we see that if the cross-ratio $\{l_1, l_2; i_a, j_a\}$ is equal to -1, the two lines l_1 and l_2 are perpendicular.

2.4.9   Quadratic transformations

A quadratic transformation is an invertible transformation between projective planes defined by polynomials of degree two. It is the simplest generalization of collineations. The simplest of all quadratic transformations, noted Σ_0, is called the *reciprocal transformation* and is defined by

$$\Sigma_0 \mathbf{x} = [x_2x_3, x_3x_1, x_1x_2]^T$$

This definition shows that Σ_0 is defined everywhere except at the points represented by $\mathbf{e}_i, i = 1, 2, 3$. They are called the *fundamental points* of the quadratic transformation. The transformation Σ_0 is its own inverse, thus explaining its name. Even though this may appear to be a very special case, it turns out to be general, thanks to the following theorem:

Theorem 2.2
Any quadratic transformation Σ can be written as the product $\mathbf{A}\Sigma_0\mathbf{B}$ of two collineations $\mathbf{A}$ and $\mathbf{B}$ with the reciprocal transformation Σ_0.

Proof   The proof is omitted here (see Semple and Kneebone [SK52])   ∎

The reader is probably already familiar with a special quadratic transformation, the inversion. This transformation is defined in the euclidean plane with an origin O, and it associates to every point M of the plane the point M' of the half-line $\langle O, M \rangle$ such that

$$OM\, OM' = a^2$$

for some scalar a (see problem 6).

2.5   The projective space

The space $\mathcal{P}^3$ is known as the *projective space*. In the following chapters, we will often model the three-dimensional euclidean space as embedded in the projective space.

2.5.1   Points, lines, and planes

A point $\mathbf{x}$ in $\mathcal{P}^3$ is defined by four numbers (x_1, x_2, x_3, and x_4), not all zero. They form a coordinate vector $\mathbf{x}$ defined up to a scale factor. In $\mathcal{P}^3$ there are objects other than just points and lines, such as planes. A plane is also defined as a four-tuple of numbers (u_1, u_2, u_3, and u_4), not all zero, which forms a coordinate vector $\mathbf{u}$ defined up to a scale factor. The equation of this plane is then

$$\sum_{i=1}^{4} u_i x_i = 0 \tag{2.10}$$

in the standard projective basis ($\mathbf{e}_1, \mathbf{e}_2, \mathbf{e}_3, \mathbf{e}_4$, and $\mathbf{e}_5$) of $\mathcal{P}^3$.

This shows that the same principle of duality that exits in $\mathcal{P}^2$ between points and lines exists in $\mathcal{P}^3$ between points and planes. A point represented by $\mathbf{x}$ can be thought of as the set of planes through it. These planes are represented by $\mathbf{u}$ satisfying $\mathbf{u}^T\mathbf{x} = 0$, which is called the *plane equation* of the point. Inversely, a plane represented by $\mathbf{u}$ can be thought of as the set of points represented by $\mathbf{x}$ and satisfying the same equation, called the *point equation* of the plane. But what about lines?

A line is defined as the set of points that are linearly dependent on two points P_1 and P_2 whose coordinate vectors in the standard projective basis are $\mathbf{x}^{(1)}$ and $\mathbf{x}^{(2)}$. We can consider the sixteen numbers

$$l_{ij} = x_i^{(1)} x_j^{(2)} - x_j^{(1)} x_i^{(2)} \qquad i, j = 1, \ldots, 4$$

Since $l_{ij} = -l_{ji}$, there are only six of these numbers that are apparently independent, for example the six numbers

$$l_{41}, l_{42}, l_{43}, l_{23}, l_{31}, \text{ and } l_{12}$$

which we can take as the components of the coordinate vector $\mathbf{l}$ of l.

These six numbers are not really independent, though, since their ratio is independent of the choice of the points P_1 and P_2. Indeed, let us define

$$\mathbf{y}^{(1)} = \alpha \mathbf{x}^{(1)} + \beta \mathbf{x}^{(2)}$$

$$\mathbf{y}^{(2)} = \alpha' \mathbf{x}^{(1)} + \beta' \mathbf{x}^{(2)}$$

Then it is easy to show that the line coordinates m_{ij} that they define satisfy

$$m_{ij} = (\alpha \beta' - \alpha' \beta) l_{ij}$$

This shows that the ratios of the l_{ij} are constant.

There is a further relation between the line coordinates that can be obtained by noticing that the 4×4 determinant $(\mathbf{x}^{(1)}, \mathbf{x}^{(2)}, \mathbf{x}^{(1)}, \mathbf{x}^{(2)})$ is identically 0. Therefore, we obtain the identity

$$S(\mathbf{l}) = l_{41} l_{23} + l_{42} l_{31} + l_{43} l_{12} = 0 \tag{2.11}$$

The six numbers l_{ij} that are connected by the relation (2.11) are referred to as the *Grassmann or Plücker coordinates* of the line (see problem 7). If we think of the vector $\mathbf{l}$ as the coordinate vector of a point in $\mathcal{P}^5$, equation (2.11) can be interpreted as the equation of a surface of degree 2 on which all points of $\mathcal{P}^5$ that represent lines of $\mathcal{P}^3$ must lie.

This representation of lines is useful in many respects. As an example, let us consider two lines l and l' represented by their Plücker coordinates $\mathbf{l}$ and $\mathbf{l}'$. The following proposition is true:

Proposition 2.5
A necessary and sufficient condition for the two lines l and l' to intersect is that their Plücker coordinates $\mathbf{l}$ and $\mathbf{l}'$ satisfy the equation

$$S(\mathbf{l}, \mathbf{l}') = (l_{41} l_{23}' + l_{41}' l_{23}) + (l_{42} l_{31}' + l_{42}' l_{31}) + (l_{43} l_{12}' + l_{43}' l_{12}) = 0 \tag{2.12}$$

Proof Let P_1, P_2 (P_1', P_2', respectively) be two points of l (l') with coordinate vectors $\mathbf{x}^{(1)}, \mathbf{x}^{(2)}$ ($\mathbf{x}'^{(1)}, \mathbf{x}'^{(2)}$). A necessary and sufficient condition for the two lines to intersect is that the 4×4 determinant $(\mathbf{x}^{(1)}, \mathbf{x}^{(2)}, \mathbf{x}'^{(1)}, \mathbf{x}'^{(2)})$ is equal to 0. By expanding this determinant and equating it to 0, we have the equivalent of equation (2.12). ∎

Finally, with respect to duality, since a line can be defined either as two points or as the intersection of two planes, it is transformed into a line by duality. Indeed, two points become two planes whose intersection is a line, and two planes become two points, which also define a line.

2.5.2   The plane at infinity

Among all possible planes, the one whose equation is $x_4 = 0$ is called the *plane at infinity* or π_∞ of $\mathcal{P}^3$. The reason for this terminology, just as in the case of $\mathcal{P}^2$, is that it is possible to think of the projective space as containing the usual affine space under the correspondence $[X_1, X_2, X_3]^T \to [X_1, X_2, X_3, 1]^T$ or $X_1 \mathbf{e}_1 + X_2 \mathbf{e}_2 + X_3 \mathbf{e}_3 + \mathbf{e}_4$. This is a one-to-one correspondence between the affine space and the projective space minus the plane at infinity of equation $x_4 = 0$. For each projective point of coordinates (x_1, x_2, x_3, x_4) not in that plane, we have

$$X_1 = \frac{x_1}{x_4} \quad X_2 = \frac{x_2}{x_4} \quad X_3 = \frac{x_3}{x_4}$$

Each plane of equation (2.10) intersects the plane at infinity along a line that is its line at infinity.

As in the case of the projective plane, it is often useful to think of the points in the plane at infinity as the set of directions of the underlying affine space. For example, the point of projective coordinates $[x_1, x_2, x_3, 0]^T$ represents the direction parallel to the vector $[x_1, x_2, x_3]^T$, and indeed it does not matter whether x_1, x_2, and x_3 are defined up to a scale factor, since the direction does not change.

2.5.3   The cross-ratio of four planes

Let us generalize the notion of cross-ratio, which was introduced for four points of $\mathcal{P}^1$ and four lines of $\mathcal{P}^2$ intersecting at a point, to four

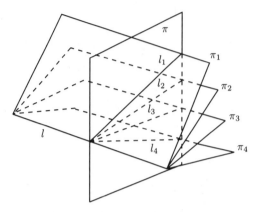

Figure 2.3 Cross-ratio of four planes: $\{\pi_1, \pi_2; \pi_3, \pi_4\} = \{l_1, l_2; l_3, l_4\}$.

planes of $\mathcal{P}^3$ intersecting at a line. Given four planes π_1, π_2, π_3, and π_4 of $\mathcal{P}^3$ that intersect at a line l, their cross-ratio $\{\pi_1, \pi_2; \pi_3, \pi_4\}$ is defined as the cross-ratio $\{l_1, l_2; l_3, l_4\}$ of their four lines of intersection with any plane π (see figure 2.3). Of course this is independent of the choice of π.

2.5.4 Pencils of planes

The structure that is analogous to the pencil of lines of $\mathcal{P}^2$ is the *pencil of planes*, the set of all the planes that intersect at a given line. This structure is also a projective space of dimension 1, an analog to the space $\mathcal{P}^1$ since, using the principle of duality, a pencil of planes is projectively equivalent to a set of points on the same line (this line is the dual of the line of intersection of the planes).

2.5.5 Collineations of $\mathcal{P}^3$

Collineations of $\mathcal{P}^3$ are defined by 4×4 invertible matrices defined up to a scale factor. According to proposition 2.1, such a collineation is defined by five pairs of corresponding points. Collineations transform points, lines, planes, and pencils of planes into points, lines, planes, and pencils of planes, preserving cross-ratios.

2.5.6   Quadrics

The discussion of conics in $\mathcal{P}^2$ found in section 2.4.6 can be carried over to $\mathcal{P}^3$.

2.5.6.1   *Definition of a quadric*

A quadric is a surface of $\mathcal{P}^3$ defined by the locus of points that satisfy the equation

$$S = \sum_{i,j=1}^{4} a_{ij}x_i x_j = 0$$

where the scalars a_{ij} satisfy $a_{ij} = a_{ji}$ for all i, j and form a 4×4 symmetric matrix $\mathbf{A}$. We can rewrite this equation in matrix form as

$$S(\mathbf{x}) = \mathbf{x}^T \mathbf{A} \mathbf{x} = 0$$

A quadric thus depends upon nine independent parameters.

2.5.6.2   *Classification of quadrics*

We can apply exactly the same reasoning to quadrics that we applied to conics in section 2.4.6.4. If the rank of matrix $\mathbf{A}$ is 4, the quadric is said to be *proper*. If it is equal to 3, then after a change of coordinates we can write the equation as

$$d_1 x_1^2 + d_2 x_2^2 + d_3 x_3^2 = 0$$

The quadric contains the point e_4, and if P is a point on the quadric, it is easy to see that the line $\langle e_4, P \rangle$ is also contained in the quadric. This is called a proper cone with vertex e_4.

When the rank of $\mathbf{A}$ is equal to 2, the equation of S can be written as

$$d_1 x_1^2 + d_2 x_2^2 = 0$$

This is the equation of a pair of planes that meet in the line $\langle e_3, e_4 \rangle$. When the rank of $\mathbf{A}$ is equal to 1, the quadric is reduced to a plane taken twice.

2.5.6.3 *Intersection of a quadric with a plane*

Consider a quadric S and a plane π. We assume that we have changed coordinates so that the equation of the plane is $x_4 = 0$. The intersection is a curve given by

$$\sum_{i,j=1}^{4} a_{ij} x_i x_j = 0 = x_4$$

and is therefore a conic in π. If S is proper, this conic is degenerate if and only if the plane is tangent to S.

2.5.6.4 *Intersection of a quadric with a line*

Let Q and R be two points of the space represented by $\mathbf{y}$ and $\mathbf{z}$, respectively. A variable point on the line $\langle Q, R \rangle$ is represented by $\mathbf{y} + \theta \mathbf{z}$, and this point lies on the quadric S if and only if

$$S(\mathbf{y} + \theta \mathbf{z}) = 0$$

We can expand this and group terms of similar degrees in θ as follows:

$$S(\mathbf{y}) + 2\theta S(\mathbf{y}, \mathbf{z}) + \theta^2 S(\mathbf{z}) = 0 \tag{2.13}$$

where

$$S(\mathbf{y}, \mathbf{z}) = \mathbf{y}^T \mathbf{A} \mathbf{z}$$

Therefore, in general, there are two points of intersection of the line $\langle Q, R \rangle$ with the quadric S. These points can be real or complex, distinct or identical, and are obtained by solving the quadratic equation (2.13).

2.5.6.5 *The tangent cone to a quadric from a point*

The line $\langle Q, R \rangle$ is tangent to S when the discriminant of the quadratic equation (2.13) is equal to 0:

$$S(\mathbf{y}, \mathbf{z})^2 - S(\mathbf{y}) S(\mathbf{z}) = 0 \tag{2.14}$$

This equation has an interesting interpretation. If we keep Q fixed and let R vary while keeping the line $\langle Q, R \rangle$ tangent to S, then equation(2.14), when considered as an equation in $\mathbf{z}$, is the equation of the tangents to S

drawn from Q. Since this equation is quadratic, we conclude that it is a quadric. Since this quadric contains the point Q and all lines $\langle Q, R \rangle$, it is a cone, called the *tangent cone* to S from Q.

2.5.7   Affine transformations of the space

In a fashion similar to that in the case of the projective plane, we can consider the subset of the projective group that preserves the plane at infinity. This set is a subgroup of the projective group called the *affine group*, and the transformations can be written in the same way as in equation (2.7):

$$\mathbf{X}' = \mathbf{B}\mathbf{X} + \mathbf{b} \tag{2.15}$$

where matrix $\mathbf{B}$ is 3×3 and has rank 3, and $\mathbf{b}$ is a 3×1 vector.

2.5.8   Euclidean transformations of the space: the absolute conic

We can also further specialize the affine transformations and require that they leave a special conic invariant. This conic, Ω, is obtained as the intersection of the quadric of equation $\sum_{i=1}^{4} x_i^2 = 0$ with π_∞:

$$\sum_{i=1}^{4} x_i^2 = x_4 = 0$$

The conic Ω is also called the *absolute conic*. Note that, in π_∞, Ω can be interpreted as a circle of radius $i = \sqrt{-1}$, an imaginary circle. It is not difficult to show that the affine transformations that keep Ω invariant can be written

$$\mathbf{X}' = c\mathbf{C}\mathbf{X} + \mathbf{b} \tag{2.16}$$

where $c > 0$ and $\mathbf{C}$ is orthogonal, i.e., satisfies the equation $\mathbf{C}\mathbf{C}^T = \mathbf{I}$ (see problem 12). As in the two-dimensional case, this subset of the affine group is a subgroup called the *similitude group*. Similarly, the subset of the similitude group where $c = 1$ is also a subgroup called the *euclidean group*.

Just as the absolute points are used to define angles in the affine plane embedded in $\mathcal{P}^2$, the absolute conic Ω is used to define angles in the affine 3-space embedded in $\mathcal{P}^3$. The angle α between two planes π_1 and

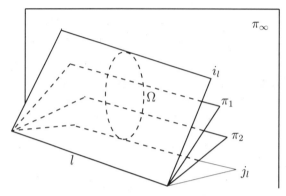

Figure 2.4 The angle between the two planes π_1 and π_2 is a simple function of the cross-ratio $(\pi_1, \pi_2; i_l, j_l)$, where i_l and j_l are the two tangent planes from l to the absolute conic Ω.

π_2 can be defined by considering their line of intersection l and the two planes i_l and j_l going through l and tangent to the absolute conic Ω (see figure 2.4). The angle is again a simple function of the cross-ratio $\{\pi_1, \pi_2; i_l, j_l\}$:

$$\alpha = \frac{1}{2i} \log(\{\pi_1, \pi_2; i_l, j_l\})$$

2.6 Problems

1. Verify the statement in section 2.3.3 about the invariance of the cross-ratio of four points.

2. Show that all circles of the two-dimensional euclidean plane pass through the absolute points and that all spheres of the three-dimensional euclidean space contain the absolute conic.

3. Verify the Laguerre formula by taking two affine lines with equations

$$\begin{cases} X_2 = a_1 X_1 \\ X_2 = a_2 X_1 \end{cases}$$

4. Prove algebraically the assertion of proposition 2.4 about the intersection of two lines of $\mathcal{P}^2$. Where do parallel affine lines intersect?

5. Prove that the definition of the cross-ratio of four lines given in section 2.4.3 is independent of the choice of the intersecting line.

6. Show that the product of the collineation **A** defined by

$$A = \begin{bmatrix} 1 & 0 & 0 \\ 0 & -1 & 0 \\ 0 & 0 & 1 \end{bmatrix}$$

with the reciprocal transformation with base points e_1 and **i** and **j** the absolute points is an inversion.

7. Suppose that the points P_1 and P_2 that define the line l in section 2.5.1 are not in the plane at infinity $x_4 = 0$. Show that the first three coordinates of **l**, the six-dimensional vector of Plücker coordinates, are those of the vector $P_1 P_2$ and that the last three coordinates are those of the vector $OP_1 \wedge OP_2$, where O is the origin of the euclidean space, represented by e_4.

8. In section 2.4.8 we considered the affine transformations that kept the absolute points i and j individually invariant. If we also allow transformations that exchange them, show that we obtain transformations such as

$$X' = c \begin{bmatrix} \cos \alpha & \sin \alpha \\ \sin \alpha & -\cos \alpha \end{bmatrix} X + b$$

with $c > 0$ and $0 \leq \alpha < 2\pi$. What is the geometric interpretation of this transformation?

9. If we represent the points of the affine plane with complex numbers, show that equation (2.8) can be written as

$$z' = c e^{i\alpha} z + b$$

a. Using this formula, verify the group structure.

b. Write the transformation defined in problem 8 using complex numbers.

c. To which class of transformations does the product of two such transformations belong?

     d. Give the inverse of a transformation defined in problem 8.

     e. Conclude that the set of transformations defined in problem 8 and those of question a form a group.

10. Verify the Laguerre formula for planes.

11. Could you suggest (and prove) a projective formula (i.e., with a cross-ratio in it) for the angle of two lines in 3-D space?

12. Prove equation (2.16).

3   Modeling and Calibrating Cameras

3.1   A guide to this chapter

This chapter contains three sections. The first section, which should be read thoroughly, establishes the fundamental properties of the pinhole camera considered as a (projective) geometric engine. The second section explores the effect of changing coordinate systems in the world or in the retina. In particular, it gives a detailed interpretation of the intrinsic parameters of a camera in relation to the somewhat mysterious entity that we called the absolute conic in chapter 2. The practical reader may skip this section almost entirely and look only at equations (3.20) and (3.21).

The third section studies the practical problem of calibrating a real camera with a theoretical as well as a concrete eye. It contains a characterization of the configuration of degenerate reference points that do not yield a unique solution to the calibration problem. Since these configurations, which are described in proposition 3.1, are extremely unlikely to occur, the proposition can be skipped the first time; however, proposition 3.2 is important, and an understanding of it is necessary in order to avoid gross errors.

3.2   Modeling cameras

Since one of the goals of this book is to develop methods for performing metric measurements from images, and since very often these images

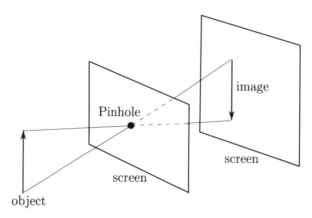

Figure 3.1   Image formation in a pinhole camera.

have been acquired using television or photographic cameras, we want to spend some time defining accurate quantitative models of these devices. There is a deep relationship between these models and projective geometry, and many of the ideas developed in the previous chapter will be put to use. The reader should be familiar with the contents of sections 2.4.1, 2.4.2, and 2.5.1.

In this chapter and in the remainder of the book, we will be using the ˜ notation to indicate projective quantities when there is a possibility of confusing them with affine or metric quantities. For example, x̃ denotes a projective coordinate vector, which is defined up to a multiplicative nonzero scalar, and **x** denotes a vector of R^n.

3.2.1   A simple camera model

We will look at a camera model first from the geometric standpoint, then from the physical standpoint.

3.2.1.1   A geometric model

Let us consider the system depicted in figure 3.1. It consists of two screens. A small hole has been punched in the first screen, and through this hole some of the rays of light emitted or reflected by the object pass,

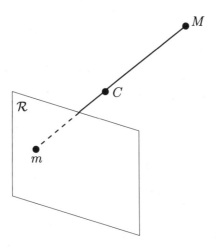

Figure 3.2   The pinhole camera model.

forming an inverted image of that object on the second screen. A beautiful picture taken with such a device can be found in the book by Jenkins and White [JW76].

We can directly build a geometric model of the pinhole camera as indicated in figure 3.2. It consists of a plane $\mathcal{R}$ called the *retinal plane* in which the image is formed through an operation called a *perspective projection*: a point C, the *optical center*, located at a distance f, the *focal length* of the optical system, is used to form the image m in the retinal plane of the 3-D point M as the intersection of the line $\langle C, M \rangle$ with the plane $\mathcal{R}$.

The *optical axis* is the line going through the optical center C and perpendicular to $\mathcal{R}$, which it pierces at a point c. Another plane of interest (see figure 3.3) is the plane $\mathcal{F}$ going through C and parallel to $\mathcal{R}$. It is called the *focal plane*. Points M situated in the focal plane do not have an image in the retinal plane since the line $\langle C, M \rangle$ is parallel to this plane and thus does not intersect it. To speak projectively, it intersects it at infinity. We return to this phenomenon in a later section. It is remarkable that such a simple system can accurately model the geometry and optics of most of the modern Vidicon, CCD, and CID cameras.

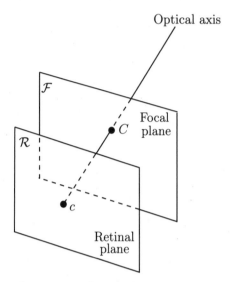

Figure 3.3   The optical axis, focal plane, and retinal plane.

3.2.1.2   *A physical model*

Next we will relate the amount of light that is reflected and emitted at a point on an object to the brightness of the image of that point in the retinal plane. The amount of light falling on a surface is called the *irradiance*, and it is measured in W×m^{-2}, watts per square meter. The amount of light radiated from a surface is called the *radiance*, and it is measured in W×m^{-2} × sr^{-1}, watts per square meter per steradian.[1] A simple computation that can be found, for example in the book by Horn [Hor86], shows that the relationship between the image irradiance E and the scene radiance L is a very simple linear relationship:

$$E = L\frac{\pi}{4}(\frac{d}{f})^2 \cos^4 \alpha$$

The parameters involved in this equation are defined in figure 3.4.

---

1. The steradian is the unit used to measure solid angles.

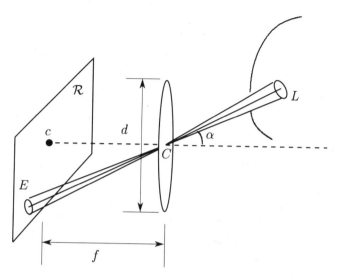

Figure 3.4 The relationship between image irradiance and scene radiance, which is linear.

3.2.2 The perspective projection matrix

We will now study our camera model in further detail. We can choose the coordinate system (C, x, y, z) for the three-dimensional space and (c, u, v) for the retinal plane as indicated in figure 3.5. The coordinate system (C, x, y, z) is called the *standard coordinate system* of the camera. From this figure it should be clear that the relationship between image coordinates and 3-D space coordinates can be written as

$$-\frac{f}{z} = \frac{u}{x} = \frac{v}{y} \tag{3.1}$$

which can be rewritten linearly as

$$\begin{bmatrix} U \\ V \\ S \end{bmatrix} = \begin{bmatrix} -f & 0 & 0 & 0 \\ 0 & -f & 0 & 0 \\ 0 & 0 & 1 & 0 \end{bmatrix} \begin{bmatrix} x \\ y \\ z \\ 1 \end{bmatrix} \tag{3.2}$$

where

$$u = U/S \quad v = V/S \qquad \text{if } S \neq 0 \tag{3.3}$$

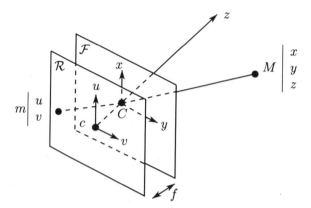

Figure 3.5 The focal plane (x, y) is parallel to the retinal plane (u, v) and at a distance f from it; f is the focal length.

Equations (3.3) should remind the reader of the equations (2.4). These equations allow us to interpret U, V, and S as the projective coordinates of a point in the retina. If $S = 0$, i.e., if $z = 0$, the 3-D point is in the focal plane of the camera. Thus the coordinates u and v are not defined, and the corresponding point is at infinity. We can convince ourselves of this by taking the point M out of the focal plane but placing it arbitrarily close to this plane (see figure 3.6). The points such that $S = 0$ are called *points at infinity* of the retinal plane. $S = 0$ is the equation of the line at infinity of the retinal plane, and this line is the "image" of the focal plane.

Note that equation (3.2) is projective, i.e., it is defined up to a scale factor, and we can rewrite it by using the projective coordinates $(X, Y, Z,$ and $T)$ of M:

$$\begin{bmatrix} U \\ V \\ S \end{bmatrix} = \begin{bmatrix} -f & 0 & 0 & 0 \\ 0 & -f & 0 & 0 \\ 0 & 0 & 1 & 0 \end{bmatrix} \begin{bmatrix} X \\ Y \\ Z \\ T \end{bmatrix} \tag{3.4}$$

The above formula expresses the fact that the relationship between image and space coordinates is linear in projective coordinates and can be written in matrix form as

$$\tilde{\mathbf{m}} = \tilde{\mathbf{P}}\tilde{\mathbf{M}} \tag{3.5}$$

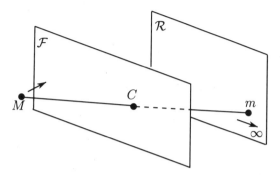

Figure 3.6 When M gets closer to the focal plane, its perspective projection m in the retinal plane goes to ∞.

where $\tilde{\mathbf{m}} = [U, V, S]^T$ and $\tilde{\mathbf{M}} = [X, Y, Z, T]^T$. A camera can be considered as a system that performs a linear projective transformation from the projective space $\mathcal{P}^3$ into the projective plane $\mathcal{P}^2$. This is one of the many examples in which the use of projective geometry makes things simpler: Instead of dealing with the nonlinear equations (3.1), we can use the linear relation (3.5) and the power of linear algebra.

It is easy to convince ourselves that relation (3.5) still holds true with different matrices $\tilde{\mathbf{P}}$ and for any choice of the 3-D and retinal plane coordinate systems. We sometimes refer to the 3-D coordinate system as the *world coordinate system*.

We can give a geometric interpretation of the row vectors of matrix $\tilde{\mathbf{P}}$. We write this matrix in two different ways:

$$\tilde{\mathbf{P}} = \begin{bmatrix} \tilde{\mathbf{Q}}_1^T \\ \tilde{\mathbf{Q}}_2^T \\ \tilde{\mathbf{Q}}_3^T \end{bmatrix} = \begin{bmatrix} \mathbf{q}_1^T \ q_{14} \\ \mathbf{q}_2^T \ q_{24} \\ \mathbf{q}_3^T \ q_{34} \end{bmatrix} \tag{3.6}$$

where $\tilde{\mathbf{Q}}_i, i = 1, 2, 3$ are 4×1 vectors and $\tilde{\mathbf{Q}}_i^T = [\mathbf{q}_i^T, q_{i4}]$. Each such vector represents a projective plane with point equation $\tilde{\mathbf{Q}}_i^T \tilde{\mathbf{M}} = 0$. According to equation (3.4) the plane of equation $\tilde{\mathbf{Q}}_3^T \tilde{\mathbf{M}} = 0$ corresponds to points in the retinal plane such that $S = 0$, i.e., points at ∞. Therefore this is the focal plane. The plane of equation $\tilde{\mathbf{Q}}_1^T \tilde{\mathbf{M}} = 0$ and equation $\tilde{\mathbf{Q}}_2^T \tilde{\mathbf{M}} = 0$ corresponds to points in the retinal plane such that $U = 0$ and $V = 0$, respectively. The intersection of these two planes is the line going through the optical center C of the camera and the origin o in the retinal

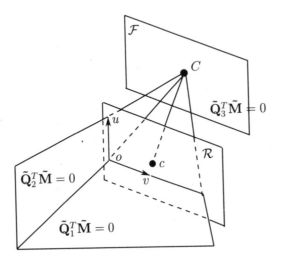

Figure 3.7 The row vectors of matrix $\tilde{\mathbf{P}}$ define the focal plane and the line joining the optical center to the origin of the coordinates in the retinal plane.

plane. Note that this line of intersection is not, in general, the optical axis of the camera. This is shown in figure 3.7.

From the perspective projection matrix $\tilde{\mathbf{P}}$ we can compute some useful information:

- One very useful piece of information in many applications is the optical center C of the camera. According to figure 3.7, C is defined as the intersection of the three planes of equations $\tilde{\mathbf{Q}}_i^T\tilde{\mathbf{M}} = 0$. Therefore it is obtained by solving the system of three linear equations

$$\tilde{\mathbf{P}}\begin{bmatrix} C \\ 1 \end{bmatrix} = \mathbf{0}$$

If we write the 3×4 matrix $\tilde{\mathbf{P}}$ as $\begin{bmatrix} \mathbf{P} & \tilde{\mathbf{p}} \end{bmatrix}$, where $\mathbf{P}$ is a 3×3 matrix and $\tilde{\mathbf{p}}$ a 3×1 vector, and assume that the rank of $\mathbf{P}$ is 3, this equation can be rewritten as

$$C = -\mathbf{P}^{-1}\tilde{\mathbf{p}} \tag{3.7}$$

The careful reader may be a bit concerned by the fact that we are extracting from a matrix $\tilde{\mathbf{P}}$, which is defined only up to a scale factor, the euclidean coordinates of a point. But notice that if $\tilde{\mathbf{P}}$ is replaced with $\lambda\tilde{\mathbf{P}}$, $\tilde{\mathbf{p}}$ with $\lambda\tilde{\mathbf{p}}$, and $\mathbf{P}^{-1}$ with $1/\lambda\mathbf{P}^{-1}$, the result is that the point $\mathbf{C}$ does not change, as is required.

- Another useful piece of information is the equation of the 3-D line $\langle C, m \rangle$ defined by a pixel m and the optical center C. This is called the *optical ray* defined by m. From the previous analysis we know a point on the line, namely C. Another point is the point at infinity, $\tilde{\mathbf{D}}$, of the line whose projective coordinates are $[\mathbf{D}^T, 0]^T$. This point satisfies equation (3.5), and therefore $\mathbf{D}$ is given by

$$\mathbf{D} = \mathbf{P}^{-1}\tilde{\mathbf{m}} \tag{3.8}$$

Note that $\mathbf{D}$ is parallel to the vector $\mathbf{Cm}$. A point M on the line is thus given by $\mathbf{M} = \mathbf{P}^{-1}(-\tilde{\mathbf{p}} + \lambda\tilde{\mathbf{m}})$ where λ varies between $-\infty$ and $+\infty$.

3.3   Changing coordinate systems

The purpose of this section is to describe how matrix $\tilde{\mathbf{P}}$ varies when we change the retinal plane and world coordinate systems, which will reveal more of the interesting structure of that matrix and will allow us to define intrinsic and extrinsic parameters. This information is quite important since in practical applications these changes of coordinate systems occur quite often.

3.3.1   Changing coordinates in the retinal plane

Let us consider the effect on the perspective projection matrix $\tilde{\mathbf{P}}$ of changing the origin of the image coordinate system and the units on the u and v axes. These units are determined by the sampling rates for Vidicon cameras or the sensitive cells size for CCD or CID cameras.

3.3.1.1   *The intrinsic parameters and the normalized camera*

The corresponding situation is shown in figure 3.8. The old coordinate system is centered at the intersection c of the optical axis with the retinal plane, and it has the same units on both axes. We go from the old coordinate system to the new coordinate system, which is centered at

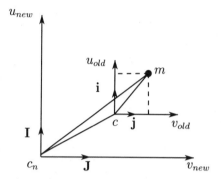

Figure 3.8 Changing coordinate systems in the retinal plane.

a point c_n in the image (usually one of the corners) and will sometimes have different units on both axes due to the electronics of acquisition. For a pixel m we have

$$\mathbf{c}_n\mathbf{m} = \mathbf{c}_n\mathbf{c} + \mathbf{cm} \tag{3.9}$$

Writing $\mathbf{cm} = u_{old}\mathbf{i} + v_{old}\mathbf{j}$ in the old coordinate system and introducing the scaling from the old coordinate system $(\mathbf{i}, \mathbf{j})$ to the new $(\mathbf{I}, \mathbf{J})$, we have $\mathbf{i} = \mathbf{sI}$ and $\mathbf{j} = \mathbf{sJ}$ with

$$\mathbf{s} = \begin{bmatrix} k_u & 0 \\ 0 & k_v \end{bmatrix}$$

We can denote $\mathbf{c}_n\mathbf{c}$ by $\mathbf{t}$ in the new coordinate system, and this allows us to rewrite equation (3.9) in projective coordinates as

$$\tilde{\mathbf{m}}_{new} = \tilde{\mathbf{H}}\tilde{\mathbf{m}}_{old} \tag{3.10}$$

where the 3×3 matrix $\tilde{\mathbf{H}}$ is given by

$$\begin{bmatrix} \mathbf{s} & \mathbf{t} \\ \mathbf{0}_2^T & 1 \end{bmatrix}$$

Note that matrix $\tilde{\mathbf{H}}$ defines a collineation of the retinal plane considered as a projective plane. This collineation preserves the line at infinity and is therefore an affine transformation (see section 2.4.7).

Since, according to equation (3.5), we have

$$\tilde{\mathbf{m}}_{old} = \tilde{\mathbf{P}}_{old}\tilde{\mathbf{M}}$$

we conclude that

$$\tilde{\mathbf{m}}_{new} = \tilde{\mathbf{H}}\tilde{\mathbf{P}}_{old}\tilde{\mathbf{M}}$$

and thus

$$\tilde{\mathbf{P}}_{new} = \tilde{\mathbf{H}}\tilde{\mathbf{P}}_{old} \tag{3.11}$$

If we denote the coordinates of **t** by u_0 and v_0, then according to equations (3.4) and (3.11) the most general matrix $\tilde{\mathbf{P}}$, when the world reference frame is the standard coordinate system of the camera (figure 3.5), can be written as

$$\tilde{\mathbf{P}} = \begin{bmatrix} -fk_u & 0 & u_0 & 0 \\ 0 & -fk_v & v_0 & 0 \\ 0 & 0 & 1 & 0 \end{bmatrix} \tag{3.12}$$

Let $\alpha_u = -fk_u$ and $\alpha_v = -fk_v$. The parameters α_u, α_v, u_0, and v_0 do not depend on the position and orientation of the camera in space, and they are thus called *intrinsic*.

We will now define a special coordinate system that allows us to normalize the retinal coordinates. This coordinate system is called the *normalized coordinate system* of the camera, and it is widely used in motion and stereo applications because it allows us to ignore the specific characteristics of the cameras and to think in terms of ideal systems. Given a matrix $\tilde{\mathbf{P}}$ defined by equation (3.12), we change the retinal coordinate system so that matrix $\tilde{\mathbf{P}}$ can be written

$$\begin{bmatrix} 1 & 0 & 0 & 0 \\ 0 & 1 & 0 & 0 \\ 0 & 0 & 1 & 0 \end{bmatrix} \tag{3.13}$$

According to equations (3.11) and (3.12) the corresponding matrix $\tilde{\mathbf{H}}$ is given by

$$\tilde{\mathbf{H}} = \begin{bmatrix} \dfrac{1}{\alpha_u} & 0 & -\dfrac{u_0}{\alpha_u} \\ 0 & \dfrac{1}{\alpha_v} & -\dfrac{v_0}{\alpha_v} \\ 0 & 0 & 1 \end{bmatrix} \tag{3.14}$$

Therefore, according to equation (3.10), the new retinal coordinates are given by

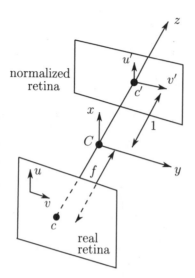

Figure 3.9 Relationship between the real and normalized retinal planes.

$$u' = \frac{u - u_0}{\alpha_u}$$

$$v' = \frac{v - v_0}{\alpha_v}$$

(3.15)

There are two important conclusions that we can draw from these algebraic manipulations.

- First, we have developed a geometric interpretation. If we consider the plane parallel to the retinal plane and at a unit distance from the optical center, this plane, together with the optical center, defines a "normalized" camera (see figure 3.9). Note that this plane is on the other side of C with respect to the retinal plane, producing an inverted image compared to the original one.

- Second, we have an interpretation of the dimensions of k_u, k_v, α_u, and α_v. Indeed, let us write the projection equation using equation (3.12):

$$\begin{bmatrix} U \\ V \\ S \end{bmatrix} = \begin{bmatrix} -fk_u & 0 & u_0 & 0 \\ 0 & -fk_v & v_0 & 0 \\ 0 & 0 & 1 & 0 \end{bmatrix} \begin{bmatrix} x \\ y \\ z \\ 1 \end{bmatrix}$$

Recall that, if $S \neq 0$, then $u = \frac{U}{S}$ and $v = \frac{V}{S}$. When we express the quantities x, y, z, and f in units of length (meters, for example) and u and v in pixel units, then the equations

$$u = \frac{U}{S} = -fk_u \frac{x}{z} + u_0$$

$$v = \frac{V}{S} = -fk_v \frac{y}{z} + v_0$$

show that k_u and k_v are expressed in units of pixel$\times m^{-1}$, and α_u and α_v are expressed in pixels. The quantities $1/k_u$ and $1/k_v$ can be interpreted as the size in meters of the horizontal and vertical pixels, respectively; the parameters α_u and α_v can be interpreted as the size of the focal length in horizontal and vertical pixels, respectively.

3.3.1.2   *What are the intrinsic parameters used for?*

Knowledge of the intrinsic parameters allows us to perform metric measurements with a camera, i.e., to compute the angle between the rays Cm and Cn determined by two pixels m and n. The easiest way to see this is to consider the absolute conic Ω introduced in chapter 2. This conic plays the role of a calibration pattern because its image ω is independent of the camera's position and orientation and depends only upon the intrinsic parameters of the camera.

Let the camera $(\mathbf{C}, \mathcal{R})$ undergo a rigid motion D, i.e., a combination of rotation and translation; $\mathbf{C}$ is the optical center and $\mathcal{R}$ the retinal plane. The new position of the camera is $(D(\mathbf{C}), D(\mathcal{R}))$. Let ω_1 and ω_2 be the images of Ω in $\mathcal{R}$ and $D(\mathcal{R})$, respectively. Then ω_2, regarded as a conic in $D(\mathcal{R})$, is the image of $D(\Omega)$. But we have seen in chapter 2 that rigid motions of the Euclidean space are a subset of the group of collineations of the projective space that leave the absolute conic invariant. Thus $D(\Omega) = \Omega$ and $\omega_1 = \omega_2$ as required. It follows that ω is determined by the camera's intrinsic parameters. Let us examine this in more detail.

We can choose the world coordinate as in figure 3.5 and use equation (3.12) to define $\tilde{\mathbf{P}}$. The equation of Ω (see section 2.5.8) is

$$X^2 + Y^2 + Z^2 = 0 = T \tag{3.16}$$

The images $\tilde{m}$ of the points $\tilde{M}$ of Ω satisfy the equation

$$\tilde{m} = \tilde{P}\tilde{M} = PM$$

since $\tilde{M} = \begin{bmatrix} M \\ 0 \end{bmatrix}$ where P is the leftmost 3×3 submatrix of $\tilde{P}$. Therefore

$$M = P^{-1}\tilde{m}$$

and since, according to equation (3.16), $M^T M = 0$, the equation of ω is

$$\tilde{m}^T P^{-1T} P^{-1} \tilde{m} = 0$$

Using equation (3.12), this is found by simple computation to be equivalent to

$$\tilde{m}^T \begin{bmatrix} \frac{1}{\alpha_u^2} & 0 & -\frac{u_0}{\alpha_u^2} \\ 0 & \frac{1}{\alpha_v^2} & -\frac{v_0}{\alpha_v^2} \\ -\frac{u_0}{\alpha_u^2} & -\frac{v_0}{\alpha_v^2} & 1 + \frac{u_0^2}{\alpha_u^2} + \frac{v_0^2}{\alpha_v^2} \end{bmatrix} \tilde{m} = 0 \tag{3.17}$$

Going to pixel coordinates, this can be rewritten as

$$\left(\frac{u - u_0}{\alpha_u}\right)^2 + \left(\frac{v - v_0}{\alpha_v}\right)^2 + 1 = 0$$

This equation shows that ω determines the intrinsic parameters and vice versa.[2]

Let us now prove that ω allows us to compute the angles between two optical rays $\langle C, m \rangle$ and $\langle C, n \rangle$ for two pixels m and n. Let M and N be the intersections of $\langle C, m \rangle$ and $\langle C, n \rangle$ with the plane at infinity, and let A and B be the two intersections of the line $\langle M, N \rangle$ with Ω. The angle between $\langle C, m \rangle$ and $\langle C, n \rangle$ is given by the Laguerre formula $\frac{1}{2i} \log(\{M, N; A, B\})$ (see chapter 2, equation (2.9)). The reason for this is that the line at infinity of the plane defined by the three points C, m, n is the intersection of that plane with the plane at infinity, i.e., the line $\langle M, N \rangle$. The absolute points are the intersections A and B of that line with the absolute conic Ω. The cross-ratio $\{M, N; A, B\}$ is preserved under the projection to the

---

2. This is also true in the more general case discussed in section 3.4.1.2.

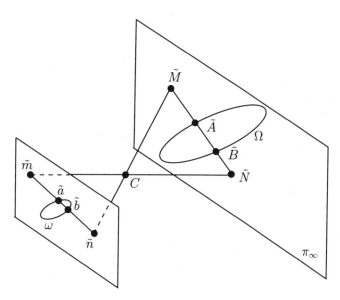

Figure 3.10 How to compute the angle between the optical rays $\langle C, m \rangle$ and $\langle C, n \rangle$ using the image of the absolute conic.

retinal plane, and thus the angle between $\langle C, m \rangle$ and $\langle C, n \rangle$ is given by $\frac{1}{2i} \log(\{m, n; a, b\})$, where the representations of the projective points a, b, A, B are related by $\tilde{a} = \tilde{P}\tilde{A}$ and $\tilde{b} = \tilde{P}\tilde{B}$. Since a and b are the two intersections of the line $\langle m, n \rangle$ with ω, this shows that the angle can be computed only from the image ω of the absolute conic, and this ends the proof. The situation is depicted in figure 3.10.

Let u, v be the pixel coordinates of m, and let u', v' be those of n. The line $\langle m, n \rangle$ is represented by $\tilde{m} + \theta \tilde{n}$. The variable θ is a projective parameter of that line. Point m has a projective parameter 0, and point n has a projective parameter equal to ∞. The reader should not worry about this, since the magic of the cross-ratio will take care of it. In order to compute the projective parameters of $\tilde{a}$ and $\tilde{b}$ we apply equation (2.5), with S given by equation (3.17). The projective parameters are the roots of the quadratic equation

$$S(\tilde{m}) + 2\theta S(\tilde{m}, \tilde{n}) + S(\tilde{n})\theta^2 = 0$$

Let θ_0 and $\overline{\theta_0}$ be the two roots, which are complex conjuguate. According to equation (2.2), we have

$$\{\tilde{m}, \tilde{n}; \tilde{a}, \tilde{b}\} = \frac{0 - \theta_0}{0 - \overline{\theta_0}} : \frac{\infty - \theta_0}{\infty - \overline{\theta_0}}$$

The ratio containing ∞ is equal to 1 (that is the magic); therefore

$$\{\tilde{m}, \tilde{n}; \tilde{a}, \tilde{b}\} = \frac{\theta_0}{\overline{\theta_0}} = e^{2iArg(\theta_0)}$$

where $Arg(\theta_0)$ is the argument of the complex number θ_0. We will let the reader finish the computation in problem 1.

3.3.2　Changing the world reference frame

Just as it is important to study how the matrix $\tilde{\mathbf{P}}$ changes when we change the image coordinate system, it is likewise important for many applications to study how the matrix $\tilde{\mathbf{P}}$ varies when we change the 3-D coordinate system.

3.3.2.1　Extrinsic parameters

As shown in figure 3.11, we go from the old coordinate system centered at the optical center C to the new coordinate system centered at O by a rotation $\mathbf{R}$ followed by a translation $\mathbf{T} = \mathbf{CO}$. Following the notation of the same figure, and similar to the retinal case, we have

$$\mathbf{CM} = \mathbf{CO} + \mathbf{OM}$$

We express $\mathbf{OM}$ in the new coordinate system as follows:

$$\mathbf{OM} = x_{new}\mathbf{I} + y_{new}\mathbf{J} + z_{new}\mathbf{K}$$

and then introduce the rotation matrix $\mathbf{R}$ from the old coordinate system to the new, yielding

$$\mathbf{I} = \mathbf{Ri} \qquad \mathbf{J} = \mathbf{Rj} \qquad \mathbf{K} = \mathbf{Rk}$$

Finally, denoting the vector $\mathbf{CO}$ in the old coordinate system as $\mathbf{t} = [t_x, t_y, t_z]^T$, we have

$$\mathbf{CM} = \mathbf{t} + \mathbf{R} \begin{bmatrix} x_{new} \\ y_{new} \\ z_{new} \end{bmatrix}$$

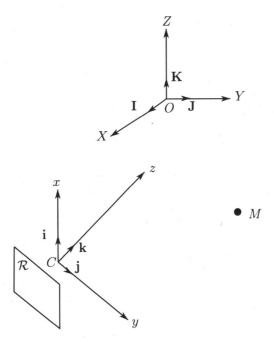

Figure 3.11   Changing coordinate systems in 3-D space.

In projective coordinates this gives

$$\tilde{\mathbf{M}}_{old} = \tilde{\mathbf{K}}\tilde{\mathbf{M}}_{new} \tag{3.18}$$

where the 4×4 matrix $\tilde{\mathbf{K}}$ is given by

$$\tilde{\mathbf{K}} = \begin{bmatrix} \mathbf{R} & \mathbf{t} \\ \mathbf{0}_3^T & 1 \end{bmatrix}$$

Matrix $\tilde{\mathbf{K}}$ represents a collineation that preserves the plane at infinity and the absolute conic. It is a Euclidean transformation of the three-dimensional space considered as a subspace of the projective space (see chapter 2). The matrices $\mathbf{R}$ and $\mathbf{T}$ describe the position and orientation of the camera with respect to the new world coordinate system. They are called the *extrinsic* parameters of the camera.

Using equations (3.5) and (3.18), respectively, we have

$$\tilde{\mathbf{m}} = \tilde{\mathbf{P}}_{old}\tilde{\mathbf{M}}_{old}$$

$$\tilde{\mathbf{m}} = \tilde{\mathbf{P}}_{old}\tilde{\mathbf{K}}\tilde{\mathbf{M}}_{new}$$

Therefore we have

$$\tilde{\mathbf{P}}_{new} = \tilde{\mathbf{P}}_{old}\tilde{\mathbf{K}} \qquad (3.19)$$

This tells us how the perspective projection matrix $\tilde{\mathbf{P}}$ changes when we change coordinate systems in the three-dimensional space: We simply multiply it on the right by the corresponding euclidean transformation of the projective space. If we now combine equations (3.11) and (3.19), we obtain the more general equation

$$\tilde{\mathbf{P}}_{new} = \tilde{\mathbf{H}}\tilde{\mathbf{P}}_{old}\tilde{\mathbf{K}} \qquad (3.20)$$

Equation (3.20) describes how the perspective projection matrix $\tilde{\mathbf{P}}$ changes when we change coordinate systems in the retinal plane or in 3-D space.

3.3.2.2 *The general form of matrix* $\tilde{\mathbf{P}}$

The camera can be considered as a system that depends upon the intrinsic and the extrinsic parameters. There are four intrinsic parameters: the scale factors α_u and α_v and the coordinates u_0 and v_0 of the intersection of the optical axis with the image plane. There are six extrinsic parameters, three for the rotation and three for the translation, which define the transformation from the world coordinate system (the one centered at $\mathbf{O}$ in figure 3.11) to the standard coordinate system of the camera .

If we use the value of $\tilde{\mathbf{P}}_{old}$ given in equation (3.12), we can write the general form of matrix $\tilde{\mathbf{P}}$ as a function of the intrinsic and extrinsic parameters:

$$\tilde{\mathbf{P}} = \begin{bmatrix} \alpha_u\mathbf{r}_1 + u_0\mathbf{r}_3 & \alpha_u t_x + u_0 t_z \\ \alpha_v\mathbf{r}_2 + v_0\mathbf{r}_3 & \alpha_v t_y + v_0 t_z \\ \mathbf{r}_3 & t_z \end{bmatrix} \qquad (3.21)$$

The vectors $\mathbf{r}_1, \mathbf{r}_2, \mathbf{r}_3$ are the row vectors of matrix $\mathbf{R}$. Note that matrix $\tilde{\mathbf{P}}$ is of rank 3 since, if α_u and α_v are not zero, matrix $\mathbf{P}$ is of rank 3.

3.3.2.3   *An application: orthographic projection*

As an application of this, let us consider the translation of $-f$ along the z-axis of the standard coordinate system (figure 3.5). This translation brings the focal plane onto the retinal plane. In the standard coordinate system the matrix $\tilde{\mathbf{P}}$ is given by equation (3.2). Therefore the new perspective projection matrix, according to equation (3.19), is given by

$$\tilde{\mathbf{P}} = \begin{bmatrix} -f & 0 & 0 & 0 \\ 0 & -f & 0 & 0 \\ 0 & 0 & 1 & -f \end{bmatrix}$$

Since $\tilde{\mathbf{P}}$ is defined up to a scale factor, this is the same as

$$\tilde{\mathbf{P}} = \begin{bmatrix} 1 & 0 & 0 & 0 \\ 0 & 1 & 0 & 0 \\ 0 & 0 & -\frac{1}{f} & 1 \end{bmatrix}$$

If we now let f go to infinity, the matrix becomes

$$\tilde{\mathbf{P}} = \begin{bmatrix} 1 & 0 & 0 & 0 \\ 0 & 1 & 0 & 0 \\ 0 & 0 & 0 & 1 \end{bmatrix}$$

With the notations of section 3.2.2, this defines a transformation $U = x, V = y, S = 1$, and therefore $u = x$ and $v = y$. This is known as an *orthographic projection* parallel to the z-axis. It appears as the limit of the general perspective projection when the focal length f becomes large with respect to the distance z of the camera from the object.

3.4   Calibrating cameras

Calibration is the process of estimating the intrinsic and extrinsic parameters of a camera. It can be thought of as a two-stage process:

1. Estimating matrix $\tilde{\mathbf{P}}$.
2. Estimating the intrinsic and extrinsic parameters from $\tilde{\mathbf{P}}$.

For some applications, the second stage may not be necessary. Stereo is such an application, as we will see in chapter 6.

3.4.1   Estimation of the perspective projection matrix $\tilde{\mathbf{P}}$

Since we wish to estimate matrix $\tilde{\mathbf{P}}$ and then possibly compute from the result the values of the intrinsic and extrinsic parameters, it is important to study the conditions under which a 3×4 matrix $\tilde{\mathbf{P}}$ can be written in the form of equation (3.21). In doing this we will discover some important constraints that have not always been taken into account in the literature.

3.4.1.1   *Constraints on* $\tilde{\mathbf{P}}$

Clearly, not any 3×4 matrix $\tilde{\mathbf{P}}$ can be written in the form of equation (3.21). Indeed, this matrix depends upon ten parameters, whereas a general projective 3×4 matrix depends upon eleven parameters. In fact, we have the following theorem:

Theorem 3.1
Let $\tilde{\mathbf{P}}$ be a 3×4 matrix defined by equation (3.6) such that $\operatorname{rank}(\mathbf{P}) = 3$. There exist four sets of extrinsic and intrinsic parameters such that $\tilde{\mathbf{P}}$ can be written as equation (3.21) if and only if the following two constraints are satisfied:

$$\|\mathbf{q}_3\| = 1 \tag{3.22}$$

$$(\mathbf{q}_1 \wedge \mathbf{q}_3) \cdot (\mathbf{q}_2 \wedge \mathbf{q}_3) = 0 \tag{3.23}$$

Proof   The *if* condition is satisfied if equations (3.22) and (3.23) are true if $\tilde{\mathbf{P}}$ is written in the form of equation (3.21). The proof of the *only if* condition is obtained as follows. Using equation (3.21) and the fact that matrix $\tilde{\mathbf{P}}$ is known up to a scale factor ε that must be ± 1 because of equation (3.22), we can compute a set of intrinsic and extrinsic parameters. The resolution proceeds as follows. By comparing the third rows in equations (3.6) and (3.21), we obtain

$$t_z = \varepsilon q_{34}$$
$$\mathbf{r}_3 = \varepsilon \mathbf{q}_3^T \tag{3.24}$$

Taking the inner products of $\mathbf{q}_3$ with $\mathbf{q}_1$ and $\mathbf{q}_2$ yields u_0 and v_0:

$$u_0 = \mathbf{q}_1^T \mathbf{q}_3$$
$$v_0 = \mathbf{q}_2^T \mathbf{q}_3$$

(3.25)

Computing the squared magnitudes of $\mathbf{q}_1$ and $\mathbf{q}_2$ yields

$$\alpha_u = \varepsilon_u \sqrt{\mathbf{q}_1^T \mathbf{q}_1 - u_0^2}$$

$$\alpha_v = \varepsilon_v \sqrt{\mathbf{q}_2^T \mathbf{q}_2 - v_0^2}$$

where ε_u and ε_v are equal to ± 1. Using the previous values for u_0 and v_0 and taking into account equation (3.22), these equations can be further simplified as

$$\alpha_u = \varepsilon_u \|\mathbf{q}_1 \wedge \mathbf{q}_3\|$$

$$\alpha_v = \varepsilon_v \|\mathbf{q}_2 \wedge \mathbf{q}_3\|$$

(3.26)

We can then compute $\mathbf{r}_1, \mathbf{r}_2, t_x$, and t_y:

$$\mathbf{r}_1 = \varepsilon(\mathbf{q}_1^T - u_0\mathbf{q}_3^T)/\alpha_u$$

$$\mathbf{r}_2 = \varepsilon(\mathbf{q}_2^T - v_0\mathbf{q}_3^T)/\alpha_v$$

$$t_x = \varepsilon(q_{14} - u_0 t_z)/\alpha_u$$

$$t_y = \varepsilon(q_{24} - v_0 t_z)/\alpha_v$$

(3.27)

Because of equation (3.22), the expressions for $\mathbf{r}_1$ and $\mathbf{r}_2$ can also be written as

$$\mathbf{r}_1^T = \varepsilon\varepsilon_u \mathbf{q}_3 \wedge \frac{(\mathbf{q}_1 \wedge \mathbf{q}_3)}{\|\mathbf{q}_1 \wedge \mathbf{q}_3\|} \qquad \mathbf{r}_2^T = \varepsilon\varepsilon_v \mathbf{q}_3 \wedge \frac{(\mathbf{q}_2 \wedge \mathbf{q}_3)}{\|\mathbf{q}_2 \wedge \mathbf{q}_3\|}$$

The parameters α_u and α_v are different from zero, as required, because $\text{rank}(\mathbf{P}) = 3$. It is easy to verify that $\|\mathbf{r}_i\|^2 = 1$ for $i = 1, 2, 3$ and that $\mathbf{r}_i \mathbf{r}_3^T = 0$ for $i = 1, 2$. But, $\mathbf{r}_1 \mathbf{r}_2^T \neq 0$ in general. Indeed

$$\mathbf{r}_1 \mathbf{r}_2^T = \frac{(\mathbf{q}_3 \wedge (\mathbf{q}_1 \wedge \mathbf{q}_3)) \cdot (\mathbf{q}_3 \wedge (\mathbf{q}_2 \wedge \mathbf{q}_3))}{\|\mathbf{q}_1 \wedge \mathbf{q}_3\| \|\mathbf{q}_2 \wedge \mathbf{q}_3\|}$$

Using standard properties of determinants, the numerator of this expression is equal to

$$\mathbf{q}_3 \cdot ((\mathbf{q}_2 \wedge \mathbf{q}_3) \wedge (\mathbf{q}_3 \wedge (\mathbf{q}_1 \wedge \mathbf{q}_3)))$$

Again using equation (3.22), this is equal to

$$(\mathbf{q}_1 \wedge \mathbf{q}_3) \cdot (\mathbf{q}_2 \wedge \mathbf{q}_3)$$

Finally, we have

$$\mathbf{r}_1 \mathbf{r}_2^T = \varepsilon_u \varepsilon_v \frac{(\mathbf{q}_1 \wedge \mathbf{q}_3) \cdot (\mathbf{q}_2 \wedge \mathbf{q}_3)}{\|\mathbf{q}_1 \wedge \mathbf{q}_3\| \|\mathbf{q}_2 \wedge \mathbf{q}_3\|} \qquad (3.28)$$

The geometric interpretation of this equation is straightforward. The direction of the line of equation ($u = 0$) ($v = 0$, respectively) in the retinal plane is that of the intersection of the focal plane of equation $\tilde{\mathbf{Q}}_3^T \tilde{\mathbf{M}} = 0$ with the plane of equation $\tilde{\mathbf{Q}}_1^T \tilde{\mathbf{M}} = 0$ ($\tilde{\mathbf{Q}}_2^T \tilde{\mathbf{M}} = 0$, respectively). This direction is therefore given by the cross-product $\mathbf{q}_1 \wedge \mathbf{q}_3$ ($\mathbf{q}_2 \wedge \mathbf{q}_3$, respectively). The cosine of the angle between those two lines is therefore precisely the right-hand side of equation (3.28). Thus, the residual term $\mathbf{r}_1 \mathbf{r}_2^T$ is the cosine of the angle (defined modulo π) between the two axes $u = 0$ and $v = 0$ in the retinal plane. For CCD cameras, these axes have a physical meaning: They are determined by the light-sensitive cells of the retina.

If the constraint (3.23) is satisfied, we see that we have several solutions for the intrinsic and extrinsic parameters, depending on the values of $\varepsilon, \varepsilon_u, \varepsilon_v$. The only further condition is that the determinant of $\mathbf{r}_1, \mathbf{r}_2, \mathbf{r}_3$ is one in order for the matrix $\mathbf{R}$ to be properly orthogonal. Since this determinant is proportional to $\varepsilon \varepsilon_u \varepsilon_v$, there are only four possibilities. From a practical standpoint, it is often the case that we know whether the origin of coordinates is in front of the camera ($t_z > 0$) or behind it ($t_z < 0$). This fixes ε and leaves only two solutions corresponding to inverting the u and v axes. ∎

Having precisely characterized the conditions under which a 3×4 matrix can be written as equation (3.21), we are well armed to design calibration algorithms. We will assume that we are given the 3-D coordinate vectors $\mathbf{M}_i$ of N reference points M_i as well as the 2-D retinal coordinates (u_i, v_i) of their images and consider the problem of estimating $\tilde{\mathbf{P}}$ from these measurements. In practice, as shown in chapter 6, these points are parts of a special pattern. We can think of several methods for obtaining the coefficients of matrix $\tilde{\mathbf{P}}$. We will first consider linear methods.

3.4.1.2   *Linear methods for estimating* $\tilde{P}$

The idea is to write the relationship between the affine coordinates of the 3-D and 2-D points M_i and m_i linearly so that least-squares methods can be used. For every reference point M_i we obtain from equations (3.5) and (3.6) two linear equations in the unknowns $\mathbf{q}_m$ and q_{m4} ($m = 1, 2, 3$):

$$\mathbf{q}_1^T\mathbf{M}_i - u_i\mathbf{q}_3^T\mathbf{M}_i + q_{14} - u_iq_{34} = 0$$

$$\mathbf{q}_2^T\mathbf{M}_i - v_i\mathbf{q}_3^T\mathbf{M}_i + q_{24} - v_iq_{34} = 0 \tag{3.29}$$

For N points, we obtain a system of $2N$ homogeneous linear equations

$$\mathbf{Aq} = \mathbf{0} \tag{3.30}$$

where $\mathbf{A}$ is a $2N \times 12$ matrix depending on the 3-D and 2-D coordinates of the reference points, and $\mathbf{q}$ is the 12×1 vector $[\mathbf{q}_1^T, q_{14}, \mathbf{q}_2^T, q_{24}, \mathbf{q}_3^T, q_{34}]^T$. The vector $\mathbf{q}$ is defined up to a scale factor, and the rank of $\mathbf{A}$ is equal to 11 in general (see below). As a result, constraints must be imposed on $\mathbf{q}$ to avoid the solution $\mathbf{q} = \mathbf{0}$, which is not physically significant.

It is natural to use the two constraints of theorem 3.1. Let us discuss the first constraint:

$$\|\mathbf{q}_3\|^2 = 1$$

This equation is invariant with respect to changes of world reference frame (see problem 4). Minimizing $\|\mathbf{Aq}\|^2$ subject to this constraint is achieved by using the results described in appendix A, and it involves finding the eigenvectors of a 3×3 matrix and inverting a 9×9 matrix (see problem 3). In what follows, we assume that matrix $\tilde{P}$ has been obtained in this manner. This means that we can get a closed-form expression of the solution (or almost one).

In the same way, the constraint $(\mathbf{q}_1 \wedge \mathbf{q}_3) \cdot (\mathbf{q}_2 \wedge \mathbf{q}_3) = 0$ is invariant with respect to changes in the world reference frame. Unfortunately, it is a polynomial of degree 4 in $\mathbf{q}$, and therefore no closed-form solution to the minimization problem can be found. Of course, minimizing $\|\mathbf{Aq}\|^2$ subject to the constraint (3.22) does not guarantee that the constraint (3.23) is satisfied. In order to take it into account, we can assume that we have neglected a physical parameter in our analysis. The physical parameter comes from the fact that the pixel grid may not be exactly

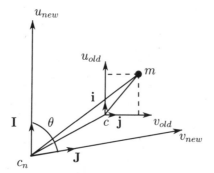

Figure 3.12   The retinal coordinate system may not even be orthogonal.

orthogonal, and that leads us to introduce an extra parameter, the angle θ between the two vectors **I** and **J**, still assuming that **I**, for example, is parallel to **i** (see figure 3.12). We have therefore increased the number of intrinsic parameters by one and can thus decrease the number of constraints on matrix $\tilde{\mathbf{P}}$ by one.[3] The relation between $(\mathbf{i}, \mathbf{j})$ and $(\mathbf{I}, \mathbf{J})$ can be written as

$$\mathbf{i} = \mathbf{s}\mathbf{I} \quad \text{and} \quad \mathbf{j} = \mathbf{s}\mathbf{J}$$

From figure 3.12, it is clear that

$$\mathbf{I} = \frac{\mathbf{i}}{k_u} \qquad \mathbf{J} = \frac{\mathbf{i}\cos\theta + \mathbf{j}\sin\theta}{k_v}$$

Therefore

$$\mathbf{s} = \begin{bmatrix} k_u & -\dfrac{k_u}{\tan\theta} \\ 0 & \dfrac{k_v}{\sin\theta} \end{bmatrix}$$

In this case we can work out a set of equations similar to equations (3.15). Indeed, the most general matrix $\tilde{\mathbf{P}}$ can be written as

---

3. We could also say that, since it is equivalent to know the intrinsic parameters or the image of the absolute conic, and since a general conic depends upon five parameters (see section 2.4.6), five intrinsic parameters are necessary.

$$\tilde{\mathbf{P}} = \begin{bmatrix} -fk_u & fk_u \cot\theta & u_0 & 0 \\ 0 & -\dfrac{fk_v}{\sin\theta} & v_0 & 0 \\ 0 & 0 & 1 & 0 \end{bmatrix} \tag{3.31}$$

Just as before, we let $\alpha_u = -fk_u$ and $\alpha_v = -fk_v$, and from this we can write the equations of the "normalized" retinal coordinates:

$$\begin{cases} u' = \dfrac{u-u_0}{\alpha_u} + \dfrac{(v-v_0)\cos\theta}{\alpha_v} & \equiv & au + bv + c \\ v' = \dfrac{(v-v_0)\sin\theta}{\alpha_v} & \equiv & dv + e \end{cases} \tag{3.32}$$

Matrix $\tilde{\mathbf{P}}$ is now given by

$$\tilde{\mathbf{P}} = \begin{bmatrix} \alpha_u \mathbf{r}_1 - \dfrac{\alpha_u}{\tan\theta}\mathbf{r}_2 + u_0\mathbf{r}_3 & \alpha_u t_x - \dfrac{\alpha_u}{\tan\theta}t_y + u_0 t_z \\ \dfrac{\alpha_v}{\sin\theta}\mathbf{r}_2 + v_0\mathbf{r}_3 & \dfrac{\alpha_v}{\sin\theta}t_y + v_0 t_z \\ \mathbf{r}_3 & t_z \end{bmatrix} = \begin{bmatrix} \mathbf{q}_1^T & q_{14} \\ \mathbf{q}_2^T & q_{24} \\ \mathbf{q}_3^T & q_{34} \end{bmatrix} \tag{3.33}$$

We can now state a theorem similar to theorem 3.1:

Theorem 3.2

Let $\tilde{\mathbf{P}}$ be a 3×4 matrix such that $\mathrm{rank}(\mathbf{P}) = 3$. There exist four sets of extrinsic and intrinsic parameters such that $\tilde{\mathbf{P}}$ can be written as equation (3.33) if and only if the constraint (3.22) is satisfied.

Proof The *if* condition is satisfied if equation (3.22) is true if $\tilde{\mathbf{P}}$ is written in the form of equation (3.33).

The proof of the *only if* condition is obtained as follows. Solving for $\mathbf{r}_3$, u_0, v_0, and t_z yields

$$\mathbf{r}_3 = \varepsilon \mathbf{q}_3^T$$
$$u_0 = \mathbf{q}_1^T \mathbf{q}_3$$
$$v_0 = \mathbf{q}_2^T \mathbf{q}_3 \tag{3.34}$$
$$t_z = \varepsilon q_{34}$$

Following the analysis performed in the proof of theorem 3.1, we have

$$\cos\theta = -\varepsilon_u \varepsilon_v \frac{(\mathbf{q}_1 \wedge \mathbf{q}_3) \cdot (\mathbf{q}_2 \wedge \mathbf{q}_3)}{\|\mathbf{q}_1 \wedge \mathbf{q}_3\| \|\mathbf{q}_2 \wedge \mathbf{q}_3\|}$$

This determines a unique value of θ strictly between 0 and π since rank($\mathbf{P}$) = 3. The other parameters are determined as follows:

$$\alpha_u = \varepsilon_u \sqrt{\mathbf{q}_1^T \mathbf{q}_1 - u_0^2} \sin \theta = \varepsilon_u \|\mathbf{q}_1 \wedge \mathbf{q}_3\| \sin \theta$$

$$\alpha_v = \varepsilon_v \sqrt{\mathbf{q}_2^T \mathbf{q}_2 - v_0^2} \sin \theta = \varepsilon_v \|\mathbf{q}_2 \wedge \mathbf{q}_3\| \sin \theta$$

$$\mathbf{r}_2 = \varepsilon (\mathbf{q}_2^T - v_0 \mathbf{q}_3^T) \frac{\sin \theta}{\alpha_v} = \varepsilon \varepsilon_v \mathbf{q}_3 \wedge \frac{(\mathbf{q}_2 \wedge \mathbf{q}_3)}{\|\mathbf{q}_2 \wedge \mathbf{q}_3\|}$$

$$\mathbf{r}_1 = \varepsilon (\mathbf{q}_1^T + (\mathbf{q}_2^T - v_0 \mathbf{q}_3^T) \frac{\alpha_u}{\alpha_v} \cos \theta - u_0 \mathbf{q}_3^T) \frac{1}{\alpha_u} = \qquad (3.35)$$

$$\frac{\varepsilon}{\sin \theta} (\varepsilon_u \mathbf{q}_3 \wedge \frac{(\mathbf{q}_1 \wedge \mathbf{q}_3)}{\|\mathbf{q}_1 \wedge \mathbf{q}_3\|} + \varepsilon_v \mathbf{q}_3 \wedge \frac{(\mathbf{q}_2 \wedge \mathbf{q}_3)}{\|\mathbf{q}_2 \wedge \mathbf{q}_3\|} \cos \theta)$$

$$t_y = \varepsilon (q_{24} - v_0 q_{34}) \frac{\sin \theta}{\alpha_v}$$

$$t_x = \varepsilon (q_{14} + (q_{24} - v_0 q_{34}) \frac{\alpha_u}{\alpha_v} \cos \theta - u_0 q_{34}) \frac{1}{\alpha_u}$$

It can be verified that $\mathbf{r}_i \mathbf{r}_j^T = \delta_{ij}$ for $i, j = 1, 2, 3$. The determinant of $\mathbf{R}$ is easily shown to be equal to $\varepsilon \varepsilon_u \varepsilon_v \text{sign}(\det(\mathbf{q}_1, \mathbf{q}_2, \mathbf{q}_3))$. There are therefore four possibilities corresponding to the four choices of ε, ε_u, and ε_v such that this determinant is equal to 1. ∎

3.4.1.3 *Questions of rank*

How can we choose the reference points? Can they be chosen arbitrarily? Are there any forbidden configurations? Those are the questions that we will answer now. We will do this by studying the rank of the matrix $\mathbf{A}$ as a function of the configuration of the points M_i. The answers to these questions are of practical relevance since the rank of $\mathbf{A}$ determines the number of solutions to the problem of minimizing $\|\mathbf{Aq}\|^2$ subject to the constraints (3.22) and (3.23). It would be reassuring to know that the solution is unique.

We know that the rank of an $n \times m$ matrix $\mathbf{A}$ is related to the dimension of its nullspace by the relation

$$\text{rank}(\mathbf{A}) + \text{null}(\mathbf{A}) = m \qquad (3.36)$$

Here we have $m = 12$ and consider the following cases:

- rank($\mathbf{A}$) = 12. Then, according to equation (3.36), the nullspace of $\mathbf{A}$ is reduced to $\mathbf{0}$ and the *only* solution to $\mathbf{Aq} = \mathbf{0}$ is $\mathbf{0}$, which is not very meaningful. We will show below that the highest possible value for rank(**A**) is 11.

■ rank(**A**) = 11. Then the nullspace is of dimension 1 and there is a unique (up to scale factor) solution to equation (3.30).

■ rank(**A**) < 11. Then the nullspace is of dimension greater than 1 and there is an infinite number of solutions to equation (3.30). We will show below that if the reference points M_i are in a plane, then rank(**A**) = 8.

Let us prove the following proposition:

Proposition 3.1
For N points ($N \geq 6$) in general position (to be made more precise in the proof), we have rank(**A**) = 11.

Proof   It is of course sufficient to show this proposition to be true when the coordinate systems are those in figure 3.9. We assume that $z \neq 0$ and write

$$u = \frac{x}{z}$$

$$v = \frac{y}{z} \tag{3.37}$$

Let us consider N points M_i of coordinates x_i, y_i, z_i. After some permutation of rows, matrix **A** can be written as N rows of the type

$$[x_i, y_i,, z_i, 1, 0, 0, 0, 0, -\frac{x_i^2}{z_i}, -\frac{x_i y_i}{z_i}, -x_i, -\frac{x_i}{z_i}]$$

and N rows of the type

$$[0, 0, 0, 0, x_i, y_i, z_i, 1, -\frac{x_i y_i}{z_i}, -\frac{y_i^2}{z_i}, -y_i, -\frac{y_i}{z_i}]$$

Therefore **A** is the product **DA′** where $\mathbf{D} = \mathrm{diag}(1/z_1, \ldots 1/z_N, 1/z_1, \ldots, 1/z_N)$ and **A′** has N rows of the type

$$[x_i z_i, y_i z_i, z_i^2, z_i, 0, 0, 0, 0, -x_i^2, -x_i y_i, -x_i z_i, -x_i]$$

and N of the type

$$[0, 0, 0, 0, x_i z_i, y_i z_i, z_i^2, z_i, -x_i y_i, -y_i^2, -y_i z_i, -y_i]$$

Since all z_i are different from 0, we have $\text{rank}(A) = \text{rank}(A')$. By inspection, it is clear that the first column of A' plus its sixth column plus its eleventh column is equal to 0. Therefore $\text{rank}(A') \leq 11$. Let us prove that it is equal to 11.

Let c_j, $j = 1, \ldots, 11$, be the first ten and the twelfth column vectors of matrix A'. We want to prove that a relation such as

$$\sum_{j=1}^{11} \lambda_j c_j = 0 \tag{3.38}$$

implies that $\lambda_j = 0$, $j = 1, \ldots, 11$. But equation (3.38) is equivalent to the N relations

$$\lambda_1 x_i z_i + \lambda_2 y_i z_i + \lambda_3 z_i^2 + \lambda_4 z_i$$
$$- \lambda_9 x_i^2 - \lambda_{10} x_i y_i - \lambda_{11} x_i = 0 \qquad i = 1, \ldots, N \tag{3.39}$$

and the N relations

$$\lambda_5 x_i z_i + \lambda_6 y_i z_i + \lambda_7 z_i^2 + \lambda_8 z_i$$
$$- \lambda_9 x_i y_i - \lambda_{10} y_i^2 - \lambda_{11} y_i = 0 \qquad i = 1, \ldots, N \tag{3.40}$$

From the fact that the polynomials xz, yz, z, z^2, x^2, and xy in the three variables $(x, y,$ and $z)$ and x are linearly independent, as are the polynomials xz, yz, z, z^2, xy, y^2, and y, we conclude that, if the reference points are in general positions, the equations (3.39) imply that

$$\lambda_1 = \cdots = \lambda_4 = \lambda_9 = \cdots = \lambda_{11} = 0$$

and the equations (3.40) imply that

$$\lambda_5 = \cdots = \lambda_8 = \lambda_9 = \cdots = \lambda_{11} = 0$$

Therefore, $\text{rank}(A) = 11$.

We can now define what we mean by *general position*. Here it means that not all of the points fall on either of the quadric surfaces whose equations are given by equations (3.39) and (3.40). Each of these quadrics is defined by seven parameters ($\lambda_1, \lambda_2, \lambda_3, \lambda_4, \lambda_9, \lambda_{10}$, and λ_{11} for the first one, and $\lambda_5, \lambda_6, \lambda_7, \lambda_8, \lambda_9, \lambda_{10}$, and λ_{11} for the second one). Therefore six points are necessary to define each of them. If we choose six points at random, they define two quadrics through the equations (3.39) and (3.40).

But in general the coefficients λ_9, λ_{10}, and λ_{11} will be different for the two quadrics, and therefore the only solution to the systems (3.39) and (3.40) of twelve linear equations in $\lambda_1, \ldots, \lambda_{11}$ will be $\lambda_i = 0$, $i = 1, \ldots, 11$. If they are equal, it means that the points M_i fall on the intersection of these two quadrics. In general, the intersection of two quadrics is a *quartic curve* (i.e., a curve of degree four) but in our case we can see by inspection that both quadrics contain the line defined as the intersection of the two planes of equations $z = 0$ and $\lambda_9 x + \lambda_{10} y + \lambda_{11} = 0$. Therefore their intersection is the union of this line and a curve of degree 3, called a *twisted cubic*, which goes through the origin. It passes through the origin since, in general, the origin does not belong to the previous line (except if $\lambda_{11} = 0$) and belongs to the intersection.

The fact that a twisted cubic is defined by six points is a result of projective geometry (see problem 5). This means that, in general, seven points chosen at random do not fall on a twisted cubic. In our case, if we choose six points at random and include the origin (which is the optical center of the camera), we have seven points which therefore cannot fall on the twisted cubic part of the intersection of our two quadrics. Neither can they fall on the linear part of the intersection, since it lies in the plane $z = 0$ and we have assumed that none of the points are in that plane. The conclusion is that six points taken at random do not fall in a configuration such that rank($\mathbf{A}$) is less than 11. Therefore, unless the 3-D reference points used for calibration fall on a twisted cubic curve that happens to go through the optical center of the camera, a situation very unlikely to occur, rank(A) = 11 and the solution to the calibration problem is essentially unique. The existence of this twisted cubic curve was first reported in the computer vision literature by Thomas Buchanan [Buc88]. ∎

Using the same techniques as those used in the proof of proposition 3.1, the following can be shown (see problem 6):

Proposition 3.2
For N coplanar points ($N \geq 4$) in general position, we have rank($\mathbf{A}$) = 8.

Therefore, the 3-D reference points used for calibration should not be chosen to lie in the same plane; in this configuration the calibration will not work.

3.4.1.4 *Nonlinear methods for estimating* $\tilde{\mathbf{P}}$

According to the previous analysis, either we solve the constrained minimization problem

$$\min_{\mathbf{q}} \|\mathbf{A}\mathbf{q}\|^2$$

subject to   (3.41)

$$\|\mathbf{q}_3\|^2 = 1$$

for which there is a closed-form expression, and recover eleven intrinsic and extrinsic parameters through equations (3.34) and (3.35), or we solve the following constrained minimization problem:

$$\min_{\mathbf{q}} \|\mathbf{A}\mathbf{q}\|^2$$

subject to

$$\|\mathbf{q}_3\|^2 = 1$$ (3.42)

and

$$(\mathbf{q}_1 \wedge \mathbf{q}_3) \cdot (\mathbf{q}_2 \wedge \mathbf{q}_3) = 0$$

From the solution to the minimization we can recover ten intrinsic and extrinsic parameters using the equations (3.24) and (3.27). Note that in the second case there is no closed-form expression for the solution, and therefore we must use iterative methods.

We might as well completely abandon the idea of the linear approach (i.e., starting with equations (3.29)). Indeed, when minimizing the criterion obtained from those equations, we are not minimizing the distance in the retina between the points m_i and the reprojected points M_i, which is the actual physical quantity we are interested in minimizing. In order to minimize this quantity, we have to consider the criterion

$$C = \sum_{i=1}^{N} \|\frac{\mathbf{q}_1^T \mathbf{M}_i + q_{14}}{\mathbf{q}_3^T \mathbf{M}_i + q_{34}} - u_i\|^2 + \|\frac{\mathbf{q}_2^T \mathbf{M}_i + q_{24}}{\mathbf{q}_3^T \mathbf{M}_i + q_{34}} - v_i\|^2 \qquad (3.43)$$

We can thus minimize C with respect to $\mathbf{q}$ subject to the constraint (3.22) and compute the extrinsic and intrinsic parameters using equations (3.34) and (3.35), or we can minimize it subject to constraints (3.22) and (3.23) and recover them using equations given in the proof of theorem 3.1.

Another way of attacking the problem is to perform the minimization directly with respect to the intrinsic and extrinsic parameters and consider C as a function of those parameters rather than of the coefficients of matrix $\tilde{\mathbf{P}}$. The optimization is then performed directly on the parameters of interest. In the next section, we will compare the performances of some of these approaches.

3.4.2 Some numerical examples

We do not show here the actual setup for the calibration, since this is done in chapter 6. We give the results of the calibration procedure using the linear method of section 3.4.1.2, in which five intrinsic parameters are considered, and the nonlinear method of section 3.4.1.4, which minimizes the criterion of equation (3.43) with respect to the eleven intrinsic and extrinsic parameters. Those results are presented in table 3.1. Several comments can be made. First, the two methods yield very similar results. We will see in a moment when they differ. Second, the parameter $\cos\theta$ that measures the angle between the u and v axes in the retinal plane is quite small, indicating that, for this camera at any rate, the hypothesis that they are orthogonal is quite good.

Table 3.1 Results of calibration using the two methods explained in the text.

Variable	Linear method	Nonlinear method
R	$\begin{bmatrix} .494922 & -0.0992085 & -.863255 \\ -.148033 & .969312 & -.196267 \\ .856235 & .224927 & .465048 \end{bmatrix}$	$\begin{bmatrix} .494856 & -0.0991567 & -.863299 \\ -.147975 & .969343 & -.196158 \\ .856283 & .224817 & .465012 \end{bmatrix}$
Axis of rotation	$[-.237829, .970916, 0.0275689]^T$	$[-.2377, .970947, 0.0275651]^T$
Angle of rotation	5.19562 degrees	5.19558 degrees
T	$[-427.482, -26.6806, -450.265]^T$	$[-427.753, -26.7242, -451.451]^T$
α_u	673.362	673.941
α_v	990.996	992.101
u_0	243.373	244.285
v_0	262.6	262.802
$\cos\theta$	-4.63662e-07	-1.51437e-07

To further compare the two methods, we have perturbed the data in the following manner: Noise has been added to the pixel coordinates of the reference points. The noise is gaussian and independent, and its standard deviation varies between 0 (for no noise) and 3 pixels. We have generated a large number of independently perturbed sets of reference points and calibrated from each of those sets. The values of the extrinsic and intrinsic parameters are plotted in the graphs of figures 3.13 and 3.14. The dotted curves represent the performances of the linear method, and the continuous curves represent the performances of the nonlinear method, which clearly appears to be more robust.

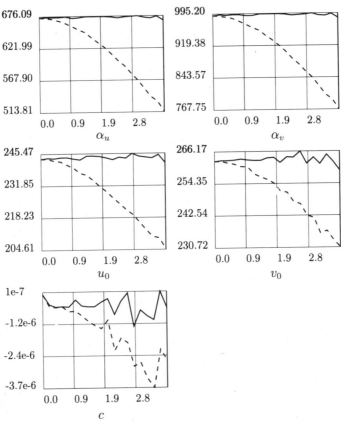

Figure 3.13 How the intrinsic parameters vary with the pixel noise.

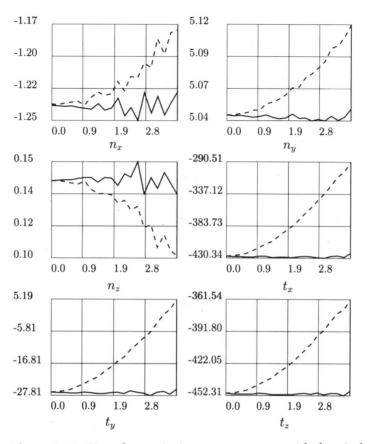

Figure 3.14 How the extrinsic parameters vary with the pixel noise.

The somewhat parabolic trend of the curves in dotted lines is explained in section 5.6.

3.4.3 Conclusion and more references

Having finished this chapter, the reader may have mixed feelings. First, the reader may have a deeper understanding of the geometric engine called a pinhole camera and its intimate connection with projective geometry. Second, the reader may be wondering which method to use for calibration. The author's experience is that the linear method of minimizing optimization problem (3.41) is very simple and gives results that are just as good as those obtained by minimizing criterion (3.43), provided that a bit of care is taken in setting up the calibration pattern. If the intrinsic and extrinsic parameters are needed, they should be reconstructed from equations (3.34) and (3.35).

The practical problem of camera calibration has been present in computer vision since the early days of its application to three-dimensional analysis [Sob74, FB81b]. Essentially at the same time, photogrammeters were busy solving the identical problem in their own context [AAK71, Bro71, Fai75, Won75, Oka81, Oka84]. Good descriptions of the problems and of some of their solutions can be found viewed from the standpoint of photogrammetry in the books of Zeller [Zel52] and Wolf [Wol83] and from the standpoint of computer vision in the books by Duda and Hart [DH73] and by Horn [Hor86] as well as in the paper by Holt and Netravali [HN91].

But the fundamental instability of the problem, which will become clearer in chapter 7, has delayed the availability of a robust and flexible technique, even though some good attempts have been made at solving the problem [FT86, Tsa86, Tsa87, Tsa89]. But there is a need for still a special calibration pattern in the field of view, which is cumbersome for many applications. Some recent ideas make us think that we may be able to eliminate this constraint in the near future [MA90, Spa91, FLM92, Fau92].

3.5 Problems

1. Finish the computation of the tangent of the angle between the lines $\langle C, m \rangle$ and $\langle C, n \rangle$ that was started in section 3.3.1.2.

2. Redo the computation of the equation of ω as a function of the intrinsic parameters with the more general value of matrix $\tilde{\mathbf{P}}$ given in equation (3.31).

3. Using the results of appendix A, show how to solve the optimization problem (3.41).

4. Show that constraints (3.22) and (3.23) are invariant to changes in the world coordinate system.

5. Prove that a twisted cubic is determined by six points.

6. Prove proposition 3.2.

7. This problem investigates the possibility of using three-dimensional lines as references in the calibration process rather than points as in section 3.4. Let L be a three-dimensional line defined by its direction (i.e., its intersection $\tilde{L}$ with π_∞) and another point $\tilde{M}$, not at infinity. Let l be the retinal image of the line represented by the 3×1 vector $\mathbf{u}$. Write two linear equations in the coefficients of the perspective projection matrix $\tilde{P}$ similar to equations (3.29), expressing the fact that the images of $\tilde{L}$ and $\tilde{M}$ belong to l.

8. This problem investigates a curious property of vanishing points that has been studied by Caprile and Torre [CT90]. In projective geometry, parallel lines intersect at a point situated in π_∞ for lines of $\mathcal{P}^3$, and on l_∞ for $\mathcal{P}^2$. This property of intersecting at a point is preserved by perspective projection, and therefore the images of parallel three-dimensional lines intersect at a point in the retinal plane. This point, which is the image of the common point at infinity of the three-dimensional lines, is called the *vanishing point* of their images. Now let us assume that we have three sets of three-dimensional parallel lines with the further property that their three directions are mutually perpendicular (in practice, those lines could be painted on three faces of a cube). Let m, n, and q be the corresponding vanishing points in the retina.

   a. Let C be the optical center of the camera. Show that the three angles (Cm, Cn), (Cn, Cq), and (Cq, Cm) are equal to $\frac{\pi}{2}$.

   b. Let c be the orthocenter of the triangle mnq (i.e., the point of intersection of its three heights). Show that the line Cc is perpendicular to the retinal plane. What conclusion can you draw from this?

   c. Let us assume that we know the intrinsic parameters of the camera so that we can change coordinate systems in the retinal plane using the matrix $\tilde{H}$ given in equation (3.14). Show that matrix $\tilde{P}$ can be written as

$$\tilde{\mathbf{P}} = \begin{bmatrix} \mathbf{R} & \mathbf{T} \\ \mathbf{0}_3^T & 1 \end{bmatrix}$$

Find a method for recovering the rotation matrix $\mathbf{R}$ from the three vanishing points m, n, p. Can you generalize it to more than three points?

4   Edge Detection

4.1   Introduction and precursors

4.1.1   What are edges?

For a person, it is usually very easy to find the contours of objects in a scene. The corresponding operation is extremely difficult for a computer. There are several reasons for this.

1. The first reason has to do with language. When we talk about contours of objects, we assume that the notion of object is well understood, but in fact it is one of the goals of computer vision to identify objects in scenes. Therefore the idea of contour cannot be defined through a definition of the idea of object since that would be creating a vicious circle.

2. Even if we use a more physical definition of an edge as a discontinuity of some sort of the image intensity function, we still have the problem of measurement noise, which is the second reason that the detection of edges in an image is a difficult task. Indeed, detecting discontinuities of image intensity can be achieved mathematically by computing derivatives of this function. The detection of edges is difficult, however, because this intensity is a physical measurement that is subject to noise (see section 4.2); moreover, the operation of derivation is prone to enhancing that noise. This problem is made even worse by the fact that the images that are generally processed have been both sampled and quantized.

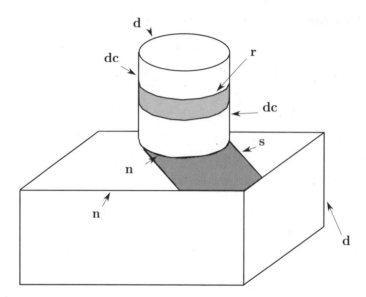

Figure 4.1   Edges in an image have different physical sources.

3. A third difficulty related to edges is that there are, so to speak, differ-
    ent sources of edges in a scene. Some edges come from shadows cast
    by objects, some from variations in the reflectance of objects, some
    from variations in the texture of objects, and some from variations
    in depth. As an example of this, figure 4.1 shows a scene composed
    of a cylindrical object with a dark belt standing on a polyhedral table.
    Edges labelled *d* are caused by discontinuities of the distance of the
    objects to the camera together with a discontinuity of the normal to
    the object surface. Edges labelled *dc* are caused by discontinuities
    of the distance of the objects to the camera, but the normal to the
    object is continuous. Edges labelled *n* are caused by a discontinuity
    of the normal to the object, while those labelled *r* are caused by a
    change of the reflectance of the object with no change of its geomet-
    rical properties. In a similar fashion, those labelled *s* are caused by
    the shadow of the cylinder cast on the table. All these distinct physi-
    cal processes may produce edges. But if we want to relate edges in an
    image to objects in a scene, we must be capable of identifying these
    various sorts of edges.

Given these preliminary words of caution, we will look at some of the precursors for detecting edges.

4.1.2   Early edge detectors

All the earlier edge detectors tried to tackle the two problems of computing some derivatives of the image intensity and of being robust to noise. These two requirements, as will be shown later, are contradictory, and various tradeoffs have been proposed to achieve a balance between accurate detection of edges and robustness to noise.

The idea of using derivatives of the image intensity function to enhance the detection of edges can be viewed from several standpoints:

- In the signal domain, an edge in some direction corresponds to a large local variation of the intensity function in a direction perpendicular to the edge. Computing such a derivative therefore replaces the problem of detecting an edge with the problem of detecting a local extremum.

- In the frequency domain, a derivative operator can be viewed as a high-frequency booster ($\sin \omega x$ becomes $\omega \cos \omega x$), and therefore such an operator will enhance edges more than flat areas.

Note that these simple ideas do not take the noise into account.

The general paradigm is a two-step method that has been used in the past and, as we will see, is still being used today:

1. Enhance the presence of edges in the original intensity image $f(x, y)$, thus creating a new image $g(x, y)$ where edges are more conspicuous. Large values of g indicate the likelihood of the presence of an edge.[1]

2. Threshold $g(x, y)$ to make an edge/no-edge decision, yielding a binary edge map $f_e(x, y)$.

This paradigm is described in figure 4.2.

---

1. This applies also to the case, discussed later, where edges are detected by zero-crossings of the second-order derivative of the image intensity via a simple change of variable.

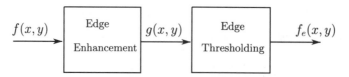

Figure 4.2   A simple paradigm for edge detection.

4.1.2.1 *Discrete approximations of derivatives*

Most of the early edge detectors have used some simple discrete approximations of continuous derivatives. Partial derivatives $\frac{\partial f}{\partial x}$ and $\frac{\partial f}{\partial y}$ of the intensity function $f(x, y)$ can be approximated with finite differences:

$$\frac{\partial f}{\partial x}(x, y) \simeq \Delta_x f(x, y) = f(x + 1, y) - f(x, y)$$

$$\frac{\partial f}{\partial y}(x, y) \simeq \Delta_y f(x, y) = f(x, y + 1) - f(x, y)$$

If we view the intensity function $f(x, y)$ as a surface in R^3 given by its equation $z = f(x, y)$, the three-dimensional vector $\mathbf{G} = [\frac{\partial f}{\partial x}, \frac{\partial f}{\partial y}, -1]^T$ is normal to that surface, and its magnitude is related to its local steepness. Since the z-coordinate of $\mathbf{G}$ is constant, its projection $\mathbf{g} = [\frac{\partial f}{\partial x}, \frac{\partial f}{\partial y}]^T$ on the (x, y) plane carries exactly the same information and points toward the direction of maximum intensity change, while its norm is an indication of the rate of change in this direction[2] and is called the image gradient. This implies in particular that $\mathbf{g}$ is orthogonal to the direction of edges. In practice, $\mathbf{g}$ is approximated by $[\Delta_x, \Delta_y]^T$. It also allows us to compute the rate of intensity changes in any direction, not only the direction of maximal change, simply by projecting it onto that direction: If $D_\theta f$ denotes the partial derivative in the direction θ, we have $D_\theta f = \nabla f \cdot \mathbf{u}_\theta = \mathbf{g} \cdot \mathbf{u}_\theta$, where $\mathbf{u}_\theta$ is the unit vector in the direction θ[3]. We will see more about the differential properties of the image intensity function in section 4.2.4.2.

---

2. $\mathbf{g}$ is also denoted by ∇f.

3. More generally, the derivative of f in the direction of a vector $\mathbf{u}$ (not necessarily of unit length) is noted $D_\mathbf{u} f$ and is equal to $\nabla f \cdot \mathbf{u}$. In particular, we will consider $D_\mathbf{g} f$, the derivative of f in the direction of the gradient.

Table 4.1 Examples of common discrete differential operators.

operator	impulse response
Δ_x	$\begin{bmatrix} 1 & -1 \end{bmatrix}$
Δ_y	$\begin{bmatrix} 1 \\ -1 \end{bmatrix}$
Δ_x^2	$\begin{bmatrix} 1 & -2 & 1 \end{bmatrix}$
Δ_y^2	$\begin{bmatrix} 1 \\ -2 \\ 1 \end{bmatrix}$
$\Delta_x^2 + \Delta_y^2$	$\begin{bmatrix} 0 & 1 & 0 \\ 1 & -4 & 1 \\ 0 & 1 & 0 \end{bmatrix}$

Higher-order derivatives are also useful; for example, we know that, wherever an intensity change occurs in some direction, there is a corresponding peak in the first directional derivative or, equivalently, a zero-crossing in the second directional derivative. The task of detecting intensity changes is thus reduced to the task of finding the zero-crossings of the second derivative in the appropriate direction. This is one of the ideas of the Marr-Hildreth edge detector, which is further described in section 4.2.2.

Derivatives of the form $\frac{\partial^{m+n} f}{\partial x^m \partial y^n}$ can be approximated by concatenating the difference operators Δ_x and Δ_y. For example:

$$\frac{\partial^2 f}{\partial x^2} \simeq \Delta_x^2 f = \Delta_x(\Delta_x f) = f(x+2, y) - 2f(x+1, y) + f(x, y)$$

Approximations of derivatives with finite differences are linear and shift-invariant operators and can be considered as discrete convolution kernels. Table 4.1 shows a few examples.

4.1.2.2   *Taking noise into account: "smooth derivatives"*

Assume that the image $I(x, y)$ is corrupted by an additive noise $N(x, y)$, which we assume to be white, zero-mean, stationary, and of standard deviation σ. We measure $J(x, y) = I(x, y) + N(x, y)$. If we smooth J with a simple average

$$\bar{J}(x, y) = \frac{1}{(2N + 1)^2} \sum_{i=-N}^{i=N} \sum_{j=-N}^{j=N} J(x + i, y + j)$$

the noise in $\bar{J}$ has a variance of $\frac{\sigma^2}{2N+1}$, but of course I has been modified.

More generally, if we assume that N is stationary and zero-mean, with an autocorrelation function $\Lambda(\tau, \mu)$, and convolve J with an impulse response $h(x, y)$, the noise in $\bar{J}$ has an autocorrelation equal to $\Lambda \otimes (h \otimes h_-)$, where $h_-(x, y) = h(-x, -y)$ (see problem 3). In terms of power spectrum (the Fourier transform of the autocorrelation function), if P_N is the power spectrum of N, it becomes $P_N | H |^2$ in $\bar{J}$, where H is the Fourier transform of h. If P_N has a high frequency content, then, by taking for h a low-pass filter, one reduces the high frequency content of N (but, alas, also that of the image I). Therefore, as in many engineering situations, we are confronted with a tradeoff problem: If we achieve too much low-pass filtering, we will eliminate most of the noise, but we will also blur the edges; on the other hand, cutting back on the filtering will preserve both edges and noise.

Since the low-pass filtering operation is also linear and shift-invariant, by combining it with a derivation operation we obtain again a linear shift-invariant operation that is represented by a convolution. Moreover, since convolution is a commutative operation, the order of operations is irrelevant. To make this clearer, let us take an example. If we blur the image with the impulse response

$$\begin{bmatrix} 1 & 1 \\ 1 & 1 \\ 1 & 1 \end{bmatrix}$$

and then compute Δ_x on the resulting image, the corresponding total impulse response is 3×3:

$$\begin{bmatrix} 1 & 0 & -1 \\ 1 & 0 & -1 \\ 1 & 0 & -1 \end{bmatrix}$$

This is one of Prewitt's masks, which are discussed in the next section.

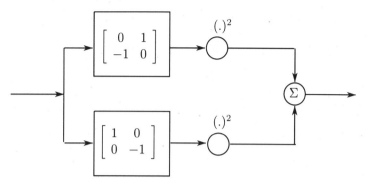

Figure 4.3   The Roberts operator.

Another example is obtained by smoothing the image with the impulse response

$$\begin{bmatrix} 1 & 2 & 1 \\ 1 & 2 & 1 \end{bmatrix}$$

and then computing Δ_y of the result. The corresponding impulse response is

$$\begin{bmatrix} 1 & 2 & 1 \\ 0 & 0 & 0 \\ -1 & -2 & -1 \end{bmatrix}$$

which is one of Sobel's masks, also discussed in the next section.

4.1.2.3   A few "classical operators"

We will now tie some of the previous ideas to some edge operators that have proven to be useful in practice.

1.   The Roberts operator [Rob65] is described in figure 4.3, which shows that this operator computes $D_{45}f$ and $D_{135}f$ (see footnote 3), and then the euclidean norm of the discrete gradient.

2.   Sobel's and Prewitt's operators [Sob78, Pre70] are described in figure 4.4, which shows that they compute the horizontal and vertical

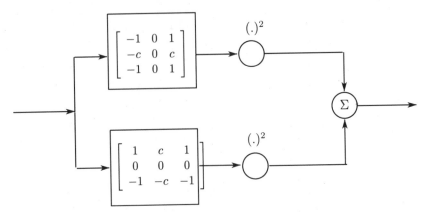

Figure 4.4   Sobel's ($c = 2$) and Prewitt's ($c = 1$) operators.

components of a smooth gradient, and then combine them to yield the euclidean norm of this vector.

4.1.3   Measuring the quality of an edge detector

The idea of measuring the quality of an edge detector is an old one, and Abdou and Pratt [Abd78] have used it to define a figure of merit for comparing edge detectors. The idea is not to use the figure of merit to design the edge detector, as will be done in Section 4.3, but to use it to select the best among existing detectors. Figure 4.5 shows a number of defects from which a detector can suffer. The figure of merit proposed by Abdou and Pratt is

$$F = \frac{1}{max(I_I, I_A)} \sum_{i=1}^{I_A} \frac{1}{1 + \alpha d^2(i)}$$

where I_I is the ideal number of edge points, I_A is the actual number of edge points, $d(i)$ is the shortest distance of the ith actual edge point to an ideal edge point, and α is a positive constant. The figure of merit F is less than or equal to 1, with equality when $I_I = I_A$ and $d(i) = 0$ for all i. Using a measure of the quality of an edge detector in its design has proven to be extremely powerful, as is shown in section 4.3.

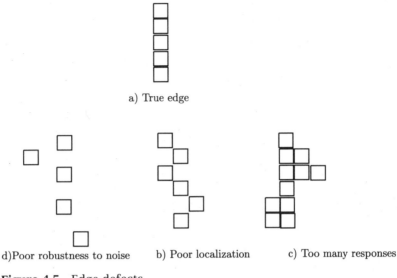

a) True edge

d)Poor robustness to noise   b) Poor localization   c) Too many responses

Figure 4.5   Edge defects.

4.2   Computing derivatives and smoothing

In the previous section we have shown the need to compute smoothed derivatives of the image. We will now study this problem in greater detail.

4.2.1   Differentiation as an ill-posed problem

One way of realizing that differentiation is indeed quite sensitive to noise is to consider a signal $s(x)$ perturbed by a sinusoidal noise:

$$S(x) = s(x) + \varepsilon \sin(\omega x)$$

If ε is sufficiently small, $S(x)$ and $s(x)$ are very close to each other (in the mean-square sense, for example[4]). Taking the derivative with respect to x, we obtain

$$S'(x) = s'(x) + \varepsilon \omega \cos(\omega x)$$

---

4. $\lim_{a \to \infty} \int_{-a}^{a} (S(x) - s(x))^2 \, dx = \frac{\varepsilon^2}{2}$

If ω is large enough, then the sinusoidal term may completely dominate the signal. The fact that high-frequency noise can hurt operations like deconvolution has been known for decades both to mathematicians and to electrical engineers. Powerful tools like the Wiener filter have been heavily used in problems such as image restoration [AH77]. Unfortunately, this formulation models both the signal s and the noise as stochastic processes and assumes some statistical knowledge about both of them. Usually stationary Gaussian processes are assumed, but these are not well suited for modeling images, especially near edges that signify an abrupt change in the statistical properties of the underlying process and therefore imply nonstationarity. Another point is that this formulation is equivalent to maximizing the signal-to-noise ratio; but, as we will see in section 4.3, there are other criteria that are also important and are not taken into account by this approach.

The previous discussion points to the fact that the problem of differentiation is ill-posed. An ill-posed problem can be defined in contrast to a well-posed problem. In 1923, Hadamard [Had23] introduced the definition of a well-posed mathematical problem as one whose solution (1) exists, (2) is unique, and (3) is robust against noise (i.e., depends continuously on the data). Differentiation can be seen as a linear inversion problem of finding $f(x)$, given

$$g(x) = \int Y(x - y)f(y)\,dy \tag{4.1}$$

where $Y(x)$ is the step function, sometimes also known as the Heaviside function, defined as follows:

$$Y(x) = \begin{cases} 1 & x > 0 \\ 0 & x \le 0 \end{cases}$$

It is well known that, if the linear operator applied to the data (here the convolution with $Y(x)$) is not well behaved, then the corresponding inversion problem is not well-posed, but rather is ill-posed.

Methods for transforming ill-posed problems into well-posed ones have recently been developed [TA77]. The idea is, given the problem of finding $\mathbf{f}$ from the data $\mathbf{g}$ such that $\mathbf{g} = \mathbf{Af}$, to set up a mean-square problem involving the sum of two terms:

$$\min_{\mathbf{f}}(\|\mathbf{g} - \mathbf{Af}\| + \lambda\|\mathbf{Pf}\|) \tag{4.2}$$

where **P** is a regularization operator that is intended to impose smoothness on the solution **f**. This technique has been used in the restoration of images [AH77, Pra78]. There are other ways of regularizing an ill-posed problem but, as pointed out by Torre and Poggio [TP86], the most useful one for computer vision is the one above.

The basic result of these methods is that, for convolution equations such as (4.1), regularization is achieved by filtering $g(x)$ with a smooth low-pass filter, and differentiation is performed on the smoothed version of $g(x)$. In order to be stabilizing, the filters must satisfy a number of properties described by Torre and Poggio [TP86] that are not very constraining. Therefore, the theory validates the intuitive ideas used in the design of the early edge detectors.

We have seen that, in order to be more robust to noise, differentiation has to be performed on a smooth version of the signal. We will now discuss two related ways of smoothing, smoothing by filtering and smoothing by approximation. Each case is illustrated by an example of an edge detector.

4.2.2   Smoothing by filtering: the Marr-Hildreth detector

Filtering is commonly used to smooth the data before differentiating it. There are a number of possible filters.

- Band-limited filters can eliminate noise with known frequency content. The corresponding impulse responses are infinite and may therefore pose some problems of implementation (see section 4.4). Examples of such filters are the prolate spheroidal functions [LP61], which satisfy all regularization properties given in the article by Torre and Poggio [TP86], and the Wiener filter in the case of a pink noise image model with an independent additive white noise.

- We can also use support-limited filters or finite impulse response (FIR) filters. They are interesting from the computational standpoint, but in general fail to satisfy the regularization properties because of their infinite frequency support.

- Another class of filters that can be considered as a compromise between the first two classes is the class of filters that minimize uncertainty. The tradeoff between space and frequency spreads can be made precise by defining the uncertainty ΔU of a function f as the product [5]:

$$\Delta U = \Omega X$$

where Ω and X are the spreads in the frequency and space domains, respectively:

$$X^2 = \frac{\int (x - x_m)^2 f^2(x)\, dx}{\int f^2(x)\, dx} \qquad x_m = \int x f^2(x)\, dx \qquad (4.3)$$

$$\Omega^2 = \frac{\int (\omega - \omega_m)^2 F^2(\omega)\, d\omega}{\int F^2(\omega)\, d\omega} \qquad \omega_m = \int \omega F^2(\omega)\, d\omega$$

F is the Fourier transform of f. The uncertainty ΔU is known to be always larger than or equal to 1/2. This is the uncertainty relation

$$\Delta U \geq \frac{1}{2} \qquad (4.4)$$

The class of real functions that minimizes it is the class of Gaussian functions $\frac{1}{\sqrt{2\pi\sigma^2}} \exp(-x^2/\sigma^2)$. An example of the use of this property of the Gaussian function is the Marr-Hildreth detector.

The use of the Gaussian function as a prefilter before differentiation has been proposed by Marr and Hildreth [MH80] on the grounds that edges are features in images that are both spatially localized (local features) and localized in frequency (i.e., they occur at a certain scale). The prefilter should therefore be localized both spatially and in the frequency domain. This is of course impossible because of the uncertainty relation (4.4), but the Gaussian is the best among all possible functions to meet that criterion.

The image is thus smoothed with a filter given by [6]

$$G_\sigma(r) = \frac{1}{2\pi\sigma^2} e^{-\frac{r^2}{2\sigma^2}}$$

---

5. f is assumed to be square-integrable, i.e., $\int |f(x)|^2\, dx < \infty$.

6. This is a good example of an impulse response that is both isotropic (a function of r only) and separable (the product of a function of x and a function of y).

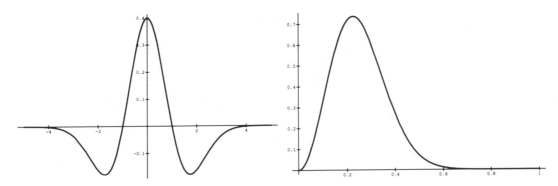

Figure 4.6 The function $D^2 G_\sigma(x)$ and its Fourier transform.

where $r^2 = x^2 + y^2$. Whenever an intensity change occurs in one direction, there will be a corresponding peak in the first directional derivative, or equivalently, a zero-crossing in the second directional derivative. The task of detecting intensity changes can thus be reduced to the task of finding the zero-crossings of the second derivative D^2_θ of the intensity in the appropriate direction θ. That is to say, we seek the zero-crossings in

$$D^2_\theta f(x, y) = D^2_\theta (G_\sigma(r) \otimes f(x, y)) = D^2_\theta G_\sigma(r) \otimes f(x, y)$$

because of the derivation theorem for a convolution. In one dimension

$$D^2 G_\sigma(x) = G''_\sigma(x) = -\frac{1}{\sqrt{2\pi}\sigma^3}(1 - \frac{x^2}{\sigma^2})e^{-\frac{x^2}{2\sigma^2}}$$

The function $D^2 G_\sigma(x)$, which is shown in figure 4.6 along with its Fourier transform, looks like a Mexican hat. It is an approximate bandpass operator. The surface $D^2_{45} G(r)$ is shown in figure 4.7.

The orientation θ that is of interest is that which is orthogonal to the local orientation of the zero-crossings. If we assume that this orientation is that of the gradient **g** of the smooth image, we are then led to finding the zero-crossings of the function $D^2_g f_s(x, y)$, where $f_s(x, y) = G_\sigma(r) \otimes f(x, y)$. We then end up with a scheme that is very similar to the ones described in sections 4.2.4.1 and 4.5. Note that in this last section we show that the normal to the edge curve is in general not parallel to **g**.

If we do not make this assumption, we have to compute a number of directional derivatives. Since convolutions are relatively expensive, it

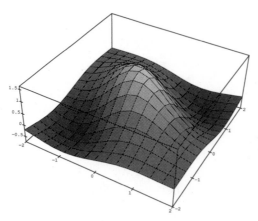

Figure 4.7   The surface $D^2_{45}G(r)$ (see text).

would greatly reduce the computational burden if their number could be decreased by using just one orientation-independent operator, for example. This immediately points toward the Laplacian. The condition under which it can be used is that the intensity variation in $G_\sigma \otimes f$ is linear along, but not necessarily near, a line of zero-crossings. In that case, the zero values of the Laplacian will detect and accurately locate the zero-crossings. Edges are detected as the pixels satisfying

$$\nabla^2 G_\sigma \otimes f(x, y) = 0 \tag{4.5}$$

This condition of linear variation is approximately satisfied in practice. In principle, however, if the intensity varies along an edge in a very nonlinear way, the Laplacian will see the zero-crossings displaced to one side (see figure 4.8). This figure shows a vertical step edge modulated vertically by a nonlinear function; the intensity variation along the edge is not linear. The results of the computation of the zero-crossings of the Laplacian are shown at the right side of the figure, and a closer view at the bottom shows the horizontal displacement of the edge.

The results of applying this operator to the image of figure 4.9 are shown in figure 4.10. Obviously there are too many zero-crossings that have no obvious perceptual significance; some sort of thresholding must take place in order to obtain the result of figure 4.11. The thresholding that has taken place is explained in more detail in section 4.5.

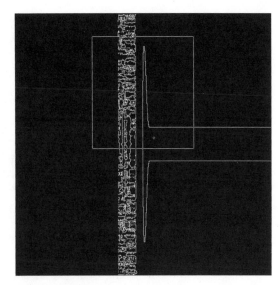

Nonlinear intensity variation along the edge.   Zero-crossings of the Laplacian, $\sigma=32$.

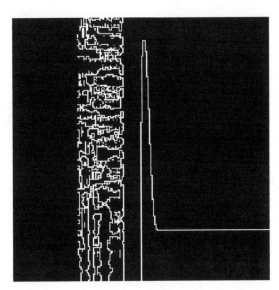

A closer view of the detected vertical edge showing the displacement.

Figure 4.8   An instance in which the Laplacian's detection is in error.

Figure 4.9 A picture of an office scene.

4.2.3 Some useful results from the calculus of variations

In some of the forthcoming sections we are going to need some simple results from the calculus of variations. Suppose we are given a function Φ from $R \times \underbrace{R \times \cdots \times R}_{n+1}$ into R, which we assume to be of class C^k. For a given function $S : R \to R$ of class C^n, we consider $(x, S(x), S'(x), \ldots, S^{(n)}(x))$ and compute the number

$$\varphi(S) = \int_a^b \Phi(x, S(x), S'(x), \ldots, S^{(n)}(x)) \, dx$$

This number depends upon the choice of S. If we consider the set of functions S such that $S(a) = \alpha$ and $S(b) = \beta$ for two given real numbers α and β, we are interested in determining, among all functions S satisfying those two conditions, those for which φ is extremal.

A *necessary* condition for this is that the functions satisfy the Euler-Lagrange equation

Zero crossings of $\nabla^2 G$ with $\sigma{=}1$.

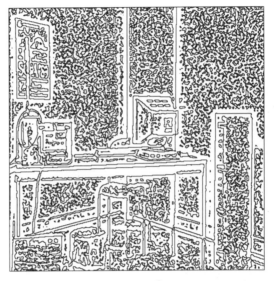

Zero crossings of $\nabla^2 G$ with $\sigma{=}2$.

Zero crossings of $\nabla^2 G$ with $\sigma{=}3$.

Figure 4.10   The zero-crossings of the Marr-Hildreth operator applied to the image in figure 4.9.

$\sigma=1$ $T_h = 15$ and $T_l = 5$.

$\sigma=2$ $T_h = 15$ and $T_l = 5$.

$\sigma=3$ $T_h = 15$ and $T_l = 5$.

Figure 4.11 Only the zero-crossings of the image in figure 4.9 for which the magnitude of the gradient is above a certain threshold have been retained.

$$\frac{\partial \Phi}{\partial S}(x, S(x), S'(x), \ldots, S^{(n)}(x))$$

$$- \frac{d}{dx} \frac{\partial \Phi}{\partial S'}(x, S(x), S'(x), \ldots, S^{(n)}(x)) \ldots \tag{4.6}$$

$$+ (-1)^n \frac{d^n}{dx^n} \frac{\partial \Phi}{\partial S^{(n)}}(x, S(x), S'(x), \ldots, S^{(n)}(x)) = 0$$

This a differential equation of order $2n$ in S. The method additionally applies, via the Lagrange multipliers idea, to the case where S also satisfies constraints of the type

$$\int_a^b C_i(x, S(x), S'(x), \ldots, S^{(n)}(x)) \, dx = c_i \qquad i = 1, \ldots, p$$

We can define the new criterion as

$$\psi(S) = \int_a^b [\Phi(x, S(x), S'(x), \ldots, S^{(n)}(x))$$

$$+ \Sigma_{i=1}^p \lambda_i C_i(x, S(x), S'(x), \ldots, S^{(n)}(x))] \, dx$$

where the λ_i's are the unknown Lagrange multipliers, and compute the new Euler-Lagrange equation.

4.2.4 Smoothing by approximation

The idea is to first approximate the data to be differentiated with a smooth function whose analytical form is known, and then to perform the differentiation on the analytical form of the best approximating function. The problem of approximation can be cast in the regularization framework. Suppose we are given n samples $f_1, \ldots, f_n$ of the signal $f(x)$ and we want to approximate at points $x_1, \ldots, x_n$. We look for a smooth function $S(x)$, for example a polynomial of degree $\leq p$, that minimizes

$$\sum (f_k - S(x_k))^2$$

If no further constraint is imposed on S, it is well known that the solution may oscillate wildly, depending on the amount of noise that is present in the data. In order to regularize the problem, we can add a term that forces the variation of the second derivative of S to be small. This corresponds to choosing $P = d^2/dx^2$ in equation (4.2). The criterion to be minimized with respect to S is now

$$\sum (f_k - S(x_k))^2 + \lambda \int S''(x)^2 \, dx$$

The solution to this problem is to convolve the initial data with a filter whose impulse response is a cubic spline [PVY85] (for a proof of this, see also problem 1). The derivative f_k' of the data at point k can then be obtained as $S'(x_k)$, which is the same as convolving the data with the derivative of a cubic spline.

We can solve the same problem in the continuous domain, i.e., we can look for the function $S(x)$ that minimizes

$$\int [(f(x) - S(x))^2 + \lambda (S''(x))^2] \, dx$$

The corresponding Euler-Lagrange equation is

$$\lambda S^{(4)}(x) + S(x) = f(x)$$

We find that S is given by $f \otimes R(x, \mu)$ [PVY85], with

$$R(x, \mu) = \frac{\mu}{2\sqrt{2}} e^{-\frac{|x|\mu}{\sqrt{2}}} (\cos \frac{|x|\mu}{\sqrt{2}} + \sin \frac{|x|\mu}{\sqrt{2}})$$
$$\lambda \mu^4 = 1 \tag{4.7}$$

This function appears again in section 4.4.2. For a proof of this result, see also problem 7.

4.2.4.1   The Haralick edge detector

The idea of smoothing the data by approximation was proposed by Robert Haralick [Har84] , who used separable Chebychev polynomials to approximate the image intensity surface f over a $P \times P$ neighborhood ($P = 3, 4$). More precisely, take n polynomials $P_k(x, y)$, $1 \le k \le n$ satisfying the orthogonal property

$$\sum_{(x,y)\in R} P_k(x, y) P_l(x, y) = 0 \quad \text{if } k \ne l$$

where R represents the $P \times P$ neighborhood.

We approximate the image $f(x, y)$ in R as

$$S(x, y) = \sum_{k=1}^{n} a_k P_k(x, y)$$

and minimize

$$\sum_{(x,y)\in R} (f(x,y) - S(x,y))^2$$

with respect to $a_1, \ldots, a_n$. The result is given (see problem 2) by

$$a_k = \frac{\sum_{(x,y)\in R} P_k(x,y) f(x,y)}{\sum_{(x,y)\in R} P_k^2(x,y)}$$

This shows that each coefficient a_k is obtained by a linear combination of the image values with the function $Q_k(x,y) = \dfrac{P_k(x,y)}{\sum_{(x,y)\in R} P_k^2(x,y)}$. Derivatives of f are then approximated with derivatives of S. In particular, Haralick proposed finding the edges as the zero-crossings of $D_g^2 f$, i.e., of $D_g^2 S$. We will see more of this idea in section 4.5.2 [7].

4.2.4.2 *The second derivative in the direction of the gradient and the Laplacian*

Let us study the relationship between the zero-crossings of the second derivative $D_g^2 f$ of the intensity function f in the direction of the gradient g and those of the Laplacian. We know what a first-order directional derivative is (see section 4.1.2.1), but what is a second directional derivative? If we consider a function $f : R^n \to R$, a point M of R^n represented by the vector $\mathbf{M}$, and an n-dimensional vector $\mathbf{u}$, we can consider the restriction of the function f to the line of R^n defined by the point M and the vector $\mathbf{u}$. This is a function that we call r from R to R defined by $r(x) = f(\mathbf{M} + x\mathbf{u})$. The first-order derivative of r at $x = 0$ is equal to the directional derivative $D_{\mathbf{u}} f$ of f in the direction $\mathbf{u}$, and its second-order derivative at $x = 0$ is equal, by definition, to the second directional derivative $D_{\mathbf{u}}^2 f$ of f in the direction of the vector $\mathbf{u}$. If we do a second-order Taylor series expansion of r in the vicinity of 0, we will get the expression of $D_{\mathbf{u}}^2 f$. Indeed, we have

$$r(x) = r(0) + x r'(0) + \frac{x^2}{2} r''(0) + \varepsilon(x^2)$$

$$= f(\mathbf{M}) + x \nabla f \cdot \mathbf{u} + \frac{x^2}{2} \mathbf{u}^T \mathbf{H} \mathbf{u} + \varepsilon(x^2)$$

---

7. $D_g f$ is the derivative in the direction of the gradient $D_g f = \nabla f \cdot \mathbf{g} = \mathbf{g} \cdot \mathbf{g} = \|\mathbf{g}\|^2$.

where **H** is the Hessian of f evaluated at **M**. From this it follows that

$$D_{\mathbf{u}}^2 f = \mathbf{u}^T \mathbf{H} \mathbf{u}$$

In the case where f is the image intensity function, we immediately have

$$D_{\mathbf{g}}^2 f = \mathbf{g}^T \mathbf{H} \mathbf{g} = f_x^2 f_{xx} + 2 f_x f_y f_{xy} + f_y^2 f_{yy} \tag{4.8}$$

The second derivative in the direction $\mathbf{g}_\top = [-f_y, f_x]^T$ orthogonal to the gradient **g** is given by

$$D_{\mathbf{g}_\top}^2 f = \mathbf{g}_\top^T \mathbf{H} \mathbf{g}_\top = f_y^2 f_{xx} - 2 f_x f_y f_{xy} + f_x^2 f_{yy} \tag{4.9}$$

This yields a simple relation between the Laplacian ∇^2, $D_{\mathbf{g}}^2$, and $D_{\mathbf{g}_\top}^2$:

$$\nabla^2 = \frac{D_{\mathbf{g}}^2 + D_{\mathbf{g}_\top}^2}{\|\mathbf{g}\|^2}$$

Notice that the operators $D_{\mathbf{g}}^2$ and $D_{\mathbf{g}_\top}^2$ are in general nonlinear. If we consider the intensity surface of section 4.1.2.1, we can express its mean curvature H (see appendix C) as a function of the derivatives of f:

$$H = \frac{(1 + f_x^2) f_{yy} + (1 + f_y^2) f_{xx} - 2 f_x f_y f_{xy}}{2 g^3}$$

where $g^2 = 1 + f_x^2 + f_y^2 = 1 + \|\mathbf{g}\|^2$. A simple algebraic manipulation shows that

$$2 g^3 H = g^2 \nabla^2 f - D_{\mathbf{g}}^2 f$$

From this we immediately conclude that the zeros of $D_{\mathbf{g}}^2 f$ coincide with those of $\nabla^2 f$ if and only if the mean curvature H is zero, which in general is not true.

4.3   One-dimensional edge detection by the maxima of the first derivative

We will now present a family of edge detectors based on the detection of extrema in the output of the convolution of the image with an impulse response to be determined. Since this impulse response has no reason to be anisotropic, it must be even or odd. Because we want to detect edges as extrema in the output, the impulse response must be "derivationlike" and therefore odd. The nice thing about the approach to be described [Can83, Can86] is that it explicitly takes two factors into account in the design of the edge detector: (1) a model of the kind of edges to be detected and (2) a quantitative definition of the performance this edge detector is supposed to have (remember section 4.1.3).

Using these specifications, we derive a criterion that must be satisfied by the unknown impulse response and we minimize that criterion using techniques of variational calculus. The edge detector thus produced can be said to be optimal for the given criterion. We restrict ourselves to step edges, and our edge model is the following:

$$e(x) = AY(x) + n(x) \qquad\qquad (4.10)$$

where $n(x)$ is a stationary white noise process satisfying

$$E(n(x)) = 0$$

and

$$E(n^2(x)) = \sigma_0^2$$

Several possible criteria can be chosen to characterize the performance of an edge detector. Three such criteria are (1) good detection, i.e., robustness to noise; (2) good localization; and (3) uniqueness of response. The last criterion means that the detector should not produce multiple outputs in response to a single edge. Let us now study in detail the derivation of the filter.

4.3.1 Deriving quantitative criteria

Let $h(x)$ be the unknown impulse response, and $o(x)$ the output signal (see figure 4.12). We have

$$o(x) = \int_{-\infty}^{+\infty} e(x - y)h(y)\,dy = A \int_{-\infty}^{x} h(y)\,dy + \int_{-\infty}^{+\infty} n(x - y)h(y)\,dy$$

At $x = 0$, we have

$$o(0) = A \int_{-\infty}^{0} h(y)\,dy + \int_{-\infty}^{+\infty} n(-y)h(y)\,dy$$

This is the sum of two contributions, the signal contribution

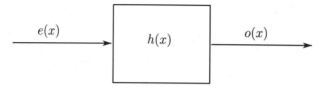

Figure 4.12   Edge detection by convolution with $h(x)$.

$$S = A \int_{-\infty}^{0} h(y)\, dy$$

and the noise contribution

$$N = \int_{-\infty}^{+\infty} h(y) n(-y)\, dy$$

4.3.1.1   Detection criterion

From the definition of the random noise $n(x)$, N is a random variable such that $E(N) = 0$ and

$$E(N^2) = \sigma_0^2 \int_{-\infty}^{+\infty} h^2(y)\, dy$$

We can therefore define the signal-to-noise ratio at $x = 0$ as[8]

$$SNR = \frac{S}{E(N^2)^{1/2}} = \frac{A}{\sigma_0} \quad \frac{\int_{-\infty}^{0} h(y)\, dy}{(\int_{-\infty}^{+\infty} h^2(y)\, dy)^{1/2}} = \frac{A}{\sigma_0} \Sigma(h)$$

This is an analytical expression for the detection criterion. If we maximize $\Sigma(h)$, the result is the standard matched filter. The derivation of this filter is interesting in its own right, since it will allow us to become more familiar with the calculus of variations.

4.3.1.2   Matched filter

For mathematical commodity, but without loss of generality, we will assume that h is nonzero only in an interval $[-W, W]$. Since h is odd, the denominator of $\Sigma(h)$ can be rewritten as

---

8. We assume that $h(x) > 0$ for $x < 0$.

$$\sqrt{2}(\int_{-W}^{0} h^2(y)\,dy)^{1/2}$$

In order to minimize $\Sigma(h)$ we can maximize

$$\int_{-W}^{0} h^2(y)\,dy$$

subject to the constraint

$$\int_{-W}^{0} h(y)\,dy = c_1$$

Applying the Lagrange multiplier idea, this is the same as maximizing

$$C(h) = \int_{-W}^{0} (h^2(y) + \lambda_1 h(y))\,dy = \int_{-W}^{0} \Phi(y,h)\,dy$$

We know from section 4.2.3 that this can be done by solving the corresponding Euler-Lagrange equation[9]

$$\Phi_h = 0$$

considered as a differential equation in h.

In this case, the Euler-Lagrange equation is very simple:

$$2h(y) + \lambda_1 = 0 \tag{4.11}$$

which shows that h is constant over the interval $[-W,0]$. The corresponding odd function is displayed in figure 4.13. This is the well-known difference of boxes used in the Herskowitz-Binford edge detector [HB80].

4.3.1.3 The localization criterion

Let us now look at the localization criterion. One possible way to make this criterion quantitative is to define it as the amount of displacement of the position x_0 of the maximum in the output $o(x)$ with respect to the true position $x = 0$ of the edge. The random variable x_0 depends on both the edge and the noise. We define the localization as the inverse of the standard deviation of x_0. A maximum in the output $o(x)$ at x_0 corresponds to a zero value of the derivative $o'(x_0)$. Let us compute $o'(x)$ as follows:

---

9. Lower indexes indicate a partial derivative.

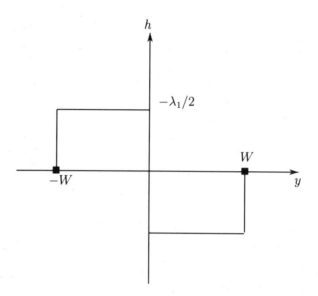

Figure 4.13   Difference of boxes.

$$o'(x) = \frac{d}{dx} \int_{-\infty}^{+\infty} e(x - y)h(y)\,dy$$

By the differentiation theorem for convolution

$$o'(x) = \int_{-\infty}^{+\infty} e(x - y)h'(y)\,dy$$

$$= A \int_{-\infty}^{+\infty} Y(x - y)h'(y)\,dy + \int_{-\infty}^{+\infty} n(x - y)h'(y)\,dy$$

Again, this is the sum of two contributions, the signal contribution

$$S(x) = A \int_{-\infty}^{+\infty} Y(x - y)h'(y)\,dy = Ah(x)$$

and the noise contribution

$$N(x) = \int_{-\infty}^{+\infty} n(x - y)h'(y)\,dy$$

From the noise definition, $N(x)$ is a Gaussian random variable such that $E(N(x)) = 0$ and

$$E(N(x)^2) = \sigma_0^2 \int_{-\infty}^{+\infty} h'^2(y)\, dy$$

Let us look at the signal part. Assuming that x_0 is close to 0, we approximate $S(x_0)$, up to the second order, as

$$S(x_0) \simeq Ah(0) + x_0 Ah'(0)$$

Note that h is odd, and therefore $h(0) = 0$, which is equal to $Ax_0 h'(0)$. Since x_0 also satisfies $o'(x_0) = 0$, we can write

$$o'(x_0) = S(x_0) + N(x_0) \approx Ax_0 h'(0) + N(x_0) = 0$$

Therefore

$$x_0 \simeq -\frac{N(x_0)}{Ah'(0)}$$

The mean of x_0 is 0, and its variance $E(x_0^2)$ is given by

$$E(x_0^2) = \frac{\sigma_0^2}{A^2} \frac{(\int_{-\infty}^{+\infty} h'^2(y)\, dy)}{h'^2(0)}$$

The localization is defined as

$$\frac{1}{E(x_0^2)^{1/2}} = \frac{A}{\sigma_0} \frac{|h'(0)|}{(\int_{-\infty}^{+\infty} h'^2(y)\, dy)^{1/2}} = \frac{A}{\sigma_0} \Lambda(h)$$

Notice that both the detection and the localization criteria are the product of a term that is a property of the signal and the noise, A/σ_0, and a term that is a property of the operator only.

The product $\Sigma\Lambda$ can be considered as a measure of both criteria that has the nice property of amplitude and scale independence, as can be verified by replacing $h(x)$ by $h_\lambda(x) = \frac{1}{\lambda} h(\frac{x}{\lambda})$. Therefore

$$\Sigma\Lambda = \frac{\int_{-\infty}^{0} h(y)\, dy}{(\int_{-\infty}^{+\infty} h^2(y)\, dy)^{1/2}} \frac{|h'(0)|}{(\int_{-\infty}^{+\infty} h'^2(y)\, dy)^{1/2}} \tag{4.12}$$

Finding the odd function h that maximizes the product $\Sigma\Lambda$ can be achieved by the calculus of variations in a way that is similar to what was done in the previous section. We assume again that h is 0 outside of the interval $[-W, +W]$, where W is a constant defining the size of the impulse response h. We then maximize

$$\int_{-W}^{0} h^2(y)\, dy$$

subject to the constraints

$$\int_{-W}^{0} h(y)\, dy = c_1,$$

$$\int_{-W}^{0} h'^2(y)\, dy = c_2,$$

and

$$h'(0) = c_3$$

Applying the results of section 4.2.3, this is the same as maximizing

$$C(h) = \int_{-W}^{0} (h^2(y) + \lambda_1 h(y) + \lambda_2 h'^2(y))\, dy = \int_{-W}^{0} \Phi(y, h, h')\, dy$$

The corresponding Euler-Lagrange equation is

$$\Phi_h - \frac{d}{dy}\Phi_h' = 2h(y) + \lambda_1 - 2\lambda_2 h''(y) = 0 \qquad (4.13)$$

This differential equation has the solution

$$h(x) = -\frac{\lambda_1}{2}\left(1 - \frac{\cosh \alpha(x + W/2)}{\cosh \alpha W/2}\right) \quad \text{on } [-W, 0]$$

where $\alpha = \lambda_2^{-1/2}$.

In particular, when α approaches infinity, λ_2 approaches 0 and equation (4.13) reduces to equation (4.11). The value of $h(x)$ approaches a constant over the range $[-W, 0]$, the signal-to-noise ratio approaches 1, and the localization term increases without bound. This function which, as we saw previously, is the optimal matched filter for the step edge model given in equation (4.10), gives the best possible signal-to-noise ratio with arbitrarily good localization. What is wrong then? Well, as shown in Figure 4.14, it tends to exhibit many maxima in its response to noisy step edges. The left part of the figure shows a step edge with noise added to it. The signal-to-noise ratio is equal to 1. The right part of the figure shows the result of applying the optimal matched filter to this noisy edge; the extra maxima are quite obvious. These extra maxima should be considered erroneous. However, we did not consider the interaction of the response at several nearby points when we constructed our crite-

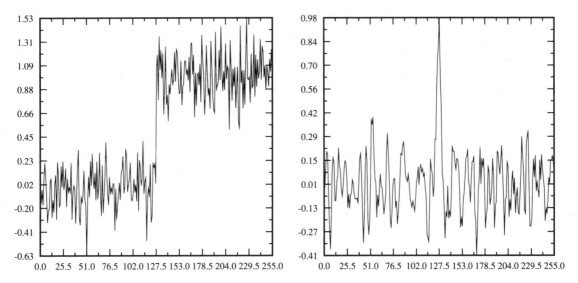

Figure 4.14 Problems with the matched filter (see text).

rion. This needs to be made explicit by adding a further constraint to the solution.

4.3.1.4 The uniqueness-of-response criterion

We need to add the requirement that h does not have "too many" responses to a single step edge in the vicinity of the step. In order to make this idea quantitative, we must obtain an expression for the distance between adjacent noise peaks in the output. We note that the mean distance between adjacent maxima in the output is twice the mean distance between adjacent zero-crossings in the derivative of the operator output. Rice [Ric45] tells us that the mean distance x_{ave} between the zero-crossings of a Gaussian random process obtained by filtering a white noise process with the impulse response $g(x)$ is equal to

$$x_{ave} = \pi \sqrt{-\frac{R_g(0)}{R_g''(0)}}$$

where $R_g(\tau) = \int_{-\infty}^{+\infty} g(x + \tau)g(x)\,dx$ is the autocorrelation function of the filtered noise. See problem 4 or the book by Papoulis [Pap65] for a proof of this formula.

Since $R_g''(\tau) = \int_{-\infty}^{+\infty} g''(x + \tau)g(x)\,dx$ and

$$R_g''(0) = \int_{-\infty}^{+\infty} g''(x)g(x)\,dx = \int_{-\infty}^{+\infty} g(x)d[g'(x)]$$

$$= [g(x)g'(x)]_{-\infty}^{+\infty} - \int_{-\infty}^{+\infty} g'^2(x)\,dx$$

assuming that g and g' are zero at infinity, we have $R_g''(0) = -\int_{-\infty}^{+\infty} g'^2(x)\,dx$, and

$$x_{ave} = \pi\left(\frac{\int_{-\infty}^{+\infty} g^2(x)\,dx}{\int_{-\infty}^{+\infty} g'^2(x)\,dx}\right)^{1/2}$$

In the case of edge detection, we are looking at maxima of the output of the convolution of the image intensity with the impulse response h or, equivalently, at zero-crossings of the convolution with h'. We thus have $g = h'$, and x_{ave} is the average distance between two extrema of $o(x)$. The average distance between two maxima of $o(x)$ is therefore equal to $2x_{ave}$. Therefore

$$x_{max} = 2x_{ave} = 2\pi\left(\frac{\int_{-\infty}^{+\infty} h'^2(x)\,dx}{\int_{-\infty}^{+\infty} h''^2(x)\,dx}\right)^{1/2} \tag{4.14}$$

4.3.2 Finding the optimal h

The optimal h can be found in several ways, depending on how we combine the three criteria. In all cases, the calculus of variations is used to derive the h that maximizes the chosen criterion. We will first discuss the original idea of Canny [Can83, Can86], which is illuminating, and then we will discuss two related approaches proposed by Deriche [Der87] and Spacek [Spa85].

4.3.2.1 *Canny's approach*

Canny maximizes the criterion $\Sigma\Lambda$ subject to the constraint $x_{max} = kW$, which states that the average maximum distance between two local maxima has to be some fraction of the spatial extent of the impulse response. From the beginning, therefore, the assumption is that this extent is finite, in marked contrast to Deriche's approach, which will be discussed next.

From the definition of equation (4.14), it can be seen that it adds only one constraint to the previous three:

$$\int_{-W}^{0} h''^2(y)\,dy = c_4$$

Using the same ideas, we find that we have to minimize

$$C(h) = \int_{-W}^{0} (h^2(y) + \lambda_1 h(y) + \lambda_2 h'^2(y) + \lambda_4 h''^2(y))\,dy$$

$$= \int_{-W}^{0} \Phi(y, h, h', h'')\,dy$$

The corresponding Euler-Lagrange equation is

$$\Phi_h - \frac{d}{dy}\Phi_{h'} + \frac{d^2}{dy^2}\Phi_{h''} = 0$$

This yields the following differential equation:

$$2h(x) - 2\lambda_2 h''(x) + 2\lambda_4 h''''(x) + \lambda_1 = 0$$

It can be shown [Can86] that the solution $h(x)$ of the differential equation is

$$h(x) = e^{-\alpha x}(a_1 \sin \omega x + a_2 \cos \omega x) + e^{\alpha x}(a_3 \sin \omega x + a_4 \cos \omega x) - \lambda_1/2$$

for x in $[-W, 0]$.

This is subject to the boundary conditions

$$h(0) = h(-W) = h'(-W) = 0$$

$$h'(0) = c_3$$

We have also added the condition that x_{max} is some fraction k of the operator length W:

$$x_{max} = kW$$

Then $a_1, a_2, a_3,$ and a_4 are easily computed as functions of $\alpha, \omega, c_3,$ and λ_1 [Can86]:

$$a_1 = -\frac{\lambda_1}{8(\omega^2 \sinh^2 \alpha - \alpha^2 \sin^2 \omega)} f_1(\alpha, \beta, \omega)$$

$$a_2 = -\frac{\lambda_1}{8(\omega^2 \sinh(\alpha)^2 - \alpha^2 \sin(\omega)^2)} f_2(\alpha, \beta, \omega)$$

with

$$f_1 = \alpha(\beta - \alpha)\sin 2\omega - \alpha\omega\cos 2\omega + (-2\omega^2\sinh\alpha$$

$$+ 2\alpha^2 e^{-\alpha})\sin\omega + 2\alpha\omega\sinh\alpha\cos\omega + \omega(\alpha + \beta)e^{-2\alpha} - \beta\omega$$

$$f_2 = \alpha(\beta - \alpha)\cos 2\omega + \alpha\omega\sin 2\omega - 2\alpha\omega\cosh\alpha\sin\omega$$

$$- 2\omega^2\sinh\alpha\cos\omega + 2\omega^2 e^{-\alpha}\sinh\alpha + \alpha(\alpha - \beta)$$

where $\beta = -\frac{2c_3}{\lambda_1}$. The values of a_3 and a_4 are obtained from a_1 and a_2, respectively, by changing the sign of α.

We therefore have a parameterization of h in terms of these four parameters. We still must find the values of the parameters that maximize the ratio of integrals that forms our criterion. It can be shown that this ratio is only a function of α, ω, and β. Therefore, the problem of finding the optimal filter has been reduced from an optimization problem in an infinite-dimensional space (the space of admissible functions h) to a nonlinear optimization problem in three variables α, ω, and β. Using constrained numerical optimization, Canny found that the largest value of k that could be obtained was about 3.64. The performance of the filter was then given by $\Sigma\Lambda = 1.12$. The corresponding values of α, β, and ω are

$$\alpha = 2.05220$$

$$\beta = 2.91540$$

$$\omega = 1.56939$$

which yield the following values for the coefficients a_i, $i = 1, \ldots 4$, and λ_1:

$$a_1 = .1486768717$$

$$a_2 = -.2087553476$$

$$a_3 = -1.244653939$$

$$a_4 = -.7912446531$$

$$\lambda_1 = -2$$

This optimal filter (shown in Figure 4.15) is close to the first derivative of a Gaussian

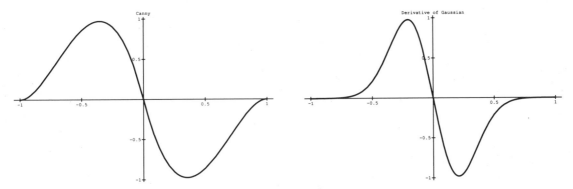

Figure 4.15 A comparison between the Canny operator and the first derivative of a Gaussian.

$$h(x) = -\frac{x}{\sigma^2} e^{-\frac{x^2}{2\sigma^2}}$$

Its performance indexes k and $\Sigma\Lambda$ are not very different (3.24 and 0.92, respectively) from the ones found by Canny.

4.3.2.2 Deriche's approach

For reasons to be described in section 4.4, Deriche was interested in impulse responses $h(x)$ with infinite support, and therefore he let W tend to infinity. Filters with such impulse responses are sometimes called IIR or infinite impulse response filters. Assuming without loss of generality that $\alpha \geq 0$, the condition $h(-\infty) = 0$ implies that $a_3 = a_4 = \lambda_1 = 0$. The other conditions imply that

$$a_2 = 0$$

$$a_1\omega = c_3$$

Therefore, if we allow IIR filters, the solution has a much simpler form:

$$h(x) = \begin{cases} a_1 e^{\alpha x} \sin \omega x & x < 0 \\ a_1 e^{-\alpha x} \sin \omega x & x \geq 0 \end{cases}$$

or

$$h(x) = a_1 e^{-\alpha |x|} \sin \omega x$$

More about this function can be found in problem 7.

We can easily compute the product $\Sigma\Lambda$ as a function of α and ω:

$$\Sigma\Lambda = \frac{2\alpha}{(\omega^2 + \alpha^2)^{1/2}}$$

Notice that it is only a function of the ratio $\omega/\alpha = t$:

$$\Sigma\Lambda = \frac{2}{(t^2 + 1)^{1/2}}$$

$\Sigma\Lambda$ is maximum and equal to 2 for $t = 0$. When we rewrite h as a function h_t of α and t as follows:

$$h_t(x) = c_3 e^{-\alpha|x|} \frac{\sin \alpha t x}{\alpha t}$$

we see that

$$\lim_{t \to 0} h_t(x) = c_3 x e^{-\alpha|x|}$$

It can be verified that this function is also a solution of the differential equation (4.13). We have obtained a function $h(x)$ of infinite spatial extent that yields a somewhat higher value for $\Sigma\Lambda$ than the Canny operator at the apparent cost of having to deal with an infinite impulse response. But see section 4.4.

4.3.2.3 Spacek's approach

Spacek very naturally extended Canny's ideas in another direction. Using the following expression giving the average distance between maxima of the filter output $o(x)$

$$x_{max}(h) = 2\pi \left(\frac{\int_{-\infty}^{+\infty} h'^2(x)\, dx}{\int_{-\infty}^{+\infty} h''^2(x)\, dx} \right)^{1/2}$$

he incorporated it into the criterion to be maximized. If we change scale, i.e., if we replace $h(x)$ by $h_\lambda(x) = \frac{1}{\lambda} h(\frac{x}{\lambda})$, x_{max} becomes

$$2\pi\lambda x_{max}(h)$$

Since the product $\Sigma(h)\Lambda(h)$ is invariant with respect to scale changes, a good candidate for the criterion is

$$C(h) = \Sigma(h)\Lambda(h)\frac{x_{max}(h)}{W}$$

Or, expressing this as a function of h and its derivatives, we have

$$C(h) = \frac{1}{W} \quad \frac{\int_{-W}^{0} h(x)\,dx}{(\int_{-W}^{0} h^2(x)\,dx)^{1/2}} \times \frac{|h'(0)|}{(\int_{-W}^{0} h''^2(x)\,dx)^{1/2}}$$

Using the same techniques as in section 4.3.1.4, we have

$$\Phi(x, h, h'') = h^2 + \lambda_1 h + \lambda_2 h''^2$$

The corresponding Euler-Lagrange equation is

$$2h(x) + \lambda_1 + 2\lambda_2 h''''(x) = 0$$

This yields the general solution

$$h(x) = (a_1 \sin \alpha x + a_2 \cos \alpha x)e^{\alpha x} + (a_3 \sin \alpha x + a_4 \cos \alpha x)e^{-\alpha x} - \lambda_1/2$$

where $a_1, a_2, a_3, a_4, \alpha$, and λ_1 are constants that are determined by the various boundary conditions and constraints that we have on h.

It is interesting to note that this solution for h is Canny's solution for $\alpha = \omega$. If we allow W to grow to infinity, the solution becomes

$$h(x) = ae^{\alpha x} \sin \alpha x$$

This is Deriche's solution for $\alpha = \omega$. For $W = 1$, Spacek found the following values:

$$a_1 = -13.3816 \qquad a_2 = 2.7953$$

$$a_3 = 0.0542 \qquad a_4 = -3.7953$$

$$\alpha = 1 \qquad \lambda_1 = -2$$

4.3.2.4 Comparing the performances of the operators

In order to compare the performances of the different operators, we have computed the values of Σ, Λ, and x_{max} for the Canny, Deriche, and Spacek operators and the first derivative of a Gaussian (FDG). Analytic expressions can be obtained for the Deriche and FDG filters as shown in table 4.2. We need to define W for an IIR filter $h(x)$ since, in particular,

Table 4.2 The performance indexes of the four filters described in the text.

	Canny	FDG	Deriche	Spacek
Σ	.6093694443	$\sqrt{\frac{2\sigma}{\sqrt{\pi}}}$	$\sqrt{\frac{2}{\alpha}}$	.6039685433
Λ	1.838076985	$\frac{2}{\sqrt{3\sigma\sqrt{\pi}}}$	$\sqrt{2\alpha}$	1.933738156
$\Sigma\Lambda$	1.120067951	$\sqrt{\frac{8}{3\pi}} = .9213177312$	2	1.167917017
x_{max}	1.200000207	$2\pi\sigma\sqrt{\frac{2}{5}}$	$\frac{2\pi}{\sqrt{5}\alpha}$	1.148754323
W	.4235557861	$\sigma\frac{\sqrt{15}}{2}$	$\frac{\sqrt{3}}{\alpha}$	.4086727170
k	2.833157395	$\frac{4\pi}{5}\sqrt{\frac{2}{3}} = 2.052079727$	$\frac{2\pi}{\sqrt{15}} = 1.622311471$	2.810939599
$\Sigma\Lambda k$	3.173328798	1.890617438	3.244622942	3.282944191

the FDG and Deriche filters are of this type. A possible way is to define W through equation (4.3)[10]:

$$W = \sqrt{\frac{\int_{-\infty}^{0} x^2 h^2(x)\, dx}{\int_{-\infty}^{0} h^2(x)\, dx}}$$

The value of the performance index $k = x_{max}/W$ is thus always well defined. This is the definition that we have used in the table. Notice that, because of that definition, W is not equal to 1 for the Canny and Spacek filters. From the table, we see that if we consider only the criterion $\Sigma\Lambda$, the operators can be ranked from best to worst as Deriche, Spacek, Canny, and FDG. If we consider the product $\Sigma\Lambda k$, then the order becomes Spacek, Deriche, Canny, and FDG.

4.4   Discrete implementations

Until now we have been working in the continuous domain. In practice we work with discrete signals and the convolution operations are discrete convolutions. For good introductions to discrete signal processing see

---

10. We have $x_m = \int_{-\infty}^{+\infty} x h^2(x)\, dx = 0$ since $h^2(x)$ is an even function.

the books by Oppenheim and Schafer and by Gold and Rabiner [OS75, GR78]. Given an impulse response $h(n)$ and an input sequence $i(n)$, the output sequence $o(n)$ is the discrete convolution $h \otimes i(n)$ of h and i:

$$o(n) = \sum_k i(k)h(n - k) = \sum_k h(k)i(n - k) \qquad (4.15)$$

The sequence h can be finite or infinite. In the second case, care has to be taken to insure the convergence of equation (4.15). The world of impulse responses is therefore divided into two classes: finite impulse responses (FIR) and infinite impulse responses (IIR).

When implementing convolutions with FIR filters, one has several possibilities. The first is to directly apply equation (4.15). If the length of h is N, to compute one output point we need to perform N multiplications and $N - 1$ additions. Another possibility is to use the Fourier transform. If we assume that the length P of the input sequence is larger than N, this technique requires $k \log_2 P$ operations per output point, where the constant k depends on the specific implementation. From this it looks as if dealing with IIR filters is an impossible task unless we truncate the IIR so that it becomes finite. It is not so if we deal with recursive filtering techniques, as we will show next.

4.4.1 Recursive systems

Suppose we have two finite sequences $a(n)$ and $b(n)$ of lengths p and q, respectively. Given an input sequence $i(n)$, let us compute the output sequence $o(n)$ as

$$o(n) = \sum_{k=0}^{p-1} a(k)i(n - k) - \sum_{l=1}^{q} b(l)o(n - l) \qquad (4.16)$$

i.e., the ouput at point n is a linear combination of the previous p input points and the previous q output points.[11] The corresponding system

---

11. Such a system is called *causal*. Noncausal systems are described by the equation

$$o(n) = \sum_{k=0}^{p-1} a(k)i(n + k) - \sum_{l=1}^{q} b(l)o(n + l)$$

is linear and stationary and therefore it is characterized by an impulse response $h(n)$:

$$o(n) = \sum_p h(k)i(n-k)$$

In the case where the sequence $b(n)$ is zero, equation (4.16) reduces to equation (4.15), with $h(n) = a(n)$. If the sequence b is nonzero, then h is infinite [OS75]. Therefore, equation (4.16) provides a way of computing the convolution of an input sequence $i(n)$ with an IIR using a finite number of operations per output point ($p + q$ multiplications and $p + q - 1$ additions). So, given an IIR $h(n)$, if its effect on an input sequence $i(n)$ can be represented as equation (4.16), and if $p + q$ is less than N (the length of the truncated version of $h(n)$ that yields a good FIR approximation to it), then we have a clear way to implement the convolution with h. The problem is that not all convolutions with a sequence $h(n)$ can be represented as equation (4.16). Fortunately, it is true in the case of Deriche filter.

In order to study recursive systems[12], the reader must be familiar with the notion of the z-transform of a sequence, which is also used in the study of the complexity of algorithms as the notion of generative sequences [Knu68]. For more details, the reader is referred to, for example, chapter 2 of the book by Oppenheim and Schafer [OS75]. If we take the z-transform of both sides of equation (4.16), we obtain

$$O(z) = I(z) \sum_{k=0}^{p-1} a(k)z^{-k} - O(z) \sum_{l=1}^{q} b(l)z^{-l}$$

Therefore

$$O(z) = \frac{\sum_{k=0}^{p-1} a(k)z^{-k}}{1 + \sum_{l=1}^{q} b(l)z^{-l}} I(z) \tag{4.17}$$

The key property of a recursive system, which is apparent from this equation, is that the ratio of the z-transforms of the output and the input is a rational function of z. Note also that, given equation (4.17), it is easy to write the recursive relationship (4.16) between the input and output sequences just by reading the coefficients of the rational function.

---

12. The word *recursive* stems from the fact that the output in equation (4.16) is computed as a linear combination of some of its previous values.

4.4.2   The recursive implementation of Deriche's filter

Let us consider the recursive implementation of Deriche's filter defined by the impulse response

$$h(n) = sne^{-\alpha|n|}$$

Let us split $h(n)$ into two parts

$$h(n) = h_+(n) + h_-(n)$$

where

$$h_+(n) = \begin{cases} sne^{-\alpha n} & n \geq 0 \\ 0 & n < 0 \end{cases}$$

and

$$h_-(n) = \begin{cases} 0 & n > 0 \\ sne^{\alpha n} & n \leq 0 \end{cases}$$

Because the z-transform is a linear operation, the z-transform $H(z)$ of $h(n)$ is the sum of the z-transform $H_+(z)$ of $h_+(n)$ and $H_-(z)$ of $h_-(n)$. Let us compute both:

$$H_+(z) = s \sum_{n=0}^{+\infty} ne^{-\alpha n}z^{-n} = sz \sum_{n=0}^{+\infty} ne^{-\alpha n}z^{-n-1} = szG_+(z)$$

Clearly

$$G_+(z) = -\frac{d}{dz}K_+(z)$$

where

$$K_+(z) = \sum_{n=0}^{+\infty} e^{-\alpha n}z^{-n} = \frac{1}{1 - e^{-\alpha}z^{-1}}$$

The series is convergent for $|z| > e^{-\alpha}$. Finally

$$H_+(z) = \frac{se^{-\alpha}z^{-1}}{(1 - e^{-\alpha}z^{-1})^2}$$

This describes a causal system with a double pole at $e^{-\alpha}$. Similarly we find that

$$H_-(z) = -\frac{se^{-\alpha}z}{(1 - e^{-\alpha}z)^2}$$

This corresponds to a noncausal system with a double pole at e^{α}. The region of convergence is $|z| < e^{\alpha}$.

From these expressions we can deduce the two corresponding recursive filters (see equation (4.17)):

$$o_+(n) = i(n-1) - b_1 o_+(n-1) - b_2 o_+(n-2)$$

$$o_-(n) = -i(n+1) - b_1 o_-(n+1) - b_2 o_-(n+2)$$

where the final output $o(n)$ is given by

$$o(n) = a(o_+(n) + o_-(n))$$

and the constants a, b_1, and b_2 have the following values:

$$a = se^{-\alpha}$$

$$b_1 = -2e^{-\alpha}$$

$$b_2 = e^{-2\alpha}$$

From this it is seen that, for the infinite impulse response $h(n)$, the result of the convolution can be computed with five multiplications and five additions for any value of α.

4.5 Two-dimensional edge detection by the maxima of the gradient magnitude

The approaches of Canny, Deriche, and Spacek all yield an impulse response that looks very much like the derivative of a smoothing function. In fact, if we compute the primitives of these impulse responses, we find very similar smoothing functions as shown in figure 4.16. Considering these functions will help us understand the two-dimensional problem in the case where we want to detect an edge in a way similar to the approach we have developed for one dimension.

4.5.1 Separable and isotropic impulse responses

In two dimensions, an edge is defined not only by its position, but also by its direction. The two-dimensional model of a step edge is shown in figure 4.17. Note that in this figure the image intensity is constant along

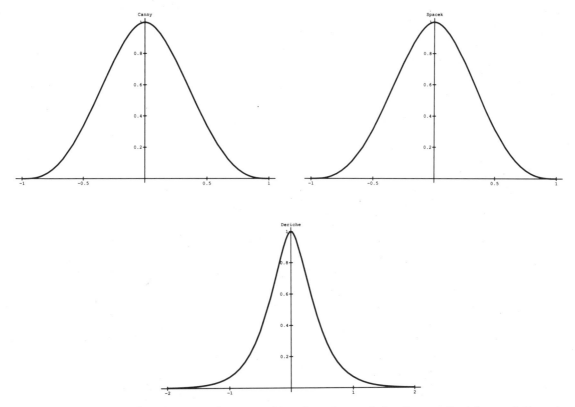

Figure 4.16 The smoothing functions of the Canny, Deriche, and Spacek filters.

the contour. We will come back to this point in the next section. It might be possible to extend the analysis we have carried out in section 4.3 to this case, but this appears to be a bit difficult analytically. Another possibility is to decide that edges will be detected as maxima of the magnitude of the gradient of the smoothed image. Thus we consider a smoothed version F of the image f, which is obtained by convolving it with a smoothing impulse response $K(x, y)$:

$$F(x, y) = f \otimes K(x, y)$$

If we consider the primitive $k(x)$ of the impulse responses $h(x)$ derived in the previous sections, a possible choice for K is $K(x, y) =$

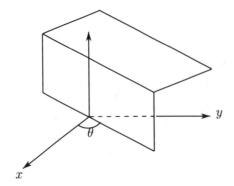

Figure 4.17 A two-dimensional constant-intensity step edge.

$k(x)k(y)$. Since $h(x) = \frac{d}{dx}k(x)$, by applying the convolution theorem to $f \otimes K(x, y)$ we have

$$\frac{\partial}{\partial x}(f \otimes K(x, y)) = f \otimes h(x)k(y)$$

$$\frac{\partial}{\partial y}(f \otimes K(x, y)) = f \otimes k(x)h(y)$$

From this it is clear that the gradient of F can be computed by convolving the rows (the columns, respectively) of f with those of h and k. The advantage of this approach is that the filtering operations required to compute the gradient of the smoothed image are separable (i.e., rows, columns), and therefore one-dimensional, which can be extremely efficient in terms of computation. The disadvantage is that the smoothing is nonisotropic: The directions 45 degrees and 135 degrees undergo more smoothing than 0 degrees and 90 degrees, and it is expected that edges in these directions will be detected more accurately than in others, the worst being the cases of 45 degrees and 135 degrees.

In order to see this better, let us assume that f is one-dimensional, i.e., $f(x, y) \equiv f(x)$. This implies[13] that

---

13. We assume that k is normalized so that $\int k(x)\, dx = 1$.

$$\begin{cases} \frac{\partial}{\partial x}(f \otimes K(x,y)) = f \otimes h(x) \\ \frac{\partial}{\partial y}(f \otimes K(x,y)) = 0 \end{cases}$$

The only nonzero component of the gradient of F is thus obtained by convolving f with h. Let us then suppose that f is rotated by 45 degrees, i.e., $f(x,y) \equiv f(x + y)$. The partial derivative in that direction is the projection of the gradient in that direction, and therefore is proportional to $(\frac{\partial}{\partial x} + \frac{\partial}{\partial y})f \otimes K(x,y)$:

$$f(x,y) \otimes [h(x)k(y) + k(x)h(y)]$$

Applying the change of variable $u = x + y$ and $v = x$, this is the same as

$$f(u) \otimes [h(v)k(u - v) + h(u - v)k(v)]$$

The equivalent impulse response in u is

$$\int (h(v)k(u - v) + h(u - v)k(v))\,dv = 2h \otimes k(u)$$

The result is proportional to

$$(f \otimes k) \otimes h(u)$$

The only nonzero component of the gradient of F is thus obtained by first smoothing f with k and then convolving the result with h. Therefore f is subjected to more smoothing in the 45 degrees direction than in the 0 degrees or 90 degrees directions (the extra smoothing corresponding to the convolution with k).

In order to alleviate this problem, we can take K to be isotropic: $K(x,y) \equiv k(r), (r = \sqrt{x^2 + y^2})$. The gradient is given by

$$\frac{\partial}{\partial x}(f \otimes k(r)) = f \otimes h(r)\frac{x}{r}$$

$$\frac{\partial}{\partial y}(f \otimes k(r)) = f \otimes h(r)\frac{y}{r}$$

The partial derivative in the direction θ is given by

$$f \otimes \frac{h(r)}{r}(x \cos \theta + y \sin \theta)$$

Suppose now that f is only a function in the direction $\theta : f(x, y) \equiv f(x \cos \theta + y \sin \theta)$. By applying the change of variable $u = x \cos \theta + y \sin \theta$ and $v = -x \sin \theta + y \cos \theta$, we obtain

$$f(u) \otimes \frac{h(\rho)}{\rho} u \quad \text{where } \rho = \sqrt{u^2 + v^2}$$

The equivalent impulse response, a function of u, is

$$u \int \frac{h(\rho)}{\rho} dv$$

which is in general different from $h(u)$. Therefore we still have the same problem as in the separable case: An edge is not detected by convolving the intensity distribution perpendicular to its direction with h. The difference is that the error is uniformly distributed in all directions. From an implementation standpoint, due to the simplicity of separable convolutions, the first solution appears more attractive.

4.5.2 Finding edge pixels

Having computed the smoothed gradient at each pixel in the image, potential edge pixels are selected by choosing those that are local maxima of the gradient magnitude in the direction of the gradient. This technique is called *nonmaxima suppression*. We assume that at an edge, the gradient **g** of F, is normal to the edge, and that its magnitude there reaches a local maximum along a cross-section of the smoothed intensity image taken along its direction. This is equivalent to saying that an edge will be detected at zero-crossings of the second derivative $D_{\mathbf{g}}^2 F$ of the smoothed intensity F in the direction of the gradient. $D_{\mathbf{g}}^2 F$ is defined as a function of F by equation (4.8).

It is worthwhile to note that this definition of an edge point does not necessarily imply that **g** is parallel to the normal of the edge curve. In order to see this, we notice that the edge curve (c) is defined by the equation

$$e(x, y) = \mathbf{g}^T \mathbf{H} \mathbf{g} = 0 \tag{4.18}$$

Therefore its normal is parallel to the vector ∇e, which is found to be equal to

$$\nabla e = (2\mathbf{H}^2 + \mathbf{R})\mathbf{g} \qquad\qquad (4.19)$$

where

$$\mathbf{R} = \begin{bmatrix} (\mathbf{H}_x\mathbf{g})^T \\ (\mathbf{H}_y\mathbf{g})^T \end{bmatrix}, \quad \mathbf{H}_x = \begin{bmatrix} F_{x^3} & F_{x^2y} \\ F_{x^2y} & F_{xy^2} \end{bmatrix}$$

is the partial derivative of the Hessian $\mathbf{H}$ with respect to x and $\mathbf{H}_y$ its derivative with respect to y.

There is no reason why the vector defined by equation (4.19) should be parallel to $\mathbf{g}$. In fact it is fairly easy to characterize those image curves that satisfy the property that their normals are parallel to the image gradient at every point. Consider figure 4.18, in which we have represented the image curve (c) in the xy-plane and the image surface (Σ) of equation $z = F(x, y)$. The curve (c) is the parallel projection of a curve (C) on the intensity surface along the z-direction. Let m be a point of (c), and let M be the corresponding point of (C). Let $\mathbf{G}$ (see section 4.1.2.1) be the gradient of the image intensity surface at M, $\mathbf{T}$ the unit vector tangent to (C), $\mathbf{t}$ the unit vector tangent to (c), and $\mathbf{g}$ the projection of $\mathbf{G}$. Since $\mathbf{G}$ is normal to the intensity surface and $\mathbf{T}$ is tangent to a curve on this surface, we have

$$\mathbf{T} \cdot \mathbf{G} = g_x T_x + g_y T_y - T_z = 0 \qquad\qquad (4.20)$$

But since $\mathbf{t}\sqrt{T_x^2 + T_y^2} = [T_x, T_y]^T$, we also have

$$(\mathbf{t} \cdot \mathbf{g})\sqrt{T_x^2 + T_y^2} = g_x T_x + g_y T_y$$

which is equal to T_z (equation (4.20)). Therefore $\mathbf{t} \cdot \mathbf{g} = 0$ is equivalent to $T_z = 0$, i.e., the curve (C) must be the intersection of the image intensity surface with a plane of constant z. This means that the intensity does not vary along (c), whose equation is therefore $F(x, y) = constant$. In practice, it is often the case that this condition is satisfied even though there may be cases where it is not.

If this is true, then, as shown in figure 4.19, it is easy to deduce a value for the curvature κ of the contour considered. Indeed, if we consider the unit normal $\mathbf{n} = \dfrac{\mathbf{g}}{\|\mathbf{g}\|}$ and the unit tangent $\mathbf{t} = \dfrac{\mathbf{g}_\top}{\|\mathbf{g}_\top\|}$, we have the following relation:

$$\mathbf{t} \cdot \mathbf{g} = 0$$

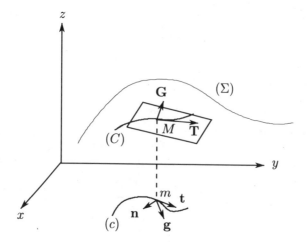

Figure 4.18   In order for **g** to be parallel to the normal **n** to (c), (C) has to be a special curve on (Σ).

Differentiating this expression with respect to the arclength s of the edge curve and using the Frenet formula (see appendix C), we obtain

$$\kappa(\mathbf{n} \cdot \mathbf{g}) + \mathbf{t}^T \mathbf{H}\mathbf{t} = 0$$

since $\frac{d\mathbf{g}}{ds} = \frac{\partial \mathbf{g}}{\partial x}\frac{dx}{ds} + \frac{\partial \mathbf{g}}{\partial y}\frac{dy}{ds} = \mathbf{H}\mathbf{t}$. Using equation (4.9), this yields

$$\kappa = -\frac{\mathbf{g}_T^T \mathbf{H}\mathbf{g}_T}{\|\mathbf{g}\|^3} = \frac{2F_x F_y F_{xy} - F_{x^2}F_y^2 - F_{y^2}F_x^2}{(F_x^2 + F_y^2)^{3/2}}$$

But because $D_{\mathbf{g}}^2 F = 0$, equation (4.8) yields

$$2F_x F_y F_{xy} = -F_x^2 F_{x^2} - F_y^2 F_{y^2}$$

which leads to

$$\kappa = -\frac{F_{x^2} + F_{y^2}}{(F_x^2 + F_y^2)^{1/2}} = -\frac{\nabla^2 F}{\|\mathbf{g}\|} \tag{4.21}$$

Equation (4.21) yields the curvature of the edge curve as a function of the image intensities. If the hypothesis that the smoothed image intensity is constant along the edge curve is not true, then the computation is more involved (see problem 5).

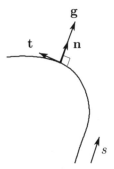

Figure 4.19 The gradient is normal to the edge, and its magnitude is maximum in that direction.

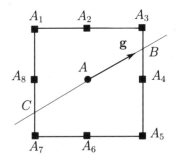

Figure 4.20 Checking whether pixel A is a local maximum of the magnitude of the gradient in the direction of the gradient.

When dealing with discrete images, the situation is as in figure 4.20: In order to decide whether pixel A is a local maximum of the gradient norm in the direction of the gradient $\mathbf{g}$, we have to do two things:

1. Decide on the size of the neighborhood of A within which we wish it to be a maximum.

2. Interpolate the gradient values that are known only at the pixels, since the direction of the gradient does not necessarily fall on real pixels.

In practice, the neighborhood is usually taken to be the 3×3 neighborhood of pixel A, and gradient values are linearly interpolated. For example, in figure 4.20 the gradient norm at pixel A is compared to the gradient norms at points B and C where they have been computed by

Local Maxima. $\alpha = 1.414$

Local Maxima. $\alpha = 1.$

Local Maxima. $\alpha = .75$

Local Maxima. $\alpha = .5$

Figure 4.21 The Deriche operator: local maxima for various scales.

linearly interpolating between the values at pixels A_3 and A_4 for B and between those at pixels A_7 and A_8 for C. Pixel A is marked as an edge pixel only if the value at A is strictly greater than the values at B and C. The result of this operation is a binary image where, for example, black pixels indicate an edge.

In figure 4.21 we show results of the Deriche edge detector applied to a variety of images and with different values of the parameter α controlling the width of the impulse response. It is clear from these results that too many edge points are being detected, especially in regions where the contrast is low. In this respect, the situation is analogous to that of figure 4.11. If we want to cut down on the number of edge pixels, we must add some thresholding operation. Thresholding is a plague that occurs in many areas in engineering, but to our knowledge it is unavoidable and must be tackled with courage. Here the idea is to keep only the edge pixels for which the gradient norm is above some threshold T. If we set T too low, then too many pixels are still present, and if we set it too high, then connected chains of edge pixels start breaking into smaller chains, which is highly undesirable (figure 4.22).

A threshold of 15 and $\alpha = 1$ A threshold of 5 and $\alpha = 1$

Figure 4.22 The difficulty of choosing the right threshold.

Figure 4.23   Hysteresis thresholding for the Deriche operator ($\alpha = 1$, $T_2 = 5$, $T_1 = 15$).

The basic question is this: How do we choose T? There is no good answer to this question, and the choice of T must be guided by the application and the lighting conditions of the scene. A variant of this thresholding idea has been introduced by Canny [Can83]. It is called *hysteresis thresholding*, and its purpose to keep the edge pixels connected as much as possible. To achieve this goal, we use two thresholds T_1 and T_2 with $T_2 < T_1$. If we think of a chain of connected edge pixels as a whole, then if for one pixel in the chain the gradient norm is higher than T_1, we will keep all pixels in the chain with a gradient norm larger than the lower threshold T_2. The result of this operation is shown in figure 4.23, which is to be compared with results of figure 4.22.

4.6   More references

The approach followed by Canny of using an edge model and of minimizing a criterion in order to find the "best" filter can be tracked further in the past, for example to Modestino and Fries [Mod77], who also proposed a recursive implementation of their filter, and to Shanmugam, Dickey, and Green [SDG79]. An interesting variation on this theme can be found in the work of Shen and Castan [SC92]. An extension of these ideas to the detection of three-dimensional edges can be found in the article by Monga, Deriche, and Rocchisani [MDR91]. Another approach, very different from the ones presented in this chapter, considers the problem of finding edge curves in an image as one of finding sequences of connected pixels maximizing some criterion defined on the discrete image considered as a graph. These curves are then found using either heuristic search techniques such as the A^* algorithm [Mar72] or dynamic programming (see chapter 6) [Mon71]. These methods can also be extended to take into account sophisticated statistical models as proposed by Basseville [BEG81, Bas81].

Variants of the idea of smoothing the data by approximation, or surface-fitting, which was presented in section 4.2.4.1, can also be found in the original paper by Hueckel [Hue71] and in a paper by Nalwa and Binford [Nal86]. Yet another very different approach is to use the so-called Hough transform [Hou62] to detect edge lines as parameterized curves [Dud72, KBS75] (see also chapter 11). Finally, there are three excellent books, one by Rosenfeld and Kak [RK82], one by Martin Levine [Lev85], and one by Anil Jain [Jai89], which cover the basic issues of image processing, including edge detection.

4.7 Problems

1. In this problem we show that the solution to the discrete smoothing problem (see section 4.2.4) is a cubic spline. Given some measurements f_k, we look for a C^2 function $S(x)$ that minimizes the following criterion:

$$C(S) = \sum_k (f_k - S(x_k))^2 + \lambda \int S''(x)^2 \, dx \qquad (4.22)$$

a. Show that the criterion (4.22) is a convex functional, i.e., that

$$C(\alpha S_1 + (1 - \alpha)S_2) \leq \alpha C(S_1) + (1 - \alpha)C(S_2)$$

for all functions S_1 and S_2, and $0 \leq \alpha \leq 1$.

b. Show that (4.22) can be written as

$$\int [\lambda S''(x)^2 + (S(x) - f(x))^2 \sum_k \delta(x - x_k)] \, dx$$

and that the corresponding Euler-Lagrange equation is

$$\lambda S^{(4)}(x) + S(x) \sum_k \delta(x - x_k) = \sum_k f_k \delta(x - x_k)$$

c. Since the criterion C is convex, the minimum of criterion (4.22) is unique. We will now show that, if the x_k are evenly spaced, S can be determined in terms of the f_k by a convolution for infinite or periodic sequences. Let $S(x) = R \otimes f(x)$. Since we know f only at the points x_k, we can take $f(x) = \sum_k f_k \delta(x - x_k)$. Show that the coefficient of f_k in the Lagrange-Euler equation is

$$\lambda R^{(4)}(x - x_k) + \sum_l R(x_l - x_k) \delta(x - x_l) - \delta(x - x_k) \tag{4.23}$$

d. Show that if the x_k are not evenly spaced these equations are inconsistent and that if they are evenly spaced they reduce to the following equation:

$$\lambda R^{(4)}(x) + \sum_l R(x_l) \delta(x - x_l) - \delta(x) = 0 \tag{4.24}$$

e. We will now show that the solutions to equation (4.24) correspond to cubic splines "stitched" together at the points x_k. Let $R_k(x)$ denote the solution in the range $x_k \leq x \leq x_{k+1}$ and write $R_k(x) = \alpha_k x^3 + \beta_k x^2 + \gamma_k x + \delta_k$. Write three algebraic conditions on the coefficients $\alpha_k, \beta_k, \gamma_k, \delta_k, \alpha_{k-1}, \beta_{k-1}, \gamma_{k-1}$, and δ_{k-1} expressing the fact that $R(x)$ is C^2 at x_k.

f. Show that $R^{(3)}(x)$ has a discontinuity of $-\frac{R(x_k)}{\lambda}$ at x_k. *Hint:* Integrate equation (4.24), and find a simple relationship between α_k and α_{k-1}.

g. Use the results of questions e and f to determine three first-order recursive relationships between β_k and β_{k-1}, γ_k and γ_{k-1}, and δ_k and δ_{k-1}.

2. Work out the minimization problem in the Haralick edge detector.

3. Let $n(x)$ be a stationary process with autocorrelation function $\Lambda_n(\tau) = E(n(x)n(x+\tau))$. If we convolve n with an impulse response $h(x)$, we obtain a new random process $m(x) = n \otimes h(x)$. Show that the autocorrelation $\Lambda_m(\tau)$ of m is equal to

$$\Lambda_n \otimes g(\tau)$$

where $g(\tau) = h \otimes h_-(\tau)$, and $h_-(\tau) = h(-\tau)$.

4. In this problem, inspired by Perona and Malik [PM90], we prove the result of Rice about the mean distance between zero-crossings of a stationary Gaussian random process (see section 4.3.1.4). Let $n(x)$ be a white stationary Gaussian process and $f(x)$ be a twice-differentiable impulse response. We will consider the filtered Gaussian process $n_f(x) = f \otimes n(x)$. We are going to compute the average spacing x_{ave} between positive-derivative zero-crossings of $n_f(x)$.

   a. A necessary and sufficient condition for x to be a positive-derivative zero of n_f is that $n_f(x) = 0$ and $n'_f(x) > 0$. Considering the function $H(n_f(x))$ and its derivative (H is the Heaviside function), build a function $s(x)$ that is infinite at the positive-derivative zeros of n_f and zero elsewhere.

   b. The quantity we want to compute is the reciprocal of the average value of $s(x)$. Using standard properties of the Fourier transform, show that

   $$E(s) = \frac{1}{4\pi^2} \int\int \frac{\partial E(e^{2\pi i(pn_f + qn'_f)})}{\partial q} \, dp\, dq$$

   c. Taking the density probability of n equal to $e^{-\frac{1}{2}n^2(t)dt}$, and letting $k = 2i\pi$, show that

   $$E(e^{2\pi i(pn_f + qn'_f)})$$

   $$= \int e^{-\frac{1}{2}\int [(n(t) - k[pf(x-t) + qf'(x-t)])^2 - k^2[pf(x-t) + qf'(x-t)]^2]dt} \, dn$$

   d. Show that this is equal to

   $$e^{\frac{1}{2}k^2(p^2 R_f(0) - q^2 R''_f(0))}$$

e. Conclude that

$$\frac{1}{E(s)} = 2\pi \sqrt{-\frac{R_f(0)}{R_f''(0)}}$$

5. Compute the curvature of the edge curve defined by equation (4.18) as a function of the smoothed intensity function $F(x, y)$ and its partial derivatives. Show that the result depends on the partial derivatives of order up to 4. *Hint*: Apply the results of appendix C.

6. Do the same exercise as described in the previous problem for the edge curve obtained by the Marr-Hildreth edge detector (equation 4.5). *Hint*: Same as for the previous problem.

7. a. Prove equation (4.7).

   b. Compute the primitive $g(x)$ of the function $h(x) = ae^{-\alpha|x|}\sin x\omega$ and verify that for $\alpha = \omega = \frac{\mu}{\sqrt{2}}$ it is the optimal smoothing of the previous question.

   c. Derive the recursive implementation of the IIR filter with impulse response $g(n), n \in Z$.

8. In this problem we will show that the edge curves detected by the Canny-Deriche-Spacek technique are the projections along the z-axis on the image plane of a very special type of curves drawn on the intensity surface (Σ) of equation $-f(x, y) + z = 0$. Consider figure 4.24, in which we have represented the tangent plane T_M to (Σ) at M, the gradient $\mathbf{G} = [-f_x, -f_y, 1]^T$, and the unit vector $\mathbf{k}$ parallel to the z-axis. To each line l of T_M going through M we associate its angle α, defined as modulo π, with the z-axis.

   a. Show that α lies between 0 and π and reaches a maximum when l is parallel to the vector $\mathbf{p} = \mathbf{G} \wedge (\mathbf{G} \wedge \mathbf{k})$. This direction is called the *direction of steepest descent* at M.

   b. Show that $\cos \alpha = -\frac{\|\mathbf{g}\|}{\sqrt{1+\|\mathbf{g}\|^2}}$ where $\mathbf{g} = [f_x, f_y]^T$.

   c. Now we want to find those points of the image intensity surface for which the function $r(x, y) \equiv \cos \alpha$ is minimal in the direction of the steepest descent. A necessary condition for this (see appendix C) is that the Lie derivative $L_\mathbf{p} r = 0$. Show that $L_\mathbf{p} r$ is proportional to $\mathbf{g}^T \mathbf{H} \mathbf{g}$ where $\mathbf{H}$ is the Hessian of $f(x, y)$, and that

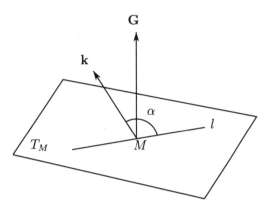

Figure 4.24 The tangent plane T_M to the intensity surface (Σ).

therefore the edge curves detected by the Canny-Deriche-Spacek method are projections along the z-axis in the image plane of curves on the image intensity surface such that the angle of steepest descent is extremal in the direction of steepest descent.

5 Representing Geometric Primitives and Their Uncertainty

In this chapter we will study in detail how to represent some fundamental geometric primitives. A *representation* is a mapping from the set of geometric primitives under study to a set of numerical parameters, a subset of R^n. The variable n is the dimension of the representation. Given the problem of choosing among several representations of a set of geometric primitives, it is important to ask the following questions [MK78, BR78]:

1. **Is the representation unique?** Does every representable geometric primitive have a unique representation? This is equivalent to saying that the previous mapping is one-to-one.

2. **Is the representation complete?** In other words, does every geometric primitive admit a representation?

3. **Is the representation minimal?** This means that the number of parameters used in the representation is minimal. This number is characteristic of the set of geometric primitives and is called its *dimension*. It is important to note that that there exist nonminimal representations whose dimensions are larger than the dimension of the set of geometric primitives.[1]

4. **Is the representation smooth?** This means that, if a geometric primitive varies smoothly, then its representation also varies smoothly.

---

1. There may also exist representations whose dimensions are smaller than the dimension of the set of geometric primitives. We exclude those from our consideration because they do not allow for the reconstruction of the primitives.

Of course, we do not always insist on having representations that satisfy all these requirements. It depends on the application.

There is a very natural way of thinking about these questions. Mathematically speaking, the relevant notion is that of a *manifold*. Rather than rediscovering this notion for every case, we will give the general definition. Interestingly enough, this notion, which is forced upon us even by examples as simple as projective points in the plane, implies that we abandon in general the simple idea of representing a set of geometric primitives by a single mapping into a set of parameters. We need several mappings and, as a consequence, a single primitive has several representations. The key idea of manifolds is that all those representations are smoothly related.

5.1   How to read this chapter

This chapter is organized into two almost independent sets of sections. In sections 5.2 to 5.5 we discuss the problems of representations, while in section 5.6 we discuss the problem of computing the uncertainty of parameters that are nonlinear functions, either explicit or implicit, of some measurements. This problem occurs often in many applications of computer vision and can be considered of great practical importance. In the case where the functions of the measurements are explicitly known, the result is summarized in equation (5.28), which gives the covariance matrix of the parameters as a function of the Jacobian matrix and the covariance matrix of the measurements. We also give a deterministic interpretation of this result that avoids the need for introducing probabilities, which we believe to be unnatural most of the time. This can be skipped on the first reading. In the frequent case where the parameters are obtained by minimizing some criterion function, the Jacobian matrix is not directly available but can be obtained by applying the implicit functions theorem. Section 5.6.4 gives an example of the application of this result to a very common practical problem and requires only some simple results from section 5.3.3.2.

The first four sections of the chapter fill two different needs. The first need is to establish a solid theoretical basis for the representation of geometric primitives such as points, lines, planes, orientations, directions, and displacements, which are routinely manipulated in computer vision problems. The second need is to give us tools for chapters 6, 8, and 11. The reader who is interested only in the tools can read the definition of a manifold in section 5.2, section 5.3.3 on the representation of 2-D lines, section 5.4.3 on the representation of planes, section 5.4.4 on the representation of 3-D lines, section 5.5.2 on quaternions, and section 5.5.4 on exponentials of antisymmetric matrices.

5.2 Manifolds

Suppose we are given a set X of primitives (see figure 5.1). It is convenient to think of those primitives as points in R^n forming a subset of that space. We assume that X is such that there exists a family U_i of open sets of R^n covering X and such that, for each U_i, there exists a one-to-one mapping φ_i from $U_i \cap X$ into R^d. The maps φ_i should be thought of as the representations of the set of primitives X. They must satisfy the following *coherence condition:*

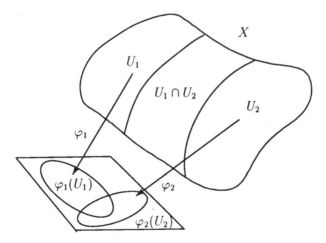

Figure 5.1   A manifold of dimension 2.

For each pair (U_i, U_j) of open sets such that $U_i \cap U_j \neq \emptyset$, the two mappings $\varphi_i \circ \varphi_j^{-1}$ and $\varphi_j \circ \varphi_i^{-1}$ from R^d into R^d are infinitely[2] differentiable, C^∞.

The set X, together with the open sets U_i and the maps φ_i, is called a C^∞ *manifold*, and d is its dimension. The situation is shown in figure 5.1. An element x of X is represented by a pair $(\mathbf{p}, i)$, where $\mathbf{p}$ is in R^d and i is the index of the map φ_i such that $\mathbf{p} = \varphi_i(x)$. To keep the geographic metaphor, the set of pairs (U_i, φ_i) is called an *atlas* of the set X. This is a bit abstract, but it is quite useful in practice. Going into the details of the theory of differential manifolds is outside the scope of this book, and we refer the interested reader to the books by Spivak, Koenderink, and Crampin and Pirani [Spi79, Koe90, CP86].

We would like to point out an easy consequence of this definition. It is known that no open set of R^n can be compact. So if the set X we want to represent is compact, we need at least two open sets U_i to cover it, and therefore at least two maps to represent it. This is one of the reasons why we have to abandon the idea of a representation as a unique mapping. We will experience this phenomenon many times, as for example when we study the unit circle as a way to represent the two-dimensional orientations.

As our first example of a differential manifold, let us consider the space R^n itself, for which an atlas is reduced to its simplest form: one open set U equal to the full space R^n, and one map φ equal to the identity.

As a second example of a manifold, let us study the case of the projective space $\mathcal{P}^n$, which was introduced in chapter 2. We choose this example because it appears several times later in this chapter under various disguises and is fundamental to an understanding of many of the representations that will be described. We remind the reader that a point x of $\mathcal{P}^n$ can be thought of as a set of $n + 1$ real numbers $x_i, i = 1, \ldots, n + 1$, not all equal to zero and defined up to multiplication by a scalar (we say *defined up to a scale factor*). If we define the subsets $U_i, i = 1, \ldots, n + 1$ of $\mathcal{P}^n$ as the sets of projective points such that $x_i \neq 0$, we obtain $n + 1$ open subsets covering $\mathcal{P}^n$:

---

2. We could impose a weaker condition, such as for the two mappings to be p times continuously differentiable, with $p \geq 0$.

$$\mathcal{P}^n = \cup_{i=1}^{n+1} U_i$$

For each set U_i we can define a mapping $\varphi_i : \mathcal{P}^n \to R^n$ as follows:

$$\varphi_i(x) = [\frac{x_1}{x_i}, \ldots, \frac{x_{i-1}}{x_i}, \frac{x_{i+1}}{x_i}, \ldots, \frac{x_{n+1}}{x_i}]^T \tag{5.1}$$

and we have the following theorem:

Theorem 5.1

The set $\mathcal{P}^n$ is a C^∞ manifold of dimension n. An atlas for this manifold is the open sets $U_i, i = 1, \ldots, n + 1$, which are defined as the points x such that the ith coordinate of their representation is nonzero, and the maps φ_i are defined by equation (5.1).

In order to prove this theorem we have to show that the coherence condition is satisfied. Let us consider U_i and U_j, $i \neq j$. Let $\mathbf{X} = [X_1, \ldots, X_n]^T$ be a point of R^n. We have the following proposition:

Proposition 5.1

The map $\varphi_j \circ \varphi_i^{-1}$ is a one-to-one C^∞ mapping from $R^n \div \{X_j = 0\}$ into $R^n \div \{X_{i-1} = 0\}$ if $j < i$ and into $R^n \div \{X_i = 0\}$ if $j > i$.

Proof The function φ_i^{-1} maps $\mathbf{X}$ onto a point x of $\mathcal{P}^n$ represented by $[X_1, \ldots, X_{i-1}, 1, X_i, \ldots, X_n]^T$. In order for this point to belong to U_j, the jth coordinate must be nonzero. If $j < i$ we have

$$\varphi_j(x) = [\frac{X_1}{X_j}, \ldots, \frac{X_{j-1}}{X_j}, \frac{X_{j+1}}{X_j}, \ldots, \frac{X_{i-1}}{X_j}, \frac{1}{X_j}, \frac{X_i}{X_j}, \ldots, \frac{X_n}{X_j}]^T$$

which shows that the $i - 1$st coordinate is nonzero and that the mapping $\varphi_j \circ \varphi_i^{-1}$ is C^∞ between R^n minus the hyperplane of equation $X_j = 0$ into R^n minus the hyperplane of equation $X_{i-1} = 0$. If $j > i$, we have

$$\varphi_j(x) = [\frac{X_1}{X_j}, \ldots, \frac{X_{i-1}}{X_j}, \frac{1}{X_j}, \frac{X_i}{X_j}, \ldots, \frac{X_{j-1}}{X_j}, \frac{X_{j+1}}{X_j}, \ldots, \frac{X_n}{X_j}]^T$$

which shows that the ith coordinate is nonzero and that the mapping $\varphi_j \circ \varphi_i^{-1}$ is C^∞ between R^n minus the hyperplane of equation $X_j = 0$ into R^n minus the hyperplane of equation $X_i = 0$. ∎

An interesting interpretation of theorem 5.1 is that, in building the atlas, we actually choose $n + 1$ different hyperplanes (of equations $x_i = 0$ $i = 1, \ldots, n$) in $\mathcal{P}^n$ and consider the $n + 1$ n-dimensional affine spaces R^n, which we consider (through the maps φ_i) as embedded in $\mathcal{P}^n$. For each of those affine spaces, the selected hyperplane can be thought of as the hyperplane at infinity, and this is of course reminiscent of the constructions in chapter 2 in which we defined the point at infinity of a projective line, the line at infinity of a projective plane, and the plane at infinity of a projective space (see sections 2.3.1, 2.4.2, and 2.5.2). The theorem tells us that $\mathcal{P}^n$ can be considered as $n + 1$ affine spaces R^n glued together by the maps φ_i. We will now study a number of simple geometric primitives from the standpoint of manifolds, first in two and then in three dimensions.

5.3   The two-dimensional case

5.3.1   Points

5.3.1.1   *Projective points*

A point m in the projective plane $\mathcal{P}^2$ (see chapter 2) is represented by three numbers ($x_1, x_2,$ and x_3), not all zero, and defined up to a scale factor. Theorem 5.1 tells us that $\mathcal{P}^2$ is a C^∞ manifold of dimension 2. An atlas for this manifold is obtained by considering the three open sets $U_i, i = 1, 2, 3$, which are defined by $x_i \neq 0, i = 1, 2, 3$. To each open set we associate the maps $\varphi_i, i = 1, 2, 3$, which are defined as

$$\varphi_1(m) = \begin{bmatrix} X_2 \\ X_3 \end{bmatrix} = \begin{bmatrix} \frac{x_2}{x_1} \\ \frac{x_3}{x_1} \end{bmatrix} \quad \varphi_2(m) = \begin{bmatrix} X_1 \\ X_3 \end{bmatrix} = \begin{bmatrix} \frac{x_1}{x_2} \\ \frac{x_3}{x_2} \end{bmatrix} \quad \varphi_3(m) = \begin{bmatrix} X_1 \\ X_2 \end{bmatrix} = \begin{bmatrix} \frac{x_1}{x_3} \\ \frac{x_2}{x_3} \end{bmatrix}$$

Proposition 5.1 tells us that those three maps are coherent.

5.3.1.2   *Euclidean points*

A euclidean point m in the euclidean plane is represented by its two coordinates (x, y) or equivalently by the complex number $z = x + iy$.

This representation is especially useful when we study the effect of a rigid displacement on points (see chapter 11 and problem 9 of chapter 2).

5.3.2 Orientations and directions

5.3.2.1 Orientations

An orientation in the plane can be thought of as a point on the unit circle S^1, and this defines a one-to-one correspondence between the set of two-dimensional orientations and the points on the unit circle. Note that, according to the remark we made in section 5.2 about compact subsets of R^n, we need at least two maps to turn S^1 into a manifold. This can be seen intuitively if we follow the naive approach, which says that orientation can be parameterized with a single parameter, such as an angle θ with $0 \leq \theta < 2\pi$. There is a problem with orientations corresponding to ε ($\varepsilon << 1$) and $2\pi - \varepsilon$, since those orientations are very similar but their representations are very different. To solve that problem, we can think of the unit circle as the union of two open sets U_1 and U_2 where U_1 is the circle minus the point $\theta = 0 \pmod{2\pi}$ and, for example, U_2 is the circle minus the point $\theta = \pi \pmod{2\pi}$. This defines two one-to-one mappings φ_1 and φ_2 from U_1 and U_2 to the open sets $]0, 2\pi[$ and $] - \pi, +\pi[$, respectively, which turn S^1 into a C^∞ manifold of dimension 1 (see problem 1).

5.3.2.2 Directions

The set of directions is obtained by considering that the orientations θ and $\theta + \pi \pmod{2\pi}$ are the same. This is equivalent to saying that the set of directions can be represented as the unit circle in which we have identified antipodal points. This space is hard to visualize, but we know from theorem 2.1 in chapter 2 that it is homeomorphic (that is, topologically equivalent) to the projective line $\mathcal{P}^1$. From theorem 5.1 we know that $\mathcal{P}^1$ is a C^∞ manifold of dimension 1. An atlas for this manifold is obtained by considering the two open sets $U_i, i = 1, 2$, which are defined by $x_i \neq 0, i = 1, 2$. To each open set we associate the maps $\varphi_i, i = 1, 2$, which are defined as

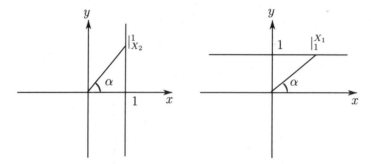

Figure 5.2   Geometric interpretation of the manifold of two-dimensional directions.

$$\varphi_1(m) = X_2 = \frac{x_2}{x_1} \qquad \varphi_2(m) = X_1 = \frac{x_1}{x_2}$$

Proposition 5.1 tells us that these two maps are coherent.

   The reader may wonder what happened to the original directions. Have they been absorbed in $\mathcal{P}^1$? In fact, things are quite simple if we think of $(1, X_2)$ and $(X_1, 1)$ as points in the plane (x, y), as shown in figure 5.2. The first map allows us to represent all directions except the one of the y-axis and $X_2 = \tan\alpha$, while the second map allows us to represent all directions except the one of the x-axis and $\frac{1}{X_1} = \tan\alpha$.

5.3.3   Lines

5.3.3.1   Projective lines

As mentioned in chapter 2, a projective line is equivalent by duality to a projective point and is represented by three numbers (u_1, u_2, and u_3), which are not all zero. These numbers define the projective equation of the line

$$u_1x_1 + u_2x_2 + u_3x_3 = 0$$

Assuming that the line of equation $x_3 = 0$ is the line at infinity, the affine equation of the line is

$$u_1x + u_2y + u_3 = 0$$

with the Cartesian coordinates $x = \frac{x_1}{x_3}$ and $y = \frac{x_2}{x_3}$. The representation (u_1, u_2, u_3) does not satisfy our requirements, since those numbers are defined up to a scale factor (nonuniqueness) and are not minimal. But, using the principle of duality, we can apply to lines exactly the same technique we applied to points (see section 5.3.1.1). This shows that the set of projective lines in $\mathcal{P}^2$ is a manifold of dimension 2.

5.3.3.2 Affine lines

The most common way to represent a line is to represent a point m of the line and its direction if the line is not oriented, or its orientation if it is. There are applications (see chapters 8 and 11) in which oriented lines occur. We previously saw that the set of orientations and the set of directions are manifolds of dimension 1. A point on a line depends upon one parameter, and therefore the set of lines is two-dimensional. Let us try to find an explicit representation that turns the set of affine lines into a manifold.

If we assume that lines are not oriented, the unit vector **n** normal to the line is not uniquely determined (since $-\mathbf{n}$ also works). We can write the equation of the line in the usual way as

$$x \cos \theta + y \sin \theta - d = 0$$

where θ is the angle of the direction of the normal with the x-axis and d is the distance of the origin to the line. The representation of the line as (θ, d) where $0 \le \theta < 2\pi$ and $d \ge 0$ is thus a representation that is minimal and complete, but unfortunately it is not unique. Indeed, if we consider the lines going through the origin, i.e., those for which $d = 0$, then $(\theta, 0)$ and $(\theta + \pi \pmod{2\pi}, 0)$ represent the same line.

To avoid these problems we must again abandon the idea of having a single mapping from the set of lines to R^2 that satisfies all of the four representational requirements and must instead define subsets of the set of lines and mappings for each of the subsets. A different mapping (representation) corresponds to each subset and, at the intersection, the mappings are coherent in the sense of the definition of manifolds. We can do this fairly simply using our experience with directions. In the case of directions we had to consider the set of directions not parallel to the x-axis and the set of directions not parallel to the y-axis. We do the same for lines. We consider the set U_1 of all lines not parallel to the x-axis. Their equation can always be written uniquely:

$$x + ay + b = 0 \qquad\qquad (5.2)$$

We represent a line not parallel to the x-axis by the pair of real numbers (a, b). This defines a map φ_1, which is one-to-one from U_1 into R^2. If we now consider the set U_2 of all lines not parallel to the y-axis, their equation can be written uniquely:

$$a'x + y + b' = 0 \qquad\qquad (5.3)$$

The representation that associates the pair of real numbers (a', b') to each line not parallel to the y-axis of equation (5.3) is a one-to-one mapping φ_2 from U_2 into R^2. We have divided the set of lines into two open subsets, and for each subset we have constructed representations.

Let us now consider the question of coherence. The intersection $U_1 \cap U_2$ is the set of lines where each line is parallel neither to the x-axis nor to the y-axis. Such a line can be represented either by equation (5.2)

$$x + ay + b = 0 \quad \text{with } a \neq 0$$

or by equation (5.3)

$$a'x + y + b' = 0 \quad \text{with } a' \neq 0$$

Let us compute a and b as functions of a' and b':

$$a = \frac{1}{a'}$$
$$\qquad\qquad (5.4)$$
$$b = \frac{b'}{a'}$$

It is clear that equations (5.4) define a mapping from an open subset of the (a', b') plane (the plane minus the b'-axis) onto an open subset of the (a, b) plane (the plane minus the b-axis), which is one-to-one and infinitely differentiable. This mapping is precisely $\varphi_1 \circ \varphi_2^{-1}$. A similar reasoning applies to $\varphi_2 \circ \varphi_1^{-1}$. We have just proved that the set of affine lines is a C^∞ manifold of dimension 2.

5.3.4   Two-dimensional displacements

A *displacement,* or *euclidean transformation,* is a transformation of the plane that preserves distances between points. In chapter 2 we have discussed the relationships between projective, affine, and euclidean transformations. These relationships are expressed in equation (2.8), in which we take $c = 1$. Every 2-D displacement can always be considered as the product of a rotation and a translation in an infinite number of ways. If we fix the center of rotation as the origin, then this decomposition is unique.

It is convenient to use complex numbers to represent points or vectors. A rotation of angle θ about the origin corresponds to multiplying by $e^{i\theta}$, and a translation $\mathbf{t} = [t_1, t_2]^T$ corresponds to adding the complex number $t = t_1 + it_2$. Therefore, the complex number $z = x + iy$ corresponds uniquely to a point M of coordinates x and y and after rotating M by θ about the origin and translating it by $\mathbf{t}$ we obtain the point M', whose complex image z' is given by

$$z' = e^{i\theta}z + t$$

We have used this idea in problem 9 of chapter 2. This makes it clear that there is a one-to-one correspondence between two-dimensional euclidean points and 2-D translations, and between two-dimensional orientations and 2-D rotations.

5.4   The three-dimensional case

5.4.1   Points

The case of a projective point m in the projective space $\mathcal{P}^3$ is dealt with in exactly the same manner as is the case of the projective plane (see section 5.3.1.1) by just adding one coordinate. Such a point is represented by four numbers ($x_1, x_2, x_3,$ and x_4), not all zero, and one can define four open sets U_i and four maps $\varphi_i, i = 1, \ldots, 4$ to construct a structure of a C^∞ manifold of dimension 3 upon $\mathcal{P}^3$. A point m in the euclidean three-dimensional space is represented by its three coordinates ($x, y,$ and z).

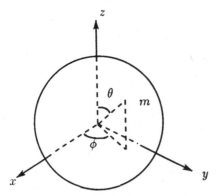

Figure 5.3 Spherical coordinates.

5.4.2 Orientations and directions

5.4.2.1 *Orientations*

An *orientation in space* can be thought of as a point on the unit sphere S^2, and there is a one-to-one correspondence between the set of three-dimensional orientations and the points on the unit sphere. Therefore, studying 3-D orientations is equivalent to studying S^2. A fairly common representation of S^2 is the so-called *spherical coordinates representation* (see figure 5.3). The angles ϕ and θ are defined as $0 \le \phi < 2\pi$ and $0 \le \theta \le \pi$. This definition does not satisfy the first of our representational requirements since, when $\theta = 0$ or π, ϕ is not defined. This cannot define a manifold since the intervals defining ϕ and θ are not open and we have only one map (see the remark at the end of the discussion on manifolds).

One way to turn S^2 into a manifold is to do a stereographic projection of the sphere to a plane as shown in figure 5.4. Consider the plane of equation $z = 0$. Now, to each point M of the open set U_1 of S^2, which is defined as the sphere minus the point A of coordinates $(0, 0,$ and $1)$, we associate the point m, which is the intersection of the line $\langle A, M \rangle$ with the plane. Analytically, if z is the z-coordinate of M, we have

$$\mathbf{m} = \frac{1}{1-z}(\mathbf{M} - z\mathbf{k}) \qquad \mathbf{M} = \frac{\|\mathbf{m}\|^2 - 1}{\|\mathbf{m}\|^2 + 1}\mathbf{k} + \frac{2}{\|\mathbf{m}\|^2 + 1}\mathbf{m} \quad .$$

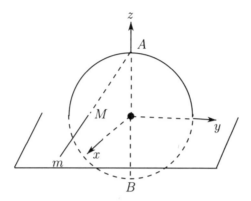

Figure 5.4   Stereographic projection.

where **k** is the unit vector along the z-axis. This defines a one-to-one mapping φ_1 between an open set U_1 of S^2 into R^2 (the first equation defines φ_1, the second φ_1^{-1}). The mapping φ_2 is defined by taking the point B of coordinates $(0, 0, \text{ and } -1)$ as the center of projection. It is easy to show that

$$\varphi_2(\mathbf{M}) = \frac{1}{1+z}(\mathbf{M} - z\mathbf{k})$$

from which it follows that $\varphi_2 \circ \varphi_1^{-1}(\mathbf{m}) = \frac{\mathbf{m}}{\|\mathbf{m}\|}$ is C^∞ in $R^2 - \mathbf{0}$, and therefore that φ_1 and φ_2 are compatible. This is applicable to the representation of orientations, and it also provides a simple correspondence between planar and spherical retinas.

5.4.2.2   Directions

The case of directions is a bit different since, just as in the two-dimensional case, we have to identify antipodal points of S^2. The same theorem applies (i.e., theorem 5.1), which means that, in that case, the set of 3-D directions is homeomorphic to the projective plane $\mathcal{P}^2$. Therefore, the question of how to represent the set of three-dimensional directions is equivalent to the question of how to represent the projective plane. We solved this problem in section 5.3.1.1. The following proposition follows:

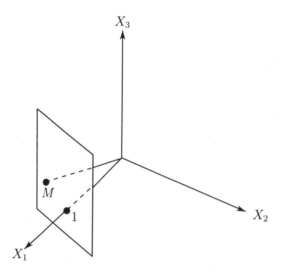

Figure 5.5 Representing all directions not parallel to the X_2X_3 plane as a point in the plane of equation $X_1 = 1$.

Proposition 5.2
The set of three-dimensional directions is a C^∞ manifold of dimension 2.

   In order to obtain a more geometric interpretation of all this using the notations of section 5.3.1.1, we can think of the point M of coordinates $(1, X_2,$ and $X_3)$ in R^3 (see figure 5.5). In this figure it clearly appears that φ_1 represents all directions except those that are parallel to the X_2X_3 plane. Similar remarks can be made for φ_2 and φ_3.

5.4.3   Planes

We can do for planes essentially the same as we did for lines in two dimensions.

5.4.3.1   *Projective planes*

As described in chapter 2, a projective plane is equivalent to a projective point and is represented by four numbers ($u_1, u_2, u_3,$ and u_4) that are not all zero. This defines the projective equation of the plane

$$u_1x_1 + u_2x_2 + u_3x_3 + u_4x_4 = 0$$

Assuming that the plane of equation $x_4 = 0$ is the plane at infinity, the affine equation of the plane is

$$u_1 x + u_2 y + u_3 z + u_4 = 0$$

with the Cartesian coordinates $x = \frac{x_1}{x_4}$, $y = \frac{x_2}{x_4}$, and $z = \frac{x_3}{x_4}$. The representation (u_1, u_2, u_3, u_4) does not satisfy our representational requirements, since the four numbers u_i are defined up to a scale factor (nonuniqueness). Neither is the representation minimal, since the set of planes is of dimension 3. In section 5.4.1 we have sketched how to construct a structure of a manifold of dimension 3 upon the set of projective points. This applies directly to this problem.

5.4.3.2 Affine planes

The simplest idea is to represent a plane as a point of the plane and the direction or orientation of its normal vector, depending upon whether or not we can define an intrinsic orientation for this normal vector. There are applications (see chapters 10 and 11) where such an intrinsic orientation can be defined.

Just as in the case of two-dimensional lines, there are problems with all the usual representations because they all try to find a single representation for planes. If we abandon this idea and use instead the manifold idea, then all problems vanish. This can be achieved in essentially the same way as for two-dimensional lines. We can introduce a satisfactory representation using as inspiration our results in response to the problem of representing three-dimensional directions. This leads us to consider planes that are not parallel to one of the axes of the coordinates:

$$x + ay + bz + c = 0 \quad \text{planes not parallel to the } x\text{-axis} \qquad (5.5)$$

$$ax + y + bz + c = 0 \quad \text{planes not parallel to the } y\text{-axis} \qquad (5.6)$$

$$ax + by + z + c = 0 \quad \text{planes not parallel to the } z\text{-axis} \qquad (5.7)$$

These equations define three open sets U_1, U_2, and U_3 of the set of planes whose union is the whole set, and in each set there is a map φ_i, $i = 1, 2, 3$ from U_i into R^3, which associates to each plane the triplet $(a, b, \text{and } c)$, which is defined by equations (5.5), (5.6), or (5.7).

As in the case of lines, let us consider the matter of coherence. The intersection of U_1 and U_2 corresponding to equations (5.5) and (5.6) is the set of planes where each plane is parallel to neither the x-axis nor to the y-axis. Such a plane can be represented either by equation (5.5)

$$x + ay + bz + c = 0 \quad \text{with } a \neq 0$$

or by equation (5.6)

$$a'x + y + b'z + c' = 0 \quad \text{with } a' \neq 0$$

Computing a, b, and c as functions of a', b', and c', we obtain

$$\begin{cases} a &= \frac{1}{a'} \\ b &= \frac{b'}{a'} \\ c &= \frac{c'}{a'} \end{cases} \tag{5.8}$$

It is clear that equations (5.8) define a mapping from an open subset of the (a', b', c') space (the space R^3 minus the plane of equation $a' = 0$) onto an open subset of the (a, b, c) space (the space R^3 minus the plane of equation $a = 0$), which is one-to-one and C^∞. Of course, the same technique can be applied to equations (5.6) and (5.7) as well as to equations (5.7) and (5.5). This proves that the set of planes is a C^∞ manifold of dimension 3.

Note that $(1, a, b)$, which represents a vector normal to the plane of equation (5.5), is analogous to $(1, X_2, X_3)$ of section 5.4.2.2. Similar remarks apply to $(a, 1, b)$ of equation (5.6) and to $(a, b, 1)$ of equation (5.7).

5.4.4   Affine lines

The usual way to represent a three-dimensional line is by specifying a point P lying on the line and its direction or orientation if the line is oriented. Of course it is a nonunique representation, since the point can be taken anywhere on the line. It is also nonminimal, since we will see in a moment that a line can be represented by four parameters. But it is complete, since every line can be expressed this way. We will make good use of this representation in chapters 8 and 11.

One way to reach our goal is to look at our results in response to the problem of representing 3-D directions. If we consider the representation of the 3-D directions obtained from their correspondence with points in $\mathcal{P}^2$, we immediately come up with the right representation: We consider the three subsets $U_i, i = 1, 2, 3$ of the set of lines that are not parallel to the xy-, yz-, and zx-planes, respectively. The three sets U_i are open and cover the set of 3-D lines. Moreover, each line in each subset is represented by four real numbers defining the maps $\varphi_i, i = 1, 2, 3$ (two for its direction, and two for the coordinates of its point of intersection with the plane to which it cannot be parallel.

In order to make all this precise, let a straight line be represented as the intersection of the two planes with equations

$$\begin{cases} x &= az + p \\ y &= bz + q \end{cases} \tag{5.9}$$

The line goes through the point P of coordinates $(p, q,$ and $0)$ and is parallel to the vector of coordinates $[a, b, 1]^T$. Lines parallel to the xy-plane cannot be represented, but any other line has a unique, smooth, and minimal representation. In order to be able to represent all lines, we have to consider the following representation:

$$\begin{cases} y &= ax + p \\ z &= bx + q \end{cases} \tag{5.10}$$

which excludes lines parallel to the yz-plane (they are parallel to the vector $[1, a, b]^T$), and the following:

$$\begin{cases} z &= ay + p \\ x &= by + q \end{cases} \tag{5.11}$$

which excludes lines parallel to the zx-plane (they are parallel to the vector $[b, 1, a]^T$).

As already stated, we have divided the set of lines into three open subsets U_1, U_2, and U_3, and for each subset we have constructed representations φ_i, $i = 1, 2, 3$. As usual, let us consider the question of coherence. The intersection of the two subsets defined by equations (5.9) and (5.10) is the set of lines which are parallel to neither the xy- nor to the yz-planes. Such lines can be represented either by equations (5.9)

$$\begin{cases} x &= az + p \\ & \qquad a \neq 0 \\ y &= bz + q \end{cases}$$

or by equations (5.10)

$$\begin{cases} y &= a'x + p' \\ & \qquad\qquad b' \neq 0 \\ z &= b'x + q' \end{cases}$$

It is easy to compute $a', b', p',$ and q' as functions of $a, b, p,$ and q:

$$a = -\frac{1}{b'} \qquad b = \frac{a'}{b'}$$

$$p = -\frac{q'}{b'} \qquad q = -\frac{a'q'}{b'} + p'$$

These functions define the mapping $\varphi_1 \circ \varphi_2^{-1}$ from an open subset of the (a', b', p', q') space (the space R^4 minus the hyperplane of equation $b' = 0$) onto an open subset of the (a, b, p, q) space (the space R^4 minus the hyperplane of equation $a = 0$), which is one-to-one and C^∞. We can apply the same technique to equations (5.10) and (5.11) and to equations (5.11) and (5.9). This proves that the set of 3-D lines is a C^∞ manifold of dimension 4. To finish the discussion on 3-D lines, we remind the reader of the Plücker coordinates that have been defined in section 2.5.1 and in problem 7 of chapter 2.

5.4.5 Quadrics

As a direct consequence of our discussion in chapter 2 of quadrics, a quadric in euclidean space can be represented by a symmetric 3×3 matrix $\mathbf{A}$, a 3×1 vector $\mathbf{v}$, and a scalar d. The equation of the quadric is then given by

$$\mathbf{x}^T \mathbf{A} \mathbf{x} + \mathbf{x}^T \mathbf{v} + d = 0$$

Notice that the representation $(\mathbf{A}, \mathbf{v}, d)$ is defined up to a scale factor.

5.5   Three-dimensional displacements

Because of the difficulty of the subject and its importance for the following chapters, we will use a whole section to discuss three-dimensional displacements. They are transformations of the euclidean 3-D space that preserve distances between points. We have dealt with them in a limited fashion in chapter 2. In particular, we have discussed the relationship between projective, affine, and euclidean transformations. This is summarized in equation (2.16), in which we take $c = 1$.

Just as in the two-dimensional case, each such transformation can be considered as a rotation about a given axis followed by a translation. Since the axis of rotation can be chosen arbitrarily (up to a translation), this decomposition is not unique (see problem 2). If we impose the condition that the axis of rotation goes through a given point (for example, the origin O of coordinates), then the decomposition is unique and we can write

$$\mathbf{OM}' = Rot(\mathbf{OM}) + \mathbf{T} \tag{5.12}$$

In this equation, Rot is a three-dimensional vector rotation that is applied to the vector $\mathbf{OM}$. The vector $\mathbf{T}$ is the translation. There is of course a one-to-one correspondence between euclidean points and translations just as in the two-dimensional case. The difficulty lies with the rotation part of the displacement. We will now study a number of ways for representing three-dimensional rotations.

5.5.1 Real orthogonal matrices

A *real orthogonal matrix* is a real square matrix $\mathbf{R}$ satisfying the constraint

$$\mathbf{RR}^T = \mathbf{I} \tag{5.13}$$

This implies that $(\det(\mathbf{R}))^2 = 1$, and therefore $\det(\mathbf{R}) = \pm 1$. It can be proven that every 3×3 orthogonal matrix of a determinant equal to 1 is the matrix of a rotation and, inversely, that every rotation can be represented by such a matrix.

Equation (5.13) implies that some very strict constraints must be satisfied by the row and column vectors of $\mathbf{R}$. More precisely, it implies that the row (column) vectors are mutually orthogonal and of unit lengths, i.e., if we denote the column vectors by $\mathbf{r}_i$ ($i = 1, 2, 3$), they satisfy the constraints

$$\mathbf{r}_i^T \mathbf{r}_j = \delta_{ij} \qquad i, j = 1, 2, 3, \quad i \le j \tag{5.14}$$

where δ_{ij} is the usual Kronecker symbol:

$$\delta_{ij} = \begin{cases} 1 & \text{if } i = j \\ 0 & \text{if } i \neq j \end{cases}$$

The relations (5.14) form a set of six independent quadratic constraints that are satisfied by the elements of an orthogonal matrix $\mathbf{R}$. Moreover, to be a rotation matrix, one must also have $\mathbf{r}_1 \cdot (\mathbf{r}_2 \wedge \mathbf{r}_3) = \det(\mathbf{R}) = 1$. Orthogonal matrices of determinant 1 clearly form a multiplicative group.

5.5.2 Quaternions

Quaternions have been found useful in robotics and computer vision [Hor86, FH86, WS91]. They can be understood very simply by looking at them as 4×1 real vectors among which we define a multiplication to turn that vector space into a noncommutative field. In order to do this, we consider a quaternion $\mathbf{q}$ as either a 4×1 vector $[q_1, q_2, q_3, q_4]^T$ or as a pair $(s, \mathbf{v})$ where s is a real number equal to q_1 and $\mathbf{v}$ is the vector $[q_2, q_3, q_4]^T$. In this notation, a quaternion is very similar to a complex number, s being like the real part and $\mathbf{v}$ like the imaginary part. A real number x is readily identified with the quaternion $(x, \mathbf{0})$, and the product of two real numbers is the real part of the the product of the corresponding quaternions:

$$(x, \mathbf{0}) \times (x', \mathbf{0}) = (xx', \mathbf{0})$$

Similarly, a 3×1 real vector $\mathbf{v}$ is readily identified with the quaternion $(0, \mathbf{v})$. We will now define the product of two quaternions $\mathbf{q}$ and $\mathbf{q}'$ as follows:

$$\mathbf{q} \times \mathbf{q}' = (ss' - \mathbf{v}.\mathbf{v}', s\mathbf{v}' + s'\mathbf{v} + \mathbf{v} \wedge \mathbf{v}') \tag{5.15}$$

The definitions of the conjugate and the magnitude of a quaternion are very similar to the ones for complex numbers:

$$\bar{\mathbf{q}} = (s, -\mathbf{v}) \quad \text{and} \quad |\mathbf{q}|^2 = \bar{\mathbf{q}} \times \mathbf{q} = \mathbf{q} \times \bar{\mathbf{q}} = (s^2 + \|\mathbf{v}\|^2, \mathbf{0}) = (\|\mathbf{q}\|^2, \mathbf{0})$$

In this formula we have used $|$ for the quaternion magnitude and $\|$ for the usual euclidean norm. It can be easily verified that the magnitude is compatible with the product in the sense that

$$|\mathbf{q} \times \mathbf{q}'| = |\mathbf{q}||\mathbf{q}'|$$

This is just about all we need to know about quaternions in order to use them to represent 3-D rotations. Indeed, a rotation of angle θ with respect to an axis $\mathbf{u}$ (a vector of length 1) can be represented by the two quaternions $\mathbf{q} = (s, \mathbf{v})$ and $-\mathbf{q} = (-s, -\mathbf{v})$, where

$$s = \cos(\theta/2)$$

$$\mathbf{v} = \sin(\theta/2)\mathbf{u}$$

(5.16)

Notice that $\|\mathbf{q}\| = 1$.

It should not be surprising that there are two quaternions for one rotation, since a rotation of angle θ with respect to an axis $\mathbf{u}$ is the same as a rotation of angle $2\pi - \theta$ with respect to the axis $-\mathbf{u}$. Looking at the previous formula, the two rotations precisely correspond to the two quaternions $\mathbf{q}$ and $-\mathbf{q}$. Inversely, for a quaternion $\mathbf{q}$ of magnitude 1, it is clear that there exists a unique rotation that is defined by the formulas (5.16).

This correspondence between rotations and quaternions of unit magnitude is even deeper, since it preserves the group operation. Indeed, given two rotations 1 and 2 and the associated quaternions $\mathbf{q}_1$ and $\mathbf{q}_2$ (for each rotation choose any one of the two possible quaternions, it does not matter which one you choose), then the product of rotation 1 and rotation 2 (that is the rotation obtained by applying first 2 and then 1) corresponds to the products $\mathbf{q}_1 \times \mathbf{q}_2$ and $-\mathbf{q}_1 \times \mathbf{q}_2$.

Since the product of rotations is not commutative unless the rotations have the same axis, this shows (as does formula (5.15)) that the product of two quaternions is also not commutative.

This correspondence between rotations and quaternions allows us to derive a very useful formula. Let $\mathbf{R}$ be the orthogonal matrix representing a rotation of angle θ with respect to an axis $\mathbf{u}$ (a vector of length 1). Let $\mathbf{q}$ be one of the two corresponding quaternions, and let $\mathbf{w}$ be a 3×1 vector. Then we can write

$$\mathbf{R}\mathbf{w} = \mathbf{q} \times \mathbf{w} \times \overline{\mathbf{q}}$$

(5.17)

In this formula, we have identified 3×1 vectors and the corresponding quaternion. In other words, the formula should read

$$(0, \mathbf{R}\mathbf{w}) = \mathbf{q} \times (0, \mathbf{w}) \times \overline{\mathbf{q}}$$

Formula (5.17) allows us to derive the relationship between the coefficients of the rotation matrix $\mathbf{R}$ and the coordinates of the quaternions $\mathbf{q}$ and $-\mathbf{q}$ representing it. If we write $\mathbf{q} = [s, l, m, n]^T$, $\mathbf{v} = [l, m, n]^T$, using the formulas in (5.15) it is easy to see that

$$\mathbf{q} \times \mathbf{w} \times \bar{\mathbf{q}} = (0, 2(\mathbf{v}.\mathbf{w})\mathbf{v} + (s^2 - \|\mathbf{v}\|^2)\mathbf{w} + 2s\mathbf{v} \wedge \mathbf{w}) \tag{5.18}$$

We can also write

$$\mathbf{v} \wedge \mathbf{w} = \tilde{\mathbf{v}}\mathbf{w}$$

with

$$\tilde{\mathbf{v}} = \begin{bmatrix} 0 & -n & m \\ n & 0 & -l \\ -m & l & 0 \end{bmatrix}$$

and

$$(\mathbf{v}.\mathbf{w})\mathbf{v} = \mathbf{A}\mathbf{w}$$

where $\mathbf{A}$ is a 3×3 matrix given by

$$\mathbf{A} = [l\mathbf{v}, m\mathbf{v}, n\mathbf{v}] = \begin{bmatrix} l^2 & lm & ln \\ lm & m^2 & mn \\ ln & mn & n^2 \end{bmatrix}$$

Writing that the imaginary part of equation (5.18) is equal to $\mathbf{R}\mathbf{w}$, we find that

$$\mathbf{R} = \begin{bmatrix} s^2 + l^2 - m^2 - n^2 & 2(lm - sn) & 2(ln + sm) \\ 2(lm + sn) & s^2 - l^2 + m^2 - n^2 & 2(mn - sl) \\ 2(ln - sm) & 2(mn + sl) & s^2 - l^2 - m^2 + n^2 \end{bmatrix} \tag{5.19}$$

From matrix (5.19) it appears that the coefficients of $\mathbf{R}$ are polynomial functions of the coordinates of $\mathbf{q}$. But remember that l, m, n, and s satisfy the relation $l^2 + m^2 + n^2 + s^2 = 1$.

5.5.3   The structure of a manifold of the set of rotations

The quaternion representation of rotations allows us to construct a structure of a manifold on the set of rotations by noticing that the set of unit quaternions is the unit sphere S^3 of R^4. We have just seen that the set of rotations is homeomorphic to S^3, where we have identified antipodal points. By again applying theorem 2.1, we can conclude that the set of 3-D rotations is homeomorphic to the projective space $\mathcal{P}^3$ for which we have already built a structure of a manifold in section 5.4.1. The open sets U_i and the maps $\varphi_i, i = 1, \ldots, 4$ have a neat interpretation in the case of rotations.

U_1 is the set of projective points x represented by $\mathbf{x} = [x_1, x_2, x_3, x_4]^T$ such that $x_1 \neq 0$ and φ_1 maps those points to the points of R^3 of coordinates ($X_2 = \frac{x_2}{x_1}, X_3 = \frac{x_3}{x_1}$, and $X_4 = \frac{x_4}{x_1}$). Reinterpreting $\mathbf{x}$ as a quaternion $(s, \mathbf{v})$, we see that $x_1 \neq 0$ is equivalent to $s \neq 0$, which, because of equations (5.16), is equivalent to $\theta \neq \pi \pmod{2\pi}$. Therefore, the set U_1 is the set of rotations whose rotation angle is different from π and, according to equations (5.16), the representation φ_1 establishes a one-to-one correspondence between those rotations and the set R^3. In this representation, each vector of R^3 can be written as $\tan(\frac{\theta}{2})\mathbf{u}$, where $\mathbf{u}$ is a unit vector parallel to the axis of rotation and θ is the angle of rotation, $0 \leq \theta < \pi$ (therefore $\tan(\frac{\theta}{2}) \geq 0$).

The sets $U_i, i = 2, 3, 4$ all exclude rotations with an angle of 0 and rotations with an axis parallel to the yz-, zx-, and xy-planes, respectively. Let us look, for example, at the map φ_2. U_2 is the set of projective points x represented by $\mathbf{x} = [x_1, x_2, x_3, x_4]^T$ such that $x_2 \neq 0$, and φ_2 maps those points to the points of R^3 of coordinates ($X_1 = \frac{x_1}{x_2}, X_3 = \frac{x_3}{x_2}, X_4 = \frac{x_4}{x_2}$). Reinterpreting $\mathbf{x}$ as a quaternion $(s, \mathbf{v})$, we see that $x_2 \neq 0$ is equivalent to $\sin \frac{\theta}{2} \neq 0$, which is equivalent to $\theta \neq 0 \pmod{2\pi}$ and $u_x \neq 0$. Therefore, it excludes the rotation of angle 0 and those with a rotation axis parallel to the yz-plane. According to equations (5.16), we have

$$X_1 = \frac{\cot \frac{\theta}{2}}{u_x} \qquad X_3 = \frac{u_y}{u_x} \qquad X_4 = \frac{u_z}{u_x}$$

If $X_1 = 0$, the rotation angle is π and the rotation axis is parallel to $[0, X_3, X_4]^T$. If $X_1 \neq 0$, the direction of the axis of rotation is given by X_3 and X_4, and its orientation is given by the sign of X_1 since $0 < \theta < \pi$ implies that $\cot \frac{\theta}{2} > 0$. Let $\varepsilon = \pm 1$ be the sign of X_1. We then have

$$u_x = \frac{\varepsilon}{\sqrt{1 + X_3^2 + X_4^2}} \qquad u_y = X_3 u_x \qquad u_z = X_4 u_x,$$

and

$$\cot\frac{\theta}{2} = \varepsilon u_x$$

which defines $0 < \theta < \pi$ (mod 2π). Similar interpretations can be derived for φ_3 and φ_4.

Finally, note that this representation of rotations provides us with a rational representation of the rotation matrix $\mathbf{R}$. Let us show this for φ_1 as an example. Let $D = \sqrt{1 + X_2^2 + X_3^2 + X_4^2}$. One of the two quaternions corresponding to the rotation represented by (X_2, X_3, X_4) is $\frac{1}{D}(1, X_2, X_3, X_4)$. This yields the values for s, l, m, and n with the notations of the previous section, which we can replace in equation (5.19) to obtain

$$\mathbf{R} = \frac{1}{1 + X_2^2 + X_3^2 + X_4^2} \begin{bmatrix} 1 + X_2^2 - X_3^2 - X_4^2 & 2(X_2 X_3 - X_4) & 2(X_2 X_4 + X_3) \\ 2(X_2 X_3 + X_4) & 1 - X_2^2 + X_3^2 - X_4^2 & 2(X_3 X_4 - X_2) \\ 2(X_2 X_4 - X_3) & 2(X_3 X_4 + X_2) & 1 - X_2^2 - X_3^2 + X_4^2 \end{bmatrix} \quad (5.20)$$

We have proved the following proposition:

Proposition 5.3
The set of three-dimensional rotations is a C^∞ manifold of dimension 3 that can be represented by an atlas of size 4.

5.5.4 Exponentials of antisymmetric matrices

There is also a deep relationship between antisymmetric matrices and rotation matrices that we will now investigate. Let $\mathbf{H}$ be a 3×3 antisymmetric matrix written as

$$\mathbf{H} = \begin{bmatrix} 0 & -c & b \\ c & 0 & -a \\ -b & a & 0 \end{bmatrix}$$

We denote by $\mathbf{r}$ the three-dimensional vector $[a, b, c]^T$. Now consider the matrix exponential $e^{\mathbf{H}}$ of $\mathbf{H}$, which is defined by the series

$$e^{\mathbf{H}} = \sum_{n=0}^{\infty} \frac{\mathbf{H}^n}{n!} \quad (5.21)$$

We have the following proposition:

Proposition 5.4
The matrix e^H is a rotation matrix. The vector **r** is parallel to its axis of rotation, and its magnitude $\|\mathbf{r}\|$ is equal to the angle of rotation (modulo 2π).

In order to prove this proposition, we need two useful lemmas.

Lemma 5.1
Let **A** and **B** be two 3×3 matrices such that

$$\mathbf{AB} = \mathbf{BA}$$

(**A** and **B** "commute"). Then,

$$e^{\mathbf{A}}e^{\mathbf{B}} = e^{\mathbf{B}}e^{\mathbf{A}} = e^{\mathbf{A}+\mathbf{B}}$$

Proof Apply the binomial formula, and use the hypothesis

$$(\mathbf{A} + \mathbf{B})^n = \sum_{i=0}^{n} \binom{n-i}{i} \mathbf{A}^{n-i}\mathbf{B}^i$$

∎

In particular, if $\mathbf{B} = -\mathbf{A}$, this shows that

$$e^{-\mathbf{A}} = (e^{\mathbf{A}})^{-1}$$

Lemma 5.2
The following relation exists between the determinant of the exponential and the trace of its exponent:

$$det(e^{\mathbf{A}}) = e^{Tr(\mathbf{A})} \tag{5.22}$$

Proof Any matrix **A** can be put in triangular form by a change of coordinates, i.e., there exists an invertible (possibly complex) matrix **P** such that $\mathbf{P}^{-1}\mathbf{AP}$ is upper-triangular:

$$\mathbf{P}^{-1}\mathbf{AP} = \begin{bmatrix} \lambda_1 & b_{12} & b_{13} \\ 0 & \lambda_2 & b_{23} \\ 0 & 0 & \lambda_3 \end{bmatrix} \tag{5.23}$$

From the definition of the exponential (equation (5.21)) we have

$$\mathbf{P}^{-1}e^{\mathbf{A}}\mathbf{P} = e^{\mathbf{P}^{-1}\mathbf{AP}} \tag{5.24}$$

Applying again the definition of the exponential we have

$$e^{\mathbf{P}^{-1}\mathbf{AP}} = \begin{bmatrix} e^{\lambda_1} & c_{12} & c_{13} \\ 0 & e^{\lambda_2} & c_{23} \\ 0 & 0 & e^{\lambda_3} \end{bmatrix} \tag{5.25}$$

From equation (5.24), $\det(e^{\mathbf{A}}) = \det(e^{\mathbf{P}^{-1}\mathbf{AP}})$, and the result follows from equations (5.23) and (5.25).   ∎

We are now ready to prove proposition 5.4:

Proof Let $\mathbf{R} = e^{\mathbf{H}}$. From the the definition of the matrix exponential, $(e^{\mathbf{H}})^T = e^{\mathbf{H}^T}$. Since $\mathbf{H}$ is antisymmetric, $e^{\mathbf{H}^T} = e^{-\mathbf{H}}$. As a consequence of lemma 5.1, $e^{-\mathbf{H}} = (e^{\mathbf{H}})^{-1}$. Thus, since $\mathbf{RR}^T = \mathbf{I}$, matrix $\mathbf{R}$ is orthogonal. From lemma 5.2, $\det(\mathbf{R}) = e^{Tr(\mathbf{H})} = e^0 = 1$. Thus $\mathbf{R}$ is a rotation matrix. We know that all vectors $\mathbf{u}$ such that $\mathbf{Ru} = \mathbf{u}$ are parallel to the rotation axis. Since $\mathbf{Hr} = \mathbf{0}$ from the definition of $\mathbf{H}$ and $\mathbf{r}$, we conclude from the definition of the matrix exponential that $\mathbf{Rr} = \mathbf{r}$ and thus that $\mathbf{r}$ is parallel to the axis of rotation. We know that the eigenvalues of a rotation matrix are $1, e^{i\theta}$, and $e^{-i\theta}$, where θ is the angle of rotation modulo 2π. It is easy to calculate the eigenvalues of matrix $\mathbf{H}$ and show that they are equal to $0, i\|\mathbf{r}\|, -i\|\mathbf{r}\|$. Thus

$$\theta = \|\mathbf{r}\| \pmod{2\pi}$$

This completes the proof of proposition 5.4   ∎

Another very useful property of $\mathbf{H}$ is given by the following proposition:

Proposition 5.5
[Rodrigues] The relationship between the antisymmetric matrix $\mathbf{H}$ and its exponential can be written

$$\mathbf{R} = e^{\mathbf{H}} = \mathbf{I} + \frac{\sin\theta}{\theta}\mathbf{H} + \frac{1-\cos\theta}{\theta^2}\mathbf{H}^2 \tag{5.26}$$

Proof It is easy to verify that $\mathbf{H}$ satisfies the following relation:

$$\mathbf{H}^3 = -\|\mathbf{r}\|^2\mathbf{H} = -\theta^2\mathbf{H}$$

This implies that

$$\mathbf{H}^{2n} = (-1)^{n-1}\theta^{2n-2}\mathbf{H}^2 \qquad n \geq 1$$

$$\mathbf{H}^{2n+1} = (-1)^n\theta^{2n}\mathbf{H} \qquad n \geq 0$$

Grouping the even and odd powers of $\mathbf{H}$ in the definition of the exponential and using the definition of sin and cos

$$\sin\theta = \sum_{n=0}^{\infty}(-1)^n\frac{\theta^{2n+1}}{n!}$$

$$\cos\theta = \sum_{n=0}^{\infty}(-1)^n\frac{\theta^{2n}}{n!}$$

we obtain equation (5.26).   ∎

This proposition is due to the French mathematician Rodrigues [Rod40]. The reader who is interested in the history of science and, in particular, in the relations between Hamilton and Rodrigues, is referred to the fascinating paper by Altmann [Alt89]. Note that, contrary to equation (5.20), equation (5.26) is not a rational representation of $\mathbf{R}$ in terms of the vector $\mathbf{r}$.

5.6 Computing uncertainty

We now want to discuss the problem of error propagation, which is basic to many questions in computer vision. We will encounter this problem in different disguises, and in the following sections we will analyze some of the most common situations. We denote by $\mathbf{x}_0$ a vector in R^n representing some measurements that we have made. From those measurements we compute a resulting vector $\mathbf{y}_0$ in R^m. The question we pose, loosely stated, is this: Knowing the uncertainty on $\mathbf{x}_0$, how do we compute the uncertainty on $\mathbf{y}_0$? Let us make the answer to this question more precise by starting with a simple case and proceeding in increasing order of difficulty.

5.6.1   When y is a known function of x

This is the simplest case in which we have a function $\mathbf{f}$ mapping R^n into R^m. The function $\mathbf{f}$ is C^1, and

$$\mathbf{y}_0 = \mathbf{f}(\mathbf{x}_0)$$

A first-order Taylor expansion of $\mathbf{f}$ in the vicinity of $\mathbf{x}_0$ yields

$$\mathbf{f}(\mathbf{x}) = \mathbf{f}(\mathbf{x}_0) + \mathbf{Df}(\mathbf{x}_0) \cdot (\mathbf{x} - \mathbf{x}_0) + \varepsilon(\|\mathbf{x} - \mathbf{x}_0\|^2) \qquad (5.27)$$

where the function $t \to \varepsilon(t)$ from R into R is such that $\lim_{t \to 0} \varepsilon(t) = 0$, and where $\mathbf{Df}(\mathbf{x}_0)$ is the derivative of $\mathbf{f}$ at $\mathbf{x}_0$, an $m \times n$ Jacobian matrix. We will now give two interpretations of equation (5.27), a probabilistic one and a deterministic one.

5.6.1.1 A probabilistic interpretation

We consider $\mathbf{x}$ to be a random vector of R^n, which we assume to have a mean of $\mathbf{x}_0$ and a covariance of $\Lambda_\mathbf{x} = E((\mathbf{x} - \mathbf{x}_0)^T(\mathbf{x} - \mathbf{x}_0))$. The vector $\mathbf{y} = \mathbf{f}(\mathbf{x})$ is also random, and we want to characterize the random variable $\mathbf{f}(\mathbf{x}) - \mathbf{f}(\mathbf{x}_0)$. Equation (5.27) immediately gives us the answer: Up to the first order, $\mathbf{f}(\mathbf{x}) - \mathbf{f}(\mathbf{x}_0)$ has zero mean and covariance

$$\Lambda_\mathbf{y} = \mathbf{Df}(\mathbf{x}_0)\Lambda_\mathbf{x}\mathbf{Df}(\mathbf{x}_0)^T \qquad (5.28)$$

The reader should be very much aware of the fact that this equation is only a first-order approximation, as he or she may be convinced by considering a pth order Taylor expansion ($p \geq 2$) instead of equation (5.27). This is precisely the problem with the dotted lines of figures 3.13 and 3.14 at the end of chapter 3, which show a parabolic trend when we increase the pixel noise. This indicates a bias that varies with this noise and is caused by the fact that, for that specific problem, the second-order term of equation (5.27) is not small compared to the first-order term.

5.6.1.2 A deterministic interpretation

There is a nonprobabilistic interpretation of matrix $\Lambda_\mathbf{x}$ that we somewhat prefer, since in practice it is more reasonable to talk about bounds on quantities than about probability density functions, which are harder to justify or estimate. Without loss of generality, let us assume that $\mathbf{x}_0 = \mathbf{0}$. The motivation is the following. For each nonrandom vector $\mathbf{z}$ of R^n, let us consider the random variable $u = (\mathbf{z}^T\mathbf{x})^2$. We have

$$E(u) = \mathbf{z}^T E(\mathbf{x}\mathbf{x}^T)\mathbf{z} = \mathbf{z}^T\Lambda_\mathbf{x}\mathbf{z}$$

Since this equation is homogeneous of degree 2 in $\mathbf{z}$, we can assume that $\mathbf{z}$ has a unit norm. What this tells us is that, if $\mathbf{x}$ is a random vector with zero mean and covariance matrix Λ_x, on the average the square of the length of its projection in a given direction $\mathbf{z}$ is $\mathbf{z}^T \Lambda_x \mathbf{z}$.

This allows us to define similar concepts in the nonrandom case. We consider the set of vectors $\mathbf{x}$ such that

$$(\mathbf{z}^T \mathbf{x})^2 \leq \mathbf{z}^T \Lambda_x \mathbf{z} \quad \text{for all vectors } \mathbf{z} \tag{5.29}$$

where Λ_x is a symmetric positive matrix. Without loss of generality, since inequality (5.29) is homogeneous of degree 2 in $\mathbf{z}$, we can restrict it to the vectors $\mathbf{z}$ of unit norm and, by a n-dimensional rotation, we can also assume that the matrix Λ_x is diagonal:

$$\Lambda_x = \text{diag}(a_1^2, \ldots, a_n^2) \tag{5.30}$$

We can then prove the following proposition:

Proposition 5.6
The set of vectors $\mathbf{x}$ satisfying inequality (5.29) for a matrix Λ_x given by equation (5.30) is the inside of the n-dimensional ellipsoid of equation

$$\begin{cases} \sum_{i=1, a_i \neq 0}^{n} \dfrac{x_i^2}{a_i^2} = 1 \\ x_i = 0 \text{ if } a_i = 0 \end{cases}$$

i.e., the set of points satisfying

$$\begin{cases} \sum_{i=1, a_i \neq 0}^{n} \dfrac{x_i^2}{a_i^2} \leq 1 \\ x_i = 0 \text{ if } a_i = 0 \end{cases}$$

Proof We will prove the proposition for $n = 2$; the proof is similar for higher values of n. Let us write $\mathbf{z} = [\cos\theta, \sin\theta]^T$. Then equation (5.29) can be written

$$(x_1 \cos\theta + x_2 \sin\theta)^2 \leq a_1^2 \cos^2\theta + a_2^2 \sin^2\theta \tag{5.31}$$

For a given value of θ, the set of vectors $\mathbf{x}$ satisfying equation (5.31) is the set of points between the two lines of equation

$$x_1 \cos\theta + x_2 \sin\theta = \pm\sqrt{a_1^2 \cos^2\theta + a_2^2 \sin^2\theta}$$

When θ varies, we have to take the intersection of all those sets. We thus obtain a convex set whose border is the envelope of either one of those lines (the set is symmetric with respect to the origin).

Using a known property of envelopes, we can write that the point m_θ, where the line l_θ of equation $x_1 \cos \theta + x_2 \sin \theta = \sqrt{a_1^2 \cos^2 \theta + a_2^2 \sin^2 \theta}$ is tangent to its envelope, which is obtained as its intersection with the line l'_θ, whose equation is the derivative with respect to θ of its equation

$$-x_1 \sin \theta + x_2 \cos \theta = \frac{(a_2^2 - a_1^2) \sin \theta \cos \theta}{\sqrt{a_1^2 \cos^2 \theta + a_2^2 \sin^2 \theta}}$$

An easy computation shows that the coordinates of the point of intersection are

$$x_1 = \frac{a_1^2 \cos \theta}{\sqrt{a_1^2 \cos^2 \theta + a_2^2 \sin^2 \theta}} \qquad x_2 = \frac{a_2^2 \sin \theta}{\sqrt{a_1^2 \cos^2 \theta + a_2^2 \sin^2 \theta}}$$

When θ varies, this point varies on the ellipse of equation

$$\frac{x_1^2}{a_1^2} + \frac{x_2^2}{a_2^2} - 1 = 0$$

∎

Note that in the case where $\Lambda_\mathbf{x}$ is symmetric positive *definite*, i.e., all scalars a_i are nonzero, then the set of vectors $\mathbf{x}$ is defined by

$$\mathbf{x}^T \Lambda_\mathbf{x}^{-1} \mathbf{x} \le 1$$

This proposition points to another interpretation of matrix $\Lambda_\mathbf{x}$: It describes bounds on the possible values of the coordinates of $\mathbf{x}$.

The proof of equation (5.28) is very similar in the nonrandom case. Using equation (5.27), we write, up to the first order,

$$(\mathbf{f}(\mathbf{x}) - \mathbf{f}(\mathbf{x}_0))(\mathbf{f}(\mathbf{x}) - \mathbf{f}(\mathbf{x}_0))^T = \mathbf{Df}(\mathbf{x}_0)(\mathbf{x} - \mathbf{x}_0)(\mathbf{x} - \mathbf{x}_0)^T \mathbf{Df}(\mathbf{x}_0)^T \qquad (5.32)$$

If the vectors $\mathbf{x}$ satisfy

$$(\mathbf{z}^T(\mathbf{x} - \mathbf{x}_0))^2 \le \mathbf{z}^T \Lambda_\mathbf{x} \mathbf{z} \qquad (5.33)$$

for all $\mathbf{z}$ in R^n, then $\mathbf{f}(\mathbf{x})$ satisfies, up to the first order,

$$(\mathbf{t}^T(\mathbf{f}(\mathbf{x}) - \mathbf{f}(\mathbf{x}_0)))^2 \le \mathbf{t}^T \Lambda_\mathbf{y} \mathbf{t}$$

for all $\mathbf{t}$ in R^m, with

$$\Lambda_\mathbf{y} = \mathbf{Df}(\mathbf{x}_0)\Lambda_\mathbf{x}\mathbf{Df}(\mathbf{x}_0)^T$$

To see this, multiply both sides of equation (5.32), on the left by $\mathbf{t}^T$ and on the right by $\mathbf{t}$ (in R^m), and apply equation (5.33) with $\mathbf{z} = \mathbf{Df}(\mathbf{x}_0)^T\mathbf{t}$. Therefore, $\Lambda_\mathbf{y}$ describes the bounds on $\mathbf{y} = \mathbf{f}(\mathbf{x})$ in the vicinity of $\mathbf{y}_0 = \mathbf{f}(\mathbf{x}_0)$ given those of $\mathbf{x}$ in the vicinity of $\mathbf{x}_0$.

5.6.2   When y has been obtained by an unconstrained minimization

This is a slightly more difficult case than the previous one but one that occurs more frequently. We consider a criterion function $C(\mathbf{x}, \mathbf{z})$, and we minimize it with respect to $\mathbf{z}$ for a given measurement vector $\mathbf{x}_0$. A minimum is obtained for $\mathbf{z} = \mathbf{y}_0$, and this defines a function $\mathbf{f}$ such that $\mathbf{y} = \mathbf{f}(\mathbf{x})$ in a neighborhood of $(\mathbf{x}_0, \mathbf{y}_0)$. The main difference from the previous case is that the function $\mathbf{f}$ is known not *explicitly* but only *implicitly* through the function C. In order to obtain our result, we need the following theorem:

Theorem 5.2
[Implicit functions theorem] Let $\Phi : (\mathbf{x}, \mathbf{y}) \to \Phi(\mathbf{x}, \mathbf{y})$ be a function of class C^∞ from an open set U of $R^n \times R^m$ into R^m. Let $(\mathbf{x}_0, \mathbf{y}_0)$ be a point of U such that $\Phi(\mathbf{x}_0, \mathbf{y}_0) = \mathbf{0}$ and such that the partial derivative $\frac{\partial \Phi}{\partial \mathbf{y}}(\mathbf{x}_0, \mathbf{y}_0))$ is one-to-one from R^m to R^m. Then there exists an open set U' of R^n containing $\mathbf{x}_0$ and an open set U'' of R^m containing $\mathbf{y}_0$ and a C^∞ mapping $\mathbf{f} : R^n \to R^m$ such that, for $(\mathbf{x}, \mathbf{y})$ in $U' \times U''$, the two relations $\Phi(\mathbf{x}, \mathbf{y}) = \mathbf{0}$ and $\mathbf{y} = \mathbf{f}(\mathbf{x})$ are equivalent. Furthermore, the derivative $\mathbf{Df}(\mathbf{x})$ of $\mathbf{f}$ is equal to $-\frac{\partial \Phi}{\partial \mathbf{y}^{-1}}\frac{\partial \Phi}{\partial \mathbf{x}}$.

Proof   The proof is outside the scope of this book. The interested reader is referred to the book by Spivak [Spi79]. ∎

We apply theorem 5.2 to obtain the following result:

Proposition 5.7
Let the criterion function $C : R^n \times R^m \to R$ be C^∞, $\mathbf{x}_0$ be the measurement vector and $\mathbf{y}_0$ be a local minimum of $C(\mathbf{x}_0, \mathbf{z})$. If the Hessian $\mathbf{H}$ of C with respect to $\mathbf{z}$ is invertible at $(\mathbf{x}, \mathbf{z}) = (\mathbf{x}_0, \mathbf{y}_0)$, then there exists an open set

U' of R^n containing $\mathbf{x}_0$ and an open set U'' of R^m containing $\mathbf{y}_0$ and a C^∞ mapping $\mathbf{f} : R^n \to R^m$ such that, for $(\mathbf{x}, \mathbf{y})$ in $U' \times U''$, the two relations "$\mathbf{y}$ is a local minimum of $C(\mathbf{x}, \mathbf{z})$ with respect to $\mathbf{z}$" and $\mathbf{y} = \mathbf{f}(\mathbf{x})$ are equivalent. Furthermore, we have the following equation:

$$\mathbf{Df}(\mathbf{x}) = -\mathbf{H}^{-1} \frac{\partial \mathbf{\Phi}}{\partial \mathbf{x}} \tag{5.34}$$

where we have taken

$$\mathbf{\Phi} = \left(\frac{\partial C}{\partial \mathbf{z}} \right)^T \qquad \text{an } m \times 1 \text{ vector}$$

$$\mathbf{H} = \frac{\partial \mathbf{\Phi}}{\partial \mathbf{z}} \qquad \text{an } m \times m \text{ matrix}$$

Proof Let us define $\mathbf{\Phi} = (\frac{\partial C}{\partial \mathbf{z}})^T$. By the definition of a local minimum, we have $\mathbf{\Phi}(\mathbf{x}_0, \mathbf{y}_0) = \mathbf{0}$. Moreover, $\frac{\partial \mathbf{\Phi}}{\partial \mathbf{z}}(\mathbf{x}_0, \mathbf{y}_0) = \mathbf{H}$ is the Hessian of C with respect to $\mathbf{z}$ at $(\mathbf{x}, \mathbf{z}) = (\mathbf{x}_0, \mathbf{y}_0)$ and is invertible. The proposition is then a direct consequence of theorem 5.2. ∎

In practice, we are given $\mathbf{x}_0$ and use some optimization method that computes $\mathbf{y}_0$. Equation (5.34) allows us to compute the derivative of $\mathbf{y}$ as a function of $\mathbf{x}$ at $\mathbf{x}_0$ from the second-order derivatives of the criterion $C(\mathbf{x}, \mathbf{z})$ with respect to $\mathbf{x}$ and $\mathbf{z}$ at $\mathbf{x} = \mathbf{x}_0$ and $\mathbf{z} = \mathbf{y}_0$. Equation (5.28) then allows us to compute the bounds on $\mathbf{y}$ knowing those on $\mathbf{x}$.

5.6.3   When y has been obtained by a constrained minimization

With the notations of the previous section, we assume that $\mathbf{y}_0$ has been obtained by minimizing the criterion function $C(\mathbf{x}_0, \mathbf{z})$ subject to some constraints:

$$\min_{\mathbf{z}} C(\mathbf{x}, \mathbf{z})$$

subject to $h_i(\mathbf{z}) = 0 \qquad i = 1, \dots, p$

We assume that the constraints are independent in the sense that the $m \times p$ Jacobian matrix $\mathbf{K} = [\frac{dh_1}{dz}^T, \dots, \frac{dh_p}{dz}^T]$ is of rank p (in particular we have $m \geq p$). We assume that a minimum has been obtained for $\mathbf{z} = \mathbf{y}_0$, and we are interested in the first-order variations of this minimum when $\mathbf{x}_0$ varies.

In order to achieve this goal, we are going to again use theorem 5.2. Using the Lagrange multipliers idea, we define a new criterion C' as

$$C'(\mathbf{x}_0, \mathbf{z}) = C(\mathbf{x}_0, \mathbf{z}) + \sum_{i=1}^{p} \lambda_i h_i(\mathbf{z})$$

Let $\boldsymbol{\lambda} = [\lambda_1, \ldots, \lambda_p]^T$. At the optimum, the derivative of C' with respect to $\mathbf{z}$ is equal to $\mathbf{0}$:

$$(\frac{\partial C'}{\partial \mathbf{z}})^T = (\frac{\partial C}{\partial \mathbf{z}})^T + \sum_{i=1}^{p} \lambda_i (\frac{dh_i}{d\mathbf{z}})^T = \mathbf{E} + \mathbf{K}\boldsymbol{\lambda} = \mathbf{0} \tag{5.35}$$

where $\mathbf{E} = (\frac{\partial C}{\partial \mathbf{z}})^T$. Let us assume without loss of generality that the first p rows of $\mathbf{K}$ are linearly independent. We can then use them to compute $\boldsymbol{\lambda}$ as a function of $\mathbf{x}_0$ and $\mathbf{z}$. More precisely, let $\mathbf{K}_1$ be the $p \times p$ matrix obtained by considering the first p rows of matrix $\mathbf{K}$, and let $\mathbf{K}_2$ be the $(m-p) \times p$ matrix obtained by considering its $m-p$ last rows. We similarly define the $p \times 1$ vector $\mathbf{E}_1$ and the $(m-p) \times 1$ vector $\mathbf{E}_2$. We have

$$\boldsymbol{\lambda} = -\mathbf{K}_1^{-1}\mathbf{E}_1 \tag{5.36}$$

We can then replace $\boldsymbol{\lambda}$ by this expression in the $m-p$ remaining equations:

$$\mathbf{K}_2\boldsymbol{\lambda} + \mathbf{E}_2 = \mathbf{0} \tag{5.37}$$

We can now define a function $\boldsymbol{\Phi}(\mathbf{x}, \mathbf{y})$ as follows. It is a mapping from $R^n \times R^m$ into R^m, with its first $m-p$ components equal to

$$-\mathbf{K}_2(\mathbf{y})\mathbf{K}_1^{-1}(\mathbf{y})\mathbf{E}_1(\mathbf{x}, \mathbf{y}) + \mathbf{E}_2(\mathbf{x}, \mathbf{y})$$

and its last p components given by $\mathbf{h}(\mathbf{y})$. This satisfies the condition $\boldsymbol{\Phi}(\mathbf{x}_0, \mathbf{y}_0) = \mathbf{0}$, and therefore, if the $m \times m$ matrix $\frac{\partial \boldsymbol{\Phi}}{\partial \mathbf{y}}(\mathbf{x}_0, \mathbf{y}_0)$ is invertible, we can apply theorem 5.2: There exist neighborhoods U' of $\mathbf{x}_0$ in R^n and U'' of $\mathbf{y}_0$ in R^m and a C^∞ mapping $\mathbf{f}: R^n \to R^m$ such that, for $(\mathbf{x}, \mathbf{y})$ in $U' \times U''$, the two relations $\boldsymbol{\Phi}(\mathbf{x}, \mathbf{y}) = \mathbf{0}$ and $\mathbf{y} = \mathbf{f}(\mathbf{x})$ are equivalent. Furthermore, the derivative $\mathbf{Df}$ of $\mathbf{f}$ is equal to $-(\frac{\partial \boldsymbol{\Phi}}{\partial \mathbf{y}})^{-1}\frac{\partial \boldsymbol{\Phi}}{\partial \mathbf{x}}$, which can be computed from the second-order derivatives of C and $\mathbf{h}$. Note that the last p rows of $\frac{\partial \boldsymbol{\Phi}}{\partial \mathbf{x}}$ are equal to $\mathbf{0}$ since $\mathbf{h}$ is not a function of $\mathbf{x}$. Therefore, in order to compute $\mathbf{Df}$, only the first $m-p$ columns of $(\frac{\partial \boldsymbol{\Phi}}{\partial \mathbf{y}})^{-1}$ have to be computed. Note also that the rank of $\mathbf{Df}$ is less than or equal to the smallest of the two numbers $m - p$ and n. In order to build an intuitive notion of what is involved, the reader is encouraged to work out the details of problem 7. See also problem 6 of chapter 8 for a more complicated example.

5.6.4 An example: computing the uncertainty of a 2-D line

In chapter 4 we discussed a number of methods for detecting edge pixels. We also know that those pixels can be linked together into sets of connected chains. It may be interesting for some applications in stereo and motion, which will be described in some of the forthcoming chapters, to perform a polygonal approximation of those chains. Given that the edge pixels are detected in the image with some uncertainty, we would like to characterize the uncertainty of the line segments. Let us thus assume that that we are given p pixels $m_i, i = 1, \ldots, p$, which are represented by their coordinate vectors $\mathbf{m}_i = [u_i, v_i]^T$, and that we approximate them by a line segment AB. The supporting line of AB is denoted by $\langle A, B \rangle$ and is represented as explained in section 5.3.3.2.

5.6.4.1 *A representation of the best supporting line*

Finding the best approximating line to a set of planar points is a classical problem (see, for example, Chapter 9 of the book by Duda and Hart [DH73] and problem 4), but we attack it here in the setting of the representation discussed in section 5.3.3.2. Remember that a line $\langle A, B \rangle$ is represented by two numbers (a, b) through two maps: φ_1, which represents all lines that are not parallel to the u-axis of equation $u + av + b = 0$, and φ_2, which represents all lines that are not parallel to the v-axis of equation $au + v + b = 0$. We will develop the computation only for φ_1, and the reader can easily transpose the results to φ_2.

The distance of a pixel m of coordinates (u, v) to the line $\langle A, B \rangle$ is

$$d(m, \langle A, B \rangle) = \frac{|u + av + b|}{\sqrt{1 + a^2}}$$

Therefore, we minimize with respect to a and b the criterion

$$C = \sum_{i=1}^{p} d^2(m_i, \langle A, B \rangle) = \frac{1}{1 + a^2} \sum_{i=1}^{p} (u_i + av_i + b)^2 \tag{5.38}$$

Computing the partial derivatives of C with respect to a and b we have

$$\frac{1}{2}\frac{\partial C}{\partial a} = -\frac{a}{(1+a^2)^2}\sum_{i=1}^{p}(u_i + av_i + b)^2 + \frac{1}{1+a^2}\sum_{i=1}^{p}v_i(u_i + av_i + b)$$

$$\frac{1}{2}\frac{\partial C}{\partial b} = \frac{1}{1+a^2}\sum_{i=1}^{p}(u_i + av_i + b)$$

Setting $\frac{\partial C}{\partial b}$ equal to 0 yields

$$b = -(\overline{u} + a\overline{v}) \tag{5.39}$$

where we have introduced the two quantities

$$\overline{u} = \frac{1}{p}\sum_{i=1}^{p}u_i \qquad \overline{v} = \frac{1}{p}\sum_{i=1}^{p}v_i$$

which are the coordinates of the center of gravity of the set of pixels. Equation (5.39) shows that the best approximating line goes through this point, since $\overline{u} + a\overline{v} + b = 0$.

Setting $\frac{\partial C}{\partial a}$ equal to 0 yields

$$\sum_{i=1}^{p}(u_i + av_i + b)(v_i - au_i - ab) = 0$$

which can be rewritten as

$$S_{uv} - a(S_{u^2} - S_{v^2}) + b\overline{v} - a^2 S_{uv} - 2ab\overline{u} - a^2 b\overline{v} - ab^2 = 0 \tag{5.40}$$

where we have introduced the three quantities

$$S_{u^2} = \frac{1}{p}\sum_{i=1}^{p}u_i^2 \qquad S_{v^2} = \frac{1}{p}\sum_{i=1}^{p}v_i^2 \qquad S_{uv} = \frac{1}{p}\sum_{i=1}^{p}u_i v_i$$

We replace b in equation (5.40) by its value from equation (5.39) and have

$$a^2(S_{uv} - \overline{u}\,\overline{v}) + a[(S_{u^2} - \overline{u}^2) - (S_{v^2} - \overline{v}^2)] - (S_{uv} - \overline{u}\,\overline{v}) = 0 \tag{5.41}$$

It is straightforward to show that $S_{u^2} - \overline{u}^2 = \frac{1}{p}\sum_{i=1}^{p}(u_i - \overline{u})^2$, which we denote as σ_u^2 (with a similar definition for σ_v^2), and that $S_{uv} - \overline{u}\,\overline{v} = \frac{1}{p}\sum_{i=1}^{p}(u_i - \overline{u})(v_i - \overline{v})$, which we denote as σ_{uv}. We can thus rewrite equation (5.41) as

$$a^2\sigma_{uv} + a(\sigma_u^2 - \sigma_v^2) - \sigma_{uv} = 0 \tag{5.42}$$

Notice that this equation is quadratic in a and always has two real roots of opposite signs. A special case occurs when $\sigma_{uv} = 0$, where there is only one zero root unless $\sigma_u^2 - \sigma_v^2 = 0$, in which case a is undefined. The corresponding values for b are obtained from equation (5.39). The correct root is the one that makes C the smallest. Assuming that σ_{uv} is not zero, we define

$$h = \frac{1}{2} \frac{\sigma_{u2} - \sigma_{v2}}{\sigma_{uv}} \tag{5.43}$$

We see that the roots of equation (5.41) are

$$a = -h \pm \sqrt{1 + h^2} \tag{5.44}$$

This completes the computation of the representation in the map defined by φ_1 of the best line approximating the p pixels m_i.

5.6.4.2 *Pixel uncertainty*

In practice, the pixels m_i are detected with some error. We can either assume that they are random with a given mean $\hat{\mathbf{m}}_i$ (the actual detected edge pixel) and covariance matrix Λ_i, or that we observe $\hat{\mathbf{m}}_i$ with some error bounds described by the matrix Λ_i, as shown in section 5.6.1.2. The question is this: What is a reasonable form for Λ_i? A simple, but commonly used form, is the following (we drop the index i for simplicity):

$$\Lambda = \begin{bmatrix} \sigma_1^2 & 0 \\ 0 & \sigma_2^2 \end{bmatrix}$$

which assumes that the axes of the ellipse of uncertainty are parallel to the u- and v-axes. Since the idea of edge direction is important, as we have seen in chapter 4, a more reasonable model is to assume that the uncertainty is σ_1^2 in the direction θ of the image intensity gradient and σ_2^2 in the perpendicular direction. This yields the following form for Λ:

$$\Lambda = \begin{bmatrix} \cos\theta & -\sin\theta \\ \sin\theta & \cos\theta \end{bmatrix} \begin{bmatrix} \sigma_1^2 & 0 \\ 0 & \sigma_2^2 \end{bmatrix} \begin{bmatrix} \cos\theta & \sin\theta \\ -\sin\theta & \cos\theta \end{bmatrix}$$

$$= \begin{bmatrix} \sigma_1^2 \cos^2\theta + \sigma_2^2 \sin^2\theta & (\sigma_1^2 - \sigma_2^2)\sin\theta\cos\theta \\ (\sigma_1^2 - \sigma_2^2)\sin\theta\cos\theta & \sigma_1^2 \sin^2\theta + \sigma_2^2 \cos^2\theta \end{bmatrix} \tag{5.45}$$

5.6.4.3 *Line uncertainty*

We have derived an analytical expression for the values of a and b representing the support line $\langle A, B \rangle$ of the best approximating line segment AB as functions of the measurements $\hat{m}_i$. Let $\mathbf{y} = [a, b]^T$ and $\mathbf{x} = [\mathbf{m}_1, \ldots, \mathbf{m}_p]^T$. The vector $\mathbf{x}_0$ is formed from the coordinates of the pixels that have actually been measured:

$$\mathbf{x}_0 = [\hat{\mathbf{m}}_1, \ldots, \hat{\mathbf{m}}_p]^T$$

Equations (5.44) and (5.39) are of the form $\mathbf{y} = \mathbf{f}(\mathbf{x})$, and we can compute the uncertainty of $\mathbf{y}$ up to the first order from the uncertainty of $\mathbf{x}$, which we can choose as equal to

$$\Lambda_{\mathbf{x}} = \text{diag}(\Lambda_1, \ldots, \Lambda_p)$$

$\Lambda_{\mathbf{x}}$ is a $2p \times 2p$ symmetric matrix whose diagonal is formed with the matrices $\Lambda_i, i = 1, \ldots, p$, which are given by equation (5.45), $\mathbf{Df}(\mathbf{x}_0)$ is a $2 \times 2p$ matrix equal to

$$\mathbf{Df}(\mathbf{x}_0) = \begin{bmatrix} \frac{\partial a}{\partial \mathbf{m}_1}, \ldots, \frac{\partial a}{\partial \mathbf{m}_n} \\ \frac{\partial b}{\partial \mathbf{m}_1}, \ldots, \frac{\partial b}{\partial \mathbf{m}_n} \end{bmatrix}$$

where all partial derivatives are evaluated at the pixels $\hat{m}_i$. If we push the computation slightly further we have

$$\frac{\partial a}{\partial \mathbf{m}_i} = \frac{\partial a}{\partial h} \frac{\partial h}{\partial \mathbf{m}_i} = \left(-1 \pm \frac{h}{\sqrt{1 + h^2}} \right) \frac{\partial h}{\partial \mathbf{m}_i}$$

$$\frac{\partial b}{\partial \mathbf{m}_i} = -\left(\frac{1}{p} \begin{bmatrix} 1 & a \end{bmatrix} + \overline{v} \frac{\partial a}{\partial \mathbf{m}_i} \right)$$

This completes the computation of the first-order approximation of the uncertainty of the representation in the map φ_1 of the best straight line approximating the p pixels $\hat{m}_i$.

We could also have saved ourselves the trouble of computing the analytical expression of $\mathbf{f}$ and trusted our favorite numerical minimization program to find the optimal a and b that minimize criterion (5.38) and then apply the results of section 5.6.2 to estimate the uncertainty. It turns out that this in fact is much simpler than the previous technique. Indeed, with the notations of that section, $\Phi = \frac{\partial C}{\partial \mathbf{z}^T}$ is a 2×1 vector, $\mathbf{H}$ is a 2×2 matrix, and $\frac{\partial \Phi}{\partial \mathbf{x}}$ is a $2 \times 2p$ vector easily computed from equation (5.38). The reader should compare the complexity of these computations with the previous ones. But remember that most of the burden has been passed over to the minimization routine.

5.7 Problems

1. Give the maps φ_1 and φ_2 corresponding to the open sets $U_1 =]0, 2\pi[$ and $U_2 =]-\pi, \pi[$ of section 5.3.2.1. Show that S^1, together with the atlas $((U_i, \varphi_i), i = 1, 2)$ is a C^∞ manifold.

2. In section 5.5 we claim that the decomposition of a 3-D displacement into a rotation and a translation is not unique and that the axis of rotation can be chosen arbitrarily. What is the effect of changing the axis of rotation in this decomposition?

3. The goal of this problem is to establish a general framework for computing derivatives of rotation matrices with respect to the parameters that are used to represent them. We restrict ourselves to minimal representations, i.e., the number of parameters is equal to 3.

   a. Suppose that the rotation matrix $\mathbf{R}$ is a C^1 function of the three-dimensional parameter vector $\alpha = [\alpha_1, \alpha_2, \alpha_3]^T$. Show that the three matrices $\mathbf{B}_i = \frac{\partial \mathbf{R}}{\partial \alpha_i} \mathbf{R}^T$, $i = 1, 2, 3$ are antisymmetric. Let $\mathbf{b}_i$ be the three vectors such that

   $$\mathbf{B}_i \mathbf{v} = \mathbf{b}_i \wedge \mathbf{v} \quad \text{for all vectors } \mathbf{v}, \quad i = 1, 2, 3$$

   If $\mathbf{M}$ is a vector representing a three-dimensional point M, show that the result of applying the 3×3 matrix $\frac{d\mathbf{RM}}{d\alpha}$ to a vector $\mathbf{v} = [v_1, v_2, v_3]^T$ is equal to

   $$\frac{d\mathbf{RM}}{d\alpha} \mathbf{v} = (\sum_{i=1}^{3} v_i \mathbf{b}_i) \wedge \mathbf{RM}$$

   b. We will now apply the result of the previous question to the case of the representation of a rotation matrix with the exponential of an antisymmetric matrix as discussed in section 5.5.4. Let $\mathbf{e}_i, i = 1, 2, 3$ be the standard basis of R^3.

i. Using the notations of section 5.5.4, show that

$$\frac{\partial \theta}{\partial a} = \frac{a}{\theta} \qquad \frac{\partial \mathbf{H}}{\partial \theta} = \tilde{\mathbf{e}}_1 \qquad \mathbf{H}\tilde{\mathbf{e}}_1\mathbf{H} = -a\mathbf{H}$$

ii. Let us rewrite Rodrigues' formula (equation 5.26) as

$$\mathbf{R} = \mathbf{I} + f(\theta)\mathbf{H} + g(\theta)\mathbf{H}^2 \tag{5.46}$$

where

$$f(\theta) = \frac{\sin\theta}{\theta} \qquad g(\theta) = \frac{1-\cos\theta}{\theta^2}$$

Show that f and g satisfy the following relation:

$$2g(\theta) - f^2(\theta) - \theta^2 g^2(\theta) = 0 \tag{5.47}$$

iii. Show that the matrix $\mathbf{B}_1$ is given by

$$\mathbf{B}_1^T = \mathbf{R}(\frac{\partial \mathbf{R}}{\partial a})^T = a\frac{\sin\theta - \theta}{\theta^3}\mathbf{H} - f(\theta)\tilde{\mathbf{e}}_1 + g(\theta)(\mathbf{H}\tilde{\mathbf{e}}_1 - \tilde{\mathbf{e}}_1\mathbf{H})$$

iv. Show that

$$\frac{d\mathbf{RM}}{d\mathbf{r}} = \mathbf{b} \wedge \mathbf{RM}$$

where

$$\mathbf{b} = \frac{1-f(\theta)}{\theta^2}(\mathbf{r.v})\mathbf{r} + f(\theta)\mathbf{v} + g(\theta)\mathbf{r}\wedge\mathbf{v}$$

4. Perform the computation that is done in section 5.6.4 with the representation (φ, ρ):

$$u\cos\varphi + v\sin\varphi - \rho = 0$$

5. Compute $\frac{\partial h}{\partial \mathbf{m}_i}$, where h is defined in section 5.6.4.1.

6. Compute the uncertainty on the endpoints A and B of a segment, assuming that they are the projections on $\langle A, B\rangle$ of m_1 and m_n (see section 5.6.4.3).

7. This problem is designed to help the reader better understand the results of section 5.6.3. Let $\mathbf{x} = [a, b]^T$ and $\mathbf{z} = [u, v]^T$. We will consider the following optimization problem:

$$\min_{\mathbf{z}} C(\mathbf{x}, \mathbf{z})$$

subject to $\|\mathbf{z}\|^2 = 1$ (5.48)

with

$$C(\mathbf{x}, \mathbf{z}) = -(\mathbf{x}^T \mathbf{z})^2$$

a. Give a geometric interpretation of this problem.

b. Show that there are, in general, two solutions given by

$$\mathbf{y} = [y_1, y_2]^T = \pm \frac{\mathbf{x}}{\|\mathbf{x}\|}$$

c. Compute $\frac{\partial \mathbf{y}}{\partial \mathbf{x}}$

d. Apply the Lagrange multiplier method to this problem, and compute the vector $(\frac{\partial C'}{\partial \mathbf{z}})^T (\mathbf{x}, \mathbf{z}, \lambda)$. Use its first component to compute λ.

e. Use your result and the second component of $(\frac{\partial C'}{\partial \mathbf{z}})^T$ to obtain a function $\psi(\mathbf{x}, \mathbf{z})$ that must be identically 0.

f. Define

$$\Phi(\mathbf{x}, \mathbf{z}) = \begin{bmatrix} \psi(\mathbf{x}, \mathbf{z}) \\ \frac{1}{2}(\mathbf{z}^T \mathbf{z} - 1) \end{bmatrix}$$

and compute $\mathbf{Df} = (\frac{\partial \Phi}{\partial \mathbf{z}})^{-1} \frac{\partial \Phi}{\partial \mathbf{x}}$. Compare your result with the result of question c. What is the rank of $\mathbf{Df}$?

8. Apply the results of section 5.6.3 to compute a first-order approximation of the bounds on the perspective projection matrix obtained by the method described in section 3.4.1.4, which consists of minimizing the criterion (3.42) subject to the constraints (3.22) and (3.23).

9. Apply the results of section 5.6.2 to compute a first-order approximation of the bounds on the intrinsic and extrinsic parameters computed by the method described in section 3.4.1.4, which consists of minimizing criterion (3.43) with respect to the intrinsic and extrinsic parameters.

6   Stereo Vision

In this chapter we deal with an important practical problem: the reconstruction of the 3-D coordinates of a number of points in a scene given several images (usually two, but see also section 6.9) obtained by cameras of known relative positions and orientations. As we will see, the main difficulty is to come up with good answers for the following so-called *correspondence problem*: Given a token in image 1, what is the corresponding token in image 2? Since there are, in general, several possibilities for the choice of the corresponding token in image 2, the stereo correspondence problem is said to be *ambiguous*, and therefore it raises a number of questions: Which tokens, which features, and which constraints can be used to reduce this ambiguity? We will now discuss the tokens, the features, and the constraints that are good candidates.

6.1   Correspondence ambiguity; tokens and features

6.1.1   Ambiguity

6.1.1.1   *The pinhole model and the correspondence problem*

One of the basic problems to be solved in stereo vision is shown in figure 6.1. Two pinhole cameras of the types discussed in chapter 3 form the images m_1 and m_2 of a physical point M. As shown in this figure, we have chosen three coordinate systems, one in each retinal plane ((u_1, v_1) and (u_2, v_2)) and one in 3-D space ((x, y, z)), which is sometimes called

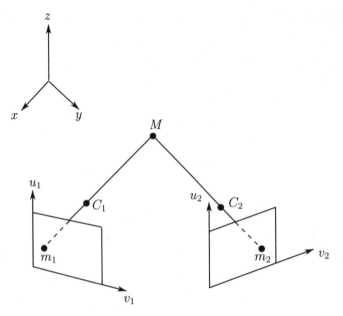

Figure 6.1   The 3-D vision problem.

the *world reference frame*. The distance between the two optical centers C_1 and C_2 is sometimes called the *baseline*.

What we observe are two images formed in the retinal planes $\mathcal{R}_1$ and $\mathcal{R}_2$. Given these two images, we want to solve two problems:

1. For a point m_1 in plane 1, decide which point m_2 in plane 2 it corresponds to. *Correspond* means that they are the images of the same physical point M. This is the *correspondence problem*.

2. Given m_1 and m_2, compute the 3-D coordinates of M in the world reference frame. This is the *reconstruction problem*.

With the simple model of figure 6.1, the second question can be answered by intersecting the lines $\langle C_1, m_1 \rangle$ and $\langle C_2, m_2 \rangle$. The result essentially depends on how accurately we have calibrated our stereo rig, i.e., how accurately we know the positions of C_1 and C_2 and the planes $\mathcal{R}_1$ and $\mathcal{R}_2$ in the world coordinate system. This is of course related to the calibration problem, which has been studied in detail in chapter 3 in the case of a single camera. We will consider the case of several cameras and how to best reconstruct points and lines in section 6.10. Note that if the positions of m_1 and m_2 are imperfectly known (which is always the case), $\langle C_1, m_1 \rangle$ and $\langle C_2, m_2 \rangle$ may not intersect.

6.1.1.2 The ambiguity of the correspondence problem

It should be clear that, unless some care is taken, the correspondence problem is ambiguous: Given a point m_1 in retina 1, it may *a priori* be put in correspondence with any point m_2 in retina 2. To solve this difficulty, we must use constraints to reduce the number of potential matches for any given point m_1. These constraints are of three basic kinds:

1. Geometric constraints imposed by the imaging system. Probably the most important such constraint is the *epipolar constraint* (see section 6.2.1), thanks to which we can transform a two-dimensional search into a one-dimensional one.

2. Geometric constraints arising from the objects being looked at. We can assume, for example, that their distance to the imaging system varies slowly almost everywhere (except at depth discontinuities). This is the origin of the disparity gradient constraint studied in section 6.2.5. Another constraint of this type arises if we assume that the objects we look at are polyhedral, as described in section 6.8.

3. Physical constraints such as those arising from models of the way objects interact with the illumination. This implies using models of the illumination sources and of the reflectances of the objects' surfaces. The simplest and most widely used model of this sort is the Lambertian model [Hor86].

Each of these constraints can be used, as will be shown next, to reduce the ambiguity of correspondence.

6.1.2 Tokens and features

Tokens used in stereo vision must be reliably extractable from images. There are a number of possible candidates:

- The simplest one is the pixel used in the correlation techniques (see section 6.4). In order to characterize pixels, we have to attach features to them. What features should we compute in both images to help resolve the correspondence problem? One condition is certainly that, if pixels m_1 and m_2 match, then their features should be the same, or approximately the same. The simplest feature we can think of is the measured radiance. But when is it the same for two corresponding pixels?

The light reflected by the surface of an object is a function of the positions of the sources, the orientation of the surface, and the viewing direction (see chapter 10 of the book by Horn [Hor86]). This behavior can be summarized in the reflectance function. For a Lambertian surface (a completely matte surface), the reflected light is the same in all directions. As a result, the intensities at two corresponding points are the same. Very few surfaces are Lambertian, however, and the extreme case is a purely glossy surface that acts like a mirror. For such a surface, the intensities at two corresponding points are most likely to be different. Between these two extremes there is an entire class of surfaces for which the reflected light varies slowly with the direction of viewing, and therefore there is a large class of surfaces for which the intensities at corresponding points are fairly close if the base line is small with respect to the viewing distance. Many of the original techniques for computing stereo correspondences are based on the idea of correlating the left and right intensity images of a stereo pair. This works well when the reflectance functions of objects are close to Lambertians, but otherwise it does not.

■ The next simplest token is the edge pixel. We can also think of grouping edge pixels together to form curves or portions of curves. The simplest curve that is invariant by perspective projection is the straight line. We will show in sections 6.7 and 6.9.1 how to use line segments as tokens in the stereo correspondence process. Curves can also be used successfully, as shown in section 6.9.2. Line segments and curves can have both geometric and intensity-based features attached to them such as length, orientation, curvature, and average contrast across them. As seen in the edge classification analysis done in chapter 4, not all edges are good for stereo. In particular, what we called *occluding edges*, i.e., depth discontinuities where the normal to the object turns away smoothly from the observer, pose a problem since in fact the two cameras do not see the same part of the object. Except for this case, edges are a very reliable source of information to guide the stereo matching process.

- Last, we can use image regions as tokens to be matched in the stereo process. Depending on how these regions are extracted, their shapes and the intensity-based feature attached to them may or may not be invariant by perspective transformation.

6.2 Constraints

6.2.1 The epipolar constraint

First we will study a very powerful constraint that arises from the geometry of stereo vision. We will use many of the results of chapter 3.

6.2.1.1 What is the epipolar constraint?

We will make a simple statement, with the help of figure 6.2. In this figure we see that, given m_1 in the retinal plane $\mathcal{R}_1$, all possible physical points M that may have produced m_1 are on the infinite half-line $\langle m_1, C_1 \rangle$. As a direct consequence, all possible matches m_2 of m_1 in the plane $\mathcal{R}_2$ are located on the image, through the second imaging system, of this infinite half-line. This image is an infinite half-line ep_2 going

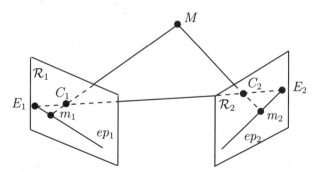

Figure 6.2 The epipolar geometry.

through the point E_2, which is the intersection of the line $\langle C_1, C_2 \rangle$ with the plane $\mathcal{R}_2$. E_2 is called the *epipole* of the second camera with respect to the first, and the line ep_2 is called the *epipolar line* of point m_1 in the retinal plane $\mathcal{R}_2$ of the second camera.

The corresponding constraint is that, for a given point m_1 in the plane $\mathcal{R}_1$, its possible matches in the plane $\mathcal{R}_2$ all lie on a line (see figure 6.2). Therefore, we have reduced the dimension of our search space from two dimensions to one. The epipolar constraint is of course symmetric and, for a point m_2 in the plane $\mathcal{R}_2$, its possible matches in the retinal plane $\mathcal{R}_1$ all lie on a line ep_1 through the epipole E_1, which is the intersection of the line $\langle C_1, C_2 \rangle$ with the plane $\mathcal{R}_1$. The lines ep_1 and ep_2 are the intersections of the plane $C_1 M C_2$, called the *epipolar plane* defined by M, with the planes $\mathcal{R}_1$ and $\mathcal{R}_2$, respectively.

Of course, when the plane $\mathcal{R}_1$ or the plane $\mathcal{R}_2$, or both, are parallel to the line $\langle C_1, C_2 \rangle$, one (or both) epipoles go to infinity and the epipolar lines in one plane (or both) become parallel. The situation where both planes are parallel to the line $\langle C_1, C_2 \rangle$ is often assumed because of its simplicity. But, in practice, it is difficult to align the two optical systems precisely and in a stable way, and we will next show that the problem of computing the epipolar lines is just as simple in the general case.

6.2.1.2 Computing the epipolar geometry

Given the two cameras 1 and 2, we know from chapter 3 that

$$\tilde{\mathbf{m}}_1 = \tilde{\mathbf{P}}_1 \tilde{\mathbf{M}} \tag{6.1}$$

and

$$\tilde{\mathbf{m}}_2 = \tilde{\mathbf{P}}_2 \tilde{\mathbf{M}} \tag{6.2}$$

As has been shown in the same chapter, the coordinates of the two optical centers, C_i $(i = 1, 2)$, in the world reference frame, are obtained by solving the following two systems of linear equations:

$$\tilde{\mathbf{P}}_i \tilde{\mathbf{M}} = \mathbf{0} \qquad i = 1, 2$$

Since each epipole E_i is the image by the ith camera of the other camera's optical center C_j $(j \neq i)$, the image coordinates of the epipoles E_i are

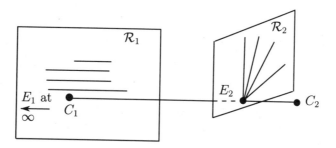

Figure 6.3 $\langle C_1, C_2 \rangle$ is parallel to the plane $\mathcal{R}_1$: E_1 is at ∞; the epipolar lines are parallel in the plane $\mathcal{R}_1$ and intersect at E_2 in the plane $\mathcal{R}_2$.

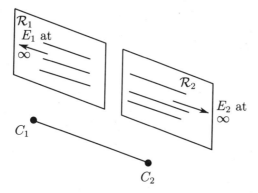

Figure 6.4 $\langle C_1, C_2 \rangle$ is parallel to the planes $\mathcal{R}_1$ and $\mathcal{R}_2$: E_1 and E_2 are at ∞; the epipolar lines are parallel in both planes $\mathcal{R}_1$ and $\mathcal{R}_2$.

obtained by applying matrices $\tilde{\mathbf{P}}_i$ to the vectors $\tilde{\mathbf{C}}_j$ ($i, j = 1, 2$, $i \neq j$). We know that there are three cases for the geometry of the epipoles:

1. Both epipoles are at a finite distance in their respective focal planes (see figure 6.2).

2. One is at a finite distance, and the other is at infinity (see figure 6.3).

3. They are both at infinity (see figure 6.4).

Let us now show how, for a given point m_1 in the plane $\mathcal{R}_1$, the corresponding epipolar line ep_1 can be computed. In order to determine a line, we need two points. One of them is the epipole E_2, which, according to equation (3.7), is given by

$$\tilde{\mathbf{e}}_2 = \tilde{\mathbf{P}}_2 \begin{bmatrix} -\mathbf{P}_1^{-1}\tilde{\mathbf{p}}_1 \\ 1 \end{bmatrix}$$

Another point is the point at infinity of the optical ray $\langle C_1, m_1 \rangle$, i.e., its point of intersection with the plane at infinity. According to equation (3.8), the image m_2 of this point in the second retinal plane is given by

$$\tilde{\mathbf{m}}_2 = \mathbf{P}_2\mathbf{P}_1^{-1}\tilde{\mathbf{m}}_1,$$

and, according to proposition 2.3, a projective representation of ep_2 is the cross-product $\tilde{\mathbf{e}}_2 \wedge \tilde{\mathbf{m}}_2$. Of course this encompasses the cases where E_2 is at either a finite or an infinite distance.

Note that the cross-product $\tilde{\mathbf{e}}_2 \wedge \tilde{\mathbf{m}}_2$ can be written as $\mathbf{F}\tilde{\mathbf{m}}_1$ where $\mathbf{F}$ is a 3×3 matrix that is easily computed as follows. Let $\tilde{\mathbf{E}}_2$ be the 3×3 antisymmetric matrix representing the cross-product with $\tilde{\mathbf{e}}_2$ (i.e., $\tilde{\mathbf{E}}_2\mathbf{x} = \tilde{\mathbf{e}}_2 \wedge \mathbf{x}$, for all vectors $\mathbf{x}$). We then have

$$\mathbf{F} = \tilde{\mathbf{E}}_2\mathbf{P}_2\mathbf{P}_1^{-1}$$

This has the advantage of vividly showing that the correspondence between a pixel and its epipolar line is linear in projective coordinates. Any pixel m_2 on the epipolar line ep_2 of m_1 satisfies the equation

$$\tilde{\mathbf{m}}_2^T\mathbf{F}\tilde{\mathbf{m}}_1 = 0 \tag{6.3}$$

We call this equation the Longuet-Higgins equation for reasons to be given in chapter 7. It shows in particular that the roles of m_1 and m_2 are symmetric and that the epipolar line of a pixel m_2 in the first retinal plane is represented by the vector $\mathbf{F}^T\tilde{\mathbf{m}}_2$.

6.2.1.3 *Working in the normalized coordinate systems*

Let us now see what kind of simplifications we obtain in the description of the epipolar geometry if we assume that we are using the normalized camera model (see sections 3.3.1.1 and 3.4.1.2) and that the world reference frame is as in figure 6.5.

Using the notation of section 3.3.2, we have $\mathbf{C}_1\mathbf{C}_2 = \mathbf{t}$ and $\mathbf{R}[\mathbf{I},\mathbf{J},\mathbf{K}] = [\mathbf{i},\mathbf{j},\mathbf{k}]$, and the matrix $\tilde{\mathbf{K}}$ is equal to

Stereo Vision

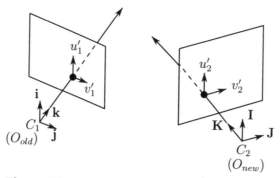

Figure 6.5 Two cameras and their normalized retinas.

$$\tilde{\mathbf{K}} = \begin{bmatrix} \mathbf{R} & \mathbf{t} \\ \mathbf{0}_3^T & 1 \end{bmatrix}$$

Matrix $\tilde{\mathbf{P}}_1$ is given by

$$\tilde{\mathbf{P}}_1 = [\mathbf{I}_3 \ \mathbf{0}]$$

where $\mathbf{I}_3$ is the 3×3 identity matrix. Matrix $\tilde{\mathbf{P}}_2$, expressed in the coordinate system C_2XYZ, is equal to $\tilde{\mathbf{P}}_1$. Therefore $\tilde{\mathbf{P}}_2$ expressed in the coordinate system C_1xyz is equal to

$$\tilde{\mathbf{P}}_1\tilde{\mathbf{K}}^{-1} = [\mathbf{R}^T \ -\mathbf{R}^T\mathbf{t}]$$

We can compute the coordinates of the epipoles E_1 and E_2:

$$\tilde{\mathbf{e}}_1 = \tilde{\mathbf{P}}_1 \begin{bmatrix} \mathbf{C}_1\mathbf{C}_2 \\ 1 \end{bmatrix} = \tilde{\mathbf{P}}_1 \begin{bmatrix} \mathbf{t} \\ 1 \end{bmatrix} = \mathbf{t}$$

$$\tilde{\mathbf{e}}_2 = \tilde{\mathbf{P}}_2 \begin{bmatrix} \mathbf{0}_3 \\ 1 \end{bmatrix} = -\mathbf{R}^T\mathbf{t}$$

Given a pixel m_1, represented by $\tilde{\mathbf{m}}_1 = [u_1', v_1', 1]^T$, its epipolar line is represented, according to the previous section, by

$$\tilde{\mathbf{e}}_2 \wedge \mathbf{P}_2\mathbf{P}_1^{-1}\tilde{\mathbf{m}}_1 = -\mathbf{R}^T\mathbf{t} \wedge \mathbf{R}^T\tilde{\mathbf{m}}_1$$

which is projectively the same as

$$\mathbf{R}^T(\mathbf{t} \wedge \tilde{\mathbf{m}}_1)$$

Similarly, given a pixel m_2, represented by $\tilde{\mathbf{m}}_2 = [u'_2, v'_2, 1]^T$, its epipolar line is represented by

$$\tilde{\mathbf{e}}_1 \wedge \mathbf{P}_1 \mathbf{P}_2^{-1} \tilde{\mathbf{m}}_2 = \mathbf{t} \wedge \mathbf{R} \tilde{\mathbf{m}}_2$$

6.2.1.4 *The epipolar line collineation*

We will finish this section with an important projective property of the sets of epipolar lines that will be used in chapter 7 for the computation of motion. If we consider the two sets of epipolar lines, they all go through the epipoles E_1 and E_2 respectively and form two pencils of lines (see chapter 2), which are examples of projective lines $\mathcal{P}^1$. Furthermore, the correspondence between the two pencils that associates to each epipolar line of the first pencil the corresponding epipolar line of the second pencil is a linear projective transformation, a collineation, or a homography. The reason for this is simple. Consider four epipolar planes that cut four corresponding epipolar lines in the two retinal planes. From the definition of the cross-ratio of four planes of a pencil that is given in section 2.5.3, the cross-ratio of the four epipolar planes is equal to the cross-ratio of the four epipolar lines they cut on both retinal planes. This means that the correspondence between the two pencils preserves cross-ratios and is therefore a collineation.

6.2.2 Uniqueness

If we limit ourselves to opaque objects, one point in the left image should have at most one match in the second image. This is not true for transparent objects. This is also not always true when we are using such tokens as line segments (see section 6.7). Nonetheless, this constraint can often be used to reduce the number of possible correspondences.

6.2.3 Continuity

The basic idea of this constraint is that the world is mostly made up of objects with smooth surfaces. This means that the *reconstruction function*, which assigns to a pair of matched pixels a 3-D point M, is smooth almost everywhere. This reconstruction function is, for historical reasons, usually summarized as a function $z = f(d)$, where z is the distance

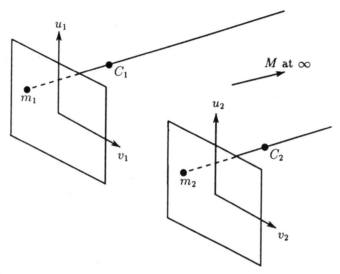

Figure 6.6   Simple disparity definition.

of M to the cameras and d is the so-called disparity. In order to precisely define the continuity constraint, we have to define *disparity*.

6.2.3.1   A definition of disparity: the parallel cameras case

Given a pixel m_1 of coordinates (u_1, v_1) in the first retinal plane and its corresponding pixel m_2 of coordinates (u_2, v_2) in the second retinal plane, disparity is defined as the difference $v_2 - v_1$. This definition implicitly assumes the camera geometry of figure 6.6 where the two retinal planes are the same. A disparity of 0 implies that the 3-D point M is at infinity. If we bring point M toward the optical center C_1 along the infinite half-line $\langle m_1, C_1 \rangle$, the disparity will increase from 0 to $+\infty$.

There is a simple relationship between disparity and the distance of the 3-D point M, with distance measured from the two optical centers (figure 6.7):

$$d = v_2 - v_1 = d_{12}f/z \tag{6.4}$$

This relation is readily obtained by noticing that the triangles $m_1 c_1 C_1$, $m_1 m M$, and $m_2 c_2 C_2$ are similar. Therefore, a fronto-parallel plane is a locus of points with constant disparity.

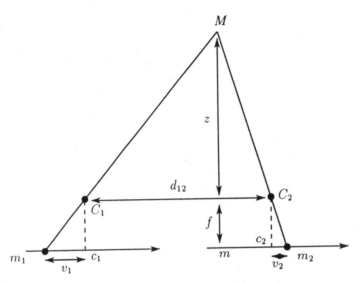

Figure 6.7   Relation between depth and disparity.

It is also easy to prove that the horizontal coordinate x of M is given by[1]

$$x = \frac{d_{12}}{2d}(v_1 + v_2) \tag{6.5}$$

It is equations (6.4) and (6.5) that are at basis of the techniques that aim at recovering surface properties of the objects being looked at from disparity measurements. The most prominent piece of work in this direction is that of Koenderink and van Doorn [KvD76], who laid out the necessary theory, as well as the work of Wildes, who has implemented some of these ideas [Wil91].

6.2.3.2   *A definition of disparity: the general case*

When we assume that the cameras are in general position, the relationship between the coordinates (u_1, v_1) and (u_2, v_2) of the two corresponding points when M is at infinity is not as simple as before. To find out

---

1. The x-axis is chosen as indicated in figure 6.14.

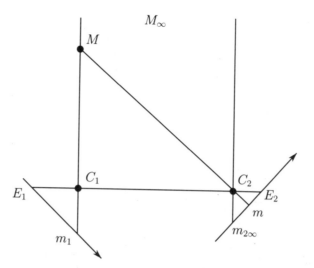

Figure 6.8   The epipolar plane configuration.

what happens, let us draw the figure in the epipolar plane $C_1C_2m_1m_2$ (figure 6.8). When M travels from infinity to C_1 along the half-line $< m_1C_1 >$, m_2 varies from $m_{2\infty}$ to the epipole E_2. What is important for the correspondence process is that the point corresponding to m_1 is to be found on the epipolar segment $E_2m_{2\infty}$.

The coordinates of $m_{2\infty}$ are easily computed from those of m_1 and the perspective projection matrices $\tilde{\mathbf{P}}_1$ and $\tilde{\mathbf{P}}_2$. The direction of the line $< C_1m_1 >$ is given by

$$\mathbf{N}_1 = \mathbf{P}_1^{-1}\tilde{\mathbf{m}}_1$$

and $m_{2\infty}$ is the image in the second retinal plane of the point at infinity $[\mathbf{N}_1^T, 0]^T$:

$$\tilde{\mathbf{m}}_{2\infty} = \mathbf{P}_2\mathbf{P}_1^{-1}\tilde{\mathbf{m}}_1$$

The situation is thus much more complex than in the previous case, and it is not reasonable to hope to obtain an exact equivalence between the two situations, i.e., to be able to define a scalar disparity as a simple function of the image coordinates of two pixels in correspondence. We prefer, in agreement with figure 6.9, to define the disparity of a point M

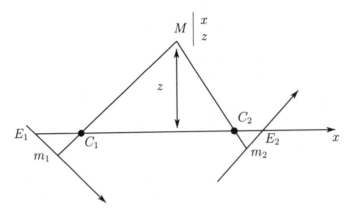

Figure 6.9   General definition of disparity.

as $d = 1/z$. Points of equal disparities are therefore on circular cylinders of axis $\langle C_1, C_2 \rangle$.

If we assume that the objects that we are looking at are smooth almost everywhere, then the disparity constraint can be introduced in the following manner. Let M be a point in 3-D space with projections m_1 and m_2 on retinas 1 and 2 with a disparity d as previously defined. Then a neighbor n_1 of m_1 in retina 1 should find a match n_2 in retina 2 with a disparity close to d. The continuity or disparity constraint is thus clearly a constraint on the smoothness of the objects being looked at. This constraint of order 0 will be made even tighter by adding a constraint on the variation of the disparity, an order 1 constraint, in section 6.2.5.

6.2.4   Ordering

Let us consider a 3-D point M and its projections m_1 and m_2 in retinas 1 and 2, respectively. Figure 6.10 shows the configuration of the corresponding epipolar plane. Now let us choose a point N in the cone defined by M, C_1, C_2 containing the base line $\langle C_1, C_2 \rangle$ (cross-hatched in figure 6.10). N has images n_1 and n_2 in retinas 1 and 2, respectively. Let us now look at the order of the images along the epipolar lines: We have (E_1, m_1, n_1) for retina 1 and (E_2, m_2, n_2) for retina 2. In other words, the images of M and N appear in the same order along the epipolar lines when N is in the previous cone. It is easy to see that the converse is true

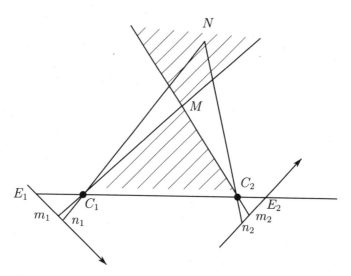

Figure 6.10   Forbidden zone attached to M_1.

when N varies in the other cone defined by M, C_1, and C_2 (the one that is not cross-hatched in figure 6.10).

There are two arguments for calling the cross-hatched zone in figure 6.10 the *forbidden zone* attached to M:

- The first (fairly weak) argument is that if the distance from M to the base line $\langle C_1, C_2 \rangle$ is large with respect to the length of $C_1 C_2$, then the angle $C_1 M C_2$ is small and the probability for a point N to fall in it is quite small (albeit nonzero).

- The second argument is that, if we assume that M and N are situated on an opaque object of nonzero thickness, as shown in figure 6.11, then M and N cannot possibly be seen simultaneously by retinas 1 and 2. Since one can easily check the fact that N is in the forbidden zone defined by M by considering the ordering of their images along the epipolar lines, this constraint can be used to eliminate matches for n_1, given the match (m_1, m_2).

In practice, it is difficult to eliminate the whole cross-hatched cone of figure 6.10 because of configurations such as the one depicted in

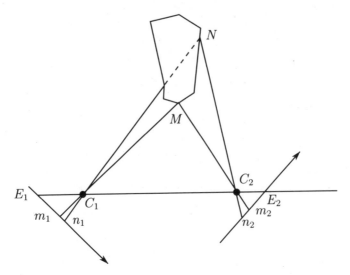

Figure 6.11 *M* and *N* are not both visible from retina 1.

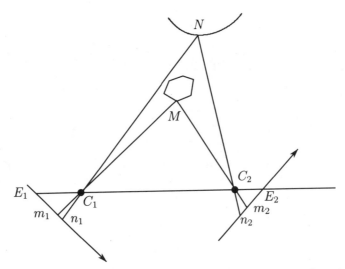

Figure 6.12 *M* and *N* do not belong to the same object: The ordering constraint does not apply.

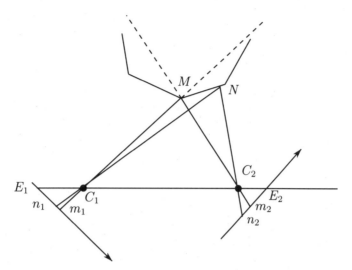

Figure 6.13   The object bulges out of the forbidden zone, and the ordering constraint applies.

figure 6.12. In this figure, the points M and N are seen to belong to two different objects to which the ordering constraint does not apply. It therefore seems more reasonable to force only the neighbors of M within a small neighborhood (for example, a disc of radius ε) to belong to the non forbidden zone. We will discuss another justification of the forbidden zone in the next section. But before doing that, we must point out the fact that the ordering constraint is in fact a constraint on the shape of the objects in disguise. Indeed, if an object bulges out of the forbidden zone, as in figure 6.13, then the constraint clearly is satisfied. This constraint essentially eliminates those objects that do not bulge out of the forbidden zone.

6.2.5   The disparity gradient

The idea of the forbidden zone is related in an interesting way to the idea of disparity gradient. Let us consider figure 6.14, where the x-axis is parallel to the v_1- and v_2-axis with its origin at o, the midpoint of the segment c_1c_2. We can imagine a virtual retina parallel to the two real ones with the optical center in O. This retina is sometimes called

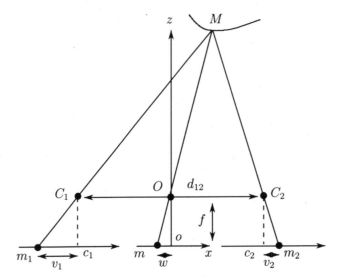

Figure 6.14   Understanding the disparity gradient.

the *cyclopean retina* [Jul71]. If M has images m_1 and m_2 in the two real retinas with coordinates v_1 and v_2, then its image m in the virtual retina has coordinate $\frac{v_1+v_2}{2}$. Assuming that the point M can vary on a smooth object defined by its equation $z = h(x)$, equations (6.4) and (6.5) show that this defines the disparity d as a smooth function of $w = \frac{v_1+v_2}{2}$. Now consider two points on the same object with cyclopean coordinates w_1 and w_2 and disparities d_1 and d_2. The magnitude of the derivative of the disparity with respect to the cyclopean coordinate, the *disparity gradient*, can be approximated as

$$DG = \left| \frac{d_1 - d_2}{w_1 - w_2} \right|$$

Using equations (6.4) and (6.5), we obtain $DG = \frac{d_{12}|z_1-z_2|}{|z_2 x_1 - z_1 x_2|}$. Experiments in psychophysics [PMF85] have led people to conjecture that human perception imposes the constraint that the disparity gradient is upper-bounded: $DG < K$. This means that, if point M on an object is perceived, points on the same object that are close to M and such that $DG > K$ are simply not perceived correctly. Let us suppose that $\mathbf{M}_1 = [x_1, z_1]^T$ is fixed, and let us

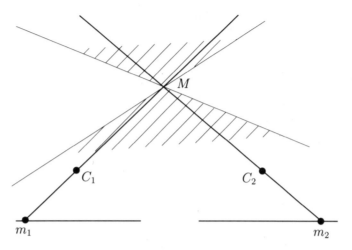

Figure 6.15 The forbidden zone obtained when $K < 2$ is larger than the usual one.

see what kind of conditions we get on $\mathbf{M}_2 = [x_2, z_2]^T$ by imposing $DG < K$. The condition $DG < K$ can be written as

$$d_{12} \mid z_1 - z_2 \mid < K \mid z_2 x_1 - z_1 x_2 \mid$$

We obtain a cone defined by the two lines of equations

$$z_1 - z_2 = \pm \frac{K}{d_{12}} (z_2 x_1 - z_1 x_2) \tag{6.6}$$

The vertex of the cone is M_1. Its complement is the cone that is forbidden in order for the disparity gradient to be less than K.

The special case $K = 2$ is interesting because the two lines are the lines $\langle C_1, m_1 \rangle$ and $\langle C_2, m_2 \rangle$ and the corresponding cone is precisely the forbidden cone (see section 6.2.4). If $K < 2$ we obtain a larger forbidden zone (see figure 6.15), and if $K > 2$ we obtain a smaller forbidden zone (see figure 6.16). Note that the disparity gradient constraint imposes a condition on the tangent to the object surface: It must lie outside of the forbidden cone (see problem 2). Therefore this is a *geometric constraint* on the kind of possible objects, i.e., the kind of objects that can be reconstructed by the stereo process. Also note that, in general, the disparity gradient constraint implies the uniqueness constraint (see problem 3).

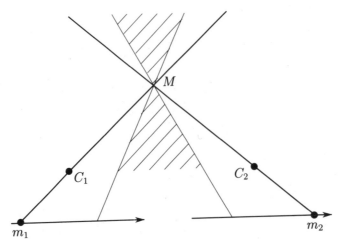

Figure 6.16 The forbidden zone obtained when $K > 2$ is smaller than the usual one.

6.2.6 Geometric constraints

We can go even further than imposing a disparity gradient limit on the scene: We can impose that the surfaces of objects locally have some known analytic form. In its simplest form, this assumption restricts objects to be locally planar, i.e., assumes that they are well approximated by their tangent planes almost everywhere except at discontinuities. This constraint is exploited in section 6.8. Notice that this is not a stronger form of the disparity gradient constraint since, for a given threshold on the disparity gradient, some planes are excluded.

Here we will study another set of geometric constraints that we will use in section 6.9. Suppose we observe a three-dimensional curve (C) with three cameras, as shown in figure 6.17. Let (c_1), (c_2), and (c_3) be its three images, and consider a point M on (C) and its images m_1, m_2, and m_3. The idea is that we can use the correspondence between m_1 and m_2 to constrain the correspondences in the third retina. More precisely, from m_1 and m_2 we can reconstruct M, and therefore, by reprojection, we can predict m_3. We call this a zero-order constraint. Next, from the tangents t_1 and t_2 to (c_1) and (c_2) at m_1 and m_2 we can predict the tangent t_3 at m_3 (first-order constraint), and from the curvatures κ_1 and κ_2 of (c_1) and

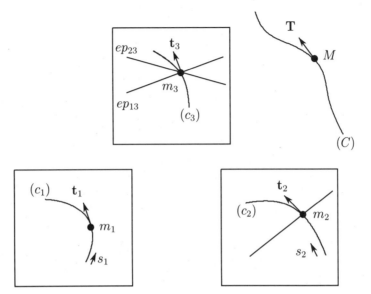

Figure 6.17 Relationships between a three-dimensional curve (C) and its images in three cameras.

(c_2) at m_1 and m_2 we can predict the curvature κ_3 at m_3 (second-order constraint).

6.2.6.1 Predicting m_3

This is a direct consequence of the epipolar geometry described in section 6.2.1: m_3 is at the intersection of ep_{13}, the epipolar line of m_1 in the third camera, and ep_{23}, the epipolar line of m_2 in the same camera.

6.2.6.2 Predicting the tangent

Let us introduce the vectors $\mathbf{U}_{t_1}$ and $\mathbf{U}_{t_2}$, as follows:

$$\mathbf{U}_{t_i} = \mathbf{C}_i \mathbf{m}_i \wedge \mathbf{t}_i \quad \text{for } i = 1, 2$$

These vectors are normal to the planes defined by the optical centers C_i, the image points m_i, and the tangents $\mathbf{t}_i$ to the curves (c_i). From elementary geometry it is clear that the unit tangent vector $\mathbf{T}$ to (C) at point M is parallel to the cross-product of U_{t_1} and U_{t_2}. This gives us the direction of that tangent. Therefore, the tangent to (c_3) at m_3 contains the image of the point at infinity on the three-dimensional tangent. This point is

$$\tilde{D} = [(U_{t_1} \wedge U_{t_2})^T, 0]^T$$

If we denote by $\tilde{P}_3$ the 3×4 perspective projection matrix for the third camera, this gives us a second point d_3 on the tangent to (c_3) at m_3. Its perspective representation (see equation (3.5)) is

$$\tilde{d}_3 = \tilde{P}_3 \tilde{D} = P_3 (U_{t_1} \wedge U_{t_2})$$

From this we can compute t_3.

This analysis, even though it is correct, is slightly misleading since in the definition of U_{t_i} we assume that both vectors are expressed in the same coordinate system (for example, the one in which the three perspective matrices $\tilde{P}_i, i = 1, 2, 3$ have been computed). Thus, if we denote by $\tilde{m}_i$ a coordinate vector of the projective point $\tilde{m}_i$ and by $\tilde{t}_i$ the vector $[t_i^T, 0]^T$, which is a coordinate vector in the direction of the tangent considered as a point at infinity, the vectors U_{t_i} can be written in the world coordinate frame as

$$U_{t_i} = (P_i^{-1} \tilde{m}_i) \wedge (P_i^{-1} \tilde{t}_i)$$

6.2.6.3 *Predicting the curvature*

We have seen that d_3 and m_3 are two points on the tangent to (c_3) at m_3. Therefore (by proposition 2.3) $\tilde{d}_3 \wedge \tilde{m}_3$ is the projective representation of that tangent. Thus the unit normal n_3 to (c_3) at m_3 is equal to

$$n_3 = \varepsilon \frac{H(\tilde{d}_3 \wedge \tilde{m}_3)}{\|H(\tilde{d}_3 \wedge \tilde{m}_3)\|} \tag{6.7}$$

where $H = \begin{bmatrix} 1 & 0 & 0 \\ 0 & 1 & 0 \\ 0 & 0 & 0 \end{bmatrix}$ and $\varepsilon = \pm 1$.

We can apply the Frenet formula $\frac{dn_3}{ds_3} = -\kappa_3 t_3$ in order to compute κ_3. By letting $X = H(\tilde{d}_3 \wedge \tilde{m}_3)$ we have, according to equation (6.7)

$$\varepsilon \frac{d\mathbf{n}_3}{ds_3} = \frac{d\mathbf{X}}{ds_3} \frac{1}{\|\mathbf{X}\|} - \frac{d\|\mathbf{X}\|}{ds_3} \frac{\mathbf{X}}{\|\mathbf{X}\|^2}$$

Since $\|\mathbf{X}\| = (\mathbf{X}^T\mathbf{X})^{\frac{1}{2}}$,

$$\frac{d\|\mathbf{X}\|}{ds_3} = (\mathbf{X}^T \frac{d\mathbf{X}}{ds_3})(\mathbf{X}^T\mathbf{X})^{-\frac{1}{2}}$$

Therefore we obtain

$$\varepsilon \frac{d\mathbf{n}_3}{ds_3} = \frac{d\mathbf{X}}{ds_3} \frac{1}{\|\mathbf{X}\|} - (\mathbf{X}^T \frac{d\mathbf{X}}{ds_3}) \frac{\mathbf{X}}{\|\mathbf{X}\|^3}$$

We have to compute $\frac{d\mathbf{X}}{ds_3}$:

$$\frac{d\mathbf{X}}{ds_3} = \mathbf{H}(\frac{d\tilde{\mathbf{d}}_3}{ds_3} \wedge \tilde{\mathbf{m}}_3 + \tilde{\mathbf{d}}_3 \wedge \begin{bmatrix} \mathbf{t}_3 \\ 0 \end{bmatrix})$$

Now let us compute $\frac{d\tilde{\mathbf{d}}_3}{ds_3}$. From the previous section, we have $\tilde{\mathbf{d}}_3 = \mathbf{P}_3(\mathbf{U}_{t_1} \wedge \mathbf{U}_{t_2})$. Thus we can write

$$\frac{d\tilde{\mathbf{d}}_3}{ds_3} = \mathbf{P}_3[(\frac{d\mathbf{U}_{t_1}}{ds_1} \wedge \mathbf{U}_{t_2})\frac{ds_1}{ds_3} + (\mathbf{U}_{t_1} \wedge \frac{d\mathbf{U}_{t_2}}{ds_2})\frac{ds_2}{ds_3}]$$

Taking $\tilde{\mathbf{m}}_i = [\mathbf{m}_i^T, 1]^T$ and using the Frenet formulas $\frac{d\mathbf{m}_i}{ds_i} = \mathbf{t}_i$ and $\frac{d\mathbf{t}_i}{ds_i} = \kappa_i\mathbf{n}_i$, we can easily find that

$$\frac{d\mathbf{U}_{t_i}}{ds_i} = \kappa_i(\mathbf{P}_i^{-1}\tilde{\mathbf{m}}_i) \wedge (\mathbf{P}_i^{-1}\begin{bmatrix} \mathbf{n}_i \\ 0 \end{bmatrix}) \qquad i = 1, 2 \tag{6.8}$$

We must now evaluate $\frac{ds_i}{ds_3}, i = 1, 2$. A simple way of doing this is to consider equation (6.3),

$$\tilde{\mathbf{m}}_3^T\mathbf{F}_{i3}\tilde{\mathbf{m}}_i = 0 \tag{6.9}$$

for $i = 1, 2$. The 3×3 matrices $\mathbf{F}_{i3}$ are equal to $\tilde{\mathbf{E}}_{3i}\mathbf{P}_3\mathbf{P}_i^{-1}$ where $\tilde{\mathbf{E}}_{3i}$ is the antisymmetric matrix representing the cross-product with a coordinate vector of the epipole of the ith camera ($i = 1, 2$) in the third camera. If we now derive equation (6.9) with respect to s_3, we obtain

$$[\mathbf{t}_3^T\ 0]^T\mathbf{F}_{i3}\tilde{\mathbf{m}}_i + \tilde{\mathbf{m}}_3^T\mathbf{F}_{i3}\begin{bmatrix}\mathbf{t}_i\\0\end{bmatrix}\frac{ds_i}{ds_3} \qquad i = 1,2$$

and this ends the computation.

6.2.7 Kinematic constraints

We will see in section 9.7 that it is also possible to add kinematic constraints to facilitate the matching process.

6.3 Rectification

The operation of *rectification* is meant to insure a simple epipolar geometry for a stereo pair. By *simple geometry* we mean that the epipoles are at infinity and that the epipolar lines are parallel to the image rows, i.e., we are in the situation illustrated by figures 6.4 and 6.6. One possible way to achieve such a result is to reproject the images onto a single plane $\mathcal{R}$ using the same optical centers, as indicated in figure 6.18. In this figure, the plane $\mathcal{R}$ is identical to the two new retinal planes $\mathcal{R}_1'$ and $\mathcal{R}_2'$. The reprojection operation works as follows: Given a pixel $m_i, i = 1, 2$ in the original retinal plane $\mathcal{R}_i, i = 1, 2$, we construct a new pixel $m_i', i = 1, 2$ by intersecting the line $\langle C_i, m_i\rangle$ with $\mathcal{R}$.

In order for the epipoles to be at ∞, the plane $\mathcal{R}$ must be parallel to the line $\langle C_1, C_2\rangle$ joining the optical centers. There is an infinity of such planes; in order to choose one among them, we need another criterion. Once the plane $\mathcal{R}$ has been chosen, having the epipolar lines parallel to the image rows is simply a matter of choosing the coordinate systems for images 1 and 2 in plane $\mathcal{R}$. Note, however, that because we are dealing with sampled images, some interpolation of the image intensities has to take place.

In order to choose the plane $\mathcal{R}$, we first notice that, among the two degrees of freedom that are left, only the orientation is relevant; the distance to the line $\langle C_1, C_2\rangle$ corresponds to a change of scale. To choose the remaining orientation parameter, we can either minimize the distortion of the projected images (see problem 5) or simply impose, as in fig-

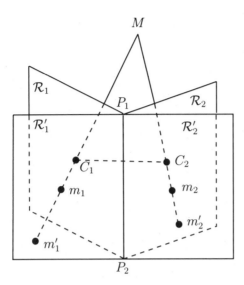

Figure 6.18 The rectification process is cast as the reprojection of the two retinas $\mathcal{R}_1$ and $\mathcal{R}_2$ onto plane $\mathcal{R}$ containing the two new retinas $\mathcal{R}_1'$ and $\mathcal{R}_2'$.

ure 6.18, the assumption that $\mathcal{R}$ is also parallel to the line $\langle P_1, P_2 \rangle$, which is the intersection of the two retinas $\mathcal{R}_1$ and $\mathcal{R}_2$.

6.4   Correlation techniques

Intensity-based area correlation techniques have been investigated extensively for commercial applications in stereophotogrammetry [KMM77, FP86], but they are also some of the oldest methods used in computer vision [Gen80].

6.4.1   The general principle of the correlation techniques

The principle of the correlation techniques is shown in figure 6.19. In order to find the coordinates of the pixel in image 2 that matches the pixel of coordinates (u_0, v_0) in image 1, we consider a rectangular window of size $(2P + 1) \times (2N + 1)$ centered at (u_0, v_0) and compute its correlation $C_{12}(\tau)$ with the second intensity image along the row $v_2 = v_0$:

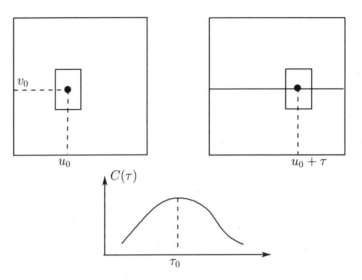

Figure 6.19   Principle of the correlation technique.

$$C_{12}(\tau) = \frac{1}{K} \sum_{u_1=-N}^{+N} \sum_{v_1=-P}^{+P} (I_1(u_1 + u_0, v_1 + v_0)$$

$$- \overline{I_1(u_0, v_0)})(I_2(u_1 + u_0 + \tau, v_1 + v_0) - \overline{I_2(u_0 + \tau, v_0)})$$

(6.10)

where

$$K = (2N + 1)(2P + 1)\sigma_1(u_0, v_0)\sigma_2(u_0 + \tau, v_0)$$

In these formulas, $\overline{I_1(u_0, v_0)}$ and $\sigma_1(u_0, v_0)$ are the mean intensity and standard deviation in image 1 at point (u_0, v_0):

$$\overline{I_1(u_0, v_0)} = \frac{1}{(2N + 1)(2P + 1)} \sum_{u_1=-N}^{+N} \sum_{v_1=-P}^{+P} I_1(u_1 + u_0, v_1 + v_0)$$

$$\sigma_1^2(u_0, v_0) = \frac{1}{(2N + 1)(2P + 1)} \sum_{u_1=-N}^{+N} \sum_{v_1=-P}^{+P} (I_1(u_1 + u_0, v_1 + v_0) - \overline{I_1(u_0, v_0)})^2$$

Similar formulas hold for $\overline{I_2(u_0 + \tau, v_0)}$ and $\sigma_2(u_0 + \tau, v_0)$. Note that, because of the normalization by σ_1 and σ_2, C_{12} lies between -1 and $+1$. I_1 and I_2 are not restricted to the original intensities, but can also be functions of those intensities as in the method described in section 6.4.2.

The curve $C_{12}(\tau)$ usually has one maximum that is reached for a value τ_0 of τ (see figure 6.19). The disparity of pixel (u_0, v_0) is taken to be τ_0. Several problems occur with this technique:

- Epipolar lines are assumed to be image rows. This implies that the images must be rectified (see the previous section).

- If the maximum of the correlation function $C_{12}(\tau)$ is not well defined, the disparity τ_0 is not very accurate.

- The disparity is assumed to be constant in the window of analysis, and therefore we may expect problems when the disparity gradient is significantly different from 0.

The third problem is by far the most important, since the underlying basic assumption is that surfaces in the scene locally have a constant disparity. According to section 6.2.3 this is equivalent to saying that they can be well represented, locally, by frontoparallel planes.

To illustrate the method, in figure 6.20 we show a stereo pair of images containing textured rocks. In figure 6.21 we show the rectified images in which the epipolar lines are the image rows. Figure 6.22 shows black and white points, which indicate agreement and disagreement between

Figure 6.20 A stereo pair of images.

Figure 6.21 The rectified stereo pair.

correlation measures. More specifically, notice that formula 6.10 is not symmetric with respect to I_1 and I_2. Therefore, we can also compute the correlation function $C_{21}(\tau)$ obtained by exchanging the roles of images 1 and 2. Figure 6.22 shows the resulting disparity map: Large disparities correspond to small values of the intensity, small disparities to large intensity values. The black pixels are those for which $C_{12}(\tau)$ and $C_{21}(\tau)$ agree. It is clear that the disagreements occur mostly near depth edges or near discontinuities of the normal where the disparity gradient is high.

In the algorithm developed by Fua [Fua91], points where C_{12} and C_{21} disagree have no disparity associated with them and the "filling in" is left to a smoothing operation that works as follows. Let $\hat{d}_{ij}$ be the estimated disparity at pixel (i, j). We approximate those estimated values with a function $S(x, y)$ which, for example, minimizes as follows:

$$\sum_{(i,j)\text{ such that }\hat{d}_{ij}\text{ exists}} (S(i, j) - \hat{d}_{ij})^2 + \lambda \int\int (\Delta S(x, y))^2 dx dy$$

where $\Delta S(x, y) = \frac{\partial^2 S}{\partial x^2} + \frac{\partial^2 S}{\partial y^2}$ is the Laplacian of S. The second term of the criterion insures the smoothness of the resulting function S. This

Figure 6.22   The agreement between C_{12} and C_{21} (see text).

is of course very similar to the problem discussed in section 4.2.4. The reconstructed depth map is shown in figure 6.23.

6.4.2   Nishihara's refinement

Nishihara [Nis84] has proposed a correlation technique based on the sign of the convolution of the images with the Laplacian of a Gaussian. The use of the Laplacian of a Gaussian is motivated by the work of Marr and Hildreth on edge detection (see chapter 4), where edges are detected as the zero-crossings of the output of such a convolution.[2] The positions of these zero-crossings in the image are quite sensitive to noise: They move by an amount that is proportional to the noise amplitude and inversely proportional to the convolution gradient at the zero-crossing [Nis84, NP82]. On the other hand, if the spacing between zero-crossings

---

2. Another notable extension of the basic correlation method is the one proposed by Kass [Kas83, Kas88], who processes the two images of the stereo pair with nearly independent linear filters and correlates the vectors of the outputs.

 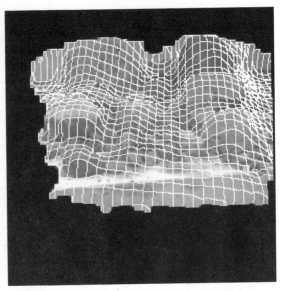

Figure 6.23 The three-dimensional reconstruction of figure 6.20. On the left is the smoothed disparity, and on the right is the disparity superimposed as a grid on one of the original images.

is relatively large compared with this amount of displacement, the region of constant sign between zeros will be stable over a large range of signal-to-noise ratios, as will be shown later. The idea is then to correlate images of the sign of the output of the convolution of the left and right image with $\nabla^2 G_\sigma$, where G_σ is a Gaussian of variance σ. As we will show later, this has the effect of sharpening the peak of the autocorrelation function.

We will now investigate the effect of noise on sign stability and the shape of the sign cross-correlation function using some simple statistical image models. Let $I(x, y)$ be an image that we model as a Gaussian process with autocorrelation $R_I(\tau_1, \tau_2)$. Then the convolution of I with the Laplacian of a Gaussian of standard deviation σ, $\nabla^2 G_\sigma$ is another image $J(x, y)$, which is also a Gaussian process with zero mean and an autocorrelation function that we will study in section 6.4.2.2.

6.4.2.1 *Sensitivity to noise*

At each pixel in the filtered image, we consider that the intensity J is a zero-mean Gaussian random variable of standard deviation σ_J (the signal) that is perturbed by a noise N that we also assume to be a zero-mean Gaussian random variable of standard deviation σ_N, independent of J. We want to compute the probability of a change of sign of J due to the addition of N. This is obviously equal to the probability that the noise value is less than minus the intensity value. This probability is given by

$$
P = \frac{2}{\sqrt{2\pi}\sigma_J} \int_0^\infty exp(-\frac{s^2}{2\sigma_J^2})ds \frac{1}{\sqrt{2\pi}\sigma_N} \int_s^\infty exp(-\frac{n^2}{2\sigma_N^2})dn
$$

$$
= \frac{1}{\pi} \int_0^\infty \int_{u\frac{\sigma_J}{\sigma_N}}^\infty exp(-\frac{u^2+v^2}{2})du dv \quad u = \frac{s}{\sigma_J}, \quad v = \frac{n}{\sigma_N}
$$

$$
= \frac{1}{\pi} \tan^{-1}(\frac{\sigma_N}{\sigma_J})
$$

Note that even when the noise and intensity levels are the same ($\sigma_N = \sigma_J$), P is only 1/4. This is the reason that the areas of constant sign in the convolved image are fairly robust to noise.

6.4.2.2 The shape of the correlation function

The second motivation for using the Laplacian of a Gaussian comes from the study of the cross-correlation function of J_1 and J_2, the filtered images of the stereo pair. Again we assume that the epipolar lines are the rows of J_1 and J_2, either through careful mechanical adjustment or after rectification (see section 6.3). In fact, for the purpose of our qualitative analysis, we might as well assume that J_2 is the same as J_1 and look at the shape of the autocorrelation of $J = \nabla^2 G_\sigma \otimes I$. We know from the theory of stochastic processes [Pap65] and from problem 3 of chapter 4 that the autocorrelation function of J is given by

$$ R_J(\tau_1, \tau_2) = H \otimes R_I(\tau_1, \tau_2) $$

where H is given by

$$ H(\tau_1, \tau_2) = \nabla^2 G_\sigma(\tau_1, \tau_2) \otimes \nabla^2 G_\sigma(-\tau_1, -\tau_2) $$

It is also known [Pap65] that the autocorrelation $R_s(\tau_1, \tau_2)$ of the sign of J obeys an arcsin law when J is a Gaussian random process:

$$ R_s(\tau_1, \tau_2) = \frac{2}{\pi} \sin^{-1}(\frac{R_J(\tau_1, \tau_2)}{R_J(0, 0)}) $$

This function is usually much more sharply peaked than R_l and thus allows for a better estimation of the disparity.

6.5 Relaxation techniques

The basic idea of the class of techniques known as *relaxation techniques* is to allow the pixels that are to be put into correspondence to make "educated guesses" as to what their match should be and then let the matches reorganize themselves by propagating some of the constraints described in section 6.2. This is one example of a class of techniques known as *relaxation labeling techniques* that have been most popular in computer vision in the mid-1970s and early-1980s. We will describe them in more detail in chapter 11. We will now present the application of those ideas to stereo vision through two algorithms.

6.5.1 The original Marr-Poggio algorithm

The *Marr-Poggio algorithm* [MP76, MP79] enforces the uniqueness and the continuity constraints. For each pixel m_i of the first image we compute an initial set of possible confidence measures $c(m_i, n_j)$ that estimate whether m_i can be put in correspondence with n_j in the second image. There are many ways of computing the c values. The simplest one is by comparing the intensity values of m_i and n_j:

$$c(m_i, n_j) = \begin{cases} 1 & \text{if the intensities at pixel } m_i \text{ in image 1 and} \\ & \text{pixel } n_j \text{ in image 2 are sufficiently close} \\ 0 & \text{otherwise} \end{cases}$$

The pixels n_j are chosen on the epipolar line of m_i, for example on the epipolar segment shown in figure 6.8. The confidence measures are then updated sequentially (but in parallel for all pixels) to enforce the continuity constraint using a formula of the type:

$$c^{(n+1)}(m_i, n_j) = \begin{cases} 1 & \text{if the number of pixels } m_i' \text{ in a neighborhood} \\ & V_i \text{ of } m_i \text{ such that } c^{(n)}(m_i', n_j') = 1 \text{ for } n_j' \text{ in a} \\ & \text{neighborhood } V_j \text{ of } n_j \text{ is above some threshold} \\ 0 & \text{otherwise} \end{cases}$$

The neighborhoods V_i and V_j are usually taken as approximations of discs of radii of a few pixels centered at m_i and n_j.

This algorithm has been tested mostly on synthetic images called *random dot stereograms*, for which it has been shown to be quite successful. In a few iterations it converges, i.e., the confidence measures remain stable. Moreover, the confidence measures are usually unambiguous in the sense that, for most pixels m_i in the first image, there is only one pixel n_j on the corresponding epipolar segment such that $c(m_i, n_j) = 1$. The point m_i is then put in correspondence with n_j. If several pixels n_j are candidates, the uniqueness constraint cannot be enforced. The algorithm does not perform as well on real images, mostly because the tokens and the features it uses (the pixel and its intensity) and the constraint it enforces (the continuity of disparity) are not sufficient to deal with most real images. Its implementation and many interesting improvements are due to Eric Grimson [Gri81a, Gri85].

6.5.2   The Pollard, Mayhew, Frisby algorithm

The Pollard, Mayhew, Frisby algorithm [PMF85] differs from the previous one on several counts, the main one being that it enforces the disparity gradient constraint (see section 6.2.5). It first extracts from both images a number of tokens, each token possibly characterized by a number of features. For example, edge points are detected and characterized by their strength and orientation. A match between a token t_i in image 1 and a token t_j in image 2 is characterized by a measure c_{ij} of its goodness by comparing the values of the features of t_i and t_j.

For each token located at pixel m_i in image 1 and every possible match n_j in image 2 (located on the epipolar segment of pixel m_i to enforce the epipolar constraint), a strength of the match $SM(m_i, n_j)$ is computed as follows. All tokens t_k located at pixels m_k within some neighborhood of m_i are considered. For each such token, the matches t_l located at pixels n_l satisfying the constraint

$$DG(m_i, n_j, m_k, n_l) < \sigma \tag{6.11}$$

are considered as candidates for supporting the match (m_i, n_j). In the case where there is more than one token l such that constraint (6.11) is satisfied, only the one with the highest value of c_{kl} is considered. The matching strength $SM(m_i, m_j)$ is then defined as

$$SM(m_i, n_j) = c_{ij} \sum_{t_k \text{ in } V_i} \frac{1}{\text{dist}(m_i, m_k)} \max_{\text{all } t_l} \frac{c_{kl}}{\text{dist}(n_j, n_l)} \sigma(DG(m_i, n_j, m_k, n_l))$$

where

$$\sigma(DG(m_i, n_j, m_k, n_l)) = \begin{cases} 1 & \text{if } DG(m_i, n_j, m_k, n_l) < \sigma \\ 0 & \text{otherwise} \end{cases}$$

This definition is nonsymmetric, and a similar expression can be computed for matches from image 2 to image 1. Tokens are then matched using an iterative winner-take-all procedure that enforces uniqueness. The method works as follows. At each iteration those matches for which the matching strength is maximum for both of the two image tokens forming them are chosen as correct. Then, because of the uniqueness constraint, all other matches associated with the two tokens in each chosen match are eliminated from further consideration. This allows further matches to be selected as correct provided that they now have the highest strengths for both constituent tokens. Typically only four or five iterations are needed to match all tokens. The algorithm has been thoroughly tested on a large number of synthetic and real images and provides accurate and reliable results.

6.6   Dynamic programming

The problem of matching primitives between images can also be cast as a problem of minimizing a cost function. Dynamic programming is a way of efficiently minimizing (or maximizing) functions of a large number of discrete variables. Successful attempts at using dynamic programming for solving the stereo matching problem are those of Baker and Binford [BB81] and Ohta and Kanade [OK85]. In both cases, they were using edges as the basic primitives.

Let us assume once again for the sake of simplicity that the epipolar lines are parallel to the scan lines, and let us consider two corresponding scanlines in the left and right images. On each scanline a number of edge pixels have been identified, and we include both ends of each scanline for convenience. Matching those edge pixels can be considered the problem of matching the intervals between them in the following manner. Let

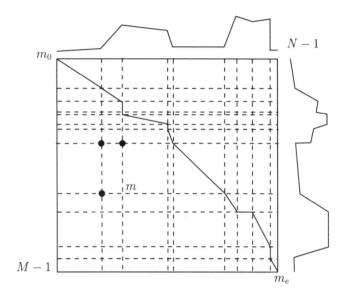

Figure 6.24 The stereo matching process can be considered finding a path in a graph.

us order the edge pixels from left to right on each scanline, and then number them from 0 to $N - 1$ on the left and from 0 to $M - 1$ on the right.

In figure 6.24 we have represented the pairs (i, j) of left and right edge pixels as points forming a two-dimensional grid. Matching the interval $[i, i']$ on the left scanline with interval $[j, j']$ on the right scanline is equivalent to drawing the line segment between points $m = (i, j)$ and $m' = (i', j')$ of the grid. The goal is then to find a sequence of such segments (a path) from point $m_0 = (0, 0)$ to point $m_e = (N - 1, M - 1)$. Constraints can be imposed on the kind of paths that are allowed by using constraints arising from stereo vision. The ordering constraint is interesting here since it is equivalent to saying that admissible paths are monotonous paths,[3] i.e., if $m = (i, j)$ and $m' = (i', j')$ are two successive points on the path, then they must satisfy $m < m'$ where $<$ is defined as

---

3. Can you see why? If not, see problem 6.

$$(i,j) < (i',j') \text{ iff } \begin{cases} i < i' \text{ and } j < j' \\ \text{or } i = i' \text{ and } j < j' \\ \text{or } j = j' \text{ and } i < i' \end{cases} \qquad (6.12)$$

Even with such a constraint there may still be a large number of admissible paths. For each such path a cost can be defined, and a best path from m_0 to m_e is defined as the one with the minimum cost. We first define the cost $c(m, m')$ of a segment between points $m = (i, j)$ and $m' = (i', j')$. Of course, there are several ways of defining such a cost; in general it should measure two things:

1. The similarity of the features at the edge pixels i in the left scanline and i' in the right. The features can be, for example, the orientation of and the intensity contrast at the edges at these two pixels.

2. The similarity of the intensities in and the lengths of the two intervals $[i, j]$ and $[i', j']$.

The minimum cost $C(m)$ of a path from m_0 to m is then recursively defined as

$$C(m) = \min_{p \text{ in } V_m} (c(p, m) + C(p))$$

where V_m is the set of nearest neighbors of m smaller than m (shown as black dots in figure 6.24).

Dynamic programming affords a way to efficiently exploit the structure of the cost function by replacing the minimization of a function of $MN - 2$ variables, $C(m_e)$, which is a function of all the vertices of the square grid, by the minimization of $MN - 1$ functions of one variable. This is done as follows:

1 Clearly, $C(m_1) = c(m_0, m_1)$

$\vdots$

n compute i_n, in V_{m_n} such that $C(m_n) = \min_{p \text{ in } V_{m_n}} (c(p, m_n) + C(p)) = c(i_n, m_n) + C(i_n)$

$\vdots$

MN-1 compute i_e in V_{m_e} such that $C(m_e) = c(i_e, m_e) + C(i_e)$

The key observation is this: If the points are considered in increasing order for the order previously defined, then at step n the required values of $C(p)$ have already been computed. This makes the minimization straightforward. The minimal cost is $C(m_e)$, and the corresponding optimal path can be found by "back tracking" the pointers. Specifically, if the last segment in the path is (i_e, m_e), then, by looking at the computation of $C(i_e)$, we find i_{e-1} for which the minimum is attained; the next-to-last segment is thus (i_{e-1}, i_e), and we can continue backtracking until we reach m_0.

So far the pairs of corresponding scanlines in the left and right images have been processed independently from the other pairs. In fact, if there is an edge extending across scanlines, the correspondences in one scanline have a strong dependency on the correspondences in the neighboring scanlines. Enforcing an inter-scanline consistency is equivalent to applying the figural continuity constraint, and there are several ways of achieving this. For example, Baker [Bak81] uses a cooperative process to detect and correct the matching results that violate the figural continuity constraint, whereas Ohta and Kanade [OK85] include it in the cost and solve a dynamic programming problem in a 3-D search space instead of the previous 2-D space.

6.7   Prediction and verification

This is our first example of a stereo algorithm where the tokens put into correspondence are of a higher symbolic level than pixels. This approach has been followed in particular by Medioni and Nevatia [MN85]. We will describe here a stereo algorithm developed by Ayache and Faverjon [AF87] that performs the matching of primitives of line segments between the two images by a technique of prediction and verification of hypotheses that is a variant of one that is used several times in this book, in particular in chapter 11. Using line segments as tokens has two advantages:

1.   The number of primitives to be matched is usually much smaller (but see the disadvantages) than, let us say the number of edge pixels.

2.   In matching symbolic primitives we can use features attached to them, such as geometric features which are robust and reliable.

Using line segments as tokens also has two disadvantages:

1. It assumes that the contours in the image are well approximated by line segments and that therefore objects in the scene are polyhedral or nearly so. If they are not, the number of line segments must increase for a given approximation tolerance, thus reducing advantage number one. In a more subtle way, if the objects are not polyhedral, then there is no guarantee that the breakpoints of the polygonal approximations in the two images of the stereo pair (the vertices of the polygons) will correspond (i.e., be on pairs of corresponding epipolar lines).

2. The density of the correspondences (and therefore of the reconstructed depth map, discussed in section 6.10) is less than the one obtained by, say, a correlation-based approach. Even though this is indeed a disadvantage of the method, the correspondences it provides are usually much more reliable and accurate than those produced by most of the correlation-based techniques, and this advantage counterbalances that disadvantage.

The first disadvantage can be alleviated by considering approximating curves rather than simply line segments as in section 6.9.2. The second disadvantage can be alleviated by the kind of interpolation techniques described in chapter 10. The method uses three constraints to reduce the size of the search space: (1) the epipolar constraint, suitably modified for the case of line segments; (2) the continuity constraint; and (3) the uniqueness constraint.

6.7.1   Building the symbolic descriptions

Both images are represented as sets of line segments. These segments are extracted by first finding edge points using one of the techniques described in chapter 4, and then approximating these points by straight line segments. Each segment is represented by a number of features, both geometric-based (coordinates of midpoint, length, orientation) and intensity-based (contrast across the segment, average intensity of image gradient along the segment, etc.). A neighborhood structure is also introduced on the two sets of segments by using buckets [AEI+85]. This means that each image is divided into nonoverlapping square windows. To each window is attached the list of segments intersecting it, and to each segment is attached the list of windows it intersects. These buckets give fast

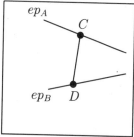
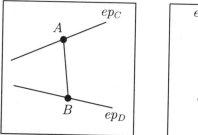

Figure 6.25   The epipolar constraint for two segments *AB* and *CD*.

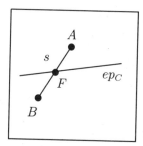
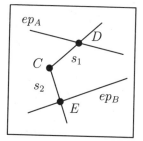

Figure 6.26   The epipolar constraint for line segments.

access to the segments that are close to a given segment and are used to implement the process of propagating the hypotheses to be described later.

6.7.2   Defining correspondences

Strictly speaking, a correspondence is a pair (L, R) of left and right segments satisfying the epipolar constraint, as shown in figure 6.25. In this figure the epipolar lines of A, B, C, and D go through points C, D, A, and B, respectively. In practice, the probability that the two polygonal approximations produce segments whose endpoints are in the same epipolar planes is very small. One is more likely to observe situations such as the one shown in figure 6.26, in which the epipolar lines of the endpoints A and B of segment AB intersect segments s_1 and s_2 at some point other than their endpoints. To satisfy the constraint, we have to create four

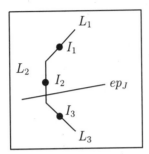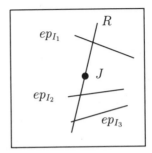

Figure 6.27   Multiple segment correspondences.

new segments, AF and FB in image 1 and CD and CE in image 2, and therefore we must change the polygonal approximations.

An acceptable correspondence (L, R) or (R, L) can be defined in several ways. In the most rigorous manner, we consider the endpoints of L; their corresponding epipolar lines intersect the line supporting R along a segment R'. The intersection R'' of R' and R must be nonempty, if the correspondence is acceptable. Using a similar procedure, the endpoints of R'' yield L'', which is included in L. The segments L'' and R'' are nonempty and have all of their points in correspondence.

Since this is bound to be a bit costly to check, we define a *modified epipolar constraint* as follows. The modified epipolar constraint for line segments implies that homologous segments have at least one analogous point. To make things simpler, this point is chosen as the midpoint of the segment, i.e., we impose the assumption that the epipolar line of the midpoint of segment L intersects segment R for the correspondence (L, R) to be possibly acceptable. This definition is not symmetric with respect to L and R, which has the advantage of potentially permitting a global match between contours that have been approximated by a different number of segments (see figure 6.27). In this figure, the four correspondences (L_1, R), (L_2, R), (L_3, R), and (R, L_2) are acceptable, but not the two correspondences (R, L_1) and (R, L_3). Finally, in order to reject a number of potentially spurious acceptable correspondences, the features of the segments are compared. To summarize, a correspondence is a pair (L, R) of left and right segments that satisfies the modified epipolar constraint. In addition, the features of the left and right segments must be sufficiently close.

6.7.3 Making hypotheses

A number of hypotheses of correspondences are made uniformly over the whole image by randomly selecting segments in the left image. In order to reduce the number of false correspondences, only segments that are neither too small (indicating poor estimation of the orientation) nor too long (likely to be broken in the right image) and have an orientation that is not too close to that of the epipolar lines are selected. The thresholds for comparing features of segments are set quite high at this stage to eliminate as many false correspondences as possible.

6.7.4 Propagating hypotheses

Once hypotheses have been made, the algorithm attempts to propagate them by traversing a graph that is used to enforce the continuity constraint. Vertices of this graph are correspondences (L, R). Two vertices are connected by an arc if and only if the distances between the midpoints of the reconstructed 3-D segments are at distances smaller than some fixed threshold ε. For each hypothesis (L, R), we consider the neighbors $L_i, i = 1, \ldots, n$ of L and the neighbors $R_j, j = 1, \ldots, m$ of R in the left and right images, respectively, obtained from the bucket structures described above. For each segment L_i in the neighborhood of L, we look to see if there exists a segment R_{i_j} in the neighborhood of R such that the distance between the midpoint of the 3-D segment reconstructed from the correspondence (L_i, R_{i_j}) to the midpoint of the 3-D segment reconstructed from the correspondence (L, R) is less than ε and whose features are sufficiently close to those of L_i. If there are several candidates, the one with the smallest 3-D distance is chosen. This process is iterated for the correspondences (L_i, R_{i_j}) until no further correspondences can be obtained. For each hypothesis (L, R), this generates a (possibly empty) sequence of correspondences (L_p, R_p).

6.7.5 Handling conflicts

A *conflict* is defined as a pair of correspondences (L, R) and (L, R') or (L, R) and (L', R). Conflicts that occur in the propagation phase are handled immediately by choosing the best correspondence in terms of its features. Conflicts that occur between two distinct components of the disparity graph are solved by comparing the sizes of the two components and erasing from the smallest one the conflicting correspondence. To avoid a dependence on the order in which the components are compared, the size comparison is based on the initial size of the components.

6.7.6 Performance

This algorithm has been used with great success on a wide variety of real images as reported in the book by Ayache [Aya89]. It is the starting point of the trinocular segment-based stereo algorithm described in section 6.9.1.

6.8   Adding the planarity constraint

In many human made environments we are bound to encounter many flat surfaces such as walls, floors, ceilings, and doors. These surfaces are planar. This implies a very strong constraint on the kind of correspondences that occur between the left and right images of a stereo pair. More precisely, if the tokens that are put into correspondence are produced by visual features situated in a plane, there exists an analytic transformation from the left image coordinates to the right image coordinates. This analytic transformation is a collineation (see chapter 2) between the two retinal planes considered as projective planes. This collineation is a function of the rotation and translation of the plane parameters from the left camera to the right camera.

6.8.1   Writing the equation

We assume that for each camera of the stereo rig we have performed the change in the retinal coordinate system described by equation (3.15) or (3.32) and that therefore we are working in the normalized retinal coordinate system for each camera. If we also assume that we are working in the normalized coordinate systems attached to each camera, then, as shown in chapter 3, this is equivalent to considering two normalized cameras with focal distances of 1 (see figure 3.9). Figure 6.28 illustrates

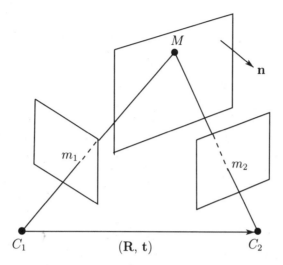

Figure 6.28   Geometry of the stereo problem when looking at a plane.

the geometry of the problem. Two cameras are forming the images of points lying in a plane. The origin of the world reference frame is at C_1 as in figure 6.5. The position and orientation of the second camera with respect to the first one is defined by the rotation matrix $\mathbf{R}$ and the translation vector $\mathbf{t}$. The plane is defined by its normal $\mathbf{n}$ in the coordinate system of the second camera and by its distance d to the origin C_2 (which we assume to be nonzero).

As we will show next, the correspondence between the two images is quite simple; it is a collineation (see chapter 2). Moreover, if we know this collineation, it allows us to compute the equation of the plane as follows:

Proposition 6.1

Let M be a point of a plane Π, whose equation is $\mathbf{n}^T\mathbf{X}_2 = d$ in the normalized coordinate system of the second camera. The images m_1 and m_2 of M in the two retinas are related by a collineation, depending only on the relative positions of the two retinas and of the plane:

$$\tilde{\mathbf{m}}_1 = \mathbf{A}\tilde{\mathbf{m}}_2 \tag{6.13}$$

Moreover, the 3×3 matrix $\mathbf{A}$ is related to the geometric parameters of the problem by the fact that it is proportional to

$$\mathbf{R} + \frac{\mathbf{t}\mathbf{n}^T}{d} \tag{6.14}$$

Proof The coordinates $\mathbf{X}_1$ and $\mathbf{X}_2$ of M in the two normalized coordinate systems of the cameras are, by definition, related by

$$\mathbf{X}_1 = \mathbf{R}\mathbf{X}_2 + \mathbf{t} \tag{6.15}$$

If M belongs to Π, defined by its normal $\mathbf{n}$ and its distance d in the normalized coordinate system of the second camera, then

$$\mathbf{n}^T\mathbf{X}_2 = d \tag{6.16}$$

Substituting equation (6.16) for equation (6.15) yields

$$\mathbf{X}_1 = (\mathbf{R} + \frac{\mathbf{t}\mathbf{n}^T}{d})\mathbf{X}_2 \tag{6.17}$$

Since we are working with normalized coordinates, the components of $\mathbf{X}_1$ and $\mathbf{X}_2$ are the projective coordinates of m_1 and m_2, and the result is proved.   ∎

Matching points or lines between the two images is almost the same. This is not surprising since, as shown in chapter 2, points and lines are projectively equivalent due to the principle of duality. We have the following proposition:

Proposition 6.2
If we consider the images of a line belonging to the same 3-D plane as in proposition 6.1, with the image lines projectively represented by $\mathbf{u}_1$ and $\mathbf{u}_2$, then

$$\mathbf{u}_2 = \mathbf{A}^T\mathbf{u}_1 \tag{6.18}$$

where $\mathbf{A}$ is the matrix defined in proposition 6.1.

Proof The equation of the first line is $\mathbf{u}_1^T\tilde{\mathbf{m}}_1 = 0$, and the equation of the second line is $\mathbf{u}_2^T\tilde{\mathbf{m}}_2 = 0$. Since $\tilde{\mathbf{m}}_1 = \mathbf{A}\tilde{\mathbf{m}}_2$, we have $\mathbf{u}_1^T\mathbf{A}\tilde{\mathbf{m}}_2 = 0$, or $(\mathbf{A}^T\mathbf{u}_1)^T\tilde{\mathbf{m}}_2 = 0$, which proves that $\mathbf{u}_2 = \mathbf{A}^T\mathbf{u}_1$.   ∎

Notice that the vector equality (6.13) is a projective equality, which is true up to a scale factor. $\mathbf{A}$ depends only upon eight independent coefficients corresponding to the eight geometric parameters of the problem, i.e., the three rotation parameters, the three coordinates of $\frac{t}{d}$, and the two parameters describing the orientation of the plane.

6.8.2   Estimating A

How can we estimate the matrix **A**? Since it represents a collineation of $\mathcal{P}^2$, we know from chapter 2 that it is determined by four pairs of corresponding points in general position, i.e., such that no three points in any image are aligned. From those four pairs we obtain **A**, which is defined up to a scale factor. By reconstructing one of the four points in three dimensions we obtain the scale factor such that **A** is equal to the expression (6.14), from which we can compute **n** and d (see problem 8). We can also estimate **A** from line correspondences, but surprisingly two pairs of corresponding lines are sufficient due to a knowledge of the epipolar geometry. On each line in the first image we can choose two points. Their corresponding points in the second image are obtained as the intersections of the epipolar lines of the two points with the corresponding line. This yields four pairs of corresponding points in general position, and therefore **A**.

6.8.3   Application to ground plane obstacle avoidance

The main application of this idea has been to obstacle avoidance. Suppose we have a vehicle moving on a locally flat surface, the ground. We can assume that, from careful calibration, the equation of that plane is known. Note that if the stereo rig is fixed with respect to the vehicle or moves with controlled motion, this knowledge is preserved over time. In order to detect potential obstacles, we can apply the collineation of matrix **A** to all pixels in image 1, thus obtaining after interpolation another image 1'. If the environment was limited to the ground plane, then the difference between the intensities of 1' and 2 should be zero, assuming Lambertian reflectance. By thresholding the magnitude of the difference image 2 minus 1', we have a simple test for the presence or absence of obstacles on the ground: Values higher than threshold signal potential obstacles. As an example, figure 6.29 shows a stereo pair of a person (his legs) standing on the floor, and next to him is a container. Figure 6.30 shows the unthresholded (left) and thresholded (right) magnitude of the difference image, in which the obstacles stand out clearly.

 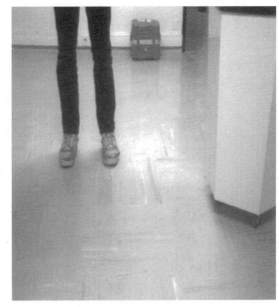

Figure 6.29   A stereo pair showing a floor and some obstacles.

6.8.4   Application to stereo

It is also possible to modify the algorithm of section 6.7 so that it takes into account the planarity constraint. The result is an algorithm that solves the stereo matching problem and at the same time finds planes. In this modified version, an hypothesis is defined as two pairs (L_1, R_1) and (L_2, R_2) of acceptable correspondences in the sense of section 6.7 that are also such that the corresponding 3-D lines are coplanar. If this hypothesis is correct, then it can be propagated by first estimating the corresponding matrix **A**, and then applying the corresponding collineation to the unmatched neighbors of L_1 and L_2. If the hypothesis is correct, then each such segment, when transformed by the collineation, is a segment in the right image that should find a match with similar features in its immediate neighborhood. If the hypothesis is not correct, there will be no such match.

When such a correspondence has been found, the estimate of matrix **A** can be updated and then applied to more segments until no more corre-

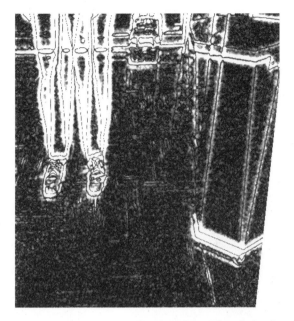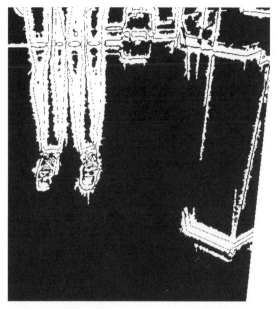

Figure 6.30   The obstacles detected in the scene of figure 6.29.

spondences can be found. Once a plane has been found by propagating an hypothesis, others can be searched for by considering different hypotheses involving segments that are still unmatched. Of course, not all such planes may be real physical surfaces, but in an indoors environment we might expect to find many physical planes using this approach. This has been implemented successfully and is described in an article by Faugeras and Lustman [FL88].

6.9   Using three cameras

The idea of using three cameras, originated by Yachida for a laser range finder system [Yac86], makes fuller use of the epipolar and geometric constraints developed in section 6.2. Let us describe the principle of the method in the case where the tokens that are matched are curves. Suppose we have identified a curve (c_1) in the first image, and suppose that it is the image of a three-dimensional curve that is a surface marking. We

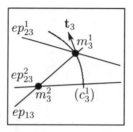

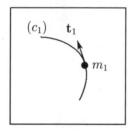

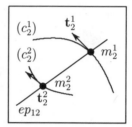

Figure 6.31   The principle of disambiguation of matches.

wish to find the corresponding curve, or segment of curve, in image 2. We choose an arbitrary point m_1 of (c_1) and consider its epipolar line ep_{12} in the second camera (see figure 6.31). Suppose this epipolar line intersects two curves (c_2^1) and (c_2^2) in image 2 at points m_2^1 and m_2^2, with unit tangent vectors $\mathbf{t}_2^1$ and $\mathbf{t}_2^2$, respectively. According to our discussion in section 6.2.6, we consider the epipolar lines ep_{13} of point m_1, and ep_{23}^1 and ep_{23}^2 of points m_2^1 and m_2^2 in image 3. We see that ep_{23}^1 and ep_{23}^2 intersect ep_{13} at points m_3^1 and m_3^2, respectively.

If (m_1, m_2^1) is the correct hypothesis, then it implies that, theoretically, we must find at point m_3^1 a curve (c_3^1) whose tangent and curvature can be computed from the tangents and curvatures of (c_1) and (c_2^1) at m_1 and m_2^1. If the hypothesis is incorrect, it may lead us to conclude several things:

1. No curve is sufficiently close to m_3^1.

2. There is a curve (c_3^1) going through m_3^1, but its tangent $\mathbf{t}_3^1$ does not have the predicted orientation.

3. There is a curve (c_3^1) going through m_3^1 and its tangent $\mathbf{t}_3^1$ has the correct orientation, but it does not have the predicted curvature.

These general ideas have been implemented in two programs, one developed by Ayache and Lustman [AL87] and the other by Robert and Faugeras [RF91] (see also the article by Kitamura and Yachida [KY90]).

6.9.1   Three cameras and line segments

The first program works on the same polygonal approximations as those described in section 6.7, thereby ignoring curvature, but performs tests 1 and 2 of the previous enumeration. The corresponding algorithm is very robust and fast for indoors scenes where long line segments frequently occur. It is described in detail in the book by Ayache [Aya89].

We will now give three examples of the performances of this algorithm in imaging three different scenes.

The office scene   Figure 6.32 shows a stereo triplet of images of an office room. Figure 6.33 shows the line segments found in the three images, figure 6.34 shows the reconstructed segments as a cross-eye stereogram that can be fused by crossing one's eyes, and figure 6.35 shows a top view of the reconstructed scene in which the cameras are located at the bottom of the figure.

The rocks scene   Figure 6.36 shows a stereo triplet of images of a scene with rocks. Figure 6.37 shows the line segments found in the three images, figure 6.38 shows the reconstructed segments as a cross-eye stereogram, and figure 6.39 shows a top view of the reconstructed scene.

The* tea box *scene   Figure 6.40 shows a stereo triplet of images of a scene with a few objects, including a box of tea. Figure 6.41 shows the line segments found in the three images, figure 6.42 shows the reconstructed segments as a cross-eye stereogram, and figure 6.43 shows a top view of the reconstructed scene.

It might be of interest to describe how the cross-eye stereograms of figures 6.34, 6.38, and 6.42 have been constructed. From the matches produced by the stereo algorithm, we can reconstruct a set of 3-D segments using techniques described at the end of this chapter in section 6.10.3. We can then reproject these 3-D segments in two planes to simulate a stereo pair. The right image is displayed on the left and the left image on the right. By crossing one's eyes, these two images can be fused to allow one to perceive depth. This is one of the techniques that is used to

Figure 6.32 A stereo triplet of an office room.

Figure 6.33   The line segments found in the images of the previous figure.

display the random dot stereograms in the book by Julesz [Jul71]. This allows us to get a vivid idea of the quality of the stereo algorithm, since the wrong matches show up as segments "floating" in space before or behind the real scene. This is especially visible in the results for the office scene and, to a lesser extent, in the results for the rocks scene. Some of these wrong matches can also be detected by looking at the top views of these reconstructed 3-D scenes (figures 6.35 and 6.39).

Figure 6.34 The three-dimensional reconstruction of the office room of figure 6.32.

Figure 6.35 A top view of the reconstructed office scene.

Figure 6.36   A stereo triplet of a scene with rocks.

Figure 6.37   The line segments found in the images of the previous figure.

6.9.2   Three cameras and curves

The main problem with the previous algorithm is that it uses polygonal approximations of the image contours. It is a very compact representation of these contours when the scene is composed of polyhedral objects, but it poses problems when this hypothesis is not satisfied, since the number of segments in the polygonal approximations will have to grow in order to keep the approximation error constant. Moreover, since we

Figure 6.38 The three-dimensional reconstruction of the rocks scene of figure 6.36.

Figure 6.39 A top view of the reconstructed rocks scene.

saw that the corresponding polygons found in two images tend not to have their vertices on corresponding epipolar lines, the results of the approximation have to be modified in the way that has been described in section 6.7.2. A final problem is that curvature is not readily available from the polygonal approximations, although it is important in using the constraint described in section 6.2.6.3.

Figure 6.40   A stereo triplet of a scene with man-made objects, including a box of tea.

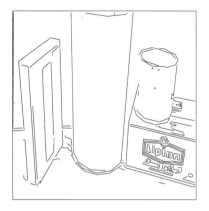

Figure 6.41   The line segments found in the images of the previous figure.

One possible way to avoid these problems is to approximate the contours with curves that are locally represented by polynomials of degree higher than 1. One example of such an approximation is the cubic B-splines, which are locally represented as polynomials of degree 3. The reader who is interested in details about splines and ways of interpolating and approximating contours with them is referred to the books by Pavlidis [Pav82] and Schumaker [Sch81]. The tangent vectors to the image curves and the curvatures are computed from these polynomials.

The method used for stereo vision proceeds by selecting at random a curve (c_1) in one of the three images, say image 1, selecting a pixel m_1 on

Figure 6.42   The three-dimensional reconstruction of the tea box scene of figure 6.40.

Figure 6.43   A top view of the reconstructed tea box scene.

that curve, and computing the tangent vector $\mathbf{t}_1$ and the curvature κ_1 at m_1 using the B-spline approximation. Next the curves in the second image that intersect the epipolar line ep_{12} of m_1 are determined. Let us denote them by $(c_2^i), i = 1, \ldots, n$. The points of intersections $m_2^i, i = 1, \ldots, n$ of ep_{12} with those curves are determined as well as the corresponding tangent vectors $\mathbf{t}_2^i$ and curvatures κ_2^i using the B-spline approximations. Each pair $(m_1, m_2^i), i = 1, \ldots, n$ satisfies the epipolar constraint and is therefore a possible correspondence. In order to reduce the ambiguity, we use the constraints described in section 6.2.6, which are explained in the following paragraph.

For each possible correspondence (m_1, m_2^i) we compute in the third image the point m_3^i of intersection between the epipolar line ep_{13} of m_1 and the epipolar line ep_{23}^i of m_2^i. We also predict the tangent vector $\mathbf{t}_{3p}^i$ and the curvature κ_{3p}^i at point m_3^i. For each point m_3^i we find the edge curve (c_3^i) that is the closest, and we eliminate the correspondences (m_1, m_2^i) by going through the following three criteria, which increase in stringency:

- If (c_3^i) is further from m_3^i than some threshold, then the correspondence is eliminated. Otherwise:

- Compute the tangent $\mathbf{t}_{3r}^i$ to (c_3^i) at the point m_{3r}^i closest to m_3^i. If $\mathbf{t}_{3r}^i$ is too different from the predicted direction $\mathbf{t}_{3p}^i$, then the correspondence is eliminated. Otherwise:

- Compute the curvature κ_{3r}^i of (c_3^i) at the point m_{3r}^i, and eliminate the correspondence if the difference with the predicted curvature κ_{3p}^i is too high.

We keep for further consideration those pixels m_1 of the first image for which there remains only one possible correspondence m_2^i in the second image after this filtering process, and the triplet (m_1, m_2^i, m_3^i) is called an hypothesis attached to the triplet of image curves $((c_1), (c_2^i),$ and $(c_3^i))$. The final step is to grow those hypotheses by performing an incremental move from m_1 on (c_1) and finding matches on (c_2^i) and (c_3^i) in the vicinity of m_2^i and m_3^i. This procedure is iterated until it fails and yields a sequence of triplets of corresponding pixels on the three image curves $((c_1), (c_2^i),$ and $(c_3^i))$.

This method has been implemented and tested on a large variety of real images. We show its results on the same images as those of the previous section.

The office scene   Figure 6.44 shows the edge curves found in the three images of figure 6.32. Figure 6.45 shows the reconstructed curves as a cross-eye stereogram that can be fused by crossing one's eyes, and figure 6.46 shows a top view of the reconstructed scene. Note that the number of false matches has decreased considerably compared to those in figures 6.34 and 6.35.

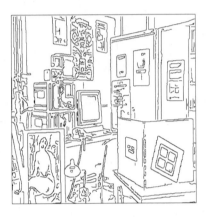

Figure 6.44   The edge curves found in the images of figure 6.32.

Figure 6.45 The three-dimensional reconstruction of the office room of figure 6.32.

Figure 6.46 A top view of the reconstructed office scene.

The rocks scene   Figure 6.47 shows the edge curves found in the three images of figure 6.36. Figure 6.48 shows the reconstructed curves as a cross-eye stereogram, and figure 6.49 shows a top view of the reconstructed scene.

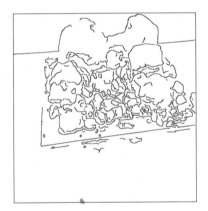

Figure 6.47   The edge curves found in the images of figure 6.36.

Figure 6.48 The three-dimensional reconstruction of the rocks scene of figure 6.36.

Figure 6.49 A top view of the reconstructed rocks scene.

The tea box scene   Figure 6.50 shows the edge curves found in the three images of figure 6.40. Figure 6.51 shows the reconstructed curves as a cross-eye stereogram, and figure 6.52 shows a top view of the reconstructed scene.

Figure 6.50   The edge curves found in the images of figure 6.40.

Figure 6.51   The three-dimensional reconstruction of the tea box scene of figure 6.40.

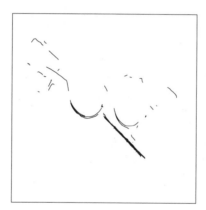

Figure 6.52   A top view of the reconstructed tea box scene.

6.10   Reconstructing points and lines in three dimensions

We will now consider the problem of reconstructing three-dimensional geometric objects from matches obtained by stereo vision. We will first describe how the calibration of the stereo rig is performed. We will then discuss the problem of reconstructing points and line segments, and the problem of computing a measure of their uncertainty. In what follows, lower indexes refer to the cameras.

6.10.1   Calibrating in the real world

In order to perform the calibration process we have described in chapter 3, we need a set of 3-D reference points. This can be achieved by using some sort of regular pattern such as the one shown in figure 6.54. The two planes are carefully assembled so that their angle is precisely known (for example 90 degrees) and the positions of the corners of the squares are also very precisely known. Those corners are used as reference 3-D points. The calibration procedure then goes as follows:

- The cameras to be calibrated (figure 6.53) acquire a picture of the calibration pattern (see figure 6.55).

- A polygonal approximation of the contours (figure 6.56) is computed, the corners are automatically extracted from this approximation (figure 6.57), and their pixel coordinates are computed.

- The intrinsic and extrinsic parameters can be computed by one of the methods described in chapter 3.

This yields the perspective matrices $\tilde{\mathbf{P}}_i$, with i varying from 1 to 2 or 3.

The quality of the calibration can be qualitatively tested by verifying that the epipolar geometry is correct. For example, figure 6.58 shows a stereo pair of images of the calibration pattern and figure 6.59 shows two corresponding epipolar lines in the left and right images. These two epipolar lines have been computed as follows. A pixel m_1 has been selected in the left image (specifically one of the two upper corners of the grid), and the equation of the corresponding epipolar line ep_2 in image 2 has been computed using the technique described in section 6.2.1.2. The equation of the corresponding epipolar line ep_1 of ep_2 can then be computed by the same method. It can be verified visually that these epipolar

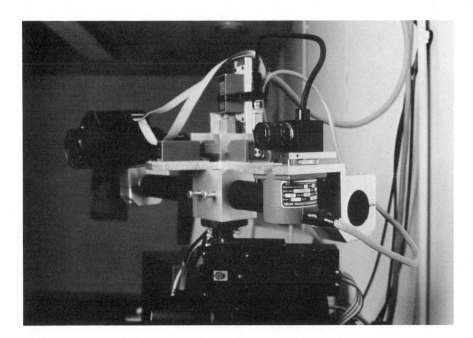

Figure 6.53   A photograph of the cameras to be calibrated.

lines go through corresponding points. Similarly, figure 6.60 shows the epipolar pencils in both images. It is apparent that all epipolar lines are convergent toward the epipoles, which are located outside of the images for the particular configuration chosen.

6.10.2   Reconstructing points

In a way that is analogous to what we did for calibration in the previous section, we can consider linear methods for which least-squares techniques apply or nonlinear methods for which more complicated minimization tools must be used.

6.10.2.1   *Linear methods*

We assume that we have n images from n cameras in which we have matched the pixels $\hat{m}_i, i = 1, \ldots, n$ of coordinates u_i, v_i. Let M be the

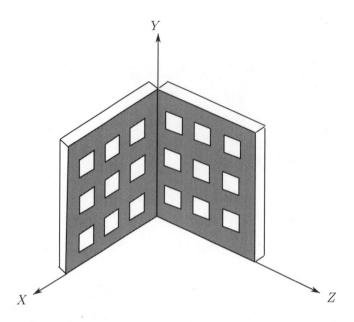

Figure 6.54 A calibration pattern: calibration points are at the intersection of the horizontal and vertical lines, which can be easily detected by simple algorithms.

Figure 6.55 An image of the calibration pattern as seen from one of the cameras.

Figure 6.56 An image of the calibration pattern with a polygonal approximation of the edges superimposed.

Figure 6.57 An image of the calibration pattern with the detected corners superimposed.

Figure 6.58 Stereo pair of the calibration pattern.

Figure 6.59 The epipolar line of a point of interest.

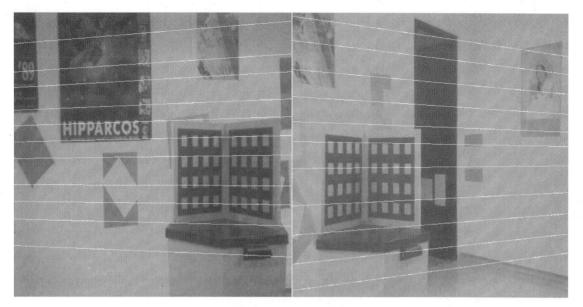

Figure 6.60 Epipolar pencil.

corresponding 3-D point that we want to reconstruct. Each camera yields two linear equations in the unknown coordinates of M, which can be written (see equations (3.29) for example)

$$\mathbf{A}_i \mathbf{M} = \mathbf{b}_i$$

where $\mathbf{A}_i$ is a 2×3 matrix involving the perspective matrix $\tilde{\mathbf{P}}_i$ of the ith camera and the coordinates of pixel $\hat{m}_i$. If we consider these $2n$ equations simultaneously, we can write

$$\mathbf{A} \mathbf{M} = \mathbf{b}$$

where $\mathbf{A}$ is a $2n \times 3$ matrix obtained by stacking the n matrices $\mathbf{A}_i$, and $\mathbf{b}$ is a $2n$-dimensional vector obtained by stacking the n vectors $\mathbf{b}_i$. The solution for $\mathbf{M}$ is, classically,

$$\mathbf{M} = (\mathbf{A}^T \mathbf{A})^{-1} \mathbf{A}^T \mathbf{b} \tag{6.19}$$

if $\text{rank}(\mathbf{A}) = 3$ which we assume to be the case.

Computing the uncertainty on M is our next goal and can be done using the analysis performed in chapter 5. We model the pixels m_i as independent random points with covariance matrices Λ_i and means $\hat{\mathbf{m}}_i$. If we denote by $\mathbf{x}$ the $2n$-dimensional vector obtained by concatenating the $\hat{\mathbf{m}}_i$, we have $\mathbf{M} = \mathbf{f}(\mathbf{x})$, where $\mathbf{f}$ is defined by equation (6.19). Therefore, according to equation (5.28), we have, up to the first order,

$$\Lambda_{\mathbf{M}} = \mathbf{Df}(\mathbf{x})\Lambda_{\mathbf{x}}\mathbf{Df}(\mathbf{x})^T$$

where $\Lambda_{\mathbf{x}} = \text{diag}(\Lambda_1, \ldots, \Lambda_n)$.

Let us now evaluate $\mathbf{Df}(\mathbf{x})$. By definition

$$\mathbf{Df}(\mathbf{x}) = [\frac{\partial \mathbf{f}}{\partial \mathbf{m}_1}(\mathbf{x}), \ldots, \frac{\partial \mathbf{f}}{\partial \mathbf{m}_n}(\mathbf{x})]$$

a $3 \times 2n$ matrix. Since $\frac{\partial \mathbf{f}}{\partial \mathbf{m}_i}(\mathbf{x})$ is a 3×2 matrix equal to $[\frac{\partial \mathbf{f}}{\partial u_i}(\mathbf{x}), \frac{\partial \mathbf{f}}{\partial v_i}(\mathbf{x})]$, we can write, according to (6.19),

$$\frac{\partial \mathbf{f}}{\partial u_i}(\mathbf{x}) = \frac{\partial (\mathbf{A}^T\mathbf{A})^{-1}}{\partial u_i}\mathbf{A}^T\mathbf{b} + (\mathbf{A}^T\mathbf{A})^{-1}\frac{\partial \mathbf{A}^T}{\partial u_i}\mathbf{b} + (\mathbf{A}^T\mathbf{A})^{-1}\mathbf{A}^T\frac{\partial \mathbf{b}}{\partial u_i}$$

with a similar formula for $\frac{\partial \mathbf{f}}{\partial v_i}$. Furthermore, we have $\frac{\partial \mathbf{A}^T}{\partial u_i} = (\frac{\partial \mathbf{A}}{\partial u_i})^T$ and[4]

$$\frac{\partial (\mathbf{A}^T\mathbf{A})^{-1}}{\partial u_i} = -(\mathbf{A}^T\mathbf{A})^{-1}\frac{\partial \mathbf{A}^T\mathbf{A}}{\partial u_i}(\mathbf{A}^T\mathbf{A})^{-1}$$

$$\frac{\partial \mathbf{A}^T\mathbf{A}}{\partial u_i} = \frac{\partial \mathbf{A}}{\partial u_i}^T\mathbf{A} + \mathbf{A}^T\frac{\partial \mathbf{A}}{\partial u_i}$$

This reduces the computation of $\mathbf{Df}(\mathbf{x})$ to that of $\frac{\partial \mathbf{A}}{\partial u_i}$, $\frac{\partial \mathbf{A}}{\partial v_i}$, $\frac{\partial \mathbf{b}}{\partial u_i}$, and $\frac{\partial \mathbf{b}}{\partial v_i}$ for $i = 1, \ldots, n$. Since $\mathbf{A}$ and $\mathbf{b}$ are affine functions of the u_i's and v_i's, those partial derivatives are very simple to compute, and this is a practical way of computing the covariance matrix $\Lambda_{\mathbf{M}}$ of the the reconstructed point M, up to a first-order approximation, from the covariance matrices of the pixels that have been matched in the n images[5] (see problem 7).

---

4. The first equation is readily obtained by taking the derivative of $(\mathbf{A}^T\mathbf{A})(\mathbf{A}^T\mathbf{A})^{-1} = \mathbf{I}$.

5. Note that, even though the computation may become a bit complicated, this method also allows us, in principle, to take into account any known uncertainty in the calibration, i.e., on the matrices $\tilde{\mathbf{P}}_i$.

6.10.2.2 *A nonlinear method*

The previous method minimizes the criterion $\|\mathbf{AM} - \mathbf{b}\|^2$ with respect to $\mathbf{M}$ in order to find the best reconstructed 3-D point. This has the advantage of providing a closed-form solution through equation (6.19), but it has the disadvantage that the criterion that is minimized does not have a good physical interpretation. An interesting variation of the previous method consists of minimizing the following criterion:

$$\sum_{i=1}^{n} \|\hat{\mathbf{m}}_i - \mathbf{m}_i\|^2 \tag{6.20}$$

where $\mathbf{m}_i$ is the 2×1 vector of coordinates of the image in the ith camera of the 3-D point M to be reconstructed. The projective coordinates of m_i are given by

$$\tilde{\mathbf{m}}_i = \tilde{\mathbf{P}}_i \tilde{\mathbf{M}}$$

and are therefore functions of M. As we said before, there does not exist any closed-form solution to the minimization of criterion (6.20), but we can use any standard iterative minimization technique such as the Newton-Raphson method which can be initialized to the solution obtained by the previous method. The first-order approximation of the covariance of M can then be computed from the results of section 5.6.2 (see problem 9). Note that all methods, linear and nonlinear, yield a reconstructed point that does not, in general, project exactly onto the measured pixel's $\hat{m}_i$.

6.10.3 Reconstructing lines

We will use the representation of lines developed in section 5.4.4 of chapter 5, in which a line is represented by four numbers a, b, p, and q, which define the equations of two planes. The two planes depend upon which of the three possible maps one is using. We are describing the computation for the first map, given that it is almost the same for the other two. Note that in practice the computation must be performed for the three maps.

Now suppose that we are given a line segment in one image. This segment defines a line l of equation $cu + dv + e = 0$. A projective representation of this line is the vector $\tilde{\mathbf{l}} = [c, d, e]^T$. The projective equation of l is $\tilde{\mathbf{l}}^T \tilde{\mathbf{m}} = 0$. Now let $\tilde{\mathbf{P}}$ be the perspective matrix of the camera obtained by calibration. We know that the relation between a 3-D point M and its image m is $\tilde{\mathbf{m}} = \tilde{\mathbf{P}}\tilde{\mathbf{M}}$. Thus, the equation $\tilde{\mathbf{l}}^T \tilde{\mathbf{m}} = 0$ of the image line l defines the equation $\tilde{\mathbf{l}}^T \tilde{\mathbf{P}} \tilde{\mathbf{M}} = 0$ of a projective plane, which is of course the plane L defined by l and the optical center of the camera. The projective representation of this plane (section 2.5.1) is the 4×1 vector

$$\tilde{\mathbf{L}} = \tilde{\mathbf{P}}^T \tilde{\mathbf{l}} \tag{6.21}$$

In the first map a line is represented as the intersection of the two planes L_1 and L_2 of equations $x = az + p$ and $y = bz + q$ whose projective representations are the 4×1 vectors $\tilde{\mathbf{L}}_1 = [1, 0, -a, -p]^T$ and $\tilde{\mathbf{L}}_2 = [0, 1, -b, -q]^T$. A line seen by one camera does not define a unique three-dimensional line, but it imposes constraints on the representation of the lines of which it might be the image (geometrically, these lines must lie in the plane previously defined). When several cameras are available, the number of constraints increases.

We can show that these constraints are linear in the coefficients a, b, p, and q of the representation. In order to do this, we note that the three planes L, L_1, and L_2 must meet along a line. This is equivalent to saying that L, for example, belongs to the pencil defined by L_1 and L_2. In terms of the projective representations, this simply means that the three projective points $\tilde{L}, \tilde{L}_1$, and $\tilde{L}_2$ of the projective space $\mathcal{P}^3$ are aligned or that the 4×3 matrix $[\tilde{\mathbf{L}}_1, \tilde{\mathbf{L}}_2, \tilde{\mathbf{L}}]$ has rank 2. This, in turn, implies that the four 3×3 subdeterminants $D_i, i = 1, \ldots, 4$ of that matrix are equal to 0. Let us write $\tilde{\mathbf{L}} = [\alpha, \beta, \gamma, \delta]^T$. Some simple algebra shows that

$$D_1 = a\alpha + b\beta + \gamma$$

$$D_2 = p\alpha + q\beta + \delta$$

$$D_3 = -b\beta + q\gamma + \alpha(aq - pb)$$

$$D_4 = a\delta - p\gamma + \beta(aq - pb)$$

Notice that $D_3 = qD_1 - bD_2$ and $D_4 = aD_2 - pD_1$. From this we conclude that writing that the four determinants are equal to 0 is equivalent to writing that D_1 and D_2 are 0, and thus we obtain the two announced linear conditions on a, b, p, and q.

The case of several cameras follows very simply. Let us call $\mathcal{L}$ the 4×1 vector $[a, b, p, q]^T$. We have just seen that a line l in one camera imposes two linear constraints on $\mathcal{L}$, which we write

$$\mathbf{A}\mathcal{L} = \mathbf{b} \qquad\qquad (6.22)$$

where $\mathbf{A}$ is the 2×4 matrix $\begin{bmatrix} \alpha & \beta & 0 & 0 \\ 0 & 0 & \alpha & \beta \end{bmatrix}$ and $\mathbf{b}$ the 2×1 vector[6] $-\begin{bmatrix} \gamma \\ \delta \end{bmatrix}$. If we have matched n segments in n cameras, therefore defining n lines l_i, we have n matrix equations

$$\mathbf{A}_i \mathcal{L} = \mathbf{b}_i \qquad i = 1, \ldots, n$$

which we can write as one single equation, similar to the case of points,

$$\mathcal{A}\mathcal{L} = \mathcal{B}$$

where $\mathcal{A}$ is a $2n \times 4$ matrix and $\mathcal{B}$ a $2n \times 1$ vector. When $n = 2$, the system has in general a unique solution $\mathcal{L} = \mathcal{A}^{-1}\mathcal{B}$. When $n \geq 3$, the system is overconstrained and the least-squares solution is

$$\mathcal{L} = (\mathcal{A}^T \mathcal{A})^{-1} \mathcal{A}^T \mathcal{B} \qquad\qquad (6.23)$$

if $\text{rank}(\mathcal{A}^T \mathcal{A}) = 4$, which we assume to be the case.

Computing the uncertainty of the representation of the 3-D line is our next goal. This is again a direct application of section 5.6. Each image line l_i is represented in one map (φ_1 or φ_2)[7] by two numbers a_i and b_i forming the vector $\mathbf{l}_i$ for which we also have a covariance matrix Λ_i (see section 5.6.4). If we denote by $\mathbf{x}$ the $2n \times 1$ vector $[\mathbf{l}_1^T, \ldots, \mathbf{l}_n^T]^T$, equation (6.23) defines a mapping $\mathbf{f}$ from $\mathbf{x}$ to the 4×1 vector $\mathcal{L}$. In fact, the analysis that was performed for points in the previous section applies almost word for word. According to equation (5.28)

$$\Lambda_{\mathcal{L}} = \mathbf{Df}(\mathbf{x})\Lambda_{\mathbf{x}}\mathbf{Df}(\mathbf{x})^T$$

---

6. A practical remark: Equation (6.22) is homogeneous in the coordinates of $\mathcal{L}$, i.e., $\mathbf{A}$ and $\mathbf{b}$ are defined up to a scale factor. Since this may cause problems, we can assume that $\bar{\mathbf{l}}$ is a normalized representation of l, i.e., is equal to $[1, a, b]^T$ in the map φ_1 and equal to $[a, 1, b]^T$ in the map φ_2 (see section 5.3.3.2 of chapter 5).

7. We assume that a map has been chosen for each 2-D line.

where $\Lambda_{\mathbf{x}} = \mathrm{diag}(\Lambda_1, \ldots, \Lambda_n)$ is a $2n \times 2n$ matrix, and

$$\mathbf{Df}(\mathbf{x}) = [\frac{\partial \mathbf{f}}{\partial \mathbf{l}_1}, \ldots, \frac{\partial \mathbf{f}}{\partial \mathbf{l}_n}]$$

is a $4 \times 2n$ matrix in which $\frac{\partial \mathbf{f}}{\partial \mathbf{l}_i} = [\frac{\partial \mathbf{f}}{\partial a_i}, \frac{\partial \mathbf{f}}{\partial b_i}]$ is a 4×2 matrix. The partial derivatives $\frac{\partial \mathbf{f}}{\partial a_i}$ and $\frac{\partial \mathbf{f}}{\partial b_i}$ are easily computed using the results of the previous section and equations (6.21) and (6.22). This completes the computation of the first-order approximation of the covariance matrix of the reconstructed 3-D line in the map φ_1.

6.11 More references

The literature on stereo vision is very extensive, and this chapter falls short of exploring all possible approaches. The reader who is interested in broadening his or her view of the problem is encouraged to read some general articles such as those by Barnard and Fischler [Bar82] and that by Binford [Bin84], which discuss complexity and constraints in stereo. Nishihara and Poggio [NP84] and Dhond and Aggarwal [DA89] also discuss many interesting aspects related to stereo and robotics. An excellent book describing the recent efforts in computational stereo in Great Britain is the one edited by John Mayhew and John Frisby [MF91]. An interesting and promising approach is to design stereo algorithms that use several of the techniques we have been describing. It is likely that this integration will add robustness and reliability. Some interesting ideas in that direction can be found in the article by Hoff and Ahuja [HA89].

6.12 Problems

1. Using the results of section 6.2.5, define the disparity d as a smooth function of w.

2. Prove from equation (6.6) that in the limit the condition on the tangent to the object is the one stated in the text, i.e., that it must lie outside the forbidden zone.

3. In this problem we will show that the disparity gradient constraint with $K < 2$ implies the uniqueness constraint. Referring to figure 6.14, assume that pixel m_1 matches m_2 and m_3. Prove that the disparity gradient of the matches (m_1, m_2) and (m_1, m_3) is equal to 2, and from this draw conclusions.

4. In section 6.2.6 we have characterized the image of a three-dimensional curve (C) in a camera, given its images in two other cameras. Using the same notations and knowing the images (c_1) and (c_2) of (C), we have characterized (c_3). Using the same ideas, compute the curvature and the torsion of (C) from (c_1) and (c_2) (use the results in appendix C).

5. This problem investigates the issue of choosing the reprojection plane for image rectification that was described in section 6.3. Let us consider figure 6.61. We assume that both cameras are referred to their normalized coordinate systems. The optical centers are C_1 and C_2, and the rigid displacement between the two normalized coordinate systems is represented by the rotation matrix $\mathbf{R}$ and the translation vector $\mathbf{t}$. In this figure we see the problem of the distortion that the rectification induces on the images. For example, the square image $abcd$ becomes the quadrilateral $ABCD$. To minimize distortion, we want this quadrilateral (and the corresponding one for the second image) to be as close as possible to the original square images. This is a way to impose a constraint on the choice of the plane $\mathcal{R}$. Let us denote by $\mathbf{n}$ its normal and by d its distance to the origin C_1 (its equation is $\mathbf{n}^T\mathbf{M} - d = 0$ in the normalized coordinate system of the first camera). The normal $\mathbf{n}$ must be such that

$$\mathbf{n}^T\mathbf{C}_1\mathbf{C}_2 = \mathbf{n}^T\mathbf{t} = 0 \tag{6.24}$$

and we can choose $d = 1$.

a. What is the equation of $\mathcal{R}$ in the normalized coordinate system of the second camera?

b. Given a pixel m in the first retina, its projection M on the plane $\mathcal{R}$ is given by

$$\mathbf{M} = \lambda\mathbf{m}$$

What is the value of λ as a function of m and $\mathbf{n}$?

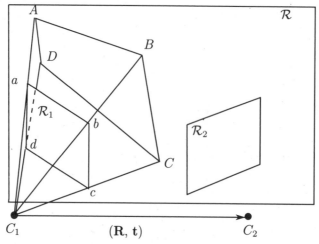

Figure 6.61   The square image *abcd* is projected as a quadrilateral *ABCD* onto the plane $\mathcal{R}$.

c. Let us denote by α, β, γ, and δ the inner products $\mathbf{n}^T\mathbf{a}, \mathbf{n}^T\mathbf{b}, \mathbf{n}^T\mathbf{c}$, and $\mathbf{n}^T\mathbf{d}$. Show that a unit norm vector $\mathbf{p}$ parallel to $\mathbf{AB}$ is

$$\mathbf{p} = \frac{\alpha\mathbf{b} - \beta\mathbf{a}}{\sqrt{\beta^2\|\mathbf{a}\|^2 + \alpha^2\|\mathbf{b}\|^2 - 2\alpha\beta\mathbf{a}^T\mathbf{b}}} \tag{6.25}$$

Give similar expressions for unit norm vectors $\mathbf{q}, \mathbf{r}$, and $\mathbf{s}$ parallel to $\mathbf{BC}, \mathbf{CD}$, and $\mathbf{DA}$.

d. We will now assume that $\mathbf{n}$ is represented in spherical coordinates (see figure 5.3). Therefore, we have $\mathbf{n} = [\sin\theta\cos\phi, \sin\theta\sin\phi, \cos\theta]^T$. Show that $\mathbf{p}$ (and therefore $\mathbf{q}, \mathbf{r}$, and $\mathbf{s}$) is a function of only $\tan\theta$ and ϕ.

e. Show that $\mathbf{p}$ is a function of only ϕ.

f. We will now introduce an index i for the camera number. A measure $D_i, i = 1, 2$ of the distortion of the ith image can be taken as how much the angles $(\mathbf{A}_i\mathbf{B}_i, \mathbf{B}_i\mathbf{C}_i), (\mathbf{B}_i\mathbf{C}_i, \mathbf{C}_i\mathbf{D}_i), (\mathbf{C}_i\mathbf{D}_i, \mathbf{D}_i\mathbf{A}_i)$, and $(\mathbf{D}_i\mathbf{A}_i, \mathbf{A}_i\mathbf{B}_i)$ differ from 90 degrees. Give a possible value for D_1.

g. Show how to compute D_2 for the second image.

h. Solve numerically for ϕ by choosing values for the coordinates of $a_i, b_i, c_i, d_i, i = 1, 2, \mathbf{t}$ and $\mathbf{R}$.

6. Show that the ordering constraint described in section 6.2.4 implies the relations (6.12).

7. Complete the computation of $\frac{\partial A}{\partial u_i}$, $\frac{\partial A}{\partial v_i}$, $\frac{\partial b}{\partial u_i}$, and $\frac{\partial b}{\partial v_i}$ as functions of the perspective matrices $\tilde{P}_i$ in section 6.10.2.1.

8. Show how the plane parameters $\mathbf{n}$ and d can be recovered from four-point correspondences in the situation described in section 6.8.

9. Using the results of section 5.6.2, compute the first-order approximation of the covariance matrix of the 3-D point M reconstructed by the method described in section 6.10.2.2.

7 Determining Discrete Motion from Points and Lines

In this chapter we will study the following problem. Given several (in practice two or three) views of a scene containing moving objects, and given a number of matched points or lines, which are all images of points and lines located on the same moving object, what is the possibility of recovering the motion of the object and the distance of the points or lines to the camera? In fact, for convenience we will study the dual problem where the camera is moving in an otherwise static environment. We will not discuss the problem of obtaining the matches themselves, which will be studied in detail in the next chapter.

7.1 How to read this chapter

This chapter can be seen as a complement of chapters 3 and 6. In chapter 6 we assumed that we had a calibrated rig of two or three cameras and investigated ways of establishing correspondences between the images that were supposed to have been acquired simultaneously. In this chapter we will consider a single moving camera in a static environment. We will assume that the intrinsic parameters (see chapter 3) are known, but that the camera's motion is unknown. We will then consider two or three images taken by the camera at two or three time instants and assume that we are given a number of token matches between the images. The main purpose of this chapter is to investigate the number of rigid displacements of the camera compatible with the matches. This chapter's title could also have been "Relative Extrinsic Camera Calibration." This problem is fairly complex and, at least in the case where the tokens are lines, is still largely unsolved. The chapter is divided into six main sections.

After a short introduction, section 7.3 will be devoted to the best-understood case where the tokens are points. In this case, two views are sufficient to obtain the camera displacement. We will begin with a thorough study of the constraint on the displacement that is imposed by one match and derive many properties of the so-called *essential matrix* that naturally arises from this constraint. On the first reading the reader can skip section 7.3.1.2, where the properties of the essential matrix are studied from the standpoint of algebraic geometry; those results are necessary only for section 7.3.5.2. We will then investigate ways of recovering the camera displacement from a number of point matches. In the case of the minimum number of points, five, we will give a proof that the number of solutions is at most ten. The proof is constructive, yields an algorithm for computing these solutions, and uses all the results of chapter 1. On the first reading, the reader may read only section 7.3.2.9. We will then discuss how we can obtain simpler algorithms by increasing the number of points. One of these algorithms is quite practical even in the presence of measurement noise. In the last part of this section we will explore the intriguing question of whether these simple algorithms can be fooled by some special configurations of the imaged points for which there may exist several solutions to the motion problem. This question has a long-standing history in photogrammetry and has been solved later and independently by computer vision researchers. The main answer is found in section 7.3.5.1, and the characterization of the number of solutions in section 7.3.5.2, which draws on the results of section 7.3.1.2; this can also be skipped on the first reading.

The fourth section is devoted to the much less well understood case where the tokens are lines. The higher degree of complexity of this case stems from the fact that three views of a line are necessary to constrain the displacement, instead of two as in the previous case. The results of this section will be used in chapter 9, but section 7.4.2 can be skipped on the first reading. The fifth section investigates how adding a constraint on the imaged points and lines, namely that they lie in a plane, can simplify the problem. In this planar case, the problem can be solved completely from two views for points and lines using elementary matrix algebra.

7.2   Introduction

Let us assume that we have a camera that is moving continuously in a static environment and following some unknown trajectory. We will consider the images obtained at a number of time instants $t_0, t_1, \ldots, t_{n-1}$ and assume that we can extract from these n images a number of tokens (points and lines) and match them between the images. For example, we will assume that we have a number of n-tuples of pixels $(m_0, m_1, \ldots, m_{n-1})$, m_i belonging to the ith image and that we know that they are all images of the same physical point in the scene. Similarly, we have a number of image lines $(l_0, l_1, \ldots, l_{n-1})$, l_i belonging to the ith image, and we know that they are all images of the same physical line in the scene.

Between the instants t_i and t_{i+1}, the camera moves along its unknown trajectory. In this chapter we will ignore the details of this trajectory and the way the camera moves along it; we are interested only in the set of finite rigid displacements D_i that bring the camera from its position and orientation at time t_i to its new position and orientation at time t_{i+1}.

We will also assume for convenience (even though it is not necessary, as problem 1 demonstrates), that we are working with the camera in a normalized coordinate system (see section 3.3.1.1). We have seen in this chapter that this implies calibrating the camera and computing its intrinsic parameters. Those, in turn, define a transformation from pixel coordinates to normalized pixel coordinates. This transformation defines a normalized camera with unit focal length and a coordinate system $Cxyz$ centered at the optical center (see figure 3.9). The motion of the camera is the motion of that coordinate system, and we will describe D_i as a rotation of matrix $\mathbf{R}_i$ around an axis going through C_i followed by the translation $\mathbf{C}_i\mathbf{C}_{i+1}$.

7.3   Determining camera displacement from point correspondences

We will first consider the case where the tokens are points. Let C be the optical center of the camera at the first time instant, C' at the second time instant, $\mathbf{R}$ the rotation matrix describing the rotation of the camera between the two time instants, and $\mathbf{t}$ the vector $\mathbf{CC'}$. Given a vector $\mathbf{x}$

expressed in the coordinate system of the camera at the second time instant, it is equal to $\mathbf{Rx}$ in the coordinate system of the camera at the first time instant.

As shown in figure 7.1, the 3-D point M has images m and m' at two consecutive time instants. Knowing that m and m' are correspondences, what constraint on $\mathbf{R}$ and $\mathbf{t}$ can we derive? From figure 7.1 it is clear that m and m' are in correspondence if and only if the three vectors $\mathbf{Cm}$, $\mathbf{C'm'}$, and $\mathbf{CC'}$ are coplanar. We write $\mathbf{m}$ for $\mathbf{Cm}$, and $\mathbf{m'}$ for $\mathbf{Cm'}$. The constraint can be written in the coordinate system of the first camera as

$$\mathbf{m} \cdot (\mathbf{t} \wedge \mathbf{Rm'}) = 0 \tag{7.1}$$

We introduce the antisymmetric matrix $\mathbf{T}$:

$$\mathbf{T} = \begin{bmatrix} 0 & -t_3 & t_2 \\ t_3 & 0 & -t_1 \\ -t_2 & t_1 & 0 \end{bmatrix}$$

Matrix $\mathbf{T}$ is such that $\mathbf{Tx} = \mathbf{t} \wedge \mathbf{x}$ for all vectors $\mathbf{x}$. Letting $\mathbf{E} = \mathbf{TR}$, equation (7.1) can be rewritten as

$$\mathbf{m}^T \mathbf{Em'} = 0 \tag{7.2}$$

The matrix $\mathbf{E}$ is called the *essential matrix* and has a number of important properties.

1. It is at the basis of a method for characterizing the complexity of the "motion-from-points" problem [Dem88]. This is the problem, given a number of point matches in two images taken at two different time instants, of characterizing the number of rigid displacements that are compatible with these matches (see section 7.3.2 for an in-depth discussion of this problem).

2. It is very useful for characterizing "degenerate" configurations of points (see section 7.3.5).

3. It is also at the basis of a linear method for computing the displacements D_i (the "eight-points algorithm" seen in section 7.3.3.1).

Notice that equation (7.1) is homogeneous with respect to $\mathbf{t}$. This reflects the fact that scale is undetermined: We cannot recover the absolute scale of the scene without an extra yardstick, such as knowing the distance in

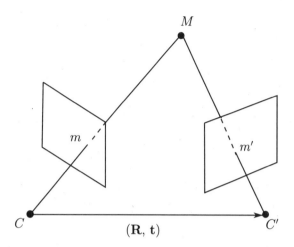

Figure 7.1 Constraint on the motion parameters derived from point matches.

space between two points. Also note that in the case where there is no translation, $\mathbf{t} = \mathbf{0}$, equation (7.1) is identically 0. Even though one may be able to recover $\mathbf{R}$, this yields no information about the depth of points in the scene (see problem 2). For this reason we assume in what follows that $\mathbf{t} \neq \mathbf{0}$.

7.3.1 Properties of essential matrices

We will characterize the set of essential matrices from two different viewpoints. The question that we will ask is the following: Given a 3×3 matrix $\mathbf{E}$, when can it be decomposed as the product of an antisymmetric matrix $\mathbf{T}$ and a rotation matrix $\mathbf{R}$? That is to say, when can it be considered as arising from a camera displacement? We will first answer this question by "elementary" means using the singular value decomposition of $\mathbf{E}$ [GF83], and we will then sketch a more advanced approach based on algebraic geometry.

7.3.1.1 A characterization of the essential matrices based on linear algebra

We are going to prove the following theorem [HF89, FM90, May90b]:

Theorem 7.1

A real 3×3 matrix $\mathbf{E}$ can be decomposed as the product $\mathbf{TR}$ of an antisymmetric matrix $\mathbf{T}$ and a rotation matrix $\mathbf{R}$ if and only if it has one singular value equal to 0 and the other two singular values equal to each other.

In order to prove this theorem, we must first prove two lemmas, which are useful by themselves:

Lemma 7.1

The essential matrix $\mathbf{E} = \mathbf{TR}$ satisfies $\mathbf{E}^T \mathbf{t} = 0$.

Proof $\mathbf{E}^T_{\cdot} = \mathbf{R}^T \mathbf{T}^T = -\mathbf{R}^T \mathbf{T}$. Therefore $\mathbf{E}^T \mathbf{t} = -\mathbf{R}^T (\mathbf{T} \mathbf{t}) = -\mathbf{R}^T (\mathbf{t} \wedge \mathbf{t}) = \mathbf{0}$. ∎

One consequence of lemma 7.1 is that the rank of the matrix $\mathbf{E}$ is less than or equal to 2, and therefore $\det(\mathbf{E}) = 0$.

Lemma 7.2

The essential matrix $\mathbf{E} = \mathbf{TR}$ is such that $\mathbf{EE}^T$ depends only on the translation vector $\mathbf{t}$.

Proof Clearly, we have

$$\mathbf{EE}^T = \mathbf{TRR}^T \mathbf{T}^T = -\mathbf{T}^2 = \begin{bmatrix} t_3^2 + t_2^2 & -t_1 t_2 & -t_1 t_3 \\ -t_2 t_1 & t_1^2 + t_3^2 & -t_2 t_3 \\ -t_3 t_1 & -t_3 t_2 & t_2^2 + t_1^2 \end{bmatrix} = (\mathbf{t}^T \mathbf{t})\mathbf{I} - \mathbf{t}\mathbf{t}^T$$

∎

We can now prove theorem 7.1:

Proof From lemma 7.1 we have concluded that $det(\mathbf{E}) = 0$, and therefore at least one singular value of $\mathbf{E}$ is equal to 0. A consequence of lemma 7.2 is that the essential matrix $\mathbf{E}$ has two equal singular values. In detail, let $\mathbf{U}$ be a rotation matrix such that $\mathbf{U}\mathbf{t} = [1, 0, 0]^T$ ($\mathbf{t}$ can be assumed to be of unit length since we know that it can be recovered only up to a scale factor). Then

$$\mathbf{UTT}^T \mathbf{U}^T = \mathbf{U}(\mathbf{I} - \mathbf{t}\mathbf{t}^T)\mathbf{U}^T = \mathbf{I} - (\mathbf{U}\mathbf{t})(\mathbf{U}\mathbf{t})^T = \begin{bmatrix} 0 & 0 & 0 \\ 0 & 1 & 0 \\ 0 & 0 & 1 \end{bmatrix} \equiv \mathbf{A}$$

Thus

$$\mathbf{U}\mathbf{E}\mathbf{E}^T\mathbf{U}^T = \mathbf{U}\mathbf{T}\mathbf{T}^T\mathbf{U}^T = \mathbf{A}$$

The matrices $\mathbf{E}$ and $\mathbf{A}$ have the same singular values.

We have just proved the *only if* part of the theorem. Let us prove the *if* part. If $\mathbf{E}$ has one singular value equal to zero and two singular values equal to $\sigma \neq 0$, then there exists a rotation matrix $\mathbf{U}$ such that

$$\mathbf{E}\mathbf{E}^T = \mathbf{U}\begin{bmatrix} 0 & 0 & 0 \\ 0 & \sigma^2 & 0 \\ 0 & 0 & \sigma^2 \end{bmatrix}\mathbf{U}^T$$

Thus

$$(\sigma^{-1}\mathbf{U}^T\mathbf{E})(\sigma^{-1}\mathbf{U}^T\mathbf{E})^T = \mathbf{A} \tag{7.3}$$

Let $\mathbf{F} = \sigma^{-1}\mathbf{U}^T\mathbf{E}$, and let $\mathbf{f}_1^T, \mathbf{f}_2^T$, and $\mathbf{f}_3^T$ be the row vectors of $\mathbf{F}$. From equation (7.3) we have

$$\mathbf{f}_1^T\mathbf{f}_1 = 0 \quad \text{and therefore} \quad \mathbf{f}_1 = \mathbf{0}$$

$$\mathbf{f}_2^T\mathbf{f}_2 = \mathbf{f}_3^T\mathbf{f}_3 = 1 \quad \text{and} \quad \mathbf{f}_2^T\mathbf{f}_3 = 0 \tag{7.4}$$

Matrix $\mathbf{F}$ is therefore "almost" orthogonal. It is easy to construct a rotation matrix $\mathbf{F}'$ such that $\mathbf{F}\mathbf{F}'^T = \mathbf{A}$. Indeed, we can choose the row vectors $\mathbf{f}_1'^T, \mathbf{f}_2'^T$, and $\mathbf{f}_3'^T$ of $\mathbf{F}'$ such that

$$\mathbf{f}_1' = \mathbf{f}_2 \wedge \mathbf{f}_3$$

$$\mathbf{f}_2' = \mathbf{f}_2$$

$$\mathbf{f}_3' = \mathbf{f}_3$$

We can therefore write

$$\mathbf{F} = \mathbf{A}\mathbf{F}'$$

We notice that matrix $\mathbf{A}$ can be written as

$$\mathbf{A} = \begin{bmatrix} 0 & 0 & 0 \\ 0 & 0 & -1 \\ 0 & 1 & 0 \end{bmatrix}\begin{bmatrix} 1 & 0 & 0 \\ 0 & 0 & 1 \\ 0 & -1 & 0 \end{bmatrix} = \mathbf{T}'\mathbf{R}'$$

where $\mathbf{T}'$ is an antisymmetric matrix and $\mathbf{R}'$ is a rotation matrix. We now have

$$\sigma^{-1}\mathbf{U}^T\mathbf{E} = \mathbf{F} = \mathbf{AF}' = \mathbf{T}'\mathbf{R}'\mathbf{F}'$$

and thus

$$\mathbf{E} = \mathbf{U}(\sigma\mathbf{T}')\mathbf{R}'\mathbf{F}' = (\mathbf{U}(\sigma\mathbf{T}')\mathbf{U}^T)(\mathbf{U}\mathbf{R}'\mathbf{F}')$$

The result follows since $\mathbf{U}(\sigma\mathbf{T}')\mathbf{U}^T$ is antisymmetric, and $\mathbf{U}\mathbf{R}'\mathbf{F}'$ is a rotation matrix. ∎

We will now derive the conditions on the coefficients of $\mathbf{EE}^T$ that are equivalent to the equality of its two nonzero singular values. We will define the coefficients a, b, and c of the characteristic polynomial of $\mathbf{EE}^T$ by

$$\det(\mathbf{EE}^T - \lambda\mathbf{I}) = -\lambda^3 + a\lambda^2 + b\lambda + c$$

Since $c = \det(\mathbf{EE}^T) = \det^2(\mathbf{E})$, we have $c = 0$. Therefore the condition we seek is equivalent to writing that the quadratic equation $-\lambda^2 + a\lambda + b$ has two equal roots:

$$a^2 + 4b = 0$$

If we define a_i, b_i by

$$\mathbf{EE}^T = \begin{bmatrix} a_1 & b_3 & b_2 \\ b_3 & a_2 & b_1 \\ b_2 & b_1 & a_3 \end{bmatrix} \tag{7.5}$$

then it is easy to show that

$$a = a_1 + a_2 + a_3$$

$$b = b_1^2 + b_2^2 + b_3^2 - a_1 a_2 - a_2 a_3 - a_3 a_1$$

Therefore:

$$a^2 + 4b = (a_1 + a_2 + a_3)^2 + 4(b_1^2 + b_2^2 + b_3^2 - a_1 a_2 - a_2 a_3 - a_3 a_1) \tag{7.6}$$

We can combine equation (7.6) and theorem 7.1 to obtain the following result:

Proposition 7.1
A real 3×3 matrix $\mathbf{E}$ with row vectors $\mathbf{e}_i^T$ can be decomposed as the product $\mathbf{TR}$ of an antisymmetric matrix $\mathbf{T}$ and a rotation matrix $\mathbf{R}$ if and only if

$$\mathbf{e}_1^T (\mathbf{e}_2 \wedge \mathbf{e}_3) = 0 \tag{7.7}$$

$$(\|\mathbf{e}_1\|^2 + \|\mathbf{e}_2\|^2 + \|\mathbf{e}_3\|^2)^2 = 4(\|\mathbf{e}_1 \wedge \mathbf{e}_2\|^2 + \|\mathbf{e}_2 \wedge \mathbf{e}_3\|^2 + \|\mathbf{e}_3 \wedge \mathbf{e}_1\|^2) \tag{7.8}$$

Proof Equation (7.7) is equivalent to $\det(\mathbf{E}) = 0$. On expressing the a_i's and the b_i's of (7.5) as functions of the $\mathbf{e}_i$, equation (7.6) yields

$$(\|\mathbf{e}_1\|^2 + \|\mathbf{e}_2\|^2 + \|\mathbf{e}_3\|^2)^2 + 4((\mathbf{e}_2^T \mathbf{e}_1)^2 + (\mathbf{e}_3^T \mathbf{e}_1)^2 + (\mathbf{e}_1^T \mathbf{e}_2)^2$$

$$- \|\mathbf{e}_1\|^2 \|\mathbf{e}_2\|^2 - \|\mathbf{e}_2\|^2 \|\mathbf{e}_3\|^2 - \|\mathbf{e}_3\|^2 \|\mathbf{e}_1\|^2) = 0$$

from which (7.8) follows. ∎

Even though proposition 7.1 has a nice interpretation in terms of the row vectors of matrix $\mathbf{E}$, it can also be expressed differently:

Proposition 7.2
A real 3×3 matrix $\mathbf{E}$ with row vectors $\mathbf{e}_i^T$ can be decomposed as the product $\mathbf{TR}$ of an antisymmetric matrix $\mathbf{T}$ and a rotation matrix $\mathbf{R}$ if and only if

$$\det(\mathbf{E}) = 0 \tag{7.9}$$

$$f(\mathbf{E}) \equiv \frac{1}{2} \mathrm{Tr}^2(\mathbf{EE}^T) - \mathrm{Tr}((\mathbf{EE}^T)^2) = 0 \tag{7.10}$$

Proof Notice that

$$\mathrm{Tr}(\mathbf{EE}^T)^2 - 2\mathrm{Tr}((\mathbf{EE}^T)^2) = -(a^2 + 4b) \qquad\qquad ∎$$

Note that equations (7.7) and (7.9) are cubic in the coefficients of $\mathbf{E}$, whereas equations (7.8) and (7.10) are biquadratic.

7.3.1.2 A characterization of the essential matrices based on algebraic geometry

Another approach for studying the $\mathbf{E}$ matrices is to consider them as vectors in a projective space of dimension 8, $\mathcal{P}^8$ (see chapter 2). Because of the two algebraic constraints (equations (7.9) and (7.10)) that must be satisfied by any essential matrix, they must lie in some manifold $\mathcal{M}$ of $\mathcal{P}^8$ (see appendix B for the definition of an algebraic manifold). In order to obtain a general characterization of $\mathcal{M}$, it is necessary to drop the (implicit) assumption that the essential matrices have real coefficients. We will therefore assume that they can have complex coefficients. This does not change the definition of a rotation matrix, which must still satisfy $\mathbf{RR}^T = \mathbf{I}$ and $\det(\mathbf{R}) = 1$. We then have the following proposition [Dem88]:

Proposition 7.3

[Demazure] The manifold $\mathcal{M}$ of complex essential matrices is characterized by the nine polynomial equations of degree 3:

$$\mathbf{F(E)} \equiv \frac{1}{2} Tr(\mathbf{EE}^T)\mathbf{E} - \mathbf{EE}^T\mathbf{E} = 0 \qquad (7.11)$$

Proof We will prove only the *if* part. Using lemma 7.2 we can write

$$\frac{1}{2}\text{Tr}(\mathbf{EE}^T)\mathbf{I} - \mathbf{EE}^T = \mathbf{tt}^T$$

We multiply on the right by $\mathbf{E}$ and use proposition 7.1 to obtain

$$\frac{1}{2}\text{Tr}(\mathbf{EE}^T)\mathbf{E} - \mathbf{EE}^T\mathbf{E} = 0$$

The components of equation (7.11) yield nine homogeneous polynomial equations of degree 3, which must be satisfied by the coefficients of $\mathbf{E}$. Conversely, any matrix that satisfies (7.11) is an essential matrix [Dem88]. Demazure shows that the equations of (7.11) are linearly independent and that they define the algebraic manifold $\mathcal{M}$ of essential matrices.   ∎

We note that the condition $\det(\mathbf{E}) = 0$ follows from (7.11). The proof by contradiction is straightforward. Suppose that $\mathbf{E}$ is a matrix satisfying (7.11) such that $\det(\mathbf{E}) \neq 0$. Then $\mathbf{E}$ is invertible, and thus (7.11) yields $\frac{1}{2}\text{Tr}(\mathbf{EE}^T)\mathbf{I} = \mathbf{EE}^T$. It follows that $\frac{3}{2}\text{Tr}(\mathbf{EE}^T) = \text{Tr}(\mathbf{EE}^T)$, and so $\text{Tr}(\mathbf{EE}^T) = 0$. On substituting $\text{Tr}(\mathbf{EE}^T) = 0$ into (7.11) and taking determinants we obtain $\det(\mathbf{E})^3 = 0$, contradicting the hypothesis that $\det(\mathbf{E}) \neq 0$.

7.3.1.3 Resolving an apparent contradiction

We have an apparent contradiction, since in proposition 7.2 we characterized the real points of the manifold $\mathcal{M}$ with two real equations (7.9) and

(7.10), and in proposition 7.3 we characterized them with the nine equations (7.11). The difference between the two propositions is that the first one deals with the real situation, while the second deals with the complex (and therefore also the real) situation. The contradiction is resolved by demonstrating that a real matrix satisfies equation (7.11) if and only if it satisfies equations (7.9) and (7.10). We note that $Tr(\mathbf{F}(\mathbf{E})\mathbf{F}(\mathbf{E})^T)$ is the sum of the squares of the entries of the left-hand side of (7.11). We offer the following proposition:

Proposition 7.4
The function $\mathbf{F}$ defined in proposition 7.3 satisfies

$$Tr(\mathbf{F}(\mathbf{E})\mathbf{F}(\mathbf{E})^T) = -\frac{1}{2}Tr(\mathbf{E}\mathbf{E}^T)Tr(\mathbf{F}(\mathbf{E})\mathbf{E}^T) + 3det(\mathbf{E})^2 \qquad (7.12)$$

Before we prove this proposition, let us see how it resolves the contradiction. If $\mathbf{E}$ is a real essential matrix, then $\mathbf{F}(\mathbf{E}) = 0$ and $det(\mathbf{E}) = 0$, and therefore $f(\mathbf{E}) = 0$. Reciprocally, if $f(\mathbf{E}) = det(\mathbf{E}) = 0$ and $\mathbf{E}$ is real, we have $\sum_{i,j=1}^{3} F_{ij}(\mathbf{E})^2 = 0$. Since the F_{ij}'s are real, each one is equal to 0 and $\mathbf{F}(\mathbf{E}) = 0$. Therefore $\mathbf{E}$ is an essential matrix because of proposition 7.3. This resolves the contradiction. Let us now prove proposition 7.4.

Proof   We write

$$\mathbf{F}(\mathbf{E}) = (\frac{1}{2}\text{Tr}(\mathbf{E}\mathbf{E}^T)\mathbf{I} - \mathbf{E}\mathbf{E}^T)\mathbf{E}$$

Letting $\mathbf{B} = \mathbf{E}\mathbf{E}^T$, we can write the two equations as follows:

$$\mathbf{F}(\mathbf{E})\mathbf{E}^T = (\frac{1}{2}\text{Tr}(\mathbf{B}) - \mathbf{B})\mathbf{B}$$

$$\mathbf{F}(\mathbf{E})\mathbf{F}(\mathbf{E})^T = \frac{1}{4}\text{Tr}(\mathbf{B})^2\mathbf{B} - \text{Tr}(\mathbf{B})\mathbf{B}^2 + \mathbf{B}^3$$

Taking the trace of the first equation, we obtain

$$\text{Tr}(\mathbf{F}(\mathbf{E})\mathbf{E}^T) = \frac{1}{2}\tau_1^2 - \tau_2 \qquad (7.13)$$

where $\tau_1 = \text{Tr}(\mathbf{B})$ and $\tau_2 = \text{Tr}(\mathbf{B}^2)$. Taking the trace of the second equation, we obtain

$$\text{Tr}(\mathbf{F}(\mathbf{E})\mathbf{F}(\mathbf{E})^T) = \frac{1}{4}\tau_1^3 - \tau_1\tau_2 + \tau_3 \tag{7.14}$$

where $\tau_3 = \text{Tr}(\mathbf{B}^3)$. We recall Newton's formula (see problem 3):

$$\tau_3 = -\frac{1}{2}\tau_1^3 + \frac{3}{2}\tau_1\tau_2 + 3\det(\mathbf{B}) \tag{7.15}$$

On combining equations (7.13), (7.14), (7.15), we obtain equation (7.12). It follows from (7.12) and the definition of $f(\mathbf{E})$ given in (7.10) that

$$\text{Tr}(\mathbf{F}(\mathbf{E})\mathbf{F}(\mathbf{E})^T) = -\frac{1}{2}\text{Tr}(\mathbf{E}\mathbf{E}^T)f(\mathbf{E}) + 3\det(\mathbf{E})^2$$

∎

7.3.2 Determining number of solutions: the five-points algorithm

In this section, we will investigate the question of how to determine the number of solutions to the motion problem for n point correspondences. We will ask and answer two questions:

- What is the minimum value of n?
- For this minimum value, how many different displacements are there that are compatible with the matches?

Since the dimensionality of the problem is five, namely three parameters for the rotation and two for the translation, which is defined up to a scale factor, and since we obtain one equation, namely (7.1), for each correspondence, the minimum number of correspondences is five. This is the answer to the first question. We will show that the maximum number of displacement solutions is ten, and we will give an algorithm for computing all solutions. This comes as a surprise, because ten is a fairly large number and this indicates that the problem is rather complex.

This problem has a very long history. We have been able to trace it back to Chasles [Cha55], who posed it in the following manner: "On donne dans le même plan deux systèmes de sept points chacun et qui se correspondent. Faire passer par chacun de ces systèmes un faisceau de sept

rayons, de telle sorte que les deux faisceaux soient homographiques."[1]
In terms of computer vision, we think of the two sets of points as pixels
in the two retinas and of the unknown points as the two epipoles. The
collineation referred to in the statement of the problem is the one that
relates the two sets of epipolar lines (see section 6.2.1.4).

The problem was solved by Hesse [Hes63]. A detailed analysis and solution of Chasles' problem can be found in an article by Sturm [Stu69].
The final word on this is that there exist three solutions in general, real or
complex, which can be found as a subset of the intersection of two planar
cubics (see problem 4). Unfortunately this does not solve our particular
problem, since there is no guarantee that the corresponding transformation from the first camera to the second is a rigid displacement. This
means that, if M is a reconstructed point with $\mathbf{M}$ its representation in
the coordinate system of the first camera, and if $\mathbf{M}'$ is its representation
in the coordinate system of the second camera, in the rigid case we can
write

$$\mathbf{M} = \mathbf{R}\mathbf{M}' + \mathbf{t}$$

or, projectively

$$\tilde{\mathbf{M}} = \mathbf{A}\tilde{\mathbf{M}}'$$

where matrix $\mathbf{A}$ is equal to

$$\begin{bmatrix} \mathbf{R} & \mathbf{t} \\ \mathbf{0} & 1 \end{bmatrix} \tag{7.16}$$

In the case of Chasles' problem, there is no guarantee that matrix $\mathbf{A}$ is
of the form of equation (7.16) but is a general collineation of $\mathcal{P}^3$. We
will now describe another approach to solving Chasles' problem incorpo-
rating the rigidity constraint. When we introduce the rigidity constraint,
fewer than seven correspondences (i.e., five) are sufficient because more
equations are available, as we will see.

The problem was solved in 1913 by Erwin Kruppa [Kru13], who found
that there were in general at most eleven solutions, real or complex. In

---

1. "We are given, in a plane, two sets of seven points in correspondence. For each
set, find a point such that the two sets of seven lines they define are related by a
collineation."

what follows we will derive Kruppa's equations and show that in fact there are in general ten solutions. The interest of Kruppa's method is that it allows us to construct the solutions explicitly: It is an algorithm. As we will also see, the ten solutions for the epipoles correspond to twenty rigid motions from camera 1 to camera 2 since each pair of epipoles yields two rigid motions (the so-called twin pairs). Among those twenty solutions at most ten are physically possible in the sense that they yield reconstructed points that are in front of both cameras. The details of the proof may not be of interest to the reader who is not mathematically inclined, who may go directly to section 7.3.2.9, where we summarize the algorithm. Note that the proof uses many of the results of projective geometry that have been introduced in chapter 2 and can therefore be considered as an exercise in applying the projective ideas to a computer vision problem.

7.3.2.1 *Enforcing the rigidity constraint*

To enforce the rigidity constraint let us look at figure 7.2 and notice that, by construction in the case of a rigid camera motion, the plane angles (xCm, xCp) and $(x'C'm', x'C'p')$ are equal. According to the projective definition of the angle between two planes given in chapter 2, we must introduce the absolute conic, Ω. Considering the images ω and ω' of Ω in the two retinal planes, let u, v be the two tangents from x to ω, and let u', v' be the two tangents from x' to ω'. If we want to enforce the equality of the two previous plane angles, a necessary condition is that the cross-ratios $\{\langle x, m \rangle, \langle x, p \rangle; u, v\}$ and $\{\langle x', m' \rangle, \langle x', p' \rangle; u', v'\}$ are equal. This implies that these tangents correspond to each other in the epipolar line collineation. This is shown in figure 7.3.

The precise correspondence of the tangents is immaterial in the sense that we could have either $u \overline{\wedge} u'$, $v \overline{\wedge} v'$ or $u \overline{\wedge} v'$, $v \overline{\wedge} u'$. For this reason we will refer to corresponding pairs of tangents without making the correspondence explicit.

7.3.2.2 *Determining intersections of the epipolar lines with $\langle \mathbf{a}, \mathbf{b} \rangle$*

Let $a\overline{\wedge}a'$, $b\overline{\wedge}b'$, $c\overline{\wedge}c'$, $d\overline{\wedge}d'$, $e\overline{\wedge}e'$ be five pairs of corresponding image points, and let x, x' be the unknown epipoles. Let $l_a, l_b, \ldots$ be the epipolar lines $\langle x, a \rangle, \langle x, b \rangle, \ldots$. After a change of projective coordinates (see section 2.2.2), we can assume that the points a, b, c, and d form the standard projective basis $\mathbf{e}_i$, $i = 1, \ldots, 4$:

$$\mathbf{a} = \begin{bmatrix} 1 \\ 0 \\ 0 \end{bmatrix} \qquad \mathbf{b} = \begin{bmatrix} 0 \\ 1 \\ 0 \end{bmatrix} \qquad \mathbf{c} = \begin{bmatrix} 0 \\ 0 \\ 1 \end{bmatrix} \qquad \mathbf{d} = \begin{bmatrix} 1 \\ 1 \\ 1 \end{bmatrix} \tag{7.17}$$

Let the image ω of the absolute conic in the first retinal plane $\mathcal{R}$ have the equation

$$\mathbf{y}^T \mathbf{A} \mathbf{y} = \sum_{i=1}^{3} a_{ik} y_i y_k = 0 \quad \text{with} \quad a_{ik} = a_{ki}$$

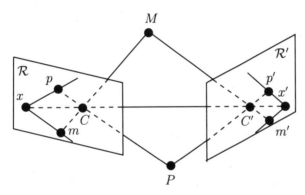

Figure 7.2 The plane angles (xCm, xCp) and $(x'C'm', x'C'p')$ are equal.

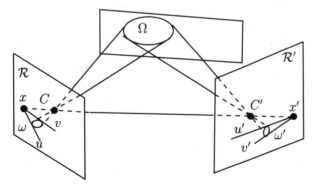

Figure 7.3 The images of the absolute conic Ω.

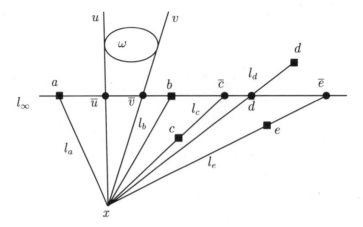

Figure 7.4 The situation in the image plane at the first time instant.

We use the same notation for the second retinal plane $\mathcal{R}'$ by adding $'$ whenever required.

The idea is to consider the intersections of the epipolar lines with the lines $\langle a, b \rangle$ and $\langle a', b' \rangle$ and to write down the conditions that these intersections are homographically related. Note that $\langle a, b \rangle$ is the line at infinity of $\mathcal{R}$, and so is $\langle a', b' \rangle$ for $\mathcal{R}'$. In effect, $\langle a, b \rangle$, $\langle a', b' \rangle$ provide a convenient set of coordinates for the two pencils of epipolar lines. We know seven epipolar lines in each retinal plane, five from the image points and 2 from the tangents to the image of the absolute conic. Let the epipolar lines $l_a, l_b,\ l_c, l_d$, and l_e intersect $\langle a, b \rangle$ at $\mathbf{a}, \mathbf{b}$, $\bar{\mathbf{c}}, \bar{\mathbf{d}}$, and $\bar{\mathbf{e}}$, respectively, as depicted in figure 7.4. Then $\bar{\mathbf{u}}$ and $\bar{\mathbf{v}}$ are the intersections of the tangents u and v drawn from the epipole $\mathbf{x}$ to the image ω of the absolute conic Ω. The coordinates of $\mathbf{a}, \mathbf{b},\ \bar{\mathbf{c}}, \bar{\mathbf{d}},\ \bar{\mathbf{e}}$ as points of $\langle a, b \rangle$ are given by

$$\mathbf{a} = [1, 0]^T \qquad\qquad \mathbf{b} = [0, 1]^T$$
$$\bar{\mathbf{c}} = [x_1, x_2]^T \qquad\qquad \bar{\mathbf{d}} = [x_1 - x_3, x_2 - x_3]^T$$
$$\bar{\mathbf{e}} = [x_1 e_3 - x_3 e_1, x_2 e_3 - x_3 e_2]^T$$

In order to find the intersection with $\langle a, b \rangle$ of the two tangents u and v to ω drawn from x, we apply equation (2.6), which gives us the equations of u and v:

$$(\mathbf{x}^T \mathbf{A} \mathbf{y})^2 = (\mathbf{x}^T \mathbf{A} \mathbf{x})(\mathbf{y}^T \mathbf{A} \mathbf{y}) \tag{7.18}$$

It follows from equation (7.18), after applying some algebra, that the coordinates y_1, y_2 on $\langle a, b \rangle$ of the intersections $\bar{\mathbf{u}}$ and $\bar{\mathbf{v}}$ of the tangents u and v from x to ω satisfy the following equation:

$$A_{11} y_1^2 + 2A_{12} y_1 y_2 + A_{22} y_2^2 = 0 \tag{7.19}$$

The coefficients A_{ij} are quadratic functions of $\mathbf{x}$:

$$A_{11} = \delta_{12} x_2^2 + \delta_{31} x_3^2 + 2\delta_1 x_2 x_3$$

$$A_{22} = \delta_{12} x_1^2 + \delta_{23} x_3^2 + 2\delta_2 x_1 x_3$$

$$A_{12} = \delta_3 x_3^2 - \delta_{12} x_1 x_2 - \delta_1 x_1 x_3 - \delta_2 x_2 x_3$$

and the coefficients δ_i and δ_{ij} are quadratic functions of the a_{ij}. Specifically,

$$\delta_1 = a_{12} a_{13} - a_{11} a_{23}$$

with δ_2 and δ_3 obtained by circular permutations of the indices. Similarly,

$$\delta_{12} = a_{12}^2 - a_{11} a_{22}$$

with δ_{23} and δ_{31} obtained by circular permutations of the indices. Note that if we denote by $\mathbf{A}^*$ the matrix of cofactors of $\mathbf{A}$, we have

$$\mathbf{A}^* = \begin{bmatrix} -\delta_{23} & \delta_3 & \delta_2 \\ \delta_3 & -\delta_{13} & \delta_1 \\ \delta_2 & \delta_1 & -\delta_{12} \end{bmatrix}$$

We now have to express that there exists a collineation between $\langle a, b \rangle$ and $\langle a', b' \rangle$ such that $a \barwedge a'$, $b \barwedge b'$, $\bar{c} \barwedge \bar{c}'$, $\bar{d} \barwedge \bar{d}'$, $\bar{e} \barwedge \bar{e}'$, and $(\bar{u}, \bar{v}) \barwedge (\bar{u}', \bar{v}')$. Since a collineation on a projective line is determined by three point correspondences, and since we have seven, we obtain four equations. Since we have four unknowns, two for the (projective) coordinates of $\mathbf{x}$ and two for those of $\mathbf{x}'$, we should be able to solve the problem. The situation in the second image plane is shown in figure 7.5, where we see that $\bar{c}', \bar{d}', \bar{e}'$ are the intersections of the epipolar lines $\langle x', c' \rangle, \langle x', d' \rangle$, and $\langle x', e' \rangle$ with the line at infinity $\langle a', b' \rangle$ and that $\bar{u}'$ and $\bar{v}'$ are the intersections of the tangents u' and v' drawn from the epipole x' to the image ω' of the absolute conic Ω.

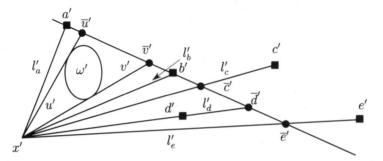

Figure 7.5 The situation in the image plane at the second time instant.

7.3.2.3 *Writing the equations*

The collineation $\mathbf{H}$ between $\langle \mathbf{a}, \mathbf{b} \rangle$ and $\langle \mathbf{a}', \mathbf{b}' \rangle$ satisfies $\mathbf{a} \overline{\wedge} \mathbf{a}'$ and $\mathbf{b} \overline{\wedge} \mathbf{b}'$, and as a result it has a very simple form:

$$\rho \mathbf{y}' = \mathbf{H} \mathbf{y} = \begin{bmatrix} \alpha & 0 \\ 0 & \beta \end{bmatrix} \mathbf{y} \tag{7.20}$$

Applying this to the points $\bar{\mathbf{c}}, \bar{\mathbf{d}}$, and $\bar{\mathbf{e}}$ we have

$$\begin{cases} \lambda x_1' = \alpha x_1 \\ \lambda x_2' = \beta x_2 \end{cases} \qquad \begin{cases} \mu(x_1' - x_3') = \alpha(x_1 - x_3) \\ \mu(x_2' - x_3') = \beta(x_2 - x_3) \end{cases}$$

$$\begin{cases} \nu(x_1' e_3' - x_3' e_1') = \alpha(x_1 e_3 - x_3 e_1) \\ \nu(x_2' e_3' - x_3' e_2') = \beta(x_2 e_3 - x_3 e_2) \end{cases}$$

where λ, μ, and ν are nonzero unknowns. Taking ratios we eliminate $\alpha, \beta, \lambda, \mu$, and ν:

$$\frac{x_1' - x_3'}{x_2' - x_3'} \times \frac{x_2'}{x_1'} = \frac{x_1 - x_3}{x_2 - x_3} \times \frac{x_2}{x_1} \tag{7.21}$$

$$\frac{x_1' e_3' - x_3' e_1'}{x_2' e_3' - x_3' e_2'} \times \frac{x_2'}{x_1'} = \frac{x_1 e_3 - x_3 e_1}{x_2 e_3 - x_3 e_2} \times \frac{x_2}{x_1} \tag{7.22}$$

To apply $\mathbf{H}$ to the pairs $(\bar{\mathbf{u}}, \bar{\mathbf{v}})$ and $(\bar{\mathbf{u}}', \bar{\mathbf{v}}')$ we start from

$$A_{11}' y_1'^2 + 2 A_{12}' y_1' y_2' + A_{22}' y_2'^2 = 0$$

Using the definition of **H** (equation (7.20)), we obtain

$$\alpha^2 A'_{11} y_1^2 + 2\alpha\beta A'_{12} y_1 y_2 + \beta^2 A'_{22} y_2^2 = 0$$

which should have the same roots as equation (7.19). This implies that

$$\begin{cases} \sigma A_{11} &= \alpha^2 A'_{11} \\ \sigma A_{22} &= \beta^2 A'_{22} \\ \sigma A_{12} &= \alpha\beta A'_{12} \end{cases}$$

Where σ is a nonzero unknown. Again, we can eliminate $\sigma, \alpha,$ and β:

$$\frac{A_{11}}{A_{12}} \times \frac{x_1}{x_2} = \frac{A'_{11}}{A'_{12}} \times \frac{x'_1}{x'_2} \tag{7.23}$$

$$\frac{A_{22}}{A_{12}} \times \frac{x_2}{x_1} = \frac{A'_{22}}{A'_{12}} \times \frac{x'_2}{x'_1} \tag{7.24}$$

We have thus obtained our four equations ((7.21) through (7.24)).

7.3.2.4 *Simplifying the equations*

We can simplify equations (7.21)–(7.24) by applying the changes of variables Φ, Φ' defined by

$$\mathbf{x} = \Phi\mathbf{u} \equiv (u_2 u_3, u_3 u_1, u_1 u_2)^T$$

$$\mathbf{x}' = \Phi'\mathbf{u}' \equiv (u'_2 u'_3, u'_3 u'_1, u'_1 u'_2)^T$$

Note that Φ and Φ' are the reciprocal transformations defined in section 2.4.9. In particular, they are self-inverse. On applying Φ and Φ' to equations (7.21) and (7.22) we obtain, after cancelling $u_1 u_2 u_3$ and $u'_1 u'_2 u'_3$,

$$\frac{u_3 - u_1}{u_3 - u_2} = \frac{u'_3 - u'_1}{u'_3 - u'_2} \tag{7.25}$$

$$\frac{u_3 e_3 - u_1 e_1}{u_3 e_3 - u_2 e_2} = \frac{u'_3 e'_3 - u'_1 e'_1}{u'_3 e'_3 - u'_2 e'_2} \tag{7.26}$$

On applying Φ and Φ' to equation (7.23) we obtain, after cancelling $u_1^2 u_2 u_3$ and $u_1'^2 u'_2 u'_3$,

$$\frac{\delta_{12}u_3^2 + \delta_{13}u_2^2 + 2\delta_1 u_3 u_2}{\delta_3 u_1 u_2 - \delta_{12}u_3^2 - \delta_1 u_2 u_3 - \delta_2 u_1 u_3} =$$

$$\frac{\delta'_{12}u'^2_3 + \delta'_{13}u'^2_2 + 2\delta'_1 u'_3 u'_2}{\delta'_3 u'_1 u'_2 - \delta'_{12}u'^2_3 - \delta'_1 u'_2 u'_3 - \delta'_2 u'_1 u'_3} \tag{7.27}$$

On applying Φ and Φ' to equation (7.24) and after cancelling $u_1 u_2^2 u_3$ and $u'_1 u'^2_2 u'_3$, we obtain

$$\frac{\delta_{12}u_3^2 + \delta_{23}u_1^2 + 2\delta_2 u_1 u_3}{\delta_3 u_1 u_2 - \delta_{12}u_3^2 - \delta_1 u_2 u_3 - \delta_2 u_1 u_3} =$$

$$\frac{\delta'_{12}u'^2_3 + \delta'_{23}u'^2_1 + 2\delta'_2 u'_1 u'_3}{\delta'_3 u'_1 u'_2 - \delta'_{12}u'^2_3 - \delta'_1 u'_2 u'_3 - \delta'_2 u'_1 u'_3} \tag{7.28}$$

7.3.2.5 Finding the solutions in one retinal plane

We must now find a way of eliminating $\mathbf{u}'$ from equations (7.25)–(7.28). We notice that (7.25) and (7.26) together define a transformation Σ from the plane (u_1, u_2, u_3) to the plane (u'_1, u'_2, u'_3). After applying some algebra, it can be shown that Σ is given by

$$\mathbf{u}' = \Sigma \mathbf{u} = \begin{bmatrix} e'_2 [eu]_2 [1u]_3 - e'_3 [eu]_3 [1u]_2 \\ e'_3 [eu]_3 [1u]_1 - e'_1 [eu]_1 [1u]_3 \\ e'_1 [eu]_1 [1u]_2 - e'_2 [eu]_2 [1u]_1 \end{bmatrix} \tag{7.29}$$

in which we have used

$$[eu]_1 = e_2 u_2 - e_3 u_3 \qquad [1u]_1 = u_2 - u_3$$

The terms $[eu]_2, [1u]_2$ and $[eu]_3, [1u]_3$ are obtained by circular permutations. Σ is, like Φ and Φ', a quadratic transformation (see problem 7).

If we now use equation (7.29) to substitute for u'_1, u'_2, u'_3 in (7.27) and (7.28), we obtain two homogeneous polynomial equations of degree 6 in u_1, u_2, and u_3, which we denote by $A(\mathbf{u}) = 0$, $B(\mathbf{u}) = 0$. Each equation represents a sextic curve in the plane (u_1, u_2, u_3), and the solutions for $\mathbf{u} = \Phi^{-1}\mathbf{x} = \Phi\mathbf{x}$ are among the points of intersection of these two sextics. Let us call them $\mathcal{A}$ and $\mathcal{B}$. Algebraic geometry (see the book by Semple and Kneebone [SK52] and appendix B) tells us that the number of intersections of two algebraic curves of degrees m and n is mn. We may therefore have here as many as thirty-six solutions, real or complex. We are now going to see that not all these solutions are possible and that twenty-six of them can be eliminated, leaving only ten.

7.3.2.6 *Eliminating impossible solutions*

There are three sources of impossible solutions:

1. Those that make the products $u_1 u_2 u_3$ and $u'_1 u'_2 u'_3$ (by which we simplified our equations to obtain equations (7.27) and (7.28)) equal to 0.

2. The points $\mathbf{m}$ such that $\Sigma \mathbf{m} = [0,0,0]^T$. Such points are called the *fundamental points* of Σ (see chapter 9 of Semple and Kneebone [SK52] and chapter 2 of the present volume).

3. If we denote by D and D' the denominators of the left- and right-hand sides of equations (7.27) and (7.28), then the points of intersection of the curves of equations $D(\mathbf{u}) = 0$ and $D'(\Sigma \mathbf{u}) = 0$ are impossible solutions.

Let us consider each case in turn.

Case 1: In order for the product $u_1 u_2 u_3$ to be equal to 0, at least one of the factors has to be equal to 0. If we assume that $u_3 = 0$, then we can show, using a system for symbolic computation, that in the equation of $\mathcal{A}$ the coefficients of the terms in u_1^6, u_1^5, and u_1^4 are equal to zero. This indicates that the point $[1,0,0]^T$ is on $\mathcal{A}$ and has order 3 (see appendix B). In addition, the point $[0,1,0]^T$ is on $\mathcal{A}$ with order 1, since the coefficient of u_3^6 is zero. Similarly, it can be shown that $[1,0,0]^T$ is of order 1 and that $[0,1,0]^T$ is of order 3 on $\mathcal{B}$. It can also be verified that the point $[0,0,1]^T$ is of order 1 on both curves and that no other point with one zero coordinate is, in general, in the intersection of $\mathcal{A}$ and $\mathcal{B}$. Therefore we have the following, in which we show the u- and x-coordinates of the points and their orders on $\mathcal{A}$ and $\mathcal{B}$:

$\mathbf{u}$	$[1,0,0]^T$	$[0,1,0]^T$	$[0,0,1]^T$
$\mathbf{x}$	$[0,1,1]^T$	$[1,0,1]^T$	$[1,1,0]^T$
$\mathcal{A}$	3	1	1
$\mathcal{B}$	1	3	1

These three points are included in the intersection of $\mathcal{A}$ and $\mathcal{B}$ but do not, in general, yield solutions to the motion problem. Counting the orders (see appendix B), we see that we have eliminated $3 \times 1 + 3 \times 1 + 1 \times 1 = 7$ solutions.

Case 2: We have to find the fundamental points of the quadratic transformation Σ. There are three such points in general (see chapter 2), which we can easily discover. Let us define two 3×3 matrices $\mathbf{X}$ and $\mathbf{Y}$ by

$$\mathbf{Xu} = \begin{bmatrix} [1u]_1 \\ [1u]_2 \\ [1u]_3 \end{bmatrix} \qquad \mathbf{Yu} = \begin{bmatrix} e_1'[eu]_1 \\ e_2'[eu]_2 \\ e_3'[eu]_3 \end{bmatrix}$$

The matrices $\mathbf{X}, \mathbf{Y}$ are

$$\mathbf{X} = \begin{bmatrix} 0 & 1 & -1 \\ -1 & 0 & 1 \\ 1 & -1 & 0 \end{bmatrix} \qquad \mathbf{Y} = \begin{bmatrix} 0 & e_1'e_2 & -e_1'e_3 \\ -e_2'e_1 & 0 & e_2'e_3 \\ e_3'e_1 & -e_3'e_2 & 0 \end{bmatrix}$$

and we have

$$\Sigma\mathbf{u} = \mathbf{Yu} \wedge \mathbf{Xu}$$

The fundamental points are therefore those points $\mathbf{u}$ such that $\mathbf{Yu} = 0$ or $\mathbf{Xu} = 0$, or such that $\mathbf{Xu}$ and $\mathbf{Yu}$ are parallel. The case $\mathbf{Xu} = \mathbf{0}$ corresponds to the fundamental point $\mathbf{d} = [1, 1, 1]^T$, which has the same x- and u-coordinates. The case $\mathbf{Yu} = \mathbf{0}$ corresponds to the fundamental point $[1/e_1, 1/e_2, 1/e_3]^T$. This is point $\mathbf{e}$. The third case is solved as follows. Let $\mathbf{p}$ be a point such that

$$\mathbf{Xp} = \lambda\mathbf{Yp}$$

This is equivalent to

$$(\mathbf{X} - \lambda\mathbf{Y})\mathbf{p} = 0 \tag{7.30}$$

The values of λ for which the determinant of $\mathbf{X} - \lambda\mathbf{Y}$ is equal to 0 are $\lambda = 0$ (corresponding to $\mathbf{X}$), $\lambda = \infty$ (corresponding to $\mathbf{Y}$), and a third value, λ_0, which can be computed, using a system such as MAPLE.[2] For this

---

2. MAPLE is a system of algebraic computation that has been developed since 1980 by the Symbolic Computation Group at the University of Waterloo.

value, it can be verified that the rank of $\mathbf{X} - \lambda_0\mathbf{Y}$ is, in general, 2 and that $\mathbf{p}$ is represented by any vector in the null space that is of dimension 1. Notice that the coordinates of $\mathbf{p}$ can be explicitly computed as functions of the coordinates of $\mathbf{e}$ and $\mathbf{e}'$ (see problem 6). Again using the power of algebraic computation, it is easy to show that the three points $\mathbf{d}, \mathbf{e}$, and $\mathbf{p}$ are points of order 2 on $\mathcal{A}$ and $\mathcal{B}$.

	d	**e**	**p**
$\mathcal{A}$	2	2	2
$\mathcal{B}$	2	2	2

These three points are included in the intersection of $\mathcal{A}$ and $\mathcal{B}$, but they do not, in general, yield solutions to the motion problem. Counting the orders, we see that we have eliminated 12 solutions (this corresponds to the case of figure B.3 of appendix B).

Case 3: The curve of equation $D(\mathbf{u}) = 0$ is a conic, and $D'(\Sigma\mathbf{u}) = 0$ is a quartic, since $D'(\mathbf{u}')$ is of degree 2 in $\mathbf{u}'$ and $\mathbf{u}' = \Sigma\mathbf{u}$ is of degree 2 in $\mathbf{u}$. These two curves have, in general, eight intersections, among which are included, as can be verified, the points $[1, 0, 0]^T$ and $[0, 1, 0]^T$, which have already been removed in case 1. Since each of the remaining six points is of order 1 on $\mathcal{A}$ and $\mathcal{B}$, we have obtained six more solutions that we must eliminate.

Adding the impossible solutions obtained in cases 1, 2, and 3, we obtain a total of twenty-five. There remain eleven intersections of $\mathcal{A}$ and $\mathcal{B}$ to consider.

7.3.2.7 *Kruppa's spurious solution*

$\mathcal{A}$ and $\mathcal{B}$ not only intersect at $[0, 0, 1]^T$, but they are tangential there, since the coefficients of u_3^5 in $A(\mathbf{u})$ and $B(\mathbf{u})$ are equal. Again, this can be verified using MAPLE. The equation of the common tangent at $[0, 0, 1]^T$ is the coefficient of u_3^5, a linear polynomial in u_1 and u_2. It follows that $[0, 0, 1]^T$ must count twice in the intersection and not once (this corresponds to the case of figure B.2 of appendix B); this eliminates one further solution, and so the number of solutions is reduced from 36 to 10, real or complex, for $\mathbf{u}$. The x-solutions are obtained as $\mathbf{x} = \Phi\mathbf{u}$ and the x'-solutions as $\mathbf{x}' = \Phi'\Sigma\mathbf{u}$. The fact that $\mathcal{A}$ and $\mathcal{B}$ are tangent at $[0, 0, 1]^T$ had been overlooked by Kruppa [Kru13].

7.3.2.8   *Recovering the motion parameters*

We have seen that the five-points method yields pairs of epipoles $\mathbf{x}$, $\mathbf{x}'$ compatible with a given set of five image correspondences. We will now describe a method for recovering the rigid motion $(\mathbf{R}, \mathbf{t})$ between the two positions of the camera from $\mathbf{x}$ and $\mathbf{x}'$. In addition to $\mathbf{x}$, $\mathbf{x}'$ we require one pair $\mathbf{a}\overline{\wedge}\mathbf{a}'$ of corresponding points. It follows from the definitions of $\mathbf{R}$, $\mathbf{t}$ and $\mathbf{x}$, $\mathbf{x}'$ (see section 6.2.1.2) that

$$\mathbf{x} = \mathbf{t} \quad \text{and} \quad \mathbf{x}' = -\mathbf{R}^T\mathbf{t}$$

Since we know $\mathbf{x}$, we know the direction of $\mathbf{t}$. Let $\mathbf{S}$ be a rotation through 180 degrees such that $\mathbf{St} = \mathbf{R}^T\mathbf{t}$. To fix ideas, let the axis of $\mathbf{S}$ be the bisector of $\mathbf{t}$ and $\mathbf{R}^T\mathbf{t}$, and let $\mathbf{U} = \mathbf{RS}$. It follows from the construction of $\mathbf{S}$ that $\mathbf{U}$ has a known axis $\mathbf{t}$, since $\mathbf{Ut} = \mathbf{RSt} = \mathbf{t}$. The angle of rotation θ of $\mathbf{U}$ is unknown.

We have $\mathbf{a}\overline{\wedge}\mathbf{a}'$, and thus $\mathbf{a}'^T\mathbf{Ea} = 0$ (equation (7.1)), where $\mathbf{E} = \mathbf{TR}$ is the essential matrix associated with $\mathbf{R}$, $\mathbf{t}$. It follows that $\mathbf{a}'^T\mathbf{TRSSa} = 0$ (since $\mathbf{S}^2 = \mathbf{I}$), and so

$$(\mathbf{a}'^T\mathbf{T})\mathbf{U}(\mathbf{Sa}) = 0 \tag{7.31}$$

We assume that $\|\mathbf{t}\| = 1$ and write Rodrigues' formula for the rotation matrix $\mathbf{U}$ (equation (5.26)):

$$\mathbf{U} = \mathbf{I} + \mathbf{T}\sin\theta + (1 - \cos\theta)\mathbf{T}^2$$

Thus

$$(\mathbf{a}'^T\mathbf{T})\mathbf{U}(\mathbf{Sa}) = 0 = \mathbf{a}'^T\mathbf{TSa} + (\mathbf{a}'^T\mathbf{T}^2\mathbf{Sa})\sin\theta + ((\mathbf{a}'^T\mathbf{T}^3\mathbf{Sa})(1 - \cos\theta)$$

Using the fact that $\mathbf{T}^3 = -\mathbf{T}$ (which was used in the proof of proposition 5.5), this can be rewritten as

$$(\mathbf{a}'^T\mathbf{T}^2\mathbf{Sa})\sin\theta + (\mathbf{a}'^T\mathbf{TSa})\cos\theta = 0 \tag{7.32}$$

The vectors $\mathbf{a}, \mathbf{a}'$ and the matrices $\mathbf{T}$ and $\mathbf{S}$ are known, and so we can solve equation (7.32) for θ. Two solutions are obtained that differ by 180 degrees, corresponding to the fact that the second camera can be rotated in two ways about $\mathbf{t}$. Having found θ and hence $\mathbf{U}$, we recover $\mathbf{R}$ using the equation $\mathbf{R} = \mathbf{US}$.

Thus five point correspondences yield at most ten real solutions for the epipoles. But each solution induces two distinct rigid motions and the total number of rigid motions is therefore twenty. This analysis does not take into account the fact that the solutions should yield reconstructed points that are in front of the cameras, even though this is an important practical issue. However, we can say that, if a solution reconstructs all points in front of the two cameras, then the solution differing by a rotation of 180 degrees does not.

7.3.2.9 *A summary of the five-points algorithm*

To summarize all this, we have obtained the following algorithm:

1. Compute in each retinal plane the collineations $\mathbf{A}$ and $\mathbf{A}'$ such that the points $a, b, c,$ and d and $a', b', c',$ and d' become the standard projective bases. Compute the new projective coordinates of e and e'. This is done using the results of sections 2.2.2 and 2.2.3. We are now using the x- and x'-coordinates, respectively.

2. In each plane apply the reciprocal transformation Σ_0. We are now using the u- and u'-coordinates, respectively.

3. Transform the u'-plane to the u-plane by the quadratic transformation Σ defined by equation (7.29).

4. Compute the u-coordinates of the thirty-six points of intersection of the sextics $\mathcal{A}$ and $\mathcal{B}$. Throw away the twenty-six spurious solutions as explained in section 7.3.2.6. The remaining ten are the u-coordinates of the epipoles.

5. Apply Σ to these ten points to obtain the u'-coordinates of the corresponding epipoles in the second plane.

6. Apply Σ_0 and $\mathbf{A}^{-1}$ to the ten points in the first plane to obtain the pixel coordinates of the epipoles there, and apply Σ_0 and $\mathbf{A}'^{-1}$ to the ten points in the second plane to obtain the pixel coordinates of the epipoles there.

7. Recover the displacement parameters, i.e., the rotation matrices and the directions of the translation vectors, using the technique explained in section 7.3.2.8.

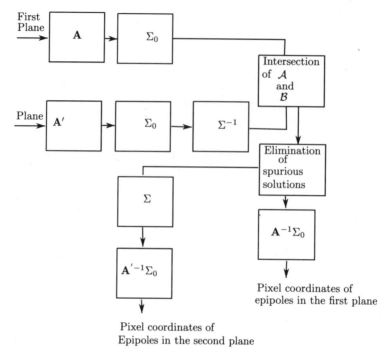

Figure 7.6   The five-points algorithm.

This algorithm is summarized in figure 7.6. This algorithm has been implemented in MAPLE and tested on a large number of examples [FM90, FM91].

7.3.3   Other techniques for estimating displacement

The previous approach, the five-points algorithm, is highly nonlinear since it requires solving for the roots of a tenth-degree polynomial. Since in practice we are interested only in the solution corresponding to the actual displacement, it is natural to explore the possibility of reducing the number of solutions, and perhaps the complexity of the resolution method, by increasing the number of points. One such method was proposed by Longuet-Higgins [LH81]. It builds on the fact that equation (7.2) is linear and homogeneous with respect to the coefficients of **E**. Therefore, if eight such equations are available, one may hope that we can solve for those coefficients.

7.3.3.1 The eight-point algorithm

The approach consists of first estimating the essential matrix $\mathbf{E}$, and then recovering $\mathbf{t}$ and $\mathbf{R}$ from $\mathbf{E}$. We notice that equation (7.2) is linear in the coefficients of the essential matrix. Calling $\mathbf{X}$ the 9×1 vector $[\mathbf{e}_1^T, \mathbf{e}_2^T, \mathbf{e}_3^T]^T$, (7.2) can be written as

$$\mathbf{a}^T \mathbf{X} = 0 \tag{7.33}$$

where $\mathbf{a}$ is the 9×1 vector $[x\mathbf{m}'^T \quad y\mathbf{m}'^T \quad \mathbf{m}'^T]^T$ (remember that $\mathbf{m} = [x, y, 1]^T$ and $\mathbf{m}' = [x', y', 1]^T$ since we are using the normalized coordinate system).

If we have n point correspondences, each yields one equation like (7.33) and we can combine them as follows:

$$\mathbf{A}_n \mathbf{X} = \mathbf{O} \tag{7.34}$$

where $\mathbf{A}_n$ is an $n \times 9$ matrix:

$$\mathbf{A}_n = \begin{bmatrix} \mathbf{a}_1^T \\ \vdots \\ \mathbf{a}_n^T \end{bmatrix}$$

Since $\mathbf{E}$ is defined, like $\mathbf{t}$, up to a scale factor, there are actually only eight unknowns, so the smallest value of n for which we can hope to estimate $\mathbf{X}$ is $n = 8$. Assuming that there exist configurations of points $M_1, ..., M_8$, in 3-D space such that the corresponding matrix $\mathbf{A}_8$ is of rank 8, then we can solve equation (7.34) for $\mathbf{X}$. This point is discussed later at greater length. Assuming, without loss of generality, that the first eight columns of $\mathbf{A}_8$ are linearly independent, we can write (7.34) as

$$\mathbf{A}_8' \mathbf{X}' = -X_9 \mathbf{C}_9 \tag{7.35}$$

where $\mathbf{A}_8'$ is the 8×8 matrix made of the first eight column vectors of $\mathbf{A}_8$, $\mathbf{X}'$ is the 8×1 vector made up of the first eight components of $\mathbf{X}$, and $\mathbf{C}_9$ is the ninth column vector of $\mathbf{A}_8$. This yields

$$\mathbf{X}' = -X_9 (\mathbf{A}_8')^{-1} \mathbf{C}_9$$

Therefore, we have estimated the essential matrix.

7.3.3.2 *When does it fail?*

The method obviously fails when the rank of $\mathbf{A}'_8$ is less than 8. A row of that matrix can be written:

$$\frac{1}{ZZ'}[XX', XY', XZ', YX', YY', YZ', ZX', ZY']$$

where $\mathbf{M} = [X, Y, Z]^T$ and $\mathbf{M}' = [X', Y', Z']^T$ are the 3-D coordinates in the standard coordinate systems attached to each camera of the corresponding points (we assume that Z and Z' are different from 0, i.e., that M does not lie in any of the two focal planes). To say that the rank of $\mathbf{A}'_8$ is less than eight is equivalent to saying that there exist eight numbers $\lambda_i, i = 1, \ldots 8$ such that

$$\lambda_1 XX' + \lambda_2 XY' + \lambda_3 XZ' + \lambda_4 YX' + \lambda_5 YY' + \lambda_6 YZ' + \lambda_7 ZX' + \lambda_8 ZY' = 0$$

Note that there is no ZZ' term. This can be written in matrix form as

$$\mathbf{M}^T \mathbf{Q} \mathbf{M}' = 0$$

where

$$\mathbf{Q} = \begin{bmatrix} \lambda_1 & \lambda_2 & \lambda_3 \\ \lambda_4 & \lambda_5 & \lambda_6 \\ \lambda_7 & \lambda_8 & 0 \end{bmatrix}$$

Or, using the fact that $\mathbf{M}' = \mathbf{R}^T(\mathbf{M} - \mathbf{t})$, we can write

$$\mathbf{M}^T \mathbf{Q} \mathbf{R}^T(\mathbf{M} - \mathbf{t})$$

This last equation is the equation in the first coordinate system of a quadric going through the points $\mathbf{M} = \mathbf{0}$ and $\mathbf{M} = \mathbf{t}$, i.e., the two optical centers.

Conversely, for given values of $\mathbf{R}$ and $\mathbf{t}$, if the 3-D points M lie on a quadric going through the origin and the point represented by $\mathbf{t}$, there exists a matrix $\mathbf{Q}'$ such that $\mathbf{M}^T \mathbf{Q}'(\mathbf{M} - \mathbf{t}) = 0$ and such that $\mathbf{M}^T \mathbf{Q} \mathbf{M}' = 0$, with $\mathbf{Q} = \mathbf{Q}'\mathbf{R}$ and $\mathbf{M}' = \mathbf{R}^T(\mathbf{M} - \mathbf{t})$. This implies that the rank of $\mathbf{A}'_8$ is less than 8 and that the eight-point algorithm fails. Does this situation often arise? Luckily the answer is no, because a quadric depends on nine parameters and is therefore determined by nine points. In general, ten points do not fall on the same quadric, and since in our case we have ten points, the eight object points plus the two optical centers, we can be assured that the previous situation is extremely unlikely.

7.3.3.3 *Recovering the motion parameters*

From the essential matrix, we can recover $\mathbf{t}$ and $\mathbf{R}$ as follows. We call $\mathbf{c}_i$ and $\mathbf{r}_i, i = 1, 2, 3$ the column vectors of $\mathbf{E}$ and $\mathbf{R}$. The equation $\mathbf{E} = \mathbf{TR}$ implies that $\mathbf{c}_i = \mathbf{t} \wedge \mathbf{r}_i$ for all i. The three column vectors of $\mathbf{E}$ are perpendicular to $\mathbf{t}$, and therefore $\mathbf{t}$ is parallel to the cross product of any two of the $\mathbf{c}_i$'s. This determines $\mathbf{t}$ up to the sign. For example:

$$\mathbf{t} = \pm \mathbf{c}_1 \wedge \mathbf{c}_2$$

The sign is determined if we know the sign of one of the components of $\mathbf{t}$, for example t_3.

From $\mathbf{t}$ we can recover $\mathbf{R}$ as follows. From the relations $\mathbf{c}_i = \mathbf{t} \wedge \mathbf{r}_i$ we obtain $\mathbf{c}_i \wedge \mathbf{c}_{i+1} = (\mathbf{r}_{i+2} \cdot \mathbf{t})\mathbf{t}$ for $i = 1, 2, 3$, where $\mathbf{r}_{i+2} = \mathbf{r}_{((i+1)\bmod 3)+1}$. The matrix of cofactors $\mathbf{E}^*$ of $\mathbf{E}$ is given by

$$\mathbf{E}^* = [\mathbf{c}_2 \wedge \mathbf{c}_3, \mathbf{c}_3 \wedge \mathbf{c}_1, \mathbf{c}_1 \wedge \mathbf{c}_2]^T$$

which can be rewritten as

$$\mathbf{E}^* = [(\mathbf{r}_1 \cdot \mathbf{t})\mathbf{t}, (\mathbf{r}_2 \cdot \mathbf{t})\mathbf{t}, (\mathbf{r}_3 \cdot \mathbf{t})\mathbf{t}]^T = (\mathbf{t}(\mathbf{R}^T\mathbf{t})^T)^T = (\mathbf{t}\mathbf{t}^T\mathbf{R})^T$$

But since we also have (from proposition 7.2)

$$\mathbf{TE} = \mathbf{T}^2\mathbf{R} = \mathbf{t}\mathbf{t}^T\mathbf{R} - (\mathbf{t} \cdot \mathbf{t})\mathbf{R}$$

we conclude that

$$(\mathbf{t} \cdot \mathbf{t})\mathbf{R} = \mathbf{E}^{*T} - \mathbf{TE} \qquad (7.36)$$

which yields $\mathbf{R}$ as a function of $\mathbf{E}$ and $\mathbf{t}$.

7.3.3.4 *A more robust version of the eight-point algorithm*

The eight-point algorithm works in two steps: (1) Estimate $\mathbf{E}$ from point correspondences and (2) estimate $\mathbf{R}$ and $\mathbf{t}$ from $\mathbf{E}$. Its sensitivity to noise is quite high. One way to decrease this problem is to use more points in the estimation of $\mathbf{E}$. Going back to equation (7.34) and assuming, without loss of generality, that its first eight columns are linearly independent, we can rewrite it as

$$\mathbf{A}'_n \mathbf{X}' = -X_9 \mathbf{C}_9 \tag{7.37}$$

where $\mathbf{A}'_n$ is the $n \times 8$ matrix made up of the first eight column vectors of $\mathbf{A}_n$; $\mathbf{X}'$ is defined as in equation (7.35), as the 8×1 vector made of the first eight components of $\mathbf{X}$; and $\mathbf{C}_9$ is the ninth column vector of $\mathbf{A}_n$. Multiplying both sides of equation (7.37) by $\mathbf{A}'^T_n$ we obtain

$$(\mathbf{A}'^T_n \mathbf{A}'_n) \mathbf{X}' = -X_9 \mathbf{A}'^T_n \mathbf{C}_9$$

Since the 8×8 matrix $\mathbf{A}'^T_n \mathbf{A}'_n$ is of rank 8, this yields

$$\mathbf{X}' = -X_9 (\mathbf{A}'^T_n \mathbf{A}'_n)^{-1} \mathbf{A}'^T_n \mathbf{C}_9$$

This solves the problem of using more than eight points in the estimation of $\mathbf{E}$ when no noise is present. When noise is present, equation (7.34) is only approximately satisfied, and we can reformulate the problem as that of finding the vector $\mathbf{X}$ that minimizes the norm of $\mathbf{A}_n \mathbf{X}$. In order to eliminate the solution $\mathbf{X} = \mathbf{0}$, we must assume that the norm of $\mathbf{X}$ is not zero. In fact, since $\mathbf{E} = \mathbf{TR}$, it is easy to show that $\|\mathbf{X}\|^2 = 2\|\mathbf{t}\|^2$. Taking $\|\mathbf{t}\|$ equal to 1 (remember that $\mathbf{t}$ is defined up to a scale factor) the problem can be reformulated as that of finding the vectors $\mathbf{X}$ that minimize the norm of $\mathbf{A}_n \mathbf{X}$ subject to the constraint that their squared norm is equal to 2.

$$\min_{\mathbf{X}} \|\mathbf{A}_n \mathbf{X}\|^2$$
subject to $\|\mathbf{X}\|^2 = 2$

According to appendix A, the solution is the eigenvector of norm $\sqrt{2}$ of the 9×9 matrix $\mathbf{A}^T_n \mathbf{A}_n$ corresponding to the smallest eigenvalue. Therefore, the solution is unique if the eigenspace associated to this eigenvalue is of dimension 1.

The computation of $\mathbf{t}$ and $\mathbf{R}$ can also be performed to take noise into account. Indeed, from proposition 7.1 it can be seen that $\mathbf{t}$ is the solution of the following meansquare problem:

$$\min_{\mathbf{t}} \|\mathbf{E}^T \mathbf{t}\|^2$$
subject to $\|\mathbf{t}\|^2 = 1$

The solution is the unit norm eigenvector of matrix $\mathbf{EE}^T$ corresponding to the smallest eigenvalue.

To find the rotation matrix $\mathbf{R}$, we have to solve the following mean-square problem:

$$\min_{\mathbf{R}} \|\mathbf{E} - \mathbf{TR}\|^2 \text{subject to } \mathbf{R}^T\mathbf{R} = \mathbf{I} \text{ and } \det(\mathbf{R}) = 1$$

Since $\mathbf{E} - \mathbf{TR} = (\mathbf{ER}^T - \mathbf{T})\mathbf{R}$, $\|\mathbf{E} - \mathbf{TR}\|^2 = \|\mathbf{ER}^T - \mathbf{T}\|^2$. On the other hand, the matrix $\mathbf{ER}^T$ is equal to $[\mathbf{Re}_1\mathbf{Re}_2\mathbf{Re}_3]$ where the $\mathbf{e}_i^T$'s are the row vectors of matrix $\mathbf{E}$. Therefore, the problem is

$$\min_{\mathbf{R}} \sum_{i=1}^{3} \|\mathbf{Re}_i - \mathbf{t}_i\|^2$$

subject to $\mathbf{R}^T\mathbf{R} = \mathbf{I}$ and $\det(\mathbf{R}) = 1$

where $\mathbf{t}_i$ is the ith column vector of matrix $\mathbf{T}$. This problem is solved in chapter 11 using quaternions, and in general the solution is unique.

7.3.3.5 *Estimating displacement directly*

The method described in sections 7.3.3.1 and 7.3.3.4 is indirect in that it first tries to estimate the essential matrix $\mathbf{E}$ and then recovers the motion parameters $\mathbf{R}$ and $\mathbf{t}$ by linear methods. The indirectness buys simplicity. Notice that the estimation of the $\mathbf{E}$ matrix in these sections is linear only by omission. Indeed, we saw in section 7.3.1 that, in order to be a "valid" $\mathbf{E}$ matrix, $\mathbf{E}$ has to satisfy two constraints, which are polynomials of degrees 3 and 4 of its coefficients. If we impose these constraints on $\mathbf{E}$, then we lose the simplicity of the linear estimation method. So the reader may be tempted to wonder, since simplicity is lost anyway, why we don't stick to the original unknowns, i.e., the motion parameters $\mathbf{R}$ and $\mathbf{t}$. Using equation (7.1), this leads to the minimization of the following function of $\mathbf{R}$ and $\mathbf{t}$ (subject to the constraint $\|\mathbf{t}\|^2 = 1$), which we call the Longuet-Higgins criterion:

$$LH(\mathbf{R}, \mathbf{t}) = \sum_{i=1}^{n} (\mathbf{m}_i.(\mathbf{t} \wedge \mathbf{Rm}_i'))^2 \tag{7.38}$$

Unfortunately, there is no closed-form solution for the minimization of equation (7.38), and nonlinear minimization methods must be used.

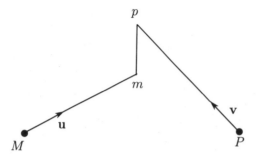

Figure 7.7   The shortest distance between two lines.

7.3.3.6   *Two geometric interpretations of the Longuet-Higgins criterion*

Let us give two geometrical interpretations of criterion (7.38). Given two lines in 3-D space, each one defined by a point and a vector as in figure 7.7, the direction of their common perpendicular is that of the cross-product $\mathbf{u} \wedge \mathbf{v}$. Their shortest distance mp is the projection of MP on this direction. Therefore we can write

$$mp = \left| \mathbf{MP} \cdot \frac{\mathbf{u} \wedge \mathbf{v}}{\|\mathbf{u} \wedge \mathbf{v}\|} \right|$$

Applying this to the situation of figure 7.1, the shortest distance between the two lines $\langle C, m \rangle$ and $\langle C', m' \rangle$ is

$$\left| \mathbf{CC'} \cdot \frac{\mathbf{m} \wedge \mathbf{Rm'}}{\|\mathbf{m} \wedge \mathbf{Rm'}\|} \right|$$

which is the same as

$$\left| \mathbf{t} \cdot \frac{\mathbf{m} \wedge \mathbf{Rm'}}{\|\mathbf{m} \wedge \mathbf{Rm'}\|} \right| = \frac{|\mathbf{m} \cdot (\mathbf{t} \wedge \mathbf{Rm'})|}{\|\mathbf{m} \wedge \mathbf{Rm'}\|}$$

Denoting by d_i the shortest distance between the lines $\langle C, m_i \rangle$ and $\langle C', m_i' \rangle$, criterion (7.38) can be rewritten as

$$\sum_{i=1}^{n} \alpha_i d_i^2 \tag{7.39}$$

where $\alpha_i = \|\mathbf{m}_i \wedge \mathbf{m}'_i\|^2$. Then α_i is equal to $\|\mathbf{m}_i\|^2\|\mathbf{m}'_i\|^2 \sin^2 \theta_i$, θ_i being the angle of the two vectors $\mathbf{m}_i$ and $\mathbf{m}'_i$. The values $\|\mathbf{m}_i\|^2$ and $\|\mathbf{m}'_i\|^2$ do not vary much when M_i varies in space, but $\sin^2 \theta_i$ varies, between 0 for a point M_i that is far to a maximum value determined by the relative positions of the two cameras. Therefore, points that are at a greater distance are weighted less than points that are closer by this criterion.

There is an alternative way to look at criterion (7.38). Given two points m and m', which are images of the same physical point, we can pose the problem of estimating $\mathbf{R}$ and $\mathbf{t}$ as that of minimizing, for example, the distance of m' to the epipolar line ep of m. This is shown in figure 7.8. Using the results of section 6.2.1.3, the projective equation of ep is

$$(\mathbf{R}^T\mathbf{t} \wedge \mathbf{R}^T\mathbf{m}) \cdot \tilde{\mathbf{m}}' = 0 \tag{7.40}$$

where $\tilde{\mathbf{m}}' = [X', Y', Z']^T$ is the projective representation of an image point m' in the coordinate system attached to the second camera. If $Z' \neq 0$, equation (7.40) is equivalent to

$$\mathbf{m} \cdot (\mathbf{t} \wedge \mathbf{R}\mathbf{m}') = 0$$

which is precisely equation (7.1). The distance d' of m' to this line is given by

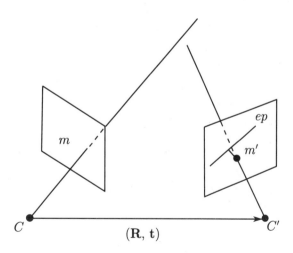

Figure 7.8 Computing the distance to the epipolar line.

$$\frac{\mid \mathbf{m} \cdot (\mathbf{t} \wedge \mathbf{Rm'}) \mid}{\beta}$$

where β is a normalizing factor equal to the norm of the vector formed with the first two coordinates of the vector $\mathbf{R}^T(\mathbf{t} \wedge \mathbf{m})$.

A special case arises when β is equal to 0, i.e., when the first two components of this vector are equal to 0. Since it is normal to the epipolar plane (it is the vector $\mathbf{t} \wedge \mathbf{m}$ expressed in the coordinate system of the second camera), this is equivalent to saying that this plane is parallel to the retinal plane of the second camera, and indeed, in this case, the epipolar line does not exist (it is at infinity). Another degeneracy occurs when $\mathbf{t} \wedge \mathbf{m} = \mathbf{0}$, i.e., when $\mathbf{m}$ is parallel to the direction of translation. In that case, the epipolar plane is not defined. Given a number of point correspondences m_i, m'_i, $i = 1, \ldots, n$, and denoting by d'_i the distance of m'_i to the epipolar line of m_i, the Longuet-Higgins criterion can be written as

$$\sum_{i=1}^{n} \beta_i d'^2_i$$

where the β_i are defined as above.

7.3.4 Conclusion

The reader may wonder which technique to use among those which have been proposed to solve the problem of displacement from points. The five-points algorithm can clearly be used only in the case where five matches are available. Our implementation has shown that it is quite sensitive to small perturbations in the pixel coordinates of the matched points. It should be considered more as a proof of the complexity of the problem than as a way of solving it. The same is true, to a smaller extent, of the various versions of the eight-point algorithm described in sections 7.3.3.1 and 7.3.3.4. We have found that the minimization of the epipolar distance criterion with respect to the displacement parameters described in section 7.3.3.6 has yielded by far the best and most stable results [Har87, TVDF89].

7.3.5 Degenerate cases

At this point, the reader may be wondering whether there are any configurations of points such that there are always several solutions to the

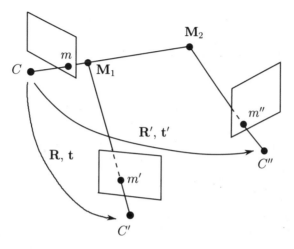

Figure 7.9 Two motions yielding the same images.

problem of motion from points, even if an arbitrarily large number of correspondences is available. The answer to this question is yes, such sets of degenerate points exist and, for points in such a configuration, there exist at most three distinct camera displacements that are compatible with the correspondences. We will show this using two different and complementary approaches.

7.3.5.1 *When degenerate points lie on a quadric*

Let us assume that there exist two distinct camera motions $(\mathbf{R}, \mathbf{t})$ and $(\mathbf{R}', \mathbf{t}')$ such that equation (7.1) is true for an arbitrary number of pairs of points $\mathbf{m}, \mathbf{m}'$. We will show that a different reconstruction corresponds to each camera motion and that each reconstructed object is a quadric. Let us denote by $\mathbf{M}_1$ and $\mathbf{M}_2$ the two coordinate vectors, expressed in the normalized coordinate system of the first camera that corresponds to the reconstructed points whose image is m. The points M_1 and M_2 are on the optical ray $\langle C, m \rangle$. Let $\mathbf{M}'_1$ and $\mathbf{M}'_2$ be the corresponding coordinate vectors of the points M_1 and M_2 expressed in the normalized camera after the first and second motion, respectively. The points M_1 and M_2 are on the optical rays $\langle C', m' \rangle$ and $\langle C'', m'' \rangle$, respectively. The situation is depicted in figure 7.9.

Equation (7.1) can be written for the first camera motion as

$$\mathbf{m} \cdot (\mathbf{t} \wedge \mathbf{Rm'}) = 0$$

By definition of the ambiguity, $\mathbf{m'} = \mathbf{m''}$, where the two vectors are expressed in the local coordinate systems attached to the camera after the two motions. The previous equation can be rewritten as

$$\mathbf{M}_2 \cdot (\mathbf{t} \wedge \mathbf{RM'}_2) = 0$$

Using the fact that $\mathbf{M'}_2 = \mathbf{R'}^T(\mathbf{M}_2 - \mathbf{t'})$, we obtain the following equation:

$$\mathbf{M}_2^T \mathbf{E} \mathbf{R'}^T (\mathbf{M}_2 - \mathbf{t'}) = 0 \qquad (7.41)$$

This is the equation of a quadric surface going through the points $\mathbf{M}_2 = \mathbf{0}$ and $\mathbf{M}_2 = \mathbf{t'}$, i.e., the optical centers of the first camera and the second camera after the second motion. It also contains the line $\mathbf{M}_2 = \lambda\mathbf{t}$ because of lemma 7.1, and therefore it goes through the optical center of the second camera after the first motion. This quadric is the locus of the ambiguous points as reconstructed from the second camera motion. Following Longuet-Higgins, [LH88], we call such a quadric a *Maybank quadric*.

Exchanging the roles of the first and the second camera motions, we obtain the equation of another quadric:

$$\mathbf{M}_1^T \mathbf{E'} \mathbf{R}^T (\mathbf{M}_1 - \mathbf{t}) = 0 \qquad (7.42)$$

This quadric is the locus of the ambiguous points as reconstructed from the first camera motion. These results were well known to the old photogrammeters [Fin97, Kra40, Wun41, Hof50, Zel52, Wol83] and has been independently "rediscovered" by a number of computer vision people, such as Longuet-Higgins, Maybank, Horn, and Negahdaripour [LH88, May90a, Hor87, Hor90, Neg89]. It is very nicely presented in the framework of projective geometry in a book by Maybank [May92].

7.3.5.2 *How many distinct ambiguous motions are there?*

Now that we know where the 3-D points must lie in order for the problem to be ambiguous, we may wonder how many ambiguous motions there may be. Even though the main result, that there are three such motions, can be derived by continuing the previous approach as in the work of Longuet-Higgins [LH88], we prefer to use the manifold $\mathcal{M}$ of essential matrices defined in section 7.3.1.3 to obtain this result. The question is the same as asking how many essential matrices $\mathbf{E}_i$ can satisfy such that

$$\mathbf{m}^T\mathbf{E}_i\mathbf{m}' = 0 \qquad\qquad (7.43)$$

for pairs of corresponding points $\mathbf{m} \leftrightarrow \mathbf{m}'$ where $\mathbf{m}$, $\mathbf{m}'$ range over open subsets of the retinal planes. The solution requires the following two propositions:

Proposition 7.5

[Maybank] Let $\mathbf{E}$ be an essential matrix, and let $\mathbf{B}$ be an arbitrary matrix. Then $\mathbf{Em} \wedge \mathbf{Bm} = 0$ for all $\mathbf{m}$ if and only if $\mathbf{B} = \lambda\mathbf{E}$ for some scalar λ.

Proof If $\mathbf{B} = \lambda\mathbf{E}$, then $\mathbf{Em} \wedge \mathbf{Bm} = \mathbf{0}$ for all $\mathbf{m}$. Conversely, let $\mathbf{E} = \mathbf{TR}$. Then

$$\mathbf{Em} \wedge \mathbf{Bm} = (\mathbf{m}^T\mathbf{B}^T\mathbf{t})\mathbf{Rm} - (\mathbf{m}^T\mathbf{B}^T\mathbf{Rm})\mathbf{t} = 0$$

for all $\mathbf{m}$. The vectors $\mathbf{Rm}$ and $\mathbf{t}$ are, in general, linearly independent. Therefore, for all $\mathbf{m}$

$$\mathbf{m}^T\mathbf{B}^T\mathbf{t} = 0 \qquad \text{and} \qquad \mathbf{m}^T\mathbf{B}^T\mathbf{Rm} = 0$$

and, as a result, $\mathbf{B}^T\mathbf{t} = 0$ and $\mathbf{B}^T\mathbf{R}$ is antisymmetric. It follows that $\mathbf{R}^T\mathbf{B}$ is antisymmetric, and thus $\mathbf{R}(\mathbf{R}^T\mathbf{B})\mathbf{R}^T = \mathbf{BR}^T$ is antisymmetric. Let $\mathbf{B} = \mathbf{T}'\mathbf{R}$, where $\mathbf{T}'$ is antisymmetric. Then

$$\mathbf{t}^T\mathbf{T}'\mathbf{R} = \mathbf{t}^T\mathbf{B} = (\mathbf{B}^T\mathbf{t})^T = \mathbf{0}$$

This implies that $\mathbf{t}^T\mathbf{T}' = \mathbf{0}$. Hence $\mathbf{T}' = \lambda\mathbf{T}$ for some scalar λ. The result follows. ∎

Proposition 7.6

[Maybank] Let $\mathbf{E}_1$, $\mathbf{E}_2$, and $\mathbf{E}_3$ be essential matrices such that $\mathbf{m}^T\mathbf{E}_i\mathbf{m}' = 0$ for i = 1,2,3, where $\mathbf{m} \leftrightarrow \mathbf{m}'$ and $\mathbf{m}$, $\mathbf{m}'$ both range over open subsets of the retinal planes modeled as two projective planes $\mathcal{P}^2$. Then $\mathbf{E}_1$, $\mathbf{E}_2$, and $\mathbf{E}_3$ are linearly dependent.

Proof The result holds if two of the $\mathbf{E}_i$ are dependent, and so we suppose that no two of the $\mathbf{E}_i$ are dependent. We then define a transformation Σ between open subsets of $\mathcal{P}^2$ as $\Sigma\mathbf{m}' = \mathbf{m}$. The points $\mathbf{E}_1\mathbf{m}'$, $\mathbf{E}_2\mathbf{m}'$, and $\mathbf{E}_3\mathbf{m}'$ are orthogonal to $\mathbf{m}$, and by proposition 7.5 no two of $\mathbf{E}_1\mathbf{m}'$, $\mathbf{E}_2\mathbf{m}'$, and $\mathbf{E}_3\mathbf{m}'$ are, in general, parallel. We thus obtain

$$\Sigma\mathbf{m}' = \mathbf{E}_1\mathbf{m}' \wedge \mathbf{E}_2\mathbf{m}' = \mathbf{E}_1\mathbf{m}' \wedge \mathbf{E}_3\mathbf{m}' \qquad\qquad (7.44)$$

for almost all $\mathbf{m}'$. This defines Σ by polynomial equations of degree 2 in $\mathbf{m}'$. Suppose that the equations defining Σ have a common factor of degree 1. Then $\mathbf{m} \leftrightarrow \mathbf{m}'$ is linear, and there exists an invertible matrix $\mathbf{A}$ such that $\mathbf{m} = \mathbf{A}\mathbf{m}'$. We obtain $\mathbf{m}'^T\mathbf{A}^T\mathbf{E}_i\mathbf{m}' = 0$ for all $\mathbf{m}'$, showing that the $\mathbf{A}^T\mathbf{E}_i$ are antisymmetric. Let $\mathbf{A}^T\mathbf{E}_i = \mathbf{T}_i$ for $i = 1, 2, 3$, and let $\mathbf{t}_i$ be the vector corresponding to the antisymmetric matrix $\mathbf{T}_i$. Then Σ is undefined at each $\mathbf{t}_i$ since $\mathbf{E}_i\mathbf{t}_i = \mathbf{A}^{-1T}\mathbf{T}_i\mathbf{t}_i = \mathbf{0}$. By hypothesis, the equations defining Σ have a common factor of degree 1. The $\mathbf{t}_i$ are zeros of this common factor, and therefore they are collinear, and this implies that the $\mathbf{T}_i$ are linearly dependent. As a result, the $\mathbf{E}_i$ are linearly dependent as required.

If the equations defining Σ do not have a common factor of degree 1, then $\mathbf{m} \leftrightarrow \mathbf{m}'$ is quadratic. It follows from the symmetry between $\mathbf{m}$ and $\mathbf{m}'$ that Σ has an inverse; this makes Σ an example of a quadratic transformation as defined in chapter 2. Let $\mathbf{n}'$ be a fixed point of $\mathcal{P}^2$ such that Σ is defined at $\mathbf{n}'$. Then $\mathbf{E}_1\mathbf{n}'$, $\mathbf{E}_2\mathbf{n}'$, and $\mathbf{E}_3\mathbf{n}'$ are linearly dependent, and so there exist coefficients a_1, a_2, and a_3, possibly depending on $\mathbf{n}'$, such that

$$a_1\mathbf{E}_1\mathbf{n}' + a_2\mathbf{E}_2\mathbf{n}' + a_3\mathbf{E}_3\mathbf{n}' = 0$$

We define the matrix $\mathbf{G}$ by

$$\mathbf{G} \equiv a_1\mathbf{E}_1 + a_2\mathbf{E}_2 + a_3\mathbf{E}_3$$

and define a transformation Φ from $\mathcal{P}^2$ to $\mathcal{P}^2$ by

$$\Phi\mathbf{m}' = \mathbf{E}_1\mathbf{m}' \wedge \mathbf{G}\mathbf{m}' = \mathbf{E}_1\mathbf{m}' \wedge (a_2\mathbf{E}_2 + a_3\mathbf{E}_3)\mathbf{m}'$$

The vectors $\mathbf{E}_1\mathbf{m}' \wedge \mathbf{E}_2\mathbf{m}'$ and $\mathbf{E}_1\mathbf{m}' \wedge \mathbf{E}_3\mathbf{m}'$ are parallel. This means that either $\Phi = \Sigma$ or $\Phi = 0$. The case $\Phi = \Sigma$ does not apply since $\Phi\mathbf{n}' = 0$, $\Sigma\mathbf{n}' \neq 0$, and thus $\Phi = 0$. It follows that $\mathbf{E}_1\mathbf{m}'$ and $(a_2\mathbf{E}_2 + a_3\mathbf{E}_3)\mathbf{m}'$ are parallel for all $\mathbf{m}'$, and so, by proposition 7.5, $\mathbf{E}_1$ and $a_2\mathbf{E}_2 + a_3\mathbf{E}_3$ are linearly dependent.   ∎

Let us go back to the question of how many essential matrices $\mathbf{E}_i$ can satisfy equation (7.43). We can state the following theorem:

Theorem 7.2
If the 3-D points lie on a Maybank quadric, there may be as many as three distinct camera motions that yield the same image of those points.

Proof Proposition 7.6 tells us that all those matrices are on a projective line of $\mathcal{P}^8$. Therefore, the question is equivalent to asking how many points of intersection a general line can have with $\mathcal{M}$, the manifold of essential matrices. Since we saw that the equations of $\mathcal{M}$ are of degree 3 (proposition 7.3), the number of intersections of a line with $\mathcal{M}$ is at most 3, which corresponds to the result obtained by the previously cited authors.   ∎

7.3.5.3 *Interpretation in terms of quadratic transformations*

In the case where the 3-D points lie on a Maybank quadric, the correspondence between the two image planes is a quadratic transformation. This is to be compared to the case studied in section 6.8 where the 3-D points were located in a plane. We saw that the two images were related by a collineation. This can be shown very simply as follows. If the 3-D points lie on a Maybank quadric, there exist two distinct essential matrices $\mathbf{E}_1$ and $\mathbf{E}_2$ such that

$$\mathbf{m}^T\mathbf{E}_1\mathbf{m}' = 0 \quad \text{and} \quad \mathbf{m}^T\mathbf{E}_2\mathbf{m}' = 0$$

for all pairs $(\mathbf{m}, \mathbf{m}')$ of corresponding points. But this means that $\mathbf{m}'$ is parallel to the cross-product of $\mathbf{E}_1^T\mathbf{m}$ and $\mathbf{E}_2^T\mathbf{m}$ or, projectively

$$\mathbf{m}' = \mathbf{E}_1^T\mathbf{m} \wedge \mathbf{E}_2^T\mathbf{m} = \Sigma\mathbf{m} \tag{7.45}$$

Equation (7.45) defines a quadratic transformation because it is of degree 2 in the coordinates of m and it is invertible. Indeed, the same reasoning shows that

$$\mathbf{m} = \mathbf{E}_1\mathbf{m}' \wedge \mathbf{E}_2\mathbf{m}' = \Sigma^{-1}\mathbf{m}'$$

The three fundamental points of the quadratic transformations Σ and Σ^{-1} are the epipoles in the first and second images, respectively, corresponding to the three possible camera displacements.

7.4 Determining displacement from line correspondences

Using lines as tokens to determine displacement is another interesting possibility, since edge segments can be reliably extracted from images through polygonal approximations to form a robust source of tokens.

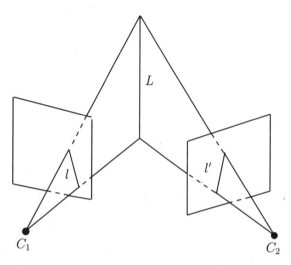

Figure 7.10 Two frames are not sufficient to constrain motion.

This approach has been explored by a number of investigators [LH86a, LH86b, LH88b, FLT87, LHD90, SA90]. But it comes as a bit of a surprise that the problem is significantly more difficult to analyze than the corresponding one with points. One of the reasons for this difficulty is the following. Unlike the case for points, which was previously analyzed, matching two lines in two frames as the images of the same 3-D line does not constrain the rigid displacement between those frames, as is shown in figure 7.10. Indeed, as can be seen from that figure, matching l and l' simply defines a 3-D line L but puts no constraint on the relative positions of C and C' (compare this figure with figure 7.1). Therefore, we need at least three views to constrain the motion. Let us consider the situation of figure 7.11.

7.4.1   Writing the equations

As we know from projective geometry (see chapter 2), a plane can be thought of as a point in projective space $\mathcal{P}^3$. The condition that three planes are in the same pencil (i.e., that they intersect along the same line) is equivalent to the condition that their representative points are aligned. If we denote those three points by $\mathbf{P}, \mathbf{P}'$, and $\mathbf{P}''$, this is equivalent to the algebraic condition that the 4×3 matrix with those vectors as column

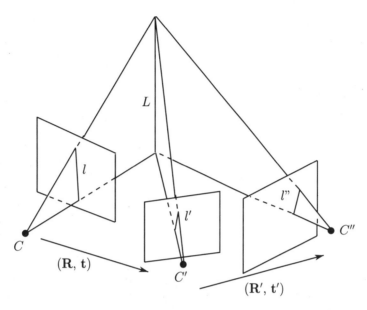

Figure 7.11   Three frames provide constraints about motion.

vectors is of rank 2 (a rank of 1 would imply that the three planes are identical). This in turn implies, as is well known from linear algebra, that all four 3×3 determinants extracted from that matrix are equal to zero. Note that this is a slightly more general situation than the one described in section 6.10.3, where we had natural analytical expressions for $\mathbf{P}, \mathbf{P}'$, and $\mathbf{P}''$. But, as shown in the next proposition, it remains true that only two of those determinants are independent.

Proposition 7.7

Given three 4×1 vectors $\mathbf{P}, \mathbf{P}'$, and $\mathbf{P}''$, the condition that they form a 4×3 matrix of rank 2 is equivalent to two relations between their coordinates.

Proof   If the rank of the matrix is 2, we can write that there exist three real numbers α, β, and γ, not all zero, such that $\alpha\mathbf{P} + \beta\mathbf{P}' + \gamma\mathbf{P}'' = 0$. This can be considered as system of homogeneous linear equations in α, β, and γ. Since the rank of the matrix of that system is equal to 2 by definition, there exists a 2×2 determinant different from 0. The corresponding two equations allow us to determine α, β, and γ up to a scale factor. Replacing them by those values in the remaining two equations yields two relations as requested. ■

Let us be more precise and take a closer look at the equations. We represent the rigid displacement of the camera from the first position to the second by the rotation **R** and the translation **t**, which are expressed in the normalized coordinate system attached to the camera in the first position. Similarly, we represent the rigid displacement from the second position to the third by the rotation **R′** and the translation **t′**, which are expressed in the normalized coordinate system attached to the camera in the second position. Let us denote by **n**, **n′**, and **n″** the normals to the three planes $(C, l), (C', l')$, and (C'', l''), each expressed in the normalized coordinate system of each camera. It is easy to see that those vectors are simply the coefficients of the projective equations of the lines l, l', and l''.

In the normalized coordinate system attached to the camera in its first position, we can show that the three vectors **P**, **P′**, and **P″** can be written as[3]:

$$\mathbf{P} = \begin{bmatrix} \mathbf{n} \\ 0 \end{bmatrix} \quad \mathbf{P}' = \begin{bmatrix} \mathbf{Rn'} \\ -\mathbf{t}^T\mathbf{Rn'} \end{bmatrix} \quad \mathbf{P}'' = \begin{bmatrix} \mathbf{RR'n''} \\ -(\mathbf{t} + \mathbf{Rt'})^T\mathbf{RR'n''} \end{bmatrix} \tag{7.46}$$

Among the four determinants mentioned above, there is one that depends only upon the two rotations:

$$\mathbf{n} \cdot (\mathbf{Rn'} \wedge \mathbf{RR'n''}) \tag{7.47}$$

The other three all involve a mixture of translation and rotation. We let $\mathbf{m'} = \mathbf{Rn'}$, $\mathbf{m''} = \mathbf{RR'n''}$, and $\mathbf{t''} = \mathbf{t} + \mathbf{Rt'}$. The three determinants involving the translations contain the last row of the matrix $[\mathbf{P}, \mathbf{P'}, \mathbf{P''}]$, which is equal to $[0, -\mathbf{t}^T\mathbf{m'}, -\mathbf{t''}^T\mathbf{m''}]$. If we compute the values of those determinants by expanding them with respect to this row, we find that they can be written as

$$(\mathbf{t}^T\mathbf{m'})(\mathbf{n} \wedge \mathbf{m''})_i = (\mathbf{t''}^T\mathbf{m''})(\mathbf{n} \wedge \mathbf{m'})_i \ \ i = 1, 2, 3 \tag{7.48}$$

where the index i indicates the corresponding coordinate in the coordinate system of the first camera.

---

3. Prove it. See problem 5 if you cannot.

By construction, $\mathbf{n} \wedge \mathbf{m}'$ and $\mathbf{n} \wedge \mathbf{m}''$ are parallel to the 3-D line L. If $\mathbf{u}$ is a unit vector parallel to L, we have

$$\mathbf{n} \wedge \mathbf{m}' = \varepsilon' \|\mathbf{n} \wedge \mathbf{m}'\|\mathbf{u}$$

$$\mathbf{n} \wedge \mathbf{m}'' = \varepsilon'' \|\mathbf{n} \wedge \mathbf{m}''\|\mathbf{u}$$

where ε' and ε'' are equal to ± 1. The equations (7.48) are thus equivalent to the single equation

$$|\mathbf{t}^T\mathbf{m}'| \, \|\mathbf{n} \wedge \mathbf{m}''\| = |\mathbf{t}''^T\mathbf{m}''| \, \|\mathbf{n} \wedge \mathbf{m}'\| \tag{7.49}$$

If we do a bit of counting of equations and unknowns, as in the case of points, we see that there are six unknowns for the two rotations and five for the two translations, which are defined up to a common scale factor. This gives a total of eleven unknowns. Since each correspondence in the three views yields two equations as we have just shown, we conclude that the minimum number of line correspondences for which we may hope to solve the motion problem is six.

7.4.2 A geometric interpretation

Equation (7.47) can be given an interesting geometric interpretation. We have seen $\mathbf{n}, \mathbf{n}'$, and $\mathbf{n}''$ as the projective representations of the three image lines l, l', and l''. We now think of matrix $\mathbf{R}$ not as defining a rotation from the first to the second camera, but as defining a collineation between two projective planes (the retinal planes of the camera in its second and first positions, or rather their duals). We do the same for matrix $\mathbf{RR}'$ (which defines a collineation between the duals of the retinal planes of the camera in its third and first positions). What equation (7.47) expresses is the fact that the three lines $l, \mathbf{R}l'$, and $\mathbf{RR}'l''$ intersect at a point d, as shown in figure 7.12. This point is the image of the point at infinity of the 3-D line L, its vanishing point (see problem 8 of chapter 3). It gives us the direction of that line in the coordinate system of the first camera. Indeed, the vectors $\mathbf{Rn}'$ and $\mathbf{RR}'\mathbf{n}''$, for example, are normal to the planes (C', l') and (C'', l''). Therefore, their cross-product is parallel to L. But this is also the projective representation of the point of intersection of the two lines $\mathbf{R}l'$ and $\mathbf{RR}'l''$, i.e., point d in figure 7.12 (proposition 2.4).

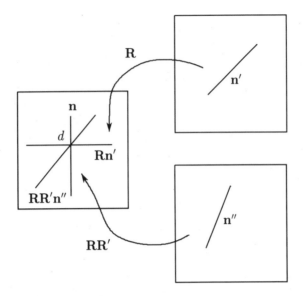

Figure 7.12   A geometric interpretation of equation 7.47.

7.4.3   Solving for the motion parameters

At the time of this writing, there is no known analog for lines to the five-points algorithm of section 7.3.2 (it would be called the six-lines algorithm). But there is an analog to the eight-points algorithm of section 7.3.3.1. This has been worked out by Liu and Huang [LH88a] and requires thirteen triples of line correspondences. But we do not know how many distinct solutions there may be when six triples of line correspondences are available. It is likely, though, that the solution is unique since we have one more equation, i.e., twelve, than the minimum required, i.e., eleven.

When there are more than six triples, the problem can be solved in two steps by minimization techniques:

Step 1:   Find two rotation matrices **R** and **R′** that minimize

$$\sum_{i=1}^{N} (\mathbf{n}_i^T (\mathbf{R}\mathbf{n}_i' \wedge \mathbf{R}\mathbf{R}'\mathbf{n}_i''))^2$$

No closed-form solution is known for this problem.

Step 2: Assuming that the solution of the previous problem is $\hat{\mathbf{R}}, \hat{\mathbf{R}}'$, find a pair $(\mathbf{t}, \mathbf{t}'')$ of vectors that minimize

$$\sum_{i=1}^{N} (\,|\, \mathbf{t}^T \mathbf{m}_i' \,|\, \|\mathbf{n}_i \wedge \mathbf{m}_i''\| - |\, \mathbf{t}''^T \mathbf{m}_i'' \,|\, \|\mathbf{n}_i \wedge \mathbf{m}_i'\|\,)^2$$

subject to the constraint $\|\mathbf{t}\|^2 + \|\mathbf{t}''\|^2 = 1$. We have $\mathbf{m}_i' = \hat{\mathbf{R}}\mathbf{n}_i'$, $\mathbf{m}_i'' = \hat{\mathbf{R}}\hat{\mathbf{R}}'\mathbf{n}_i''$, and $\mathbf{t}'' = \mathbf{t} + \hat{\mathbf{R}}\mathbf{t}'$. There is no closed-form solution for this problem either.

7.4.4 A degenerate case

We saw in section 7.3.5 that there are configurations of points for which there are always several solutions to the the motion-from-point problem, even if an arbitrarily large number of correspondences is available. There is a similar but more complicated problem with regard to lines. Indeed, the previous method fails in the following situation. Suppose that the three cameras are in general positions, and consider three pixels m, m', and m'' with the same image coordinates. The three optical rays $r = \langle C, m \rangle, r' = \langle C', m' \rangle$, and $r'' = \langle C'', m'' \rangle$ are in general skew. Let us consider a line L of 3-space intersecting r, r', r'' and its images l, l', and l''. If we draw them in the first retina, for example, they intersect at m. This is true for all lines L and all pixels m, m', and m'' as defined above. The set Γ of all such lines defeats the algorithm, since equation (7.47) is satisfied for $\mathbf{R} = \mathbf{R}\mathbf{R}' = \mathbf{I}$, which is wrong since we have assumed that the cameras were in general position. There are always at least two solutions to the motion-from-lines problem regardless of the number of available line correspondences. For fixed m, m' and m'', the set of all lines of 3-space meeting the three optical rays r, r', and r'' is a one-parameter family lying on a ruled quadric. The set Γ lies in the union of all these quadrics and has been studied by Buchanan [Buc92]. Problem 8 gives an algebraic characterization of Γ.

7.5 Determining the displacement of a planar patch

As in chapter 6, another potentially useful constraint is to limit the geometric complexity of the scenes and to assume that the kinds of surfaces that are present are *a priori* limited. For example, we could assume that they are well approximated by second-degree surfaces, i.e., quadrics.

Even though this might be an interesting line of approach for a number of industrial scenes, it is appealing to consider first an even simpler case where we assume that the surfaces present in the scene are planar. This is quite acceptable for many practical applications, such as for a mobile vehicle in an urban or building environment where streets, walls, ceilings, and floors are fairly common. This approach has been followed in particular by Tsai and Huang [TH82] and by Faugeras and Lustman [FL88].

7.5.1 Solving the decomposition problem

In section 6.8 we established the fundamental equation of the problem. Referring to figure 6.28, the main result is that, if the moving camera is looking at a plane, the correspondence between the two retinal planes is a collineation; the matrix $\mathbf{A}$ of this collineation can be expressed very simply as a function of the motion $(\mathbf{R}, \mathbf{t})$ from the first position of the camera and the representation $(\mathbf{n}, d)$ of the plane. Note that this representation is in the coordinate system attached to the camera in its second position, which means that the representation in the coordinate system attached to the camera in its first position is $(\mathbf{Rn}, d + \mathbf{Rn}^T \mathbf{t})$. For convenience we can rewrite equation (6.14) as

$$\mathbf{A} = d\mathbf{R} + \mathbf{tn}^T \tag{7.50}$$

In chapter 6, $\mathbf{R}$ and $\mathbf{t}$ were known by calibration. Here they are not. We will show how we can estimate them, as well as $\mathbf{n}$ and d, from matrix $\mathbf{A}$. The estimation of $\mathbf{A}$ from point and line correspondences between the two views is treated in problem 9.

Theorem 7.3
Equation (7.50) has, in general, four different solutions. It has only two if and only if $\mathbf{A}$ has a singular value of multiplicity 2. The problem is partially undetermined if and only if $\mathbf{A}$ has a singular value of multiplicity 3.

Proof Using the singular value decomposition, $\mathbf{A}$ can always be decomposed as $\mathbf{A} = \mathbf{U}\mathbf{D}\mathbf{V}^T$, where $\mathbf{D}$ is a diagonal matrix and $\mathbf{U}$ and $\mathbf{V}$ are orthogonal matrices (satisfying $\mathbf{U}^T\mathbf{U} = \mathbf{V}^T\mathbf{V} = \mathbf{I}$). The diagonal elements of $\mathbf{D}, d_i, i = 1, 2, 3$ are the square roots of the eigenvalues of $\mathbf{AA}^T$. We sort them in decreasing order:

$d_1 \geq d_2 \geq d_3$

Using this decomposition, we obtain the new equation

$$\mathbf{D} = d'\mathbf{R}' + \mathbf{t}'\mathbf{n}'^T \tag{7.51}$$

Now $\mathbf{R}$, $\mathbf{t}$, and $\mathbf{n}$ are related to $\mathbf{R}'$, $\mathbf{t}'$, and $\mathbf{n}'$ by

$$\left\{ \begin{array}{l} \mathbf{R} = s\mathbf{U}\mathbf{R}'\mathbf{V}^T \\ \mathbf{t} = \mathbf{U}\mathbf{t}' \\ \mathbf{n} = \mathbf{V}\mathbf{n}' \\ d = sd' \\ s = \det(\mathbf{U})\det(\mathbf{V}) \end{array} \right. \tag{7.52}$$

Notice that $\mathbf{R}'$ is a rotation (i.e., $\det(\mathbf{R}') = 1$).

Using the canonical basis $(\mathbf{e}_1, \mathbf{e}_2, \mathbf{e}_3)$ and writing $\mathbf{n}' = x_1\mathbf{e}_1 + x_2\mathbf{e}_2 + x_3\mathbf{e}_3$, equation (7.51) gives us three vector equations:

$$d_i\mathbf{e}_i = d'\mathbf{R}'\mathbf{e}_i + \mathbf{t}'x_i \quad \text{for } i = 1, 2, 3 \tag{7.53}$$

Since $\mathbf{n}$ has a unit norm and $\mathbf{V}$ is orthogonal, $\mathbf{n}'$ also has a unit norm: $\sum_{i=1}^{3} x_i^2 = 1$. Eliminating $\mathbf{t}'$ finally yields

$$d'\mathbf{R}'(x_j\mathbf{e}_i - x_i\mathbf{e}_j) = d_ix_j\mathbf{e}_i - d_jx_i\mathbf{e}_j \quad \text{for } i \neq j \tag{7.54}$$

Because $\mathbf{R}'$ preserves the vector norm, we obtain the following set of equations:

$$\left\{ \begin{array}{l} (d'^2 - d_2^2)x_1^2 + (d'^2 - d_1^2)x_2^2 = 0 \\ (d'^2 - d_3^2)x_2^2 + (d'^2 - d_2^2)x_3^2 = 0 \\ (d'^2 - d_1^2)x_3^2 + (d'^2 - d_3^2)x_1^2 = 0 \end{array} \right. \tag{7.55}$$

This can be considered a linear system in the unknowns x_1^2, x_2^2, and x_3^2. Since it must have a nonzero solution, its determinant must be zero:

$$(d'^2 - d_1^2)(d'^2 - d_2^2)(d'^2 - d_3^2) = 0$$

Therefore we obtain different cases according to the order of multiplicity of the singular values of $\mathbf{A}$. There are only three possibilities:

All singular values are different:

$d_1 \neq d_2 \neq d_3$ and $d' = \pm d_2$

Two singular values are equal:

$d_1 = d_2 \neq d_3$ or $d_1 \neq d_2 = d_3$ and $d' = \pm d_2$

For this case, we consider only the case $d_1 = d_2$, because the case $d_2 = d_3$ is symmetrical.

All singular values are equal:

$d_1 = d_2 = d_3$ and $d' = \pm d_2$

The solutions $d' = \pm d_1$ and $d' = \pm d_3$ are indeed impossible; as an example we will prove it for case 1. Assuming $d' = d_1$, the equations (7.55) yield

$$x_1 = 0 \quad \text{and} \quad (d_1^2 - d_3^2)x_2^2 + (d_1^2 - d_2^2)x_3^2 = 0$$

Since $d_1 > d_2 > d_3$, this implies $x_2 = x_3 = 0$, which is impossible because $\mathbf{n}'$ has a unit norm. If $d_1 \neq d_3$, as in cases 1 and 2 above, we can compute x_1, x_2, and x_3 using the equations (7.55) and remembering that $\mathbf{n}'$ has a unit norm

$$\begin{cases} x_1 &= \varepsilon_1 \sqrt{\dfrac{d_1^2 - d_2^2}{d_1^2 - d_3^2}} \\ x_2 &= 0 \qquad\qquad \varepsilon_1, \varepsilon_3 = \pm 1 \\ x_3 &= \varepsilon_3 \sqrt{\dfrac{d_2^2 - d_3^2}{d_1^2 - d_3^2}} \end{cases} \tag{7.56}$$

Let us now study the three cases in detail. The study is divided into two parts, depending on the sign of d'.

Case $d' > 0$:

All singular values are different:
We know that $d' = d_2$. Referring to equations (7.53), we obtain $\mathbf{R}'\mathbf{e}_2 = \mathbf{e}_2$. $\mathbf{R}'$ is a rotation of axis $\mathbf{e}_2$. We can compute the matrix $\mathbf{R}'$ as

$$\begin{bmatrix} \cos\theta & 0 & -\sin\theta \\ 0 & 1 & 0 \\ \sin\theta & 0 & \cos\theta \end{bmatrix}$$

Using equations (7.54) and (7.56), we find

$$\begin{cases} \sin\theta &= (d_1 - d_3)\dfrac{x_1 x_3}{d_2} &= \varepsilon_1\varepsilon_3\dfrac{\sqrt{(d_1^2 - d_2^2)(d_2^2 - d_3^2)}}{(d_1 + d_3)d_2} \\[2mm] \cos\theta &= \dfrac{d_1 x_3^2 + d_3 x_1^2}{d_2} &= \dfrac{d_2^2 + d_1 d_3}{(d_1 + d_3)d_2} \end{cases} \qquad (7.57)$$

Substituting these values into equations (7.53) yields

$$\mathbf{t'} = (d_1 - d_3)\begin{bmatrix} x_1 \\ 0 \\ -x_3 \end{bmatrix} \qquad (7.58)$$

The four solutions provided by the four pairs of values for ε_1 and ε_3 are reduced to two by imposing the assumption that the coordinate of **Rn** along the z-axis is the negative of the normal to the plane (i.e., **Rn** points toward the camera).

Two singular values are equal:
We have $d' = d_1 = d_2$. In this case, we obtain $x_1 = x_2 = 0$ and $x_3 = \varepsilon_3 = \pm 1$.
  From equations (7.54) and (7.53) we then get

$$\begin{cases} \mathbf{R'} &= \mathbf{I} \\ \mathbf{t'} &= (d_3 - d_1)\mathbf{n'} \end{cases}$$

The two solutions are here reduced to one by imposing the same constraint on the normal **n** as in the previous case.

All singular values are equal:
We have $d' = d_1 = d_2 = d_3$. Here x_1, x_2, and x_3 are undefined, and the equations (7.54) and (7.53) provide us with

$$\begin{cases} \mathbf{R'} = \mathbf{I} \\ \mathbf{t'} = 0 \end{cases}$$

In this case, the motion is a pure rotation and the normal to the plane remains undefined.

Case $d' < 0$:

All singular values are different:
We have $d' = -d_2$. The equations (7.53) yield $\mathbf{R'e_2} = -\mathbf{e_2}$, which implies that $\mathbf{R'}$ is a symmetry (i.e., a rotation of angle π) with respect to an axis **v** perpendicular to $\mathbf{e_2}$, i.e., in the plane $(\mathbf{e_1}, \mathbf{e_3})$. Let $\varphi/2$ be the angle between $\mathbf{e_1}$ and **v**. The rotation $\mathbf{R'}$ can be written as

$$\begin{bmatrix} \cos\varphi & 0 & \sin\varphi \\ 0 & -1 & 0 \\ \sin\varphi & 0 & -\cos\varphi \end{bmatrix}$$

with

$$\begin{cases} \sin\varphi = \dfrac{d_1 + d_3}{d_2} x_1 x_3 = \varepsilon_1 \varepsilon_3 \dfrac{\sqrt{(d_1^2 - d_2^2)(d_2^2 - d_3^2)}}{(d_1 - d_3)d_2} \\[3mm] \cos\varphi = \dfrac{d_3 x_1^2 - d_1 x_3^2}{d_2} = \dfrac{d_1 d_3 - d_2^2}{(d_1 - d_3)d_2} \end{cases} \tag{7.59}$$

Substituting these values into equations (7.53) yields

$$\mathbf{t}' = (d_1 + d_3) \begin{bmatrix} x_1 \\ 0 \\ x_3 \end{bmatrix} \tag{7.60}$$

Again, the four solutions are reduced to two by imposing the same constraint on the normal.

Two singular values are equal:

We have $d' = -d_1 = -d_2$. We also have, once more, $x_1 = x_2 = 0$ and $x_3 = \varepsilon_3 = \pm 1$. $\mathbf{R}'$ is therefore a symmetry with respect to $\mathbf{e}_3$:

$$\begin{cases} \mathbf{R}' = \begin{bmatrix} -1 & 0 & 0 \\ 0 & -1 & 0 \\ 0 & 0 & 1 \end{bmatrix} \\ \mathbf{t}' = (d_3 + d_1)\mathbf{n}' \end{cases}$$

Again, the two solutions are reduced to one by imposing the constraint on the normal to the plane.

All singular values are equal:

We have $d' = -d_1 = -d_2 = -d_3$. The equations (7.51) imply that $\mathbf{R}'\mathbf{x} = -\mathbf{x}$ for all vectors $\mathbf{x}$ in the plane orthogonal to $\mathbf{n}'$. $\mathbf{R}'$ is therefore a symmetry with respect to the axis $\mathbf{n}'$. Therefore, $\mathbf{R}' = -\mathbf{I} + 2\mathbf{n}'\mathbf{n}'^T$ and, according to equation (7.51), $\mathbf{t}' = -2d'\mathbf{n}'$. ∎

Since we have *a priori* no way of knowing the sign of d', we have a total of four solutions when the singular values are distinct, two solutions when two singular values are equal, and an indetermination when the three are equal. But, among the four solutions, only two are possible if we go back to the physical interpretation of the problem, as we will show next.

Proposition 7.8
For the observed points seen by the two cameras (i.e., the points in front of the cameras), the decomposition problem has in fact only two physical solutions in the general case and one solution when there is a double singular value.

Proof Let M be a point in the plane that is visible by the two cameras, and let Z_1 and Z_2 be the z-coordinates of M in the coordinate frames attached to the two positions of the camera. The constraint of visibility by the two cameras enforces $Z_1 > 0$ and $Z_2 > 0$. Using equations (6.15) and (7.50), we obtain

$$d\mathbf{X}_1 = d\mathbf{R}\mathbf{X}_2 + d\mathbf{t} = (\mathbf{A} - \mathbf{t}\mathbf{n}^T)\mathbf{X}_2 + d\mathbf{t} = \mathbf{A}\mathbf{X}_2 - \mathbf{t}(\mathbf{n}^T\mathbf{X}_2 - d) = \mathbf{A}\mathbf{X}_2$$

and thus

$$\frac{Z_1}{Z_2} = \frac{a_{31}x_2 + a_{32}y_2 + a_{33}}{d} > 0$$

This shows that, if we know $\mathbf{A}$ and $\mathbf{m}_2$, the image of M in the second camera, then we can determine the sign of d. As $d = sd'$ and since s is determined by $\mathbf{A}$, we have only two solutions, corresponding to $d' > 0$ and $d' < 0$.   ∎

7.5.2   The degenerate cases

Let us study in more detail the degenerate cases, that is, the cases where there are singular values with an order of multiplicity greater than 1.

Proposition 7.9
$\mathbf{A}$ has two equal singular values if and only if $\mathbf{t} \wedge \mathbf{R}\mathbf{n} = 0$, which means that the translation is normal to the plane, as shown in figure 7.13. $\mathbf{A}$ has three equal singular values if and only if either the translation is zero (as in the case of pure rotation, for example), or $\mathbf{t} = -2d\mathbf{R}\mathbf{n}$ (as when a transparent plane is observed from the two opposite sides and from the same distance, as shown in figure 7.14).

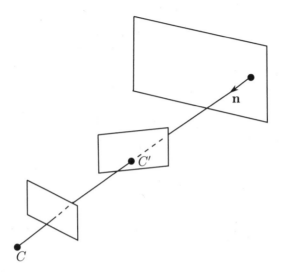

Figure 7.13   An example of double degeneracy.

Proof

Double singular value:

the singular values are the square roots of the eigenvalues of $\mathbf{A}\mathbf{A}^T$. From equation (7.50), we have

$$\mathbf{A}\mathbf{A}^T\mathbf{x} = d^2\mathbf{x} + (\mathbf{t} \cdot \mathbf{x})\mathbf{t} + d(\mathbf{Rn} \cdot \mathbf{x})\mathbf{t} + d(\mathbf{t} \cdot \mathbf{x})\mathbf{Rn}$$

If $\mathbf{t} = \lambda\mathbf{Rn}$, it is clear that the plane orthogonal to $\mathbf{t}$ is a plane of eigenvectors of $\mathbf{A}\mathbf{A}^T$ for the eigenvalue d^2. Reciprocally, if there is a double singular value, we have proved that:

- if $d' > 0$, $\mathbf{R}' = \mathbf{I}$ and $\mathbf{t}' = (d_3 - d_1)\mathbf{n}'$, so that the equations (7.52) yield

$$\mathbf{Rn} = s\mathbf{U}\mathbf{R}'\mathbf{V}^t\mathbf{V}\mathbf{n}' = \pm\frac{s}{d_3 - d_1}\mathbf{U}\mathbf{t}' = \pm\frac{s}{d_3 - d_1}\mathbf{t}$$

- if $d' < 0$, $\mathbf{n}' = \pm\mathbf{e}_3$, $\mathbf{R}'\mathbf{e}_3 = \mathbf{e}_3$ and $\mathbf{t}' = (d_1 + d_3)\mathbf{n}'$, so that the same equations as above show the result.

Triple singular value:

If d' is positive, we have shown that $\mathbf{t}' = 0$, and therefore $\mathbf{t} = 0$. Reciprocally, if $\mathbf{t} = 0$, then $\mathbf{A} = d\mathbf{R}$ and $\mathbf{A}\mathbf{A}^T = d^2\mathbf{I}$ and all the singular values are equal to d. If d' is negative, we have shown that $\mathbf{t}' = -2d'\mathbf{n}'$ and that $\mathbf{R}'\mathbf{n}' = \mathbf{n}'$. It follows that

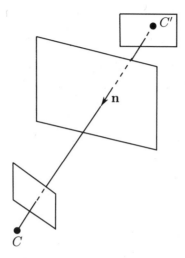

Figure 7.14   An example of triple degeneracy.

$$\mathbf{t} = \mathbf{U}\mathbf{t}' = -2d'\mathbf{U}\mathbf{R}'\mathbf{n}' = -2d'\mathbf{U}\mathbf{R}'\mathbf{V}^T\mathbf{n} = -2sd'\mathbf{R}\mathbf{n} = -2d\mathbf{R}\mathbf{n}$$

Reciprocally, if $\mathbf{t} = -2d\mathbf{R}\mathbf{n}$, then $\mathbf{A} = d\mathbf{R} - 2d\mathbf{R}\mathbf{n}\mathbf{n}^T = d\mathbf{R}(\mathbf{I} - 2\mathbf{n}\mathbf{n}^T)$ and $\mathbf{A}^T\mathbf{A} = d^2\mathbf{I}$, which ends the proof.   ∎

7.6   Problems

1. Suppose that at time t_0 the camera is calibrated, and let $\tilde{\mathbf{P}}_0$ be the corresponding perspective projection matrix. Show that equation (7.1) can be written

   $$(\mathbf{P}_0^{-1}\tilde{\mathbf{m}}) \cdot (\mathbf{t} \wedge \mathbf{R}(\mathbf{P}_0^{-1}\tilde{\mathbf{m}}')) = 0$$

   where $\tilde{\mathbf{m}}$ and $\tilde{\mathbf{m}}'$ are projective representations of the pixels m and m'.

2. When the translation is 0, equation (7.1) is identically 0. Show that in this case the rotation matrix $\mathbf{R}$ can, in general, be determined from three point matches.

3. Show that n complex numbers x_i satisfy the following relation:

$$\sum_{i=1}^{n} x_i^3 = -\frac{1}{2}(\sum_{i=1}^{n} x_i)^3 + \frac{3}{2}(\sum_{i=1}^{n} x_i)(\sum_{i=1}^{n} x_i^2) + 3 \sum_{i,j,k \text{ all different}} x_i x_j x_k$$

Deduce from this equation (7.15).

4. This problem develops Sturm's method for solving Chasles' problem. Let $\mathbf{p}_i \leftrightarrow \mathbf{p}'_i, i = 1, \ldots, 7$ be a set of image correspondences. We know that $\mathbf{x}$ and $\mathbf{x}'$ are epipoles compatible with the image correspondences if and only if

$$\langle \mathbf{x}, \mathbf{p}_i \rangle \overline{\wedge} \langle \mathbf{x}', \mathbf{p}'_i \rangle \qquad i = 1, \ldots, 7$$

a. Let $\mathbf{q}$ be a point. Show that the line $\langle \mathbf{x}, \mathbf{q} \rangle$ meets $\langle \mathbf{p}_1, \mathbf{p}_2 \rangle$ at the point $\mathbf{p}$ given by

$$\mathbf{p} = (\mathbf{x} \wedge \mathbf{q}) \wedge (\mathbf{p}_1 \wedge \mathbf{p}_2) = (\mathbf{p}_2, \mathbf{x}, \mathbf{q})\mathbf{p}_1 - (\mathbf{p}_1, \mathbf{x}, \mathbf{q})\mathbf{p}_2$$

Show that $\langle \mathbf{p}_1, \mathbf{p}_2 \rangle$ can be parameterized by the projective parameter $\theta_p = \frac{(\mathbf{p}_2, \mathbf{x}, \mathbf{q})}{(\mathbf{p}_1, \mathbf{x}, \mathbf{q})}$ and that $\theta_{p_1} = \infty$ and $\theta_{p_2} = 0$.

b. Compute the cross-ratio $\{\langle \mathbf{x}, \mathbf{q} \rangle, \langle \mathbf{x}, \mathbf{p}_3 \rangle; \langle \mathbf{x}, \mathbf{p}_1 \rangle, \langle \mathbf{x}, \mathbf{p}_2 \rangle\}$ of the four lines $\langle \mathbf{x}, \mathbf{q} \rangle, \langle \mathbf{x}, \mathbf{p}_3 \rangle, \langle \mathbf{x}, \mathbf{p}_1 \rangle$, and $\langle \mathbf{x}, \mathbf{p}_2 \rangle$.

c. We will now show that the first six correspondences constrain $\mathbf{x}$ to lie on a cubic curve. Write three equations relating $\mathbf{x}$ and $\mathbf{x}'$.

d. Perform a change of projective basis in the two retinal planes so that

$$\mathbf{p}_1 = \mathbf{p}'_1 = [1, 0, 0]^T \quad \mathbf{p}_2 = \mathbf{p}'_2 = [0, 1, 0]^T$$
$$\mathbf{p}_3 = \mathbf{p}'_3 = [0, 0, 1]^T \quad \mathbf{p}_4 = \mathbf{p}'_4 = [1, 1, 1]^T$$

Show that the three equations you were asked to write in problem 4(c) become

$$\frac{p_1^{(i)} x_3 - p_3^{(i)} x_1}{p_3^{(i)} x_2 - p_2^{(i)} x_3} \times \frac{x_2}{x_1} = \frac{p_1^{(i)'} x'_3 - p_3^{(i)'} x'_1}{p_3^{(i)'} x'_2 - p_2^{(i)'} x'_3} \times \frac{x'_2}{x'_1} \qquad i = 4, 5, 6$$

e. Apply the two quadratic transformations Φ and Φ' defined by

$$\mathbf{u} = \Phi \mathbf{x} = [x_2 x_3, x_3 x_1, x_1 x_2]^T$$
$$\mathbf{u}' = \Phi' \mathbf{x}' = [x'_2 x'_3, x'_3 x'_1, x'_1 x'_2]^T$$

and show that the three equations you have written can be written as

$$\frac{p_1^{(i)} u_1 - p_3^{(i)} u_3}{p_3^{(i)} u_3 - p_2^{(i)} u_2} = \frac{p_1^{(i)'} u_1' - p_3^{(i)'} u_3'}{p_3^{(i)'} u_3' - p_2^{(i)'} u_2'} \qquad i = 4, 5, 6$$

f. Write these three equations as

$$\mathbf{a}_i(\mathbf{u}) \cdot \mathbf{u}' = 0 \qquad i = 4, 5, 6$$

where $\mathbf{a}_i(\mathbf{u})$ is a 3×1 vector. Conclude that $\mathbf{u}$ has to lie on a planar curve of degree 3.

g. Show that this cubic curve defines a cubic for $\mathbf{x}$. Let $g(\mathbf{x}) = 0$ be its equation.

h. Show that the cubic of equation $g(\mathbf{x}) = 0$ passes through the six points $\mathbf{p}_i, i = 1, \ldots, 6$. Show that it also passes through the three points $\mathbf{b}_i, i = 1, 2, 3$ such that

$$\mathbf{a}_4(\Phi \mathbf{b}_1) = \lambda_1 \mathbf{a}_5(\Phi \mathbf{b}_1) \ \lambda_1 \neq 0$$

$$\mathbf{a}_5(\Phi \mathbf{b}_2) = \lambda_2 \mathbf{a}_6(\Phi \mathbf{b}_2) \ \lambda_2 \neq 0$$

$$\mathbf{a}_6(\Phi \mathbf{b}_3) = \lambda_3 \mathbf{a}_4(\Phi \mathbf{b}_3) \ \lambda_3 \neq 0$$

i. If we now consider the correspondence $\mathbf{p}_7 \overline{\wedge} \mathbf{p}_7'$, show that this constrains $\mathbf{x}$ to lie on another cubic curve and that these two cubics have six points in common.

j. Conclude that, in general, there are three solutions to Chasles' problem

5. Show that the expressions for $\mathbf{P}'$ and $\mathbf{P}''$ given in equations (7.46) are correct.

6. Compute the value of λ_0, the third value for which the determinant of matrix $\mathbf{X} - \lambda \mathbf{Y}$ of equation 7.30 is 0. Also compute a corresponding vector of the nullspace. *Hint*: use a system for algebraic computation.

7. Verify that the quadratic transformation Σ defined by equations (7.29) can be written as

$$\Sigma = \mathbf{A} \Sigma_0 \mathbf{B}$$

where **A** and **B** are the 3×3 matrices representing collineations, and Σ_0 represents the reciprocal transformation (theorem 2.2).

8. The goal of this problem is to give an algebraic characterization of the set Γ of section 7.4.4.

   a. Let $\mathbf{q}_1, \mathbf{q}_2$, and $\mathbf{q}_3$ denote the Plücker coordinates (see section 2.5.1) of three rays r_1, r_2, and r_3 through C, not all in a plane. What are the Plücker coordinates of a general ray through C?

   b. Let $\mathbf{q}'_1, \mathbf{q}'_2, \mathbf{q}'_3$ and $\mathbf{q}''_1, \mathbf{q}''_2, \mathbf{q}''_3$ be the Plücker coordinates of rays r'_1, r'_2, r'_3 and r''_1, r''_2, r''_3, respectively, through C' (respectively, C'') homologous to r_1, r_2, and r_3. This means that the image coordinates of their points of intersection with the second retinal plane (respectively, the third) are equal to those of the intersections of r_1, r_2, and r_3 with the first retinal plane. Let r, r', and r'' be three general homologous rays with Plücker coordinates $\mathbf{q}, \mathbf{q}'$, and $\mathbf{q}''$ and let L be a line of Plücker coordinates $\mathbf{p}$ intersecting r, r', and r''. What are the necessary and sufficient conditions that are satisfied by $\mathbf{p}$?

   c. Find a polynomial equation that is satisfied by all lines of Γ.

9. This problem discusses how matrix **A** of section 7.5 can be recovered from point and line correspondences.

   a. Given a pair of matched pixels (m_1, m_2), write two linear equations that must be satisfied by the coefficients of **A**.

   b. Given a pair of matched lines (l_1, l_2), write two linear equations that must be satisfied by the coefficients of **A**.

   c. Propose a procedure for estimating **A** when a sufficient number of point and line matches have been established.

8 Tracking Tokens over Time

In this chapter we will study the problem of tracking tokens, such as points or lines, over time. We will consider this problem both as a two-dimensional problem, tracking tokens in a sequence of images, and as a three-dimensional problem, tracking tokens in a sequence of stereo frames.

8.1 Introduction

In the previous chapter we studied the problem of estimating the motion of a camera moving in a static environment (or of estimating the motion of an object observed by a static camera) from a number of token matches. Rather than motion, we should actually have been talking about displacement, since we were really analyzing a small number of snapshots taken at different time instants. We were also assuming that the matches were given to us. In this chapter we would like to look at the motion problem from a slightly different viewpoint; in particular, we want to perform the analysis continuously. In order to do this we have to introduce some new tools: recursive least-squares methods and Kalman filtering. These methods will be quite useful for other applications as well (see chapter 11).

We will present these tools in a fairly systematic manner. One of the key problems in many dynamic computer vision questions is that of minimizing at a certain time a criterion that depends upon measurements that have been made previously, as well as upon some measurements that we are currently performing or will be performing. For the sake of efficiency, it is important to avoid going over the complete minimization process each time a new measurement is performed. It is also important to have an idea of how the next measurement will change the current estimate of the quantities with respect to those that we are minimizing. The first point hints at the concept of *recursivity*, the second at the concept of *prediction*. Those are two ideas that are central to the theory of deterministic recursive least-squares estimation and to its probabilistic analog, the theory of the Kalman filter. Fortunately, both theories lead to the same set of equations. Section 8.2 presents both of these theories, but the emphasis is on the deterministic least-squares approach for the reasons previously stated: We believe that in most cases probabilities are not necessary, and they may even be cumbersome in many computer vision problems. The reader who is interested only in using the results may find it sufficient to read the introduction of that section and go directly to the equations (8.31)–(8.34) and section 8.2.2.

In section 8.3 we will study the problem of tracking two-dimensional tokens (lines and points) in the image without attempting to relate this motion to the corresponding three-dimensional motion. This is done in the next chapter. We will then extend the ideas developed in the two-dimensional case to three dimensions in section 8.4 and will show that they can serve as the basis of a very simple method for estimating three-dimensional motions by tracking three-dimensional tokens obtained, for example, from stereo vision. One of the main advantages of this method is that it can easily deal with the motions of multiple objects.

The method for tracking two-dimensional tokens can be used to provide matches for the techniques developed in the previous chapter, but care must be taken before applying these methods to estimate displacements in order to guarantee that the hypothesis of a single motion is satisfied.

8.2 Recursive least-squares and Kalman filtering methods

We are going to study systems that can be defined by n parameters. We think of these parameters as forming a vector $\mathbf{a}$ of dimension n called the *state vector*. The parameters are usually not directly observable, but can be probed through measurements represented by $\mathbf{x}$, a vector of size m. The relationship between the measurements and the state vector is called the *measurement equation* $\mathbf{f}(\mathbf{x}, \mathbf{a})$, which is usually vector-valued. The measurement equation $\mathbf{f}$ maps the product $R^m \times R^n$ into R^p. In our applications this function is almost always nonlinear, even though the linear case is extremely important since it provides the general paradigm for the nonlinear case. For this reason, we will study the linear case in detail before we see how it can be extended to the nonlinear case. Our presentation is largely inspired by the one proposed by Sorenson [Sorwn].

We will assume that we are dealing with a discrete set of measurement equations and use the index i to index them. Therefore, we will talk about the measurement equation

$$\mathbf{f}_i(\mathbf{x}_i, \mathbf{a}_i) = \mathbf{0} \tag{8.1}$$

where i varies over, for example, the set of integers. We also need to define how the state $\mathbf{a}_i$ varies with i. We will assume that the *state model* is linear and is defined by the following equation[1]:

$$\mathbf{a}_i = \mathbf{\Phi}_{i,i-1}\mathbf{a}_{i-1} + \mathbf{w}_{i-1} \tag{8.2}$$

where $\mathbf{\Phi}_{i,i-1}$ is an $n \times n$ matrix and $\mathbf{w}_{i-1}$ represents errors or uncertainties in the model. This equation is sometimes also called the *plant equation*.

Depending upon our point of view, we may or may not give a probabilistic interpretation to the measurements and to the state vectors. It is our opinion that in computer vision the deterministic interpretation is better because it is usually artificial to assume that the quantities we deal with are random. Fortunately, both approaches yield the same set of equations.

8.2.1   Deterministic least-squares

8.2.1.1   *A constant-state model and linear measurement equation*

General analysis   A special case occurs when $\mathbf{\Phi}_{i,i-1}$ is the identity matrix and $\mathbf{w}_{i-1}$ is zero; in that case the state vector is constant, but unknown. The problem is, given $N + 1$ measurement equations (8.1), to find $\mathbf{a}$ that minimizes

---

1. A more general case is discussed in section 8.2.2.

$$\frac{1}{2}\Sigma_{i=0}^{N}\mathbf{f}_i^{T}(\mathbf{x}_i,\mathbf{a})\mathbf{f}_i(\mathbf{x}_i,\mathbf{a}) \tag{8.3}$$

By combining the $N + 1$ measurement vectors $\mathbf{x}_i$ into one $m(N + 1)$ vector $\mathbf{x}$ and the $N + 1$ measurement equations $\mathbf{f}_i(\mathbf{x}_i,\mathbf{a})$ into one $p(N + 1)$ measurement equation $\mathbf{f}$, we then have to find the best $\mathbf{a}$ that minimizes

$$C = \frac{1}{2}\mathbf{f}^{T}(\mathbf{x},\mathbf{a})\mathbf{f}(\mathbf{x},\mathbf{a})$$

A necessary condition for C to be minimized is that

$$\frac{\partial \mathbf{f}}{\partial \mathbf{a}}^{T}\mathbf{f}(\mathbf{x},\mathbf{a}) = \mathbf{0} \tag{8.4}$$

In general, it is not possible to solve equation (8.4) explicitly for $\mathbf{a}$. However, if $\mathbf{f}$ is linear

$$\mathbf{f}(\mathbf{x},\mathbf{a}) = \mathbf{x} - \mathbf{H}\mathbf{a} = \mathbf{0} \tag{8.5}$$

In this case, $\frac{\partial \mathbf{f}}{\partial \mathbf{a}} = -\mathbf{H}$, and equation (8.4) becomes

$$\mathbf{H}^{T}\mathbf{H}\mathbf{a} = \mathbf{H}^{T}\mathbf{x} \tag{8.6}$$

Supposing that $\mathbf{H}^{T}\mathbf{H}$ has an inverse, the solution $\hat{\mathbf{a}}$ of equation (8.6) is given by

$$\hat{\mathbf{a}} = (\mathbf{H}^{T}\mathbf{H})^{-1}\mathbf{H}^{T}\mathbf{x} \tag{8.7}$$

It comes as no surprise that we find the standard solution to the problem $\min_{\mathbf{a}} \|\mathbf{x} - \mathbf{H}\mathbf{a}\|^2$. Observe that in equation (8.7) an $n \times n$ matrix has to be inverted and all measurements have to be gathered and processed before the result can be computed.

A recursive solution   It is possible to solve equation (8.3) *recursively* without having to wait until all data have been collected and without having to reprocess old data when new data is obtained. Of course this is of utmost importance in the case of computer vision, and in particular in the case of dynamic vision. Suppose that $\hat{\mathbf{a}}_{i-1}$ is the estimate of $\mathbf{a}$ based upon the $i - 1$ first measurement equations (8.5), and suppose that we obtain the ith measurement equation. Let

$$C_i = \frac{1}{2}\Sigma_{k=0}^{i}(\mathbf{x}_k - \mathbf{H}_k\mathbf{a})^T(\mathbf{x}_k - \mathbf{H}_k\mathbf{a})$$

(8.8)

We have, of course

$$C_i = C_{i-1} + \frac{1}{2}(\mathbf{x}_i - \mathbf{H}_i\mathbf{a})^T(\mathbf{x}_i - \mathbf{H}_i\mathbf{a})$$

Taking the derivative with respect to **a**, we obtain

$$\frac{\partial C_i}{\partial \mathbf{a}} = \frac{\partial C_{i-1}}{\partial \mathbf{a}} - \mathbf{H}_i^T\mathbf{x}_i + \mathbf{H}_i^T\mathbf{H}_i\mathbf{a} = \mathbf{0}$$

(8.9)

Now we let

$$\mathbf{H}^{(i-1)} = \begin{bmatrix} \mathbf{H}_0 \\ \mathbf{H}_1 \\ \vdots \\ \mathbf{H}_{i-1} \end{bmatrix}$$

Note that

$$\mathbf{H}^{iT}\mathbf{H}^{i} = \mathbf{H}^{(i-1)T}\mathbf{H}^{(i-1)} + \mathbf{H}_i^T\mathbf{H}_i$$

(8.10)

Now condition (8.9) becomes

$$\mathbf{H}^{(i-1)T}\mathbf{H}^{(i-1)}\mathbf{a} - \mathbf{H}^{(i-1)T}\mathbf{x}^{i-1} - \mathbf{H}_i^T\mathbf{x}_i + \mathbf{H}_i^T\mathbf{H}_i\mathbf{a} = \mathbf{0}$$

where

$$\mathbf{x}^{i-1} = \begin{bmatrix} \mathbf{x}_0 \\ \mathbf{x}_1 \\ \vdots \\ \mathbf{x}_{i-1} \end{bmatrix}$$

since, according to equation (8.7), $\hat{\mathbf{a}}_{i-1} = (\mathbf{H}^{(i-1)T}\mathbf{H}^{(i-1)})^{-1}\mathbf{H}^{(i-1)T}\mathbf{x}^{(i-1)}$, this can be rewritten as

$$(\mathbf{H}^{(i-1)T}\mathbf{H}^{(i-1)} + \mathbf{H}_i^T\mathbf{H}_i)\mathbf{a} = \mathbf{H}^{(i-1)T}\mathbf{H}^{(i-1)}\hat{\mathbf{a}}_{i-1} + \mathbf{H}_i^T\mathbf{x}_i$$

(8.11)

Let

$$\mathbf{P}_i^{-1} = \mathbf{H}^{iT}\mathbf{H}^{i}$$

Because of equation (8.10), $\mathbf{P}_i^{-1}$ satisfies the following recursive equation:

$$\mathbf{P}_i^{-1} = \mathbf{P}_{i-1}^{-1} + \mathbf{H}_i^T \mathbf{H}_i \qquad (8.12)$$

Then equation (8.11) becomes

$$\mathbf{P}_i^{-1}\hat{\mathbf{a}}_i = \mathbf{P}_{i-1}^{-1}\hat{\mathbf{a}}_{i-1} + \mathbf{H}_i^T \mathbf{x}_i$$

and, assuming that $\mathbf{P}_i^{-1}$ has an inverse, we obtain

$$\hat{\mathbf{a}}_i = \mathbf{P}_i \mathbf{P}_{i-1}^{-1}\hat{\mathbf{a}}_{i-1} + \mathbf{P}_i \mathbf{H}_i^T \mathbf{x}_i \qquad (8.13)$$

The matrix inversion lemma (see problem 1) yields

$$\mathbf{P}_i = (\mathbf{P}_{i-1}^{-1} + \mathbf{H}_i^T \mathbf{H}_i)^{-1} = \mathbf{P}_{i-1} - \mathbf{P}_{i-1}\mathbf{H}_i^T (\mathbf{I} + \mathbf{H}_i \mathbf{P}_{i-1}\mathbf{H}_i^T)^{-1}\mathbf{H}_i \mathbf{P}_{i-1}$$

Thus, multiplying on the right by $\mathbf{P}_{i-1}^{-1}$ we have

$$\mathbf{P}_i \mathbf{P}_{i-1}^{-1} = \mathbf{I} - \mathbf{P}_{i-1}\mathbf{H}_i^T (\mathbf{I} + \mathbf{H}_i \mathbf{P}_{i-1}\mathbf{H}_i^T)^{-1}\mathbf{H}_i = \mathbf{I} - \mathbf{K}_i \mathbf{H}_i$$

where

$$\mathbf{K}_i = \mathbf{P}_{i-1}\mathbf{H}_i^T (\mathbf{H}_i \mathbf{P}_{i-1}\mathbf{H}_i^T + \mathbf{I})^{-1}$$

Using equation (8.12) together with the fact that $\mathbf{K}_i \mathbf{H}_i = \mathbf{I} - \mathbf{P}_i \mathbf{P}_{i-1}^{-1}$, we have

$$\mathbf{K}_i \mathbf{H}_i = \mathbf{P}_i \mathbf{H}_i^T \mathbf{H}_i$$

It follows that, if $\text{rank}(\mathbf{H}_i) = m$,

$$\mathbf{K}_i = \mathbf{P}_i \mathbf{H}_i^T \qquad (8.14)$$

and therefore equation (8.13) becomes

$$\hat{\mathbf{a}}_i = \hat{\mathbf{a}}_{i-1} + \mathbf{K}_i (\mathbf{x}_i - \mathbf{H}_i \hat{\mathbf{a}}_{i-1}) \qquad (8.15)$$

This equation is precisely the answer to our initial question. It shows how to compute the best estimate of the state, $\hat{\mathbf{a}}_i$, after i measurements have been made, from the previous state $\hat{\mathbf{a}}_{i-1}$, the ith measurement $\mathbf{x}_i$, the measurement matrix $\mathbf{H}_i$, and the matrix $\mathbf{K}_i$ given by equation (8.14). Equation (8.12) tells us how to compute $\mathbf{P}_i$ from $\mathbf{P}_{i-1}$ and the measurement matrix $\mathbf{H}_i$.

The weighted least-squares case   A simple and useful generalization of this analysis is when some measurement errors are given more weight

Tracking Tokens over Time

than others. This is the same as rewriting the cost function C_i as

$$C_i = \frac{1}{2}\Sigma_{k=0}^i (\mathbf{x}_k - \mathbf{H}_k\mathbf{a})^T \mathbf{R}_k^{-1}(\mathbf{x}_k - \mathbf{H}_k\mathbf{a})$$

where the weight matrices $\mathbf{R}_k^{-1}$ are symmetric positive definite. It is easy to show that the weighting matrix $\mathbf{R}_i^{-1}$ modifies only $\mathbf{P}_i$ and $\mathbf{K}_i$:

$$\mathbf{P}_i = (\mathbf{P}_{i-1}^{-1} + \mathbf{H}_i^T\mathbf{R}_i^{-1}\mathbf{H}_i)^{-1} \tag{8.16}$$

$$\mathbf{K}_i = \mathbf{P}_{i-1}\mathbf{H}_i^T(\mathbf{H}_i\mathbf{P}_{i-1}\mathbf{H}_i^T + \mathbf{R}_i)^{-1} = \mathbf{P}_i\mathbf{H}_i^T\mathbf{R}_i^{-1} \tag{8.17}$$

8.2.1.2 A linear state model and measurement equations

Definition

We go back to the more general case where the state model is linear and is given by equation (8.2). We now minimize the criterion C_N, which is given by

$$C_N = \frac{1}{2}(\mathbf{a}_0 - \mathbf{b}_0)^T\mathbf{M}_0^{-1}(\mathbf{a}_0 - \mathbf{b}_0) + \frac{1}{2}\Sigma_{i=0}^N(\mathbf{x}_i - \mathbf{H}_i\mathbf{a}_i)^T\mathbf{R}_i^{-1}(\mathbf{x}_i - \mathbf{H}_i\mathbf{a}_i)$$

$$+ \frac{1}{2}\Sigma_{i=0}^{N-1}\mathbf{w}_i^T\mathbf{Q}_i^{-1}\mathbf{w}_i \tag{8.18}$$

with respect to the sequence $\mathbf{a}_i$, $i = 0, \ldots, N$, subject to the constraints

$$\mathbf{a}_i = \mathbf{\Phi}_{i,i-1}\mathbf{a}_{i-1} + \mathbf{w}_{i-1} \quad \text{for } i = 1, \ldots, N$$

Matrixes $\mathbf{M}_0^{-1}$, $\mathbf{R}_i^{-1}$, $i = 0, \ldots, N$, and $\mathbf{Q}_i^{-1}$, $i = 0, \ldots, N - 1$ are symmetric and positive definite. As explained in the previous section, the matrices $\mathbf{R}_i^{-1}$ can be considered weights on the measurements. Similarly, the matrices $\mathbf{Q}_i^{-1}$ are weights on the errors of the state model (8.2), $\mathbf{b}_0$ is an initial estimate of the state $\mathbf{a}_0$, and $\mathbf{M}_0^{-1}$ is a weight on that estimate.

To shorten the formulas, we will adopt the notation

$$\mathbf{x}^T\mathbf{A}\mathbf{x} = \|\mathbf{x}\|_{\mathbf{A}}^2$$

This allows us to rewrite equation (8.18) as

$$C_N = \frac{1}{2}\|\mathbf{a}_0 - \mathbf{b}_0\|_{\mathbf{M}_0^{-1}}^2 + \frac{1}{2}\Sigma_{i=0}^N\|\mathbf{x}_i - \mathbf{H}_i\mathbf{a}_i\|_{\mathbf{R}_i^{-1}}^2 + \frac{1}{2}\Sigma_{i=0}^{N-1}\|\mathbf{w}_i\|_{\mathbf{Q}_i^{-1}}^2$$

One measurement   In order to obtain a recursive solution to this problem, we will consider the cost function after the first measurement has been obtained:

$$C_0 = \frac{1}{2}\|\mathbf{a}_0 - \mathbf{b}_0\|^2_{\mathbf{M}_0^{-1}} + \frac{1}{2}\|\mathbf{x}_0 - \mathbf{H}_0\mathbf{a}_0\|^2_{\mathbf{R}_0^{-1}} \qquad (8.19)$$

We will choose the value $\hat{\mathbf{a}}_0$ of $\mathbf{a}_0$ that minimizes C_0. It satisfies the condition

$$\frac{\partial C_0}{\partial \mathbf{a}_0}(\hat{\mathbf{a}}_0) = \mathbf{0} = \mathbf{M}_0^{-1}(\hat{\mathbf{a}}_0 - \mathbf{b}_0) - \mathbf{H}_0^T\mathbf{R}_0^{-1}(\mathbf{x}_0 - \mathbf{H}_0\hat{\mathbf{a}}_0)$$

Solving for $\hat{\mathbf{a}}_0$, we obtain

$$(\mathbf{M}_0^{-1} + \mathbf{H}_0^T\mathbf{R}_0^{-1}\mathbf{H}_0)\hat{\mathbf{a}}_0 = \mathbf{M}_0^{-1}\mathbf{b}_0 + \mathbf{H}_0^T\mathbf{R}_0^{-1}\mathbf{x}_0$$

or

$$\hat{\mathbf{a}}_0 = (\mathbf{M}_0^{-1} + \mathbf{H}_0^T\mathbf{R}_0^{-1}\mathbf{H}_0)^{-1}(\mathbf{M}_0^{-1}\mathbf{b}_0 + \mathbf{H}_0^T\mathbf{R}_0^{-1}\mathbf{x}_0) \qquad (8.20)$$

Thanks to the matrix inversion lemma, we can let

$$\mathbf{P}_0 = (\mathbf{M}_0^{-1} + \mathbf{H}_0^T\mathbf{R}_0^{-1}\mathbf{H}_0)^{-1} = \mathbf{M}_0 - \mathbf{M}_0\mathbf{H}_0^T(\mathbf{H}_0\mathbf{M}_0\mathbf{H}_0^T + \mathbf{R}_0)^{-1}\mathbf{H}_0\mathbf{M}_0 \qquad (8.21)$$

Using equation (8.21), equation (8.20) becomes

$$\hat{\mathbf{a}}_0 = \mathbf{b}_0 - \mathbf{M}_0\mathbf{H}_0^T(\mathbf{H}_0\mathbf{M}_0\mathbf{H}_0^T + \mathbf{R}_0)^{-1}\mathbf{H}_0\mathbf{b}_0 + \mathbf{P}_0\mathbf{H}_0^T\mathbf{R}_0^{-1}\mathbf{x}_0 \qquad (8.22)$$

Using equation (8.17) to define $\mathbf{K}_0$ (in which $\mathbf{P}_{-1} = \mathbf{M}_0$), we obtain

$$\hat{\mathbf{a}}_0 = \mathbf{b}_0 + \mathbf{K}_0(\mathbf{x}_0 - \mathbf{H}_0\mathbf{b}_0) \qquad (8.23)$$

Two measurements and generalization to an arbitrary stage   Now suppose there are two measurements. The cost function C_1 is given by

$$C_1 = \frac{1}{2}\|\mathbf{a}_0 - \mathbf{b}_0\|^2_{\mathbf{M}_0^{-1}} + \frac{1}{2}\Sigma_{i=0}^1\|\mathbf{x}_i - \mathbf{H}_i\mathbf{a}_i\|^2_{\mathbf{R}_i^{-1}} + \frac{1}{2}\|\mathbf{w}_0\|^2_{\mathbf{Q}_0^{-1}} \qquad (8.24)$$

in which $\mathbf{a}_1$, $\mathbf{a}_0$, and $\mathbf{w}_0$ are related by

$$\mathbf{a}_1 = \mathbf{\Phi}_{1,0}\mathbf{a}_0 + \mathbf{w}_0$$

Expanding the Taylor series of C_0 in the vicinity of $\hat{\mathbf{a}}_0$, we obtain

$$C_0 = \|\hat{\mathbf{a}}_0 - \mathbf{b}_0\|^2_{\mathbf{M}_0^{-1}} + \frac{1}{2}\|\mathbf{x}_0 - \mathbf{H}_0\hat{\mathbf{a}}_0\|^2_{\mathbf{R}_0^{-1}} + \frac{\partial C_0}{\partial \mathbf{a}_0}(\hat{\mathbf{a}}_0)(\mathbf{a}_0 - \hat{\mathbf{a}}_0)$$

$$+ \frac{1}{2}(\mathbf{a}_0 - \hat{\mathbf{a}}_0)^T \frac{\partial^2 C_0}{\partial \mathbf{a}_0^2}(\hat{\mathbf{a}}_0)(\mathbf{a}_0 - \hat{\mathbf{a}}_0)$$

which is exact since C_0 is a quadratic function of $\mathbf{a}_0$. But we know that $\frac{\partial C_0}{\partial \mathbf{a}_0}(\hat{\mathbf{a}}_0) = \mathbf{0}$, and it is easy to show that

$$\frac{\partial^2 C_0}{\partial \mathbf{a}_0^2} = \mathbf{P}_0^{-1}$$

So

$$C_0 = \|\hat{\mathbf{a}}_0 - \mathbf{b}_0\|^2_{\mathbf{M}_0^{-1}} + \|\mathbf{x}_0 - \mathbf{H}_0\hat{\mathbf{a}}_0\|^2_{\mathbf{R}_0^{-1}} + \frac{1}{2}\|\mathbf{a}_0 - \hat{\mathbf{a}}_0\|^2_{\mathbf{P}_0^{-1}} =$$

$$L_0 + \frac{1}{2}\|\mathbf{a}_0 - \hat{\mathbf{a}}_0\|^2_{\mathbf{P}_0^{-1}}$$

(8.25)

where L_0 is independent of $\mathbf{a}_0$.

We can now rewrite C_1 as follows:

$$C_1 = L_0 + \frac{1}{2}\|\mathbf{a}_0 - \hat{\mathbf{a}}_0\|^2_{\mathbf{P}_0^{-1}} + \frac{1}{2}\|\mathbf{x}_1 - \mathbf{H}_1\mathbf{a}_1\|^2_{\mathbf{R}_1^{-1}} + \frac{1}{2}\|\mathbf{w}_0\|^2_{\mathbf{Q}_0^{-1}}$$

By eliminating $\mathbf{a}_0$ through the state equation and assuming that the inverse of $\mathbf{\Phi}_{1,0}$ exists and is $\mathbf{\Phi}_{0,1}$, we obtain

$$C_1 = L_0 + \frac{1}{2}\|\mathbf{\Phi}_{0,1}(\mathbf{a}_1 - \mathbf{w}_0) - \hat{\mathbf{a}}_0\|^2_{\mathbf{P}_0^{-1}} + \frac{1}{2}\|\mathbf{x}_1 - \mathbf{H}_1\mathbf{a}_1\|^2_{\mathbf{R}_1^{-1}} + \frac{1}{2}\|\mathbf{w}_0\|^2_{\mathbf{Q}_0^{-1}}$$

Now we choose $\mathbf{w}_0$ to minimize C_1:

$$\frac{\partial C_1}{\partial \mathbf{w}_0} = \mathbf{0} = -\mathbf{\Phi}_{0,1}^T\mathbf{P}_0^{-1}(\mathbf{\Phi}_{0,1}(\mathbf{a}_1 - \mathbf{w}_0) - \hat{\mathbf{a}}_0) + \mathbf{Q}_0^{-1}\mathbf{w}_0$$

Solving for $\mathbf{w}_0$, we obtain

$$(\mathbf{Q}_0^{-1} + \mathbf{\Phi}_{0,1}^T\mathbf{P}_0^{-1}\mathbf{\Phi}_{0,1})\mathbf{w}_0 = \mathbf{\Phi}_{0,1}^T\mathbf{P}_0^{-1}(\mathbf{\Phi}_{0,1}\mathbf{a}_1 - \hat{\mathbf{a}}_0) = \mathbf{\Phi}_{0,1}^T\mathbf{P}_0^{-1}\mathbf{\Phi}_{0,1}(\mathbf{a}_1 - \mathbf{\Phi}_{1,0}\hat{\mathbf{a}}_0)$$

so that

$$\mathbf{\Phi}_{0,1}^T(\mathbf{\Phi}_{1,0}^T\mathbf{Q}_0^{-1}\mathbf{\Phi}_{1,0} + \mathbf{P}_0^{-1})\mathbf{\Phi}_{0,1}\mathbf{w}_0 = \mathbf{\Phi}_{0,1}^T\mathbf{P}_0^{-1}\mathbf{\Phi}_{0,1}(\mathbf{a}_1 - \mathbf{\Phi}_{1,0}\hat{\mathbf{a}}_0)$$

Solving for $\hat{\mathbf{w}}_0$, we have

$$\hat{\mathbf{w}}_0 = \boldsymbol{\Phi}_{1,0}(\boldsymbol{\Phi}_{1,0}^T\mathbf{Q}_0^{-1}\boldsymbol{\Phi}_{1,0} + \mathbf{P}_0^{-1})^{-1}\mathbf{P}_0^{-1}\boldsymbol{\Phi}_{0,1}(\mathbf{a}_1 - \boldsymbol{\Phi}_{1,0}\hat{\mathbf{a}}_0)$$

Applying the matrix inversion lemma again yields

$$(\boldsymbol{\Phi}_{1,0}^T\mathbf{Q}_0^{-1}\boldsymbol{\Phi}_{1,0} + \mathbf{P}_0^{-1})^{-1} = \mathbf{P}_0 - \mathbf{P}_0\boldsymbol{\Phi}_{1,0}^T(\mathbf{Q}_0 + \boldsymbol{\Phi}_{1,0}\mathbf{P}_0\boldsymbol{\Phi}_{1,0}^T)^{-1}\boldsymbol{\Phi}_{1,0}\mathbf{P}_0$$

and

$$\hat{\mathbf{w}}_0 = (\mathbf{I} - \boldsymbol{\Phi}_{1,0}\mathbf{P}_0\boldsymbol{\Phi}_{1,0}^T(\mathbf{Q}_0 + \boldsymbol{\Phi}_{1,0}\mathbf{P}_0\boldsymbol{\Phi}_{1,0}^T)^{-1})(\mathbf{a}_1 - \boldsymbol{\Phi}_{1,0}\hat{\mathbf{a}}_0) \qquad (8.26)$$

which is a fairly ugly expression. Now let

$$\mathbf{P}_1' = \mathbf{Q}_0 + \boldsymbol{\Phi}_{1,0}\mathbf{P}_0\boldsymbol{\Phi}_{1,0}^T$$

Notice that this implies that

$$\mathbf{I} - \boldsymbol{\Phi}_{1,0}\mathbf{P}_0\boldsymbol{\Phi}_{1,0}^T\mathbf{P}_1'^{-1} = \mathbf{Q}_0\mathbf{P}_1'^{-1} \qquad (8.27)$$

and therefore equation (8.26) can be written as

$$\hat{\mathbf{w}}_0 = \mathbf{Q}_0\mathbf{P}_1'^{-1}(\mathbf{a}_1 - \boldsymbol{\Phi}_{1,0}\hat{\mathbf{a}}_0) \qquad (8.28)$$

Now we perform a bit of algebraic manipulation for C_1 to obtain a form similar to that of equation (8.19):

$$\|\boldsymbol{\Phi}_{0,1}(\mathbf{a}_1 - \hat{\mathbf{w}}_0) - \hat{\mathbf{a}}_0\|^2_{\mathbf{P}_0^{-1}} = \|\mathbf{a}_1 - \hat{\mathbf{w}}_0 - \boldsymbol{\Phi}_{1,0}\hat{\mathbf{a}}_0\|^2_{\boldsymbol{\Phi}_{0,1}^T\mathbf{P}_0^{-1}\boldsymbol{\Phi}_{0,1}}$$

By replacing $\hat{\mathbf{w}}_0$ by its value obtained from equation (8.26), we obtain

$$\|\mathbf{a}_1 - \hat{\mathbf{w}}_0 - \boldsymbol{\Phi}_{1,0}\hat{\mathbf{a}}_0\|^2_{\boldsymbol{\Phi}_{0,1}^T\mathbf{P}_0^{-1}\boldsymbol{\Phi}_{0,1}}$$

$$= \|\mathbf{a}_1 - \boldsymbol{\Phi}_{1,0}\hat{\mathbf{a}}_0\|^2_{\mathbf{P}_1'^{-1}\boldsymbol{\Phi}_{1,0}\mathbf{P}_0\boldsymbol{\Phi}_{1,0}^T(\boldsymbol{\Phi}_{0,1}^T\mathbf{P}_0^{-1}\boldsymbol{\Phi}_{0,1})\boldsymbol{\Phi}_{1,0}\mathbf{P}_0\boldsymbol{\Phi}_{1,0}^T\mathbf{P}_1'^{-1}}$$

which is equal to

$$\|\mathbf{a}_1 - \boldsymbol{\Phi}_{1,0}\hat{\mathbf{a}}_0\|^2_{\mathbf{P}_1'^{-1}\boldsymbol{\Phi}_{1,0}\mathbf{P}_0\boldsymbol{\Phi}_{1,0}^T\mathbf{P}_1'^{-1}}$$

Now, because of equation (8.27),

$$\|\boldsymbol{\Phi}_{0,1}(\mathbf{a}_1 - \mathbf{w}_0) - \hat{\mathbf{a}}_0\|^2_{\mathbf{P}_0^{-1}} = \|\mathbf{a}_1 - \boldsymbol{\Phi}_{1,0}\hat{\mathbf{a}}_0\|^2_{(\mathbf{P}_1'^{-1} - \mathbf{P}_1'^{-1}\mathbf{Q}_0\mathbf{P}_1'^{-1})}$$

$$= \|\mathbf{a}_1 - \boldsymbol{\Phi}_{1,0}\hat{\mathbf{a}}_0\|^2_{\mathbf{P}_1'^{-1}} - \|\mathbf{a}_1 - \boldsymbol{\Phi}_{1,0}\hat{\mathbf{a}}_0\|^2_{\mathbf{P}_1'^{-1}\mathbf{Q}_0\mathbf{P}_1'^{-1}}$$

In addition, using equation (8.28), we have

$$\|\hat{\mathbf{w}}_0\|_{\mathbf{Q}_0^{-1}}^2 = \|\mathbf{a}_1 - \boldsymbol{\Phi}_{1,0}\hat{\mathbf{a}}_0\|_{\mathbf{P}_1'^{-1}\mathbf{Q}_0\mathbf{P}_1'^{-1}}^2$$

which leaves us with the equation

$$C_1 = L_0 + \frac{1}{2}\|\mathbf{a}_1 - \boldsymbol{\Phi}_{1,0}\hat{\mathbf{a}}_0\|_{\mathbf{P}_1'^{-1}}^2 + \frac{1}{2}\|\mathbf{x}_1 - \mathbf{H}_1\mathbf{a}_1\|_{\mathbf{R}_1^{-1}}^2 \tag{8.29}$$

This equation has essentially the same form as equation (8.19), since L_0 does not depend upon $\mathbf{a}_1$. Therefore it follows from equation (8.23) that

$$\hat{\mathbf{a}}_1 = \boldsymbol{\Phi}_{1,0}\hat{\mathbf{a}}_0 + \mathbf{K}_1(\mathbf{x}_1 - \mathbf{H}_1\boldsymbol{\Phi}_{1,0}\hat{\mathbf{a}}_0)$$

where

$$\mathbf{K}_1 = \mathbf{P}_1'\mathbf{H}_1^T(\mathbf{H}_1\mathbf{P}_1'\mathbf{H}_1^T + \mathbf{R}_1)^{-1}$$

Using the same techniques as those that led to equation (8.25), we obtain

$$C_1 = L_1 + \frac{1}{2}\|\mathbf{a}_1 - \hat{\mathbf{a}}_1\|_{\mathbf{P}_1^{-1}}^2 \tag{8.30}$$

where

$$\mathbf{P}_1^{-1} = (\mathbf{P}_1'^{-1} + \mathbf{H}_1^T\mathbf{R}_1\mathbf{H}_1)^{-1} = \frac{\partial^2 C_1}{\partial \mathbf{a}_1^2}$$

and L_1 is independent of $\mathbf{a}_1$. It follows that

$$\mathbf{P}_1 = \mathbf{P}_1' - \mathbf{K}_1\mathbf{H}_1\mathbf{P}_1'$$

The generalization to an arbitrary stage follows, and we obtain the famous Kalman equations :

$$\hat{\mathbf{a}}_i = \boldsymbol{\Phi}_{i,i-1}\hat{\mathbf{a}}_{i-1} + \mathbf{K}_i(\mathbf{x}_i - \mathbf{H}_i\boldsymbol{\Phi}_{i,i-1}\hat{\mathbf{a}}_{i-1}) \tag{8.31}$$

$$\mathbf{K}_i = \mathbf{P}_i'\mathbf{H}_i^T(\mathbf{H}_i\mathbf{P}_i'\mathbf{H}_i^T + \mathbf{R}_i)^{-1} \tag{8.32}$$

$$\mathbf{P}_i' = \boldsymbol{\Phi}_{i,i-1}\mathbf{P}_{i-1}\boldsymbol{\Phi}_{i,i-1}^T + \mathbf{Q}_{i-1} \tag{8.33}$$

$$\mathbf{P}_i = \mathbf{P}_i' - \mathbf{K}_i\mathbf{H}_i\mathbf{P}_i' \tag{8.34}$$

These equations allow us to sequentially compute the best set of state estimates starting from $i = 1$. State $\hat{\mathbf{a}}_0$ is defined by equation (8.23). These equations are precisely the answer to our question. Equation (8.31) tells us how to compute the best state estimate, $\hat{\mathbf{a}}_i$, after i measurements have been made, from the previous state $\hat{\mathbf{a}}_{i-1}$, the ith measurement $\mathbf{x}_i$, the measurement matrix $\mathbf{H}_i$, and the matrix $\mathbf{K}_i$. Equations (8.32)-(8.34) tell us how to compute matrix $\mathbf{K}_i$, sometimes called the *Kalman gain*. Note that, in order to compute the Kalman gain, we have to invert an $m \times m$ matrix instead of an $n \times n$ matrix in the nonrecursive case. In practice, m is often less than n.

An interpretation of matrices $\mathbf{P}_i$ and $\mathbf{P}'_i$ There is an interesting interpretation of the matrices $\mathbf{P}_i$ and $\mathbf{P}'_i$. Equation (8.30) can be generalized to an arbitrary stage and written as

$$C_i = L_i + \frac{1}{2}\|\mathbf{a}_i - \hat{\mathbf{a}}_i\|^2_{\mathbf{P}_i^{-1}}$$

where L_i is independent of $\mathbf{a}_i$. Thus, once $\hat{\mathbf{a}}_0,\ldots,\hat{\mathbf{a}}_{i-1}$ have been determined, the value of criterion C_i is bounded by $\frac{1}{2}\|\mathbf{a}_i - \hat{\mathbf{a}}_i\|^2_{\mathbf{P}_i^{-1}}$. Consider the set of the $\mathbf{a}_i$ defined by

$$\|\mathbf{a}_i - \hat{\mathbf{a}}_i\|^2_{\mathbf{P}_i^{-1}} \leq 1$$

This set is the inside of the ellipsoid discussed in section 5.6, and we know that for those $\mathbf{a}_i$'s we have

$$(\mathbf{x}^T(\mathbf{a}_i - \hat{\mathbf{a}}_i))^2 \leq \mathbf{x}^T\mathbf{P}_i\mathbf{x} \qquad \forall \mathbf{x} \in R^n$$

Therefore, matrix $\mathbf{P}_i$ gives the bounds on the $\mathbf{a}_i - \hat{\mathbf{a}}_i$'s such that the error C_i is not more than half its minimum value L_i.

If we now look at equation (8.31), we see that $\mathbf{\Phi}_{i,i-1}\hat{\mathbf{a}}_{i-1}$ can be considered the best prediction of the new state $\hat{\mathbf{a}}_i$ after i measurements have been made and before the $(i + 1)$ first one has been performed. According to equation (8.29) and its generalization to stage $i + 1$:

$$C_i = L_{i-1} + \frac{1}{2}\|\mathbf{a}_i - \mathbf{\Phi}_{i,i-1}\hat{\mathbf{a}}_{i-1}\|^2_{\mathbf{P}_i'^{-1}} + \frac{1}{2}\|\mathbf{x}_i - \mathbf{H}_i\mathbf{a}_i\|^2_{\mathbf{R}_i^{-1}}$$

Matrix $\mathbf{P}'_i$ can be considered to define a bound on $\mathbf{a}_i - \mathbf{\Phi}_{i,i-1}\hat{\mathbf{a}}_{i-1}$. This property is used in sections 8.3 and 8.4 to restrict the number of potential matches in tracking applications.

8.2.2 Kalman filtering

Most of what has been said in the case of deterministic least-squares carries over to the case where the measurements $\mathbf{x}_i$ are distorted by random noise. More specifically, let us assume the fairly general case in which the state evolves according to

$$\mathbf{a}_i = \mathbf{g}_i(\mathbf{a}_{i-1}, \mathbf{w}_{i-1}) \tag{8.35}$$

The state has an initial state $\mathbf{a}_0$, which is a random variable with a known probability density function, say $p(\mathbf{a}_0)$. The term $\mathbf{w}_{i-1}$ represents a sample of a random sequence with a known probability density function. We assume that the $\mathbf{w}_i$ are independent and constitute a *white-noise sequence*:

$$p(\mathbf{w}_0, \mathbf{w}_1, \ldots, \mathbf{w}_i) = p(\mathbf{w}_0)p(\mathbf{w}_1) \ldots p(\mathbf{w}_i)$$

The state is observed through the measurement equation

$$\mathbf{f}_i(\mathbf{x}_i, \mathbf{a}_i, \mathbf{v}_i) = \mathbf{0} \tag{8.36}$$

where the $\mathbf{v}_i$ are a white-noise sequence for which the probability density function is known:

$$p(\mathbf{v}_0, \mathbf{v}_1, \ldots, \mathbf{v}_i) = p(\mathbf{v}_0)p(\mathbf{v}_1) \ldots p(\mathbf{v}_i)$$

The problem is then to estimate $\mathbf{a}_i$ from the measurements $\mathbf{x}_i$. If $\hat{\mathbf{a}}_i$ is some estimator of $\mathbf{a}_i$, the error committed by this estimator is

$$\mathbf{e}_i = \mathbf{a}_i - \hat{\mathbf{a}}_i$$

If we define the cost function[2]

$$L(\mathbf{e}_i) = E(\mathbf{e}_i^T \mathbf{e}_i)$$

then it can be shown that the first moment[3] of the *a posteriori* density function $p(\mathbf{a}_i \mid \mathbf{x}^i)$ minimizes this cost function. This is called the *minimum variance* estimate of $\mathbf{a}_i$. We can even show that this is true of the following classes of criteria [May79, volume 1, p.232]:

---

2. *E* denotes the expected value.

3. $\hat{\mathbf{a}}_i = \int \mathbf{a}_i p(\mathbf{a}_i \mid \mathbf{x}^i) d\mathbf{a}_i$.

$$L(\mathbf{e}_i) = E(\mathbf{e}_i^T \mathbf{M}_i \mathbf{e}_i)$$
$$L(\mathbf{e}_i) = E(C(\mathbf{e}_i))$$

where $\mathbf{M}_i$ is an arbitrary symmetric positive semi-definite matrix, and $C(.)$ is symmetric and nondecreasing:

$$C(\mathbf{0}) = 0$$
$$C(\mathbf{e}) = C(-\mathbf{e})$$
$$C(\mathbf{e}_1) \geq C(\mathbf{e}_2) \text{ if } \|\mathbf{e}_1\| \geq \|\mathbf{e}_2\|$$

This result is therefore quite general, but in practice the probability density function $p(\mathbf{a}_i \mid \mathbf{x}^i)$ is unknown and difficult to estimate except in the following case.

8.2.2.1 *Linear Gaussian systems*

We will now restrict ourselves to the case of linear Gaussian systems where the plant and measurement equations (8.35) and (8.36) are linear:

$$\mathbf{a}_i = \mathbf{\Phi}_{i,i-1}\mathbf{a}_{i-1} + \mathbf{w}_{i-1}$$

$$\mathbf{x}_i = \mathbf{H}_i\mathbf{a}_i + \mathbf{v}_i$$

The initial state is a Gaussian random variable with density function

$$p(\mathbf{a}_0) = k_0 \exp(-\frac{1}{2}(\mathbf{a}_0 - \mathbf{b}_0)^T \mathbf{M}_0^{-1}(\mathbf{a}_0 - \mathbf{b}_0))$$

We will also assume that $\mathbf{w}_i$ and $\mathbf{v}_i$ have Gaussian distributions

$$p(\mathbf{w}_i) = k_w \exp(-\frac{1}{2}\mathbf{w}_i^T \mathbf{Q}_i^{-1}\mathbf{w}_i)$$

$$p(\mathbf{v}_i) = k_v \exp(-\frac{1}{2}\mathbf{v}_i^T \mathbf{R}_i^{-1}\mathbf{v}_i)$$

For this linear Gaussian system, the *a posteriori* density function is characterized by the following properties:

1. The *a posteriori* density $p(\mathbf{a}_i \mid \mathbf{x}^i)$ is Gaussian:

    $$p(\mathbf{a}_i \mid \mathbf{x}^i) = [(2\pi)^n \mid \mathbf{P}_i \mid]^{-\frac{1}{2}} \exp(-\frac{1}{2}(\mathbf{a}_i - \hat{\mathbf{a}}_i)^T \mathbf{P}_i^{-1}(\mathbf{a}_i - \hat{\mathbf{a}}_i))$$

    where $\mid \mathbf{P}_i \mid$ is the determinant of matrix $\mathbf{P}_i$.

2. The mean value $\hat{\mathbf{a}}_i$ is given by

   $$\hat{\mathbf{a}}_i = \hat{\mathbf{a}}_i' + \mathbf{K}_i(\mathbf{x}_i - \mathbf{H}_i\hat{\mathbf{a}}_i')$$

   The value $\hat{\mathbf{a}}_i'$ is the mean value of the prediction density $p(\mathbf{a}_i \mid \mathbf{x}^{i-1})$ and is given by

   $$\hat{\mathbf{a}}_i' = E(\mathbf{a}_i \mid \mathbf{x}^{i-1}) = \int \mathbf{a}_i p(\mathbf{a}_i \mid \mathbf{x}^{i-1}) d\mathbf{a}_i = \mathbf{\Phi}_{i,i-1}\hat{\mathbf{a}}_{i-1}$$

3. The prediction density $p(\mathbf{a}_i \mid \mathbf{x}^{i-1})$, which is the probability density of the state given that i measurements have been performed, is also Gaussian, with covariance $\mathbf{P}_i'$:

   $$\mathbf{P}_i' = E((\mathbf{a}_i - \mathbf{a}_i')^T(\mathbf{a}_i - \mathbf{a}_i') \mid \mathbf{x}^{i-1}) = \mathbf{\Phi}_{i,i-1}\mathbf{P}_{i-1}\mathbf{\Phi}_{i,i-1}^T + \mathbf{Q}_{i-1}$$

4. $\mathbf{K}_i$ is a gain matrix defined by

   $$\mathbf{K}_i = \mathbf{P}_i'\mathbf{H}_i^T(\mathbf{H}_i\mathbf{P}_i'\mathbf{H}_i^T + \mathbf{R}_i)^{-1}$$

5. The covariance matrix $\mathbf{P}_i$ of $p(\mathbf{a}_i \mid \mathbf{x}^i)$ is given by

   $$\mathbf{P}_i = E((\mathbf{a}_i - \hat{\mathbf{a}}_i)^T(\mathbf{a}_i - \hat{\mathbf{a}}_i) \mid \mathbf{x}^i) = \mathbf{P}_i' - \mathbf{K}_i\mathbf{H}_i\mathbf{P}_i'$$

6. If we assume that the first measurement occurs at 0, we have

   $$\hat{\mathbf{a}}_0 = \mathbf{b}_0 + \mathbf{K}_0(\mathbf{x}_0 - \mathbf{H}_0\mathbf{b}_0)$$

   $$\mathbf{K}_0 = \mathbf{M}_0\mathbf{H}_0^T(\mathbf{H}_0\mathbf{M}_0\mathbf{H}_0^T + \mathbf{R}_0)$$

   $$\mathbf{P}_0 = \mathbf{M}_0 - \mathbf{K}_0\mathbf{H}_0\mathbf{M}_0$$

It is remarkable to note that the equations that describe the evolution of the mean and covariance matrix of the minimum variance estimator in the case of linear Gaussian systems are identical to those obtained in the recursive solution of the deterministic least-squares problem for a linear state model and measurement equations.

This analysis provides a probabilistic interpretation of equations (8.31)–(8.34). In particular, note the interpretation of matrices $\mathbf{P}_i'$ and $\mathbf{P}_i$ in terms of the covariance matrix of the state $\mathbf{a}_i$, given the i ($i + 1$, respectively) first measurements. Also note the interpretation of $\mathbf{\Phi}_{i,i-1}\hat{\mathbf{a}}_{i-1}$ as the mean value of the prediction density, i.e., the density of the state, given the first i measurements. In practice, $\mathbf{\Phi}_{i,i-1}\hat{\mathbf{a}}_{i-1}$ is used to predict the state of the system before the $(i+1)$st measurement has been performed, and $\mathbf{P}'_i$ is used to restrict the number of potential matches in tracking applications such as those described in later sections.

8.2.2.2   *How important is the Gaussian assumption?*

Since in practice the Gaussian assumption is usually difficult to justify, it is worthwhile to ask how important this assumption is for the previous results to hold. If we restrict ourselves to estimators of the state that are linear functions of the measurements $\mathbf{x}^i$, then the Gaussian assumption is unnecessary. More precisely, we have the following proposition (see appendix 7A of the book by Jazwinski [Jaz70]):

Proposition 8.1
The minimum variance estimate in the Gaussian case, defined by properties 1-6 of the previous section, is also the linear minimum variance estimator in the general case, without any assumption of Gaussianness.

This proposition says that, if the state is estimated as a linear function of the measurements, then the estimator developed for the Gaussian case is the best one in that class even if the Gaussian assumption is not satisfied. Note that we still require that the sequences $\mathbf{v}_i$ and $\mathbf{w}_i$ be white and that there may exist nonlinear estimators with a smaller variance than that of the linear estimator.

8.2.2.3   *Dealing with the nonlinear case: the extended Kalman filter*

In our applications we often deal with the case where the state equation is linear but the measurement equations are not. Let us go back to equation (8.36) and assume additive noise:

$$\mathbf{f}_i(\mathbf{x}_i, \mathbf{a}_i, \mathbf{v}_i) \equiv \mathbf{f}_i(\mathbf{x}_i + \mathbf{v}_i, \mathbf{a}_i) = \mathbf{0}$$

The first-order Taylor series expansion in the vicinity of $(\mathbf{x}_i, \mathbf{\Phi}_{i,i-1}\hat{\mathbf{a}}_{i-1})$ is

$$\mathbf{f}_i(\mathbf{x}_i + \mathbf{v}_i, \mathbf{a}_i) = 0 = \mathbf{f}_i(\mathbf{x}_i, \Phi_{i,i-1}\hat{\mathbf{a}}_{i-1}) + \frac{\partial \mathbf{f}_i}{\partial \mathbf{x}_i} \cdot \mathbf{v}_i + \frac{\partial \mathbf{f}_i}{\partial \mathbf{a}_i} \cdot (\mathbf{a}_i - \Phi_{i,i-1}\hat{\mathbf{a}}_{i-1}) \quad (8.37)$$

where all partial derivatives are evaluated at $(\mathbf{x}_i, \Phi_{i,i-1}\hat{\mathbf{a}}_{i-1})$. This equation can be rewritten as a linear measurement equation $\mathbf{x}'_i = \mathbf{H}_i \mathbf{a}_i + \mathbf{v}'_i$ with

$$\mathbf{x}'_i = \frac{\partial \mathbf{f}_i}{\partial \mathbf{a}_i} \Phi_{i,i-1}\hat{\mathbf{a}}_{i-1} - \mathbf{f}_i$$

$$\mathbf{H}_i = \frac{\partial \mathbf{f}_i}{\partial \mathbf{a}_i} \tag{8.38}$$

$$\mathbf{v}'_i = \frac{\partial \mathbf{f}_i}{\partial \mathbf{x}_i} \mathbf{v}_i$$

The variable $\mathbf{v}'_i$ is also a zero-mean Gaussian random variable with covariance matrix $\frac{\partial \mathbf{f}_i}{\partial \mathbf{x}_i} \mathbf{R}_i \frac{\partial \mathbf{f}_i}{\partial \mathbf{x}_i}^T$. Therefore, by *linearizing* the $(i + 1)$st measurement equation in the vicinity of the $(i + 1)$st measurement and the predicted state after the first i measurements, we end up in a situation where all the previous results for the linear case can be applied. The price we have to pay for this simplification is that we cannot prove either optimality or even convergence: The estimator that we build may diverge! We are nonetheless going to use this technique in the next sections because it is very efficient and robust in practice and does not suffer from the problems that in theory may occur.

8.2.2.4 *Choosing a measurement equation*

In all the examples we study in this chapter and in chapter 11, the measurement equation $\mathbf{f}_i$ will not be given, but rather we will have a number of "possible" measurement equations $(\mathbf{f}_i^1, \mathbf{f}_i^2, \ldots, \mathbf{f}_i^q)$. We would like to order them so as to choose from them a few best. To do this, we use the expansion (8.37), which shows that, up to the first order, $\mathbf{f}_i(\mathbf{x}_i, \Phi_{i,i-1}\hat{\mathbf{a}}_{i-1})$ is a zero-mean Gaussian random variable with covariance matrix

$$\Lambda_i = \frac{\partial \mathbf{f}_i}{\partial \mathbf{a}_i} \mathbf{P}'_i \frac{\partial \mathbf{f}_i}{\partial \mathbf{a}_i}^T + \frac{\partial \mathbf{f}_i}{\partial \mathbf{x}_i} \mathbf{R}_i \frac{\partial \mathbf{f}_i}{\partial \mathbf{x}_i}^T \tag{8.39}$$

We will now introduce the so-called *Mahalanobis distance:*

$$d_i(\mathbf{x}_i, \mathbf{\Phi}_{i,i-1}\hat{\mathbf{a}}_{i-1}) = \mathbf{f}_i(\mathbf{x}_i, \mathbf{\Phi}_{i,i-1}\hat{\mathbf{a}}_{i-1})^T \Lambda_i^{-1} \mathbf{f}_i(\mathbf{x}_i, \mathbf{\Phi}_{i,i-1}\hat{\mathbf{a}}_{i-1}) \qquad (8.40)$$

This is a random variable which, up to the first order, is a χ^2 with p_i degrees of freedom (p_i is the dimension of Λ_i). We thus have q random variables with known distributions and can look up in statistical tables confidence thresholds (which depend on the value p_i) such that the probability that d_i is less than the threshold is, for example, 95 percent. The plausible measurement equations are then those for which the distance d_i^j is less than the threshold. This result is used heavily in sections 8.3 and 8.4.

8.3   Two-dimensional token tracking

As a first application of the tools developed in the previous sections, we will study the problem of *tracking* tokens in a sequence of images. To be concrete, these tokens will be line segments that have been extracted by the processes we have described in chapter 4. By *tracking* we mean the ability to identify a given segment in an image as the same one as another segment in the previous image. Underlying all this is the assumption that both segments are the projections in the image of the same physical segment in the scene. If we assume that the motion of the segments is due only to the motion of the camera, as in chapter 7, the tracking will provide us with matches from which the parameters of the motion can be determined using the techniques developed in that chapter. This idea is explained in figure 8.1, where the matches between segments at times t, $t + n\Delta t$, and $t + m\Delta t$ can be used to compute the rigid motion of the camera between these time instants and to reconstruct depth, up to a scale factor, for those segments that have been matched. But note that the assumption that the motion of the segments is due only to the motion of the camera is not necessary for the tracking. According to the analysis of the previous section, we must now choose the state and determine the plant equation and the measurement equations for this specific problem.

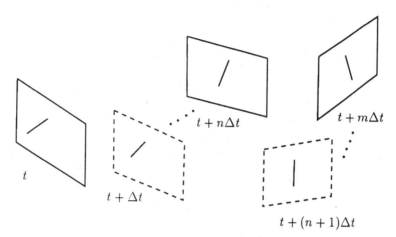

Figure 8.1   Tracking tokens provides matches.

8.3.1   Choosing a representation of two-dimensional line segments

In chapter 5 we studied a representation of 2-D lines by two numbers (a, b) such that the equation of the line is $x + ay + b = 0$ or $ax + y + b = 0$ depending upon which of the two maps, φ_1 or φ_2, we are using. In φ_1 the lines parallel to the x-axis cannot be represented, and in φ_2 the lines parallel to the y-axis cannot be represented. Problem 6 of the same chapter shows how to compute the weight (covariance) matrix of the endpoints m_1 and m_2 of the segment (a 4×4 matrix).

One possible representation of a line segment is therefore the four-dimensional vector $[\mathbf{m}_1^T, \mathbf{m}_2^T]^T$. This assumes that segments are oriented (otherwise $[\mathbf{m}_1^T, \mathbf{m}_2^T]^T$ represents the same segment as $[\mathbf{m}_2^T, \mathbf{m}_1^T]^T$). If they are not, we can use the direction, midpoint, and length representation, expressed as the vector $[a, b, y, l]^T$, where y is the ordinate of the midpoint and l the length of the segment. This is for the map φ_1. For φ_2 we would use $[a, b, x, l]^T$, where x is the abscissa of the midpoint. Of course, weight (covariance) matrices for these representations can also be computed up to the first order using the techniques of chapter 5. In what follows we denote by $\mathbf{r}$ the representation vector chosen and by $\mathbf{R}$ the corresponding covariance matrix.

8.3.2   The plant and measurement equations

We define the state of the segment as the vector

$$\mathbf{a} = \begin{bmatrix} \mathbf{r} \\ \dot{\mathbf{r}} \\ \ddot{\mathbf{r}} \end{bmatrix} \tag{8.41}$$

This vector is, in general, a twelve-dimensional vector.[4] The components $\dot{\mathbf{r}}$ and $\ddot{\mathbf{r}}$ are the first- and second-order time derivatives of the vector $\mathbf{r}$. The plant equation is simply

$$\mathbf{a}_i = \mathbf{\Phi}_{i,i-1}\mathbf{a}_{i-1} + \mathbf{w}_i$$

where matrix $\mathbf{\Phi}_{i,i-1}$ is

$$\mathbf{\Phi}_{i,i-1} = \begin{bmatrix} \mathbf{I}_4 & \mathbf{I}_4\Delta t & \frac{1}{2}\mathbf{I}_4(\Delta t)^2 \\ \mathbf{0}_4 & \mathbf{I}_4 & \mathbf{I}_4\Delta t \\ \mathbf{0}_4 & \mathbf{0}_4 & \mathbf{I}_4 \end{bmatrix}$$

$\mathbf{I}_4$ is the 4×4 identity matrix. This equation simply means that we assume that the kinematics of the segment representation have a constant acceleration. Simpler (constant-velocity) or more complicated kinematic models could be considered. The equation $\mathbf{w}_i$ represents the error in the modeling.

Let S_0 be a segment represented by $\mathbf{r}_0$ at time i, and let its state be $\mathbf{a}$. We predict its representation at time $i + 1$ to be

$$\mathbf{r}'_0 = [\mathbf{I}_4\ \mathbf{I}_4\Delta t\ \frac{1}{2}\mathbf{I}_4(\Delta t)^2]\mathbf{a} = \mathbf{Ha}$$

A measurement is the identification of the "virtual" or "predicted" segment represented by $\mathbf{r}'_0$ with a real segment S_1 at time $i + 1$, which is represented by $\mathbf{r}_1$. The measurement vector is thus $\mathbf{x} = \mathbf{r}_1$, and the measurement equation is

$$\mathbf{x} = \mathbf{r}_1 = \mathbf{r}'_0 = \mathbf{Ha} + \mathbf{v}$$

---

4. When the $[a,b,x,l]^T$ or $[a,b,y,l]^T$ representation is used, sometimes the length is ignored and the state becomes nine-dimensional.

The measurement error is represented by $\mathbf{v}$. To finish our modeling, we must define the weight (covariance) matrices $\mathbf{Q}_i$ and $\mathbf{R}_i$. $\mathbf{R}_i$ is related to our representation of line segments, and we have discussed in section 8.3.1 how to choose it. Matrixes $\mathbf{Q}_i$ are chosen by the user. We are therefore in exactly the case of linear plant and measurement equations, studied in section 8.2.1.2, and we can apply the results obtained there in a straightforward manner.

8.3.3   Running the process

Let us now see how all this can be used to track a segment in a sequence of images.

8.3.3.1   *Initialization*

At time 0 we consider a segment S represented by $\mathbf{r}_0$ with the state vector $\mathbf{b}_0$ and weight matrix $\mathbf{M}_0$. The choice of $\mathbf{b}_0$ and $\mathbf{M}_0$ depends upon the *a priori* information. In practice, when nothing is known one often takes $\mathbf{b}_0 = [\mathbf{r}_0^T, \mathbf{0}, \mathbf{0}]^T$, that is, we consider that S is not moving, and that

$$
\mathbf{M}_0 = \begin{bmatrix} \mathbf{R}_0 & \mathbf{0} & & \\ & \lambda_1^2 & & \\ \mathbf{0} & & \ddots & \\ & & & \lambda_8^2 \end{bmatrix}
$$

The diagonal elements λ_i^2 are fairly big, reflecting the fact that we know nothing about the kinematics of the segment. $\mathbf{R}_0$ is the bound on the representation $\mathbf{r}_0$.

We use the analysis of section 8.2.2.4 to determine the candidate segments at time 1. If S_i is the ith segment at time 1 represented by $(\mathbf{r}_1^i, \mathbf{R}_1^i)$, we consider the "possible" measurement equations

$$\mathbf{r}_1^i - \mathbf{H}\mathbf{b}_0 = \mathbf{0}$$

Following the analysis of section 8.2.2.4, we compute the covariance matrices

$$\Lambda_0^i = \mathbf{H}\mathbf{M}_0\mathbf{H}^T + \mathbf{R}_1^i$$

and the Mahalanobis distances

$$d_0^i = (\mathbf{r}_1^i - \mathbf{H}\mathbf{b}_0)^T (\Lambda_0^i)^{-1} (\mathbf{r}_1^i - \mathbf{H}\mathbf{b}_0)$$

for all segments in the image at time 1. Those segments whose distances are smaller than a fixed threshold are kept as matches. Each match defines a token, and we can update the state using equation (8.23) as follows:

$$\hat{\mathbf{a}}_0^i = \mathbf{b}_0 + \mathbf{K}_0^i (\mathbf{r}_1^i - \mathbf{H}\mathbf{b}_0)$$

in which

$$\mathbf{K}_0^i = \mathbf{M}_0 \mathbf{H} (\mathbf{H}\mathbf{M}_0\mathbf{H}^T + \mathbf{R}_1^i)^{-1}$$

The bound on $\hat{\mathbf{a}}_0^i$ is defined by

$$\mathbf{P}_0^i = (\mathbf{M}_0^{-1} + \mathbf{H}^T (\mathbf{R}_1^i)^{-1} \mathbf{H})^{-1}$$

8.3.3.2 Continuous processing

The continuous processing is not very different from the initialization. We do the reasoning at time 2, but the generalization to an arbitrary stage follows. Let S be a token at time 1 represented by $(\mathbf{r}_1, \mathbf{R}_1)$, whose state is $\hat{\mathbf{a}}_0$ with weight $\mathbf{P}_0$. First we make a prediction by computing the state $\hat{\mathbf{a}}_1' = \mathbf{\Phi}_{1,0}\hat{\mathbf{a}}_0$ and its weight $\mathbf{P}_1'$ (using equation (8.33)). Then we determine the candidate segments at time 2 as follows.

If S_i is the ith segment detected in the image at time 2, represented by $(\mathbf{r}_2^i, \mathbf{R}_2^i)$, we consider the "possible" measurement equations

$$\mathbf{r}_2^i - \mathbf{H}\hat{\mathbf{a}}_1' = \mathbf{0}$$

We compute the covariance matrices

$$\Lambda_1^i = \mathbf{H}\mathbf{P}_1'\mathbf{H}^T + \mathbf{R}_2^i$$

and then the Mahalanobis distances

$$d_1^i = (\mathbf{r}_2^i - \mathbf{H}\hat{\mathbf{a}}_1')^T (\Lambda_1^i)^{-1} (\mathbf{r}_2^i - \mathbf{H}\hat{\mathbf{a}}_1')$$

for all segments in the image at time 2. Those segments whose distances are smaller than a fixed threshold are kept as matches. Each match provides an updating of the state using equations (8.31)–(8.34)

$$\hat{\mathbf{a}}_1^i = \hat{\mathbf{a}}_1' + \mathbf{K}_1^i (\mathbf{r}_2^i - \mathbf{H}\hat{\mathbf{a}}_1')$$

where

$$\mathbf{K}_1^i = \mathbf{P}_1' \mathbf{H}^T (\mathbf{H}\mathbf{P}_1' \mathbf{H}^T + \mathbf{R}_2^i)^{-1}$$

The weight of the new state is given by

$$\mathbf{P}_1^i = \mathbf{P}_1' - \mathbf{K}_1^i \mathbf{H}\mathbf{P}_1'$$

8.3.3.3 *Several matches*

Retaining several matches is possible and often desirable, especially in the case where the diagonal elements of the weight (covariance) matrices are big. In that case there may be several good candidates to the match, and the best one may not always be the right one. Keeping several candidates increases the probability of having the right match, as the wrong matches will not find further matches at the next time instants because they provide wrong estimates of the kinematics. Therefore we need a mechanism, a memory, to keep track of the number of times a given token has found matches in the past. A token that has not found matches for some time should disappear. Even though this has not been implemented in the instantiation of the two-dimensional token tracker described in the article by Deriche and Faugeras [DF90], it should be easy to do. On the other hand, it has been implemented in the case of the three-dimensional tracker, which we will describe in section 8.4.

8.3.4 An example

We will show an example of a sequence of frames taken by one camera mounted on a mobile robot moving down a hallway (see figures 8.2 and 8.3). The segments that are tracked by the algorithm are overlaid on the images together with their internal numbers. When two segments have the same number in two different frames, it is because the tracker thinks they are the same segment at different time instants. We will show eight different frames.

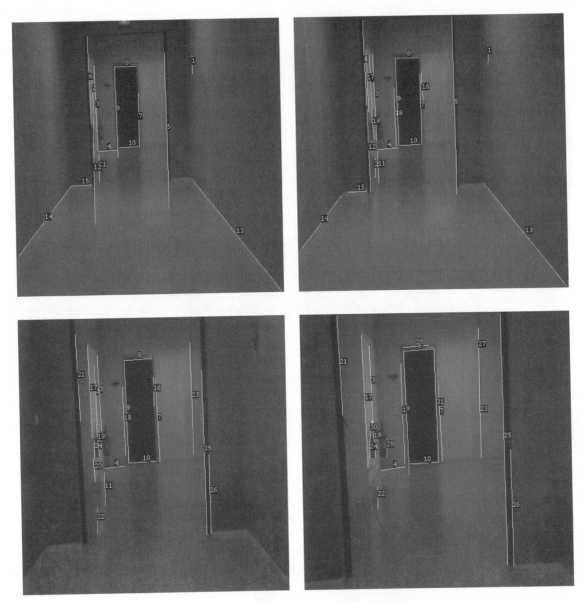

Figure 8.2   The first four frames of the hallway scene.

Figure 8.3   The last four frames of the hallway scene.

8.4   Three-dimensional token tracking

As a second application of the tools developed in the beginning of this chapter, we will now study the problem of tracking tokens in three dimensions. We will assume that we have a sequence of stereo frames from which we will compute, using the algorithms described in chapter 6, a sequence of three-dimensional frames. To be concrete, these three-dimensional frames will consist of sets of three-dimensional line segments. By *tracking* we mean the ability to follow the motion of a given segment and to estimate its kinematics. Since much more information is available than in the previous two-dimensional example, we may expect to be able to solve much more difficult problems. Indeed, we will directly estimate the three-dimensional kinematics of the line segments and will be able to cope with the problem of multiple-object motion. This three-dimensional tracker has been developed by Zhengyou Zhang as part of his Ph.D. work [Zha90]. Just as we have done previously, we must now choose the state and determine the plant and the measurement equations.

8.4.1   A bit of kinematics

We know from elementary kinematics that the motions of the points of a moving rigid body are conveniently described by a six-dimensional entity called a *screw*, which is defined at every point P of space and noted $S(P) = (\Omega, \mathbf{V}(P))$. Ω is called the *angular velocity*, and $\mathbf{V}(P)$ is the *velocity of the point* of the solid in motion coinciding with P. The kinematic screw at one point entirely describes the motion of the solid since, at every point M, the velocity of the point of the solid coinciding with M is given by

$$\mathbf{V}(M) = \mathbf{V}(P) + \Omega \wedge \mathbf{PM} \tag{8.42}$$

Letting P be at the origin O of our coordinate system, we write $\mathbf{V}(P) = \mathbf{V}$, $\mathbf{OM} = \mathbf{M}$, $\mathbf{V}(M) = \dot{\mathbf{M}}$ and rewrite equation (8.42) as

$$\dot{\mathbf{M}} = \mathbf{V} + \Omega \wedge \mathbf{M} \tag{8.43}$$

If we assume that $\mathbf{V}$ and Ω are known functions of time, then equation

(8.43) appears as a first-order linear differential equation in **M**. No closed form solution, in general, exists for this equation, except when Ω is not a function of time (motion with constant angular velocity), in which case the solution is given by

$$\mathbf{M}(t) = e^{(t-t_0)\tilde{\Omega}}\mathbf{M}(t_0) + \int_{t_0}^{t} e^{(t-s)\tilde{\Omega}}\mathbf{V}(s)ds \tag{8.44}$$

where $\tilde{\Omega}$ is the antisymmetric matrix representing the cross-product with Ω ($\tilde{\Omega}\mathbf{x} = \Omega \wedge \mathbf{x}$). Thus, according to section 5.5.4, $e^{(t-t_0)\tilde{\Omega}}$ and $e^{(t-s)\tilde{\Omega}}$ are rotation matrices.

We can obtain slightly more detailed results that are useful in practice by making assumptions about the functional form of $\mathbf{V}(s)$. For example, we may assume that it is a polynomial in s:

$$\mathbf{V}(s) = \sum_{i=0}^{n} \mathbf{V}_i s^i$$

Using Rodrigues' equation (5.26) we can write

$$e^{(t-s)\tilde{\Omega}} = \mathbf{I} + \frac{\sin((t-s)\|\Omega\|)}{\|\Omega\|}\tilde{\Omega} + \frac{1 - \cos((t-s)\|\Omega\|)}{\|\Omega\|^2}\tilde{\Omega}^2$$

From this it is clear that, in order to compute the integral $\int_{t_0}^{t} e^{(t-s)\tilde{\Omega}}\mathbf{V}(s)\,ds$, which appears in equation (8.44), we need to compute the integrals

$$L_i = \int_{t_0}^{t} s^i \sin((t-s)\|\Omega\|)ds$$

$$M_i = \int_{t_0}^{t} s^i \cos((t-s)\|\Omega\|)ds$$

It is simple to show that this can be done in closed form (see problem 4). For the special cases $n = 0, 1$ (constant velocity and constant acceleration) we have the following result:

Proposition 8.2
When $\mathbf{V}(s) = \mathbf{V} + s\mathbf{A}$, the trajectory of the point M is given by

$$\mathbf{M}(t) = \mathbf{U}_0\mathbf{M}(t_0) + \mathbf{U}_1\mathbf{V} + \mathbf{U}_2\mathbf{A} \tag{8.45}$$

with the following values for the matrices $\mathbf{U}_i$, $i = 0, 1, 2$

$$\mathbf{U}_0 = \mathbf{I} + \frac{\sin((t - t_0)\|\Omega\|)}{\|\Omega\|}\tilde{\Omega} + \frac{1 - \cos((t - t_0)\|\Omega\|)}{\|\Omega\|^2}\tilde{\Omega}^2$$

$$\mathbf{U}_1 = \mathbf{I}(t - t_0) + \frac{1 - \cos((t - t_0)\|\Omega\|)}{\|\Omega\|^2}\tilde{\Omega} + \frac{(t - t_0)\|\Omega\| - \sin((t - t_0)\|\Omega\|)}{\|\Omega\|^3}\tilde{\Omega}^2$$

$$\mathbf{U}_2 = \mathbf{I}\frac{(t - t_0)^2}{2} + \frac{(t - t_0)\|\Omega\| - \sin((t - t_0)\|\Omega\|)}{\|\Omega\|^3}\tilde{\Omega} +$$

$$\frac{((t - t_0)\|\Omega\|)^2 - 2(1 - \cos((t - t_0)\|\Omega\|))}{2\|\Omega\|^4}\tilde{\Omega}^2$$

Proof The proof is a direct consequence of problem 4.   ■

8.4.2 Choosing a representation of three-dimensional line segments

In chapter 5 we studied a representation of 3-D lines by four numbers ($a, b, p,$ and q) such that the equations of the line are ($x = az + p, y = bz + q$) in the first map φ_1, with the two other maps obtained by exchanging the roles played by $x, y,$ and z. In φ_1 lines perpendicular to the z-axis cannot be represented, while in φ_2 and φ_3 it is the lines perpendicular to the x- and y-axis, respectively, that cannot be represented. From this representation, it is not too difficult to compute the weight (covariance) matrix of the endpoints M_1 and M_2 of a line segment, a 6×6 matrix (see problem 6).

One possible representation of a line segment is therefore the six-dimensional vector $[\mathbf{M}_1^T, \mathbf{M}_2^T]^T$. Just as in the two-dimensional case, this assumes that segments are oriented. If they are not, we can use the representation of direction, midpoint and length which is the vector $[a, b, \mathbf{M}^T, l]^T$, where $\mathbf{M}$ is the representation of the midpoint and l is the length of the segment. Of course, weight (covariance) matrices for these representations can be computed up to first order using the techniques of chapter 5. In what follows, we will denote by $\mathbf{r}$ the representation vector, and we will let $\mathbf{C}$ be the corresponding covariance matrix.

8.4.3 The plant and measurement equations

Contrary to the two-dimensional case, the state of the segment is directly related to the kinematic screw of the solid to which we assume it is attached. We define it to be the vector

$$\mathbf{a} = \begin{bmatrix} \Omega \\ \mathbf{V} \\ \mathbf{V}^{(1)} \\ \vdots \mathbf{V}^{(n)} \end{bmatrix} \tag{8.46}$$

which is a $3(n + 2)$-dimensional vector in which $\mathbf{V}^{(i)}$ represents the ith order time derivative of $\mathbf{V}$. In practice, $n = 1$ or 0. The plant equation is then

$$\mathbf{a}_i = \Phi_{i,i-1}\mathbf{a}_{i-1} + \mathbf{w}_i$$

This assumes that the angular velocity is constant. We could use more elaborate models, but we would lose the closed-form expressions of proposition 8.2.

Matrix $\Phi_{i,i-1}$, in the case where $n = 1$, is given by

$$\Phi_{i,i-1} = \begin{bmatrix} \mathbf{I}_3 & \mathbf{0}_3 & \mathbf{0}_3 \\ \mathbf{0}_3 & \mathbf{I}_3 & \mathbf{I}_3\Delta t \\ \mathbf{0}_3 & \mathbf{0}_3 & \mathbf{I}_3 \end{bmatrix}$$

A measurement is the identification of a segment S_1 at time t_{i-1} with a segment S_2 at time t_i. Assuming that S_1 is represented by $\mathbf{r}_1$ and S_2 by $\mathbf{r}_2$, the measurement vector is $\mathbf{x} = \begin{bmatrix} \mathbf{r}_1 \\ \mathbf{r}_2 \end{bmatrix}$ and the measurement equation is

$$\mathbf{f}_i(\mathbf{x}, \mathbf{a}) \equiv D_{i,i-1}\mathbf{r}_1 - \mathbf{r}_2 \qquad i \geq 1$$

where $D_{i,i-1}$ represents the effect on the representation vector $\mathbf{r}_1$ of the rigid motion between t_{i-1} and t_i and is a function of the state $\mathbf{a}$, which we will now describe. The case $i = 0$ is studied in section 8.4.4.1.

8.4.3.1 Transforming the direction

Let $\mathbf{u}_1$ be the direction of S_1 and suppose, for simplicity, but without loss of generality, that it can be represented in the map φ_i in which $\mathbf{u}_2$, the direction of S_2, can also be represented. According to our constant angular velocity model, the direction of S_1 at time t_i will be $\mathbf{U}_0\mathbf{u}_1$, and we must have

$$\varphi_i(\mathbf{U}_0\mathbf{u}_1) = \varphi_i(\mathbf{u}_2) \qquad i = 1, 2, 3 \tag{8.47}$$

More precisely, suppose that $i = 1$. If (a_1, b_1) is the representation of the direction of S_1 and (a_2, b_2) is that for S_2, we have

$$\mathbf{U_0} \begin{bmatrix} a_1 \\ b_1 \\ 1 \end{bmatrix} \wedge \begin{bmatrix} a_2 \\ b_2 \\ 1 \end{bmatrix} = \mathbf{0} \tag{8.48}$$

which expresses the fact that the directions are the same. Note that this is equivalent to two scalar equations. This is the first piece of the measurement equation, which concerns the directions.

8.4.3.2 *Transforming the midpoint*

Let M_1 be the midpoint of S_1. In the constant acceleration model, at time t_i it becomes $\mathbf{U_0}M_1 + \mathbf{U_1}V + \mathbf{U_2}A$, and we must have

$$\mathbf{U_0}M_1 + \mathbf{U_1}V + \mathbf{U_2}A = M_2 \tag{8.49}$$

This is the second piece of the measurement equation, which concerns the midpoints.

8.4.3.3 *Transforming the length*

The length of the segment is invariant, and therefore the measurement equation is

$$l_1 = l_2 \tag{8.50}$$

8.4.4 Running the process

We are now ready to put all this together in order to track a line segment in a sequence of three-dimensional frames. The situation is somewhat similar to that of section 8.3 except for the fact that the measurement equations (8.47)–(8.50) are nonlinear. Therefore, the linearization method of section 8.2.2.3 has to be used.

8.4.4.1 *Initialization*

At time 0, let us consider a segment S represented by the vector $\mathbf{r_0}$ with covariance matrix $\mathbf{C_0}$. Let $\mathbf{b_0}$ be our initial estimate of its state, and let $\mathbf{M_0}$ be its weight matrix. If we have no *a priori* information, we assume that $\mathbf{b_0} = \mathbf{0}$, i.e., we consider that S is not moving and that $\mathbf{M_0}$ diagonal. We then use the analysis described in section 8.2.2.4 to determine the candidate segments at time 1. If S_i is the ith segment at time 1 represented by $(\mathbf{r}_1^i, \mathbf{C}_1^i)$, we consider the "possible" measurement equations

$$\mathbf{f}_0^i(\mathbf{x}_0^i, \mathbf{b}_0) = \mathbf{0}$$

where $\mathbf{x}_0^i = [\mathbf{r}_0^T, \mathbf{r}_1^{iT}]^T$ has weight matrix

$$\mathbf{R}_0^i = \begin{bmatrix} \mathbf{C}_0 & \mathbf{0} \\ \mathbf{0} & \mathbf{C}_1^i \end{bmatrix}$$

From equations (8.47)–(8.49) we can compute the covariance matrices (see problem 5) as follows:

$$\Lambda_0^i = \frac{\partial \mathbf{f}_0^i}{\partial \mathbf{a}} \mathbf{M}_0 \frac{\partial \mathbf{f}_0^i}{\partial \mathbf{a}}^T + \frac{\partial \mathbf{f}_0^i}{\partial \mathbf{x}} \mathbf{R}_0^i \frac{\partial \mathbf{f}_0^i}{\partial \mathbf{x}}^T$$

where each partial derivative is evaluated at $(\mathbf{x}_0^i, \mathbf{b}_0)$. We then compute the Mahalanobis distances

$$d_0^i = \mathbf{f}_0^i(\mathbf{x}_0^i, \mathbf{b}_0)^T (\Lambda_0^i)^{-1} \mathbf{f}_0^i(\mathbf{x}_0^i, \mathbf{b}_0)$$

for all segments in the 3-D frame at time 1. Those segments with distances smaller than a fixed threshold are kept as matches.

Each match defines a token, and we update the state using equation (8.23) as follows:

$$\hat{\mathbf{a}}_0^i = \mathbf{b}_0 + \mathbf{K}_0^i(\mathbf{x}_0^i - \mathbf{H}_0^i \mathbf{b}_0)$$

in which

$$\mathbf{H}_0^i = \frac{\partial \mathbf{f}_0^i}{\partial \mathbf{a}}(\mathbf{x}_0^i, \mathbf{b}_0)$$

and

$$\mathbf{K}_0^i = \mathbf{M}_0 \mathbf{H}_0^i (\mathbf{H}_0^i \mathbf{M}_0 \mathbf{H}_0^{iT} + \mathbf{R}_0^i)^{-1}$$

The weight on $\hat{\mathbf{a}}_0^i$ is the matrix $\mathbf{P}_0^i = (\mathbf{M}_0^{-1} + \mathbf{H}_0^{iT}(\mathbf{R}_0^i)^{-1}\mathbf{H}_0^i)^{-1}$.

8.4.4.2 Continuous processing

Just as in the two-dimensional case, we do the reasoning at time 2, but the generalization to an arbitrary stage follows. Let S be a token at time 1 represented by $(\mathbf{r}_1, \mathbf{C}_1)$ with state $\hat{\mathbf{a}}_0$ and with weight $\mathbf{P}_0$. We make a prediction by computing the state $\hat{\mathbf{a}}_1' = \Phi_{1,0}\hat{\mathbf{a}}_0$ and its weight $\mathbf{P}_1'$ (using equation (8.33)). We then determine the candidate segments at time 2.

If S_i is the ith segment at time 2 represented by $(\mathbf{r}_2^i, \mathbf{C}_2^i)$, we consider the "possible" measurement equations

$$\mathbf{f}_1^i(\mathbf{x}_1^i, \hat{\mathbf{a}}_1') = \mathbf{0}$$

where $\mathbf{x}_1^i = [\mathbf{r}_1^T, \mathbf{r}_2^{iT}]^T$ has weight matrix

$$\mathbf{R}_1^i = \begin{bmatrix} \mathbf{C}_1 & \mathbf{0} \\ \mathbf{0} & \mathbf{C}_2^i \end{bmatrix}$$

and $\hat{\mathbf{a}}_1'$ has weight matrix $\mathbf{P}_1'$. Just as in the previous section, we select matches based on the Mahalanobis distance and update the state using equations (8.31)–(8.34). We have

$$\hat{\mathbf{a}}_1^i = \hat{\mathbf{a}}_1' + \mathbf{K}_1^i(\mathbf{x}_1^i - \mathbf{H}_1^i\hat{\mathbf{a}}_1')$$

in which

$$\mathbf{H}_1^i = \frac{\partial \mathbf{f}_1^i}{\partial \mathbf{a}}(\mathbf{x}_1^i, \hat{\mathbf{a}}_1')$$

and

$$\mathbf{K}_1^i = \mathbf{P}_1'\mathbf{H}_1^{iT}(\mathbf{H}_1^i\mathbf{P}_1'\mathbf{H}_1^{iT} + \mathbf{R}_1^i)^{-1}$$

The weight of the new state $\hat{\mathbf{a}}_1^i$ is the matrix $\mathbf{P}_1^i = \mathbf{P}_1' - \mathbf{K}_1^i\mathbf{H}_1^i\mathbf{P}_1'$.

8.4.5 An example

We will show one example of the results of the three-dimensional token tracker in a case where the scene can be represented fairly accurately with line segments. The scene contains two boxes standing on a table. The table can rotate about a vertical axis and translate along the same axis, as is explained in figure 8.4. A sequence of ten stereo triplets has been acquired while the table has been moving up and rotating as indicated in the same figure. Figure 8.5 shows the first and last images of the sequence formed by the first camera of the stereo rig. From this sequence we have generated ten three-dimensional stereo frames to which we have applied the tracker described previously.

In figure 8.6 we show a comparison between the first stereo frame and the second. The picture at the top of the figure is a reprojection in the first camera of the 3-D segments of the two frames. The bottom part of the figure is a cross-eye stereogram that shows the two stereo frames. In both cases segments of the first frame are in solid lines, while those of

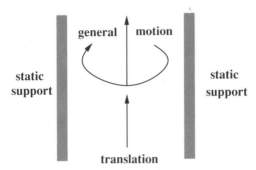

Figure 8.4   The table can rotate about and translate along a vertical axis.

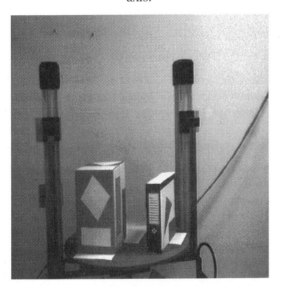 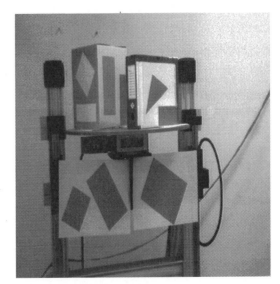

Figure 8.5   The images taken by the first camera at t_1 and t_{10}.

the second frame are in dotted lines. The next figure, figure 8.7, shows a comparison between the first stereo frame and the tenth. Using the same format, figure 8.8 shows the superposition of the frame predicted at time t_3 (solid lines), and the observed frame at time t_3 (dotted lines). It can be seen that, except for those segments that just appeared at the bottom of the frame and for which too few observations have been made to build a correct kinematic model, the agreement between the real and predicted tokens is very good. Using the same format, figure 8.9 shows the superposition of the frame predicted at time t_{10} (solid lines) and

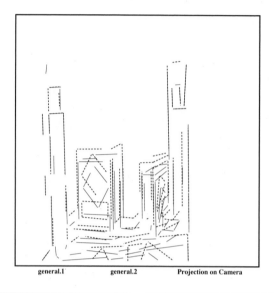

general.1   general.2   Projection on Camera

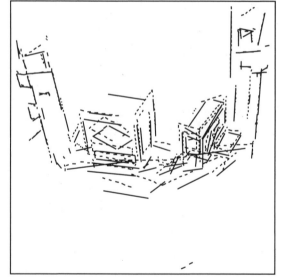
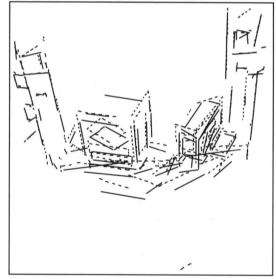

Figure 8.6   The superposition of the first frame (in solid lines) and the tenth frame (in dashed lines).

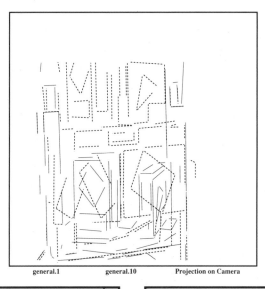

general.1   general.10   Projection on Camera

Figure 8.7   The superposition of the first frame (in solid lines) and the tenth frame (in dashed lines).

TR.general.2.pred   TR.general.3   Projection on Camera

Figure 8.8 The superposition of the third predicted frame (in solid lines) and the third observed frame (in dashed lines).

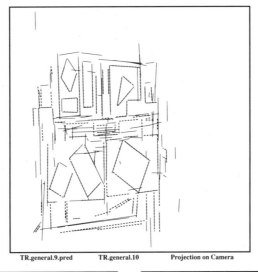

TR.general.9.pred   TR.general.10   Projection on Camera

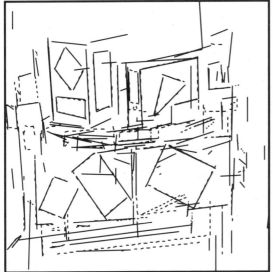

Figure 8.9 The superposition of the tenth predicted frame (in solid lines) and the tenth observed frame (in dashed lines).

the observed frame at time t_{10} (dotted lines). It can be seen that, for the majority of segments, the agreement between the real and predicted tokens is very good.

8.5   Conclusion and references

The problem of tracking tokens in sequences of images or in sequences of stereo frames has received considerable attention in the last few years, and the use of the Kalman or extended Kalman filters or equivalently of recursive least-squares estimation theory has now become standard. The applications of these methods to the 2D-2D and 3D-3D tracking problems described in sections 8.3 and 8.4 have not been as numerous as their applications to the 2D-3D tracking problem in which the observations are made in the image and the tracking is done in three dimensions.

Examples of the 2D-2D problem can be found [SM82, LY82, SJ87, Hwa89, DF90, GV91]. Examples of the 3D-3D problem are difficult to find (see the article by Young and Chellappa [YC90] for an exception, although the matching problem is avoided), and the interested reader is referred to the book by Zhang and Faugeras [ZF92b]. Examples of the 2D-3D problem are by far the most common. Token-based approaches [BC86, WHA87, Dic87, ER87, DG88b, DG88a, BC89, MCB89, SP90, BCC90, Riv90, DM92] as well as intensity-based approaches in the case of known or partially known motion have been developed [HW88, MSK88].

The two key ideas that were mentioned at the onset of this chapter, those of *recursive parameter estimation* and of the *prediction of parameter values*, have proved to be extremely important for solving dynamic vision problems. Note that, as is often the case, these ideas had been in use for a long time in other fields as described, for example, in the excellent book by Bar-Shalom *et al.* [BF88].

8.6   Problems

1. The purpose of this exercise is to demonstrate the matrix inversion lemma. Let $\mathbf{A}, \mathbf{B}$ be two $n \times n$ invertible matrices, $\mathbf{C}$ a $p \times n$ matrix, and $\mathbf{D}$ a $p \times p$ invertible matrix. We will prove that if

$$\mathbf{A}^{-1} = \mathbf{B}^{-1} + \mathbf{C}^T\mathbf{D}^{-1}\mathbf{C} \qquad\qquad (8.51)$$

then we also have

$$\mathbf{A} = \mathbf{B} - \mathbf{B}\mathbf{C}^T(\mathbf{C}\mathbf{B}\mathbf{C}^T + \mathbf{D})^{-1}\mathbf{C}\mathbf{B} \qquad\qquad (8.52)$$

a. Multiply equation (8.51) on the left by matrix **A** and the result on the right by matrix **B** to obtain

$$\mathbf{B} = \mathbf{A} + \mathbf{A}\mathbf{C}^T\mathbf{D}^{-1}\mathbf{C}\mathbf{B} \qquad\qquad (8.53)$$

b. Multiply equation (8.53) on the right by $\mathbf{C}^T$, and factor out $\mathbf{A}\mathbf{C}^T\mathbf{D}^{-1}$. Multiply the equation on the right by the inverse of $\mathbf{D} + \mathbf{C}\mathbf{B}\mathbf{C}^T$ and obtain

$$\mathbf{A}\mathbf{C}^T\mathbf{D}^{-1} = \mathbf{B}\mathbf{C}^T(\mathbf{D} + \mathbf{C}\mathbf{B}\mathbf{C}^T)^{-1}$$

c. Multiply the previous equation on the right by **CB** and subtract it from **B**. Conclude by using equation (8.53).

2. The midpoint M of segment M_1M_2 is represented by

$$\mathbf{M} = \frac{\mathbf{M}_1 + \mathbf{M}_2}{2}$$

If the endpoints have covariance matrices Λ_1 and Λ_2 and are independent, what is the covariance matrix of M?

3. The length L of the segment M_1M_2 is equal to $\|\mathbf{M}_1\mathbf{M}_2\|$; up to a first-order approximation, what is its variance?

4. Compute the integrals L_i and M_i as defined in section 8.4.1.

5. Compute the derivatives $\frac{\partial \mathbf{f}}{\partial \mathbf{a}}$ and $\frac{\partial \mathbf{f}}{\partial \mathbf{x}}$ in the case of 3-D segments.

6. This problem is a generalization of section 5.6.4. Given p points M_i in 3-space, we are going to compute the line best approximating these points, i.e., the line L such that the sum of the squared distances of the data points to the line is minimized.

a. We will represent L with a point **P** and a unit vector **u** parallel to L. Show that the sum of the squared distances of the points M_i to L is given by

$$C(\mathbf{P}, \mathbf{u}) = \sum_{i=1}^{p} [\|\mathbf{PM}_i\|^2 - (\mathbf{PM}_i \cdot \mathbf{u})^2]$$

b. Show that L goes through the center of gravity of the points M_i.

c. Show that the direction of L is parallel to the eigenvector of the covariance matrix of the set of points corresponding to the *largest* eigenvalue.

d. Use the technique of section 5.6.3 to estimate the uncertainty of L given the uncertainty of the 3-D points M_i.

9   Motion Fields of Curves

In this chapter we will adopt an even more continuous approach than in the previous chapter, and we will study the problem of computing the three-dimensional motion and structure of a moving curve. We will begin with a special case, that of a straight line. We will then treat the general case. But before we go into these topics, we would like to briefly discuss the general notion of optical flow.

9.1   How to read this chapter

This chapter is organized in six sections. In section 9.2 we will introduce the ideas of optical flow and motion field and stress their difference based on the motion constraint equation (9.1). We will then explain how, in the case of rigid 3-D motion, the kinematic screw can be recovered from the motion fields measured at a number of pixels (at least five), as well as the corresponding depths, up to a scale factor. We will also briefly describe how the aperture problem, which arises from equation (9.1), can be solved by "inventing" an approximate motion field.

The rest of the chapter is devoted to showing that this is in fact an impossible task since the complete motion field is not computable from the sequence of images, at least for smooth curves, unless more hypotheses are introduced, such as the assumption that the 3-D motion is rigid. In section 9.3 we will restrict our study of the motion field to the case of a moving 3-D curve with no assumption of rigidity. We will consider its camera image, a 2-D curve, which contains all the available information about the 3-D shape and motion. We will then introduce the spatiotemporal surface generated by this image curve in the three-dimensional space obtained by adding a time axis to the two image axes. This surface has been introduced initially by Baker and Bolles [BB89]. We will characterize it completely through differential geometry and show that the motion field cannot be recovered from it and, as a consequence, that the motion field cannot be recovered from the image curve either.

In proving this result, we will introduce some important ideas. First we will present the idea of apparent and real motion fields, where the real motion field is identical to the motion field. Second we will develop the idea that these two motion fields, when thought of as vectors tangent to the spatiotemporal surface, define differential operators that have intuitive interpretations: The apparent motion field (respectively, the real motion field) corresponds to differentiating functions defined on the image curve (and therefore in the image) with respect to time while keeping the image curve (respectively, the 3-D curve) arclength constant. These two motion fields have the same component along the normal to the image curve but, in general, different components along the tangent. One of the main results of this section is that only the tangential component of the apparent motion field and the common normal component can be recovered from the image, not the tangential component of the real motion field. The reader who is uninterested in mathematical details may just want to read section 9.3.1 for the notations, equations (9.12) and (9.13), proposition 9.3, and theorem 9.1, which are necessary to understand the following sections.

In the next two sections we will restrict our attention even further to the case of rigidly moving curves. In section 9.4 we will first consider the case of straight lines for two reasons. First, it turns out that the case of straight lines almost entirely contains the case of general curves. Second, there is a neat generalization to the instantaneous case of the problem studied in section 7.4 in the discrete case. Again, the reader who is not interested in mathematical details can read only section 9.4.1 for notations and then jump directly to equations (9.36) and (9.38) and to propositions 9.8 and 9.9, which entirely characterize the motion of a 3-D straight line.

In section 9.5 we will attack the most general problem of the motion of a 3-D curve. The key difference of this problem from the case of straight lines is that the time derivatives of image quantities that appear in the two main equations, (9.44) and (9.45), now depend on both the choice of a point on the image curve and on our ability to track it over time. This is equivalent to knowing the full real motion field, and we will show in section 9.3 that this is not possible. Using the tools developed in that section, and in particular equation (9.13), we will show that the tangential component of the real motion field and its time derivative appear in the equations. We will also show that these quantities can be eliminated from the equations (9.44) and (9.45). The resulting equations can be called the fundamental equations of the motion of rigid 3-D curves. Again, the reader who is uninterested in mathematical details can read only theorem 9.4.

In section 9.6 we will give some examples, and in the final section we will show how the theory developed so far finds an unexpected and easy application to the correspondence problem in stereo vision: It provides constraints to eliminate wrong correspondences resulting from the fact that these wrong matches would yield nonrigidly moving 3-D curves.

9.2   Optical flow and the motion field

The concept of *optical flow* was introduced by Gibson [Gib50] and is based upon the idea that there is a relationship between the temporal variations of the image intensity at one point of the retinal plane and the motion of the camera and the motions and the shapes of the objects present in the scene. As we will see in a moment, the relationship is not very simple.

9.2.1   Optical flow

Let us consider the image intensity $I(x, y, \tau)$ at pixel m of coordinates (x, y) in the retinal plane at time τ. The point m is the image of a 3-D point M moving in the scene with a velocity $\mathbf{V}_M$. The velocity of m is $\mathbf{v}_m = [v_x, v_y]^T = \dot{\mathbf{m}}$ (see figure 9.1). If we take the total time derivative $\dot{I}$ of I with respect to time, we obtain

$$\dot{I} = \frac{\partial I}{\partial x}\frac{dx}{d\tau} + \frac{\partial I}{\partial y}\frac{dy}{d\tau} + \frac{\partial I}{\partial \tau}$$

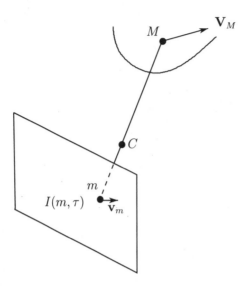

Figure 9.1   Optical flow.

Now, by definition, $\frac{dx}{d\tau} = V_x$, and $\frac{dy}{d\tau} = V_y$; therefore the previous equation can be rewritten as

$$\dot{I} = \frac{\partial I}{\partial x} V_x + \frac{\partial I}{\partial y} V_y + \frac{\partial I}{\partial \tau} = \nabla I \cdot \mathbf{v}_m + \frac{\partial I}{\partial \tau}$$

This formula involves no approximations, but it involves one quantity, $\dot{I}$, which cannot be computed simply from the sequence of images. In fact, in order to compute it we need to introduce models of the scene reflectance.

Before doing this, we will define optical flow. Assuming that $\dot{I} = 0$, we immediately obtain the so-called *motion constraint equation*

$$\nabla I \cdot \mathbf{v}_m + \frac{\partial I}{\partial \tau} = 0 \tag{9.1}$$

which has been presented by many authors as a constraint on the velocity $\mathbf{v}_m$. Why is this a constraint? Because equation (9.1) imposes the assumption that $\mathbf{v}_m$ lies on a straight line whose normal is parallel to the image gradient ∇I at m. But there is a hidden problem here, namely the fact that we have made the assumption that $\dot{I} = 0$. As we will show next, this assumption is largely wrong, and in fact equation (9.1) should

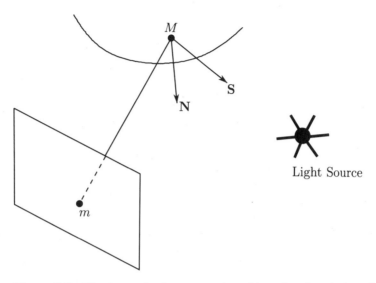

Figure 9.2   The intensity image produced by a Lambertian surface.

be considered not as a constraint on the image velocity field $\mathbf{v}_m$, but as the definition of a new image vector field $\mathbf{v}_m^o$, the optical flow, parallel to ∇I:

$$\mathbf{v}_m^o = -\frac{\frac{\partial I}{\partial \tau}}{\|\nabla I\|} \frac{\nabla I}{\|\nabla I\|} \tag{9.2}$$

Following Horn [Hor86][12], we draw a sharp distinction between the motion field $\mathbf{v}_m$ and the optical flow field $\mathbf{v}_m^o$. Note that $\mathbf{v}_m^o$ can be computed from a sequence of images.

9.2.2   The case of a Lambertian surface

For a Lambertian surface, the image intensity has the following expression (refer to figure 9.2):

$$I(m, \tau) = \rho \mathbf{S}(M, \tau) \cdot \mathbf{N}(M) \tag{9.3}$$

where ρ is a constant parameter called the *albedo*, $\mathbf{S}$ is a unit vector in the direction of the illumination source assumed to be reduced to a point, and $\mathbf{N}$ is the unit vector normal to the object surface at point M. Assuming that the object is moving rigidly with a kinematic screw $(\mathbf{\Omega}, \mathbf{V})$

with respect to some point of reference, it is easy to compute $\dot{I}$:

$$\dot{I} = \rho \left(\frac{d\mathbf{S}}{d\tau} \cdot \mathbf{N} + \mathbf{S} \cdot \frac{d\mathbf{N}}{d\tau} \right)$$

Since the unit normal $\mathbf{N}$ moves with the object, $\frac{d\mathbf{N}}{d\tau} = \Omega \wedge \mathbf{N}$. Therefore

$$\dot{I} = \rho \left(\frac{d\mathbf{S}}{d\tau} \cdot \mathbf{N} + (\mathbf{S}, \Omega, \mathbf{N}) \right)$$

where $(\mathbf{S}, \Omega, \mathbf{N})$ is the determinant of the three vectors $\mathbf{S}$, Ω, and $\mathbf{N}$. Now, if we assume that the illumination source is at infinity and does not move, then the vector field $\mathbf{S}$ is constant, and this reduces to

$$\dot{I} = \rho (\mathbf{S}, \Omega, \mathbf{N})$$

which is, in general, nonzero if the angular velocity is nonzero. Therefore, even for a Lambertian surface that is not purely translating, the motion constraint equation does not hold. This has been acknowledged only recently [VP89], and it raises some serious questions, as we will point out next, about the validity of a number of algorithms that are based on the motion constraint equation (9.1).

9.2.3 The motion field

According to the previous discussion, the motion field $\mathbf{v}_m$ is the time derivative $\dot{\mathbf{m}}$ of the representation $\mathbf{m}$ of pixel m. Looking at figure 9.1, we can write

$$\mathbf{M} = z\mathbf{m}$$

Taking the time derivative of both sides, we have

$$\dot{\mathbf{M}} = \dot{z}\mathbf{m} + z\dot{\mathbf{m}} \tag{9.4}$$

Or, if $\mathbf{k}$ is the unit vector along the z-axis, we get

$$\mathbf{V}_M = (\mathbf{V}_M^T \mathbf{k})\mathbf{m} + z\mathbf{v}_m$$

From this equation we can deduce the relationship between the motion field $\mathbf{v}_m$, the 3-D velocity field $\mathbf{V}_M$ and the depth z:

$$\mathbf{v}_m = \frac{1}{z}(\mathbf{V}_M - (\mathbf{V}_M^T \mathbf{k})\mathbf{m})$$

The right-hand side is a function of $\frac{\mathbf{v}_M}{z}$, the 3-D velocity field scaled by the inverse of the depth of the point. If we assume that this field is obtained from a kinematic screw $(\Omega, \mathbf{V})$ where Ω is the angular velocity and $\mathbf{V}$ the linear velocity, we have

$$\mathbf{v}_m = \frac{1}{z}(\mathbf{V} - (\mathbf{V}^T\mathbf{k})\mathbf{m}) + \Omega \wedge \mathbf{m} - (\mathbf{k}, \Omega, \mathbf{m})\mathbf{m} \tag{9.5}$$

which shows that the motion field is a function of $\frac{\mathbf{v}}{z}$ and Ω.

If we have n pixels $m_1, \ldots, m_n$ at which we know the motion fields $\mathbf{v}_{m_1}, \ldots, \mathbf{v}_{m_n}$, and if we assume that the n corresponding 3-D points $M_1, \ldots, M_n$ belong to the same object moving rigidly with the kinematic screw $(\Omega, \mathbf{V})$, we have $2n$ equations in the unknowns $(\Omega^T, \mathbf{V}^T, z_1, \ldots, z_n)$. To solve for those unknowns is to solve the so-called *motion and structure problem*. A closer look at equation (9.5) shows that the problem is homogeneous in $(\mathbf{V}^T, z_1, \ldots, z_n)$, and therefore the total number of unknowns is $3 + 2 + n = n + 5$. Intuitively, this says that the solution to the motion and structure problem cannot provide us with both the absolute depth of the 3-D points and their linear velocity. It is only the relative information that we can hope to recover from the measurements of the motion field.

A naive counting of the equations tells us that, if n is larger than or equal to 5, we may be able to solve the problem. Note that the equations are linear in Ω, but nonlinear in $(\mathbf{V}^T, z_1, \ldots, z_n)$. Another way to obtain the same result, which is interesting in its own right, is to eliminate the depth z from the equations as follows. Going back to equation (9.4), we replace $\dot{\mathbf{M}}$ with $\mathbf{V} + \tilde{\Omega}\mathbf{M}$, $\dot{\mathbf{m}}$ by $\mathbf{v}_m$ and then multiply both sides by $\tilde{\mathbf{V}}$:

$$\tilde{\mathbf{V}}\tilde{\Omega}\mathbf{M} = \dot{z}\tilde{\mathbf{V}}\mathbf{m} + z\tilde{\mathbf{V}}\mathbf{v}_m$$

If we now take the inner product of both sides with $\mathbf{m}$, we eliminate $\dot{z}$ and we can divide by z:

$$\mathbf{m}^T\tilde{\mathbf{V}}\tilde{\Omega}\mathbf{m} = \mathbf{m}^T\tilde{\mathbf{V}}\mathbf{v}_m \tag{9.6}$$

This is a homogeneous equation that is linear in $\mathbf{V}$, linear in Ω, and quadratic in both $\mathbf{V}$ and Ω. The depth z does not appear in it. Five pixels are, in principle, sufficient to compute Ω and $\mathbf{V}$, with the linear velocity defined up to a nonzero scale factor. It can be shown that in that case the number of solutions is, in general, equal to ten, just as in the discrete case studied in section 7.3.2 [May90c]. Maybank [May87] and Heeger and Jepson [HJ92] have shown how to use equation (9.6) to robustly compute **V** and Ω from the knowledge of the motion field at a number of image pixels. Depth can then be recovered from equation (9.5), for example.

The main difficulty is not in solving this system of nonlinear equations, but in actually computing the motion field $\mathbf{v}_m$ at a sufficiently large number of points. So far the standard approach to this problem in computer vision has been to identify $\mathbf{v}_m^o$, the optical flow field defined by equation (9.2), with the projection of the motion field $\mathbf{v}_m$ along the direction of the gradient

$$\mathbf{v}_m^o = \mathbf{v}_m^T \frac{\nabla I}{\|\nabla I\|}$$

This equation assumes that $\dot{I}$ is equal to 0, which, as we saw in the previous section, is not true in general. Assuming that it is true yields a linear constraint on the two coordinates of $\mathbf{v}_m$ and therefore only one equation at every pixel, which is obtained by projecting the two sides of (9.5) along the direction of the image gradient. The motion and structure problem is thus impossible to solve, since n points yield n equations in $n + 5$ unknowns. This is the mathematical statement of the aperture problem: The motion field is not fully defined at each pixel since we have only one equation, equation (9.1), between its two coordinates. In order to solve this new problem, researchers have tried to "invent" a motion field, close to the real one if possible, by imposing a smoothness constraint.

The idea is to find a smooth field $\hat{\mathbf{v}}_m$ whose component along the direction of the image gradient is as close as possible to the measured optical flow $\mathbf{v}_m^o$. This can be expressed mathematically as the following minimization problem:

$$\min_{\mathbf{v}_m} \int \int ((\mathbf{v}_m^T \mathbf{n} - \mathbf{v}_m^o)^2 + \lambda Tr(D\mathbf{v}_m(D\mathbf{v}_m)^T))dxdy \qquad (9.7)$$

where $\mathbf{n} = \frac{\nabla I}{\|\nabla I\|}$ and $D\mathbf{v}_m$ is the derivative of the function $(x, y) \rightarrow \mathbf{v}_m(x, y)$ at the pixel m of coordinates (x, y). If we write $\mathbf{v}_m = [v_{m_1}, v_{m_2}]^T$, we have

$$D\mathbf{v}_m = \begin{bmatrix} \frac{\partial v_{m_1}}{\partial x} & \frac{\partial v_{m_1}}{\partial y} \\ \frac{\partial v_{m_2}}{\partial x} & \frac{\partial v_{m_2}}{\partial y} \end{bmatrix}$$

The criterion (9.7) is the sum of two terms: The first term imposes the condition that the component of the "invented" field $\hat{\mathbf{v}}_m$ along $\mathbf{n}$ is as close as possible to the measurements $\mathbf{v}_m^o$, and the second term controls, through the parameter λ, its smoothness. A detailed analysis of the possible solutions to this minimization problem can be found in the work of Horn [Hor86], and Ellen Hildreth developed a related approach for the image contours [Hil84]. Of course there is no guarantee that the computed field $\hat{\mathbf{v}}_m$ is close to the motion field $\mathbf{v}_m$, and in fact it is, in general, different.

Another quite different approach to the estimation of the motion field has been proposed by by Girosi, Verri, and Torre [T88, VGT89, VGT90]. It has its roots in the work of Nagel [Nag83, Nag85a, Nag85b, Nag86, Nag87], who has investigated in great depth the use of Taylor series expansions of the image intensity function of a higher order than the one provided by the basic motion constraint equation (9.1). The idea is to replace the motion constraint equation (9.1) by another one that fully determines the "motion field" at each pixel. For example, take the constraint that the total derivative of the image spatial gradient is equal to 0:

$$\dot{\nabla} I = \mathbf{0} \tag{9.8}$$

This equation can also be written as

$$\mathbf{H}\mathbf{v}_m = \frac{\partial \nabla I}{\partial \tau}$$

where $\mathbf{H}$ is the Hessian of the image intensity function. This shows that, wherever in the image this Hessian is invertible (has a nonzero determinant), $\mathbf{v}_m$ can be computed as

$$\mathbf{v}_m = \mathbf{H}^{-1} \frac{\partial \nabla I}{\partial \tau}$$

But again, as in the case of equation (9.1), equation (9.8) holds only in very special cases, and the motion field computed by the previous equation is only an approximation of the real one. In the remainder of this chapter, we are going to investigate in great depth the relationship between $\mathbf{v}_m$ and $\mathbf{V}_M$.

9.3   The motion fields of a curve

We will now assume that we observe in a sequence of images a family (c_τ) of curves, where τ denotes the time, which we assume to be the perspective projection in the retina of a 3-D curve (C) that moves in space. If we consider the three-dimensional space (x, y, τ), this family of curves sweeps in that space a surface (Σ) defined as the set of points $((c_\tau), \tau)$ (see figure 9.3). We call (Σ) the *spatio-temporal surface* generated by the curves (c_τ).

9.3.1   Definitions and notations

At a given time instant τ, let us consider the observed curve (c_τ). Its arclength s can be computed, and (c_τ) can be parameterized by s and τ: It is the set of points $m(s, \tau)$ in the retinal plane. The corresponding points P on (Σ) are represented by the vector $\mathbf{P} = (\mathbf{m}^T(s, \tau), \tau)^T$. Let S be an arclength defined along the 3-D curve (C). We will assume that the motion of (C) preserves the arclength. This rules out elastic motions, but allows ropelike and rigid motions. We call such motions *isometric motions*. Observe that the arclength s of (c_τ) is a function $s(S, \tau)$ of the

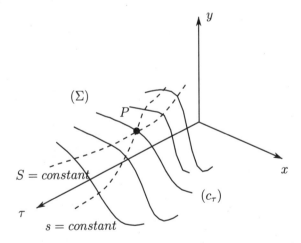

Figure 9.3   Definition of the spatiotemporal surface (Σ).

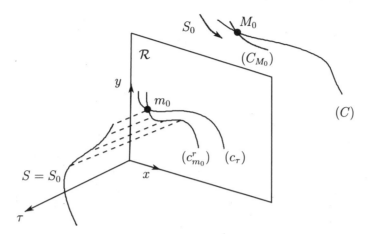

Figure 9.4 Projection in the image plane, parallel to the τ-axis, of the curve $S = S_0$ of the surface (Σ): $(c^r_{m_0})$ is the "real" trajectory of m_0.

arclength S of the 3-D curve (C) and of the time τ, and that the two parameters (S, τ) can be used to parameterize (Σ) in a neighborhood of P. Of course, the function $s(S, \tau)$ is unknown.

As shown in figure 9.3, we can consider on (Σ) the curves defined by $s = constant$ or $S = constant$. These curves are, in general, different, and their projections, parallel to the τ-axis, in the retinal or (x, y)-plane have an important physical interpretation related to our upcoming definition of the motion fields. Indeed, as shown in figure 9.4, suppose that we choose a point M_0 on (C) and fix its arclength S_0 at time τ. When (C) moves, this point follows a trajectory (C_{M_0}) in 3-D space and its image m_0 follows a trajectory $(c^r_{m_0})$ in the retinal plane. This last curve is the projection in the retinal plane, parallel to the τ-axis, of the curve defined by $S = S_0$ on the surface (Σ). We call it the "real" trajectory of m_0 because it is the retinal image of (C_{M_0}), which is the trajectory of a physical point attached to (C).

We can also consider the same projection of another curve defined on (Σ) by $s = s_0$. The corresponding curve $(c^a_{m_0})$ in the retinal plane is the trajectory of the image point m_0 of arclength s_0 on (c_τ). We call this curve the "apparent" trajectory of m_0 (see figure 9.5) because it is not, in general, the retinal image of a physical point attached to (C). The

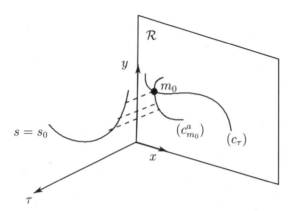

Figure 9.5 Projection in the image plane, parallel to the τ-axis, of the curve $s = s_0$ of the surface (Σ): $(c^a_{m_0})$ is the "apparent" trajectory of m_0.

mathematical reason why these two curves are different is that the first one is defined by $S = S_0$, while the second is defined by $s(S, \tau) = s_0$.

Let us now define precisely what we mean by *motion fields*. If we consider figure 9.6, point m on (c_τ) is the image of point M on (C). This point has a 3-D velocity $\mathbf{V}_M$ whose projection in the retina is the *real motion field* $\mathbf{v}_r$ (r for *real*). Mathematically speaking:

- $\mathbf{v}_r$ is the partial derivative of $\mathbf{m}(s, \tau)$ with respect to time when S is kept constant or, in other words, its total time derivative $\dot{\mathbf{m}}$.

- The *apparent motion field* $\mathbf{v}_a$ (a for *apparent*) of $\mathbf{m}(s, \tau)$ is the partial derivative with respect to time when s is kept constant, $\frac{\partial \mathbf{m}}{\partial \tau} = \mathbf{m}_\tau$.

These two quantities are, in general, distinct. To relate this to the previous discussion about the curves $S = S_0$ and $s = s_0$ of (Σ), the vector $\mathbf{v}_a$ is tangent to the "apparent" trajectory of m, while $\mathbf{v}_r$ is tangent to the "real" one. This is summarized in figure 9.7.

We will now make an important statement. All the information about the motion of points of (c_τ) (and of the 3-D points of (C) that project onto them) is entirely contained in the surface (Σ). Since (Σ) is intrinsically characterized, up to a rigid motion, by its first and second fundamental forms and by the Gauss and Codazzi-Mainardi equations (see appendix C), they are all we need to characterize the motion fields of (c_τ) and the motion of (C). Our main conclusion will be that only the apparent motion field can be recovered from (Σ).

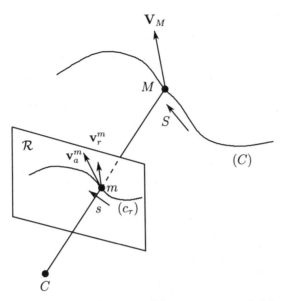

Figure 9.6   Definition of the two motion fields, the real and the apparent.

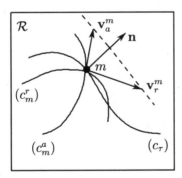

Figure 9.7   Comparison of the two motion fields and the real and apparent trajectories. Here **n** is the normal to (c_τ).

9.3.2   Characterization of the spatiotemporal surface (Σ)

In this section we will compute the first and second fundamental forms and the Codazzi-Mainardi equations of the spatiotemporal surface (Σ). On the way, we will be gleaning a number of interesting facts related to the motion and deformation of the curve (c_τ). We will often use the following result about functions defined on (c_τ) and thus on (Σ). Given a function f of the variables s and τ, f is a function on (c_τ). It is also a function f' of S and τ, and therefore it also defines a function on (Σ). We will have to compute $\frac{\partial f'}{\partial S}$ and $\frac{\partial f'}{\partial \tau}$. The second derivative is also called the *total time derivative* of f with respect to time, $\dot{f}$; introducing $u = \frac{\partial s}{\partial S}$ and $v = \frac{\partial s}{\partial \tau}$, we have the following equations:

$$f'_S = \frac{\partial f'}{\partial S} = u\frac{\partial f}{\partial s} = uf_s \qquad \dot{f} = \frac{\partial f'}{\partial \tau} = f'_\tau = v\frac{\partial f}{\partial s} + \frac{\partial f}{\partial \tau} = vf_s + f_\tau \tag{9.9}$$

The reader should carefully note that, when we write $\frac{\partial f'}{\partial \tau}$ in the second set of equations (9.9), this is a partial derivative at $S = constant$ whereas, when we write $\frac{\partial f}{\partial \tau}$, this is a derivative at $s = constant$. Following these notations, we denote by $\mathbf{P}(s, \tau) = [\mathbf{m}^T(s, \tau), \tau]^T$ the generic point of (Σ) and by $\mathbf{P}'(S, \tau) = [\mathbf{m}'^T(S, \tau), \tau]^T$ the same point considered as a function of S and τ.

9.3.2.1   The first fundamental form of the spatiotemporal surface (Σ)

Using equations (9.9) and the first two-dimensional Frenet formula, we can write

$$\mathbf{P}'_S = u\mathbf{P}_S = u\begin{bmatrix} \mathbf{m}_s \\ 0 \end{bmatrix} = \begin{bmatrix} u\mathbf{t} \\ 0 \end{bmatrix} \tag{9.10}$$

$$\mathbf{P}'_\tau = v\mathbf{P}_S + \mathbf{P}_\tau = v\begin{bmatrix} \mathbf{m}_s \\ 0 \end{bmatrix} + \begin{bmatrix} \mathbf{m}_\tau \\ 1 \end{bmatrix} = \begin{bmatrix} v\mathbf{t} + \mathbf{v}_a \\ 1 \end{bmatrix} \tag{9.11}$$

in which $\mathbf{t}$ is the unit tangent vector to (c_τ) at m. Let us define $\mathbf{V}_a$ as $[\mathbf{v}_a^T, 1]^T$, a three-dimensional vector. We can now write the apparent motion field $\mathbf{v}_a$ in the Frenet frame $\mathbf{t}, \mathbf{n}$, where $\mathbf{n}$ is the unit normal vector to (c_τ) at m:

$$\mathbf{v}_a = \alpha\mathbf{t} + \beta\mathbf{n} \tag{9.12}$$

We call α and β the *tangential apparent motion field* and the *normal apparent motion field*, respectively. We see from equation (9.11) that $\mathbf{P}'_\tau = [(\nu + \alpha)\mathbf{t}^T + \beta\mathbf{n}^T, 1]^T$. But, by definition, $\mathbf{P}'_\tau = [\mathbf{m}'^T_\tau, 1]^T = [\dot{\mathbf{m}}^T, 1]^T = [\mathbf{v}^T_r, 1]^T$. Therefore the quantity $\nu + \alpha$ is the tangential real motion field, which we denote by w, and β is the normal real motion field. The real and apparent motion fields have the same component along $\mathbf{n}$: we call it the normal motion field (see figure 9.7). According to all this, the real motion field is given by

$$\mathbf{v}_r = w\mathbf{t} + \beta\mathbf{n} \tag{9.13}$$

We also define $\mathbf{V}_r$ as $[\mathbf{v}^T_r, 1]^T = \mathbf{P}'_\tau$.

Let us now consider the tangent plane T_P to the spatiotemporal surface (Σ) at P. By definition, it is spanned by the two vectors $\mathbf{P}'_S$ and $\mathbf{P}'_\tau$ (see appendix C). Examining these two vectors, we see that the vectors $\mathbf{t}_0 = [\mathbf{t}^T, 0]^T$ and $\mathbf{n}_\beta = [\beta\mathbf{n}^T, 1]^T$, which are orthogonal, also span T_P since $\mathbf{P}'_S = u\mathbf{t}_0$ and $\mathbf{P}'_\tau = \mathbf{V}_r = w\mathbf{t}_0 + \mathbf{n}_\beta$ (see figure 9.8). From this follows the fact that

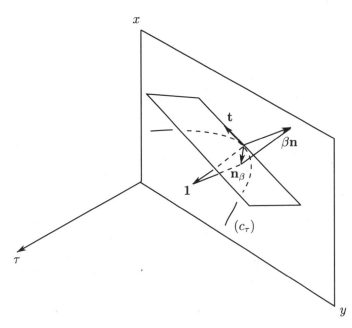

Figure 9.8 The vectors $\mathbf{t}_0$ and $\mathbf{n}_\beta$ span the tangent plane T_P to Σ.

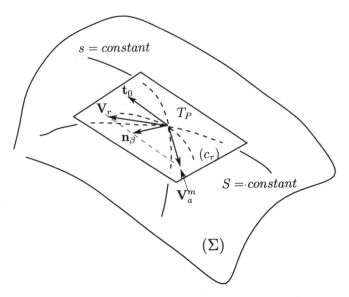

Figure 9.9   Various vectors of the tangent plane T_P to (Σ).

the two vectors $\mathbf{V}_r = w\mathbf{t}_0 + \mathbf{n}_\beta$ and $\mathbf{V}_a = \alpha\mathbf{t}_0 + \mathbf{n}_\beta$ belong to T_P and define on (Σ) two tangent vector fields. The relationship between these vectors of (T_P) is shown in figure 9.9. Expanding on this idea, we can give a geometric interpretation both of the operation of the partial derivative $\frac{\partial}{\partial\tau}$ when the image arclength s is kept constant and of the total time derivative. Given a function f of s and τ into R, this induces a function F on (Σ), which is given by $f(s,\tau) = F(\mathbf{P}(s,\tau))$. The derivative $\frac{\partial f}{\partial\tau}$ is the directional derivative of F in T_P along $\mathbf{V}_a$, which we denote by $L_{\mathbf{V}_a}F$. This is called the *Lie derivative* of the function F with respect to the tangent field $\mathbf{V}_a$ (see appendix C). It satisfies the following linear property:

$$L_{\mathbf{V}_a} = L_{\alpha\mathbf{t}_0 + \mathbf{n}_\beta} = \alpha L_{\mathbf{t}_0} + L_{\mathbf{n}_\beta}$$

Thus

$$\frac{\partial f}{\partial\tau} = L_{\mathbf{V}_a}f = \alpha L_{\mathbf{t}_0}F + L_{\mathbf{n}_\beta}F$$

$L_{\mathbf{t}_0}F$ is simply $\frac{\partial f}{\partial s}$, and we can write $L_{\mathbf{n}_\beta}F = \partial_{\mathbf{n}_\beta}f$. How we compute this quantity is shown in figure 9.10. We consider the normal $\mathbf{n}$ at the point m of the curve (c_τ). At time $\tau + d\tau$, the curve $(c_{\tau+d\tau})$ is intersected by

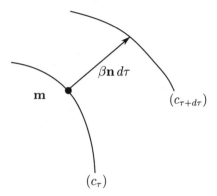

Figure 9.10 A geometric interpretation of $\partial_{\mathbf{n}_\beta}$ (see text).

the line defined by m and $\mathbf{n}$ at a point represented by $\mathbf{m} + \beta\mathbf{n}d\tau$, and we have

$$\partial_{\mathbf{n}_\beta} f = \lim_{d\tau \to 0} \frac{f(\mathbf{m} + \beta\mathbf{n}d\tau) - f(\mathbf{m})}{d\tau}$$

Thus we write

$$\frac{\partial f}{\partial \tau} = \alpha \frac{\partial f}{\partial s} + \partial_{\mathbf{n}_\beta} f \tag{9.14}$$

Similarly, we have

$$L_{\mathbf{v}_r} = L_{w\mathbf{t}_0 + \mathbf{n}_\beta} = w L_{\mathbf{t}_0} + L_{\mathbf{n}_\beta}$$

and therefore

$$\dot{f} = L_{\mathbf{v}_r} f = w \frac{\partial f}{\partial s} + \partial_{\mathbf{n}_\beta} f \tag{9.15}$$

Equations (9.14) and (9.15) have the advantage that they express $\frac{\partial f}{\partial \tau}$ and $\dot{f}$ as functions of $\frac{\partial f}{\partial s}$ and $\partial_{\mathbf{n}_\beta} f$ and of the two unknown tangential motion fields, the apparent one α and the real one w. Values for $\frac{\partial f}{\partial s}$ and $\partial_{\mathbf{n}_\beta}$ can be computed from the sequence of image curves (for $\partial_{\mathbf{n}_\beta}$ we need to know β, but in a moment we will show that it can be estimated from (Σ)). Equations (9.14) and (9.15) also hold for functions f into R^p. We will frequently be using the cases $p = 2, 3$ in what follows.

From equations (9.10) and (9.11) and equation C.3 of appendix C, we can compute the coefficients of the first fundamental form:

Proposition 9.1
The coefficients of the first fundamental form in the basis $(\mathbf{P}'_S, \mathbf{P}'_\tau)$ of T_P
are given by

$$E = u^2 \quad F = uw \quad G = 1 + w^2 + \beta^2 \tag{9.16}$$

We can also compute these coefficients in the basis $(\mathbf{t}_0, \mathbf{n}_\beta)$:

Proposition 9.2
The coefficients of the first fundamental form in the basis $(\mathbf{t}_0, \mathbf{n}_\beta)$ of T_P
are given by

$$E' = 1 \quad F' = 0 \quad G' = 1 + \beta^2$$

Proof With the notations of appendix C, let us denote φ as the linear
mapping $T_P \to T_P$ such that $\Phi_1 \mathbf{x} = \varphi(\mathbf{x}) \cdot \mathbf{x}$ for all $\mathbf{x}$ of T_P. Since we have

$$\mathbf{t}_0 = \frac{1}{u}\mathbf{P}'_S \quad \mathbf{n}_\beta = -\frac{w}{u}\mathbf{P}'_S + \mathbf{P}'_\tau$$

we immediately have $E' = \Phi_1 \mathbf{t}_0 = \frac{1}{u^2}\Phi_1 \mathbf{P}'_S = \frac{E}{u^2} = 1$, $G' = \Phi_1 \mathbf{n}_\beta = \frac{w^2}{u^2}E - 2\frac{w}{u}F + G = 1 + \beta^2$ and $F' = \varphi(\mathbf{t}_0) \cdot \mathbf{n}_\beta = -\frac{w}{u^2}E + \frac{1}{u}F = 0$. ∎

We can also compute a normal $\mathbf{N}_P$ to (Σ), which will be needed for the
second fundamental form.

$$\mathbf{N}_P = \mathbf{t}_0 \wedge \mathbf{n}_\beta = \begin{bmatrix} \mathbf{t} \\ 0 \end{bmatrix} \wedge \begin{bmatrix} \beta\mathbf{n} \\ 1 \end{bmatrix}$$

Let $\mathbf{t} = [t_x, t_y]^T$. Then $\mathbf{n} = \varepsilon[t_y, -t_x]^T$, where $\varepsilon = \pm 1$. The cross-product
that appeared in the previous equation is therefore equal to

$$\begin{bmatrix} t_y \\ -t_x \\ -\varepsilon\beta \end{bmatrix} = \varepsilon \begin{bmatrix} \mathbf{n} \\ -\beta \end{bmatrix}$$

Finally

$$\mathbf{N}_P = \varepsilon \begin{bmatrix} \mathbf{n} \\ -\beta \end{bmatrix}$$

Given a normal $\mathbf{N}_P$ to the spatiotemporal surface (Σ), whose coordinates
in the coordinate system $(\mathbf{t}, \mathbf{n}, \boldsymbol{\tau})$ ($\boldsymbol{\tau}$ is the unit vector defining the τ-axis)
are denoted by $N_\mathbf{t}, N_\mathbf{n}, N_\tau$, we have

$$\beta = -\frac{N_\tau}{N_\mathbf{n}} \qquad N_\mathbf{t} = 0$$

We have thus proved the following proposition:

Proposition 9.3
The normal to the spatiotemporal surface (Σ) yields an estimate of the *normal motion field* β as

$$\beta = -\frac{N_\tau}{N_\mathbf{n}} \tag{9.17}$$

In what follows we take $\mathbf{N}_P = \begin{bmatrix} \mathbf{n} \\ -\beta \end{bmatrix}$, since $\mathbf{N}_P$ is defined up to a scale factor.

9.3.2.2   The second fundamental form of the spatiotemporal surface (Σ)

We denote $\frac{\partial^2 s}{\partial S^2}$ by u_S, $\frac{\partial^2 s}{\partial \tau^2}$ by v_τ, $\frac{\partial^2 s}{\partial \tau \partial S}$ by u_τ, and $\frac{\partial^2 s}{\partial S \partial \tau}$ by v_S. We are going to compute $\frac{\partial^2 \mathbf{P}'}{\partial S^2}$, $\frac{\partial^2 \mathbf{P}'}{\partial \tau^2}$, and $\frac{\partial^2 \mathbf{P}'}{\partial S \partial \tau}$. Starting with the last one and using equation (9.11) and the first equation (9.9), we deduce that

$$\frac{\partial^2 \mathbf{P}'}{\partial S \partial \tau} = \begin{bmatrix} v_S \mathbf{t} + u(v\kappa\mathbf{n} + \frac{\partial \mathbf{v}_a}{\partial s}) \\ 0 \end{bmatrix}$$

Let us now evaluate $\frac{\partial \mathbf{v}_a}{\partial s}$. From the definition of $\mathbf{v}_a$ (equation (9.12)) and the two-dimensional Frenet formulas (C.1), we infer that

$$\frac{\partial \mathbf{v}_a}{\partial s} = (\frac{\partial \alpha}{\partial s} - \kappa\beta)\mathbf{t} + (\kappa\alpha + \frac{\partial \beta}{\partial s})\mathbf{n} \tag{9.18}$$

Thus

$$\frac{\partial^2 \mathbf{P}'}{\partial S \partial \tau} = \begin{bmatrix} (v_S + u(\frac{\partial \alpha}{\partial s} - \kappa\beta))\mathbf{t} + u(\kappa w + \frac{\partial \beta}{\partial s})\mathbf{n} \\ 0 \end{bmatrix} \tag{9.19}$$

Let us now compute $\frac{\partial^2 \mathbf{p}'}{\partial \tau \partial S}$. From equation (9.10), we deduce that

$$\frac{\partial^2 \mathbf{P}'}{\partial \tau \partial S} = \begin{bmatrix} u_\tau \mathbf{t} + u\dot{\mathbf{t}} \\ 0 \end{bmatrix} \tag{9.20}$$

Using the derivation rule (9.15), we can write

$$\dot{\mathbf{t}} = w\frac{\partial \mathbf{t}}{\partial s} + \partial_{\mathbf{n}_\beta}\mathbf{t} = \kappa w \mathbf{n} + \partial_{\mathbf{n}_\beta}\mathbf{t} \tag{9.21}$$

The vector $\partial_{\mathbf{n}_\beta}\mathbf{t}$ is a derivative of the unit vector $\mathbf{t}$. It is therefore perpendicular to $\mathbf{t}$ and is in the plane defined by $\mathbf{n}$ and $\boldsymbol{\tau}$. We write

$$\partial_{\mathbf{n}_\beta}\mathbf{t} = \varphi\mathbf{n} + \psi\boldsymbol{\tau} \tag{9.22}$$

Therefore, equation (9.21) yields

$$\dot{\mathbf{t}} = (\kappa w + \varphi)\mathbf{n} + \psi\boldsymbol{\tau} \tag{9.23}$$

From the Schwarz equality, $\frac{\partial^2 \mathbf{p}'}{\partial s \partial \tau} = \frac{\partial^2 \mathbf{p}'}{\partial \tau \partial s}$ and $u_\tau = v_s$. We conclude, by equating equations (9.19) and (9.20), that, if $u \neq 0$, $\psi = 0$, $\frac{\partial \alpha}{\partial s} = \kappa\beta$, and $\varphi = \frac{\partial \beta}{\partial s}$. We call φ the *β-curvature* of (c_τ), while κ is the *space curvature*. Of course, we also have

$$\partial_{\mathbf{n}_\beta}\mathbf{n} = -\varphi\mathbf{t} \tag{9.24}$$

We have proved the following theorem:

Theorem 9.1
The tangential apparent motion field α and the β-curvature φ satisfy

$$\frac{\partial \alpha}{\partial s} = \kappa\beta \tag{9.25}$$

$$\varphi = \frac{\partial \beta}{\partial s} \tag{9.26}$$

Equation (9.25) is instructive. Indeed, it shows that α, the tangential component of the apparent motion field $\mathbf{v}_a$, is entirely determined up to the addition of a function of time by the normal component of the motion field β and the space curvature κ of (c_τ):

$$\alpha = \int_{s_0}^{s} \kappa(y,\tau)\beta(y,\tau)dy \tag{9.27}$$

Changing the origin of arclengths from s_0 to s_1 on (c_τ) is equivalent to adding the function $\int_{s_0}^{s_1} \kappa(y,\tau)\beta(y,\tau)dy$ to α, a function that is constant on (c_τ). This is the fundamental result of this section. We have proved the following theorem:

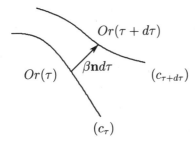

Figure 9.11   The choice of the origin of arclength on (c_τ).

Theorem 9.2
The tangential apparent motion field can be recovered from the normal flow up to the addition of a function of time through equation (9.27).

The choice of this function of time is related to the choice of the origin of arclengths at each time instant. In practice, we want this function of time to be smooth, i.e., if $Or(\tau)$ is the origin at time τ, its tangential apparent velocity is 0 by definition (equation (9.27)), and we would like the origin at time $Or(\tau + d\tau)$ to be $Or(\tau) + \beta \mathbf{n} d\tau$ (see figure 9.11). Mathematically this means that, if P_{or} is the corresponding point on (Σ), it follows a trajectory described by the following differential equation[1]:

$$\frac{dP_{or}}{d\tau}(\tau) = \mathbf{n}_\beta(\tau) \tag{9.28}$$

We know from the theory of differential equations that, if $\mathbf{n}_\beta$ is smooth enough, then equation (9.28) has a unique solution for the initial condition $P_{or}(0) = P_0$ in a neighborhood of P_0. Thus, since $\mathbf{n}_\beta(\tau)$ is known at each time instant, if we choose the origin as P_0 at time 0 we can compute what the origin is at time τ and can compute α from equation (9.27).

We will now prove an interesting relationship between the β- and space curvatures of (c_τ).

Proposition 9.4
The β- and space curvatures of (c_τ) satisfy the following equation,

---

1. Or equivalently, the point Or in the image follows a trajectory defined by $\frac{dOr}{d\tau}(\tau) = \beta \mathbf{n}$.

$$\frac{\partial \varphi}{\partial s} = \partial_{n_\beta} \kappa - \kappa^2 \beta$$

which can be rewritten as

$$\partial_{n_\beta} \kappa = \frac{\partial^2 \beta}{\partial s^2} + \kappa^2 \beta \tag{9.29}$$

Proof We compute $\frac{\partial^2 \mathbf{t}}{\partial s \partial \tau}$ and $\frac{\partial^2 \mathbf{t}}{\partial \tau \partial s}$ and write that they are equal. Using the derivation rule (9.14), we can write

$$\frac{\partial^2 \mathbf{t}}{\partial s \partial \tau} = \frac{\partial(\alpha \frac{\partial \mathbf{t}}{\partial s} + \partial_{n_\beta} \mathbf{t})}{\partial s} = \frac{\partial((\kappa \alpha + \varphi)\mathbf{n})}{\partial s}$$

Thus

$$\frac{\partial^2 \mathbf{t}}{\partial s \partial \tau} = (\frac{\partial \kappa}{\partial s} \alpha + \kappa \frac{\partial \alpha}{\partial s} + \frac{\partial \varphi}{\partial s})\mathbf{n} - \kappa(\kappa \alpha + \varphi)\mathbf{t}$$

On the other hand,

$$\frac{\partial^2 \mathbf{t}}{\partial \tau \partial s} = \frac{\partial(\kappa \mathbf{n})}{\partial \tau} = \alpha \frac{\partial(\kappa \mathbf{n})}{\partial s} + \partial_{n_\beta}(\kappa \mathbf{n})$$

thus

$$\frac{\partial^2 \mathbf{t}}{\partial \tau \partial s} = (\alpha \frac{\partial \kappa}{\partial s} + \partial_{n_\beta} \kappa)\mathbf{n} - \kappa(\kappa \alpha + \varphi)\mathbf{t}$$

From this point, together with equation (9.25) and (9.26), the announced results follow.   ∎

Just as the previous result has been obtained by writing that $\frac{\partial^2 \mathbf{t}}{\partial s \partial \tau} = \frac{\partial^2 \mathbf{t}}{\partial \tau \partial s}$, we can obtain another result by applying the same technique to the other fundamental quantity of our problem, namely β. We thus obtain the following proposition:

Proposition 9.5
The normal flow, and also the β- and spatial curvatures, satisfy the following relationship:

$$\partial_{n_\beta}(\frac{\partial \beta}{\partial s}) - \frac{\partial(\partial_{n_\beta} \beta)}{\partial s} = \kappa \beta \frac{\partial \beta}{\partial s} \tag{9.30}$$

Proof The proof is straightforward and uses the derivation rule (9.14).
∎

There is an interesting interpretation of equation (9.30) in terms of *Lie brackets* (see appendix C for a definition and some properties). Indeed, its left-hand side is recognized as the *Lie derivative* $L_{[\mathbf{n}_\beta,\mathbf{t}_0]}\beta$ of β with respect to the *Lie bracket* $[\mathbf{n}_\beta,\mathbf{t}_0]$. It is easy to show (see problem 4) that $L_{[\mathbf{n}_\beta,\mathbf{t}_0]}\beta = \frac{\partial\alpha}{\partial s}\frac{\partial\beta}{\partial s}$. Therefore, equation (9.30) can be rewritten as

$$\frac{\partial\alpha}{\partial s}\frac{\partial\beta}{\partial s} = \kappa\beta\frac{\partial\beta}{\partial s}$$

and, if $\frac{\partial\beta}{\partial s} \neq 0$, we again find equation (9.25). Equation (9.30) is not "new." It is equivalent to equation (9.25) in the case where $\frac{\partial\beta}{\partial s} \neq 0$.

Let us now evaluate $\frac{\partial^2\mathbf{P}'}{\partial s^2}$ and $\frac{\partial^2\mathbf{P}'}{\partial\tau^2}$. From equation (9.10) and the first equation of (9.9) we can derive

$$\mathbf{P}'_{s^2} = u^2\mathbf{P}_{s^2} + u_s\mathbf{P}_s = \begin{bmatrix} u^2\kappa\mathbf{n} + u_s\mathbf{t} \\ 0 \end{bmatrix}$$

From equation (9.11) we have

$$\mathbf{P}'_{\tau^2} = \begin{bmatrix} \nu_\tau\mathbf{t} + \nu\dot{\mathbf{t}} + \dot{\mathbf{v}}_a \\ 0 \end{bmatrix}$$

We have previously seen that $\dot{\mathbf{t}} = (\kappa w + \varphi)\mathbf{n}$ (equation (9.23)). Now, again using the derivation rule (9.15), we obtain

$$\dot{\mathbf{v}}_a = w\frac{\partial\mathbf{v}_a}{\partial s} + \partial_{\mathbf{n}_\beta}\mathbf{v}_a$$

We know from equations (9.18) and (9.25) that $\frac{\partial\mathbf{v}_a}{\partial s} = (\kappa\alpha + \varphi)\mathbf{n}$. We can evaluate $\partial_{\mathbf{n}_\beta}\mathbf{v}_a$:

$$\partial_{\mathbf{n}_\beta}\mathbf{v}_a = (\partial_{\mathbf{n}_\beta}\alpha - \beta\varphi)\mathbf{t} + (\alpha\varphi + \partial_{\mathbf{n}_\beta}\beta)\mathbf{n}$$

so that finally

$$\mathbf{P}'_{\tau^2} = \begin{bmatrix} (\nu_\tau + \partial_{\mathbf{n}_\beta}\alpha - \beta\varphi)\mathbf{t} + (\kappa w^2 + 2w\varphi + \partial_{\mathbf{n}_\beta}\beta)\mathbf{n} \\ 0 \end{bmatrix}$$

We can now compute the coefficients of the second fundamental form. After applying some algebra and using equation (9.26), we obtain the following:

Proposition 9.6
The coefficients of the second fundamental form in the basis $(\mathbf{P}'_S, \mathbf{P}'_\tau)$ of T_P are given by

$$L = \frac{\kappa u^2}{\sqrt{1+\beta^2}} \quad M = \frac{(\kappa w + \frac{\partial \beta}{\partial s})u}{\sqrt{1+\beta^2}} \quad N = \frac{\kappa w^2 + 2w\frac{\partial \beta}{\partial s} + \partial_{\mathbf{n}_\beta}\beta}{\sqrt{1+\beta^2}} \tag{9.31}$$

We can also compute these coefficients in the basis $(\mathbf{t}_0, \mathbf{n}_\beta)$:

Proposition 9.7
The coefficients of the second fundamental form in the basis $(\mathbf{t}_0, \mathbf{n}_\beta)$ are given by

$$L' = \frac{\kappa}{\sqrt{1+\beta^2}} \quad M' = \frac{\frac{\partial \beta}{\partial s}}{\sqrt{1+\beta^2}} \quad N' = \frac{\partial_{\mathbf{n}_\beta}\beta}{\sqrt{1+\beta^2}}$$

Proof Let us denote ψ as the linear mapping $T_P \to T_P$ such that $\Phi_2 \mathbf{x} = \psi(\mathbf{x}) \cdot \mathbf{x}$ for all $\mathbf{x}$ of T_P. Since we have

$$\mathbf{t}_0 = \frac{1}{u}\mathbf{P}'_S \quad \mathbf{n}_\beta = -\frac{w}{u}\mathbf{P}'_S + \mathbf{P}'_\tau$$

we can write $L' = \Phi_2 \mathbf{t}_0 = \frac{1}{u^2}\Phi_2 \mathbf{P}'_S = \frac{L}{u^2}$, $N' = \Phi_2 \mathbf{n}_\beta = \frac{w^2}{u^2}L - 2\frac{w}{u}M + N = \frac{\partial_{\mathbf{n}_\beta}\beta}{\sqrt{1+\beta^2}}$, and $M' = \psi(\mathbf{t}_0) \cdot \mathbf{n}_\beta = -\frac{w}{u^2}L + \frac{1}{u}\psi \mathbf{P}'_S \cdot \mathbf{P}'_\tau = -\frac{w}{u^2}L + \frac{1}{u}M = \frac{\frac{\partial \beta}{\partial s}}{\sqrt{1+\beta^2}}$　■

This proposition shows that neither u nor ν can be recovered from the first and second fundamental forms of (Σ). As a consequence, the tangential component w of the real motion field $\mathbf{v}_r$ cannot be recovered either.

9.3.2.3　The Codazzi-Mainardi equations

The reader may wonder whether we have completely characterized the spatiotemporal surface (Σ) and whether it is possible to find other relations that may yield more information than what we have found so far. The answer to this is no due to the Bonnet theorem, which is given in appendix C. We will show that, by combining equations (C.8–C.12) with the expressions (9.16) and (9.31), the Gauss and Codazzi-Mainardi equations

(C.8), (C.9), and (C.10) for (Σ) imply equations (9.29), (9.25), and (9.30). The Gauss and Codazzi-Mainardi equations can be written as

$$\frac{wu\beta}{(1+\beta^2)^{\frac{3}{2}}}(\kappa^2\beta + \frac{\partial^2\beta}{\partial s^2} - \partial_{n_\beta}\kappa) = 0$$

$$\frac{u}{(1+\beta^2)^{\frac{3}{2}}}(\kappa(1+\beta^2) - \partial_{n_\beta}\beta)(u_\tau - w_s + \kappa u\beta) = 0$$

$$\frac{u}{(1+\beta^2)^{\frac{1}{2}}}(\kappa\beta\frac{\partial\beta}{\partial s} - \partial_{n_\beta}(\frac{\partial\beta}{\partial s}) + \frac{\partial(\partial_{n_\beta}\beta)}{\partial s}) = 0$$

The first equation implies equation (9.29), and the third implies equation (9.30). But we have seen that equation (9.30) also implied equation (9.25). Now, using the facts that $w = v + \alpha$, $v_s = u_\tau$, and $\alpha_s = u\frac{\partial\alpha}{\partial s}$, we can write the second equation as

$$\frac{u^2}{(1+\beta^2)^{\frac{3}{2}}}((\kappa(1+\beta^2) - \partial_{n_\beta}\beta)(\frac{\partial\alpha}{\partial s} - \kappa\beta) = 0$$

Therefore, it appears that this equation is a consequence of the third and that the condition $\partial_{n_\beta}\beta = \kappa(1+\beta^2)$ is not necessarily true. We will show it again later in the simple case of retinal rigid motion (see section 9.6.1). From the Bonnet theorem, the two equations (9.25) and (9.29), together with those giving the coefficients of the first and second fundamental forms (equations (9.16) and (9.31)), completely characterize (Σ) up to a rigid motion.

9.3.2.4　Conclusion

There are three main consequences that we can draw from this analysis. Under the weak assumption of *isometric motion*, we have shown the following:

1. The normal motion field β can be recovered from the normal to the spatiotemporal surface (proposition 9.3).

2. The tangential apparent motion field can be recovered from the normal motion field through equation (9.27) up to the addition of a function of time, and we have seen how to eliminate this problem,

3. The tangential real motion field cannot be recovered from the spatiotemporal surface.

Therefore, the full real motion field is not computable from the observation in the image of a moving curve under the isometric assumption. In order to compute it we must add more hypotheses, for example, that the 3-D motion is rigid. This is what we will do in section 9.5. Note that this is not what has been done in the literature [HS81, Nag83, Hil84, BB83, Gon89, Bou89]. We suspect that these authors actually compute the apparent motion field, which, as we will show in section 9.6, can be quite different from the real one. In particular, we will show in problem 1 that this is indeed the case for the algorithm described in the article by Bouthemy [Bou89].

9.3.3   Interpretation in terms of image intensities

In this section our goal is to interpret the results of the previous section in terms of image intensities and, in particular, to provide means of actually computing the quantities β, $\frac{\partial \beta}{\partial s}$, $\frac{\partial^2 \beta}{\partial s^2}$, $\partial_{n_\beta} \beta$, $\partial_{n_\beta} \frac{\partial \beta}{\partial s}$, κ, and $\frac{\partial \kappa}{\partial s}$. Since the theory that has been presented deals with curves, we have to go back to how these curves are extracted in the images. In chapter 4 we discussed several approaches for detecting edge pixels. The Marr-Hildreth edge detector, for example, computes the zero-crossings in the result $J(x, y, \tau)$ of the convolution of the image $I(x, y, \tau)$ with the Laplacian of a Gaussian $\Delta G_\sigma(x, y)$, where $G_\sigma(x, y)$ is proportional to $e^{-\frac{x^2+y^2}{2\sigma^2}}$:

$$^{mh}J(x, y, \tau) = \Delta G_\sigma \otimes I(x, y, \tau)$$

Connected sets of pixels where ^{mh}J is equal to 0 can then be extracted to form a number of discrete curves[2]. They are therefore characterized by the equation

$$^{mh}J(x, y, \tau) = 0$$

This equation can be thought of as the equation of the spatiotemporal surface generated by the curves and can be used to compute the previous quantities.

---

2. The upper-index *mh* stands, of course, for Marr-Hildreth.

For example, the vector[3]

$$\mathbf{N} = \nabla_3 {}^{mh}J = \begin{bmatrix} {}^{mh}J_x \\ {}^{mh}J_y \\ {}^{mh}J_\tau \end{bmatrix}$$

is normal to that surface. The vector $\nabla_2 {}^{mh}J = \begin{bmatrix} {}^{mh}J_x \\ {}^{mh}J_y \end{bmatrix}$ is, by definition, normal to the curve (c_τ) of equation ${}^{mh}J(x, y, \tau) = 0$. Therefore, using the notations of section 9.3.2.1, we have

$$N_t = 0 \quad N_n = \varepsilon \sqrt{{}^{mh}J_x^2 + {}^{mh}J_y^2} \quad N_\tau = {}^{mh}J_\tau$$

where $\varepsilon = \pm 1$. Using equation (9.17), this yields the following expression for β:

$$\beta_{mh} = -\varepsilon \frac{{}^{mh}J_\tau}{\sqrt{{}^{mh}J_x^2 + {}^{mh}J_y^2}}$$

This is one way of detecting the curves in the image, from which we see that the computation of the normal flow β can be done directly from the image intensities.

If, instead of using the Marr-Hildreth edge detector, we use the Canny-Deriche edge detector described in chapter 4, we come up with another definition of the curves (c_τ). In that case, the image $I(x, y, \tau)$ is first smoothed with an impulse response $K(x, y)$ yielding an image $I_1(x, y, \tau)$ (section 4.5.1), and the points where the magnitude of the gradient is maximum in the direction of the gradient are marked as edges. As shown in section 4.5.2, at these points we have

$$D_g^2 I_1 = 2\mathbf{g}^T\mathbf{H}\mathbf{g} = 0$$

where $\mathbf{g} = \nabla_2 I_1$ and $\mathbf{H}$ is the Hessian of I_1. The curves (c_τ) and therefore the spatiotemporal surfaces that they generate satisfy the equation

$${}^{cd}J(x, y, \tau) = \mathbf{g}^T\mathbf{H}\mathbf{g} = 0$$

where $\mathbf{g}$ and $\mathbf{H}$ have been defined above.[4] The normal motion field is then given by

---

3. In what follows, ∇_3 represents the spatio-temporal gradient, while ∇_2 represents the image gradient.

4. The upper-index *cd* stands for Canny-Deriche.

$$\beta_{cd} = -\varepsilon \frac{{}^{cd}J_\tau}{\sqrt{{}^{cd}J_x^2 + {}^{cd}J_y^2}}$$

and is, in general, different from β_{mh}.

Before we show how to compute the other quantities, let us look at a last example of curves (c_τ). Suppose we are interested in isointensity curves that satisfy ${}^{hs}J(x, y, \tau) = I(x, y, \tau) = constant.$[5] Then using the same reasoning as before yields the following for the normal motion field:

$$\beta_{hs} = -\varepsilon \frac{I_\tau}{\sqrt{I_x^2 + I_y^2}}$$

This is the value obtained from equation (9.2). This shows that, in our formalism, the motion constraint equation is equivalent to saying that the curves (c_τ), which are considered to be the images of significant three dimensional curves are isointensity curves.

We can now go ahead and compute the quantities $\frac{\partial \beta}{\partial s}$, $\frac{\partial^2 \beta}{\partial s^2}$, $\partial_{n_\beta}\beta$, and $\partial_{n_\beta}\frac{\partial \beta}{\partial s}$. In order to do this, it is sufficient to use the correct formula for β corresponding to the definition of the curves (c_τ) that we are observing and then apply

$$\frac{\partial \beta}{\partial s} = \nabla_3 \beta \cdot \mathbf{t}_0 = \nabla_2 \beta \cdot \mathbf{t} \qquad \frac{\partial^2 \beta}{\partial s^2} = \nabla_3 \frac{\partial \beta}{\partial s} \cdot \mathbf{t}_0 = \nabla_2 \frac{\partial \beta}{\partial s} \cdot \mathbf{t}$$

$$\partial_{n_\beta}\beta = \nabla_3 \beta \cdot \mathbf{n}_\beta = \beta \nabla_2 \beta \cdot \mathbf{n} + \frac{\partial \beta}{\partial \tau} \quad \partial_{n_\beta}\frac{\partial \beta}{\partial s} = \nabla_3 \frac{\partial \beta}{\partial s} \cdot \mathbf{n}_\beta = \beta \nabla_2 \frac{\partial \beta}{\partial s} \cdot \mathbf{n} + \frac{\partial^2 \beta}{\partial \tau \partial s}$$

Note that the partial derivative $\frac{\partial}{\partial \tau}$ is taken at x and y constant.

The vectors $\mathbf{t}$ and $\mathbf{n}$ are defined as

$$\mathbf{t} = \varepsilon_1 \frac{1}{\sqrt{J_x^2 + J_y^2}} \begin{bmatrix} -J_y \\ J_x \end{bmatrix} \qquad \mathbf{n} = \varepsilon_2 \frac{1}{\sqrt{J_x^2 + J_y^2}} \begin{bmatrix} J_x \\ J_y \end{bmatrix}$$

and $\varepsilon_1, \varepsilon_2 = \pm 1$. Similar reasoning allows us to establish formulas for κ and $\frac{\partial \kappa}{\partial s}$. Note that the highest-order derivative that we need depends upon the edge detector that we use. For example, we need derivatives of order 4 if we use the Canny-Deriche or the Marr-Hildreth detectors, but only order 3 if we believe that edges are isointensity curves. This is a serious

---

5. The upper-index *hs* stands for Horn-Schunck.

practical problem, which we discussed in chapter 4. Some useful results can also be found in the work of Meer and Weiss [MW89, Wei91].

9.4 Rigid motion of a 3-D straight line

To start the study of the motion field of curves in the case of a rigid motion, we begin with the simplest example, a straight line.

9.4.1 Some issues of representation

Let us define the kind of representations that we will be using.

9.4.1.1 *Representation of a 3-D line*

We represent a straight line L in 3-D space with a direction vector $\mathbf{W} = [\alpha, \beta, \gamma]^T$ and a point M of coordinates $(x, y, \text{ and } z)$, which we will leave unspecified at the moment. $\mathbf{W}$ is defined up to a scale factor. We do not insist on having a minimal representation for the direction of L.

9.4.1.2 *Representation of a 2-D line*

A line l in the retinal plane is represented, as in chapter 5, by two numbers a and b such that the equation of the line is $x + ay + b = 0$ in the map φ_1 and $ax + y + b = 0$ in the map φ_2. These two numbers define a vector $\mathbf{n} = [1, a, b]^T$ in φ_1 or $\mathbf{n} = [a, 1, b]^T$ in φ_2, which is normal to the plane defined by l and the optical center of the camera (see figure 9.12). It is the time derivative $\dot{\mathbf{n}}$ of the vector $\mathbf{n}$ that we call the motion field of the line l. It can be estimated from the two-dimensional token-tracker described in chapter 8.

9.4.1.3 *Relations between L and l*

We will now establish the relationships between the representation of a 3-D line and its image in the retinal plane. The first relation is that the direction $\mathbf{W}$ of the line is perpendicular to the normal $\mathbf{n}$ to the plane that it defines with the optical center

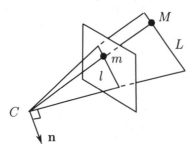

Figure 9.12   The vector **n** is normal to the plane defined by the optical center *C* of the camera and the line *l*.

$$\mathbf{W}^T\mathbf{n} = 0 \tag{9.32}$$

The second relation is that, for any point *M* of *L*, we have

$$\mathbf{M}^T\mathbf{n} = 0 \tag{9.33}$$

and therefore we also have

$$\mathbf{m}^T\mathbf{n} = 0$$

9.4.2   The first-order motion equations

We will now relate the observed parameters **n** and **ṅ** to the three-dimensional motion and structure of the line. For this, we assume that the 3-D line under consideration is attached to a rigid body whose motion is described by its instantaneous rotational velocity, **Ω**, and linear velocity, **V**, which is its kinematic screw at the origin *C*.

9.4.2.1   *The relationship between the direction of the 3-D line and its angular velocity*

Let **T** be a normalized line direction:

$$\mathbf{T} = \frac{\mathbf{W}}{\|\mathbf{W}\|}$$

Note that **T** also satisfies equation (9.32). If we recall that the velocity **Ṁ** of any point **M** attached to the rigid body is given by

$$\dot{\mathbf{M}} = \mathbf{V} + \mathbf{\Omega} \wedge \mathbf{M} \tag{9.34}$$

The normalized direction **T** satisfies a simpler differential equation:

$$\dot{\mathbf{T}} = \mathbf{\Omega} \wedge \mathbf{T} \tag{9.35}$$

We will now express **W** as a function only of the image measurements **n**, **ṅ**, and $\mathbf{\Omega}$. For this we can use equation (9.32) and take its time derivative:

$$\dot{\mathbf{n}}^T \mathbf{T} + \mathbf{n}^T \dot{\mathbf{T}} = 0$$

Replacing **Ṫ** in that equation with its value in equation (9.35), we obtain

$$\dot{\mathbf{n}}^T \mathbf{T} + (\mathbf{n}, \mathbf{\Omega}, \mathbf{T}) = 0$$

where $(\mathbf{n}, \mathbf{\Omega}, \mathbf{T})$ is the determinant of the three vectors **n**, $\mathbf{\Omega}$, and **T**. Using standard properties of determinants, this equation can be rewritten as

$$\mathbf{T}^T (\dot{\mathbf{n}} + \mathbf{n} \wedge \mathbf{\Omega}) = 0$$

Combining this with equation (9.32) shows that **T** is perpendicular to both vectors, **n** and $\dot{\mathbf{n}} + \mathbf{n} \wedge \mathbf{\Omega}$, and therefore it is proportional to their cross-product. Since **W** is a direction, i.e., is defined up to a scale factor, we can write

$$\mathbf{W} = \mathbf{n} \wedge (\mathbf{n} \wedge \mathbf{\Omega} + \dot{\mathbf{n}}) \tag{9.36}$$

Equation (9.36) is fundamental. It allows us to recover the spatial direction of a 3-D line if we know $\mathbf{\Omega}$, the representation **n** of its 2-D image, and the measured motion field **ṅ**, which can be estimated by the token tracker described in chapter 8.

9.4.2.2 *The relationship between a point of the 3-D line and its kinematic screw*

Let us recall that the velocity **Ṁ** of any point **M** attached to the rigid 3-D line is given by equation (9.34). On the other hand, the relationship between **n**, the representation of the 2-D line, and the 3-D point *M* is given by the equation (9.33). Taking the time derivative of equation (9.33) yields

$$\dot{\mathbf{n}}^T \mathbf{M} + \mathbf{n}^T \dot{\mathbf{M}} = 0$$

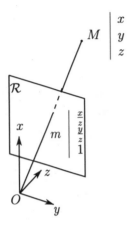

Figure 9.13   The perspective projection.

Replacing $\dot{\mathbf{M}}$ in that equation with its value from equation (9.34), we obtain

$$(\Omega \wedge \mathbf{M} + \mathbf{V})^T \mathbf{n} + \mathbf{M}^T \dot{\mathbf{n}} = 0$$

which can be rewritten as

$$\mathbf{M}^T (\mathbf{n} \wedge \Omega + \dot{\mathbf{n}}) + \mathbf{V}^T \mathbf{n} = 0$$

On the other hand, we have the perspective equation (see figure 9.13)

$$\mathbf{M} = z\mathbf{m} \qquad (9.37)$$

This leads to the following relation, which gives z as a function of Ω, $\mathbf{V}$, $\mathbf{n}$ and the 2-D motion field $\dot{\mathbf{n}}$ obtained from the line segments tracker:

$$z\mathbf{m}^T (\mathbf{n} \wedge \Omega + \dot{\mathbf{n}}) + \mathbf{V}^T \mathbf{n} = 0 \qquad (9.38)$$

A complete determination of the 3-D position of the point $\mathbf{M}$ is then obtained using relation (9.37).

9.4.3   The second-order motion equations

We will now eliminate $\mathbf{W}$ and z from equations (9.36) and (9.38) by taking another time derivative. This yields two equations linking the kinematic screw $(\Omega, \mathbf{V})$ and its time derivative $(\dot{\Omega}, \dot{\mathbf{V}})$ to quantities measured in the image by, for example, the token tracker described in the previous chapter.

9.4.3.1   *An equation between the angular velocity and acceleration*

Equation (9.36) yields one equation involving only the angular velocity Ω and the acceleration $\dot{\Omega}$. We write

$$\mathbf{W} = \|\mathbf{W}\| \frac{\mathbf{W}}{\|\mathbf{W}\|} = \|\mathbf{W}\|\mathbf{T}$$

and take the time derivative of both sides

$$\dot{\mathbf{W}} = \|\dot{\mathbf{W}}\|\mathbf{T} + \|\mathbf{W}\|\dot{\mathbf{T}} \qquad (9.39)$$

We already know that $\dot{\mathbf{T}} = \Omega \wedge \mathbf{T} = \Omega \wedge \frac{\mathbf{W}}{\|\mathbf{W}\|}$, and we have to evaluate $\|\dot{\mathbf{W}}\|$:

$$\|\mathbf{W}\| = (\mathbf{W}^T\mathbf{W})^{\frac{1}{2}}$$

Therefore

$$\|\dot{\mathbf{W}}\| = \frac{\dot{\mathbf{W}}^T\mathbf{W}}{\|\mathbf{W}\|}$$

By substituting from equation (9.39) we obtain

$$(\mathbf{W}^T\mathbf{W})\dot{\mathbf{W}} - (\dot{\mathbf{W}}^T\mathbf{W})\mathbf{W} + (\mathbf{W}^T\mathbf{W})\mathbf{W} \wedge \Omega =$$
$$(\mathbf{W}^T\mathbf{W})(\dot{\mathbf{W}} + \mathbf{W} \wedge \Omega) - (\dot{\mathbf{W}}^T\mathbf{W})\mathbf{W} = \mathbf{0} \qquad (9.40)$$

Note here that the first term of this expression is equivalent to $\mathbf{W} \wedge (\dot{\mathbf{W}} \wedge \mathbf{W})$. With this substitution we can write

$$\mathbf{W} \wedge (\dot{\mathbf{W}} \wedge \mathbf{W} + (\mathbf{W}^T\mathbf{W})\Omega) = \mathbf{0} \qquad (9.41)$$

Taking the cross-product of the second term with $\mathbf{W}$ yields

$$\mathbf{W} \wedge (\dot{\mathbf{W}} + \mathbf{W} \wedge \Omega) = \mathbf{0} \qquad (9.42)$$

since $\mathbf{W}^T\mathbf{W} \neq 0$. Equations (9.41) and (9.42) are equivalent since the first one implies the second and since, if we expand the first term of (9.42), we obtain

$$\mathbf{W} \wedge \dot{\mathbf{W}} + (\mathbf{W}^T\mathbf{\Omega})\mathbf{W} - (\mathbf{W}^T\mathbf{W})\mathbf{\Omega} = \mathbf{0}$$

Taking the cross-product with $\mathbf{W}$ gives equation (9.41).

Next we will show that equation (9.42) is equivalent to a single scalar equation.

Proposition 9.8
Equation (9.36) implies equation (9.42), which is equivalent to

$$\mu\mathbf{n} = \mathbf{0} \tag{9.43}$$

where

$$\mu = \mathbf{W}^T(2\dot{\mathbf{n}} \wedge \mathbf{\Omega} + \mathbf{n} \wedge \dot{\mathbf{\Omega}} + \ddot{\mathbf{n}} + (\mathbf{n}^T\mathbf{\Omega})\mathbf{\Omega}) \tag{9.44}$$

and where $\mathbf{W}$ is given by equation (9.36).

Proof   First we evaluate the term $\mathbf{W} \wedge \mathbf{\Omega}$ using equation (9.36):

$$\mathbf{W} \wedge \mathbf{\Omega} = (\mathbf{n} \wedge (\mathbf{n} \wedge \mathbf{\Omega} + \dot{\mathbf{n}})) \wedge \mathbf{\Omega} = (\mathbf{n}^T\mathbf{\Omega})(\mathbf{n} \wedge \mathbf{\Omega} + \dot{\mathbf{n}}) - (\dot{\mathbf{n}}^T\mathbf{\Omega})\mathbf{n}$$

Then we evaluate $\dot{\mathbf{W}}$, also using (9.36):

$$\dot{\mathbf{W}} = \dot{\mathbf{n}} \wedge (\mathbf{n} \wedge \mathbf{\Omega}) + \mathbf{n} \wedge (\dot{\mathbf{n}} \wedge \mathbf{\Omega} + \mathbf{n} \wedge \dot{\mathbf{\Omega}} + \ddot{\mathbf{n}})$$

$$= (\dot{\mathbf{n}}^T\mathbf{\Omega})\mathbf{n} - (\dot{\mathbf{n}}^T\mathbf{n})\mathbf{\Omega} + \mathbf{n} \wedge (\dot{\mathbf{n}} \wedge \mathbf{\Omega} + \mathbf{n} \wedge \dot{\mathbf{\Omega}} + \ddot{\mathbf{n}})$$

Thus

$$\dot{\mathbf{W}} + \mathbf{W} \wedge \mathbf{\Omega} = (\mathbf{n}^T\mathbf{\Omega})\dot{\mathbf{n}} - (\dot{\mathbf{n}}^T\mathbf{n})\mathbf{\Omega} + \mathbf{n} \wedge (\dot{\mathbf{n}} \wedge \mathbf{\Omega} + \mathbf{n} \wedge \dot{\mathbf{\Omega}} + \ddot{\mathbf{n}} + (\mathbf{n}^T\mathbf{\Omega})\mathbf{\Omega})$$

We recognize in the first two terms $\mathbf{n} \wedge (\dot{\mathbf{n}} \wedge \mathbf{\Omega})$ and obtain

$$\dot{\mathbf{W}} + \mathbf{W} \wedge \mathbf{\Omega} = \mathbf{n} \wedge (2\dot{\mathbf{n}} \wedge \mathbf{\Omega} + \mathbf{n} \wedge \dot{\mathbf{\Omega}} + \ddot{\mathbf{n}} + (\mathbf{n}^T\mathbf{\Omega})\mathbf{\Omega})$$

As a consequence

$$\mathbf{W} \wedge (\dot{\mathbf{W}} + \mathbf{W} \wedge \mathbf{\Omega}) = [\mathbf{W}^T(2\dot{\mathbf{n}} \wedge \mathbf{\Omega} + \mathbf{n} \wedge \dot{\mathbf{\Omega}} + \ddot{\mathbf{n}} + (\mathbf{n}^T\mathbf{\Omega})\mathbf{\Omega})]\mathbf{n}$$

since $\mathbf{W}^T\mathbf{n} = 0$ ■

We have shown that equation (9.36) yields one scalar equation, $\mu = 0$, unless $\mathbf{n} = \mathbf{0}$, which happens only if l is reduced to a point, i.e., if L goes through C, which is not a generic situation (equation (9.32)).

9.4.3.2   *An equation between* (Ω, V) *and* $(\dot{\Omega}, \dot{V})$

Equation (9.38) yields an equation involving the kinematic screw (Ω, V) and its time derivative $(\dot{\Omega}, \dot{V})$. We have the following proposition:

Proposition 9.9

Equation (9.38) implies the following scalar equation:

$$[\mathbf{m}^T(\mathbf{n} \wedge \Omega + \dot{\mathbf{n}})][V^T(\mathbf{n} \wedge \Omega + 2\dot{\mathbf{n}}) + \dot{V}^T\mathbf{n}]$$
$$- (V^T\mathbf{n})[\mathbf{m}^T(2\dot{\mathbf{n}} \wedge \Omega + \mathbf{n} \wedge \dot{\Omega} + \ddot{\mathbf{n}} + (\Omega^T\mathbf{n})\Omega)] = 0 \tag{9.45}$$

Proof   We take the time derivative of equation (9.38)

$$\dot{\mathbf{M}}^T(\mathbf{n} \wedge \Omega + \dot{\mathbf{n}}) + \mathbf{M}^T(\dot{\mathbf{n}} \wedge \Omega + \mathbf{n} \wedge \dot{\Omega} + \ddot{\mathbf{n}}) + \dot{V}^T\mathbf{n} + V^T\dot{\mathbf{n}} = 0$$

Using equations (9.34) and (9.37), we have

$$V^T(\mathbf{n} \wedge \Omega + 2\dot{\mathbf{n}}) + z\mathbf{m}^T(\dot{\mathbf{n}} \wedge \Omega + \mathbf{n} \wedge \dot{\Omega} + \ddot{\mathbf{n}} - \Omega \wedge (\mathbf{n} \wedge \Omega + \dot{\mathbf{n}}))$$
$$+ \dot{V}^T\mathbf{n} = 0 \tag{9.46}$$

We can simplify this by using equation (9.38) to replace z with its value, along with the fact that $\mathbf{m}^T\mathbf{n} = 0$. Equation (9.46) yields

$$[\mathbf{m}^T(\mathbf{n} \wedge \Omega + \dot{\mathbf{n}})][V^T(\mathbf{n} \wedge \Omega + 2\dot{\mathbf{n}}) + \dot{V}^T\mathbf{n}]$$
$$- (V^T\mathbf{n})[\mathbf{m}^T(2\dot{\mathbf{n}} \wedge \Omega + \mathbf{n} \wedge \dot{\Omega} + \ddot{\mathbf{n}} + (\Omega^T\mathbf{n})\Omega)] = 0$$

This is the announced equation.   ∎

This does not depend upon the choice of the point m on the line l. Indeed, let us choose two points m_1 and m_2 on l and show that the left-hand sides of (9.46) are the same for each. By subtracting them, we obtain

$$(\mathbf{M}_1 - \mathbf{M}_2)^T(2\dot{\mathbf{n}} \wedge \Omega + \mathbf{n} \wedge \dot{\Omega} + \ddot{\mathbf{n}} + (\Omega^T\mathbf{n})\Omega)$$

Since $\mathbf{M}_1 - \mathbf{M}_2$ is parallel to $\mathbf{W}$, this is proportional to μ and is therefore equal to 0.

9.4.3.3   *The relationship with the discrete motion case*

Note that the equations $\mu = 0$ and (9.45) are the continuous analog of equations (7.47) and (7.49) of chapter 7. Let us prove it. We consider the situation of figure 7.11 and assume that the first image has been obtained at time 0, the second at time τ_1, and the third at time τ_2. We will build upon the fact that τ_1 and τ_2 are infinitesimally small quantities. Let $\Omega(\tau)$ be the angular velocity at time τ and $\tilde{\Omega}(\tau)$ the corresponding 3×3 antisymmetric matrix. Also let $\Omega = \Omega(0)$ and $\dot{\Omega} = \dot{\Omega}(0)$. Note that the matrices $\mathbf{R}$ and $\mathbf{RR}'$ of equation (7.47) describe the displacement of the *camera*, whereas $\Omega(\tau)$ describes the motion of the rigid body to which the line L is attached. Let $\mathbf{U}(\tau)$ be the rotation matrix that represents the discrete rotation of that body between time 0 and τ. Since $\mathbf{U}(\tau)$ is orthogonal, it satisfies

$$\mathbf{U}(\tau)\mathbf{U}(\tau)^T = \mathbf{I}$$

Taking the time derivative of this equation yields

$$\frac{d\mathbf{U}}{d\tau}(\tau)\mathbf{U}(\tau)^T + \mathbf{U}(\tau)\frac{d\mathbf{U}}{d\tau}(\tau)^T = \mathbf{0}$$

Since $\frac{d\mathbf{U}}{d\tau}(\tau)^T = \frac{d\mathbf{U}^T}{d\tau}(\tau)$, this shows that the matrix $\frac{d\mathbf{U}}{d\tau}(\tau)\mathbf{U}(\tau)^T$ is antisymmetric and is, in fact, equal to $\tilde{\Omega}(\tau)$. Thus we have

$$\frac{d\mathbf{U}}{d\tau}(\tau) = \tilde{\Omega}(\tau)\mathbf{U}(\tau)$$

This gives us a differential equation that is satisfied by the rotation matrix $\mathbf{U}(\tau)$ representing the rotation between time 0 and time τ of the rigid body to which the line L is attached in the coordinate system attached to the camera at time 0. Thus the rotation matrix $\mathbf{R}(\tau)$, which represents the rotation of the camera between time 0 and time τ in the same coordinate system, satisfies the following differential equation:

$$\frac{d\mathbf{R}}{d\tau}(\tau) = -\tilde{\Omega}(\tau)\mathbf{R}(\tau) \tag{9.47}$$

where we have

$$\mathbf{R} = \mathbf{R}(\tau_1) \quad \mathbf{RR}' = \mathbf{R}(\tau_2)$$

Taking into account the fact that we are interested in infinitesimally small values of τ, we look for a solution of equation (9.47) by using a second-order Taylor series expansion

$$\mathbf{R}(\tau) = \mathbf{I} + \tau\mathbf{A} + \frac{\tau^2}{2}\mathbf{B}$$

where $\mathbf{A}$ and $\mathbf{B}$ are two unknown matrices. In order to compute them, we do a first-order Taylor series expansion of equation (9.47),

$$\frac{d\mathbf{R}}{d\tau}(\tau) = \mathbf{A} + \tau\mathbf{B} = -(\tilde{\Omega} + \tau\dot{\tilde{\Omega}})(\mathbf{I} + \tau\mathbf{A})$$

which yields

$$\mathbf{A} = -\tilde{\Omega} \quad \mathbf{B} = \tilde{\Omega}^2 - \dot{\tilde{\Omega}}$$

We can now express $\mathbf{R}$ and $\mathbf{RR'}$ up to the second order:

$$\mathbf{R} = \mathbf{I} - \tau_1\tilde{\Omega} + \frac{\tau_1^2}{2}(\tilde{\Omega}^2 - \dot{\tilde{\Omega}})$$

$$\mathbf{RR'} = \mathbf{I} - \tau_2\tilde{\Omega} + \frac{\tau_2^2}{2}(\tilde{\Omega}^2 - \dot{\tilde{\Omega}})$$

Now that we have dealt with the rotation matrices, let us deal with the normal vectors $\mathbf{n}, \mathbf{n'}$, and $\mathbf{n''}$. Using similar notations, we let $\mathbf{n}(\tau)$ be the normal vector to the plane defined by the optical center of the camera and the 3-D line L, and we let $\mathbf{n} = \mathbf{n}(0), \dot{\mathbf{n}} = \dot{\mathbf{n}}(0)$, and $\ddot{\mathbf{n}} = \ddot{\mathbf{n}}(0)$. We have $\mathbf{n'} = \mathbf{n}(\tau_1)$ and $\mathbf{n''} = \mathbf{n}(\tau_2)$. We do a second-order Taylor series expansion with both vectors and obtain

$$\mathbf{n'} = \mathbf{n}(\tau_1) = \mathbf{n} + \tau_1\dot{\mathbf{n}} + \frac{\tau_1^2}{2}\ddot{\mathbf{n}}$$

$$\mathbf{n''} = \mathbf{n}(\tau_2) = \mathbf{n} + \tau_2\dot{\mathbf{n}} + \frac{\tau_2^2}{2}\ddot{\mathbf{n}}$$

We can now compute second-order Taylor series expansions for $\mathbf{Rn'}$ and $\mathbf{RR'n''}$:

$$\mathbf{Rn'} = \mathbf{m'} = \mathbf{n} + \tau_1(\dot{\mathbf{n}} + \mathbf{n} \wedge \Omega) + \frac{\tau_1^2}{2}(2\dot{\mathbf{n}} \wedge \Omega + \mathbf{n} \wedge \dot{\Omega} + \ddot{\mathbf{n}} + \Omega \wedge (\Omega \wedge \mathbf{n}))$$

$$\mathbf{RR'n''} = \mathbf{m''} = \mathbf{n} + \tau_2(\dot{\mathbf{n}} + \mathbf{n} \wedge \Omega) + \frac{\tau_2^2}{2}(2\dot{\mathbf{n}} \wedge \Omega + \mathbf{n} \wedge \dot{\Omega} + \ddot{\mathbf{n}} + \Omega \wedge (\Omega \wedge \mathbf{n}))$$

According to equation (7.47), we have to compute the cross-product $\mathbf{Rn'} \wedge \mathbf{RR'n''}$. We do not consider the terms perpendicular to $\mathbf{n}$ since we will take the inner product with $\mathbf{n}$ and the first nonzero term is of order 3 in τ_1, τ_2:

$$\frac{\tau_1\tau_2}{2}(\tau_2 - \tau_1)(\dot{\mathbf{n}} + \mathbf{n} \wedge \Omega) \wedge (2\dot{\mathbf{n}} \wedge \Omega + \mathbf{n} \wedge \dot{\Omega} + \ddot{\mathbf{n}} + \Omega \wedge (\Omega \wedge \mathbf{n}))$$

Taking the inner product with $\mathbf{n}$ and using equation (9.36), we find that, up to the fourth order, equation (7.47) is equal to

$$\mu \frac{\tau_1 \tau_2}{2} (\tau_2 - \tau_1)$$

where μ is defined by equation (9.44).

Let us now consider the equations (7.49). In order to compute the translation vectors $\mathbf{t}$ and $\mathbf{t}''$, we introduce the linear velocity $\mathbf{V}(\tau)$ and let $\mathbf{V}(0) = \mathbf{V}$ and $\dot{\mathbf{V}}(0) = \dot{\mathbf{V}}$. The motion of a point M attached to the camera is defined by the differential equation

$$\dot{\mathbf{M}}(\tau) = -\mathbf{V}(\tau) - \Omega(\tau) \wedge \mathbf{M}(\tau) \tag{9.48}$$

We are interested in small motions of the origin, so we look at the second-order Taylor series expansion of $\mathbf{M}(\tau)$:

$$\mathbf{M}(\tau) = \tau \mathbf{a} + \frac{\tau^2}{2} \mathbf{b}$$

where $\mathbf{a}$ and $\mathbf{b}$ are constant unknown vectors. Using this expression for $\mathbf{M}(\tau)$ in equation (9.48) and expanding $\mathbf{V}(\tau)$ and $\Omega(\tau)$ up to the first order, we obtain

$$\mathbf{a} + \tau \mathbf{b} = -\mathbf{V} - \tau(\dot{\mathbf{V}} - \Omega \wedge \mathbf{a}) + o(\tau^2)$$

which yields by identification

$$\mathbf{a} = -\mathbf{V} \quad \mathbf{b} = -\dot{\mathbf{V}} - \Omega \wedge \mathbf{a} = -\dot{\mathbf{V}} + \Omega \wedge \mathbf{V}$$

Therefore, we have a second-order approximation of the trajectory of the origin:

$$\mathbf{M}(\tau) = -\mathbf{V}\tau - (\dot{\mathbf{V}} - \Omega \wedge \mathbf{V}) \frac{\tau^2}{2}$$

This allows us to write

$$\mathbf{t} = -\mathbf{V}\tau_1 - (\dot{\mathbf{V}} - \Omega \wedge \mathbf{V}) \frac{\tau_1^2}{2}$$

$$\mathbf{t}'' = -\mathbf{V}\tau_2 - (\dot{\mathbf{V}} - \Omega \wedge \mathbf{V}) \frac{\tau_2^2}{2}$$

Now, by letting $\mathbf{u} = \dot{\mathbf{n}} + \mathbf{n} \wedge \Omega$ and $\mathbf{v} = 2\dot{\mathbf{n}} \wedge \Omega + \mathbf{n} \wedge \dot{\Omega} + \ddot{\mathbf{n}} + \Omega \wedge (\Omega \wedge \mathbf{n})$, we can write

$$\mathbf{t}^T \mathbf{m}' = -(\mathbf{V}\tau_1 + (\dot{\mathbf{V}} - \Omega \wedge \mathbf{V}) \frac{\tau_1^2}{2})^T (\mathbf{n} + \tau_1 \mathbf{u} + \frac{\tau_1^2}{2} \mathbf{v})$$

$$\mathbf{t}''^T \mathbf{m}'' = -(\mathbf{V}\tau_2 + (\dot{\mathbf{V}} - \Omega \wedge \mathbf{V}) \frac{\tau_2^2}{2})^T (\mathbf{n} + \tau_2 \mathbf{u} + \frac{\tau_2^2}{2} \mathbf{v})$$

For a point m of the line l, we project the equations (7.49) on the vector $\mathbf{n} \wedge \mathbf{m}$. We have

$$\mathbf{n} \wedge \mathbf{m}' = \tau_1 \mathbf{n} \wedge \mathbf{u} + \frac{\tau_1^2}{2} \mathbf{n} \wedge \mathbf{v}$$

$$\mathbf{n} \wedge \mathbf{m}'' = \tau_2 \mathbf{n} \wedge \mathbf{u} + \frac{\tau_2^2}{2} \mathbf{n} \wedge \mathbf{v}$$

Let us now compute $(\mathbf{n} \wedge \mathbf{u}) \cdot (\mathbf{n} \wedge \mathbf{m})$. Using standard properties of determinants, this is equal to

$$(\mathbf{n} \wedge \mathbf{u}) \cdot (\mathbf{n} \wedge \mathbf{m}) = (\mathbf{n} \wedge \mathbf{u}, \mathbf{n}, \mathbf{m}) = -(\mathbf{m}, \mathbf{n}, \mathbf{n} \wedge \mathbf{u}) = (\mathbf{n} \cdot \mathbf{n})(\mathbf{m} \cdot \mathbf{u})$$

because, by definition, $\mathbf{m} \cdot \mathbf{n} = 0$. Similarly, we find that

$$(\mathbf{n} \wedge \mathbf{v}) \cdot (\mathbf{n} \wedge \mathbf{m}) = (\mathbf{n} \cdot \mathbf{n})(\mathbf{m} \cdot \mathbf{v})$$

Therefore, we also have

$$(\mathbf{n} \wedge \mathbf{m}') \cdot (\mathbf{n} \wedge \mathbf{m}) = (\mathbf{n} \cdot \mathbf{n})(\tau_1 \mathbf{m} \cdot \mathbf{u} + \frac{\tau_1^2}{2} \mathbf{m} \cdot \mathbf{v})$$

$$(\mathbf{n} \wedge \mathbf{m}'') \cdot (\mathbf{n} \wedge \mathbf{m}) = (\mathbf{n} \cdot \mathbf{n})(\tau_2 \mathbf{m} \cdot \mathbf{u} + \frac{\tau_2^2}{2} \mathbf{m} \cdot \mathbf{v})$$

The equations (7.49) projected on $\mathbf{n} \wedge \mathbf{m}$ can thus be written as

$$(\mathbf{V}\tau_1 + (\dot{\mathbf{V}} - \Omega \wedge \mathbf{V})\frac{\tau_1^2}{2})^T (\mathbf{n} + \tau_1 \mathbf{u} + \frac{\tau_1^2}{2}\mathbf{v})(\tau_2 \mathbf{m} \cdot \mathbf{u} + \frac{\tau_2^2}{2}\mathbf{m} \cdot \mathbf{v}) =$$

$$(\mathbf{V}\tau_2 + (\dot{\mathbf{V}} - \Omega \wedge \mathbf{V})\frac{\tau_2^2}{2})^T (\mathbf{n} + \tau_2 \mathbf{u} + \frac{\tau_2^2}{2}\mathbf{v})(\tau_1 \mathbf{m} \cdot \mathbf{u} + \frac{\tau_1^2}{2}\mathbf{m} \cdot \mathbf{v})$$

(we have simplified by $(\mathbf{n} \cdot \mathbf{n})$).

We expand and group terms of similar order in τ_1, τ_2 and find that the term of order 2 is identically 0, whereas the term of order 3 is

$$\frac{\tau_1 \tau_2}{2}(\tau_1 - \tau_2)[(\mathbf{m}^T \mathbf{u})[2\mathbf{V}^T \mathbf{u} + \dot{\mathbf{V}}\mathbf{n} - (\mathbf{V}, \mathbf{n}, \Omega)] - (\mathbf{V}^T \mathbf{n})(\mathbf{m}^T \mathbf{v})]$$

Notice that

$$\mathbf{V}^T \mathbf{u} = \mathbf{V}^T \dot{\mathbf{n}} + (\mathbf{V}, \mathbf{n}, \Omega)$$

From this we obtain

$$\frac{\tau_1 \tau_2}{2}(\tau_1 - \tau_2)[(\mathbf{m}^T \mathbf{u})[\mathbf{V}^T(\mathbf{n} \wedge \Omega + 2\dot{\mathbf{n}}) + \dot{\mathbf{V}}\mathbf{n}] - (\mathbf{V}^T \mathbf{n})(\mathbf{m}^T \mathbf{v})]$$

Equating this term to 0, we obtain, as announced, equation (9.45).

9.5   Rigid motion of a 3-D curve

We will now study the case of a general 3-D curve (C) moving rigidly. Let $(\Omega, \mathbf{V})$ be its kinematic screw at the optical center O of the camera. First we will derive a relation between the tangents $\mathbf{t}$ and $\mathbf{T}$ to (c_τ) and (C) and the angular velocity Ω. We will be constantly using the coordinate system $(\mathbf{t}, \mathbf{n}, \mathbf{k})$, where $\mathbf{k}$ is the unit vector along the z-axis (see figure 9.14). In this section, the third coordinate of each vector is a space coordinate (along the z-axis); previously the third coordinate was a time coordinate (along the τ-axis).

9.5.1   Stories of tangents

Let us denote by $\mathbf{U_t}$ the vector $\mathbf{m} \wedge \mathbf{t}$. This vector is normal to the plane defined by the optical center of the camera, the point m on (c_τ), and $\mathbf{t}$ (see figure 9.15). Since this plane also contains the tangent $\mathbf{T}$ to (C) at M, the 3-D point whose image is m, we have

$$\mathbf{U_t} \cdot \mathbf{T} = 0 \tag{9.49}$$

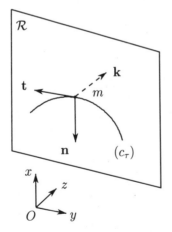

Figure 9.14   Definition of the local system of coordinates.

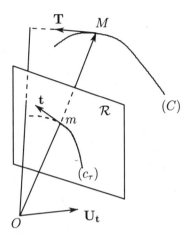

Figure 9.15   Relation between **t** and **T**.

Using exactly the same reasoning that led us to equation (9.36), we find that **T** is proportional to the cross-product **W** of $\mathbf{U_t}$ and $\dot{\mathbf{U}}_t + \mathbf{U_t} \wedge \mathbf{\Omega}$:

$$\mathbf{W} = \mathbf{U_t} \wedge (\mathbf{U_t} \wedge \mathbf{\Omega} + \dot{\mathbf{U}}_t) \tag{9.50}$$

$$\mathbf{T} = \varepsilon \frac{\mathbf{W}}{\|\mathbf{W}\|} \tag{9.51}$$

where $\varepsilon = \pm 1$. We can assume that $\varepsilon = 1$ by correctly orienting (c_τ) and (C). Let us compute $\dot{\mathbf{U}}_t$. Using the derivation rule (9.15), we write

$$\dot{\mathbf{U}}_t = w \frac{\partial \mathbf{U_t}}{\partial s} + \partial_{\mathbf{n}_\beta} \mathbf{U_t}$$

We have $\frac{\partial \mathbf{U_t}}{\partial s} = \kappa \mathbf{m} \wedge \mathbf{n}$, and we note that $\mathbf{U_n} = \mathbf{m} \wedge \mathbf{n}$. As a result we can write

$$\partial_{\mathbf{n}_\beta} \mathbf{U_t} = \partial_{\mathbf{n}_\beta} \mathbf{m} \wedge \mathbf{t} + \mathbf{m} \wedge \partial_{\mathbf{n}_\beta} \mathbf{t}$$

We know from section 9.3.2.2 that $\partial_{\mathbf{n}_\beta} \mathbf{t} = \frac{\partial \beta}{\partial s} \mathbf{n}$ and we can compute $\partial_{\mathbf{n}_\beta} \mathbf{m}$ as follows. By definition, $\dot{\mathbf{m}} = \mathbf{v}_r = w\mathbf{t} + \beta\mathbf{n}$. On the other hand, using equation 9.15,

$$\dot{\mathbf{m}} = w\mathbf{t} + \partial_{\mathbf{n}_\beta} \mathbf{m}$$

It follows that

$$\partial_{n_\beta} \mathbf{m} = \beta \mathbf{n}$$

Finally,

$$\dot{\mathbf{U}}_t = (\kappa w + \frac{\partial \beta}{\partial s}) \mathbf{U_n} - \beta \mathbf{t} \wedge \mathbf{n} \tag{9.52}$$

Equations (9.50) and (9.51) are important because in a very simple man-ner they relate $\mathbf{T}$, the tangent to the unknown 3-D curve (C), to the known vector $\mathbf{U}_t$, the angular velocity Ω, and $\dot{\mathbf{U}}_t$. Notice that this last vec-tor contains the unknown tangential real motion field w. This is the main difference from the case of straight lines.

Reproducing the same reasoning that led to equations (9.41)–(9.43), we have the following theorem:

Theorem 9.3
$\mathbf{W}$ satisfies the following equations, which are equivalent:

$$\mathbf{W} \wedge (\dot{\mathbf{W}} \wedge \mathbf{W} + (\mathbf{W}^T \mathbf{W})\Omega) = 0 \tag{9.53}$$

$$\mathbf{W} \wedge (\dot{\mathbf{W}} + \mathbf{W} \wedge \Omega) = 0 \tag{9.54}$$

$$\begin{cases} \mu \mathbf{W} = 0 \\ \mu = \mathbf{W}^T (2\dot{\mathbf{U}}_t \wedge \Omega + \mathbf{U}_t \wedge \dot{\Omega} + \ddot{\mathbf{U}}_t + (\mathbf{U}_t^T \Omega)\Omega) \end{cases} \tag{9.55}$$

$\mathbf{W}$ is given by equation (9.50).

Equations (9.53)–(9.55) are fundamental: They express the relationship between the unknown geometry and motion of the 3-D curve (C) and the geometry and motion of the 2-D curve (c_τ). In order to exploit them, we have to compute $\ddot{\mathbf{U}}_t$. Again we use equation (9.15):

$$\ddot{\mathbf{U}}_t = (w^2 \frac{\partial \kappa}{\partial s} + w(\partial_{n_\beta}\kappa + \frac{\partial^2 \beta}{\partial s^2}) + \partial_{n_\beta}\frac{\partial \beta}{\partial s} + \kappa \dot{w})\mathbf{U_n}$$

$$+ (\kappa w + \frac{\partial \beta}{\partial s})\dot{\mathbf{U}}_n - (w\frac{\partial \beta}{\partial s} + \partial_{n_\beta}\beta)\mathbf{t} \wedge \mathbf{n}$$

Now, since

$$\dot{\mathbf{U}}_n = -(\kappa w + \frac{\partial \beta}{\partial s})\mathbf{U}_t + w\mathbf{t} \wedge \mathbf{n} \tag{9.56}$$

we eventually have

$$\ddot{\mathbf{U}}_t = (w^2 \frac{\partial \kappa}{\partial s} + w(\partial_{\mathbf{n}_\beta} \kappa + \frac{\partial^2 \beta}{\partial s^2}) + \partial_{\mathbf{n}_\beta} \frac{\partial \beta}{\partial s} + \kappa \dot{w}) \mathbf{U}_n$$

$$\qquad (9.57)$$

$$- (\kappa w + \frac{\partial \beta}{\partial s})^2 \mathbf{U}_t + (\kappa w^2 - \partial_{\mathbf{n}_\beta} \beta) \mathbf{t} \wedge \mathbf{n}$$

Notice that equations (9.53)–(9.55) involve w and $\dot{w}$, the real tangential motion field and its total time derivative, as well as $\dot{\Omega}$, the angular acceleration. Again, the presence of w and $\dot{w}$ in the equations is the essential difference from the case of a straight line.

9.5.2   Writing an equation that involves point m

As a direct consequence of section 9.4.3.2 we obtain an equation that involves the image point m. Equation (9.45) can be written with the notations of this section as follows:

$$(\mathbf{m}^T(\mathbf{U}_t \wedge \Omega + \dot{\mathbf{U}}_t))(\mathbf{V}^T(\mathbf{U}_t \wedge \Omega + 2\dot{\mathbf{U}}_t) + \dot{\mathbf{V}}^T \mathbf{U}_t)$$

$$\qquad (9.58)$$

$$- (\mathbf{V}^T \mathbf{U}_t)(\mathbf{m}^T(2\dot{\mathbf{U}}_t \wedge \Omega + \mathbf{U}_t \wedge \dot{\Omega} + \ddot{\mathbf{U}}_t + (\mathbf{U}_t^T \Omega)\Omega))$$

This equation also involves w and $\dot{w}$, the real tangential motion field and its total time derivative, as well as the kinematic screw $(\Omega, \mathbf{V})$ and its time derivative $(\dot{\Omega}, \dot{\mathbf{V}})$.

9.5.3   The Frenet frame of the curve (C)

Equations (9.53)-(9.55) characterize the motion of the tangent $\mathbf{T}$ to the curve (C). But we know that we can also define a normal $\mathbf{N}$ and a binormal $\mathbf{B} = \mathbf{T} \wedge \mathbf{N}$ to (C), these three vectors forming the Frenet frame at point M. In order to fully characterize the motion of (C), we must also study the motion of either $\mathbf{N}$ or $\mathbf{B}$. $\mathbf{B}$ is simpler to study, but no new equation can be obtained from it. In order to see it, let us compute $\mathbf{N}$.

We rewrite equation (9.51) as $\|\mathbf{W}\|\mathbf{T} = \mathbf{W}$ and take its derivative with respect to S; using the second of the three-dimensional Frenet formulas (C.2), we have

$$u \frac{\partial \|\mathbf{W}\|}{\partial s} \mathbf{T} + \Gamma \|\mathbf{W}\| \mathbf{N} = u \frac{\partial \mathbf{W}}{\partial s}$$

$$\qquad (9.59)$$

where Γ is the curvature of (C). Since $\|W\| = (W \cdot W)^{1/2}$, we have

$$\frac{\partial \|W\|}{\partial s} = \frac{W \cdot \frac{\partial W}{\partial s}}{\|W\|} \tag{9.60}$$

Substituting this into equation (9.59) and doing some algebra yields

$$\Gamma N = \frac{u}{(W \cdot W)^{3/2}} W \wedge (\frac{\partial W}{\partial s} \wedge W)$$

This yields the direction W_N of the normal N as

$$W_N = W \wedge (\frac{\partial W}{\partial s} \wedge W) \tag{9.61}$$

The direction of B is therefore

$$W_B = W \wedge \frac{\partial W}{\partial s} \tag{9.62}$$

Thus, we can compute the directions of the normal N and the binormal B from the direction W of the tangent T using equations (9.61) and (9.62). The computation of the curvature and the torsion is studied in problem 2. The motion of N and B do not yield any new equation relating the kinematic screw (Ω, V) and its derivative $(\dot{\Omega}, \dot{V})$ (see problem 5).

9.5.4   Using the perspective equation

We are now going to again use the perspective equation (9.37) (see figure 9.13)

$$z m = M$$

to obtain a number of interesting relations. Taking the total derivative of equation (9.37) with respect to time and applying our derivation rule yields

$$V_{Mz} m + z(w t + \beta n) = V_M \tag{9.63}$$

where the vector V_M is the three-dimensional velocity of point M, which is of course equal to $V + \Omega \wedge M$. Projecting this vector equation onto t and n yields two scalar equations:

$$z(w + \Omega \cdot b) = V_t - (m \cdot t)V_z = -\varepsilon U_n \cdot V \tag{9.64}$$

$$z(\beta - \mathbf{\Omega} \cdot \mathbf{a}) = V_n - (\mathbf{m} \cdot \mathbf{n})V_z = \varepsilon \mathbf{U_t} \cdot \mathbf{V} \tag{9.65}$$

where $\mathbf{a}$ and $\mathbf{b}$ are given by

$$\mathbf{a} = \mathbf{m} \wedge \mathbf{U_t} \tag{9.66}$$
$$\tag{9.67}$$
$$\mathbf{b} = \mathbf{m} \wedge \mathbf{U_n}$$

$V_t = \mathbf{V} \cdot \mathbf{t}$, $V_n = \mathbf{V} \cdot \mathbf{n}$, and ε is defined by $\mathbf{t} \wedge \mathbf{n} = \varepsilon \mathbf{k}$. They are fundamental in the sense that they express the relationship between the unknown 3-D motion of a point and its observed 2-D motion.

Notice that we can eliminate z between (9.64) and (9.65) and obtain the value of the tangential real optical flow w as a function of $\mathbf{\Omega}$ and $\mathbf{V}$:

$$w = (\beta - \mathbf{\Omega} \cdot \mathbf{a}) f(\mathbf{V}) - \mathbf{\Omega} \cdot \mathbf{b} \tag{9.68}$$

where we have

$$f(\mathbf{V}) = \frac{V_t - (\mathbf{m} \cdot \mathbf{t})V_z}{V_n - (\mathbf{m} \cdot \mathbf{n})V_z} = -\frac{\mathbf{U_n} \cdot \mathbf{V}}{\mathbf{U_t} \cdot \mathbf{V}} \tag{9.69}$$

We assume that $V_n - (\mathbf{m} \cdot \mathbf{n})V_z \neq 0$.

9.5.5   Closing the loop, or finding the kinematic screw

The basic idea is to combine equations (9.55) and (9.58), which tie together the local structure of (C) at M (its tangent) and the fact that we have rigid motion, with equation (9.68), which is a pure expression of the kinematics of the point M without any reference to the fact that it belongs to a curve. We take the total time derivative $\dot{w}$ of w, using equation (9.68). In doing this, we introduce the accelerations $\dot{\mathbf{\Omega}}$ and $\dot{\mathbf{V}}$. If we now replace w and $\dot{w}$ with these values in equations (9.55) and (9.58), we obtain two polynomial equations in $\mathbf{\Omega}$, $\mathbf{V}$, $\dot{\mathbf{\Omega}}$, and $\dot{\mathbf{V}}$, with coefficients depending on the observed geometry and motion of the 2-D curve. Two such equations are obtained at each point of (c_τ).

This step is crucial. This is where we combine the structural information about the geometry of (C) embedded in equation (9.53) with purely kinematic information about the motion of its points embedded in equation (9.63). This eliminates the need to estimate the real tangential motion field w and its time derivative $\dot{w}$. Thus we have the following theorem:

Theorem 9.4

At each point of (c_τ) we can write two polynomial equations in the coordinates of $\Omega, \mathbf{V}, \dot{\Omega}$, and $\dot{\mathbf{V}}$ with coefficients that are polynomials in quantities that can be measured from the spatiotemporal surface (Σ):

$$\beta \quad \frac{\partial \beta}{\partial s} \quad \frac{\partial^2 \beta}{\partial s^2} \quad \partial_{\mathbf{n}_\beta} \beta \quad \partial_{\mathbf{n}_\beta} \frac{\partial \beta}{\partial s}$$

$$\kappa \quad \frac{\partial \kappa}{\partial s} \quad \partial_{\mathbf{n}_\beta} \kappa$$

These polynomials are obtained by eliminating w and $\dot{w}$ between equations (9.55), (9.58), (9.68), and (9.70). The total degree is 6 for the first equation, 4 for the second. The equations are homogeneous in $(\mathbf{V}, \dot{\mathbf{V}})$ and of degree 4 for the first and 2 for the second. The degrees in $\mathbf{V}$ are 4 for the first one, 2 for the second. Both equations are linear in $\dot{\mathbf{V}}$ and $\dot{\Omega}$. The degree in $(\Omega, \dot{\Omega})$ is 3 for the first equation, 2 for the second. The degrees in Ω are 3 for the first equation, 2 for the second.

The fact that these equations are homogeneous in $(\mathbf{V}, \dot{\mathbf{V}})$ is another manifestation of the fact that we cannot recover absolute 3-D velocities through monocular motion. Thus, N points on (c_τ) provide $2N$ equations in the eleven unknowns Ω, $\mathbf{V}$, $\dot{\Omega}$, and $\dot{\mathbf{V}}$. Therefore, in some cases we should expect to be able to find a finite number of solutions. Degenerate cases where such solutions do not exist can be easily found: Straight lines, for example [FDN89], are notorious for being degenerate from that standpoint. The problem of studying the cases of degeneracy is outside the scope of this book. Ignoring for the moment these difficulties (but not underestimating them), we can state one major conjecture/result:

Conjecture 9.1

The kinematic screw $\Omega, \mathbf{V}$ and its time derivative $\dot{\Omega}, \dot{\mathbf{V}}$ of a rigidly moving 3-D curve can, in general, be estimated from the observation of the spatiotemporal surface generated by its retinal image by solving a system of polynomial equations. Depth can then be recovered at each point using equation (9.65). The tangent to the curve can be recovered at each point using equation (9.50).

Notice that we never actually compute the tangential real motion field w. It is used just as an intermediate unknown and then is eliminated as quickly as possible, making it irrelevant. Of course, if it is needed, it can be recovered afterwards from equation (9.64).

To be thorough, we will show how to compute $\dot{w}$. Using equations (9.68) and (9.15), we can write

$$\dot{w} = (w\frac{\partial \beta}{\partial s} + \partial_{n_\beta}\beta - \dot{\Omega}\cdot\mathbf{a} - \Omega\cdot\dot{\mathbf{a}})f(\mathbf{V})$$
$$+ (\beta - \Omega\cdot\mathbf{a})\dot{f}(\mathbf{V}) - \dot{\Omega}\cdot\mathbf{b} - \Omega\cdot\dot{\mathbf{b}}$$

(9.70)

From equations (9.66) and (9.67), we deduce that

$$\dot{\mathbf{a}} = (w\mathbf{t} + \beta\mathbf{n}) \wedge \mathbf{U_t} + \mathbf{m} \wedge \dot{\mathbf{U}}_t$$

and

$$\dot{\mathbf{b}} = (w\mathbf{t} + \beta\mathbf{n}) \wedge \mathbf{U_n} + \mathbf{m} \wedge \dot{\mathbf{U}}_n$$

We have already computed $\dot{\mathbf{U}}_t$ and $\dot{\mathbf{U}}_n$ (equations (9.52) and (9.56)). Therefore

$$\dot{\mathbf{a}} = (w\mathbf{t} + \beta\mathbf{n}) \wedge \mathbf{U_t} + (\kappa w + \frac{\partial \beta}{\partial s})\mathbf{b} - \beta\mathbf{m} \wedge (\mathbf{t} \wedge \mathbf{n})$$

(9.71)

$$\dot{\mathbf{b}} = (w\mathbf{t} + \beta\mathbf{n}) \wedge \mathbf{U_n} - (\kappa w + \frac{\partial \beta}{\partial s})\mathbf{a} + w\mathbf{m} \wedge (\mathbf{t} \wedge \mathbf{n})$$

(9.72)

Finally, we have to compute $\dot{f}(\mathbf{V})$. From its definition (equation (9.69)), we deduce that

$$\dot{f}(\mathbf{V}) = \frac{(\dot{\mathbf{V}}\cdot\mathbf{U_t}+\mathbf{V}\cdot\dot{\mathbf{U}}_t)(\mathbf{V}\cdot\mathbf{U_n})-(\dot{\mathbf{V}}\cdot\mathbf{U_n}+\mathbf{V}\cdot\dot{\mathbf{U}}_n)(\mathbf{V}\cdot\mathbf{U_t})}{(\mathbf{V}\cdot\mathbf{U_t})^2}$$

(9.73)

9.6   Some simple examples

In this section we will describe in more detail a number of cases that are simpler than the general motion cases we have studied so far. As a first example, we will consider the case where the observed motion is in a plane parallel to the retinal plane. We will show that in this case the apparent and real motion fields are identical. As a second example, we will consider the case of a pure translational motion for which there are only six unknowns, $\mathbf{V}$ and $\dot{\mathbf{V}}$. As a third example, we will examine the case of the ego-motion of a mobile robot moving on a flat ground, which we assume to be the xy-plane, with two degrees of translational freedom and one degree of rotational freedom and also a total of six unknowns, $V_x, V_y, \dot{V}_x, \dot{V}_y, \Omega_z,$ and $\dot{\Omega}_z$. For these last two cases we will show that, if the curve (C) is a circle, the solution to the motion is essentially unique, thereby increasing our belief in conjecture 9.1.

9.6.1 The example of a motion parallel to the retinal plane

Let us consider the simple case in which the motion of (C) is in a plane parallel to the retinal plane. In this case, the apparent and real optical flows are in general identical.[6] If d is the distance of the plane to the retina, the motion of m is described by

$$\mathbf{v}_m = \mathbf{v}_m^a = \mathbf{v}_m^r = \frac{\mathbf{V}}{d} + \Omega \times \mathbf{m}$$

where $\mathbf{V}$ is parallel to the retinal plane and Ω is perpendicular to it (see figure 9.16). From the definitions of $\mathbf{v}_m^a$ and $\mathbf{v}_m^r$ (equations (9.12) and (9.13)), this implies that

$$\alpha = w = \frac{\mathbf{V}}{d} \cdot \mathbf{t} + \Omega \cdot \mathbf{U_t} \tag{9.74}$$

and

$$\beta = \frac{\mathbf{V}}{d} \cdot \mathbf{n} + \Omega \cdot \mathbf{U_n} \tag{9.75}$$

Differentiating equation (9.74) with respect to s, we readily obtain

$$\frac{\partial \alpha}{\partial s} = \frac{\partial w}{\partial s} = \kappa(\frac{\mathbf{V}}{d} \cdot \mathbf{n} + \Omega \cdot \mathbf{U_n}) = \kappa \beta$$

which is of course equation (9.25). This is an interesting result that says that, for a rigid planar motion parallel to the retinal plane, the derivative of the tangential velocity of a point on the curve with respect to arclength is equal to the product of the curvature with the normal velocity at that point. For such motions, the aperture problem does not exist since the tangential real motion field can be recovered from the normal field.

---

6. There are some degenerate cases, such as a circle whose center is on the optical axis, for which it is not possible to measure the rotation in the image plane.

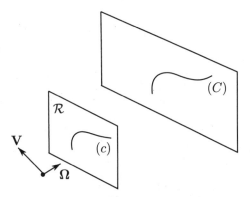

Figure 9.16 When the 3-D motion is in a plane parallel to the retinal plane, the apparent and real motion fields are identical.

The simplicity of this case allows us to verify that the condition $\partial_{n_\beta}\beta = \kappa(1 + \beta^2)$ that we met in section 9.3.2.3 is not satisfied. Using equation (9.15), we can write

$$\dot{\beta} = w\frac{\partial\beta}{\partial s} + \partial_{n_\beta}\beta$$

Now we compute $\dot{\beta}$ and $\partial_{n_\beta}\beta$ from equation (9.75). After applying some algebra, we find that (we omit d for simplicity)

$$\dot{\beta} = \dot{\mathbf{V}} \cdot \mathbf{n} + \dot{\Omega} \cdot \mathbf{U_n} - (\kappa w + \frac{\partial\beta}{\partial s})\mathbf{V} \cdot \mathbf{t} + \Omega \cdot \dot{\mathbf{U}}_n$$

Using equation (9.56) for $\dot{\mathbf{U}}_n$ and equation (9.74)

$$\dot{\beta} = \dot{\mathbf{V}} \cdot \mathbf{n} + \dot{\Omega} \cdot \mathbf{U_n} - w(\kappa w + \frac{\partial\beta}{\partial s}) + w\Omega \cdot (\mathbf{t} \wedge \mathbf{n})$$

We can also compute $\frac{\partial\beta}{\partial s}$:

$$\frac{\partial\beta}{\partial s} = -\kappa w + \Omega \cdot (\mathbf{t} \wedge \mathbf{n})$$

Replacing this expression in the expression of $\dot{\beta}$ yields

$$\dot{\beta} = \dot{\mathbf{V}} \cdot \mathbf{n} + \dot{\Omega} \cdot \mathbf{U_n}$$

and we obtain

$$\partial_{n_\beta}\beta = \dot{\mathbf{V}} \cdot \mathbf{n} + \dot{\Omega} \cdot \mathbf{U_n} + \kappa w^2 - w\Omega \cdot (\mathbf{t} \wedge \mathbf{n})$$

Thus we notice that $\partial_{n_\beta}\beta$ involves the accelerations $\dot{\mathbf{V}}$ and $\dot{\Omega}$, whereas the term $\kappa(1 + \beta^2)$ involves only velocities. Therefore, in general, $\partial_{n_\beta}\beta \neq \kappa(1 + \beta^2)$, which confirms our analysis of section 9.3.2.3.

What happens if we tilt the plane of the motion? Equation (9.82) of section 9.7.3 provides an immediate answer. Let us rewrite this equation as

$$u = \frac{\partial s}{\partial S} = -\varepsilon\frac{\mathbf{U_n} \cdot \mathbf{T}}{z} = \varepsilon\frac{(\mathbf{m}, \mathbf{T}, \mathbf{n})}{z}$$

If we take the derivative u_τ of u with respect to time, because of the Schwarz equality, we obtain v_S, the derivative of $v = \frac{\partial s}{\partial \tau}$ with respect to S. As soon as z is not constant and $\mathbf{T}$ is different from $\mathbf{t}$, this derivative is in general not zero, which shows that v is not constant and that $w = v + \alpha$ is different from α.

9.6.2   The example of a pure translational motion

In this case there are only five unknowns, $\mathbf{V}$ and $\dot{\mathbf{V}}$. In the example we present, we have[7] $\mathbf{V} = [1, 0, 13.8]^T$, and $\dot{\mathbf{V}} = [0, 0, 6]^T$ and we observe at time $\tau = 2.3$ a circle of center $C = [\tau, 2, 2\tau^2]^T$ and radius 10. We solve the system of six equations in five unknowns obtained by considering three points on the observed ellipse and obtain two solutions. One of them is the correct solution, but the second one is incorrect and yields a reconstructed curve that is a hyperbola. The results appear in figure 9.17, which shows the reconstructed curves and the real one. The left side of the figure shows a perfect superposition between the real and the reconstructed curves, while the right side shows the difference between the extra solution and the real one. In this case the computed motion is $\mathbf{V} = [1, 1.176, 7.845]^T$ and $\dot{\mathbf{V}} = [10.394, 7.132, 74.422]^T$. If we now add a second circle, not in the same plane as the first, and if we move with the same rigid motion and choose one point among the three on this circle, then the solution to the motion is unique.

---

7. We normalize so that $V_x = 1$.

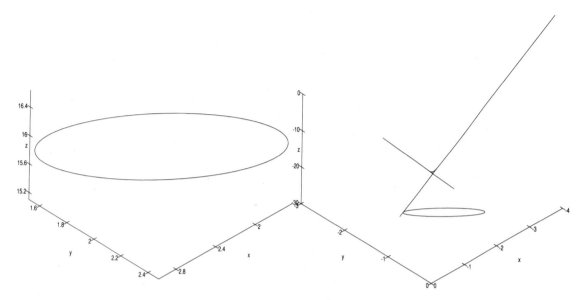

Figure 9.17 The reconstructed curves corresponding to the two solutions of the motion equations. The left side is the correct solution; the right side shows the superposition of the correct one and the incorrect one, which is a hyperbola.

It is important to note that this experiment and the one described in the next section are only simulations, since the coefficients of the polynomial equations are not estimated from the spatiotemporal surface but are computed analytically. Then what does it tell us? Clearly it does not tell us anything about the numerical stability of the problem; that issue is outside the scope of this book. However, it does tell us that the number of "ghost" solutions is very small, and in the case of two circles, equal to 0, even though this is the case of a very simple planar curve. Our guess is that, for more general curves, the solution will in general be unique.

9.6.3   The example of a mobile robot moving on a flat ground

We can also solve the case of a mobile robot moving on a flat ground with two translational degrees of freedom (x and y) and one rota-

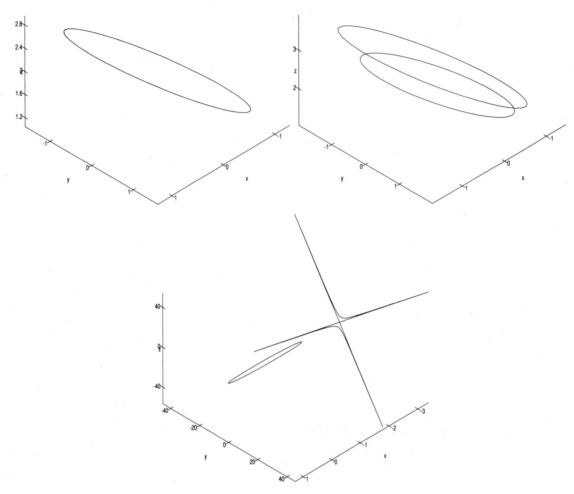

Figure 9.18   The reconstructed curves corresponding to the three solutions of the motion equations. The top left is the correct solution; the bottom and top right show the superposition of the correct one and the incorrect ones.

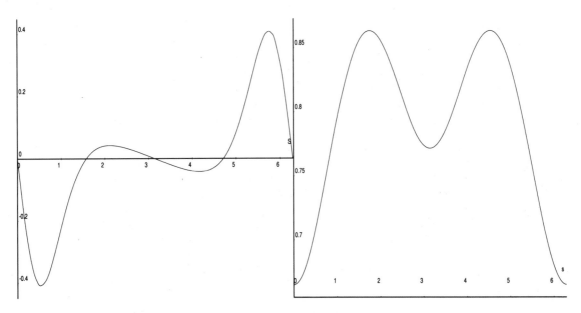

Figure 9.19 A plot of the real (left) and apparent (right) motion fields along the observed ellipse.

tional degree of freedom (z). Just as previously we can work with one and two (noncoplanar) circles. In the second case we find that the solution is unique. In the first case we find three distinct solutions. The first solution is correct, with $V_x = 1, V_y = 0, \dot{V}_x = 0.385, \dot{V}_y = 0, \Omega_z = 1.3$, and $\dot{\Omega}_z = 0.5$. The reconstructed curve is shown at the top left of figure 9.18. The second solution is incorrect, with $V_x = 1, V_y = -0.047, \dot{V}_x = -0.292, \dot{V}_y = -0.097, \Omega_z = 1.130$, and $\dot{\Omega}_z = 0$. The reconstructed curve is a circle, which is shown with the correct one at the top right of the same figure. The third solution is also incorrect, with $V_x = 1, V_y = -1.400, \dot{V}_x = -1.242, \dot{V}_y = -2.281, \Omega_z = 0$, and $\dot{\Omega}_z = 0.063$. The reconstructed curve is a hyperbola, which is shown with the correct one in the bottom part of the same figure. In figure 9.19 we compare the apparent and real motion fields along the observed ellipse. The difference between the two is apparent. Just as in the previous example, if we add a second circle that is not coplanar with the first one but moving with the same motion, we find a unique solution.

9.7   Constraining stereo matches

The previous analysis can be put to use to constrain stereo matches in the following manner. Let us consider the situation of figure 9.20, in which we observe with a stereo rig the motion of the rigid three-dimensional curve (C). Let M be a point on this curve, and let m_1 and m_2 be its images in each of the two retinal planes. We call (c_1) and (c_2) the two images of (C). Quantities related to the first and second cameras are indexed by 1 and 2, respectively. The rig is calibrated so that we can express all vectors in the standard coordinate system attached to the first camera.

In particular, for the kinematic screw we have

$$\mathbf{\Omega}_2 = \mathbf{R}^T \mathbf{\Omega}$$

$$\mathbf{V}_2 = \mathbf{R}^T(\mathbf{V} + \mathbf{\Omega} \wedge \mathbf{Tr})$$

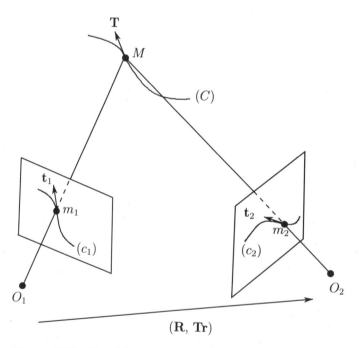

Figure 9.20   Matching two curves in stereo.

9.7.1   Constraints from the tangents

It is clear geometrically that the direction $\mathbf{W}$ of the unit tangent vector $\mathbf{T}$ to (C) at M is parallel to[8] $\mathbf{U}_{t_1} \wedge \mathbf{U}_{t_2}$. But, according to equation (9.50), it is also parallel to $\mathbf{U}_{t_i} \wedge (\dot{\mathbf{U}}_{t_i} + \mathbf{U}_{t_i} \wedge \Omega), i = 1, 2$. Therefore we can write the two equations

$$(\mathbf{U}_{t_1} \wedge \mathbf{U}_{t_2}) \wedge (\mathbf{U}_{t_i} \wedge (\dot{\mathbf{U}}_{t_i} + \mathbf{U}_{t_i} \wedge \Omega)) = \mathbf{0}, i = 1, 2$$

We expand the triple cross-product and notice that $\mathbf{U}_{t_i}^T (\mathbf{U}_{t_1} \wedge \mathbf{U}_{t_2}) = 0, i = 1, 2$:

$$[(\mathbf{U}_{t_1} \wedge \mathbf{U}_{t_2})^T (\dot{\mathbf{U}}_{t_i} + \mathbf{U}_{t_i} \wedge \Omega)]\mathbf{U}_{t_i} = \mathbf{0}, i = 1, 2$$

Expanding the inner product yields

$$(\Omega, \mathbf{U}_{t_i}, \mathbf{U}_{t_1} \wedge \mathbf{U}_{t_2}) = (\dot{\mathbf{U}}_{t_i}, \mathbf{U}_{t_1}, \mathbf{U}_{t_2}) \qquad i = 1, 2 \tag{9.76}$$

These two equations describe the projection of the angular velocity Ω in the plane defined by $\mathbf{U}_{t_1}$ and $\mathbf{U}_{t_2}$, i.e., the plane normal to $\mathbf{T}$. They are linear in Ω and in the two tangential motion fields w_1 and w_2 at m_1 and m_2.

9.7.2   Constraints from the points

We write equations (9.64) and (9.65) for the two cameras. For the first camera we obtain

$$z(w_1 + \Omega^T \mathbf{b}_1) = -\varepsilon_1 \mathbf{V} \cdot \mathbf{U}_{\mathbf{n}_1} \tag{9.77}$$

$$z(\beta_1 + \Omega^T \mathbf{a}_1) = \varepsilon_1 \mathbf{V} \cdot \mathbf{U}_{t_1} \tag{9.78}$$

and for the second camera we have

$$z_2(w_2 + \Omega_2^T \mathbf{b}_2) = -\varepsilon_2 \mathbf{V}_2 \cdot \mathbf{U}_{\mathbf{n}_2} \tag{9.79}$$

$$z_2(\beta_2 + \Omega_2^T \mathbf{a}_2) = \varepsilon_2 \mathbf{V}_2 \cdot \mathbf{U}_{t_2} \tag{9.80}$$

The value of z_2 is obtained from the following equation:

---

8. We assume that $\mathbf{U}_{t_1} \wedge \mathbf{U}_{t_2}$ is expressed in the coordinate system attached to the first camera, i.e., we take $\mathbf{U}_{t_2} = \tilde{\mathbf{R}}(\mathbf{m}_2 \wedge \mathbf{t}_2)$.

$\mathbf{M}_2 = \mathbf{R}^T(\mathbf{M} - \mathbf{Tr})$.

Equations (9.77)-(9.80) are four linear equations in the components of the kinematic screw $(\Omega, \mathbf{V})$ and the tangential motion fields w_1 and w_2. We have a total of six linear equations.

9.7.3   A constraint from the binormal

In section 9.5.3 we saw that the binormal $\mathbf{B}$ to (C) was parallel to $\mathbf{W} \wedge \frac{\partial \mathbf{W}}{\partial s}$. We can therefore write that the vectors $(\mathbf{U}_{t_1} \wedge \mathbf{U}_{t_2}) \wedge \frac{\partial \mathbf{W}_1}{\partial s_1}$ and $(\mathbf{U}_{t_1} \wedge \mathbf{U}_{t_2}) \wedge \frac{\partial \mathbf{W}_2}{\partial s_2}$ are parallel, where $\mathbf{W}_1$ and $\mathbf{W}_2$ are given by equation (9.50). Computing the cross-product of these two vectors, we have

$$(\mathbf{U}_{t_1} \wedge \mathbf{U}_{t_2}, \frac{\partial \mathbf{W}_1}{\partial s_1}, \frac{\partial \mathbf{W}_2}{\partial s_2})\mathbf{U}_{t_1} \wedge \mathbf{U}_{t_2}$$

We therefore obtain one equation from the binormal to (C):

$$(\mathbf{U}_{t_1} \wedge \mathbf{U}_{t_2}, \frac{\partial \mathbf{W}_1}{\partial s_1}, \frac{\partial \mathbf{W}_2}{\partial s_2}) = 0 \tag{9.81}$$

In order to exploit it, we need to evaluate the two vectors $\frac{\partial \mathbf{W}_i}{\partial s_i}, i = 1, 2$. Let us do it for $i = 1$ and drop the index for a moment. From equation (9.50), we can write

$$\frac{\partial \mathbf{W}}{\partial s} = \kappa \mathbf{U_n} \wedge (\mathbf{U}_t \wedge \Omega + \dot{\mathbf{U}}_t) + \mathbf{U}_t \wedge (\kappa \mathbf{U_n} \wedge \Omega + \frac{\partial \dot{\mathbf{U}}_t}{\partial s})$$

From the definition of the Lie bracket given in appendix C, we can prove that $L_{[t_0, v_m^r]} = (\frac{\partial w}{\partial s} - \kappa \beta)L_{t_0}$ and that

$$\frac{\partial \dot{\mathbf{U}}_t}{\partial s} = \overline{\frac{\partial \mathbf{U}_t}{\partial s}} + (\frac{\partial w}{\partial s} - \kappa \beta)\frac{\partial \mathbf{U}_t}{\partial s}$$

Using the fact that $\frac{\partial \mathbf{U}_t}{\partial s} = \kappa \mathbf{U_n}$, we can write

$$\frac{\partial \dot{\mathbf{U}}_t}{\partial s} = \overline{\kappa \mathbf{U_n}} + \kappa(\frac{\partial w}{\partial s} - \kappa \beta)\mathbf{U_n} = \dot{\kappa}\mathbf{U_n} + \kappa\dot{\mathbf{U}}_n + \kappa(\frac{\partial w}{\partial s} - \kappa \beta)\mathbf{U_n}$$

$$= (\dot{\kappa} + \kappa(\frac{\partial w}{\partial s} - \kappa \beta))\mathbf{U_n} + \kappa\dot{\mathbf{U}}_n$$

From equation (9.56) and $\dot{\kappa} = w\frac{\partial \kappa}{\partial s} + \partial_{\mathbf{n}_\beta}\kappa$ we obtain

$$\frac{\partial \dot{\mathbf{U}}_{\mathbf{t}}}{\partial s} = -\kappa(\kappa w + \frac{\partial \beta}{\partial s})\mathbf{U}_{\mathbf{t}} + (w\frac{\partial \kappa}{\partial s} + \kappa\frac{\partial w}{\partial s} + \partial_{\mathbf{n}_\beta}\kappa - \kappa^2\beta)\mathbf{U}_{\mathbf{n}} + \kappa w\mathbf{t} \wedge \mathbf{n}$$

Finally, using equation (9.29) we obtain

$$\frac{\partial \dot{\mathbf{U}}_{\mathbf{t}}}{\partial s} = -\kappa(\kappa w + \frac{\partial \beta}{\partial s})\mathbf{U}_{\mathbf{t}} + (w\frac{\partial \kappa}{\partial s} + \kappa\frac{\partial w}{\partial s} + \frac{\partial^2 \beta}{\partial s^2})\mathbf{U}_{\mathbf{n}} + \kappa w\mathbf{t} \wedge \mathbf{n}$$

The only term that remains to be estimated is $\frac{\partial w}{\partial s}$. We can do it using equation (9.64). Indeed, we take the derivative of that equation with respect to s:

$$\frac{T_z}{u}(w + \mathbf{\Omega} \cdot \mathbf{b}) + z(\frac{\partial w}{\partial s} + \mathbf{\Omega} \cdot \frac{\partial \mathbf{b}}{\partial s}) = \varepsilon(\kappa\mathbf{U}_{\mathbf{t}} \cdot \mathbf{V} - V_z)$$

If we take the derivative of the perspective equation $\mathbf{M} = z\mathbf{m}$ with respect to S (see problem 2), we obtain

$$T_z\mathbf{m} + uz\mathbf{t} = \mathbf{T}$$

Projecting this equation on $\mathbf{t}$ yields:

$$uz\|\mathbf{W}\| = \mathbf{W} \cdot (\mathbf{t} - (\mathbf{m} \cdot \mathbf{t})\mathbf{k} = -\varepsilon\mathbf{U}_{\mathbf{n}} \cdot \mathbf{W} \tag{9.82}$$

By taking $\mathbf{W} = \mathbf{U}_{\mathbf{t}_1} \wedge \mathbf{U}_{\mathbf{t}_2}$ and $\mathbf{T} = \frac{\mathbf{U}_{\mathbf{t}_1} \wedge \mathbf{U}_{\mathbf{t}_2}}{\|\mathbf{U}_{\mathbf{t}_1} \wedge \mathbf{U}_{\mathbf{t}_2}\|}$, equation (9.82) yields

$$uz = -\varepsilon(\mathbf{U}_{\mathbf{n}}, \mathbf{U}_{\mathbf{t}_1}, \mathbf{U}_{\mathbf{t}_2})$$

and therefore

$$\frac{T_z}{u} = -\frac{\varepsilon z(\mathbf{U}_{\mathbf{t}_1} \wedge \mathbf{U}_{\mathbf{t}_2})_z}{(\mathbf{U}_{\mathbf{n}}, \mathbf{U}_{\mathbf{t}_1}, \mathbf{U}_{\mathbf{t}_2})}$$

Let us call A the quantity $-\frac{(\mathbf{U}_{\mathbf{t}_1} \wedge \mathbf{U}_{\mathbf{t}_2})_z}{(\mathbf{U}_{\mathbf{n}}, \mathbf{U}_{\mathbf{t}_1}, \mathbf{U}_{\mathbf{t}_2})}$. Now we have

$$Az(w + \mathbf{\Omega} \cdot \mathbf{b}) + z(\frac{\partial w}{\partial s} + \mathbf{\Omega} \cdot \frac{\partial \mathbf{b}}{\partial s}) = \kappa\mathbf{U}_{\mathbf{t}} \cdot \mathbf{V} - V_z$$

From equation (9.64)

$$z(\frac{\partial w}{\partial s} + \mathbf{\Omega} \cdot \frac{\partial \mathbf{b}}{\partial s}) = \kappa\mathbf{U}_{\mathbf{t}} \cdot \mathbf{V} - V_z - A\mathbf{U}_{\mathbf{n}} \cdot \mathbf{V}$$

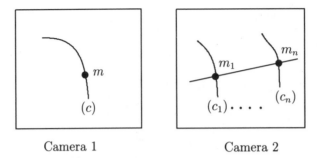

Camera 1   Camera 2

Figure 9.21 n possible hypotheses for matching curve (c) in image 1 to a curve in image 2.

which provides an expression for $\frac{\partial w}{\partial s}$ that is linear in $(\Omega, \mathbf{V})$. From this we can conclude that equation (9.81) is at most of degree 2 in the coordinates of $(\Omega, \mathbf{V})$.

9.7.4 How to use this information

Suppose we are trying to do stereo from curves as in section 6.9.2 of chapter 6. At each time instant we extract a number of curves in each image, and for each of these curves we construct the corresponding spatiotemporal surfaces. Let (c) be a curve in image 1, and let $(c_1), \ldots, (c_n)$ n be possible candidates in image 2 (see figure 9.21). Let m be a point on (c), and let $m_1, \ldots, m_n$ be the corresponding points on $(c_1), \ldots, (c_n)$, which are obtained by intersecting them with the epipolar line of m.

For each pair of hypothesis $((c), (c_i))$, if we assume that the corresponding 3-D curve (C_i) moves rigidly, we can write for each pair of corresponding points (m, m_i) on (c) and (c_i) seven equations in the eight unknowns $(\Omega, \mathbf{V})$, w_m, and w_{m_i}, the tangential motion fields. If we now choose another point p on (c) and consider the corresponding points p_i on (c_i), we can write for each hypothesis $((c), (c_i))$ fourteen equations in the ten unknowns $(\Omega, \mathbf{V})$, w_m, w_{m_i}, w_p, and w_{p_i}, twelve of them linear. If we assume that the rank of the system of twelve linear equations is 10, this provides two constraints as follows. Assuming, without loss of generality, that the first ten equations are independent, we can compute $(\Omega, \mathbf{V})$, w_m, w_{m_i}, w_p, and w_{p_i} from them. The two constraints are obtained by replacing the unknowns with their computed values in the last two equations. Two other constraints are obtained by doing the same with the two nonlinear equations. These constraints should be satisfied only for the correct hypothesis since there is, in general, no reason for an incorrect match to yield a three-dimensional curve moving rigidly.

9.8　More references

The work on optical flow is extensive, and it is out of the question to discuss and cite it all. The problem of the reliable estimation of optical flow has received enormous attention, and two techniques are worth mentioning: The one developed by Anandan [Ana89] is based on time correlation at various spatial resolution; the method developed by Heeger [Hee88], which is more biologically oriented, is based upon the combination of the outputs of a set of spatiotemporal motion-energy filters.

Much of the work that has not been mentioned in this chapter has been devoted to the study of the properties of the real motion field and how they relate to scene motion and structure, assuming that they can be reliably computed from the images. Probably the most prominent efforts in this direction have been those of Koenderink and vanDoorn [KvD75, KvD78, Koe86], of Longuet-Higgins and Prazdny [LP80, Pra83], and of Maybank [May87].

Some authors have investigated methods for approximating the motion field locally by regular functions, as have Haralick and Lee [HL83] and also Waxman, Kamgar-Parsi, and Subbarao [WKS87, Sub88], who used quadratic approximations to the motion field and showed how to solve the motion and structure problem under this simplifying hypothesis, assuming as always that the real motion field can be achieved.

The work on the flow generated by contours is much scarcer. Apart from the pioneering work of Ellen Hildreth [Hil84], which was somewhat generalized by D'Hayer [DHa86], a notable exception is the work of Fredrik Bergholm [Ber89b, Ber89a, BC91], who has studied ambiguous planar curves, i.e., planar space curves for which no unique motion can be recovered from the normal flow. Interesting results about the interpretation of visual motion can be found in the book by Murray and Buxton [MB90].

9.9 Problems

1. In his 1986 paper [Bou86], Bouthemy proposed a method for reconstructing the motion field $\mathbf{v}_m$ along an image curve (c) from the estimation $\hat{\beta}$ of the normal field. In order to achieve this, he used a recursive formula, which he derived from the theory of stochastic gradient. The details of the derivation are irrelevant here. The formula is

$$\mathbf{v}_m(s+1) = \mathbf{v}_m(s) - y\mathbf{n}(s)(\mathbf{v}_m(s) \cdot \mathbf{n}(s) - \hat{\beta}(s)) \qquad (9.83)$$

where s is the arclength along (c), $\mathbf{n}$ the normal, and y a coefficient that is constant along (c). Let $\mathbf{t}$ be the tangent to (c). Show that the computed motion field approximately satisfies equation (9.25).

2. In this problem we will show how to compute the curvature and torsion of the curve (C).

   a. Show that taking the derivative of equation (9.37) with respect to S yields

   $$T_z\mathbf{m} + uz\mathbf{t} = \mathbf{T} \qquad (9.84)$$

   where $T_z = \mathbf{T} \cdot \mathbf{k}$.

   b. Show that the projection of this equation along the tangent $\mathbf{t}$ to (c_τ) yields

   $$uz\|\mathbf{W}\| = \mathbf{W} \cdot \mathbf{t} - (\mathbf{m} \cdot \mathbf{t})W_z = -\mathbf{U_n} \cdot \mathbf{W} \qquad (9.85)$$

   c. Show that

   $$\mathbf{U_n} \cdot \mathbf{W} = \beta - \varepsilon\Omega \cdot \mathbf{a}$$

   d. Show that the projection of equation (9.84) along the tangent $\mathbf{n}$ to (c_τ) yields $0 = 0$.

   e. Express the curvature Γ of (C) as a function of $\mathbf{W}$ and z.

   f. Let $x = \|\mathbf{W} \wedge \frac{\partial \mathbf{W}}{\partial s}\|$. We have $x\mathbf{B} = \varepsilon\mathbf{W} \wedge \frac{\partial \mathbf{W}}{\partial s}$, where $\varepsilon = \pm 1$. Show that the third three-dimensional Frenet formula yields

   $$\rho x = \varepsilon u(\mathbf{N}, \mathbf{W}, \frac{\partial^2 \mathbf{W}}{\partial s^2})$$

Conclude that

$$\rho = -\frac{u\|\mathbf{W}\|}{x^2}\left(\mathbf{W}, \frac{\partial \mathbf{W}}{\partial s}, \frac{\partial^2 \mathbf{W}}{\partial s^2}\right)$$

3. In section 9.6.1, we have shown that, in the case where the rigid motion of (C) takes place in a plane parallel to the retinal plane, the apparent and real motion fields are the same. Show that this is also true for an isometric motion of (C) in such a plane.

4. In this problem we will compute the Lie bracket $L_{[\mathbf{n}_\beta, \mathbf{t}_0]}$. We will use the notations of appendix C. If $\mathbf{X}(u^1, u^2)$ and $\mathbf{Y}(u^1, u^2)$ are two vector fields tangent to (Σ), the Lie bracket $[\mathbf{X}, \mathbf{Y}]$ of $\mathbf{X}$ and $\mathbf{Y}$ is defined by its coordinates in the tangent plane T_P by the formulas (see equations (C.13) of appendix C):

$$[\mathbf{X}, \mathbf{Y}]^i = X^j \frac{\partial Y^i}{\partial u^j} - Y^j \frac{\partial X^i}{\partial u^j} \tag{9.86}$$

where we have used the Einstein convention.

a. Express $\mathbf{n}_\beta$ and $\mathbf{t}_0$ in the coordinate system defined by $\mathbf{P}'_S$ and $\mathbf{P}'_\tau$ (we have $u^1 = S$ and $u^2 = \tau$).

b. Using equations (9.86), compute $[\mathbf{n}_\beta, \mathbf{t}_0]^1$ and $[\mathbf{n}_\beta, \mathbf{t}_0]^2$.

c. Using the facts that $w = v + \alpha$ and $v_S = u_\tau$ and the first of the derivation rules (9.14), show that

$$[\mathbf{n}_\beta, \mathbf{t}_0]^1 = \frac{1}{u}\frac{\partial \alpha}{\partial s}$$

Conclude, i.e., give the expression of $L_{[\mathbf{n}_\beta, \mathbf{t}_0]}$.

5. In this problem we will study the motion of $\mathbf{W}_B$ defined in section 9.5.3 and show that it does not provide any new equation if equation (9.54) is satisfied.

a. Show that the analysis of section 9.4.3.1 proves that $\mathbf{W}_B$ satisfies equation (9.42)

$$\mathbf{W}_B \wedge (\dot{\mathbf{W}}_B + \mathbf{W}_B \wedge \Omega) = \mathbf{0}$$

b. Let $\mathbf{Y} = \frac{\partial \mathbf{w}}{\partial s}$. Show that

$$\mathbf{W_B} \wedge (\dot{\mathbf{W}}_\mathbf{B} + \mathbf{W_B} \wedge \Omega) = (\mathbf{Y}^T(\mathbf{W} \wedge (\dot{\mathbf{W}} + \mathbf{W} \wedge \Omega)))\mathbf{Y}$$
$$+ (\mathbf{W}^T(\mathbf{Y} \wedge (\dot{\mathbf{Y}} + \mathbf{Y} \wedge \Omega)))\mathbf{W}$$

c. Compute $\dot{\mathbf{Y}} = \frac{d(\frac{\partial \mathbf{W}}{\partial s})}{d\tau}$. *Hint*: use the fact that it is different from $\frac{\partial \dot{\mathbf{W}}}{\partial s}$ and that the difference between the two is given by $L_{[v_r,t_0]}\mathbf{W}$. Since $\mathbf{V}_r = w\mathbf{t}_0 + \mathbf{n}_\beta$, show that

$$L_{[v_r,t_0]} = L_{[n_\beta,t_0]} - \frac{\partial w}{\partial s}L_{t_0} = (\kappa\beta - \frac{\partial w}{\partial s})L_{t_0}$$

d. Show that

$$\mathbf{W} \wedge (\dot{\mathbf{Y}} + \mathbf{Y} \wedge \Omega) = -\mathbf{Y} \wedge (\dot{\mathbf{W}} + \mathbf{W} \wedge \Omega + (\kappa\beta - \frac{\partial w}{\partial s})\mathbf{W})$$

Conclude that $\mathbf{W}^T(\mathbf{Y} \wedge (\dot{\mathbf{Y}} + \mathbf{Y} \wedge \Omega)) = 0$ and that the binormal does not bring in more information if the equation (9.54) for the tangent is satisfied.

e. Show that this implies that the normal to (C) does not bring in any more information either.

10 Interpolating and Approximating Three-Dimensional Data

10.1 The status of the problem

In the previous chapters, we have studied a number of techniques for obtaining 3-D data using stereo vision and motion. In chapter 11 we will discuss techniques based on using active sensing devices such as laser range finders. All these measurements have a purpose: to build a representation of the environment to achieve some task such as obstacle avoidance, trajectory planning, recognition of places or objects, manipulation, etc. The question of which representation is suitable for which task is not an innocent one, since it relates to the complexity of the processing that is necessary in order to obtain the representation from the measurements. If we follow the principle of economy, also known in physics as the *principle of minimal energy*, we would like to have representations as simple as possible in order to accomplish the task at hand. This idea and its possible consequence, that many tasks may require only simple representations, and perhaps even no representation at all, has been proposed and developed by Brooks [Bro91]. Nonetheless, the relationship between task requirements and representation still remains to be analyzed.

Two basic questions must be considered:

1. What information must be present in the representation for a given task?

2. What is the accuracy with which this information must be computed?

We believe, as many authors do [Mar82], that the answer to question 1 is that all the information necessary for solving the task should be made explicit in the representation. We believe that the answer to the accuracy question does not lie in racing toward ever more accurate data, but rather in carefully evaluating the sources of errors and uncertainty and quantitatively characterizing these sources. The representation must contain, for example, geometric information, but also uncertainty information. In other words, we believe it is fundamental that representations always contain not only measurements, but also a characterization of the uncertainty on these measurements. We have developed this point in detail in chapters 5 and 8.

In this chapter we will focus on the problems of deciding what kind of 3-D information must be represented to solve the problems of obstacle avoidance, navigation, and object or place identification. It is probably the case that the first two tasks do not require as detailed descriptions as the other two, and for this reason we will present several variants of the same ideas that can accommodate various densities in the raw 3-D measurements. The idea is that simpler tasks require less dense measurements.

Badler, Bajcsy, and Solina [BR78, BS87] and Marr and Nishihara [MK78] discuss a number of important points that must be addressed when judging the suitability of shape representations for the tasks we have discussed:

1. **What are the primitive elements in the representation?**

    Obstacle avoidance and navigation require a volumetric representation; therefore, volumes must be primitive elements. Identification, on the other hand, requires surface models: Surfaces and significant curves on surfaces must also be present in the representation. This is a preliminary analysis, and we must define what the primitive volume-, surface-, and curve-elements should be.

2. **What is the coordinate system in which those primitives are specified?**

    Typically a representation is viewer- or object-centered. When we are measuring object shapes with our sensors, we are operating within a viewer-centered coordinate system, or within a number of viewer-centered coordinate systems if our sensors are allowed to move around (see chapter 7). On the other hand, models of places or objects are described in an object-centered coordinate system, which is usually different from the viewer-centered one. One of the problems related to the identification is to establish the correspondence between the two types of coordinate systems. This correspondence can be either a rigid transformation if objects are rigid, or a more general one if they are not.

So the question of the appropriate coordinate system in which to describe things is really the question of how the primitive elements in the representation change when submitted to an allowable transformation. To take a concrete simple example, let us assume that we are interested in representing the 2-D shape of figure 10.1. If we use a quadtree representation [HS79, Sam80, Sam89], the shape will change considerably when we apply translations and rotations. For instance, we have applied a horizontal translation of one pixel to the shape in figure 10.1 and displayed the new quadtree representation in figure 10.2. It is clear that the simple geometric relation between figures 10.1.a and 10.2.a is considerably more obscure in figures 10.1.b and 10.2.b.

On the other hand, we could have represented the square in figure 10.1.a by the list of its edges represented by their endpoints, along with an array containing the coordinates of those endpoints:

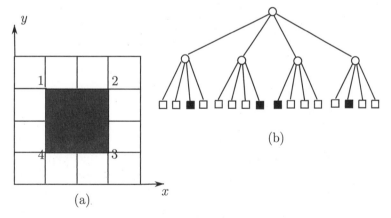

(b)

(a)

Figure 10.1 A simple shape and its associated quadtree.

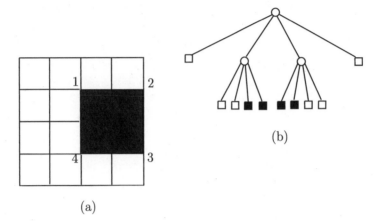

(b)

(a)

Figure 10.2 The square of figure 10.1 translated by $[0,1]^T$ and its associated quadtree. Note the dissimilarity between 10.1.b and 10.2.b.

Edges

edge	vertices	
1	1	2
2	2	3
3	3	4
4	4	1

Endpoints

vertex	coordinates	
1	1	3
2	3	3
3	3	1
4	1	1

The representation of the shape in figure 10.2.a has the same list of edges as in figure 10.1.a, and below is shown the list of the coordinates of the endpoints to which we have applied the same transformation as before (here a translation $[1,0]^T$):

Endpoints

vertex	coordinates	
1	2	3
2	4	3
3	4	1
4	2	1

It is clear that the second representation supports rigid transformations much better than the first one.

3. **How are the primitive elements organized in a description?**
This question points to the idea of the structure of the representation. It is just as fundamental as the first question, since it has a direct impact on the kind of algorithms that will be easy or difficult to run on the representation. In fact, we may think of a representation as a ternary object composed of the *primitive elements*, their *relations*, which are made explicit by the structure, and the *algorithms* that operate on the structure. This topic is discussed at great length, mostly for 2-D image analysis, in a book by Pavlidis [Pav77], and it overlaps considerably with the area of computer science known as data structures [Knu68, AHU74], as with the emerging discipline of computational geometry [PS85]. We will deal with these issues in some amount of detail later in this chapter, but right now let us bring up a simple point related to the idea of hierarchy.

The original, and fairly vague, idea is that of describing things at a variety of levels. In general, each level may require completely different conceptual tools for the analysis. A standard example is that of a computer, which may be described at the operating system level by studying how various programs are executed and how they interact among themselves and with the users. But the computer can also be described at the architectural level by studying the various hardware pieces, such as the CPU, memories, buses, and disks and how they interact with programs and among themselves. The computer can also be described at the register level by studying the structure of these hardware pieces, which can be described at the component level, electrical level, electronic level, etc.

We see two main ideas emerging from this example. The first is that of zooming in on a complex reality and deciding (maybe somewhat arbitrarily) to isolate levels of descriptions at which things are homogeneous and primitive elements can be identified. The second idea is that of including the levels of description. This may be somewhat misleading, and it carries the risk that we will take for granted the implicit assumption that the understanding of what is going on at one level can be obtained from the descriptions at lower levels. We call this the *fine-to-coarse assumption.* This is the same as saying that understanding quantum mechanics allows us to understand human psychology. This is an extreme example to illustrate this assumption, which is sometimes called the *reductionist assumption.*

In computer vision the notion of hierarchy, at least in shape representation, is usually attached to the notion of resolution: Shapes can be described with various amounts of detail, and the fine-to-coarse assumption is true most of the time. That is to say that the description at a coarser level can be computed from the description at finer levels. In fact, the hierarchy is used opposite to the way it was used in the quantum mechanics example: We use coarse level descriptions to prepare for and reduce the complexity of the work to be done at lower levels. Returning to the previous example, in the computer vision paradigm we would understand quantum mechanics by means of human psychology.

Two important questions related to the idea of the structure of a description have been briefly mentioned previously but are worth making more explicit:

4. **What operations on the representation are natural, and which ones are difficult?**

   Translated in terms of algorithms, this question can be rephrased as follows: What is the complexity of the algorithms that can run on the representation? In this chapter we will make some effort to characterize the complexity of the algorithms that are described.

5. **What is the construction and storage cost associated with the representation?**

   These are very natural questions in the areas of data structures and computational geometry. We will try to answer them as precisely as possible in the various examples that we will present. It is our belief that computer vision should invest more in the complexity analysis of the various structures and algorithms that it proposes and manipulates.

If we consider a representation as a mapping r of a set of shapes (defined by the application) into a set of structures, we may ask another type of question related to the properties of the mapping r. For example:

6. **What class of shapes is the representation designed for?**
   In particular, does there exist a well-defined description for each shape in the class of shapes in which we are interested? Stated another way, this question asks where the mapping r is well defined. For example, if we assume that the set of all shapes is the set of all closed subsets of the usual three-dimensional euclidean space, which is indeed a very large set, we might want to concentrate on a subset of these shapes defined as the bounded closed sets (therefore compact) with a boundary that is twice continuously differentiable (i.e., smooth shapes). This would exclude, in particular, all polyhedra, for which the differentiability condition of the boundary is not satisfied at edges or vertices.

   Once the domain of definition of r has been agreed upon, we can define r itself: We can give, for each shape in the set under consideration, the way to construct its *unique* representation.[1] If we now add more structure to the set of shapes — for example, if we define a topology [Mat75, Mum87], which may or may not be reducible to a distance (for example the Hausdorff distance)[2] — we can then talk about differences between shapes and how they are reflected by differences between their representations. A typical question would be:

7. **Do differences between descriptions reflect the relative importance of differences between the shapes?**
   This question has to do with the continuity of the function r. If the topology on the set of shapes is defined in such a way that for the task at hand it reflects well the degree of difference between shapes,

---

1. Note that the uniqueness assumption is not necessary (see chapter 5).
2. The Hausdorff distance is defined in section 10.3.

and if r is continuous, this sensitivity to the interesting differences will be carried over to the set of representations.

If we again examine our tasks (obstacle avoidance, navigation, and object identification) in the light of these questions, we can come up with a number of useful requirements for the kind of representations we will be dealing with. First, since in general multiple views obtained from a variety of viewpoints are available, they must have good properties with respect to rigid motions (see the example of figures 10.1 and 10.2). Second, since we want to deal both with free space for obstacle avoidance and trajectory planning and with boundaries of objects for identification, they should include volumes and surfaces as primitive elements. Third, the representation should be robust to the number of measurements in the following sense:

- It should be usable when only sparse data is available, and it should converge toward the true volumes and surfaces when the density increases.

- Conversely, if a large number of data measurements is available, the representation should be easy to simplify in places where the measurements are redundant (for example, where curvature variations are small).

Fourth, and related to the previous point, we would like the representations to be easily updatable when new data becomes available, a property we might want to call *dynamic flexibility*. Fifth, we want the complexity of computing the representations to be small for obvious reasons of efficiency.

To summarize all this, the representation should (1) allow for easy assessment of rigid motions, (2) be volume- and surface-oriented, (3) work for both sparse and dense data, (4) be capable of being (intelligently) simplified by throwing away data, (5) be easy to update when new data becomes available, and (6) facilitate efficient computation. What we propose to do is to use a triangulation of our data points as a basis to support a number of other representations. The triangulation will establish neighborhood relations between the measurements, which are a first step toward the recovery of more complex shape characteristics of the underlying objects. This discrete topology will then be used to construct other less detailed representations, making explicit different aspects such as smooth patches, curves, medial axes of free space, etc.

10.2   How to read this chapter

After this introduction we will dive into the problem of shape topologies in section 10.3. This is important to understand the relationship between the shapes that we want to represent and the approximations that we propose more clearly. We will use the theory proposed by Matheron [Mat75] to define topologies on sets of shapes. But an understanding of this section is required only for the theoretical sections, 10.4.2 and 10.4.3, which deal with the approximation properties of the Delaunay triangulation. The reader who is uninterested in mathematical details may look just at theorems 10.3 and 10.4, which state the two main results. Section 10.4 deals with the properties of the Delaunay triangulation of a set of points. Section 10.4.1 explains the relationship between the Delaunay triangulation and the Voronoi diagram, and sections 10.4.4 and 10.4.5 deal with the problems of actually computing the Delaunay triangulation of a set of points and analyzing of the complexity of the algorithm.

Section 10.5 is a generalization to the case where we are given line segments instead of points and where we want these line segments to be edges of the Delaunay triangulation of their endpoints. The reason for this is explained in section 10.6. This question arises because, as seen in chapter 6, some of the algorithms that reconstruct 3-D data actually produce line segments. We will present a simple algorithm to guarantee that this condition is satisfied by adding a few points to the line segments, and we will analyze the complexity of this algorithm. We will take this opportunity to introduce a theoretical tool that we believe is very important in the analysis of geometric algorithms: the theory of random closed sets, which we restrict to one single but very useful theorem, theorem 10.5. The next section shows how to use some of the previous tools to build polyhedral interpolations of 3-D data. Many real examples are presented. The final section, section 10.7, describes some simple ways of building higher-order approximations of 3-D data with planes and quadrics. Again, many real examples are presented.

10.3   Shape topologies

In order to discuss questions of approximations of shapes and limits of shapes, we need to introduce a topology on the set of shapes. We assume that the reader has some familiarity with elementary topology.

10.3.1   The Hausdorff distance

First we will consider the set $\mathcal{K}$ of nonempty compact sets of R^n with the usual euclidean distance d. We can define a distance, called the Hausdorff distance, between two compact sets K_1 and K_2 as

$$h(K_1, K_2) = \sup(\rho(K_1, K_2), \rho(K_2, K_1)) \tag{10.1}$$

where $\rho(K_1, K_2) = \sup_{x \in K_1} d(x, K_2)$. An equivalent definition that is very useful in practice is

$$h(K_1, K_2) = \inf_{\varepsilon}\{\varepsilon : K_1 \subset K_2 \oplus B_\varepsilon, \text{ and } K_2 \subset K_1 \oplus B_\varepsilon\} \tag{10.2}$$

where B_ε is the closed ball of radius ε and $\oplus$ is the Minkowski sum of two sets defined by

$$K_1 \oplus K_2 = \{\mathbf{a} + \mathbf{b}, \ \mathbf{a} \in K_1 \text{ and } \mathbf{b} \in K_2\}$$

An example of the effect of the $\oplus$ operator is given in figure 10.3. A proof that this indeed defines a distance can be found by working out problem 1.

Note that the Hausdorff metric ignores the empty set $\varnothing$. Indeed, relations (10.1) and (10.2) do not make any sense if K_1 or K_2 is the empty set. The assumption that the sets are closed is also important, as is seen by taking $K_2 = \mathring{K}_1$ for a compact set K_1 with a nonempty interior[3] (for example, a closed disk). In this case $h(K_1, K_2) = 0$ even though K_1 is distinct from K_2, which contradicts the definition of a distance. The assumption that the sets are compact and therefore bounded is also essential, as is seen in the example of two lines in a plane at a nonzero angle. Clearly,

---

3. The notation $\mathring{A}$ for a subset A, of R^n means the interior of A, the largest open subset of A or the union of all open subsets of A. Similarly, the notation $\overline{A}$ means the closure of A, the smallest closed set containing A, or the intersection of all closed sets containing A.

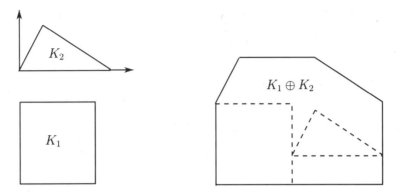

Figure 10.3   An example of the Minkowski sum of two compact sets.

$h(K_1, K_2) = \infty$ for each nonzero value of the angle between the two lines, whereas $h(K_1, K_2) = 0$ when this angle is zero. Thus the Hausdorff distance is not continuous, which is a contradiction.

The Hausdorff distance defines a topology on the set $\mathcal{K}' = \mathcal{K} \div \emptyset$ of nonempty compact sets, but the problem with this topology is that $\mathcal{K}'$ itself is not compact. The reason is that there are sequences of compact sets that converge toward infinite and therefore noncompact sets. As an example, consider in the plane the sequence of closed squares $(Sq_n), n \geq 1$ whose vertices have coordinates $(-n, 0), (n, 0), (n, n)$, and $(-n, n)$. This sequence converges toward the closed half-plane defined by $y \geq 0$, which is not compact. In order to avoid these kinds of problems, we will enlarge the set $\mathcal{K}$ and consider the set of all closed sets of R^n.

10.3.2   The hit-or-miss topology

Consider the set $\mathcal{F}$ of closed sets which is larger than $\mathcal{K}$, and define a topology, called the *hit-or-miss topology* [Mat75] as follows:

Definition 10.1
We call the hit-or-miss topology on $\mathcal{F}$ the topology $T_{\mathcal{F}}$ generated by the neighborhoods

$$\mathcal{F}_{G_1, G_2, \ldots, G_p}^K = \{F \in \mathcal{F} : F \cap K = \emptyset \text{ and } F \cap G_i \neq \emptyset, i = 1, \ldots, p\}$$

where p is an integer, K is a compact set, and $G_i, i = 1, \ldots, p$ is a finite family of open sets.

From this definition, the following fundamental theorem can be proved:

Theorem 10.1
The set $\mathcal{F}$ with the topology $T_{\mathcal{F}}$ is compact and separable.

Proof   The proof of this theorem is outside the scope of this book, but it can be found in the book by Matheron [Mat75]. The fact that $\mathcal{F}$ is compact implies that it is Hausdorff. Here the name *Hausdorff* does not refer to the previously defined Hausdorff distance, but to the fact that, given two distinct points of $\mathcal{F}$, there exist two neighborhoods of these points with an empty intersection. A *Hausdorff space* is sometimes also called a *separated space:* The two neighborhoods separate the two points. *Separable* means that there exists a countable set of open sets such that each open set for $T_{\mathcal{F}}$ is the union of such sets. Most usual spaces are separable (in particular R^n). An important consequence of separability is that the properties of convergence can be studied only on sequences.   ∎

We can develop a more intuitive grasp of what convergence of closed sets means through the following theorem:

Theorem 10.2
A sequence (F_i) of closed sets converges toward F if and only if the following conditions are met simultaneously:

1. For each point x in F, there exists a point x_i in F_i for i that is large enough that $x_i \to x$ in the usual euclidean sense.

2. (F_{i_k}) is a subsequence of (F_i), and x_{i_k} is a point in F_{i_k}. If $x_{i_k} \to x$, then $x \in F$.

Proof   Again, the proof of this theorem is outside the scope of this book, but it can be found in the book by Matheron [Mat75].   ∎

We will use this theorem in section 10.4 to discuss questions related to the approximation of skeletons. Now we will use it to define two closed sets associated with the sequence (F_i). These two sets will allow us to more precisely analyze the process of set convergence.

Definition 10.2
Let (F_i) be a sequence of closed sets. The lower limit of (F_i), denoted by $\underline{\lim}F_i$, is the set of all limits of points x_i in F_i or, equivalently, the largest

closed set satisfying the first condition of theorem 10.2. The upper limit of (F_i), denoted by $\overline{\lim}F_i$, is the set of all cluster points[4] of sequences of points x_i in F_i or, equivalently, the smallest closed set verifying the second criterion of theorem 10.2.

We have $\underline{\lim} F_i \subset \overline{\lim} F_i$ for a general sequence (not necessarily converging) of closed sets (F_i), and the fact that the sequence is converging toward the closed set F is equivalent to $\underline{\lim} F_i = \overline{\lim} F_i$.

Now that we have defined a topology on $\mathcal{F}$, we may want to see what happens when we reduce it to the set $\mathcal{K}$ of compact sets on which we already have a topology induced by the Hausdorff distance. The relationship between the two topologies is described by the following proposition:

Proposition 10.1

Let (K_i) be a sequence of compact sets in $\mathcal{K}$. It converges in $\mathcal{K}$ if and only if the two following conditions are met:

1. (K_i) converges in $\mathcal{F}$ according to the topology $\mathcal{T}_{\mathcal{F}}$.
2. There exists K in $\mathcal{K}$ such that $K_i \subset K$ for all i.

In other words, the topology induced by the Hausdorff distance does not "see" points at infinity. This is the reason for keeping all K_i of the proposition within a fixed, compact set K. As an example, if we consider in R the sequence of points (x_i) of coordinate i, this is a sequence of compact sets that does not converge in $\mathcal{K}$ because the points go to infinity, but the set does converge in $\mathcal{F}$ toward the empty set $\varnothing$.

10.4   Delaunay triangulation

Let us now assume that we have measured 3-D points on the surfaces of a set of objects that we assume to be locally smooth; we have no *a priori* connectivity information and want to connect points that are neighbors on the surface by line segments in a meaningful fashion. If we do that

---

4. A *cluster point of a sequence* is a point such that each of its neighborhoods contains an infinite number of points of the sequence. As a consequence of this, there exists a subsequence of the original sequence converging toward the cluster point.

without caution, we will obtain something that resembles, but is not necessarily, a polyhedral structure (i.e., some faces may intersect along lines that are not edges). Let us assume for the moment that we can guarantee that we will obtain a polyhedron. There are many different possible polyhedra, but we are interested in those that respect the topology of the underlying surfaces and are minimal in the sense that they contain the smallest possible number of edges. To be more specific, let us further assume that we restrict ourselves to simplicial polyhedra, i.e. those defined by a set of triangles $\mathcal{T}$. We do not lose any generality by doing this since, if a polyhedron is not simplicial, we can always triangulate its faces to make it simplicial.

Not all sets of triangles define valid polyhedra, and in order to do so they must satisfy the following three properties:

1. Two triangles are either disjoint, have one vertex in common, or have two vertices and therefore the entire edge joining them in common.

2. $\mathcal{T}$ is connected.

3. For every vertex v of each triangle in $\mathcal{T}$, the edges opposite v in the triangles of $\mathcal{T}$ that have v as a vertex form a simple polygon.

Of course, given a set of points, there are many such polyhedra, and computing all of them is a formidable task. We are interested only in those that correctly approximate the underlying surface. The word correctly has to be made more precise by defining criteria for good approximation. But since, in practice, the underlying surface is not available, this is a difficult way to go and we will not follow it. A degraded version of this idea is to assume some property of the underlying surface, for example, local smoothness, and to look for polyhedra that minimize curvature.

There exists a geometric structure, the *Delaunay triangulation*, which provides simplicial polyhedral approximations of surfaces that are closely related to their metric properties. This structure has been proposed by mathematicians such as Delaunay and Voronoi and studied by researchers in combinatorics and computational geometry. It is intimately related to another structure, the *Voronoi diagram*, which has also received considerable attention. It is also a global structure that allows for the extraction of a minimal representation of the shape that is guaranteed to converge toward the true surface when the number of samples increases. Finally, it is both a surface and a volume representation.

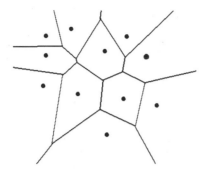

Figure 10.4   Voronoi diagram of a set of points.

We will now study Delaunay triangulations and Voronoi diagrams in more detail. Our exposition is mostly inspired by the one found in the book by Preparata and Shamos [PS85].

10.4.1   Voronoi diagrams and Delaunay triangulations

Let $d(P, Q)$ denote the usual euclidean distance between points, and let S be a set of n points $M_1, M_2, \ldots, M_n$. The Voronoi diagram of S is a set V of n convex polyhedra $V_1, V_2, \ldots, V_n$ that cover the whole space. V_i consists of all the points that are closer to M_i than to any other point in S:

$$V_i = \{P \text{ such that } d(P, M_i) \le d(P, M_j) \text{ for all } j = 1, \ldots, n\}$$

An example of the Voronoi diagram of a set of points in the plane is given in figure 10.4.

The sets V_i are convex polyhedra, and they are the intersection of the $n - 1$ half-spaces H_{ij} defined by

$$H_{ij} = \{P \text{ such that } d(P, M_i) \le d(P, M_j)\} \ j = 1, \ldots, n; j \ne i$$

Because things are very much alike in two and three dimensions (in fact, in k dimensions for $k \ge 2$), we will denote by k the dimension of the space (in our case $k = 2, 3$). Let us assume that no $k + 2$ points of the original set S are cospherical ($k = 3$) or cocircular ($k = 2$). This condition, as shown in the next proposition, is imposed in order to avoid degeneracies. In the 2-D case a degeneracy occurs when more than three Voronoi polygons meet at one vertex. In the 3-D case a degeneracy occurs when more than four Voronoi polyhedra meet at one vertex. In three dimensions (and higher, of course) we can also have lower-order degeneracies, as when more than three Voronoi polyhedra share an edge. However, the existence of a lower-order degeneracy implies the existence of a higher-order degeneracy. Indeed, in the 3-D case, if four Voronoi polyhedra share an edge, then at least five polyhedra must share each vertex at the end of that edge.

Let us give a property of the Voronoi diagram of a set of points that clarifies its relationship with the idea of *nearest neighbors*.

Definition 10.3

Given a point M in a finite set S, its nearest neighbors P are defined as the set N_M:

$$N_M = \{P : P \in S, d(M,P) = \min_{N \in S \div M} d(M,N)\}$$

As pointed out by Preparata and Shamos [PS85], this relation is not necessarily symmetric. Also, although a point can have every other point as a nearest neighbor, it can be the nearest neighbor of at most six points in dimension 2 and 12 in dimension 3 [HC52].

Proposition 10.2

Each nearest neighbor of a point M_i in S defines a face ($k = 3$) or an edge ($k = 2$) of V_i.

Proof Let M_j be a nearest neighbor of M_i, and let P be the midpoint of their adjoining segment. Suppose that M_j does not define a face ($k = 3$) or an edge ($k = 2$) of V_i. Then P does not lie on the boundary of V_i; it therefore lies outside the boundary, and (see figure 10.5) M_iP intersects the boundary of V_i at a point Q on the bisector of, let us say, M_iM_k. Then

$$M_iM_k \le 2M_iQ < M_iM_j$$

and M_j is not a nearest neighbor of M_i, which is a contradiction.   ∎

There is also an interesting relationship between the Voronoi diagram and the convex hull:

Proposition 10.3

A polyhedron V_i is unbounded if and only if the point M_i belongs to the boundary of the convex hull of S.

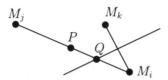

Figure 10.5   Proof of proposition 10.2.

Proof   We prove that polyhedron V_i is bounded if and only if point M_i does not belong to the boundary of the convex hull of S. First, if V_i is bounded, let $f_1, ..., f_k$ be the set of its faces. Each face $f_h (h = 1, ..., k)$ belongs to the bisector of a segment $M_i M_h, M_h$ in S. We then construct the following polyhedron with vertices $M_h, h = 1, ..., k$: We draw a face between M_h, $M_{h'}$, and $M_{h''}$ if and only if f_h, $f_{h'}$ and $f_{h''}$ are adjacent (have a common vertex). Clearly, M_i is interior to this polyhedron and is therefore not on the convex hull of S.

Inversely, let us assume that M_i is not on the convex hull of S. It is not difficult to show that there exists a triangle ($k = 2$) or a tetrahedron ($k = 3$) with vertices in S containing M_i. Let us do the proof for $k = 3$, which we transpose directly from the proof given by Preparata and Shamos [PS85, p. 202]. We denote by M_1, M_2, M_3, and M_4 the vertices of the tetrahedron containing M. The trick is to consider the four spheres $B_4 \equiv B(M_i, M_1, M_2, M_3)$, $B_1 \equiv B(M_i, M_2, M_3, M_4)$, $B_2 \equiv B(M_i, M_3, M_4, M_1)$, and $B_3 \equiv B(M_i, M_4, M_1, M_2)$ and a sphere B enclosing them. We will prove that any point P that lies outside of B is closer to M_1, M_2, M_3, or M_4 than it is to M_i.

Suppose, without loss of generality, that P is closer to M_1, that is, that $d(P, M_1) \leq d(P, M_k)$, $k = 2, 3, 4$. We will show that $d(P, M_i) > d(P, M_1)$. We assume the reverse and obtain a contradiction. Indeed, if $d(P, M_i) \leq d(P, M_1)$, P belongs to the Voronoi tetrahedron of M_i in the set $\{M_i, M_1, M_2, M_3, M_4\}$. This tetrahedron is bounded since its vertices are the centers of the spheres B_k, $k = 1, ..., 4$ and are included in their union. Therefore P belongs to that union, which is a contradiction (see figure 10.6 for the 2-D case). Therefore no point outside B can belong to the Voronoi polyhedron of M_i, which must be included in B and thus is bounded.   ■

Let us now consider the geometric dual of V that is obtained by linking with a straight line segment any two points of S whose Voronoi polyhe-

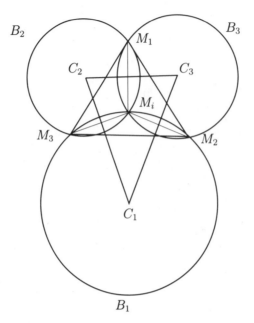

Figure 10.6   Proof of proposition 10.3.

dra are adjacent. The resulting structure is a triangulation of the original set of points, i.e., it partitions the convex hull of S into triangles (tetrahedra) determined by the points of S. The proof of this is not very simple, and the two-dimensional version of it can be found in the book by Preparata and Shamos [PS85]. The Delaunay triangulation of the points in figure 10.4 is shown in figure 10.7. This leads to the following definition:

Definition 10.4
The Delaunay triangulation of a set of points is obtained by joining by a straight line segment two points whose Voronoi polyhedra (triangles) share a face (an edge).

There is a useful characterization of the Delaunay triangulation of a set of points that can be obtained from the following property of the Voronoi diagram:

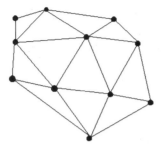

Figure 10.7   The Delaunay triangulation of the points of figure 10.4.

Proposition 10.4

Every vertex in the Voronoi diagram is the common intersection of exactly $k + 1$ edges of the diagram.

Proof This is because we have assumed that no $k + 2$ points in the original set are cospherical.   ∎

This property implies that the Voronoi vertices are the centers of circles ($k = 2$) or spheres ($k = 3$) defined by $k + 1$ points of the original set. These circles and spheres, which we will call the *Delaunay circles and spheres*, have the following fundamental property:

Proposition 10.5

For every vertex v of the Voronoi diagram of S, the corresponding Delaunay sphere (circle) contains no other point of S.

Proof Let us suppose that the $k + 1$ points defining the Delaunay sphere (circle) are $M_1, M_2, ..., M_{k+1}$ and that M_n is inside the sphere. This implies that v is strictly closer to M_n than to any of M_i ($i = 1, ..., k + 1$). Therefore v belongs to V_n and not to the V_i's ($i = 1, ..., k + 1$), which is a contradiction since v belongs to the intersection of the V_i's ($i = 1, ..., k + 1$).   ∎

This property is characteristic of the Delaunay triangulation in the sense that, if a triangulation of a set of points is such that the spheres (circles) circumscribing the tetrahedra (triangles) of the triangulation have no other points of the set in their interior, then it arises by duality from the Voronoi diagram of the points.

From proposition 10.5 follows the next proposition:

Proposition 10.6

Two points M_i and M_j determine an edge of the Delaunay triangulation if and only if there exists a sphere (circle) through these two points that does not contain any other point of the set in its interior.

Proof   The proof is obvious.   ∎

In particular, and we will use this property in section 10.5, this is true if the ball $B(M_i, M_j)$ of diameter $M_i M_j$ does not contain any other point in its interior. This property is related to another interesting structure called the *Gabriel graph* [GS69, MS80], which is defined in problem 6.

10.4.2   Delaunay triangulations and skeletons

There is an interesting relationship between the Delaunay triangulation of a set of points on the boundary of an object and the skeleton of that object. The *skeleton of a shape* has been widely studied in computer vision, pattern recognition, and mathematical morphology [Blu78, Ser82, Nac82, BA84]. Let us first give its definition:

Definition 10.5

Let X be an object. Let the interior skeleton $Sk_{int}(X)$ of X be the closure of $B_{max_{int}}$, the set of the centers of the maximal balls included in X. Formally, we have

$$B_{max_{int}} = \{x, \exists r_x > 0, B(x, r_x) \subset X \text{ and if } B'(x', r') \subset X \text{ and}$$

$$B(x, r_x) \subset B'(x', r') \text{ then } x' = x, r' = r_x\}$$

$$Sk_{int}(X) = \overline{B_{max_{int}}}$$

Similarly, the exterior skeleton $Sk_{ext}(X)$ is defined from the maximal balls included in $\overline{X^c}$, and the skeleton $Sk(X)$ is the union of $Sk_{int}(X)$ and $Sk_{ext}(X)$.

Now suppose that we are given an object X and points measured on its boundary ∂X. We can compute the Delaunay triangulation of this set of points and consider the centers of the spheres circumscribed to each Delaunay simplex. We can clearly see in figure 10.8 that the centers approximate the skeleton of the object. This qualitative remark can be

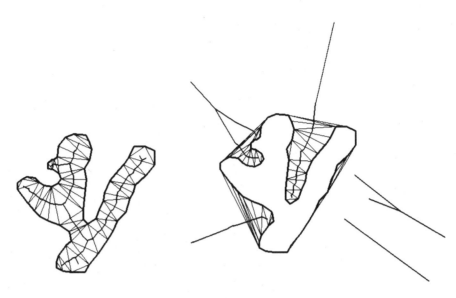

Figure 10.8 The skeleton of the object X is approximated by the centers of the Delaunay circles.

made more precise, and it can be shown that, when the density of points measured on ∂X increases, the set of the centers of the Delaunay spheres converges toward the skeleton of X. In order to do this, we must define the class of objects we are considering. For convenience, we will assume that the objects X are compact, with boundaries ∂X that are C^3 (three times continuously differentiable). We also need to quantify the idea of having many points measured on the object. In order to do this, we will define the notion of the density of points on ∂X:

Definition 10.6

Let $\mathcal{P}$ be a set of n points $M_i, i = 1, \ldots, n$ of ∂X. $\mathcal{P}$ is said to have density $\frac{1}{\varepsilon}$ if and only if for all points M of ∂X there is a $j, 1 \le j \le n$, such that M_j is within $B(M, \varepsilon)$, the open ball of center M and radius ε.

This gives a precise meaning to sentences such as "the density of points on ∂X increases without bounds."

We will now consider a sequence $\mathcal{P}_i$ of sets of points of ∂X of density $\frac{1}{\varepsilon_i}$ that are denser and denser ($\lim_{i \to \infty} \varepsilon_i = 0$). Letting $DelSk_i(X)$ be the set of the centers of the Delaunay spheres of $\mathcal{P}_i$, we have the following theorem [Sch89]:

Theorem 10.3

[Schmitt] Under the previous conditions, if ∂X is C^3, then

$$\lim_{i \to \infty} DelSk_i(X) = Sk(X)$$

The limit is taken in the sense of the hit-or-miss topology for closed sets defined in section 10.3.2.

In order to prove this proposition, we use theorem 10.2 to show that $\overline{\lim} \, DelSk_i(X) \subset Bmax(X)$ and $Bmax(X) \subset \underline{\lim} \, DelSk_i(X)$. $Bmax(X)$ is defined as the union of $Bmax_{int}(X)$ and $Bmax_{ext}(X)$. We will first prove the following proposition:

Proposition 10.7

Let (B_i) be a sequence of Delaunay balls, where B_i is a Delaunay ball of the set $\mathcal{P}_i$ of center S_i. If B is a cluster point of the sequence (B_i), B is maximal in X or in $\overline{X^c}$ or, equivalently:

$$\overline{\lim} \, S_i \subset Bmax(X)$$

Proof The key idea of the proof is to notice that when i grows larger and larger, the Delaunay balls are "almost" maximal. Since $B_i = B(S_i, r_i)$ is a Delaunay ball of the set $\mathcal{P}_i$ of density $\frac{1}{\varepsilon_i}$, the ball $B(S_i, r_i - \varepsilon_i)$ does not intersect ∂X. If it did, it would be at points outside the set $\mathcal{P}_i$ because of proposition 10.5. Let M be such a point. The ball of center M and radius ε_i is included in the Delaunay ball B_i and therefore does not contain any point of $\mathcal{P}_i$ (proposition 10.5), contradicting the definition of a set of density $\frac{1}{\varepsilon_i}$. Therefore, the ball $B(S_i, r_i - \varepsilon_i)$ is included in X or $\overline{X^c}$.

Because the set of closed sets $\mathcal{F}$ is compact (theorem 10.1), any sequence of closed sets has a cluster point. Let B be a cluster point of the sequence (B_i). There exists a subsequence (B_{i_p}) converging toward B. By again extracting a subsequence, we can assume from the above that all balls $B(S_{i_p}, r_{i_p} - \varepsilon_{i_p})$ are included in X or $\overline{X^c}$. Since $\lim_{i_p \to \infty} B(S_{i_p}, r_{i_p} - \varepsilon_{i_p}) = B$ and since taking the limit preserves set inclusions, we have either $B \subset X$ or $B \subset \overline{X^c}$. We will now prove that B is maximal.

Assume, for example, that $B \subset X$, and let B' be a ball such that $B \subset B' \subset X$. We will show that $B = B'$. Let us denote by $M_{i_p}^0, \ldots, M_{i_p}^k$ ($k = 2$ or

3) the vertices of the Delaunay simplex defining B_{i_p}. Because of proposition 10.2, we can assume that those $k + 1$ sequences of points converge toward $M^0, \ldots, M^k$ (we can extract another subsequence if necessary), which are in B. They are also on ∂X since the points $M_{i_p}^0, \ldots, M_{i_p}^k$ are on ∂X. Two cases are possible:

All limits are the same

$M^0 = \cdots = M^k = M$. Let us orient ∂X so that the normal at M points toward X. When we have $k + 1$ points of ∂X converging toward M, the limit of the balls defined by these points is osculating to ∂X. Let us separately consider the cases $k = 2$ and $k = 3$.

$k = 2$

Let κ be the curvature of ∂X at M, and let B_M be the osculating circle. We have $B = B_M$, and therefore $\kappa > 0$ because of the way we have oriented the normal; $\kappa = 0$ would imply that a half-plane would be included in X, which we have assumed to be compact and therefore bounded. If $R = 1/\kappa$ is the radius of B, it is known that R is the maximal radius of a disk containing M and included in X, and therefore B is maximal.[5]

$k = 3$

Let κ_1 and κ_2 be the principal curvatures of ∂X at M. Let M_1 (respectively, M_2) be the points of the normal to ∂X of abscissa κ_1 (respectively, κ_2). All spheres centered at a point P of the line segment $\langle M_1, M_2 \rangle$ (including the endpoints) and going through M are osculating to ∂X. If $\kappa_1 \kappa_2 < 0$, M is hyperbolic and we assume that $\kappa_1 > 0$. Let B_{M_1} be the osculating sphere to ∂X at M centered at M_1. The same reasoning used in the 2-D case shows that $B = B_{M_1}$ and is maximal.[6] If $\kappa_1 \kappa_2 > 0$, M is elliptic and we assume that $0 < \kappa_2 < \kappa_1$. It can be shown that the only sphere osculating to ∂X and included in X is B_{M_1} and that $R_1 = 1/\kappa_1$ is the maximum radius

---

5. Note that M is a bit special. Indeed, it is known that, at a generic point on a curve, the osculating circle B_M crosses the curve at M, and therefore $B_M \not\subset X$ and $B_M \not\subset \overline{X^c}$. In order for this to be true, a condition on the third derivative of the curve at M has to be true (see problem 9).

6. Note that, contrary to the 2-D case, the point M does not have to be special on ∂X (see problem 10).

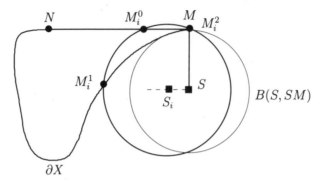

Figure 10.9   The hypothesis that ∂X is C^3 is essential to the proof of proposition 10.7. This is an example of a sequence such that $\lim S_i$ does not belong to $Bmax(X)$.

of a sphere going through M and included in X (see also problem 10). Therefore, again we conclude that $B = B_{M_1}$ and is maximal.

At least two limits are different

We know that these points are on the boundaries of B and X. They must also be on the boundary of B' since $B \subset B' \subset X$. This implies that $B = B'$ since two balls with at least two points of their borders in common cannot be included in each other. B is maximal in X.
This ends the proof.   ∎

Note that the assumption that ∂X is C^3 is essential to the proof. If we assume that it is only piecewise smooth, problems can occur at cusps. For example, figure 10.9 shows an example of an object X that is piecewise C^3 and has a cusp at M where a line segment NM and an arc of a C^3 curve are tangent. The osculating circle to the curve at M has center S. We will consider the sequence of circles (B_i) defined as follows. For a point S_i of the line going through the center S of the osculating circle and parallel to MN sufficiently close to S, the circle of center S_i going through $M \equiv M_i^2$ intersects MN at M_i^0 and the other part of ∂X at M_i^1. The limit of the sequence of balls $B(M_i^0, M_i^1, M_i^2)$ is the osculating circle, which is not maximal in X^c.

We will now prove the second proposition that is necessary to complete the proof of theorem 10.3:

Proposition 10.8
$Bmax(X) \subset \underline{\lim} S_i$.

Proof According to definition 10.2 and theorem 10.2, we must prove that, for all maximal balls $B = B(M, r)$ in X or $\overline{X^c}$, there exists a sequence $(B_i = B(M_i, r_i))$ of Delaunay balls such that $M_i \to M$. Let $A = B \cap \partial X$. The interior of B is included in the interior of X and thus does not contain any points of the sets $\mathcal{P}_i$. Therefore, for each index i we can find a maximal open ball $\mathring{B}_i$ in $\mathcal{P}_i^c$ such that $\mathring{B} \subset \mathring{B}_i$. This implies, by taking the topological closure, that $A \subset B \subset B_i$. ∂B_i contains some points in $\mathcal{P}_i$, but $\mathring{B}_i$ does not. Let $\mathcal{Q}_i$ be the set of those points. If B_i is not a Delaunay ball of $\mathcal{P}_i$, we can increase its diameter while keeping the points in $\mathcal{Q}_i$ on its boundary until it becomes a Delaunay ball of $\mathcal{P}_i$, which we will call B_i' (note that B_i' may have infinite radius). The center M_i of B_i is in B_i' because we have increased the diameter of B_i.

Let B^0 be a cluster point of the sequence (B_i). Using an argument similar to the one used in the beginning of the proof of the previous proposition, we can guarantee that $B^0 \subset X$ or $\overline{X^c}$. Then $A \subset B \subset B^0 \subset X$ or $\overline{X^c}$. Because B is maximal, B is the unique cluster point of the sequence (B_i) which, as a consequence, converges toward B. Furthermore, the sequence of points (M_i) converges toward M, the center of B. Let B' be a cluster point of the sequence (B_i'). Because M_i is in B_i', M is in B'. From the previous proposition, we know that B' is maximal. If ∂X is C^2, there exist only two maximal balls with nonzero radii containing A, one of them in X, the other in $\overline{X^c}$. Because $A \subset B'$, B' is one of those two balls. Since M is in B', $B' = B$. Thus, each cluster point of the sequence (B_i') is in B, which proves that $B_i' \to B$ and ends the proof. ∎

Note that the assumption that ∂X is C^2 is essential in the above proof. If we assume that ∂X is a polygon and is therefore piecewise C^∞, there may be points of the skeleton that are not reached by the limits of the centers of the Delaunay spheres as shown in figure 10.10.

In this figure, the local shape of the skeleton of X is the line $\langle A, B \rangle$; but it is clear that the points of the open segment AB, represented in dotted line in the figure, cannot be reached by the limits of the centers of the Delaunay spheres. To understand how AB is defined, see problem 8.

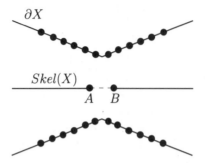

Figure 10.10 The open segment AB of the skeleton cannot be reached by the centers of the Delaunay spheres.

10.4.3 Delaunay triangulation and the polyhedral approximation of shapes

In this section, we want to make more precise the idea that the shape of an object can be closely approximated by a subset of the Delaunay triangulation of a set of points on the surface. In particular, we want to show that, under some conditions, a polyhedron extracted from the Delaunay triangulation of the set of points is homeomorphic to the surface of the object. This property is used in section 10.6.

In the previous section we have defined the density of a set of points on ∂X. We also need the notion of thickness of X, which is related to the minimal size of the maximal balls contained in the object or in its complement. More precisely:

Definition 10.7
The thickness e of an object X is the real positive number such that any maximal ball included in X or in $\overline{X^c}$ has a radius larger than or equal to e.

We can now relate the quality of the approximation of ∂X by the Delaunay triangulation of a set of points $\mathcal{P}$ of ∂X to the curvature of ∂X, the thickness of X, and the density $1/\varepsilon$ of $\mathcal{P}$:

Theorem 10.4
If the thickness of X is strictly greater than e and the set of points $\mathcal{P}$ has density $\frac{1}{\varepsilon}$ such that $e > \frac{\varepsilon}{\sin(\sqrt{2}/2)} > \varepsilon$, then there exists an approximating

polyhedron $\mathcal{P}_a$ which is included in the Delaunay triangulation of the points in $\mathcal{P}$ that is homeomorphic to ∂X.

Proof We will prove this theorem in the planar case. First we choose an origin and an arclength s on ∂X, and we order the points P_i of $\mathcal{P}$ according to their arclength. Let there be n points in $\mathcal{P}$ that are indexed from 1 to n. Their arclengths are $s_1 \leq s_2 \leq \cdots \leq s_n$. When we talk about the arc $P_i P_{i+1}$ of ∂X, we assume that $P_{n+1} = P_1$. Finally, let γ be the mapping from R^+ to ∂X. It satisfies

$$\gamma(s_i) = \mathbf{P}_i \qquad i = 1, \ldots, n$$

$$\|\gamma'(s)\| = 1$$

We begin by stating that, for each point M of ∂X, there exists at least two maximal circles going through that point, one included in X and the other in $\overline{X^c}$. These circles must be tangent to ∂X at M, and therefore their radii must be smaller than the radius of curvature of ∂X at M. But since their radii are also larger than e, we conclude that the radius of curvature is also larger than e at every point of ∂X.   ■

We will next prove that the distance between two consecutive points of $\mathcal{P}$ is less than 2ε:

Proposition 10.9
We have

$$d(P_i, P_{i+1}) \leq 2\varepsilon \qquad i = 1, \ldots, n$$

Proof First we will prove that, for each point M of the arc $P_i P_{i+1}$ of ∂X, the open ball $B(M, \varepsilon)$ intersects ∂X in one and only one connected component. Let M be a point of the arc $P_i P_{i+1}$, and consider the open ball $B(M, \varepsilon)$. Let us assume that $\partial X \cap B(M, \varepsilon)$ contains two distinct connected components. By shrinking $B(M, \varepsilon)$, we can make it become tangent to that second component at S (see figure 10.11). The segment MS is normal at S to the second component.

We can now move M along MS toward S while keeping the ball centered at M tangent at S to the second component. It will eventually become tangent to the first component at a point N (see figure (10.12). This ball is entirely contained in X or $\overline{X^c}$ and is maximal by construction. Its

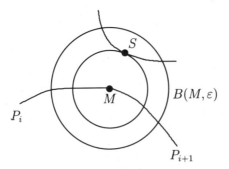

Figure 10.11   Proof of proposition 10.9.

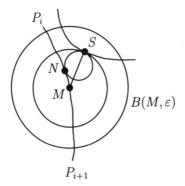

Figure 10.12   End of the proof of proposition 10.9.

radius is strictly less than ε, thus contradicting the hypothesis that the thickness of X is larger than ε.

According to the definition of the density of a set of points, $B(M, \varepsilon)$ contains at least one point of $\mathcal{P}$, and therefore it must be either P_i or P_{i+1}. If the difference in arclength between M and P_i is sufficiently close to 0, P_i is in $B(M, \varepsilon)$. If we assume that there exist points M such that $B(M, \varepsilon)$ does not contain P_i, they form an open subset of the arc $P_i P_{i+1}$. Taking its closure, we consider the point M_0 closest to P_i in terms of arclength. $\overline{B}(M_0, \varepsilon)$ contains both P_i and P_{i+1}, and therefore the euclidean distance $d(P_i, P_{i+1})$, which is less than or equal to $d(P_i, M_0) + d(M_0, P_{i+1})$, is upper-bounded by 2ε. $\blacksquare$

We will now prove that each line segment P_iP_{i+1} is a Delaunay edge of the Delaunay triangulation of $\mathcal{P}$. We will even prove that it is an arc of the Gabriel graph of $\mathcal{P}$ (see problem 6 for the definition of the Gabriel graph).

Proposition 10.10
The disk $B(P_i, P_{i+1})$ of diameter P_iP_{i+1} intersects ∂X along the arc P_iP_{i+1}.

Proof It is sufficient to show that $B(P_i, P_{i+1}) \cap \partial X$ has a unique connected component. It has at least one because, if it had zero, it would be tangent to ∂X at P_i and P_{i+1}, included in X or $\overline{X^c}$, and therefore maximal. But its radius is smaller than ε, contradicting the fact that the thickness of X is larger than ε.

It has only one because, if we consider the ball $B(R_i, \varepsilon)$ (R_i is the midpoint of the line segment P_iP_{i+1}), we can apply the same reasoning as in the proof of proposition 10.9 and conclude that this ball contains only one component of ∂X. If we now shrink this ball so that it becomes a ball of diameter P_iP_{i+1}, we will find that it also contains only one component of ∂X, namely the arc P_iP_{i+1}. In particular, it does not contain any other point of $\mathcal{P}$, and the line segment P_iP_{i+1} is therefore, according to proposition 10.5, a Delaunay edge of the Delaunay triangulation of $\mathcal{P}$. ∎

We will now prove that the polygon whose edges are the line segments P_iP_{i+1} is homeomorphic to ∂X. In order to do this, we will first give an upper bound on the lengths of the arcs P_iP_{i+1}.

Proposition 10.11
(Joël Briançon) The length of the arc P_iP_{i+1} of ∂X is upper-bounded by $2e \arcsin(\varepsilon/e)$.

Proof We will use a system of polar coordinates (ρ, θ) whose origin is the point P_i (see figure 10.13). Let M be a point of the arc P_iP_{i+1}, $\mathbf{t}$ the unit vector tangent to ∂X at M, $\mathbf{u}$ the unit vector parallel to $\mathbf{P}_i\mathbf{M}$, and φ the angle between $\mathbf{u}$ and $\mathbf{t}$. If R is the radius of curvature at M and s is the arclength along ∂X, we have the following relation:

$$\frac{d\theta}{ds} + \frac{d\varphi}{ds} = \frac{1}{R}$$

The key relation for our purpose is obtained from the previous one by taking into account the fact that $\frac{d\rho}{ds} = \cos\varphi$ and $\rho\frac{d\theta}{ds} = \sin\varphi$:

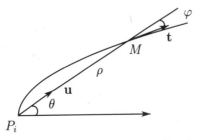

Figure 10.13   The system of polar coordinates centered at P_i.

$$\frac{1}{\rho}\frac{d(\rho\sin\varphi)}{d\rho}=\frac{1}{R}\leq\frac{1}{e}$$

We then integrate once to obtain

$$\rho\sin\varphi\leq\frac{\rho^2}{2e}$$

Since $\frac{d\rho}{ds}=\cos\varphi$, we have

$$\frac{d\rho}{ds}\geq\sqrt{1-\frac{\rho^2}{4e^2}}$$

This yields

$$s\leq 2e\arcsin(\frac{\rho}{2e})$$

Because we have previously proved that the distance $d(P_i, P_{i+1})$ is less than 2ε, the conclusion follows.   ∎

This proposition shows that, according to intuition, if the radius of curvature of a curve is lower-bounded at each point, the the curve cannot "zigzag" too much.

We are now in a position to prove the following:

Proposition 10.12
The arc P_iP_{i+1} is strictly monotonous along the line segment P_iP_{i+1}.

This means that all lines perpendicular to the line segment P_iP_{i+1} intersect the arc P_iP_{i+1} at one and only one point and are never tangent to this arc. Therefore, the projection from the arc to the line segment is one-to-one and continuous, as well as its inverse, and we have proved proposition 10.4.

Let us now prove proposition 10.12:

Proof If the projection from the arc P_iP_{i+1} is not one-to-one, there exists at least one point Q of the line segment P_iP_{i+1} such that the line perpendicular to P_iP_{i+1} at Q intersects the arc in at least two points R and S. Consider the subarc $C - RS$ of the arc P_iP_{i+1}. There exists a point M_1 of C where the tangent is parallel to the line $\langle R, S \rangle$, which is therefore perpendicular to the line segment P_iP_{i+1}. Therefore, if the projection is not one-to-one there exists at least one point of the arc with a tangent perpendicular to the line segment P_iP_{i+1}. There always exists a point M_2 on the arc P_iP_{i+1} such that the tangent is parallel to $\langle P_i, P_{i+1} \rangle$. We will now show that the existence of these two points implies a contradiction to the previous proposition. In other words, this is not compatible with the upper bound that we have established on the length of the arc P_iP_{i+1}.

Let s_1 and s_2 be the arclengths of M_1 and M_2. Since the two tangents are perpendicular, we have

$$\| \boldsymbol{\gamma}'(s_1) - \boldsymbol{\gamma}'(s_2) \| = \sqrt{2} \tag{10.3}$$

But we also have

$$\| \boldsymbol{\gamma}'(s_1) - \boldsymbol{\gamma}'(s_2) \| \leq \max_s \| \boldsymbol{\gamma}''(s) \| \, | s_1 - s_2 |$$

and we know that $\| \boldsymbol{\gamma}''(s) \| = \frac{1}{R} \leq \frac{1}{e}$ and, from the previous proposition, that $| s_1 - s_2 | \leq 2e \arcsin(\frac{\varepsilon}{e})$. Combining all this yields

$$\| \boldsymbol{\gamma}'(s_1) - \boldsymbol{\gamma}'(s_2) \| \leq 2 \arcsin(\frac{\varepsilon}{e})$$

which is strictly less than $\sqrt{2}$ because of our hypothesis on e. This contradicts equation (10.3). Thus the projection is one-to-one and obviously continuous both ways. ■

10.4.4   Computing the Delaunay triangulation of a set of points

We have seen that, from the standpoint of computational complexity, there is an equivalence between the computation of the Voronoi diagram and the computation of the Delaunay triangulation of a set of points.

More precisely, there is an $O(n)$ algorithm[7] that builds the Voronoi diagram of n points, given their Delaunay triangulation, and an $O(n)$ algorithm that builds the Delaunay triangulation of n points, given their Voronoi diagram.

In the planar case, there exists an $O(n \log n)$ algorithm for constructing the Voronoi diagram of a set of n points [PS85]. In 3-D space, things are a little bit more complicated. The reason for this is that, unlike the planar case where the Delaunay triangulation is a planar graph and is composed of at most $O(n)$ triangles (see problem 2), in the 3-D case the number of tetrahedra can be as large as $O(n^2)$ (see problem 3). Therefore there is no hope of ever obtaining an $O(n \log n)$ algorithm in three dimensions. On the other hand, the planar $O(n \log n)$ algorithm uses the technique of divide and conquer to obtain its performance and therefore processes all the points at the same time. Very often in practice one is interested in algorithms that work incrementally, adding points when new measurements become available. We will now describe such an algorithm [Bow81, Wat81, Boi84]. We will do it in three dimensions, although the translation of the algorithm to two dimensions is obvious and is left to the reader.

We will assume, without loss of generality, that the set of measured points falls within a cube of known size, and we will initialize the process with a Delaunay triangulation of its eight vertices. At each iteration we keep a list of the simplexes (tetrahedra) S_i in the triangulation as well as the centers C_i and radii R_i of their circumscribed spheres. Each new point M will fall within at least one of those spheres; if it falls within p of them, all the p corresponding simplexes must be deleted from the triangulation because of proposition 10.5, and new simplexes must be formed with M as a vertex. These new simplexes can be formed very simply by considering all faces of the erased simplexes, eliminating those that are shared by two erased simplexes, and adding every simplex consisting of one remaining face and point M. It is guaranteed that each such simplex is a Delaunay simplex, i.e., its circumscribed sphere does not contain any other data point (see problem 4). Figure 10.14 shows the process at work in the two-dimensional case.

---

7. A function $f(n)$ is $O(g(n))$ if there exists a positive constant c and an integer n_0 such that $f(n) \leq cg(n)$ for all $n \geq n_0$

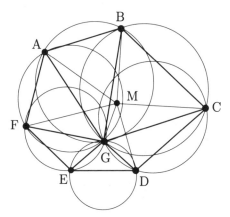

Figure 10.14 Since M falls in the discs of triangles $AFG, AGB, BGC,$ and CDG, these four simplexes are deleted. Face AG is common to AFG and AGB. It is deleted, as are GB and GC, and the six simplexes $MAB, MBC, MCD,$ $MDG, MGF,$ and MFA are added to the list of Delaunay simplexes.

Finding the spheres into which the point M falls is easily done by computing the differences $d^2(M, C_i) - R_i^2$, for $i = 1, ..., n$, if there are currently n simplexes in the triangulation. A negative value indicates that M is inside the sphere. The algorithm thus proceeds as follows:

- **Input:** A series of points M falling within a given cube.
- **Output:** A Delaunay triangulation of these points and the eight vertices of the cube.

1. **Initialization:** Compute a Delaunay triangulation of the cube vertices, as well as the centers and radii of the circumscribed spheres.

2. **Find the spheres:** The current point to be inserted is M; the current triangulation has n simplexes. For $i = 1$ to n, if $d^2(M, C_i) - R_i^2$ is negative, then flag the ith simplex S_i.

3. **Update the triangulation:** For all flagged simplexes, construct the list of their faces. Remove from the list each face that appears twice, then with each remaining face form a simplex with M and insert it in the triangulation. Erase from the triangulation all flagged simplexes. Go to step 2.

The key point in favor of this algorithm is that step 3 is in general very local: Point M "interacts" with only a few existing Delaunay tetrahedra, and the updating of the triangulation is both local and very simple.

Degeneracies may (and do) occur when the point M appears to be on the surface of a Delaunay sphere due to the limited accuracy of the computation of the floating point. Several strategies are then possible. We can slightly perturb the point's coordinates so that the degeneracy disappears and insert it regularly, or we can leave it as it is, although in that case the updating of the triangulation becomes a bit difficult and the triangulation is no longer unique. Suppose that, instead of adding a new point, we want to erase a point like M in figure 10.14. We have only to remove all triangles adjacent to M from the triangulation, remove M, and compute the Delaunay triangulation of the polygon that surrounded M (polygon $ABCDGF$ in figure 10.14). Therefore the operation of erasing a point, just like adding one, is also in general quite local (see problem 5).

10.4.5 Complexity analysis

The complexity of the previous algorithm is dominated by that of steps 2 and 3. The basic question, therefore, is this: How many simplexes are present in the Delaunay triangulation of k points? We saw in the previous section that this number is $O(k)$ in the planar case, but may be $O(k^2)$ in the three-dimensional case. Therefore, the algorithm for computing the Delaunay triangulation has a worst-case complexity of $O(n^2)$ in the planar case and $O(n^3)$ in the three-dimensional case since, at each iteration, in the worst case the inserted point may interact with all existing simplexes.

We may think that we could save time by improving step 2 a little. Indeed, it looks as if we would not need to check all existing simplexes to locate those whose circumscribed balls contain the points to be inserted. This is due to the fact that this set of simplexes is face-connected. Therefore, if we can find one simplex whose circumscribed ball contains the point, all the others can be found by propagation of connected components. The complexity of step 2 becomes the sum of two contributions:

1. Find a simplex whose circumscribed ball contains the point.

2. From this simplex, find all the others.

To implement step 1 above, one might think of considering the last point inserted, P, and follow the segment PM, checking each time it crosses the boundary of a simplex. The last simplex found contains M. If points P and M are sufficiently close, the number of tetrahedra crossed in this fashion can be fairly small (but the worst case is still $O(k)$ in the plane and $O(k^2)$ in the 3-D case). Step 2 above is implemented by a standard propagation of connected components, and its complexity is exactly equal to the number of simplexes whose circumscribed balls contain M. Unfortunately, this number can be $O(k^2)$ in the three-dimensional case and $O(k)$ in the planar case. The global worst-case complexity of the algorithm is thus unchanged.

In practice, we are more interested in what happens on the average. If we experimentally measure the behavior of the algorithm when we increase the number of points, we observe a curve similar to that of figure 10.15, which is very close to a straight line. This experimentally observed linear variation in the number of tetrahedra is confirmed

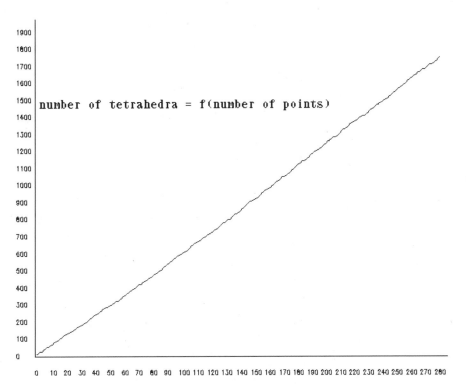

Figure 10.15 The number of tetrahedra is a linear function of the number of points inserted.

theoretically. Indeed, it is proved in the book by Santalo [San76] that, for a uniform distribution of points in 3-D space, the average number of Delaunay simplexes is proportional to the density of points, and is therefore $O(n)$ and not $O(n^2)$. The overall average complexity of the algorithm is thus $O(n^2)$ in two and three dimensions. Recently, randomization methods have been introduced in computational geometry with optimal average time performance, i.e., $O(n \log n)$ [DMT90].

10.5   Constrained Delaunay triangulation

As we previously saw (in chapter 6, for example), there may be cases where we do not deal only with points, but also with line segments. If we compute the Delaunay triangulation of the segments' endpoints, the segments may not always be Delaunay edges, as is shown in figure 10.16 for the planar case. This may cause problems, as is shown in section 10.6, if we want to use the Delaunay triangulation of the set of endpoints to represent the surface of the objects on which the segments have been measured.

It is possible, nonetheless, to modify the initial segments by adding more points on those segments in such a way that the resulting Delaunay triangulation is guaranteed to contain the new set of segments as Delaunay edges. The basis of the method is to use proposition 10.6 and add as many points as necessary to the line segments, thereby creating new segments, so that the open balls with those segments for diameters do not contain any other points of the extended set. As an example, if in figure 10.17 we add the two points M and N to the segment AC, the segments AM, MN, and NC are Delaunay edges of the triangulation of the six points $ABCDMN$.

10.5.1   Computing the constrained Delaunay triangulation of a set of line segments

We will now describe a method that starts with a set of line segments forming a set of nonintersecting polygonal lines and adds points to those line segments in a way that guarantees that the resulting line segments are all part of a Delaunay triangulation of the augmented set of points.

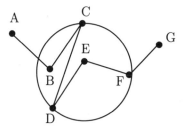

Figure 10.16   Segment *CD* is not a Delaunay edge because all circles going through *C* and *D* contain at least two other data points.

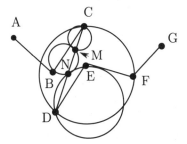

Figure 10.17   Adding points *M* and *N* to segment *CD* makes segments *CM*, *MN*, and *ND* Delaunay edges.

For each segment *MN*, the open ball $B(M,N)$ of diameter *MN* plays an important role: We call neighbors of the segment *MN* those segments intersecting $B(M,N)$. They are computed as follows:

- For a given segment *PQ*, if *P* or *Q* is in $B(M,N)$, then *PQ* is a neighbor of *MN*.

- Otherwise, we compute the distance *d* of the center of $B(M,N)$ to the line supporting *PQ*.

- If that distance is less than the radius of $B(M,N)$, and if the projection of the center of $B(M,N)$ on the line falls between *P* and *Q*, then *PQ* is a neighbor of *MN* (see figure 10.18).

We process the segments sequentially and construct two sets of segments. One set, called *Closed* and initially empty, contains all segments

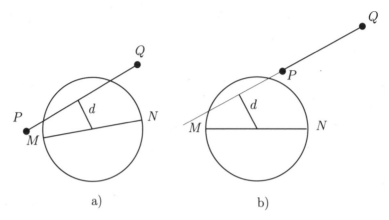

Figure 10.18 *PQ* is a neighbor of *MN* in case (a) but not in case (b).

that are guaranteed to be Delaunay edges. The other set, called *Open*, contains the segments that still need to processed. Initially, all segments are in the *Open* set.

Let *MN* be a segment in the *Open* set. If it has no neighbors, we insert it in the *Closed* set. If it has neighbors, we consider the two largest balls B_M and B_N centered on the segment *MN*, the first going through *M*, the second through *N*, and not intersecting the neighbors of *MN*. A special treatment must be applied to the segments *RM* and *SN* that are adjacent to *MN* at *M* and *N*, if there are any: B_M (B_N, respectively) must not contain *R* (*S*). These two balls can be computed in a time that is proportional to the number of neighbors of the segment *MN*.

Two cases are possible:

$$B_M \cap B_N = \varnothing$$

Such a situation is shown in figure 10.19. Let *P* and *Q* be the second intersections of B_M and B_N with *MN*, respectively. If neither *M* nor *N* has a segment adjacent to it, then B_M and B_N are empty and, according to proposition 10.6, the segments *MP* and *QN* will be Delaunay edges. We add both of them to the set *Closed* and add the segment *PQ* to the set *Open*.

If, for example, *RM* is adjacent to *MN*, two cases are possible:

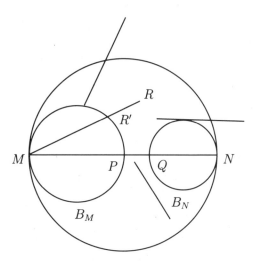

Figure 10.19   The case where $B_M \cap B_N = \varnothing$.

R *is on the boundary of* B_M

The triangle MPR is a Delaunay triangle because of proposition 10.5. We erase the segment MR from the set *Open* and add it to the set *Closed*.

R *is outside* B_M

Let R' be the intersection of MR with the boundary of B_M. Then we can add MR' to the set *Closed*, erase MR from the set *Open*, and add RR' to the set *Open*. The case where SN is adjacent to MN is treated similarly.

$B_M \cap B_N \neq \varnothing$

Such a situation is shown in figure 10.20. Let T be the midpoint of the segment PQ. We can clearly add the segments MT and TN to the set *Closed*. If MR is adjacent to MN, let R' be the intersection of the segment MR with the boundary of $B(M,T)$, the open ball of diameter MT. Then we can add MR' to the set *Closed* and RR' to the set *Open*. The case where QN is adjacent to MN is treated similarly.

Note that, each time a new segment is inserted into the set *Open*, its neighbors must be computed; this can be easily done from the set of neighbors of MN.

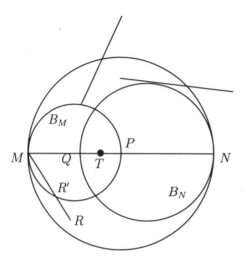

Figure 10.20   The case where $B_M \cap B_N \neq \varnothing$.

The previous description can be expressed in algorithmic form as follows. We use the two segment lists *Open* and *Closed*.

- **Input:** A set of segments S.
- **Output:** A set of segments S' such that each segment s' in S' is included in a segment s of S, the Delaunay triangulation of their endpoints: All segments in S' are Delaunay edges.

1. **Initialization:** Compute the neighbors of each segment of S. Insert all segments of S into *Open*, and initialize *Closed* to NIL (the empty list).

2. **Process *Open*:** While *Open* is not NIL, execute steps 3–6. Take the first segment MN of the list, and compute the balls B_M and B_N. If $B_M \cap B_N = \varnothing$, then go to step 3; otherwise go to step 4.

3. $B_M \cap B_N = \varnothing$: Insert MP and NQ into *Closed*. Compute the neighbors of PQ, and insert them into *Open*.

4. $B_M \cap B_N \neq \varnothing$: Let T be the midpoint of PQ. Add MT and TN to *Closed*. Let B_M (B_N, respectively) become $B(M, T)$, $(B(N, T))$.

5. MR **adjacent to** MN: If R is on the boundary of B_M, then enter MR into *Closed*; otherwise compute R', the intersection of MR with the boundary of B_M, and enter MR' into *Closed*. Compute the neighbors of RR', and enter RR' into *Open*.

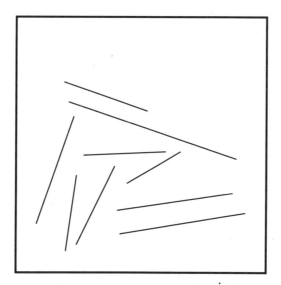

Figure 10.21   Initial set of segments to be triangulated.

6.   *NQ* **adjacent to** *MN*: If *Q* is on the boundary of B_N, then enter *NQ* into *Closed*; otherwise compute Q', the intersection of *NQ* with the boundary of B_N, and enter NQ' into *Closed*. Compute the neighbors of QQ', and enter QQ' into *Open*.

7.   **Compute Delaunay:** Compute the Delaunay triangulation of the endpoints of the segments in *Closed*.

As an example of this procedure, look at figures 10.21, 10.22, and 10.23, which show, respectively, a set of segments, the Delaunay triangulation of the segments' endpoints, and the Delaunay triangulation of the extended set of points obtained by adding new points to the initial segments. Five of the initial nine segments are not Delaunay edges in the initial triangulation, and all segments are Delaunay edges after more points have been added.

10.5.2   Complexity analysis

The complexity of this algorithm is the sum of two contributions:

1.   Computing the Delaunay triangulation of $O(n)$ points. We have seen in section 10.4.4 that this is worst-case $O(n^2)$ in the planar case

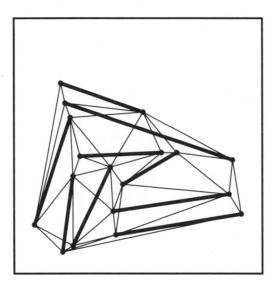

Figure 10.22   Unconstrained triangulation of the segments of figure
10.21.

and $O(n^3)$ in the three-dimensional case if we use the sequential
algorithm for the Delaunay triangulation. In practice, we have seen
that this algorithm is in fact quadratic.

2. Adding the points to the segments in order to guarantee that all seg-
    ments are Delaunay edges. This step is dominated by the computa-
    tion of the neighbors of $O(n)$ segments, which is *a priori* $O(n^2)$.

In order to reduce the computation time, we use *bucketing techniques*,
which we have also used in chapter 6. The idea of using buckets in this
case is clearly motivated by the fact that we do not need to compare
the distance of each segment MN to every other segment. The segments
that must be considered are those intersecting the sphere whose diameter is the segment MN. The bucketing technique relies on dividing the
space into cubic or parallelepipedic buckets and then computing for each
sphere and for each segment the buckets they intersect. We then compute the distances of the segment MN with each segment that may intersect the sphere of diameter MN. These candidate segments are those
that have at least one bucket in common with those that intersect the
sphere of diameter MN.

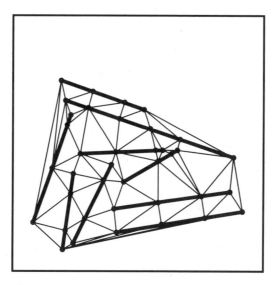

Figure 10.23   Constrained triangulation of the segments of figure 10.21.

The worst case of this approach is still $O(n^2)$, but let us look at the average case, which is in practice more interesting. In order to do this, we have to more precisely define the notion of random segment. We will take this opportunity to introduce a very powerful tool for which we can find many applications. Even though the underlying theory is difficult, its use is very simple. Therefore, we will present only the ideas and the results and let the interested reader read the books by Matheron and Serra [Mat75, Ser82].

10.5.2.1 *Random closed sets*

In order to formalize the idea of a random shape we will use the concepts introduced in section 10.3. The hit-or-miss topology $T_{\mathcal{F}}$ over the set of closed sets $\mathcal{F}$ is used to define a new set σ_f by taking enumerable unions and intersections of open subsets of $\mathcal{F}$. The elements of σ_f can be thought of as events, i.e., as sets of possible shapes whose probabilities we want to measure. Accordingly, these sets are called *measurable*, and the pair $(\mathcal{F}, \sigma_f)$ is called a *measurable space*. A shape probability can then be defined as an application $P : (\mathcal{F}, \sigma_f) \rightarrow [0; 1]$ that satisfies the following conditions:

1. $P(\mathcal{F}) = 1$.

2. $P(\cup_{i \in I} A_i) = \sum_{i \in I} P(A_i)$ for each enumerable set of measurable sets A_i such that $A_i \cap A_j = \varnothing$ if $i \neq j$.

This leads us to a definition:

Definition 10.8

A random closed set (RACS) is a triplet $(\mathcal{F}, \sigma_f, P)$ where P is a probability on the measurable space $(\mathcal{F}, \sigma_f)$.

We will now introduce a special type of RACS, the Boolean model; it will allow us to model random distributions of shapes. A Boolean model is the superposition of two processes:

1.   A point process (the *seed*), which follows a Poisson distribution, i.e., the probability of finding n points in a unit volume is $\frac{\rho^n}{n!} e^{-\rho}$. The value ρ is called the *intensity* of the Poisson process.

2.   A shape process (the *primary grain*), which is a RACS.

More precisely, if X' is the primary grain representing the shape process, and if $\rho \in R^{+*}$ is the intensity of the seed, the Boolean model X is the RACS with a realization given by

$$X = \cup_{x \in \mathcal{P}} X'_x$$

where $\mathcal{P}$ is a realization of a Poisson point process of intensity ρ, and $X'_x = \{\mathbf{x} + \mathbf{y} : \mathbf{y} \in X'\}$ is the translation of X' by $\mathbf{x}$. We assume that the sets $(X'_x)_{x \in \mathcal{P}}$ are drawn independently (see figure 10.24).

The following theorem describes the number of primary grains that intersect a deterministic compact set K:

Theorem 10.5

The number of primary grains intersecting the deterministic compact set K is a random variable with a Poisson random distribution of intensity

$$\rho' = \rho E(V(X' \oplus \check{K}))$$

where $\check{K}$ is the symmetric set of K with respect to the origin, $\oplus$ is the Minkowski sum defined in section 10.3, $V(X' \oplus \check{K})$ is the volume of $X' \oplus \check{K}$, and E denotes the expected value.

Proof   The proof of this theorem is outside the scope of this book, but it can be found in the work of Prêteux and Schmitt [PS88].   ∎

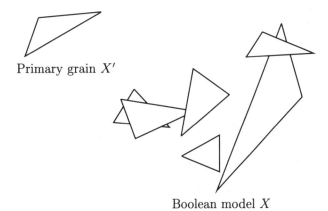

Primary grain X'

Boolean model X

Figure 10.24 An example of boolean schema. The primary grain is a triangle. The shape and orientation of the triangles as well as their positions in the plane vary randomly.

10.5.2.2   *An application to bucketing*

Coming back to our bucketing problem, we will model our observed line segments as the realization of a Boolean model. The seed has intensity ρ and is the midpoint of the primary grain, a segment of average length $\bar{l}$ whose direction is assumed to be uniformly distributed between 0 and 2π. A direct application of theorem 10.5 yields the following:

K is a circle of radius r: The average number $\overline{ns}$ of line segments that intersect K is equal to (see figure 10.25)

$$\overline{ns} = \rho r(2\bar{l} + \pi r)$$

K is a sphere of radius r: The average number $\overline{ns}$ of line segments that intersect K is equal to

$$\overline{ns} = \pi \rho r^2 (\bar{l} + \frac{4}{3} r)$$

These results allow us to compute the average number of operations that are required in order to compute the neighbors of n segments whose lengths we assume are uniformly distributed with an average value $\bar{l}$. Therefore the radius r is uniformly distributed with an average of $\frac{\bar{l}}{2}$, and

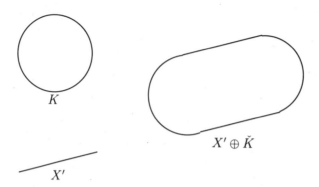

Figure 10.25   The shape of $X' \oplus \check{K}$.

the average number of operations that have to be performed to compute the neighbors of n segments is equal to

$$n\rho\bar{l}^2(1 + \tfrac{\pi}{3})   \text{ in two dimensions}$$

$$n\tfrac{2\pi\rho\bar{l}^3}{3}   \text{ in three dimensions}$$

This means that the complexity of the bucketing algorithm is linear, on the average, in the number of line segments. The careful reader will have noticed that, since the density ρ is estimated as $\frac{n}{L^3}$ in three dimensions, or $\frac{n}{L^2}$ in two dimensions (L is the size of the working volume), the complexity is in fact still $O(n^2)$. But our estimation of the constant is now accurate. Also, in practice, the ratio n/L^3 (n/L^2) is a small number compared to n.

10.6   Application: building polyhedral interpolations

We now explain how to extract a polyhedron from the Delaunay triangulation of a set of points $\mathcal{P}$ of ∂X that satisfy all the properties of proposition 10.4.

10.6.1   The visibility property

First we will define the notion of an optical ray as follows:

Figure 10.26 The figure shows the original Delaunay triangulation of the points of ∂X and the polygon approximating the surface of the object.

Definition 10.9

Let O be a point outside the object X, and let M be a point of ∂X; M is said to be visible from O if the line segment OM does not intersect ∂X at any other point. OM is called an optical ray.

This leads us to the following technique. Let $\mathcal{P}$ be a set of points on ∂X that have been measured from a number of positions O_i, $i = 1, \ldots, n$, which we assume to be in X^c. For each measured point, we know from which position (possibly several) it was measured. Thus, for each measured point M that is visible from O_i, the segment $O_i M$ is by construction an optical ray. We eliminate all triangles in the Delaunay triangulation of $\mathcal{P}$ that are intersected by $O_i M$. If the density of $\mathcal{P}$ satisfies the conditions of theorem 10.4, the boundary of the remaining simplexes is identical to the polyhedron $\mathcal{P}_a$ defined in this proposition. An example is given in figure 10.26.

This opens the possibility of *actively* exploring the shape of an object by moving a sensor around it, making sufficiently dense measurements, computing their Delaunay triangulation, and eliminating simplexes by the visibility property. In doing so, we incrementally build a polyhedron approximating the surface of the object. Of course in practice there is no way, in general, of making sure that the conditions of theorem 10.4 are satisfied. Thus we can never be sure that the polyhedron obtained is homeomorphic to the actual shape.

Figure 10.27 shows a two-dimensional example of the basic principle of the method. The environment to be explored has the shape of a maze-like deadend. Initially the robot is at the entrance of the labyrinth and

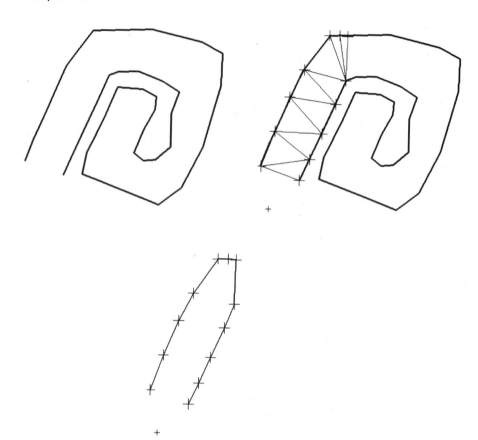

Figure 10.27 The Labyrinth to be explored by the mobile robot. The Delaunay triangulation of the first points measured by stereo. A model of the environment after removal of the empty triangles. (The robot is represented by a small cross.)

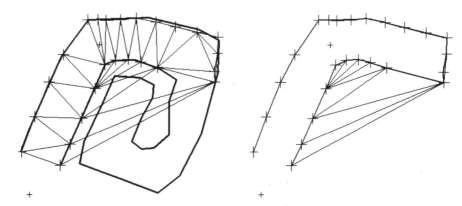

Figure 10.28 The robot has moved into free space and made more measurements. The Delaunay triangulation of the points measured in the two positions. A new model of the environment.

measures a few points on the walls, then computes the Delaunay triangulation of the measured points. The optical rays from the robot's position to the measured points are then used to mark as empty the triangles that they cross. The resulting approximation is shown in the third part of the figure. In figure 10.28 the robot has moved into the part it has determined to be free space and has made more stereo measurements. The first part of the figure shows the Delaunay triangulation of the union of the set of measured points and the new model of the environment. Finally, figure 10.29 shows the improvement of the model when the robot moves deeper into the maze.

In three-dimensional space, things are exactly the same when we deal with point measurements and very similar when we deal with three-dimensional line segments. In this case, we assume that the constrained Delaunay triangulation has been built for the set S of segments provided by stereo using the method of section 10.5 so that each segment is a Delaunay edge. The reason we assume this is explained in figure 10.30, where we show a two-dimensional example. The figure shows a polygonal object and a stereo rig represented by the large black bullet. The edges of the polygonal object have been measured by the stereo rig, and the unconstrained and constrained Delaunay triangulations of their endpoints have been computed and are shown in parts (a) and (c) of the figure, respectively. The results of eliminating all Delaunay triangles that are intersected by one or several optical rays in the unconstrained and

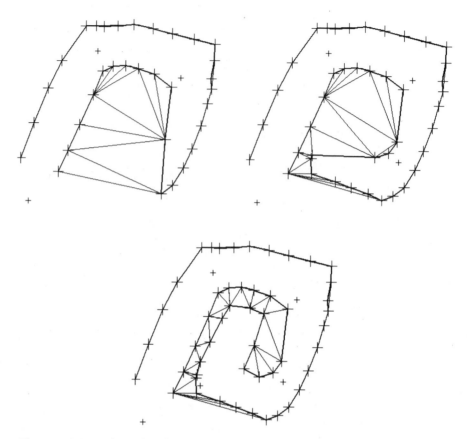

Figure 10.29 The robot has progressed farther into its environment. The evolution of its model of free space and obstacles.

constrained cases are shown in parts (b) and (d), respectively. The remaining boundary is shown in thick lines. It is clear that the method is much more accurate in (d) than in (b), where a "hole" has been punched in the boundary.

As shown in Figure 10.31, for a stereo segment MN in three dimensions, the visibility property means that all tetrahedra intersected by triangle OMN can be removed from the Delaunay triangulation, where O indicates the robot' position. We call such a triangle a *stereo triangle*. For example, the stereo triangle OMN intersects the tetrahedron $QRST$, the intersection being the triangle HIJ. Therefore, the tetrahedron $QRST$

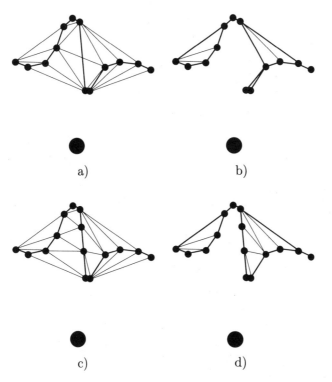

Figure 10.30   One reason for using the constrained Delaunay triangulation (see text).

can be marked as *empty* space, i.e., it can be removed from the triangulation.

10.6.2   An algorithm for simplex removal

We must deal with the question of how to efficiently detect those tetrahedra that are intersected by at least one stereo triangle OMN given the Delaunay triangulation of the endpoints of the stereo segments. We will use the fact that the set of simplexes that intersect a stereo triangle is face-connected. A method for handling this problem therefore consists of searching for each such triangle, along with a simplex that intersects

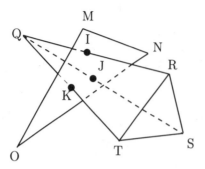

Figure 10.31   The stereo triangle PMN intersects the tetrahedron $QRST$, which can then be marked as empty.

it, and then propagating among its neighbors until it is no longer possible (a neighbor of a simplex is a simplex that shares a face with it). This guarantees that we will find all simplexes that intersect the stereo triangle.

The following algorithm uses a list of tetrahedra called *Open*, two arrays of integers called *Empty*, and an array of Booleans called *Mark*, each of which is the size of the number of tetrahedra.

10.6.2.1   The visibility algorithm

- **Input:** A set of tetrahedra and a set of stereo triangles.
- **Output:** A list of empty space tetrahedra.
- **Initialize:** Initialize the array *Empty* to 0.
- **Process stereo triangles:** For each stereo triangle T do the following:

1. **Initialize:** Find a Delaunay tetrahedron Tet that intersects T. Put it in the *Open* list. Initialize the array *Mark* to *false*.

2. **Process** *Open*: While *Open* is not empty, take the first element i of the list, set $Mark[i]$ to *true*, and increase $Empty[i]$ by one. Find the neighbors of i that intersect T, and put those that have not been marked in the *Open* list.

At the end of this algorithm, the array *Empty* contains, for each tetrahedron of the original Delaunay triangulation, the number of stereo tri-

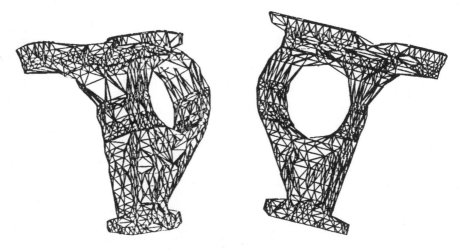

Figure 10.32   Polyhedral approximation of a foundry casting.

angles it intersects. All the simplexes for which the value of *Empty* is equal to 0 are considered to belong to the interiors of the objects, and all others are considered to belong to free space, with a probability that increases with the value stored in *Empty*.

10.6.3   Application to object modeling

This method has been applied to points measured on objects with a laser range finder as described in chapter 11, mostly to produce surface models of various industrial parts. The resulting polyhedra are shown in figures 10.32, 10.33, 10.34, and 10.35. It has also been applied to stereo results. For example, figures 10.36–10.38 show the results of the modeling for three simple objects: a sphere, a cylinder, and a cone. On top of each figure is a stereo triplet from which the algorithm described in section 6.9.1 and the reconstruction technique described in section 6.10.3 produce a set of three-dimensional line segments. A polyhedral model of the visible part of each object is displayed at the right of each figure. Note in particular that the shadows in the sphere and cylinder images have not been resolved as expected. More examples appear in chapter 11.

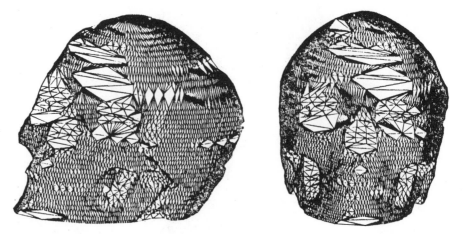

Figure 10.33 Polyhedral approximation of a face.

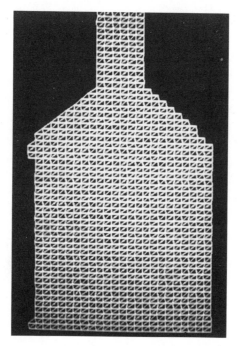

Figure 10.34 Polyhedral approximation of an oil bottle.

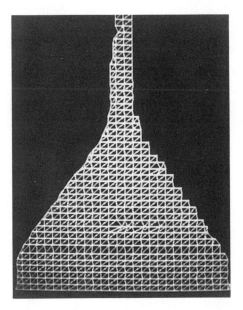

Figure 10.35   Polyhedral approximation of a funnel.

10.6.4 Application to the modeling of the environment of a mobile robot

These ideas have also been applied to model the environment of a mobile robot [FLB90]. Several 3-D reconstructions are obtained from different viewpoints by a mobile robot moving in a laboratory environment. The method for merging the different reconstructions is described in section 11.5. We will present results in two cases: first, in the case where we take one viewpoint into account for computing the approximating polyhedron; and second, in the case where we combine the results from several viewpoints.

458

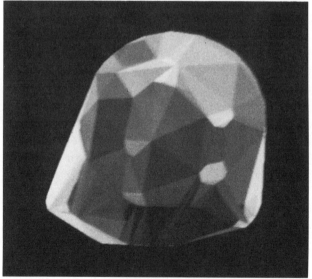

Figure 10.36 Stereo triplet of a sphere (a), and the resulting polyhedral approximation (b).

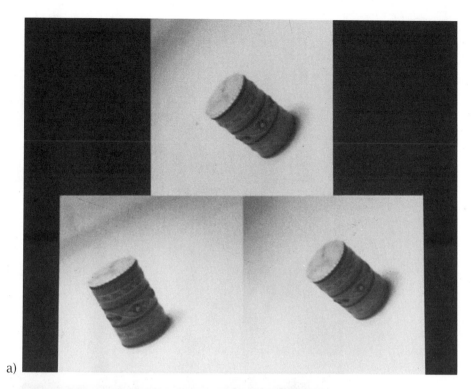

a)

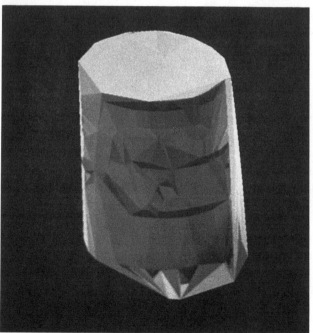

b)

Figure 10.37 Stereo triplet of a cylinder (a), and the resulting polyhedral approximation (b).

a)

b)

Figure 10.38 Stereo triplet of a cone (a), and the resulting polyhedral approximation (b).

Figure 10.39   A stereo triplet of a part of the laboratory.

10.6.4.1   Considering one viewpoint

The first image of the environment is shown in figure 10.39. The result of the stereo matcher for this scene is shown in figure 10.40, where the line segments present in the triplet images are those that have been matched. In order to display the results of the visibility algorithm, we show cross-sections of the Delaunay triangulation before and after the visibility algorithm has been applied. In figure 10.41 we show such a cross-section with a plane parallel to the floor at about table height before the visibility algorithm has been applied and after the removal of empty tetrahedra. The table is clearly visible. In order to give a more expressive representation, we have projected each visible face of the unmarked tetrahedra onto the image plane, computed the average grey level of each projected triangle in the original image, and created a synthetic image of the remaining polyhedron, with hidden surface elimination, where each visible triangle is drawn and filled with the grey level we have obtained. Such a result is given in figure 10.42, which should be compared with figure 10.39. Since we have a 3-D model of the scene, we have displayed two slightly different viewpoints.

Similar results are presented for the image of figure 10.43. The salient features of this scene are a table in the foreground and, on the right-hand side, a hallway extending a distance of about 20 meters from the camera. In the middle of the hallway, a door is half open. On the wall behind the table there is a fire extinguisher. Figure 10.44 shows the segments that have been matched by stereo, and figure 10.45 shows a cross-section of

Figure 10.40 The line segments that have been matched in the stereo triplet corresponding to figure 10.39.

the Delaunay triangulation before and after eliminating empty tetrahedra. The plane is parallel to the floor and is approximately at the height of the table, which is again clearly visible, as is the door halfway down the hallway. The camera is on the right-hand side of the figure.

10.6.4.2 *Considering several viewpoints*

In figure 10.46 we consider a second image of the scene shown in figure 10.39, taken from another viewpoint, with the three sets of segments in figure 10.47. The difference is a rotation of five degrees of the cameras with respect to a vertical axis. In figure 10.48 we also show a cross-section of the Delaunay triangulation of the combination of the two views before and after marking the empty tetrahedra. As we can see by compar-

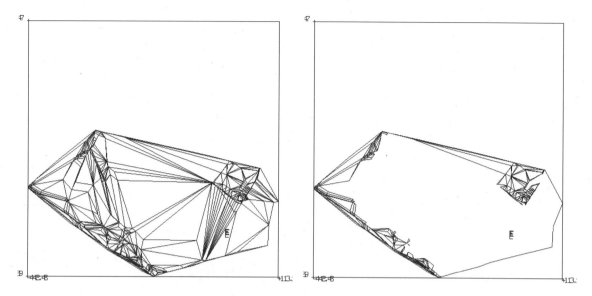

Figure 10.41 A cross-section of the Delaunay triangulation with a plane parallel to the floor before and after the removal of empty tetrahedra for the scene of figure 10.39 (using one viewpoint).

ing this figure with figure 10.41, we have a somewhat better definition of the scene. We have also built a "synthetic" image from the new polyhedral representation obtained by combining the two viewpoints as explained previously. This is shown in figure 10.49. Comparing this figure with figure 10.42 shows an improvement in the definition of the windows, the chair, and the table, as well as the details on the back wall.

Results are presented for three viewpoints by combining figures 10.43 and 10.50. The two viewpoints differ from that of figure 10.43 by two rotations of plus and minus 5 degrees with respect to a vertical axis. Figure 10.51 shows the sets of line segments for these two images, and figure 10.52 shows a cross-section of the Delaunay triangulation of the combination of the three views before and after marking the empty tetrahedra. This figure should be compared with figure 10.45. The definition has improved everywhere, including near the door. Figure 10.53 shows the corresponding "synthetic" image after merging the three views displayed from two viewpoints.

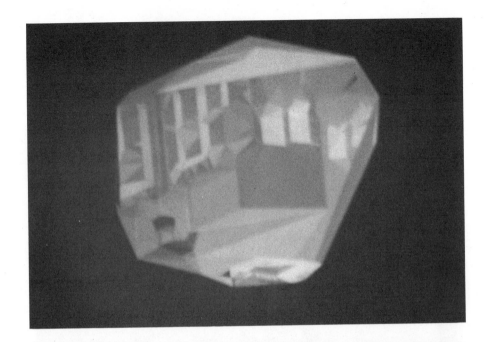

Figure 10.42 A "synthetic" image created from the polyhedral model of the scene shown in figure 10.39. The result is shown from two different viewpoints.

Figure 10.43   A stereo triplet of another part of the laboratory.

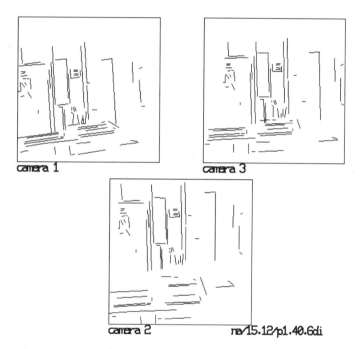

Figure 10.44   The line segments that have been matched in the stereo triplet corresponding to figure 10.43.

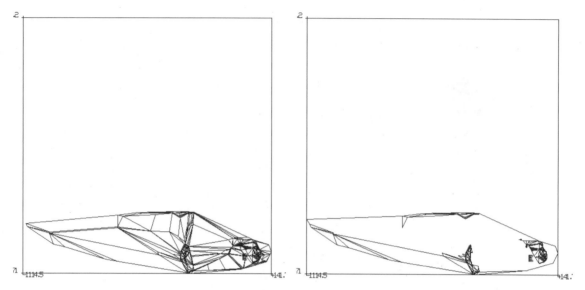

Figure 10.45 A cross-section of the Delaunay triangulation with a plane parallel to the floor before and after the removal of empty tetrahedra for the scene of figure 10.43 (using one viewpoint).

Figure 10.46 The second viewpoint corresponding to figure 10.39.

467

camera 1   camera 3

camera 2   na/15.12/p1.70.6di

Figure 10.47 The line segments that have been matched in the stereo triplet corresponding to figure 10.46.

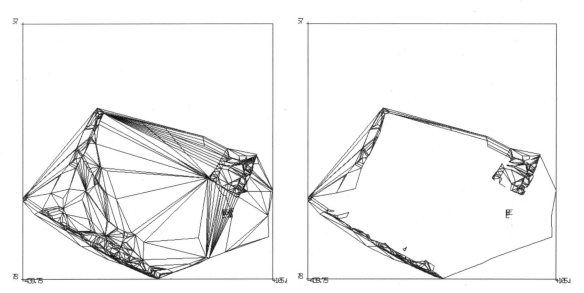

Figure 10.48 A cross-section of the Delaunay triangulation with a plane parallel to the floor before and after the removal of empty tetrahedra for the scene of figures 10.39 and 10.46 (using two viewpoints).

Figure 10.49 The "synthetic" image obtained by combining figures 10.39 and 10.46.

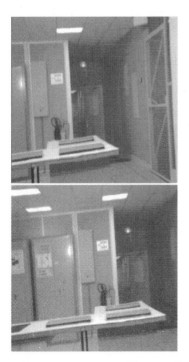

Figure 10.50 The two extra viewpoints corresponding to figure 10.43.

469

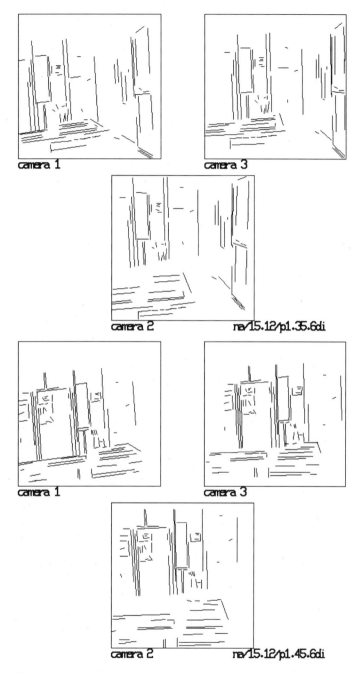

Figure 10.51 The line segments that have been matched in the stereo triplet corresponding to figure 10.49.

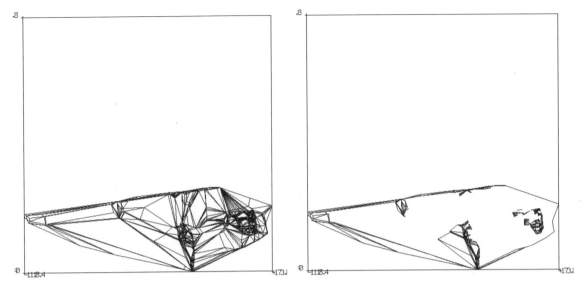

Figure 10.52 A cross-section of the Delaunay triangulation with a plane parallel to the floor before and after the removal of empty tetrahedra for the scene of figures 10.43 and 10.49 (using three viewpoints).

Figure 10.53 The "synthetic" image obtained by combining figures 10.43 and 10.49.

The careful reader will have noticed that it appears as if we were able to look behind the wall or the door. This is readily explained by the fact that for the door, for example, there are tetrahedra that link it to details in the back of the hallway; these extended tetrahedra are then intersected by one or two stereo triangles and are therefore removed. This relates to a remark we made in section 10.6 on the possibility of counting for each tetrahedron the number of stereo triangles it intersects and removing only the tetrahedra that intersect a sufficiently large number of stereo triangles. Here the number is one.

10.7   Finding surface patches

So far we have seen how to represent a set of measured points by finding a simplicial polyhedron that interpolates these points. When the density of the points is high, this polyhedron is a very fine approximation of the set of points, which may not be suitable for many applications. In this section we want to develop ways of finding surface patches. More precisely, we want them to be (1) robust to measurement noise and (2) viewer-independent.

Condition 1 implies that we cannot use high-degree polynomials since they will tend to "follow" the noise unless we use regularization techniques. Condition 2 implies that, if we approximate the points in two different coordinate systems, then the approximations should relate to each other by the same transformation as that which relates the two coordinate systems. These considerations lead us to use first- and second-degree polynomials (planes and quadrics) to approximate surface patches. This is the approach that has been followed by Oshima and Shirai and by Faugeras and Hébert [OS79, FH86], for example.

10.7.1   Surface fitting

When constructing the regions of the object that are best approximated by planes or quadrics, we have to repeatedly solve the following problem. Given a set of N points forming a region of the object surface, find the plane (quadric) that minizes the error measure

$$E = \sum_{i=1}^{N} d^2(M_i, S) \tag{10.4}$$

where the M_i's are the points in the region and d is the distance of M_i to the surface S. In the case of a plane represented by a unit normal $\mathbf{n}$ and its distance d to the origin, it is well known that $d(M_i, P) = |\mathbf{n}^T M_i + d|$. In the case of a quadric Q, there is no such simple formula relating the representation of Q and the distance d. In fact, it can be shown (see problem 11) that the distance to a quadric of a given point M is found by solving an equation of degree 8. For the sake of simplicity, as is the planar case we define as the point error measure the value

$$d^2(M_i, Q) = \frac{1}{2} M_i^T \mathbf{A} M_i + M_i^T \mathbf{v} + d = 0$$

where $\mathbf{A}$ is a symmetric 3×3 matrix, the vector $\mathbf{v}$ is a 3×1 vector, and d is a real number defining the equation of Q (see chapter 5). It can be shown (see problem 14) that, in the case of a quadric with a center, this is equal to the square of the euclidean distance between M_i and m_i, which is the intersection of the segment CM_i (C is the center of the quadric) with the quadric.

The problem is now to minimize criterion E in the case of a plane and a quadric. The case of a plane is classical (see the book by Duda and Hart [DH73] and problem 13): A normal to the best plane is an eigenvector of length one, $\mathbf{n}_{min}$, of the covariance matrix Λ of the points in the region associated with the smallest eigenvalue λ, which is also the minimum error E_{min}. The covariance matrix is given by

$$\Lambda = \frac{1}{N} \sum \mathbf{A}_i \mathbf{A}_i^T, \quad \mathbf{A}_i = \mathbf{M}_i - \mathbf{M} \quad \text{and} \quad \mathbf{M} = \frac{1}{N} \sum \mathbf{M}_i$$

The distance to the best approximating plane is given by

$$d_{min} = -\frac{1}{N} \sum_{i=1}^{N} \mathbf{n}_{min}^T \mathbf{M}_i$$

In the case of a quadric, we represent it, for the purpose of approximation, by ten numbers $a_{1,...,10}$ that are related to the previous description by the following relationships:

$$\mathbf{A} = \begin{bmatrix} a_1 & a_4/\sqrt{2} & a_5/\sqrt{2} \\ a_4/\sqrt{2} & a_2 & a_6/\sqrt{2} \\ a_5/\sqrt{2} & a_6/\sqrt{2} & a_3 \end{bmatrix}$$

$$\mathbf{v} = [a_7, a_8, a_9]^t$$

$$d = a_{10}$$

As we noted earlier, the representation of a quadric is not scale-invariant, and therefore neither is criterion E. This implies that, if we do not add a constraint on the a_i's, the minimum of E is 0, which is achieved for $a_i = 0$ for all i's. Since there does not exist a "natural" constraint like $\|\mathbf{n}\| = 1$ in the case of a quadric, several constraints can be considered. Some of the many possibilities are as follows:

1. $\sum_{i=1}^{10} a_i^2 = 1$

2. $a_{10} = 1$

3. $\text{Trace}(\mathbf{AA}^T) = \sum_{i=1}^{6} a_i^2 = 1$

From these we select the third since it is the only one of the three that is invariant with respect to rotations and translations (see problem 15). This implies that, if we use constraint 1 or 2, the solutions to the minimization of E in two different coordinate systems will not be the same quadric (see problem 16).

Let us define the vector $\mathbf{p} = [a_1, ..., a_{10}]^T$. Criterion E can be rewritten as

$$E = \sum \mathbf{p}^T \mathbf{P}_i^T \mathbf{P}_i \mathbf{p} = \mathbf{p}^T (\sum \mathbf{P}_i^T \mathbf{P}_i) \mathbf{p} = \mathbf{p}^T \mathbf{Pp}$$

where $\mathbf{P}$ is a 10×10 symmetric matrix and $\mathbf{P}_i = [x_i^2, y_i^2, z_i^2, x_i y_i, x_i z_i, y_i z_i, x_i, y_i, z_i, 1]^T$. Constraint 3 can be written as

$$\|\mathbf{Bp}\|^2 = 1$$

where $\mathbf{B}$ is a 6×10 matrix that "selects" the first six elements of vector $\mathbf{p}$. Appendix A provides the solution to this optimization problem (see also problem 17).

10.7.2   Region growing

In the computer vision literature there are two main ways of segmenting entities in a picture, such as a curve, an object, etc. [Pav77]. The first method, called the *split* technique, starts from the entire object and checks if it is homogeneous according to some criterion. If not, the object is split into a number of subobjects. The process is then applied recursively until the objects either become too small or become homogeneous. The major question, that of where to split, has not received any satisfying answer. The second method, called the *merge* technique, starts from elementary homogeneous parts of the object and attempts to merge some of them into larger parts, imposing that the new larger parts are still homogeneous according to the same criterion.

We will discuss a merging scheme, also called a *region-growing paradigm*, that starts from the simplicial polyhedron obtained, for example, by the techniques of section 10.6, and merges the initial triangular regions into larger ones that are best approximated by planes or by quadrics. Regions that are merged together must be neighbors, i.e., they must share a simple polygonal line made of edges of the initial triangles. The process stops when only one region is left or when the total approximation error, as measured by criterion E, reaches some tolerance threshold.

The object is described by a *region adjacency graph*, or RAG, in which the vertices represent the regions and the arcs indicate that two regions are adjacent. The merge procedure works as follows. At every iteration, the two adjacent regions R_i and R_j that produce the smallest error $E(R_i \cup R_j)$ are merged. This guarantees that the total error E grows as slowly as possible and can be easily implemented by maintaining a heap of all pairs of adjacent regions [AHU74, CLR90]. In this way, the best pair is always at the top of the heap. The merge consists of updating the region adjacency graph and the heap. The algorithm can be described as follows:

- **Input:** A simplicial polyhedron interpolating the data points and a tolerance T on the maximum approximation error.
- **Output:** A segmentation of the points into the regions best approximated by a plane or a quadric.

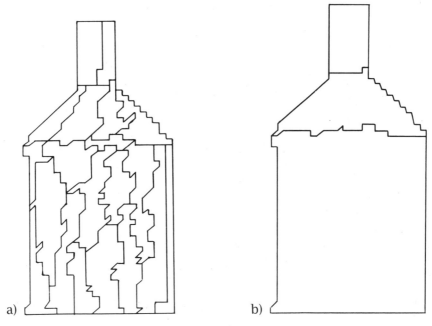

Figure 10.54 The approximation of the oil bottle of figure 10.34 with planes (a) and quadrics (b).

1. **Initialization:** Build the region adjacency graph of the set of initial triangles. Initialize the approximation error for each region to 0 (set $E^0 = 0$). For each pair of adjacent regions, compute the error for the best approximating plane (quadric). Use these values to build a heap such that the top of the heap is the pair of adjacent regions R_i, R_j with the smallest error $E_{ij} = E(R_i \cup R_j)$

2. **Iteration:** Update the total error: $E^n = E^{n-1} + E_{ij} - E_i - E_j$. If E^n is less than the tolerance T, then remove the top of the heap and update it (this involves recomputing the errors E_{ik} and E_{jl} for all regions R_k and R_l adjacent to R_i or R_j) and then reinserting the corresponding pairs into the heap). Update the RAG; otherwise stop.

The results of this segmentation program are shown in figures 10.54 and 10.55, which correspond to figures 10.34 and 10.35.

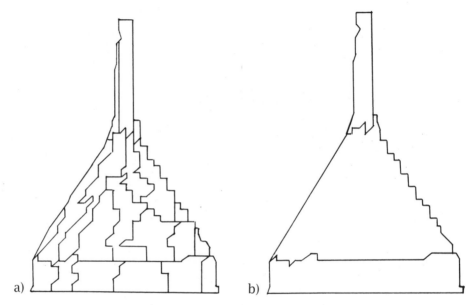

Figure 10.55 The approximation of the funnel of figure 10.35 with planes (a) and quadrics (b).

10.8   More references

The paper by Besl [Bes88] presents a good overview of the problems of geometric modeling in computer vision. The idea of skeletons discussed in section 10.4.2 is intimately related to the idea of generalized cylinders, which has been proposed by Agin [Agi72], by Binford and Nevatia [NB77], and by Marr and Nishihara [MK78]. They are at the center of the ACRONYM system, which has been developed by Brooks for the symbolic interpretation of images [Bro82]. Ways to extract generalized cylinders from range data are discussed in a paper by Nevatia and Binford [NB77, Nev82] and in one by Rao and Nevatia [RN88]. Theoretical properties of generalized cylinders have been studied by Ponce and Chelberg [Pon90, PC87].

In this chapter we have not discussed other techniques of approximation based on regularization. These techniques work well if we have data that have been obtained from one viewpoint and can therefore be described as a function $z = f(x, y)$. They have been pioneered by Grimson [Gri81b] and further refined by Terzopoulos [Ter86]. A slightly different line of attack on the same problem has been proposed by Blake and Zisserman [BZ87]. A good example of the application of some of these ideas is discussed in an article by Li [Li90]. The regularization approaches have been extended to dynamic models of approximation called snakes [KWT88]. An interesting connection between these regularization techniques and Baysian estimation, as well as a description of how to model uncertainty which is complementary to the one presented in chapter 5, can be found in the work of Szeliski [Sze90]. Another very different approach to this problem has been proposed by Sander and Zucker [San89, SZ90] who use differential geometric techniques and a relaxationlike procedure to build coherent global smooth descriptions of noisy range data.

There are some good references on the use of general ideas from differential geometry to represent shapes, for example the paper by Brady, Ponce, Yuille, and Asada [Bra85] or the one by Nalwa [Nal89], as well as the beautiful book by Koenderink [Koe90]. An interesting application to the labeling of line drawings is discussed by Malik [Mal87] and Nalwa [Nal88]. There are also some interesting ideas on the notion of deformable models, which can be found in the work of Pentland [Pen90] and are related to the previously mentioned work on snakes. Some of the concepts developed in solid modeling are also relevant to the question of shape representation in computer vision. See, for example, the articles by Brown and Requicha [Bro81, Req80].

10.9 Problems

1. a. Show that the two definitions 10.1 and 10.2 of the Hausdorff distance are equivalent.

   b. Show that the Hausdorff distance satisfies the three axioms defining a distance:
   - $h(K_1, K_2) = 0 \iff K_1 = K_2$,
   - $h(K_1, K_2) = h(K_2, K_1)$
   - $h(K_1, K_3) \le h(K_1, K_2) + h(K_2, K_3)$

2. A graph $G = (V, E)$ is said to be planar if it can be embedded in the plane without crossings. Let v, e, and f denote, respectively, the number of vertices, edges, and faces (including the single unbounded region). They are related by the classical Euler's formula [HC52]:

$$v - e + f = 2$$

Prove the following inequalities:

$$3f \leq 2e$$

$$e \leq 3v - 6$$

$$f \leq 2v - 4$$

3. This problem shows a configuration of n points such that there are $\theta(n^2)$ tetrahedra in their Delaunay triangulation. It is inspired by Preparata and Shamos [PS85]. Consider a set S_1 of n points that are uniformly placed on a circle in the (x, y) plane and centered at the origin. Next consider a set S_2 of n points that are uniformly placed on the z-axis with the median at the origin. Prove that any segment joining a point of S_1 to a point of S_2 is an edge of the Delaunay triangulation of the set $S = S_1 \cup S_2$ *Hint:* consider the planes defined by a point of S_1 and the z-axis, and compute the corresponding planar Voronoi diagrams.

4. Prove the statement made at the end of the third paragraph of section 10.4.4 about the property of the inserted point in the Delaunay triangulation.

5. Show that in order to erase a point from a Delaunay triangulation one needs only to consider all simplexes adjacent to this point, erase the point, and retriangulate only the points belonging to these simplexes. The resulting triangulation is Delaunay.

6. Let S be a set of n points M_i. The Gabriel graph of S is defined as follows. It has an edge between M_i and M_j (the straight line segment $M_i M_j$) if and only if the ball of diameter $M_i M_j$ does not contain any other point of S in its interior.

a. Show that the Gabriel graph is a subgraph of the Delaunay triangulation.

    b. Show that it can be obtained by erasing from the Delaunay triangulation all edges that do not cross their dual Voronoi edge (in two dimensions) or face (in three dimensions).

7. a. Apply theorem 10.5 to compute the average number $\overline{ns}$ of line segments intersecting a square K_a of side a. Assume that the segments are the realization of a Boolean model of intensity ρ and a primary grain defined as the set of segments with uniformly distributed length (average length $\bar{l}$) and orientation. In order to generalize this result, note that a square is equal to the Minkowski addition of two of its adjacent sides:

$$K_a = S_x \oplus S_y$$

    b. Show that the Minkowski addition is associative:

$$X \oplus (Y \oplus Z) = (X \oplus Y) \oplus Z$$

    c. Show that, if the primary grain is a convex compact of average area $\bar{A}$, then the equation $E(V(X' \oplus K_a)) = \bar{A} + a(\bar{x} + \bar{y}) + a^2$ holds, where $\bar{x}$ and $\bar{y}$ are the average lengths of its projections on the x- and y-axes.

    d. Verify your result from question a.

8. a. How are points A and B of figure 10.10 defined?

    b. If we abandon the symmetry of figure 10.10, can you describe and construct the skeleton of X?

9. Consider a planar curve (c) of class C^3 and a point m of the curve, which we assume to be the origin of arclength. Let $s \rightarrow \mathbf{y}(s)$ be a parameterization of (c) where s is the arclength, and let $\mathbf{t}$ and $\mathbf{n}$ be the tangent and normal to (c) at the origin m. We assume that the x-axis is parallel to $\mathbf{t}$ and the y-axis to $\mathbf{n}$. Let m_1 and m_2 be two points of (c) of arclengths s_1 and s_2 that are close to m, and consider the circle defined by the three points m, m_1, and m_2. The purpose of this problem is to study the limit of this circle when m_1 and m_2 converge toward m.

    a. Compute the coordinates of the center p of this circle as functions of s_1 and s_2.

b. Show that when s_1 and s_2 converge toward 0 the limit of p is the point p_0 of coordinates $[0, \frac{1}{\kappa}]^T$, where κ is the curvature of (c) at m. The circle of center p_0 and radius $\frac{1}{\kappa_0}$ is the circle osculating to (c) at m.

c. Show that in general (c) crosses its osculating circle at m.

d. Consider all the circles centered on the normal to (c) at m and going through m. Study their position with respect to (c) and characterize the osculating circle.

10. Consider a surface (S) of class C^2 and a point M on the surface, which we assume to be the origin of coordinates. Take the z-axis parallel to the normal to (S) at M and the x- and y-axes in the plane tangent to (S) at M and parallel to the two principal directions of curvature (see appendix C). We assume that the z-axis points toward the object X whose boundary is (S). A point Q of the surface in the vicinity of M has coordinates $[x, y, f(x, y)]^T$ and f satisfies

$$f(x, y) = \frac{\kappa_1}{2}x^2 + \frac{\kappa_2}{2}y^2 + o(x^2 + y^2)$$

where κ_1 and κ_2 are the two principal curvatures at M. We assume that the normal is oriented in such a way that $\kappa_2 \le \kappa_1$ and $\kappa_1 \ge 0$. We know that all the spheres centered on the z-axis at points of coordinates varying between $R_1 = \frac{1}{\kappa_1}$ and $R_2 = \frac{1}{\kappa_2}$ and going through M are osculating to (S). Ignoring the special case $\kappa_1 = \kappa_2$, study the relative positions of the osculating spheres and the surface (S).

11. Let us consider a quadric defined by its equation

$$\frac{1}{2}\mathbf{M}^T \mathbf{A} \mathbf{M} + \mathbf{M}^T \mathbf{v} + d = 0$$

and let N be a point. We want to find the shortest distance from N to the quadric surface. Let M be a variable point on the quadric, and consider the line segment NM. If the distance from N to the quadric is minimum, then the line segment NM is parallel to the normal at M to the quadric.

a. Show that this condition yields two quadratic equations in the coordinates of M.

b. Those two equations define two quadric surfaces on which M must lie. Conclude that there are in general at most eight points on the initial quadric such that NM is parallel to the normal at M to the quadric.

12. Work out the same problem as problem 11 in the plane. Show that the shortest distance from a point to a conic can be found by solving a biquadratic equation.

13. Let a plane be represented by a pair $\mathbf{n}, d$, where $\mathbf{n}$ is a unit vector perpendicular to the plane and d is the signed distance of the plane to the origin. Let M_i, $i = 1, \ldots, p$ be p points in space. We want to find the best plane approximating these p points.

   a. Consider the center of gravity M of the p points and define

   $$\mathbf{M}'_i = \mathbf{M}_i - \mathbf{M}$$

   Write criterion (10.4) as a function of the covariance matrix Λ of the p points, M, $\mathbf{n}$, and d.

   b. Show that the best approximating plane goes through M. *Hint:* compute $\frac{\partial E}{\partial d}$.

   c. Show that the best unit normal vector is an eigenvector of the covariance matrix Λ. Show that the error is equal to p times this eigenvalue.

14. The center of a quadric of equation

   $$f(N) = \frac{1}{2} \mathbf{N}^T \mathbf{A} \mathbf{N} + \mathbf{N}^T \mathbf{v} + d = 0$$

   is defined as the point C such that

   $$\mathbf{A} \mathbf{C} + \mathbf{v} = \mathbf{0}$$

   Thus it exists only for a quadric such that the rank of $\mathbf{A}$ is 3. Assume that this is true, and consider a point M. The half-line $\langle C, M \rangle$, which we parameterize as the set of points P, is represented by

   $$\mathbf{P} = \mathbf{C} + \lambda(\mathbf{M} - \mathbf{C}) \qquad \lambda \geq 0$$

   a. Show that the value of the parameter λ of the point m of intersection of the half-line $\langle C, M \rangle$ with the quadric satisfies the equation

$$\lambda^2(f(M) + k) - k = 0$$

with $k = -(d + \frac{1}{2}\mathbf{C}^T\mathbf{v})$.

b. Deduce from this result the relation

$$f(M) = k(\frac{d(C,M)^2}{d(C,m)^2} - 1)$$

c. What can you say about criterion (10.4) for a quadric with a center?

15. Prove that constraint 3 near the end of section 10.7.1 is invariant when we apply a rigid displacement to the coordinate system.

16. Solve the minimization problem (10.4) subject to constraint 2. Give an example in which the quadrics found by solving this problem in two different coordinate systems differing by a rigid displacement are not related by this displacement.

17. Show how to use appendix A to compute the vector $\mathbf{p}$ that minimizes criterion E subject to the constraint $\|\mathbf{Bp}\|^2 = 1$.

11 Recognizing and Locating Objects and Places

11.1 The status of the problems

We have seen in the previous chapters a number of ways to construct both 2-D and 3-D representations of objects in terms of geometric primitives. We have studied ways of reliably extracting these primitives from a number of sensory processes, and we would now like to address the question of how to use these representations for recognizing and locating objects or for the navigation of a robot. The difficulty of these problems is a function of several variables:

Dimensionality: Objects can be one-, two-, or three-dimensional. Examples of one-dimensional objects are waveforms of various kinds. Examples of two-dimensional objects are flat parts such as keys, coins, etc., for which the third dimension is negligible with respect to the other two. Examples of three-dimensional objects can be found by looking around.

Partial visibility: Objects can be completely visible (observed) or partially hidden. It is almost always the case in robotics applications that the objects to be dealt with are partially hidden. The fact that parts of the object may be missing seriously adds to the difficulty of recognizing them.

Rigidity: Objects can be rigid or nonrigid. Nonrigid objects range from articulated bodies, such as a robot manipulator, to continuously deformable objects, such as clouds.

Differences in classes of objects: Related to this distinction between rigid and nonrigid objects is the distinction between recognizing one instance of a specific shape, such as a given chair of known shape and dimensions, and recognizing classes of objects such as the class of chairs. An articulated object is somewhat in between in the sense that there exists an analytical parametrization of all its possible configurations, whereas very likely such a parametrization does not exist for the class of chairs.

Noise: Typically measurements in the scene are noisy. The difficulty of the problem increases with an increase in noise.

In this book we concentrate exclusively on specific instances of partially overlapping rigid 2-D and 3-D objects, mostly because the one-dimensional problem is more relevant to classical pattern recognition and the other problems are areas that are open to research. We deal explicitly with the problem of noisy measurements.

From now on we will assume that every object is defined by a model $M = (M_1, ..., M_n)$ that is composed of a number of geometric primitives M_i of the types we have described in chapter 3, and that a number of visual sensors provide us with a set of similar descriptions $S = (S_1, ..., S_p)$ for the observed scene. The *recognition* problem is then to produce a list of pairs of model/scene primitives $R_n = ((M_1, S_{i_1}), ..., (M_n, S_{i_n}))$ where the S_{i_j}'s are either scene primitives or are represented by the special symbol NIL, which indicates that the model primitive M_j is not present in the scene. Such a list is called a *recognition sequence*. The *localization* problem is to find the best rigid transformation T such that, when it is applied to the identified model primitives, it brings them as close as possible to their corresponding scene primitives. We will make heavy use of the rigidity constraint to help find the best matches between model and scene primitives.

We will begin this chapter with a description of the main approaches that have been used to attack these problems. It is the last one, the tree-search approach, on which we will focus, and we will describe in detail in the two- and three-dimensional cases.

11.2   Various approaches to the problems

The complexity of the recognition problem depends directly on the number of scene and model primitives, since the number of recognition sequences R is of the order of $(p + 1)^n$. This rapidly becomes extremely large when n and p grow larger; it is therefore usually impossible to explore all possibilities. Several approaches are possible to limit the computational explosion, and we will investigate two: the Hough transform and graph matching.

11.2.1   The Hough transform

The idea of the *Hough transform* was introduced a long time ago [Hou62, DH73] to identify simple geometric primitives such as lines in images. It has been considerably generalized to deal with any parameterized planar primitive and, in fact, any shape, planar or not [DY80, Bal81, Dav82]. It can also be used for the recognition and localization of objects by considering the space that describes the parameters of the rigid transformation.

To be more precise, let us take the example of planar rigid transformations. Each such transformation can be uniquely decomposed into a rotation around the origin and a translation. The corresponding parameter space is three-dimensional, with one dimension for the angle of rotation and two for the coordinates of the translation (see chapter 5). We can quantize this parameter space with as many levels as necessary for the purpose of estimating the transformation. Suppose, for the sake of simplicity, that we are interested in recovering only the rotation. This quantized space is then considered as a one-dimensional accumulator that is initialized to zero.

For each model primitive M_i $(i = 1..., n)$, we consider all its possible pairings (M_i, S_j) with scene primitives S_j. Continuing with our 2-D example and assuming that scene and model primitives are oriented line segments, a match determines the rotation angle, and the corresponding accumulator cell is increased by 1. After the np pairings have been considered, peaks in the accumulator indicate the best candidates for the rotation angle. The situation is depicted in figure 11.1, which shows a number of interesting phenomena. In this simple example, the scene is a rotation of -90 degrees of the model (figure 11.1.a). The primitives used in the representation are line segments, which we assume to be oriented. If we allow all possible matches (M_i, S_j), the resulting accumulator is shown in figure 11.1.b, where it can be seen that the maximum at -90 degrees is there, but it is not much higher than other peaks such as the

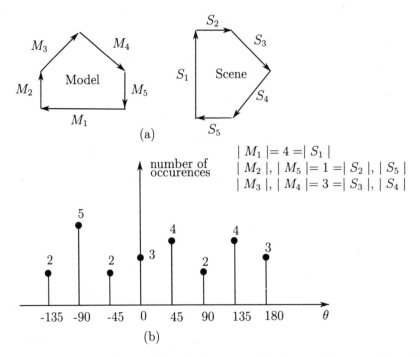

$$| M_1 | = 4 = | S_1 |$$
$$| M_2 |, | M_5 | = 1 = | S_2 |, | S_5 |$$
$$| M_3 |, | M_4 | = 3 = | S_3 |, | S_4 |$$

Figure 11.1   (a) The model and the scene. (b) The Hough accumulator for the rotation angle when we allow all possible matches between model and scene.

one at 45 degrees, for example. Note that we have ignored the length of the line segments.

In practice, even though the line segment length may be unreliable because of occlusion and/or bad segmentation, it can be useful to limit the number of potential pairings (M_i, S_j). If we authorize only matches (M_i, S_j) such that the ratio of the lengths of the shortest segment to the longest is larger than or equal to .5, we obtain the result of figure 11.2.a. If we allow only matches between segments of equal lengths, we obtain the result of figure 11.2.b. Even though things appear to work well on this simple academic example, problems occur in practical situations.

If the orientations of the scene segments are noisy because of bad sensory measurements, the right peak in the accumulator may become very blurred so that it is not easily detected. Several comparable maxima may also be present, and a verification procedure to determine the best

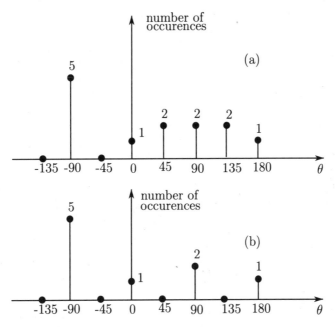

Figure 11.2 (a) The values in the Hough accumulator for the rotation angle when we allow matches between the model and the scene such that the ratio of the lengths of the shortest segment to the longest is $\geq .5$. (b) The result when we allow only matches of segments of equal length.

one must be implemented. Moreover, the value of the rotation angle for which the peak occurs may not be the best estimation of the right one, and accuracy in the localization may be poor. Therefore, the first drawback of the Hough transform is its poor ability to take into account noisy measurements. In this simple example, we had only a one-dimensional accumulator. If we include translation, the accumulator becomes three-dimensional. If we go to a three-dimensional recognition problem, the accumulator becomes six-dimensional (three dimensions for rotation and three for translation). The second drawback of the Hough transform is that we have to deal with high-dimensional accumulators.

Another problem is that some geometric primitives do not entirely constrain the transformation, so updating the accumulator may be difficult. For example, matching two points in two or three dimensions does not constrain simply the rigid transformation; matching two planes in three dimensions, as indicated in figure 11.30, only constrains the axis of rotation to lie in a plane, and thus makes updating the accumulator difficult. In order to alleviate this problem we can choose to match s-tuples of model and scene primitives, where s is the smallest value such that matching s model primitives with s scene primitives entirely determines the rigid transformation. But then the number of matches to be considered can become of the order of $n^s p^s$. As an example, in the three-dimensional case, $s = 3$ for points and planes and $s = 2$ for lines, as shown in sections 11.4.3.1 and 11.5.1.2.

Finally, the Hough transform does not take full advantage of the rigidity constraint. Indeed, if a match (M_i, S_j) is correct and determines the model-to-scene transformation, then we only have to verify this and not consider all matches (M_k, S_l) that yield other transformations. There is also no simple way to exploit any *a priori* information about the object pose in order to avoid considering all possible matches (M_i, S_j). Note that some of the problems attached to the use of the generalized Hough transform can be decreased by using *geometric hashing* [LW88, Wol90, FJ92, SM92].

11.2.2   Graph matching

If we add more structure to our model and scene descriptions, we can represent them with graphs. The nodes of these graphs represent the primitives M_i and S_j. They are labeled with features attached to the primitives. The arcs represent the relationships between these primitives. There may be many relations: for example, adjacency, "nearness," parallelism, perpendicularity, and so on.

Going back to the example of figure 11.1, if we consider the relations "adjacent" and "parallel," the graphs representing the model and the scene are shown in figure 11.3. Arcs labeled a indicate adjacency, and arcs labeled p indicate parallelism. The features attached to each segment can be, for example, the coordinates of the midpoint, the length of the segment, and its orientation. Recognizing the model M in the scene S is equivalent to finding out that the graph representing M is isomorphic to the graph representing S, i.e., that there exists a one-to-one correspondence between the nodes that preserves the graph structure.

This can be formally expressed as follows. A graph G is defined as a pair (V, E) of a set of vertices V and edges E, where E is a subset of the Cartesian product $V \times V$. Given two graphs $G_1 = (V_1, E_1)$ and $G_2 = (V_2, E_2)$,

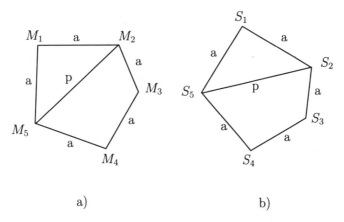

a)   b)

Figure 11.3 The two graphs associated with the model and the scene of figure 11.1.a.

an isomorphism between these two graphs is a one-to-one function f of V_1 into V_2 such that, for all edges $a_1 = (x_1, y_1)$ in E_1, $(f(x_1), f(y_1))$ is in E_2: f preserves the graph structure. Considering labeled edges where labels are taken within a finite set L is a simple extension of the previous definition. This is a somewhat unrealistic abstraction of what happens in practice because we have neglected two important factors. First, because of partial occlusion only part of the model is present in the scene. The real problem is to find a maximal subgraph isomorphism, i.e., to find the largest subgraph of M isomorphic to a subgraph of S. The second factor is related to the fact that the vertices of the graphs we manipulate are usually labeled with numerical values that are derived from the features of the corresponding geometric primitives. The values of these features should also be taken into account when we search for graph correspondences. This means that the function f above should also satisfy the condition that, when $f(x_1) = y_1$, then the features attached to x_1 should be "close" to the features of y_1. The notion of isomorphism then becomes that of ε-isomorphisn [Har79, Har80].

11.2.2.1 Maximal cliques

A *clique* of a graph is a completely connected subgraph of the graph. The idea of using maximal cliques of a graph to recognize objects has been pioneered by Ambler, Barrow, Brown, Burstall, and Popplestone

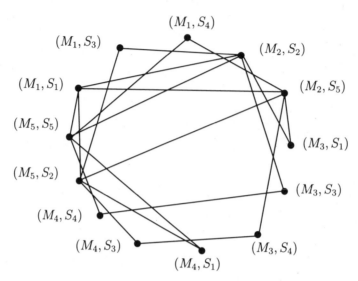

Figure 11.4   The association graph of the two graphs of figure 11.3

[Amb73]. Given the object and the scene graphs G_1 and G_2, we build the so-called *association graph* A as follows. A node a of A is a pair (M_i, S_j) such that M_i and S_j have the same features. An arc $a_1 a_2$ exists in A between the nodes $a_1 = (M_{i_1}, S_{j_1})$ and $a_2 = (M_{i_2}, S_{j_2})$ if and only if the arcs between M_{i_1} and M_{i_2} in G_1 are the same as the arcs S_{j_1} and S_{j_2} in G_2. This expresses the fact that the matches (M_{i_1}, S_{j_1}) and (M_{i_2}, S_{j_2}) are compatible. As an example, figure 11.4 shows the association graph of the two graphs of figure 11.3.

The solution to recognition problem thus appears to be equivalent to finding the largest maximal completely connected subgraph of A, i.e., the largest maximal clique. *Maximal* means that it is not possible to add another vertex to the clique without destroying the property of its being completely connected. *Largest* means that, among all maximal cliques, it is the one with the largest number of vertices. Such a clique defines a matching between the model, represented by G_1, and the scene, represented by G_2. The corresponding recognition sequence R_n is obtained from the vertices of A in the clique. Those model primitives that do not appear are matched with *NIL*. This matching is maximal in the sense that the list R_n contains the smallest possible number of symbols *NIL*; in addition, all matches (M_j, S_{i_j}) and (M_k, S_{i_k}) are compatible since the relations in G_1 between M_j and M_k are the same as the relations in G_2 between S_{i_j} and S_{i_k}. In the association graph of figure 11.4 there are two largest maximal cliques of size 3: $((M_1, S_1), (M_2, S_2), (M_5, S_5))$ and $((M_1, S_1), (M_2, S_5), (M_5, S_2))$.

If we do not put any restriction on the possible matches (M_i, S_j), the association graph A may have as many as np vertices. In this formalism, it is easy to accommodate features associated with each model/scene primitive. If $\mathbf{m}_i$ represents the features attached to scene primitive M_i and $\mathbf{s}_j$ the features attached to scene primitive S_j, it is usually true that we can compute some numerical measure $d_{ij} = d(\mathbf{m}_i, \mathbf{s}_j)$ of the difference between the feature vectors $\mathbf{m}_i$ and $\mathbf{s}_j$. We decide that the match (M_i, S_j) is allowable if d_{ij} is less than a given threshold. Otherwise, the node (M_i, S_j) does not appear in the association graph.

In a similar vein, relations between the vertices in G_1 and G_2 may not all be exact binary relations and may be thought of as having attached to them a measure of how well they are satisfied. Examples of such relations are topological relations such as close to, above, and on the right of, as well as geometric relations such as parallel or perpendicular. An arc in the association graph between (M_i, S_j) and (M_k, S_{k_j}) will appear if and only if the relations between M_i and M_k in G_1 are sufficiently similar to the relations between S_{i_j} and S_{k_j} in G_2. Here the word similar is defined by the measures attached to the relations. We will give examples of how to compute similarities in section 11.2.2.2 on relaxation labeling.

Notice that, except for simple examples, the construction of the entire association graph and the search for maximal cliques appears to be a formidable task. For instance, in the 2-D example described in section 11.3, we can easily have n and p of the order of fifty to a few hundred, leading to association graphs having tens of thousands of vertices. As shown, for example, in the books by Aho, Hopcroft, and Ullman and by Cormen, Leiserson, and Rivest [AHU74, CLR90], the clique-finding problem is NP-complete, which makes its complexity at least exponential in terms of the number of vertices of the association graph. This is yet another reason for keeping its size small.

An algorithm for finding all maximal cliques of a graph can be obtained from the following simple idea. Given a clique C and a set S of nodes including C, the cliques that include C and are included in S are obtained by choosing an element s in $S \div C$ connected to all elements of C, if there is one; each clique including C must either include s or exclude it. We then solve the two subproblems for $C \cup \{s\}$ and $S \div \{s\}$ on one hand and for C and $S \div \{s\}$ on the other. Futhermore, if we consider the set S' of nodes of G such that each s' in S' is connected to each element of C,[1] since any maximal clique included in S and containing C must include S', the problem does not need to be solved if S' is not included in S.

We therefore have the following algorithm:

- **Input**: A clique C and a set S containing C.

- **Output**: All maximal cliques containing C and included in S.

1. Compute S', the set of nodes of G connected to all elements of C.

2. If S' is not included in S, report failure.

3. If no node in $S \div C$ is connected to all elements of C, then C is maximal in S.

4. Otherwise choose s in $S \div C$ connected to all elements of C, and solve for $(C \cup \{s\}, S \div \{s\})$ and $(C, S \div \{s\})$.

In order to find all maximal cliques of a graph G, we simply apply the previous algorithm to $(\varnothing, S)$ where S is the set of all nodes in the graph. Even though this looks appealing, there are nevertheless two main difficulties with this approach:

1. Features and relations may have numerical values (and in practice they very often do) attached to them, which makes the construction of the association graph a little difficult because thresholds have to be applied in order to decide when two nodes of G_1 and G_2 can be associated to create a node in A and when nodes in A can be connected.

2. The size of A may be extremely large for many real problems, and finding all maximal cliques may be extremely time-consuming since the clique-finding problem is NP-complete.

The first problem can be solved by not thresholding the measures of goodness of fit and keeping this numerical information present. The second problem can be solved by not constructing the whole association graph at the cost of possibly missing some of the maximal cliques

---

1. We agree that when $C = \varnothing$, $S' = \varnothing$.

(and therefore some of the solutions to the matching problem). This is a common tradeoff between completeness (finding all the solutions to a combinatorial problem, even those that do not have a physical interpretation), and efficiency. We will now present two approaches to achieving this tradeoff.

11.2.2.2 Relaxation labeling

The first approach consists in associating with each node (M_i, S_j) of the association graph a measure $p_i(j)$ of how good this particular match is. This measure can be computed from a distance d_{ij} between the feature vectors $\mathbf{m}_i$ and $\mathbf{s}_j$ of M_i and S_j in many ways, using the idea that, if d_{ij} is small, then $p_i(j)$ should be large, and vice versa. It is convenient to have $0 \le p_i(j) \le 1$, and we can use a formula such as

$$p_i(j) = \frac{k_i}{1 + \alpha d_{ij}}, \tag{11.1}$$

to define it. The number α is positive, and k_i is a normalizing factor equal to

$$1 / \sum_j \frac{1}{1 + \alpha d_{ij}}$$

so that the $p_i(j)$ are between 0 and 1 and add up to 1:

$$\sum_{j=1}^{n} p_i(j) = 1 \qquad 0 \le p_i(j) \le 1$$

To each pair (M_i, S_j), (M_k, S_l) of nodes in the association graph we can also attach a measure of their compatibility, $c(i, j, k, l)$. This measure can be computed in a way similar to $p_i(j)$ by comparing the relations in G_1 between the nodes M_i and M_k with the relations in G_2 between the nodes S_j and S_l. If these relations are alike, the compatibility $c(i, j, k, l)$ is close to 1; if they are very dissimilar, it is close to 0. This is equivalent to considering a weighted association graph where an arc exists between (M_i, S_j) and (M_k, S_l) if and only if M_i and M_k are neighbors in G_1 and S_j and S_l are neighbors in G_2, with the arc weighted by the value $c(i, j, k, l)$.

For each node (M_i, S_j) in the association graph, we can consider its neighbors (M_k, S_l). Each such neighbor has a value $p_k(l)$ attached to it, and the arc between the node (M_i, S_j) and (M_k, S_l) is weighted by

$c(i,j,k,l)$. If we denote by V_{ij} the set of neighbors of (M_i, S_j) in the association graph (there are $|V_{ij}|$ such neighbors), we can define a number $q_i(j)$ as

$$q_i(j) = \frac{1}{|V_{ij}|} \sum_{(M_k, S_l) \text{ in } V_{ij}} c(i,j,k,l) p_k(l)$$

This number is an indication of how matching M_i with S_j is compatible with the structures of the graphs G_1 and G_2 in the neighborhoods of M_i and S_j. If for each match (M_k, S_l) where $p_k(l)$ is close to 1 we have the compatibility $c(i,j,k,l)$ also close to 1, then $q_i(j)$ will be close to 1. On the contrary, if $p_k(l)$ is close to 1 when $c(i,j,k,l)$ is close to 0 and vice versa, then $q_i(j)$ will be close to 0.

A measure of the consistency between the features (the $p_i(j)$) and the neighbors (the $q_i(j)$) for the match (M_i, S_j) can be taken as the product $p_i(j)q_i(j)$, which is close to 1 if and only if both factors are close to 1. We call this a *local consistency measure*. A global measure can be obtained by averaging the local measures:

$$C = \sum_{(M_i, S_j) \text{ in } A} p_i(j)q_i(j)$$

This criterion C has a nice geometric interpretation. Considering for each model element M_i the vector $\mathbf{p}_i$ of size n whose jth coordinate is $p_i(j)$ and the vector $\mathbf{q}_i$ whose jth coordinate is $q_i(j)$, then it appears that C can be rewritten as

$$C = \sum_{M_i} \mathbf{p}_i \cdot \mathbf{q}_i \tag{11.2}$$

In the *relaxation approach* the $p_i(j)$ are allowed to vary and C is considered a function of these np variables. The values computed using equation (11.1) are considered the starting point of a procedure that tries to maximize C, for example, by steepest ascent. When convergence has been obtained, each vector $\mathbf{p}_i$ is examined and its largest coordinate value is selected. Let us assume that, for each i, the vector $\mathbf{p}_i$ has one coordinate of index j_i equal to 1 and all others equal to 0. We have thus constructed the list

$$((M_1, S_{j_1}), \dots, (M_n, S_{j_n}))$$

Another procedure must be applied to decide whether or not the model can be considered to have been recognized in the scene. In particular, the number of appearances of the NIL symbol among the S_{i_j} should be sufficiently small. It is important to note that, in order to maximize C, the association graph does not have to be explicitly constructed at the cost of having to recompute the $c(i, j, k, l)$ each time they are needed. Returning again to equation (11.2), we see that each inner product $\mathbf{p}_i \cdot \mathbf{q}_i$ is maximum when $\mathbf{p}_i$ and $\mathbf{q}_i$ are parallel, i.e., when features and neighbors agree and when $\mathbf{p}_i$ is a unit vector, that is, when one of its coordinates is equal to 1 and all others are equal to 0. Notice that in this case there is no ambiguity for the match of M_i.

If we compare this method with the maximal cliques method, we see that it avoids in principle constructing the association graph. However, it does not guarantee that, after the convergence of the maximization process and after selecting for each model element M_i the scene element S_j such that $p_i(j)$ is the largest, the corresponding subgraph of the association graph will be a maximum clique. In fact, it may not even be a clique. The main problem with relaxation techniques is that all the *a priori* information has to be buried once and for all in the numbers $p_i(j)$ (equation (11.1)) and $c(i, j, k, l)$. It is then the algorithm that maximizes C that decides what the results are. In practice, these numbers are computed from the actual measurements by somewhat ad hoc formulae such as (11.1). It is not clear what impact on the results a different formula would have. And it is not always easy to embed *global* constraints, such as rigidity, in the $c(i, j, k, l)$ [BF84].

Perhaps it might be useful to emphasize that there is a huge amount of literature on relaxation labeling and its applications to computer vision. We will mention here the original paper by Rosenfeld, Hummel, and Zucker [RHZ76], which started the activity in the field with a somewhat heuristic approach to the problem. At the same time, Ullman [Ull79] was developing a different, but related, line of attack for solving the problem of matching tokens in motion analysis. This work was followed by two more theoretical papers, which attempted to lay a firmer ground for further developing the theory and the applications [FB81a, HZ83]. As shown in the influential paper by Geman and Geman [GG84], the correct setting for relaxation labeling is the theory of Markov random fields, whose application to computer vision has become quite important.

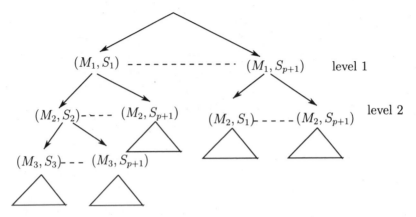

Figure 11.5 The interpretation tree.

11.2.2.3 *The tree-search approach*

Another approach to solving the recognition and localization problems is that of exploring the *interpretation tree* of figure 11.5: Level $i, i = 1, \ldots, n$ of the tree describes the possible hypotheses for the model primitive M_i, and a path from the root to a leaf is a recognition sequence. As we will see, this approach lends itself very nicely to the implementation of the rigidity constraint. The basic paradigm that we use is that of *recognizing* while *localizing*. It means that, at the same time that we are traversing the tree to compute a recognition sequence R_n, we are also computing the pose of the object, i.e., the best rigid transformation T from the model to the scene. This is achieved by using the method of prediction and verification, which we have already used for stereo in section 6.7. This approach has two important advantages:

1. It allows us to reduce the breadth of the search as follows: For every path explored from the root in the interpretation tree corresponding to a partial recognition $R_k = ((M_1, S_{i_1}), \ldots, (M_k, S_{i_k}))(k < n)$, we compute, using methods to be described later, the best rigid transformation T_k from model to scene. We can then apply T_k to the next unmatched model primitive M_{k+1} and consider as possible candidates for M_{k+1} only those unmatched scene primitives that are sufficiently close to $T_k(M_{k+1})$. This considerably reduces the breadth of the in-

terpretation tree. This is the same as predicting where M_{k+1} is in the scene (i.e., close to $T_k(M_{k+1})$) and verifying it by looking for unmatched scene primitives that are sufficiently close to it.

2. It allows us to reduce the depth of the search as follows: When we compute the best rigid transformation, we also obtain a residual error ε_k. We do not want to generate recognition sequences R_n with too large an error ε_n, so we want to be able to stop the search when ε_k grows larger than some threshold. We also want in general to recognize a sufficiently large part of an object in the scene. This implies that the number of scene primitives matched to *NIL* has to be smaller than some threshold so that, if at level k in the interpretation tree we have already gone over the threshold, it is not necessary to continue the search.

The rest of this chapter develops these ideas, which have been embedded in a number of robust systems.

11.3   Recognizing and determining the pose of 2-D objects

We will first describe a system that can recognize and locate 2-D objects from their silhouettes. The system is robust in the sense that it has been explicitly designed to cope with uneven lighting conditions including variations of contrast, shadows, and highlights; with the occurrence of touching and/or partially overlapping objects (see figure 11.6); and with the occurrence on the objects of unpredictable artifacts such as sprues or dead-heads (see figure 11.7).

11.3.1   Building models and scene descriptions

Models and scenes are represented the same way. The acquisition device is a standard television camera. Edges are found using the techniques described in chapter 4, and chains of connected edge pixels are approximated by line segments. This somewhat reduces the class of possible representable shapes to that of "fairly" polygonal objects. Most of the following ideas can be extended to curvilinear geometric primitives.

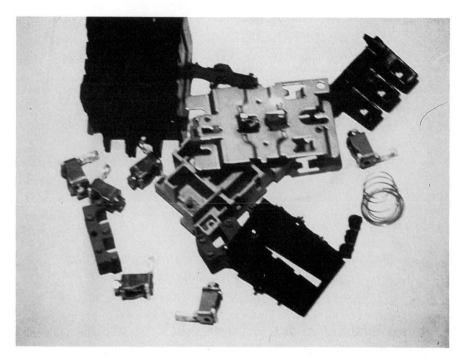

Figure 11.6 An example of the kind of scene that the recognition system can cope with.

Figure 11.8 shows two reference· parts, and figure 11.9 shows the four polygonal models corresponding to the two positions of stable equilibrium of the parts. Figure 11.10 shows some of the models for the parts of figure 11.6. The models and the scene are described in different coordinate systems, and we make the assumption that the transformation from model to scene is a rotation of angle θ around the origin, a scaling k, and a translation $\mathbf{t} = [t_1, t_2]^T$, which we represent as a 4×1 vector $\mathbf{a} = [\theta, k, t_1, t_2]^T$. Each segment is represented by a 4×1 vector $\mathbf{s} = [a, b, x, l]^T$, where the equation of the infinite line[2] supporting the segment is $ax + y + b = 0$ (see sections 5.3.3.2 and 8.3.1), x is the abscissa of the midpoint, and l is the length of the segment. To each such

---

2. We assume that the line is represented in the map φ_2 of section 5.3.3.2.

Figure 11.7 Unpredictable artifacts can be present on the objects.

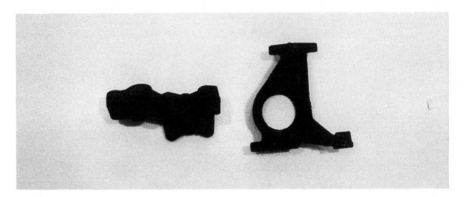

Figure 11.8 Two reference parts.

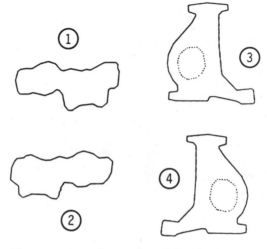

Figure 11.9   Polygonal models of the parts of figure 11.8.

representation vector is attached a covariance (weight) matrix **R** that is computed, for example, as described in chapter 5.

11.3.2   Effect of the transformation T on the representation s of a segment

We determine how the representation **s** of a segment changes when the segment is submitted to the transformation T represented by **a**. T is a collineation, or, more precisely, a similitude (see section 2.4.8). Let $\mathbf{s}' = [a', b', x', l']^T$ be the new representation. It is easy to show that

$$l' = kl \tag{11.3}$$

$$x' = k(x \cos \theta + (ax + b) \sin \theta) + t_1 \tag{11.4}$$

Let matrix **D** be defined by

$$\mathbf{D} = \begin{bmatrix} k \cos \theta & -k \sin \theta & t_1 \\ k \sin \theta & k \cos \theta & t_2 \\ 0 & 0 & 1 \end{bmatrix}$$

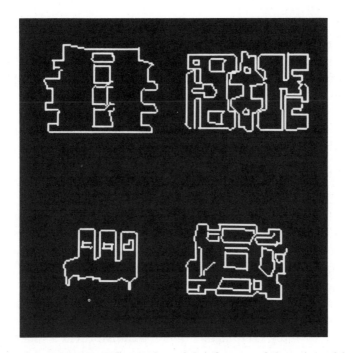

Figure 11.10   Polygonal models of some of the parts of figure 11.6.

Matrix $\mathbf{D}$ is a projective representation of the collineation T (see chapter 2). We also have

$$\mathbf{D}^{-1} = \begin{bmatrix} \frac{\cos\theta}{k} & \frac{\sin\theta}{k} & -\frac{t_1\cos\theta + t_2\sin\theta}{k} \\ -\frac{\sin\theta}{k} & \frac{\cos\theta}{k} & -\frac{-t_1\sin\theta + t_2\cos\theta}{k} \\ 0 & 0 & 1 \end{bmatrix}$$

The infinite line supporting the segment has a projective representation equal to $[a, 1, b]^T$ and thus a projective representation of the line transformed by T is $\mathbf{D}^{-1T} \begin{bmatrix} a \\ 1 \\ b \end{bmatrix}$. Therefore we have

$$a' = \frac{a\cos\theta - \sin\theta}{a\sin\theta + \cos\theta} = \frac{a - \tan\theta}{a\tan\theta + 1} \tag{11.5}$$

$$b' = \frac{t_1(\sin\theta - a\cos\theta) - t_2(\cos\theta + a\sin\theta) + bk}{a\sin\theta + \cos\theta} \tag{11.6}$$

Let us now suppose that we match a model segment represented by $\mathbf{s}$ to a scene segment represented by $\mathbf{s}'$. Equation (11.3) yields k, (11.5) yields θ $(\bmod \pi)$, and (11.4) and (11.6) yield two values for $\mathbf{t}$ corresponding to the two values of θ. Thus the match of a model segment to a scene segment defines two transformations $T^{(1)}$ and $T^{(2)}$, which are represented by the two vectors $\mathbf{b}_0^{(1)} = \mathbf{h}_1(\mathbf{s}, \mathbf{s}')$ and $\mathbf{b}_0^{(2)} = \mathbf{h}_2(\mathbf{s}, \mathbf{s}')$[3]. Using the techniques described in chapter 5, we can compute a first-order approximation $\mathbf{M}_0^{(i)}$ to the covariance (weight) matrices of $\mathbf{b}_0^{(i)}, i = 1, 2$ (see problem 2).

11.3.3   Searching the interpretation tree

Given a model segment M_1 represented by $\mathbf{s}_1$, we consider the various hypotheses (M_1, S_j), where S_j is a scene segment. As explained in the previous section, each such hypothesis defines at most two transformations $T_{0j}^{(1)}$ and $T_{0j}^{(2)}$ from the model space to the scene space. We do the reasoning for $T_{0j}^{(1)}$, which we denote by T_{0j}. Let $\mathbf{b}_{0j}$ be its representation and $\mathbf{M}_{0j}$ its covariance (weight) matrix. We traverse the tree in the following manner: Consider the next unmatched model primitive M_2 represented by $\mathbf{s}_2$, apply T_{0j} to it, and obtain a transformed segment $T_{0j}(M_2)$. For each unmatched scene segment[4] S_k represented by $\mathbf{s}'_k$, we consider equations (11.3)-(11.6) as measurement equations $\mathbf{f}(\mathbf{x}_k, \mathbf{b}_{0j})$ where $\mathbf{x}_k = [\mathbf{s}_2^T, \mathbf{s}_k'^T]^T$. We can apply the method described in chapter 8 to select those segments S_k that are good potential matches by computing a Mahalanobis distance. This is done as follows. Let Λ_{0j} be the matrix defined by

$$\Lambda_{0j} = \frac{\partial \mathbf{f}}{\partial \mathbf{a}} \mathbf{M}_{0j} \frac{\partial \mathbf{f}}{\partial \mathbf{a}}^T + \frac{\partial \mathbf{f}}{\partial \mathbf{x}} \mathbf{U}_k \frac{\partial \mathbf{f}}{\partial \mathbf{x}}^T$$

in which the partial derivatives are evaluated at $\mathbf{x} = \mathbf{x}_k$ and $\mathbf{a} = \mathbf{b}_{0j}$ and

$$\mathbf{U}_k = \begin{bmatrix} \mathbf{R}_2 & \mathbf{0} \\ \mathbf{0} & \mathbf{R}'_k \end{bmatrix}$$

is the covariance (weight) of $\mathbf{x}_k$. These matches such that the Mahalanobis distance $d_{2k} = \mathbf{f}(\mathbf{x}_k, \mathbf{b}_{0j}) \Lambda_{0j}^{-1} \mathbf{f}(\mathbf{x}_k, \mathbf{b}_{0j})^T$ is less than a given threshold pro-

---

3. If the segments are oriented, only one transformation is obtained.

4. In practice one often reduces this number by bucketing. See chapter 10.

vide a new estimate $\hat{\mathbf{a}}_0^{(k)}$ of the representation of the transformation from model to scene and a matrix $\mathbf{P}_0^{(k)}$ of its covariance (weight) matrix.

The reader will have already discovered that we are discussing here the case described in chapter 8 as the constant-state nonlinear measurement equation case. The plant equation is

$$\mathbf{a}_i = \mathbf{a}_{i-1} + \mathbf{w}_{i-1}$$

where the index i refers not to time as in chapter 8, but rather to the level in the interpretation tree. Depending on whether or not the model for the transformation T is correct, i.e., whether it represents well the transformation from model to scene, we may or may not introduce the error $\mathbf{w}_i$ and its covariance (weight) matrix $\mathbf{Q}_i$. The partial derivatives $\frac{\partial \mathbf{f}}{\partial \mathbf{a}}$ and $\frac{\partial \mathbf{f}}{\partial \mathbf{x}}$ that are needed for equations (8.38)–(8.40) can be computed from equations (11.3)–(11.6) (see problem 3).

Each nonmatched scene segment S_k whose Mahalanobis distance with $T_{0j}(M_2)$ is less than the threshold is used, as we said before, to update the estimate of T_{0j}. Those scene segments whose distance is above the threshold are not considered. We may thus considerably reduce the size of the interpretation tree explored since, for these S_k, the node (M_2, S_k) does not generate any further branches. The *NIL* label is always considered, i.e., the node (M_2, NIL) is added without changing the initial state vector $\mathbf{b}_{0j}$ and its covariance (weight) matrix $\mathbf{M}_{0j}$.

11.3.4 Finishing the search

Using the previous technique, we build a number of recognition sequences $R_n^{(i)} = ((M_1, S_{i_1}), \ldots, (M_n, S_{i_n}))$, each one characterized by a transformation $T^{(i)}$ represented by $\mathbf{a}^{(i)}$, weighted by $\mathbf{P}^{(i)}$. A total error $\varepsilon_n^{(i)}$ can be computed for each recognition sequence by expanding the measurement equation $\mathbf{f}$ in the vicinity of each $(\mathbf{x}_j, \mathbf{a}^{(i)})$, $j = 1, \ldots, n$ corresponding to the match (M_j, S_{i_j})[5]

$$d_j = \mathbf{f}(\mathbf{x}_j, \mathbf{a}^{(i)}) \Lambda_j^{-1} \mathbf{f}(\mathbf{x}_j, \mathbf{a}^{(i)})^T$$

---

5. If $S_{i_j} = NIL$ we do not compute anything and set $d_j = 0$.

where

$$\Lambda_j = \frac{\partial \mathbf{f}}{\partial \mathbf{a}} \mathbf{P}^{(i)} \frac{\partial \mathbf{f}}{\partial \mathbf{a}^T} + \frac{\partial \mathbf{f}}{\partial \mathbf{x}} \mathbf{U}_j \frac{\partial \mathbf{f}}{\partial \mathbf{x}^T}$$

In this equation, all partial derivatives are computed at $(\mathbf{x}_j, \mathbf{a}^{(i)})$ and $\mathbf{U}_j$ is the covariance (weight) matrix of $\mathbf{x}_j = [\mathbf{s}_j^T, \mathbf{s}_{i_j}'^T]^T$ equal to

$$\begin{bmatrix} \mathbf{R}_j & \mathbf{0} \\ \mathbf{0} & \mathbf{R}_{i_j}' \end{bmatrix}$$

The error corresponding to the recognition sequence $R^{(i)}$ is then

$$\varepsilon_n^{(i)} = \frac{1}{n} \sum_{j=1}^{n} d_j$$

A second measure of the quality of the sequence is $D^{(i)} = 1 - \frac{p_i}{n}$, where p_i is the number of times the symbol *NIL* occurs in the sequence $S_{i_j}, j = 1, \ldots, n$.[6] The two values $C^{(i)}$ and $D^{(i)}$ characterize the quality of the recognition sequence $R^{(i)}$. They can be used to select those that will be accepted (they have been used to define the quality measure of table 11.1).

11.3.5   Examples

The system that we have described was developed by Nicholas Ayache for his master's thesis [Aya83, AF86].

11.3.5.1   *A didactic example*

In figure 11.11 we present a simple example that demonstrates how, when exploring the interpretation tree and following the right path, the estimation of the position and orientation of the model in the scene

---

6. The number of matches can also be used to reduce the depth of the explored interpretation tree as follows. Suppose that we insist on having at least a percentage q of the model primitives recognized in the scene in order to validate a recognition sequence. If at level k in the tree the number of *NIL* symbols is larger than $\lceil nq \rceil$ for a given partial recognition sequence $R^{(i)}$, then that particular sequence can be stopped because it will never reach the threshold q.

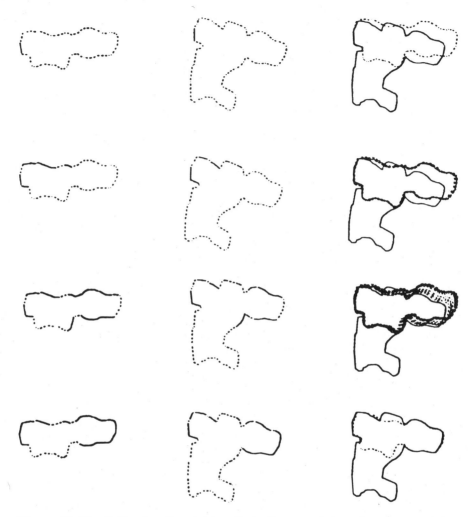

Figure 11.11 Following the right path in the search tree: improvement in the model localization.

improves, making it easier and easier to match more model primitives to scene primitives. The model is that of the left object in figure 11.8, and the scene is composed of two such objects lying on top of each other. The first column shows the model, the second one the scene. The solid lines in both columns are the segments that have been matched, the dotted lines those that have not been matched. The third column shows the scene in solid lines, and superposed on it in dotted lines is the current estimate of the position and orientation of the model in the scene. For example, the first row of the figure shows the estimation of position and orientation when only one match has been performed, and that particular match is represented in the first and second columns by the segment that is a solid line. Row four shows the final estimation of the model position and orientation in the third column, while the first and second show the segments that have been matched between the model and the scene.

11.3.5.2 *A more complicated example*

Figure 11.12 shows a bin containing the objects in figure 11.8 in two of their static equilibrium positions, the representation of the scene with polygons (containing 280 line segments), and the polygonal approximations of the four models. Note that the objects not only overlap each other, but that some of them also have sprues and dead-heads attached to them due to the casting process. After searching for the first model, it has been recognized with the best score in the position and orientation shown in figure 11.13. In this figure, both the model and the scene are represented. The solid lines in the model indicate the segments that have been matched, while the dotted lines indicate those which have not. The model has been superposed on the scene with the position and orientation calculated by the algorithm. Figures 11.14-11.16 show the analog for models two, three, and four of figure 11.9.

To give the reader a better idea of what happens in the algorithm, figure 11.17 shows the results for some wrong hypotheses. They can be compared with the correct results of figures 11.13–11.16 both visually as well as by means of the quality measures defined in section 11.3.4. These quality measures and the computing time are given in table 11.1.

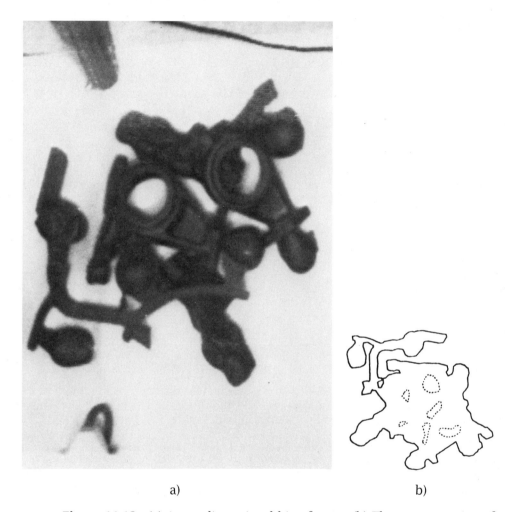

a)   b)

Figure 11.12   (a) A two-dimensional bin of parts. (b) The representation of the scene with line segments.

Figure 11.13   The first model of figure 11.9 identified in the scene of figure 11.12 and its superposition with the scene in the position and orientation calculated by the algorithm described in sections 11.3.2 – 11.3.4.

Figure 11.14   The second model of figure 11.9 identified in the scene of figure 11.12 and its superposition with the scene in the position and orientation calculated by the algorithm described in sections 11.3.2 – 11.3.4.

11.3.5.3   *Coupling perception, recognition, localization, and action*

As a final example of the two-dimensional system, we show a case where the results of the computer vision system are used as an input to drive a robot manipulator that picks up the object that has been recognized and located and repositions it somewhere else on the working bench. Figure 11.6 shows a photograph of the two-dimensional bin. The parts are from an electromechanical device. Figure 11.18 also shows the image acquired by the camera located above the bin and the polygonal approximation constructed from it, which contains 759 segments. The models for some of these parts are displayed in figure 11.10.

Figure 11.15 The third model of figure 11.9 identified in the scene of figure 11.12 and its superposition with the scene in the position and orientation calculated by the algorithm described in sections 11.3.2–11.3.4.

Figure 11.16 The fourth model of figure 11.9 identified in the scene of figure 11.12 and its superposition with the scene in the position and orientation calculated by the algorithm described in sections 11.3.2–11.3.4.

The result of the recognition and localization of the upper left-hand model in figure 11.10 in the scene is presented in figure 11.19, where the model is overlaid with the image in the position and its orientation is computed by the algorithm. Once a model has been localized in the scene, the system uses the representation of the scene of figure 11.18 and a catalog of grasping locations, which has been computed elsewhere, to check whether there is enough room to grasp a given object. Figure 11.20 shows the picking and repositioning of the object corresponding to the same model by the robot manipulator.

Table 11.1   Recognition and localization of models 1, 2, 3, and 4.

Model	Number of segments	Quality measure
1	39	54%
2	41	55%
3	50	45%
4	50	40%

11.3.6   More references

The Hough transform has been used in several systems for the recognition of planar objects [SKB82, TMV85, DRR86]. Bolles and Cain [BC82] use a combination of the hypotheses and test paradigms to obtain a reasonable number of matching hypotheses and to search for maximal cliques to prune these hypotheses. The approach is known as the *local feature focus approach*. Grimson and Lozano-Pérez search the interpretation tree while using constraints on the model, such as the constraint that it is rigid [GL84, GL87, Gri89a] or that it can vary in a way that can be parameterized with a reasonably small number of parameters [Gri89b]. But they do not attempt to facilitate the tree search by estimating the model-to-scene transformation. An excellent description and analysis, from the complexity standpoint, of the search process in the interpretation tree approach, as well as of many other related approaches, can be found in the book by Grimson [Gri90].

Schwartz and Sharir [SS87] concentrate more on the problem of the efficient estimation of the model-to-scene rigid transformation in the general case where the boundaries of objects and models are represented by general curves. A quite different approach to the problem of object recognition has been proposed by Forsyth *et al.* in which they eliminate the need to compute the pose of objects through the computation of quantities that are unaffected by object pose, perspective projection, and the intrinsic parameters of the camera [FMZ*91].

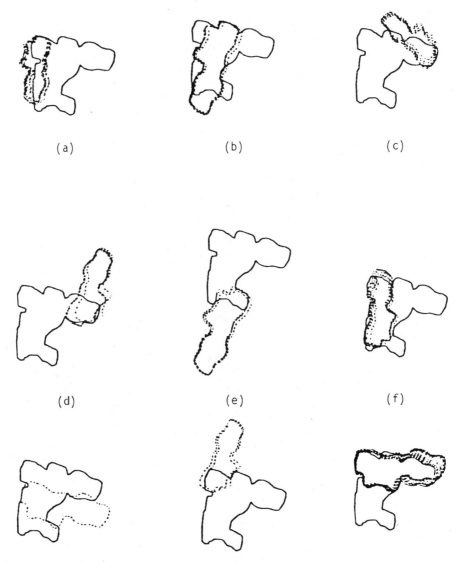

Figure 11.17 The results of some wrong hypotheses for the bin of figure 11.12 (the correct one is the one at the bottom right).

a)

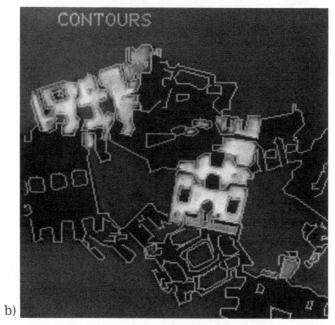

b)

Figure 11.18   The digital image of the scene of figure 11.6 (a), and its polygonal approximation (b).

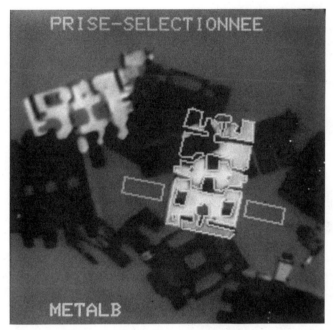

Figure 11.19   A result of the algorithm on the bin of figure 11.18.

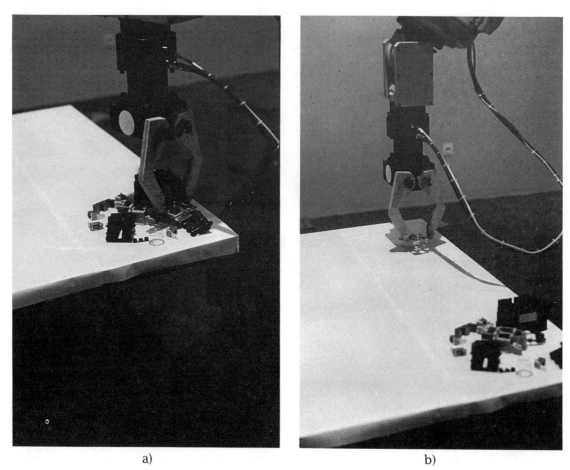

a)   b)

Figure 11.20   The robot manipulator picking up an object.

11.4   Recognizing and determining the pose of 3-D objects

Ideas very similar to those of the previous section can be applied to the problem of recognizing and locating 3D objects from 3D measurements. These measurements are obtained either from stereo and motion or from any kind of rangefinder such as the one described in the next section (see [Jar83, Kan87] for more examples). In this section we concentrate on the use of a laser rangefinder, the use of stereo will be described in section 11.5.

11.4.1   Building models and scene descriptions

We describe a triangulation laser range finder developed at INRIA. A laser source is used to produce a beam that falls on a system of moving mirrors that is used to control its direction in space. The laser beam produces a bright spot on the objects to be modeled that is imaged by a number of cameras forming a calibrated stereo rig. Since this bright spot can, in general, be accurately detected in all images, there is no ambiguity in matching, and the three-dimensional position of the spot is reconstructed by triangulation. This is the principle of *active stereo* (see figure 11.21). Two such systems have been built at INRIA by Georges Kryze and François Germain. In the first one, the laser beam can move only in a plane: There is only one mirror whose position is controlled by a galvanometer. Two cameras are used to analyze the scene (figure 11.22). Since the laser beam moves in a plane, the objects are placed on a computer-controlled table with two degrees of freedom: one rotation around a vertical axis and a translation along that same axis. The combination of these two degrees allows for the exploration of most of the surfaces of the objects (figure 11.23). A second system with two moving mirrors with their axes at right angles has also been built. This extra degree of freedom allows for the exploration of all directions of space. Three cameras are used in this case (figure 11.24).

Either one of these systems produces a set of three-dimensional points M represented by their coordinates (x, y, and z) in a coordinate system attached to the stereo rig. This set of points is processed as explained in the previous chapter; first we compute a Delaunay triangulation, and

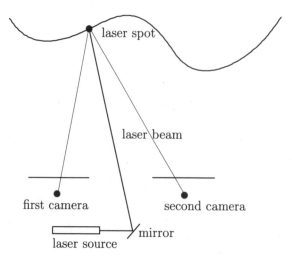

Figure 11.21 The principle of active stereo using a triangulation laser range finder.

Figure 11.22 A photograph of the first INRIA 2-D laser range finder.

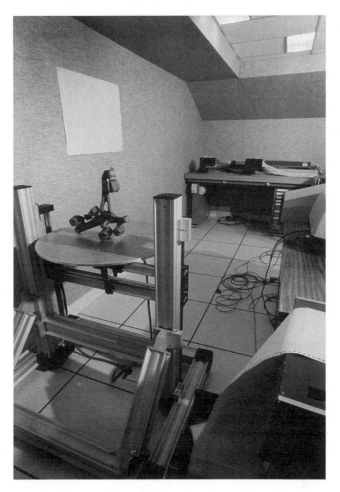

Figure 11.23   A photograph of the first INRIA 2-D laser range finder and the computer-controlled rotating table.

Figure 11.24 A photograph of the three cameras of the second INRIA 3-D laser range finder.

second we throw away the tetrahedra that are intersected by optical rays. The result is a triangulation of the surface of the object or of the scene from which we build more compact descriptions, such as approximations with planes and quadrics (see chapter 10).

As a further example, let us consider the object of figure 11.25. Figure 11.26 shows one set of measured 3-D points on its surface, figure 11.27 shows the boundary of the original Delaunay triangulation (i.e., the convex hull of the measured points), and figure 11.28 shows two views from two different viewpoints of the resulting triangulation of the object's surface. Figure 11.29 shows the approximation with larger planar faces constructed from this triangulation by the technique described in chapter 10. Dotted lines indicate hidden faces. Note that this is the three-dimensional analog of the polygonal approximations of figures 11.9 and 11.10 (in fact, one of the parts in these figures is the silhouette of the object of figure 11.25).

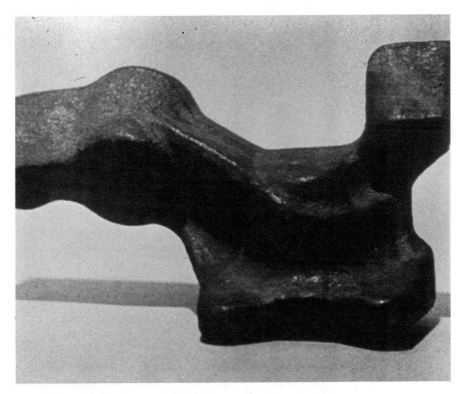

Figure 11.25   A photograph of a Renault part.

As in section 11.3, models and scenes are described in different co-ordinate systems, and we make the assumption that the transformation from model to scene is a rotation around an axis going through the origin, followed by a translation. This transformation T is represented by a six-dimensional vector $\mathbf{a} = [\mathbf{r}^T, \mathbf{t}^T]^T$, where $\mathbf{r}$ is a three-dimensional vector representing the rotation (see section 5.5.3 or 5.5.4) and $\mathbf{t}$ is the vector of translation. Each planar facet in the model and in the scene is represented by its underlying infinite plane (more detailed descriptions including the shape of the boundary could be used).

The plane is represented by a three-dimensional vector $\mathbf{p} = [a, b, c]^T$ in one of three possible maps, as explained in section 5.4.3.2. Each such plane has a covariance (weight) matrix Λ associated with it, which can be computed by the methods described in section 5.6 (see also problem 6 of chapter 8 for the case of lines).

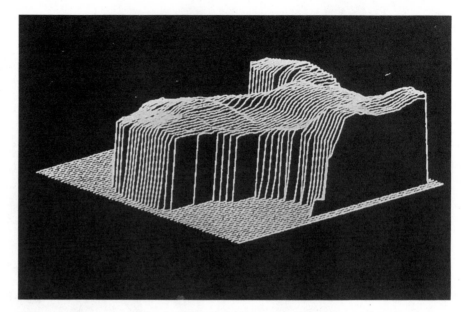

Figure 11.26 An isometric plot of the 3-D points measured by laser range finder on the surface of the Renault part.

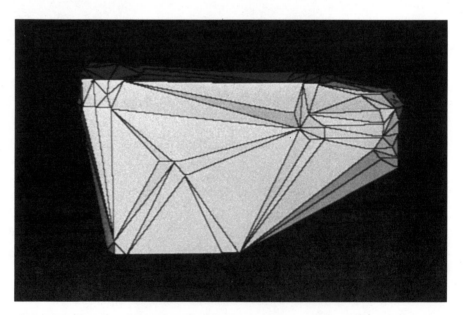

Figure 11.27 The original Delaunay triangulation of the points on the Renault part.

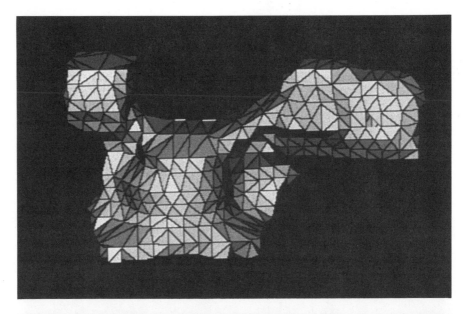

Figure 11.28   Two views of the final triangulation.

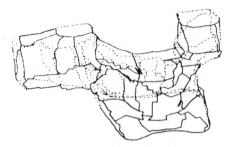

Figure 11.29   An approximation of the triangulation of figure 11.28.

11.4.2   The effect of the transformation T on a plane represented by **p**

Let **R** be the rotation matrix defining the rotation, and let us consider the 4×4 matrix **D** defined by

$$\mathbf{D} = \begin{bmatrix} \mathbf{R} & \mathbf{t} \\ \mathbf{0} & 1 \end{bmatrix}$$

The matrix **D** is a projective representation of the displacement T (see chapter 2). We have

$$\mathbf{D}^{-1} = \begin{bmatrix} \mathbf{R}^T & -\mathbf{R}^T \mathbf{t} \\ \mathbf{0} & 1 \end{bmatrix}$$

We know from chapter 5, equations (5.20) and (5.26), that **R** is a simple function of **r**. Let us suppose that the plane is represented in the map φ_1 (section 5.4.3.2). The coefficients of the equation of the transformed plane are

$$\mathbf{D}^{-1T} \begin{bmatrix} 1 \\ \mathbf{p} \end{bmatrix} \tag{11.7}$$

Let us make all this more explicit. Suppose we want to represent the transformed plane in the same map, φ_1. Let us call $\mathbf{r}_i^T, i = 1, 2, 3$ the row vectors of matrix **R**; let **m** be the vector $[1, a, b]^T$, which is normal to the plane; and let $\mathbf{p}' = [a', b', c']^T$ be the representation of the transformed plane. From equation (11.7), we can write

$$a' = \frac{\mathbf{r}_2^T \mathbf{m}}{\mathbf{r}_1^T \mathbf{m}} \tag{11.8}$$

$$b' = \frac{\mathbf{r}_3^T \mathbf{m}}{\mathbf{r}_1^T \mathbf{m}} \tag{11.9}$$

$$c' = \frac{-\mathbf{t}^T \mathbf{R} \mathbf{m} + c}{\mathbf{r}_1^T \mathbf{m}} \tag{11.10}$$

These three equations define a measurement equation $\mathbf{f}(\mathbf{x}, \mathbf{a}) = \mathbf{0}$, which arises each time we decide to match the model plane represented by $\mathbf{p}$ to the scene plane represented by $\mathbf{p}'$, where $\mathbf{x} = [\mathbf{p}^T, \mathbf{p}'^T]^T$ and $\mathbf{a}$ is the above representation of T.

11.4.3   Searching the interpretation tree

The main difference from the two-dimensional case studied in the previous section is that, in order to define the rotation part of T, we need to match two nonparallel planes in the model to two planes in the scene. The angle of the two model planes must be equal to the angle of the two scene planes. Because of errors this is rarely the case, and a best approximation must be found. We will show that there are, in general, four different rotations that are solutions to this problem.

11.4.3.1   Finding the initial rotations

Let M_1 and M_2 be the model planes, and let S_1 and S_2 be the scene planes. Let $\mathbf{n}_1, \mathbf{n}_2, \mathbf{n}'_1$, and $\mathbf{n}'_2$ be the corresponding unit normals. Note that, if there is no intrinsic way of orienting the normals, we can also use $-\mathbf{n}_1, -\mathbf{n}_2, -\mathbf{n}'_1$, and $-\mathbf{n}'_2$. For the particular sensor that we have been discussing in section 11.4.1 one knows on which side of the plane the object lies, and this defines a coherent way of orienting the normals by assuming, for example, that they point toward the outside of the object. We assume that (M_1, S_1) and (M_2, S_2) are the two matches, and we look for the rotation matrix $\mathbf{R}$ such that

$$C = \sum_{i=1}^{2} \| \varepsilon'_i \mathbf{n}'_i - \varepsilon_i \mathbf{R} \mathbf{n}_i \|^2 = 0$$

where $\varepsilon_i, \varepsilon'_i = \pm 1$. Since C can be rewritten

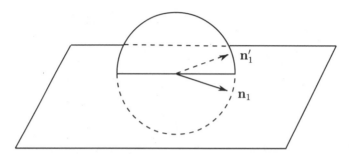

Figure 11.30 Matching two normal vectors forces the rotation axis to lie in a plane.

$$\sum_{i=1}^{2} \|\mathbf{n}'_i - \varepsilon_i \varepsilon'_i \mathbf{R} \mathbf{n}_i\|^2 = 0$$

it is clear that there are only four possibilities. That each possibility yields only one solution can be understood geometrically. Let us look at figure 11.30. From this figure it is clear that the set of rotations bringing $\mathbf{n}_1$ to $\mathbf{n}'_1$ have their axes lying in the plane of the unit circle shown in the figure. This plane is, of course, the bisector plane of the angle $(\mathbf{n}_1, \mathbf{n}'_1)$. If we now add the two vectors $\mathbf{n}_2$ and $\mathbf{n}'_2$ to this figure, they define another unit circle that will, in general, intersect the first one at two points that are antipodal on the unit sphere on which the two circles are drawn. These two points define the same rotation that brings $\mathbf{n}_1$ onto $\mathbf{n}'_1$ and $\mathbf{n}_2$ onto $\mathbf{n}'_2$.

Now we compute a representation of this rotation. In doing so we assume the more general case where we have some measurement errors, and we minimize with respect to the rotation matrix $\mathbf{R}$ the following criterion:

$$C = \sum_{i=1}^{2} \|\mathbf{n}'_i - \mathbf{R} \mathbf{n}_i\|^2$$

We denote by $\mathbf{q}$ one of the two quaternions representing $\mathbf{R}$, and we use formula (5.17) to obtain

$$C = \sum_{i=1}^{2} |\, \mathbf{n}'_i - \mathbf{q} \times \mathbf{n}_i \times \overline{\mathbf{q}} \,|^2$$

where vectors and quaternions are identified. Because $\mathbf{q}$ represents a rotation, $|\mathbf{q}|^2 = 1$. Therefore we can multiply the previous equation by $|\mathbf{q}|^2$:

$$\sum_{i=1}^{2} (|\mathbf{n}'_i - \mathbf{q} \times \mathbf{n}_i \times \overline{\mathbf{q}}| \cdot |\mathbf{q}|)^2$$

Since the magnitude of the quaternion is compatible with its product, this is the same as

$$\sum_{i=1}^{2} |\mathbf{n}'_i \times \mathbf{q} - \mathbf{q} \times \mathbf{n}_i \times \overline{\mathbf{q}} \times \mathbf{q}|^2$$

Since $\overline{\mathbf{q}} \times \mathbf{q} = |\mathbf{q}|^2 = 1$, we finally have

$$\sum_{i=1}^{2} |\mathbf{n}'_i \times \mathbf{q} - \mathbf{q} \times \mathbf{n}_i|^2 \tag{11.11}$$

It follows from the definition of the product of the quaternion given in chapter 5 that $\mathbf{n}'_i \times \mathbf{q} - \mathbf{q} \times \mathbf{n}_i$ is a linear function of the 4 coordinates of $\mathbf{q}$. Therefore, there exists a 4×4 matrix $\mathbf{A}_i$ such that

$$|\mathbf{n}'_i \times \mathbf{q} - \mathbf{q} \times \mathbf{n}_i|^2 = \mathbf{q}^T \mathbf{A}_i^T \mathbf{A}_i \mathbf{q}$$

where $\mathbf{q}$ denotes the 4×1 vector attached to the quaternion. The problem can be rewritten as

$$\min_{\mathbf{q}} \mathbf{q}^T \mathbf{A} \mathbf{q} \tag{11.12}$$

with

$$\mathbf{A} = \sum_{i=1}^{2} \mathbf{A}_i^T \mathbf{A}_i$$

and with the constraint on the vector $\mathbf{q}$ being $\|\mathbf{q}\|^2 = 1$. As shown in appendix A, the solution to problem (11.12) is the eigenvector of unit length of matrix $\mathbf{A}$ corresponding to the smallest eigenvalue.

In the noiseless case, matrix $\mathbf{A}$ is of rank 3 in general. Therefore there exists a 4×1 unit vector $\mathbf{q}_0$ such that $\mathbf{A}\mathbf{q}_0 = \mathbf{0}$. The rotation represented by $\mathbf{q}_0$ and $-\mathbf{q}_0$ is the solution to our problem. Thus, even if it is a bit tedious, we have an analytical expression for each of the four rotation solutions of our initial problem, and therefore, going back to the original representation, we can write an expression such as

$$\mathbf{r}_0^{(i)} = \mathbf{h}^{(i)}(\mathbf{p}_1, \mathbf{p}_1', \mathbf{p}_2, \mathbf{p}_2') \qquad i = 1, \ldots, 4$$

Using the methods of chapter 5 and knowing the covariance (weight) matrices $\mathbf{Q}_1, \mathbf{Q}_1', \mathbf{Q}_2, \mathbf{Q}_2'$ of $\mathbf{p}_1, \mathbf{p}_1', \mathbf{p}_2$, and $\mathbf{p}_2'$, we can compute a first-order approximation to the bound $\Lambda_0^{(i)}$ on $\mathbf{r}_0^{(i)}$. Note that the translation vector $\mathbf{t}$ cannot be computed at this stage: It can only be constrained by the two equations (11.10), in which we replace $\mathbf{R}$ by one of the computed rotation matrices.

11.4.3.2   *Continuing the search*

The continuation of the search is fairly similar to what we have described in the two-dimensional case, except for the fact that the translation is still undetermined. For the next unmatched model primitive M_3 represented by $\mathbf{p}_3$, we select those unmatched scene primitives S_k represented by $\mathbf{p}_k'$ that are possible matches as follows. We restrict our attention to the measurement equations (11.8) and (11.9), which involve only the rotation part of T, and we consider them as one measurement equation $\mathbf{f}'(\mathbf{x}, \mathbf{r})$. Linearizing $\mathbf{f}'$ in the vicinity of $\mathbf{x}_k = [\mathbf{p}_3^T, \mathbf{p}_k'^T]^T$ and $\mathbf{r}_0$, we can write

$$\mathbf{f}'(\mathbf{x}, \mathbf{r}) = \mathbf{f}'(\mathbf{x}_k, \mathbf{r}_0) + \frac{\partial \mathbf{f}'}{\partial \mathbf{x}} \cdot (\mathbf{x} - \mathbf{x}_k) + \frac{\partial \mathbf{f}'}{\partial \mathbf{r}} \cdot (\mathbf{r} - \mathbf{r}_0)$$

We define[7]

$$\Lambda_k = \frac{\partial \mathbf{f}'}{\partial \mathbf{r}} \Lambda_0 \frac{\partial \mathbf{f}'}{\partial \mathbf{r}^T} + \frac{\partial \mathbf{f}'}{\partial \mathbf{x}} \begin{bmatrix} \mathbf{Q}_3 & \mathbf{0} \\ \mathbf{0} & \mathbf{Q}_k' \end{bmatrix} \frac{\partial \mathbf{f}'}{\partial \mathbf{x}^T}$$

Only the scene primitives S_k for which the Mahalanobis distance $d_k = \mathbf{f}'(\mathbf{x}_k, \mathbf{r}_0) \Lambda_k^{-1} \mathbf{f}'^T(\mathbf{x}_k, \mathbf{r}_0)$ is less than some threshold are kept and used as follows.

First, a new estimate $\hat{\mathbf{r}}_0^{(k)}$ of the representation is obtained by applying the Kalman equations using the new measurement equation $\mathbf{f}'(\mathbf{x}_k, \mathbf{r}) = \mathbf{0}$. This also yields a bound $\mathbf{P}_0^{(k)}$ on $\hat{\mathbf{r}}_0^{(k)}$. Second, we compute an estimate $\mathbf{t}_0^{(k)}$ of the translation $\mathbf{t}$ by solving the system of linear equations (11.10) given by the three matches. Since $\mathbf{t}_0^{(k)}$ is given by a

---

7. We have changed the traditional $\mathbf{R}_3$ and $\mathbf{R}_k'$ to $\mathbf{Q}_3$ and $\mathbf{Q}_k'$ to avoid confusion with rotation matrices.

formula $\mathbf{t}_0^{(k)} = \mathbf{h}(\mathbf{p}_1, \mathbf{p}_2, \mathbf{p}_3, \mathbf{p}_1', \mathbf{p}_2', \mathbf{p}_k', \mathbf{r}_0)$, we can compute a bound[8] $\mathbf{M}_0^{(k)}$ on $\mathbf{b}_0^{(k)} = [\mathbf{r}_0^{(k)T}, \mathbf{t}_0^{(k)T}]^T$ (see problem 7). It is thus at level 4 of the interpretation tree that we can start the standard procedure. Just as in the two-dimensional case, we are in the situation of a constant-state nonlinear measurement equation.

The plant equation is

$$\mathbf{a}_i = \mathbf{a}_{i-1} + \mathbf{w}_{i-1}$$

where the index i refers to the level in the interpretation tree. The measurement equation is given by the three equations (11.8)–(11.10) from which the required derivatives $\frac{\partial \mathbf{f}}{\partial \mathbf{x}}$ and $\frac{\partial \mathbf{f}}{\partial \mathbf{a}}$ can be computed (see problem 6). The general step consists of a prediction in which we apply the current estimate T_0 of the transformation T represented by $\mathbf{b}_0$ with covariance (weight) matrix $\mathbf{M}_0$ to the next unmatched model primitive M_4. For each unmatched scene primitive S_k represented by $\mathbf{p}_k'$ we compute the Mahalanobis distance d_k using the full measurement equation $\mathbf{f}$. All the matches (M_4, S_k) for which d_k is less than the threshold are accepted, and the state is updated to $\hat{\mathbf{a}}_0^{(k)}$ with covariance (weight) matrix $\mathbf{P}_0^{(k)}$. The *NIL* match is always considered, i.e., the node (M_4, NIL) is added without changing the state $\mathbf{b}_0$.

11.4.4 Finishing the search

The process is formally exactly the same as described in section 11.3.4.

11.4.5 Examples

The system that we have described was developed by Martial Hébert for his Ph.D. thesis [Heb83, FH86]. We will show several examples of the results of his program on a variety of bins containing several parts, such as the one shown in figure 11.25. Each bin has been scanned by the laser range finder of figure 11.23. The scans are only from one viewpoint, i.e., we do not rotate the table to operate under conditions that are close to what can be found in a real application. As explained in section 11.4.1,

---

8. We neglect the fact that $\hat{\mathbf{r}}_0^{(k)}$ is itself a function of $\mathbf{p}_1, \mathbf{p}_2, \mathbf{p}_3, \mathbf{p}_1', \mathbf{p}_2'$, and $\mathbf{p}_k'$

the model of the part has been built from data obtained by combining the rotation and the translation of the table.

The scenes are "range images" that are displayed in a rather unusual manner. Since at each pixel we have the depth, it is straightforward to compute the normal to the object, which is oriented in such a way that it points toward the outside of the object. If we then project this unit vector along an axis directed toward the cameras, we obtain a value close to 1 for those pixels whose normals are pointing toward the cameras and close to 0 for those pixels whose normals are pointing at 90 degrees. Such an "image" is displayed in figure 11.31. We apply the algorithm for finding planar regions, which has been described in the previous chapter, and find a number of planar regions that are shown in figure 11.32. We then apply the algorithm described in sections 11.4.2–11.4.4 to the model of figure 11.29 and the scene represented by figure 11.32 and find the first instantiation of the model in the scene. This is shown in

Figure 11.31 The image of the normals of a first bin containing three parts (see text).

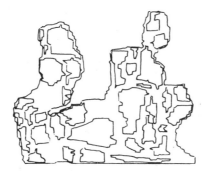

Figure 11.32   The planar regions found in the first bin.

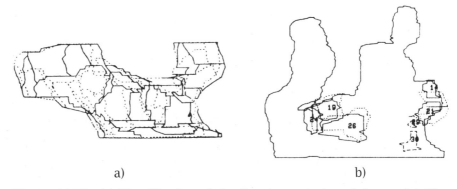

a)   b)

Figure 11.33   (a) Identification of the first instantiation of the model. The model is shown with the orientation computed by the algorithm. (b) The model faces that have been matched (dotted lines) are superposed on their corresponding scene faces (solid lines).

figure 11.33, where we show the model in the orientation computed by the algorithm and the superposition of the model on the scene, where in solid lines we show the scene primitives that have been matched to the model primitives, which are shown in light dotted lines.

Similar results are shown in figures 11.34 and 11.35. Figure 11.36 shows the "image" of a second bin containing four Renault parts. The results are presented in a different format from that used for the first bin. Figure 11.37 shows four things: The upper left corner displays in green the segmentation of the scene into planar faces. The lower left corner displays in blue the model of the Renault part, which is also segmented

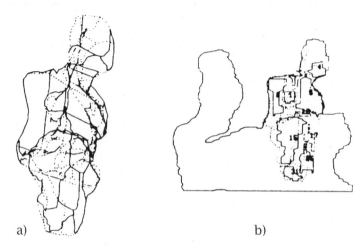

a)   b)

Figure 11.34   (a) Identification of the second instantiation of the model. The model is shown with the orientation computed by the algorithm. (b) The model faces that have been matched (dotted lines) are superposed on their corresponding scene faces (solid lines).

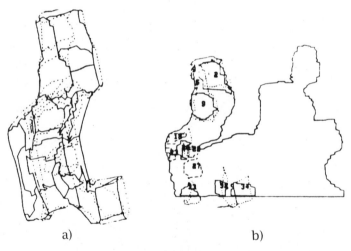

a)   b)

Figure 11.35   (a) Identification of the third instantiation of the model. The model is shown with the orientation computed by the algorithm. (b) The model faces that have been matched (dotted lines) are superposed on their corresponding scene faces (solid lines).

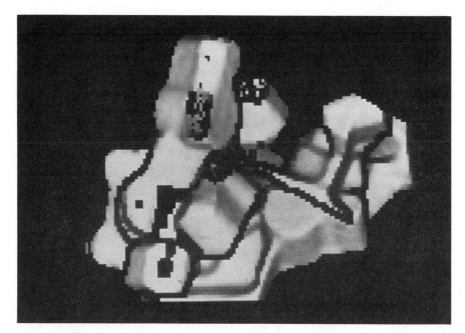

Figure 11.36 The image of the normals of a second bin containing four parts (see text).

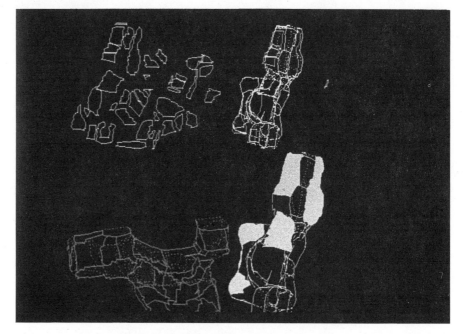

Figure 11.37 Starting from the upper left and going counterclockwise: Planar faces of the second bin, the model of the Renault part, the orientation of its first instantiation in the bin, and the superposition of the matched faces of the model and the scene.

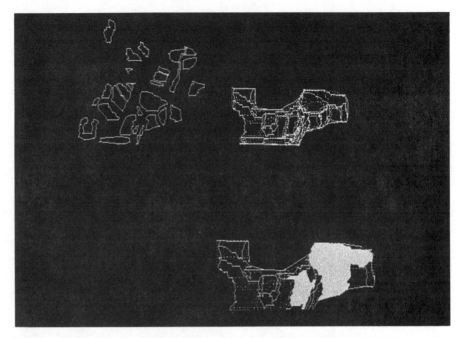

Figure 11.38 Starting from the upper left and going counterclockwise: Planar faces of the second bin, the orientation of the second instantiation of the model in the bin, and the superposition of the matched faces of the model and the scene.

into planar faces. The lower right corner shows that model in the orientation computed by the algorithm for its first instantiation in the scene; the faces that have been matched are painted green. Finally, the upper right corner shows the superposition of the faces of the model and the scene which have been matched by the algorithm. Figures 11.38–11.40 show the same results (without the model) for the instantiations 2, 3, and 4 of the model in the scene.

Computing times vary between 2 and 10 seconds on a Sun 3-50 workstation.

11.4.6 More references

The papers by Besl and Cain [BC85, Bes90] give a good overview of some of the problems and solutions in the area of three-dimensional object

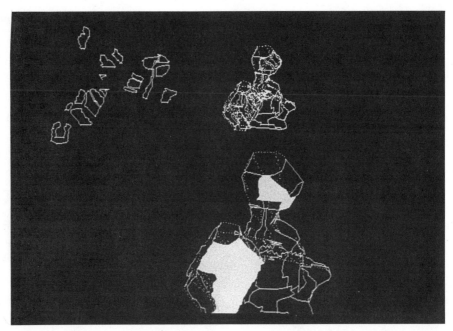

Figure 11.39 Starting from the upper left and going counterclockwise: Planar faces of the second bin, the orientation of the third instantiation of the model in the bin, and the superposition of the matched faces of the model and the scene.

recognition. Oshima and Shirai [OS83] have used the graph-matching ideas to recognize objects in range images obtained from a laser range finder. Bolles and Horaud [BH86] have used the local feature focus approach developed by Bolles and Cain [BC82] in three dimensions. Dhome and Kasvand [DK87] use a variation of the Hough transform idea to recognize polyhedra. Besl and McKay [BM92] describe a fairly general method for registering 3-D shapes.

We have not discussed the problem of recognizing and computing the pose of three-dimensional objects from 3-D models and 2-D images, but this has been and remains an active area for research by such individuals as Lowe [Low85, Low87], Dhome et al. [DRLR89], Huttenlocher and Ullman [HU87, HU90], and Worrall et al. [WBS89], all of whom use strategies similar to the one described in section 11.2.2.3. In contrast to them, Thompson and Mundy [TM87] use a variation of the Hough transform

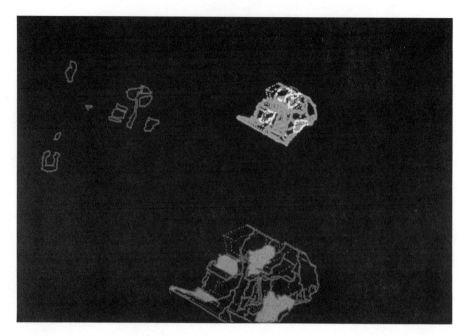

Figure 11.40 Starting from the upper left and going counterclockwise: Planar faces of the second bin, the orientation of the fourth instantiation of the model in the bin, and the superposition of the matched faces of the model and the scene.

technique. Ponce, Hoogs, and Kriegman have been using CAD models for computing the pose of 3-D objects from range data or from raw intensity images [PHK92]. Their method involves a mixture of ideas from algebra and differential geometry.

11.5   Optical navigation and model building for a mobile robot

We will now describe a computer vision system that helps a mobile robot perform a number of tasks. We will specifically address two of these tasks: optical navigation and model building. Both tasks are performed using inputs provided by the stereo vision system described in section 6.9.1. Optical navigation is concerned with the determination of the robot's ego-motion and the motions of other possibly moving bodies. The ego-motion part can be thought of as a complement to other

Figure 11.41   A photograph of the INRIA mobile robot.

sensing procedures such as odometry or inertial sensing. Model building is concerned with putting together a large number of three-dimensional views of the environment of the robot into a coherent three-dimensional wireframe model that can then be interpolated/approximated by the methods described in chapter 10. The reader will remember that this trinocular stereo system produces three-dimensional line segments with some uncertainty. Figure 11.41 shows the robot cart with the trinocular stereo rig mounted on it. The robot has two driving wheels and can move on a flat ground at a speed of up to 2 m/s. The stereo rig can rotate rigidly around a vertical axis. By combining its ego-motion with the rotation of the rig, the robot can easily "look around" to analyze its environment.

11.5.1   Optical navigation

The problem of optical navigation is conceptually very similar to the one discussed in section 11.4. For a given position of the robot, the stereo system produces a three-dimensional map of its environment. This map is a set of three-dimensional line segments $M_i, i = 1, \ldots, n$. The robot then moves a bit and produces another three-dimensional map composed of another set of three-dimensional line segments $S_k, k = 1, \ldots, p$. These segments are represented in a coordinate system that is rigidly attached to the stereo rig. Therefore, the two sets are not represented in the same coordinate system. The problem is to determine from the two sets of segments the rigid transformation from the first coordinate system to the second. In this section we will assume that nothing but the robot is moving. In the next section we will study the more general situation where other moving objects are also present.

We can clearly use the same formalism as in sections 11.3 and 11.4 and can solve the problem by building recognition sequences $R = ((M_1, S_{i_1}), \ldots, (M_n, S_{i_n}))$ and estimating the best rigid transformation T to bring the model primitive M_j (a three-dimensional line segment in the first visual map) onto the scene primitive S_{i_j} (a three-dimensional line segment in the second visual map) for $j = 1, \ldots, n$. The *NIL* label plays the same role as before. We will use the same representation of line segments as the one in section 8.4.2: direction, midpoint, and length, forming a six-dimensional vector $\mathbf{s} = [a, b, \mathbf{M}^T, l]^T$.

11.5.1.1   *The effect of the representation* T *on the representation* $\mathbf{s}$ *of a segment*

Let us assume that the transformed direction is represented in the same map, for example φ_1, as the original. Then, using $\mathbf{m} = [a, b, 1]^T$

$$a' = \frac{\mathbf{r}_1^T \mathbf{m}}{\mathbf{r}_3^T \mathbf{m}} \tag{11.13}$$

$$b' = \frac{\mathbf{r}_2^T \mathbf{m}}{\mathbf{r}_3^T \mathbf{m}} \tag{11.14}$$

$$\mathbf{M}' = \mathbf{RM} + \mathbf{t} \tag{11.15}$$

$$l' = l \tag{11.16}$$

These six equations define a measurement equation $\mathbf{f}(\mathbf{x}, \mathbf{a}) = \mathbf{0}$, where $\mathbf{x} = [\mathbf{s}^T, \mathbf{s}'^T]^T$ and $\mathbf{a}$ is the representation of T.

11.5.1.2   *Searching the interpretation tree*

The main difference from the case studied in section 11.4 is that the full transformation T is determined by matching two model primitives to two scene primitives. Indeed, let M_1 and M_2 be the two model primitives, and let S_1, S_2 be the two scene primitives. Let $\mathbf{n}_i, \mathbf{n}'_i, i = 1, 2$ be four unit vectors parallel to the segments' directions. Just as in section 11.4.3.1, the rotation matrix is obtained by solving

$$C = \sum_{i=1}^{2} \|\mathbf{n}'_i - \varepsilon'_i \varepsilon_i \mathbf{R} \mathbf{n}_i\|^2 = 0$$

in the errorless case. We know that there are four solutions in general. When errors are present, we minimize C by the same technique as in section 11.4.3.1. The translation is then

$$\mathbf{t} = \mathbf{M}'_1 - \mathbf{R}\mathbf{M}_1 = \mathbf{M}'_2 - \mathbf{R}\mathbf{M}_2$$

in the errorless case, or is obtained by minimizing

$$\sum_{i=1}^{2} \|\mathbf{t} + \mathbf{R}\mathbf{M}_i - \mathbf{M}'_i\|^2$$

when errors are present. In that case

$$\mathbf{t} = \frac{1}{2} \sum_{i=1}^{2} (\mathbf{M}'_i - \mathbf{R}\mathbf{M}_i)$$

yields an initial estimate $\mathbf{b}_0$ of the representation of T as well as a first-order approximation $\mathbf{M}_0$ of its covariance (weight) matrix. The rest of the procedure is the same as described in section 11.4.3.2, replacing the measurement equations 11.8-11.9 with 11.13-11.16.[9]

11.5.1.3   *Examples*

This system has been implemented by Ayache and Zhang [Aya88, Aya89, Zha90, ZF92a] as parts of their Ph.D. theses and has been used on the

---

9. Often equation (11.16) is not used, and equation (11.15) is replaced with $(\mathbf{M}' - \mathbf{R}\mathbf{M} - \mathbf{t}) \wedge \begin{bmatrix} a' \\ b' \\ 1 \end{bmatrix} = \mathbf{0}.$

Figure 11.42   The first view of the Modigliani scene.

INRIA mobile robot to perform optical navigation. The TINA system developed at the University of Sheffield [PPMF87] works somewhat similarly by applying the constrained search approach to stereo data developed by Grimson and Lozano-Pérez [GL84]. As a typical example, in figure 11.42 we show a picture of a scene acquired from one of the three cameras mounted on the robot. It is a fairly complex scene with a robot manipulator on the left behind a reproduction of a painting by the Italian painter Modigliani. In the center of the scene we have a table on which some sort of calibration pattern is standing. In the background we have another table supporting a workstation and, on the right, some file cabinets with posters. The stereo algorithm described in section 6.9 is applied to the triplet of images, and 261 three-dimensional line segments are reconstructed with their uncertainties. Figure 11.43 shows the results of the three-dimensional reconstruction as a cross-eye stereogram.

Figure 11.44 shows the three-dimensional reconstructed scene projected in a frontoparallel (left) and horizontal (right) plane. The triangle represents the three cameras. In both images we have displayed the

Figure 11.43 A cross-eye stereogram showing the results of the stereo reconstruction of the scene shown in figure 11.42.

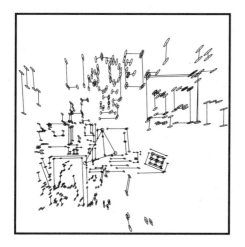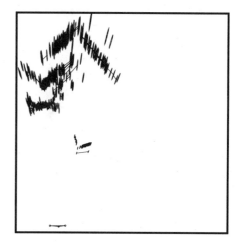

Figure 11.44 Reprojection of the three-dimensional segments of figure 11.43 in a frontoparallel (left) and horizontal (right) plane showing the ellipses of uncertainty of the endpoints.

ellipses of uncertainty that characterize the uncertainty of the endpoints of the reconstructed three-dimensional segments. As explained in chapter 6, these ellipses are the projections in the plane of projection of the ellipsoids defined by the covariance (weight) matrices of the endpoints: The larger the ellipse, the larger the uncertainty. The increase of uncertainty with the increase in distance to the cameras is clearly visible. The segments with the largest ellipses will be given the lowest weight by the Kalman filtering.

The robot then moves backward 75 cm and rotates 10 degrees. The new image seen by the same camera is shown in figure 11.45. We apply the same stereo algorithm as before and reconstruct a second three-dimensional visual map containing 250 segments. We then attempt to match this second map to the first one with the algorithm sketched previously, and 157 segments are matched. Figure 11.46 is similar to figure 11.43 and is a cross-eye stereogram showing the reconstructed three-dimensional segments from the second viewpoint.

Figure 11.47 is a cross-eye stereogram that shows the two reconstructed scenes in the same coordinate system before the estimation and compensation for the motion. The segments in the first scene are continuous; those in the second are represented by dotted lines. The difference is quite noticeable. Figure 11.48 also shows the superposition of the two scenes after compensation for the estimated robot displacement. This displacement has been applied to all segments in the first scene. If the estimation and the stereo were perfect, the transformed segments should superpose perfectly on those in the second scene. This is of course not exactly the case, but the cross-eye stereogram in figure 11.48 clearly shows the quality of the results.

Having estimated the ego-displacement of the robot, it is possible to check the accuracy of the method even further by generating a trajectory to return the robot to the initial position and orientation. We command the robot to return to what the program thinks is the original position using this computed trajectory. From that position the robot acquires a new stereo triplet. Figure 11.49 shows two images acquired by one of the three cameras: The left image is the same as figure 11.42, while the right image is what the camera sees after the robot has returned to the estimated starting point; the visual difference is quite small.

Figure 11.45   The second view of the Modigliani scene.

Figure 11.46   A cross-eye stereogram showing the results of the stereo reconstruction of the scene shown in figure 11.45.

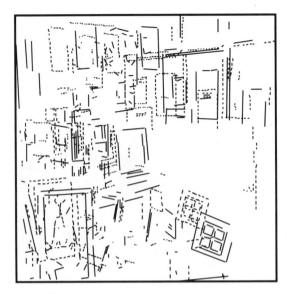

Figure 11.47 A cross-eye stereogram showing the superposition of the two scenes of figures 11.43 and 11.45 before the estimation of and compensation for the robot displacement.

Figure 11.48 A cross-eye stereogram showing the superposition of the two scenes of figures 11.43 and 11.45 after compensation for the estimated robot displacement.

Figure 11.49 A comparison between the original image (left) and the one seen by the same camera after the robot has returned to its estimated original position and orientation (right).

11.5.1.4 Determining object displacements

In the previous analysis, some model segments were matched to *NIL*. There are at least two reasons for this. The first is that because of the robot displacement they have gone out of the field of view. The second is that they belong to an object that is also moving. Determining the segments belonging to the second category and estimating their rigid displacement can be achieved as follows. Discard from the list of model and scene segments those that have already been matched, and apply the best estimate $\hat{T}$ of the robot's ego-displacement to the remaining model segments, thus obtaining a new list $M_1^{(1)}, \ldots, M_{n_1}^{(1)}$ of segments with their covariance (weight) matrices. Next, apply the search procedure again to the new model and scene lists. This can be iterated as many times as necessary.

As an example of such a process, let us consider figure 11.50. The left image in that figure shows a scene viewed from one of the cameras of the stereo rig, and the right image shows the same image after the robot has backed up and the box on the table has moved to the left

Figure 11.50 Images of the scene seen from one of the three cameras of the stereo rig before (left), and after (right) the robot and the box on the table have moved.

and toward the robot. There are therefore two rigid displacements apparent in that scene: the robot's ego-displacement and the box displacement. Figures 11.51 and 11.52 are cross-eye stereograms showing the line segments reconstructed from stereo in the first and second scenes. Figure 11.53 is also a cross-eye stereogram showing the superposition of the two reconstructed visual maps. The initial map is in solid lines, and the final map is in dotted lines.

The algorithm of this section is run a first time to estimate the ego-motion. It is applied to the first map, and the results are shown in figure 11.54. This figure is a cross-eye stereogram that shows that the displacement of the robot has been correctly estimated but that the displacement of the box has not been accounted for. We then remove the matched segments in both maps and obtain the results shown in figure 11.55. Note that in this figure we have applied the estimated ego-motion to the segments of the first visual map.

We then apply the algorithm once again to these two visual maps and obtain an estimation of the displacement of the box. The results obtained by applying this estimated motion to the first visual map are shown in figure 11.56 in the usual format. Those results are better than those

Figure 11.51 A cross-eye stereogram of the visual map corresponding to the first position of the robot.

Figure 11.52 A cross-eye stereogram of the visual map corresponding to the second position of the robot. Note that the box on the table has also moved.

Figure 11.53 A cross-eye stereogram showing the superposition of the two scenes of figure 11.50 before the estimation of and compensation for the robot and box displacements.

Figure 11.54 A cross-eye stereogram showing the superposition of the two scenes of figure 11.50 after compensation for the estimated robot displacement.

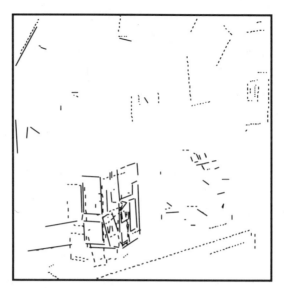

Figure 11.55 Superposition of the two reconstructed visual maps after compensation for the robot's ego-displacement estimated by the algorithm and the elimination of the segments that have been matched.

Figure 11.56 Superposition of the two reconstructed visual maps of figure 11.55 after compensation for the box displacement estimated by the algorithm and the elimination of the segments that have been matched in the first pass of ego-displacement estimation.

obtained by keeping the second-best recognition sequence after the first run of the algorithm. Indeed, in the first phase of the algorithm, we find two different rigid displacements with fairly high-quality measures. But the quality of the results for the box is decreased by the occurrence of a few wrong matches in its recognition sequence. For example, some segments in the background of the room may be matched to the wrong segments. This does not happen in the recognition sequence corresponding to the room. After we eliminate the segments in that sequence, we decrease the risk of obtaining false matches when locating the box.

11.5.2 Putting together different 3-D visual maps of the environment

We will now study the second problem, that of putting together different 3-D visual maps of the environment that the robot is exploring [AF86, ZF92a]. This problem has also been studied in a similar context by the University of Sheffield group [PPP*89]. Relevant error models have also been developed by Mathies and Shafer [MS87] and by Durrant-Whyte [Dur87]. We will assume for simplicity that only the robot is moving and that the environment is static. The process is best understood when it is described with only two visual maps, but the generalization to an arbitrary number of visual maps is straightforward.

Using the same notations as before, let $(M_1, \ldots, M_n)$ be a first visual map, and let $(S_1, \ldots, S_p)$ be a second. We assume that we have run on these two maps the process explained in section 11.5.1, constructed a recognition sequence $((M_1, S_{i_1}), \ldots, (M_n, S_{i_n}))$, and estimated the corresponding rigid transformation $\hat{T}$ and its covariance (weight) matrix $\mathbf{P}$. Those pairs of segments (M_i, S_{i_j}) such that $S_{i_j} \neq NIL$ correspond to the same physical segment seen by the vision system from two different angles. It is therefore not necessary to keep both segments in the robot's representation of the environment: They can be fused into a new unique segment.[10]

---

10. If the segments are partially occluded in *different* ways in the two views, we may not want to combine them completely, but rather combine only their orientations.

11.5.2.1 *Fusing two views*

The principle of the method for fusing two views is quite simple. Let (M, S) be such a pair of 3-D visual maps, with M represented by $\mathbf{s}$, S by $\mathbf{s}'$, and $\hat{T}$ by $\hat{\mathbf{a}}$. We can look at the measurement equations (11.13)-(11.16) in a different way from before and think of $\mathbf{s}'$ as the state $\mathbf{a}$ to be estimated and $[\mathbf{s}^T, \hat{\mathbf{a}}^T]^T$ as the measurement $\mathbf{x}$. Thus we consider $\mathbf{b}_0 = \mathbf{s}'$ as the initial estimate of the state with covariance (weight) matrix $\mathbf{M}_0 = \mathbf{R}'$, and $\mathbf{x} = [\mathbf{s}^T, \hat{\mathbf{a}}^T]^T$ as the measurement with covariance (weight) matrix[11] $\begin{bmatrix} \mathbf{R} & \mathbf{0} \\ \mathbf{0} & \mathbf{P} \end{bmatrix}$. We then use the measurement equations (11.13)-(11.16) to produce a new estimate $\hat{\mathbf{a}}_0$ of the state $\mathbf{a}$ as well as its new covariance (weight) matrix $\mathbf{P}_0$ or, to put it differently, a new estimate $\hat{\mathbf{s}}'$ of the representation of S and a new covariance (weight) matrix $\hat{\mathbf{R}}'$.

Perhaps a simpler way of looking at it is the following. The segment $\hat{T}(M)$ has a representation $\hat{\mathbf{s}}$ given by equations (11.13)–(11.16). Knowing the covariance (weight) matrix $\mathbf{R}$ on M, and $\mathbf{P}$ on $\hat{T}$, we can compute a first-order approximation of the covariance (weight) matrix $\hat{\mathbf{R}}$ on $\hat{T}(M)$ (neglecting the fact that $\hat{T}$ is a function of M) using the methods of chapter 5 (see problem 8). The fusion of $\hat{T}(M)$ and S yields a new segment $\hat{S}$, which is represented by $\hat{\mathbf{s}}'$ such that

$$\hat{\mathbf{s}}' = [\hat{\mathbf{R}}^{-1} + \mathbf{R}'^{-1}]^{-1}(\hat{\mathbf{R}}^{-1}\hat{\mathbf{s}} + \mathbf{R}'^{-1}\mathbf{s}')$$

and a covariance (weight) matrix

$$\hat{\mathbf{R}}' = [\hat{\mathbf{R}}^{-1} + \mathbf{R}'^{-1}]^{-1}$$

Figure 11.57 shows the different stages of the fusion for the midpoint. The left part shows the two segments, M (in dotted lines) and S (in solid lines), before the estimated motion has been applied to M. The ellipses represent the uncertainty of the midpoints. The middle part shows the two segments $\hat{T}(M)$ (in dotted lines) and S (in solid lines). The right part shows the fused segment $\hat{S}$ and the ellipse of uncertainty of its midpoint

---

11. Note that matrices $\mathbf{R}$ and $\mathbf{R}'$ represent covariance (weight) matrices, not rotation matrices.

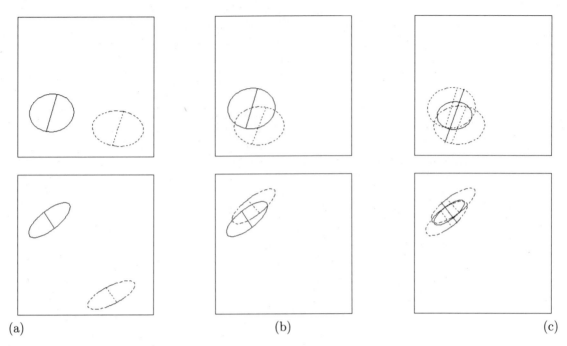

Figure 11.57 Evolution of the midpoint of a segment during fusion (see text).

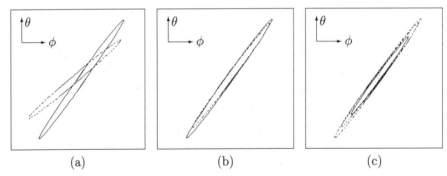

Figure 11.58 Evolution of the orientation of a segment during fusion (see text).

as a solid line together with the two original segments and their ellipses of uncertainty in dotted lines. Note the important reduction of uncertainty after fusion. Figure 11.58 shows the same stages for the segment orientations. The ellipses are represented in the (θ, Φ) plane for the spherical coordinates.

After this operation has been performed for all pairs (M, S) such that $S \neq NIL$, the environment of the robot is represented by the following:

1. $\hat{T}$, the estimate of the best rigid transformation from the first coordinate system to the second, and its covariance (weight) matrix $\mathbf{P}$.

2. A sublist $(M_{k_1}, \ldots, M_{k_q})$ of the original list of segments reconstructed in the first position of the robot and corresponding to those segments that have not been detected in the second position.

3. A sublist $(S_{l_1}, \ldots, S_{l_r})$ of the original list of segments reconstructed in the second position of the robot and corresponding to those segments that have not been detected in the first position.

4. A sublist $(S_{m_1}, \ldots, S_{m_s})$ of the original list of segments reconstructed in the second position of the robot and corresponding to the segments that have been detected in the first position. The representations of these segments have been updated using the previous rules. Their matches in the first position have been erased from the representation.

11.5.2.2   An example

A complete example will demonstrate what kind of results can be obtained using real data. In this example, the robot is moving in a room occupied by some objects. A labeled map of the room is shown in figure 11.59. A total of thirty-five stereo triplets have been acquired while the robot has been moving about the room, and hence thirty-five visual maps have reconstructed and fused pairwise. This means that, if $V_i, i = 1, \ldots, 35$ are the visual maps, we have fused V_1 and V_2 and then have fused the resulting map with V_3, etc. Some sample images of the room are shown in figure 11.60. The final result is represented in the coordinate system of V_{35}. We show a top view of it in figure 11.61 and several perspective views, represented as cross-eye stereograms, in figures 11.62 and 11.63.

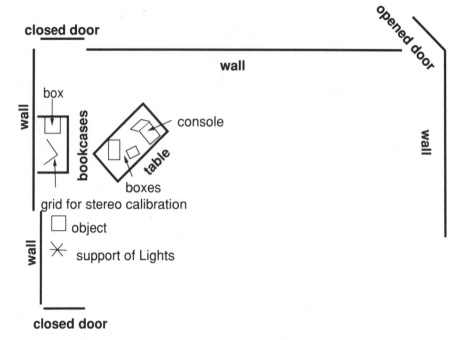

Figure 11.59   Labeled model of the room.

11.5.3   More references

The area of optical navigation and model building has been an application of computer vision from the very early days with the work of Moravec [Mor77, Mor80] and Gennery [Gen77, Gen80]. An excellent compilation of many of the important recent and not so recent articles can be found in the book edited by Iyengar and Elfes [IE91].

(a) First sample image

(b) Second sample image

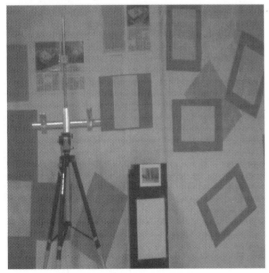

(c) Third sample image

(d) Fourth sample image

Figure 11.60   Four views of the room.

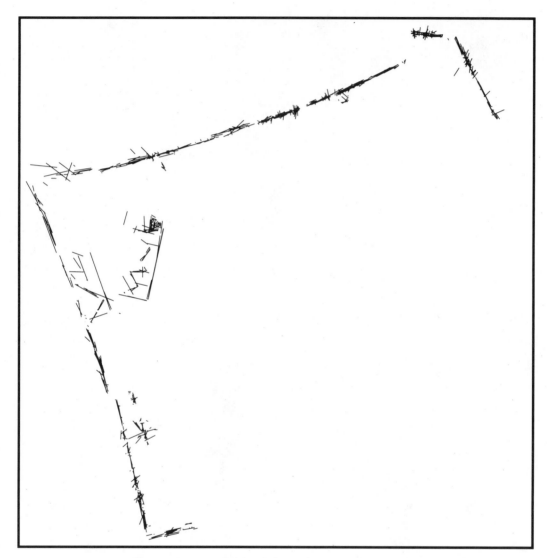

Figure 11.61 The final three-dimensional visual map of the room obtained by integrating thirty-five stereo triplets (top view).

Figure 11.62 First perspective view of the three-dimensional visual map of the room obtained by integrating thirty-five stereo triplets.

Figure 11.63 Second perspective view of the three-dimensional visual map of the room obtained by integrating thirty-five stereo triplets.

11.6 Problems

1. This problem is intended to investigate the computation of the best rigid displacement D between two sets of planar points. The points M and S in the first and second sets, respectively, are represented by the complex numbers z and Z, respectively. We assume that D is a rotation of angle θ around the origin of coordinates followed by a translation represented by the complex number t. A point M is therefore transformed into a point $M' = D(M)$, which is represented by $ze^{i\theta} + t$. Given n pairs of corresponding points, we want to find the best 2-D displacement D that minimizes the sum of the squared distances:

$$C(\theta, t) = \sum_{j=1}^{n} |z_j e^{i\theta} + t - Z_j|^2$$

Introduce the centroids $\overline{M}$ and $\overline{S}$ of the points M_j and $S_j, j = 1, \ldots, n$, represented by z and Z. Write $z_j = z + z'_j$, $Z_j = Z + Z'_j$, and show that the best displacement is given by

$$\hat{t} = Z - ze^{i\hat{\theta}}$$

$$\hat{\theta} = -Arg\left(\sum_{j=1}^{n} z'_j \overline{Z'_j}\right)$$

2. In section 11.3.2 we have derived the equations that describe the changes in the representation of a line segment when we apply to it a transformation T. Given two line segments represented by $\mathbf{s}$ and $\mathbf{s}'$, we have shown that there exist, in general, two transformations $T^{(1)}$ and $T^{(2)}$ such that $T^{(1)}\mathbf{s} = T^{(2)}\mathbf{s} = \mathbf{s}'$. These two transformations are represented by the vectors $\mathbf{b}^{(1)}$ and $\mathbf{b}^{(2)}$, which are functions of $\mathbf{s}$ and $\mathbf{s}'$.

    a. Compute $\mathbf{b}^{(1)}$ and $\mathbf{b}^{(2)}$ as functions of $\mathbf{s}$ and $\mathbf{s}'$.

    b. Given a covariance (weight) matrix $\mathbf{R}$ for $\mathbf{s}$ and $\mathbf{R}'$ for $\mathbf{s}'$, assume that the covariance (weight) matrix on $[\mathbf{s}^T, \mathbf{s}'^T]^T$ is

$$\begin{bmatrix} \mathbf{R} & \mathbf{0} \\ \mathbf{0} & \mathbf{R}' \end{bmatrix}$$

and compute the first-order approximation of the covariance (weight) matrices for $\mathbf{b}^{(1)}$ and $\mathbf{b}^{(2)}$.

3. In section 11.3.3, in order to apply the Kalman equations during the tree search we need to compute the partial derivatives $\frac{\partial \mathbf{f}}{\partial \mathbf{a}}$ and $\frac{\partial \mathbf{f}}{\partial \mathbf{b}}$, where $\mathbf{f}, \mathbf{x}$, and $\mathbf{a}$ are defined in the text. Compute these partial derivatives.

4. This problem is intended to investigate the computation of the best rigid displacement between two sets of three-dimensional points. The points M and S in the first and second sets, respectively, are represented by $\mathbf{p} = \mathbf{OM}$ and $\mathbf{q} = \mathbf{OS}$, respectively. We assume that D is a rotation around an axis going through the origin O represented by the rotation matrix $\mathbf{R}$, followed by a translation represented by the vector $\mathbf{t}$. A point M is therefore transformed by the rigid motion $(\mathbf{R}, \mathbf{t})$ into a point $M' = D(M)$ represented by $\mathbf{p}' = \mathbf{Rp} + \mathbf{t}$. Given n pairs of corresponding points, we want to find the best 3-D displacement D that minimizes the sum of the squared distances:

$$C(\mathbf{R}, \mathbf{t}) = \sum_{i=1}^{n} \|\mathbf{q}_i - \mathbf{Rp}_i - \mathbf{t}\|^2 \qquad (11.17)$$

Introduce the centroids $\overline{M}$ and $\overline{S}$ of the points M_i and $S_i, i = 1, \ldots, n$, which are represented by $\mathbf{p}$ and $\mathbf{q}$. Write $\mathbf{p}_i = \mathbf{p} + \mathbf{p}_i'$, $\mathbf{q}_i = \mathbf{q} + \mathbf{q}_i'$ and show that the best displacement is given by

$$\hat{\mathbf{t}} = \mathbf{q} - \hat{\mathbf{R}}\mathbf{p}$$

where $\hat{\mathbf{R}}$ is obtained as the minimum of the following criterion:

$$\sum_{i=1}^{n} \|\mathbf{q}_i' - \mathbf{Rp}_i'\|^2$$

How would you minimize this criterion?

5. The purpose of this problem is to study the rank of the matrices $\mathbf{A}_i^T \mathbf{A}_i$ of section 11.4.3.1 in the noiseless case.

   a. Show that the matrix $\mathbf{A}_i$ is equal to

$$\mathbf{A}_i = \begin{bmatrix} 0 & \mathbf{b}_i^T \\ -\mathbf{b}_i & \mathbf{B}_i \end{bmatrix}$$

where $\mathbf{b}_i = \mathbf{n}_i - \mathbf{n}'_i$, $\mathbf{B}_i = \tilde{\mathbf{n}}_i + \tilde{\mathbf{n}}'_i$ and the notation $\tilde{\mathbf{x}}$ indicates the 3×3 antisymmetric matrix representing the cross-product with the vector $\mathbf{x}$, i.e., $\tilde{\mathbf{x}}\mathbf{y} = \mathbf{x} \wedge \mathbf{y}$.

b. Show that

$$\mathbf{A}_i^T \mathbf{A}_i = -\mathbf{A}_i^2 = \left[\begin{array}{cc} \mathbf{b}_i^T \mathbf{b}_i & -\mathbf{b}_i^T \mathbf{B}_i \\ -\mathbf{B}_i^T \mathbf{b}_i & \mathbf{b}_i \mathbf{b}_i^T - \mathbf{B}_i^2 \end{array} \right]$$

and that

$$\mathbf{B}_i^T \mathbf{b}_i = 2\mathbf{n}_i \wedge \mathbf{n}'_i$$

c. Show that the matrix $\mathbf{A}_i^T \mathbf{A}_i$ has two distinct eigenvalues $\lambda_1 = 0$ and $\lambda_2 = \mathbf{b}_i'^T \mathbf{b}'_i + \mathbf{b}_i^T \mathbf{b}_i$, where $\mathbf{b}'_i = \mathbf{n}_i + \mathbf{n}'_i$ such that each eigensubspace is of dimension 2. Compute an orthogonal basis of eigenvectors of matrix $\mathbf{A}_i^T \mathbf{A}_i$.

6. Compute the partial derivatives $\frac{\partial \mathbf{f}'}{\partial \mathbf{x}}$ and $\frac{\partial \mathbf{f}'}{\partial \mathbf{r}}$, which are needed in section 11.4.3.2.

7. Compute the bound $\mathbf{M}_0^{(k)}$ on $\mathbf{b}_0^{(k)'} = [\mathbf{r}_0^T, \mathbf{t}_0^{(k)T}]^T$ of section 11.4.3.2.

8. Compute the first-order approximation of the covariance (weight) matrix of the transformed segment $\hat{T}(M)$ in section 11.5.2.1 knowing the covariance (weight) matrix $\mathbf{R}$ of M and $\mathbf{P}$ of $\hat{T}$.

12 Answers to Problems

12.1 Answers to problems of chapter 2

1. Take four points of projective parameters $\alpha_i, i = 1, \ldots, 4$. Their cross-ratio is equation (2.2):

$$\frac{\alpha_1 - \alpha_3}{\alpha_1 - \alpha_4} : \frac{\alpha_2 - \alpha_3}{\alpha_2 - \alpha_4}$$

If we apply a collineation to the points of the line, the projective parameter α is transformed into $\beta = \frac{a\alpha+b}{c\alpha+d}$. A simple algebraic manipulation shows that the cross-ratio of the four transformed points is the same as the one of the original points if the determinant $ad - bc$ is different from 0, which is true since the matrix of a collineation is supposed to be invertible.

2. The affine equation of a circle with center of coordinates a, b and radius R is

$$(X_1 - a)^2 + (X_2 - b)^2 - R^2 = 0$$

Its projective equation is

$$(x_1 - ax_3)^2 + (x_2 - bx_3)^2 - R^2 x_3^2 =$$
$$x_1^2 + x_2^2 + x_3((a^2 + b^2 - R^2)x_3 - 2ax_1 - 2bx_2) = 0$$

The absolute points satisfy $x_1^2 + x_2^2 = 0, x_3 = 0$ and therefore belong to the circle.

Similarly, the projective equation of a sphere with center of coordinates a, b, c and radius R can be written as

$$x_1^2 + x_2^2 + x_3^2 + x_4((a^2 + b^2 + c^2 - R^2)x_4 - 2ax_1 - 2bx_2 - 2cx_3) = 0$$

Therefore, the absolute conic of equation $x_1^2 + x_2^2 + x_3^2 = x_4 = 0$ belongs to the sphere.

3. The points at infinity of the two lines are represented by the vectors $[1, a_i, 0]^T$. The cross-ratio of those points with the absolute points is

$$\rho = \frac{a_1 - i}{a_2 - i} : \frac{a_1 + i}{a_2 + i}$$

Note that, with reference to the figure 12.1, $a_i = \tan \theta_i, i = 1, 2$. Thus we can write ρ as

$$\rho = \frac{\sin \theta_1 - i \cos \theta_1}{\sin \theta_1 + i \cos \theta_1} \cdot \frac{\sin \theta_2 + i \cos \theta_2}{\sin \theta_2 - i \cos \theta_2}$$

Since $e^{i\theta} = \cos \theta + i \sin \theta$, we have

$$\rho = e^{2i(\theta_1 - \theta_2)}$$

and $\frac{1}{2i} \log \rho = \theta_1 - \theta_2$.

4. Let l_1 and l_2 be two projective lines represented by $[u_1, u_2, u_3]^T$ and $[v_1, v_2, v_3]^T$. To find their point of intersection, we have to solve a system of linear equations:

$$\begin{cases} u_1 x_1 + u_2 x_2 + u_3 x_3 = 0 \\ v_1 x_1 + v_2 x_2 + v_3 x_3 = 0 \end{cases}$$

Solving for x_1 and x_2, we find

$$x_1 = -x_3 \frac{\begin{vmatrix} u_3 & u_2 \\ v_3 & v_2 \end{vmatrix}}{\begin{vmatrix} u_1 & u_2 \\ v_1 & v_2 \end{vmatrix}} \qquad x_2 = -x_3 \frac{\begin{vmatrix} u_1 & u_3 \\ v_1 & v_3 \end{vmatrix}}{\begin{vmatrix} u_1 & u_2 \\ v_1 & v_2 \end{vmatrix}}$$

and thus we can choose $x_1 = -\begin{vmatrix} u_3 & u_2 \\ v_3 & v_2 \end{vmatrix}$, $x_2 = -\begin{vmatrix} u_1 & u_3 \\ v_1 & v_3 \end{vmatrix}$, and $x_3 = \begin{vmatrix} u_1 & u_2 \\ v_1 & v_2 \end{vmatrix}$, which shows that $\mathbf{x} = \mathbf{l}_1 \wedge \mathbf{l}_2$.

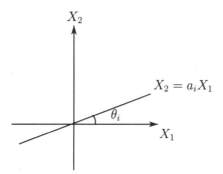

Figure 12.1 See problem 3.

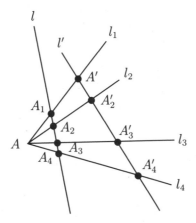

Figure 12.2 See problem 5.

If the determinant $\begin{vmatrix} u_1 & u_2 \\ v_1 & v_2 \end{vmatrix} = u_1 v_2 - u_2 v_1$ is equal to zero, the point of intersection is on l_∞. If we look at the affine lines of equations $u_1 X_1 + u_2 X_2 + u_3$ and $v_1 X_1 + v_2 X_2 + v_3$, the condition $u_1 v_2 - u_2 v_1 = 0$ means that they are parallel. Therefore, distinct parallel affine lines, considered as embedded in $\mathcal{P}^2$, intersect at infinity.

5. Let us refer to figure 12.2. Let $l_i, i = 1, \ldots, 4$ be the four lines, and let l and l' be two other lines that do not go through their common point of intersection and intersect them at $A_i, i = 1, \ldots, 4$ and

at $A'_i, i = 1, \ldots, 4$, respectively. Since we know that a pencil of lines is a $\mathcal{P}^1$, we can write

$$\mathbf{l}_3 = \alpha \mathbf{l}_1 + \mathbf{l}_2$$
$$\mathbf{l}_4 = \beta \mathbf{l}_1 + \mathbf{l}_2$$

The representation of A_i is $\mathbf{l}_i \wedge \mathbf{l}$ for $i = 1, \ldots, 4$ and the representation of A'_i is $\mathbf{l}_i \wedge \mathbf{l}'$. From the previous two equations, we have

$$\mathbf{A}_3 = \alpha \mathbf{A}_1 + \mathbf{A}_2 \quad \mathbf{A}'_3 = \alpha \mathbf{A}'_1 + \mathbf{A}'_2$$
$$\mathbf{A}_4 = \beta \mathbf{A}_1 + \mathbf{A}_2 \quad \mathbf{A}'_4 = \beta \mathbf{A}'_1 + \mathbf{A}'_2$$

From this it follows that

$$\{A_1, A_2; A_3, A_4\} = \{\infty, 0; \alpha, \beta\} = \frac{\beta}{\alpha} = \{A'_1, A'_2; A'_3, A'_4\}$$

There is another solution that has the advantage of giving a nice geometric interpretation of the cross-ratio in terms of the angles between the lines. We assume that the following is known:
Given a triangle ABC, the following equalities hold:

$$\frac{BC}{\sin BAC} = \frac{CA}{\sin CBA} = \frac{AB}{ACB}$$

Considering magnitudes only, the cross-ratio $\{A_1, A_2; A_3, A_4\}$ is equal to

$$\frac{A_1 A_3}{A_1 A_4} : \frac{A_2 A_3}{A_2 A_4}$$

If we consider the triangles $A_1 A A_3$ and $A_1 A A_2$, we can write

$$\frac{A_1 A_3}{A_2 A_3} = \left(\frac{A_1 A_3}{A A_1} : \frac{A_2 A_3}{A A_2} \right) \frac{A A_1}{A A_2} = \left(\frac{\sin A_1 A A_3}{\sin A A_3 A_1} : \frac{\sin A_2 A A_3}{\sin A A_3 A_2} \right) \frac{A A_1}{A A_2}$$

$$= \frac{A A_1}{A A_2} \frac{\sin A_1 A A_3}{\sin A_2 A A_3}$$

Similarly one proves that

$$\frac{A_1 A_4}{A_2 A_4} = \frac{A A_1}{A A_2} \frac{\sin A_1 A A_4}{\sin A_2 A A_4}$$

which yields

$$\{A_1, A_2; A_3, A_4\} = \frac{A_1 A_3}{A_2 A_3} : \frac{A_1 A_4}{A_2 A_4} = \frac{\sin A_1 A A_3}{\sin A_2 A A_3} : \frac{\sin A_1 A A_4}{\sin A_2 A A_4}$$

6. The reciprocal transformation whose fundamental points are the origin represented by $\mathbf{e}_3$ and the absolute points is defined by

$$\frac{x_1' + ix_2'}{a} = \frac{a}{x_1 + ix_2} \quad \frac{x_1' - ix_2'}{a} = \frac{a}{x_1 - ix_2} \quad x_3' = \frac{1}{x_3}$$

These equations reduce to

$$\frac{x_1'}{x_3'} = \frac{a^2 x_3 x_1}{x_1^2 + x_2^2} \quad \frac{x_2'}{x_3'} = -\frac{a^2 x_3 x_2}{x_1^2 + x_2^2}$$

If we now superimpose the collineation defined by matrix $\mathbf{A}$, we obtain the equations

$$\frac{x_1''}{x_3''} = \frac{a^2 x_3 x_1}{x_1^2 + x_2^2} \quad \frac{x_2''}{x_3''} = \frac{a^2 x_3 x_2}{x_1^2 + x_2^2}$$

which represents an inversion.

7. Just apply the definition of the l_{ij} of section 2.5.1 and divide by the product $x_4^{(1)} x_4^{(2)}$, which is different from zero by hypothesis.

8. If we allow the exchange of the absolute points represented by $\mathbf{i}$ and $\mathbf{j}$, we have, in a manner similar to section 2.4.8:

$$\frac{1}{-i} = \frac{b_{11}1 + b_{12}i + b_1 0}{b_{21}1 + b_{22}i + b_2 0}$$

$$\frac{1}{i} = \frac{b_{11}1 - b_{12}i + b_1 0}{b_{21}1 - b_{22}i + b_2 0}$$

In other words

$$(b_{11} + b_{22})i - (b_{12} - b_{21}) = 0$$

and

$$-(b_{11} + b_{22})i - (b_{12} - b_{21}) = 0$$

Therefore $b_{11} + b_{22} = b_{12} - b_{21} = 0$, and we can write

$$\mathbf{X}' = c \begin{bmatrix} \cos\alpha & \sin\alpha \\ \sin\alpha & -\cos\alpha \end{bmatrix} \mathbf{X} + \mathbf{b}$$

$c > 0, 0 \leq \alpha < 2\pi$. Since

$$\begin{bmatrix} \cos \alpha & \sin \alpha \\ \sin \alpha & -\cos \alpha \end{bmatrix} = \begin{bmatrix} 1 & 0 \\ 0 & -1 \end{bmatrix} \begin{bmatrix} \cos \alpha & \sin \alpha \\ -\sin \alpha & \cos \alpha \end{bmatrix}$$

we see that the transformation is obtained by first applying a rotation of angle α around the origin of coordinates, followed by a symmetry with respect to the x-axis, followed by a scaling by c and a translation by $\mathbf{b}$.

9.

a. Verifying the group structure is simple: The identity is obtained for $b = \alpha = 0$ and $c = 1$; the product of two transformations of the set belongs to the set as shown by taking $z_1' = c_1 e^{i\alpha_1} z + b_1$ and $z_2' = c_2 e^{i\alpha_2} z_1' + b_2$, which is equal to $c_1 c_2 e^{i(\alpha_1 + \alpha_2)} z + b_2 + b_1 c_2 e^{i\alpha_2}$; and the inverse is defined by $z = \frac{1}{c} e^{-i\alpha}(z' - b) = \frac{1}{c} e^{-i\alpha} z' - \frac{b}{c} e^{-i\alpha}$, which also belongs to the set.

b. $z' = c\overline{e^{i\alpha} z} + b$.

c. If we define $z_1' = c_1 \overline{e^{i\alpha_1} z} + b_1$ and $z_2' = c_2 \overline{e^{i\alpha_2} z_1'} + b_2$ we obtain

$$z_2' = c_1 c_2 e^{i(\alpha_1 - \alpha_2)} z + b_2 + \overline{b_1} c_2 e^{-i\alpha_2}$$

which belongs to the group of question 9a.

d. The inverse is defined by

$$z = \frac{1}{c} \overline{e^{i\alpha} z'} - \frac{\overline{b} e^{-i\alpha}}{c}$$

e. It is easy to check that the product of two transformations in the two sets belongs to the set defined in problem 8. From this the conclusion follows.

10. Refer to figures 12.3 and 12.4. Let $l_1 = \pi_1 \cap \pi_\infty$, $l_2 = \pi_2 \cap \pi_\infty$, and $P_{12} = l_1 \cap l_2$. If $l = \pi_1 \cap \pi_2$, it is clear that $P_{12} = l \cap \pi_\infty$. The angle between π_1 and π_2 is the angle between two lines h_1 and h_2 perpendicular to l at the same point (to make them coplanar). Let us now denote by H_1 and H_2 the intersections of h_1 and h_2 with π_∞; they are, of course, on l_1 and l_2, respectively. Let us also denote by i_1, j_1 and i_2, j_2 the absolute points of π_1 and π_2, which are the intersections of l_1 and l_2 with the absolute conic Ω. Since h_1 is orthogonal to l, then, because of the Laguerre formula for lines, we have $\{P_{12}, H_1; i_1, j_1\} = -1$.

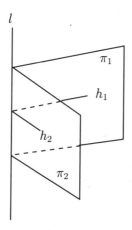

Figure 12.3 See problem 10.

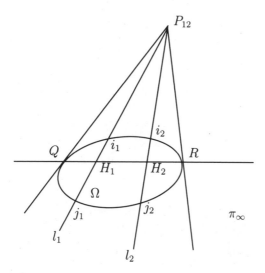

Figure 12.4 See problem 10.

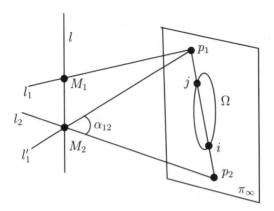

Figure 12.5   See problem 11.

Similarly, $\{P_{12}, H_2; i_2, j_2\} = -1$. Now consider the line $\langle H_1, H_2 \rangle$ and its intersections Q and R with Ω. By the Laguerre formula for lines, the angle between h_1 and h_2 is $\frac{1}{2i} \log(\{H_1, H_2; Q, R\})$.

Let us show that the cross-ratio $\{H_1, H_2; Q, R\}$ is equal to the cross-ratio of the four planes π_1, π_2, i_l, and j_l, where i_l and j_l are the two planes tangent to Ω and going through l. By the definition of the polar of a point with respect to a conic, the line $\langle H_1, H_2 \rangle$ is the polar of the point P_{12} with respect to Ω. This implies that $\langle P_{12}, Q \rangle$ and $\langle P_{12}, R \rangle$ are tangent to Ω at Q and R and are therefore the intersections of the planes i_l and j_l with π_∞. Since $\{H_1, H_2; Q, R\} = \{l_1, l_2; \langle P_{12}, Q \rangle, \langle P_{12}, R \rangle\}$, and the second cross-ratio is equal to $\{\pi_1, \pi_2; i_l, j_l\}$ as can be seen by choosing π_∞ as the cutting plane π in figure 2.3, this ends the proof.

11. Refer to figure 12.5. If the two lines l_1 and l_2 are coplanar, we know the answer. If they are not coplanar, they have a common perpendicular l which intersects l_1 in M_1 and l_2 in M_2. Let l_1' be the line parallel to l_1 going through M_2. The angle between l_1 and l_2 is equal to the angle between l_1' and l_2. Let p_2 be the point at infinity of l_2, and let p_1' be the point at infinity of l_1'. Since l_1' is parallel to l_1, $p_1' = p_1$, the point at infinity of l_1. Let i and j be the intersections of the line $\langle p_1, p_2 \rangle$ with Ω. Then $\alpha_{12} = \frac{1}{2i} \log(\{p_1, p_2; i, j\})$.

12. Equation (2.15) can be written projectively as

$$\mathbf{x}' = \begin{bmatrix} \mathbf{B} & \mathbf{b} \\ \mathbf{0} & 1 \end{bmatrix} \mathbf{x}$$

Its restriction to π_∞ of equation $x_4 = 0$ is $\mathbf{y}' = \mathbf{B}\mathbf{y}$ where $\mathbf{y} = [x_1, x_2, x_3]^T$. If the corresponding point is on Ω, it satisfies $\mathbf{y}^T\mathbf{y} = 0$. We want $\mathbf{y}'$ to also satisfy $\mathbf{y}'^T\mathbf{y}' = 0$, and we know that $\mathbf{y}'^T\mathbf{y}' = \mathbf{y}^T\mathbf{B}^T\mathbf{B}\mathbf{y}$. Let us write matrix $\mathbf{B}$ as $[\mathbf{b}_1, \mathbf{b}_2, \mathbf{b}_3]$ and choose $\mathbf{y} = [1, i, 0]^T$. We have

$$\mathbf{y}^T\mathbf{B}^T\mathbf{B}\mathbf{y} = (\mathbf{b}_1 + i\mathbf{b}_2)^T(\mathbf{b}_1 + i\mathbf{b}_2) = \mathbf{b}_1^T\mathbf{b}_1 - \mathbf{b}_2^T\mathbf{b}_2 + 2i\mathbf{b}_1^T\mathbf{b}_2$$

This must be equal to zero, which implies that

$$\begin{cases} \mathbf{b}_1^T\mathbf{b}_1 = \mathbf{b}_2^T\mathbf{b}_2 \\ \mathbf{b}_1^T\mathbf{b}_2 = 0 \end{cases}$$

Similarly, if we choose $\mathbf{y} = [1, 0, i]^T$, we obtain

$$\begin{cases} \mathbf{b}_1^T\mathbf{b}_1 = \mathbf{b}_3^T\mathbf{b}_3 \\ \mathbf{b}_1^T\mathbf{b}_3 = 0 \end{cases}$$

For $\mathbf{y} = [0, 1, i]^T$ we obtain

$$\begin{cases} \mathbf{b}_2^T\mathbf{b}_2 = \mathbf{b}_3^T\mathbf{b}_3 \\ \mathbf{b}_2^T\mathbf{b}_3 = 0 \end{cases}$$

Let $c^2 = \mathbf{b}_1^T\mathbf{b}_1 = \mathbf{b}_2^T\mathbf{b}_2 = \mathbf{b}_3^T\mathbf{b}_3$. We have proven that $\mathbf{B}^T\mathbf{B} = c^2\mathbf{I}$ and therefore that $\mathbf{B} = c\mathbf{C}$ and $\mathbf{C}^T\mathbf{C} = \mathbf{I}$.

12.2   Answers to problems of chapter 3

1. Let m and n have pixel coordinates (u, v) and (u', v'), respectively. From equation (3.17) we obtain

$$S(\tilde{\mathbf{m}}) = \left(\frac{u-u_0}{\alpha_u}\right)^2 + \left(\frac{v-v_0}{\alpha_v}\right)^2 + 1$$

$$S(\tilde{\mathbf{n}}) = \left(\frac{u'-u_0}{\alpha_u}\right)^2 + \left(\frac{v'-v_0}{\alpha_v}\right)^2 + 1$$

$$S(\tilde{\mathbf{m}}, \tilde{\mathbf{n}}) = \frac{(u-u_0)(u'-u_0)}{\alpha_u^2} + \frac{(v-v_0)(v'-v_0)}{\alpha_v^2} + 1$$

from which follows (after some algebra)

$$S(\tilde{\mathbf{m}}, \tilde{\mathbf{n}})^2 - S(\tilde{\mathbf{m}})S(\tilde{\mathbf{n}}) = -\left[\left(\frac{u - u'}{\alpha_u}\right)^2 + \left(\frac{v - v'}{\alpha_v}\right)^2 \right.$$

$$\left. + \left(\frac{uv' - u'v + u_0(v - v') - v_0(u - u')}{\alpha_u\alpha_v}\right)^2\right]$$

Let us call this quantity $-\Delta^2$. From there we can write that

$$\tan(\mathrm{Arg}(\theta_0)) = \pm\frac{\Delta}{S(\tilde{\mathbf{m}}, \tilde{\mathbf{n}})}$$

2. Using the notations of section 3.3.1.2 and equation (3.31), the matrix **P** is, in the more general case

$$\mathbf{P} = \begin{bmatrix} -\alpha_u & \alpha_u \cot\theta & u_0 \\ 0 & -\frac{\alpha_v}{\sin\theta} & v_0 \\ 0 & 0 & 1 \end{bmatrix}$$

From this expression we can compute $S(\tilde{\mathbf{m}}) = \tilde{\mathbf{m}}^T\mathbf{P}^{-1T}\mathbf{P}^{-1}\tilde{\mathbf{m}}, S(\tilde{\mathbf{n}}) = \tilde{\mathbf{n}}^T\mathbf{P}^{-1T}\mathbf{P}^{-1}\tilde{\mathbf{n}}$ and $S(\tilde{\mathbf{m}}, \tilde{\mathbf{n}}) = \tilde{\mathbf{n}}^T\mathbf{P}^{-1T}\mathbf{P}^{-1}\tilde{\mathbf{m}}$, which are found to be equal to the values computed in the previous problem with the following additive correcting terms:

$$\frac{2\cos\theta}{\alpha_u\alpha_v}(u - u_0)(v - v_0)$$

$$\frac{2\cos\theta}{\alpha_u\alpha_v}(u' - u_0)(v' - v_0)$$

$$\frac{\cos\theta}{\alpha_u\alpha_v}[(u - u_0)(v - v_0) + (u' - u_0)(v' - v_0) - (u - u')(v - v')]$$

3. From the notations of appendix A, **z** is a 3×1 vector obtained by extracting the coordinates 9 to 11 from **q**. Matrix **C** is the $2N \times 9$ submatrix of **A** corresponding to its first eight columns and its last column, and matrix **D** is the $2N \times 3$ submatrix of **A** corresponding to the other three columns. The appendix tells us that $\mathbf{q}_3$ is the eigenvector of the symmetric positive 3×3 matrix $\mathbf{D}^T(\mathbf{I} - \mathbf{C}(\mathbf{C}^T\mathbf{C})^{-1}\mathbf{C}^T)\mathbf{D}$ corresponding to the smallest eigenvalue. The remaining nine components of **q**, the vector **y** of the appendix, are then obtained from equation (A.3), for which the inversion of a 9×9 matrix is required.

4. According to equation (3.19), if **R** is the rotation matrix of the change of coordinate system, $\mathbf{q}_i$ becomes $\mathbf{R}^T\mathbf{q}_i, i = 1, 2, 3$. Therefore we have

$$\|\mathbf{R}^T\mathbf{q}_3\| = \|\mathbf{q}_3\|$$

and also

$$(\mathbf{R}^T\mathbf{q}_1 \wedge \mathbf{R}^T\mathbf{q}_3) \cdot (\mathbf{R}^T\mathbf{q}_2 \wedge \mathbf{R}^T\mathbf{q}_3) =$$
$$(\mathbf{R}^T(\mathbf{q}_1 \wedge \mathbf{q}_3)) \cdot (\mathbf{R}^T(\mathbf{q}_2 \wedge \mathbf{q}_3)) =$$
$$(\mathbf{q}_1 \wedge \mathbf{q}_3) \cdot (\mathbf{q}_2 \wedge \mathbf{q}_3)$$

5. A twisted cubic is a curve that is represented by parametric equations of the form

$$x_1 : x_2 : x_3 : x_4 = f_1(t) : f_2(t) : f_3(t) : f_4(t)$$

where the functions $f_i(t)$ are linearly independent cubic polynomials in the parameter t. The notation $x : y = z : t$ is equivalent to $x/z = y/t$. Let us choose four points of the curve as the points $\mathbf{e}_i, i = 1, \ldots, 4$ of the standard projective basis, and let us suppose that the parameter of $\mathbf{e}_i$ is $t_i, i = 1, \ldots, 4$. Then

$$f_1(t_2) = f_1(t_3) = f_1(t_4) = 0$$

and hence

$$f_1(t) = c_1(t - t_2)(t - t_3)(t - t_4)$$

We find similar expressions for $f_2, f_3,$ and f_4. The equations of the twisted cubic may accordingly be written

$$x_1 : x_2 : x_3 : x_4 = c_1(t - t_1)^{-1} : c_2(t - t_2)^{-1} : c_3(t - t_3)^{-1} : c_4(t - t_4)^{-1}$$

If we now apply the reciprocal transformation of the projective space given by

$$x_i = \frac{1}{x_i'} \qquad i = 1, \ldots, 4$$

then the twisted cubic is transformed into the line

$$x_i' = \frac{t - t_i}{c_i} \qquad i = 1, \ldots, 4$$

In this way we obtain a one-to-one correspondence between the twisted cubics going through four points and the lines of space. Since a line is determined by two points, a general twisted cubic is defined by six general points.

6. Going back to the proof of proposition 3.1, we now assume that the N points are coplanar. Then there exist four numbers a, b, c, and d, not all equal to zero, such that

$$ax_i + by_i + cz_i + d = 0 \qquad i = 1, \ldots, N$$

We see by inspection that the first four columns of matrix $\mathbf{A}$ have a rank less than or equal to 3, and that the same is true for the next four columns and for the last four. Since the linear relation between the first, sixth, and eleventh columns is still true, we see that the rank of $\mathbf{A}$ is less than or equal to $12 - 4 = 8$. Let us prove that it is in general equal to 8.

Denoting by $\mathbf{c}_j, j = 1, \ldots, 8$ the first three column vectors, followed by the fifth, sixth, seventh, ninth, and tenth, we want to prove that a relation such as

$$\sum_{j=1}^{8} \lambda_j \mathbf{c}_j = \mathbf{0} \tag{12.1}$$

implies $\lambda_j = 0, j = 1, \ldots, 8$. But equation (12.1) is equivalent to the N equations

$$\lambda_1 x_i z_i + \lambda_2 y_i z_i + \lambda_3 z_i^2 - \lambda_7 x_i^2 - \lambda_8 x_i y_i = 0 \tag{12.2}$$

and the N equations

$$\lambda_4 x_i z_i + \lambda_5 y_i z_i + \lambda_6 z_i^2 - \lambda_7 x_i y_i - \lambda_8 y_i^2 = 0 \tag{12.3}$$

We assume, without loss of generality, that $c \neq 0$ and substitute $\alpha x_i + \beta y_i + \gamma$ for z_i; we obtain for (12.2)

$$
\begin{aligned}
x_i^2(\alpha \lambda_1 + \alpha^2 \lambda_3 - \lambda_7) + y_i^2(\beta \lambda_2 + \beta^2 \lambda_3) \\
+ x_i y_i(\beta \lambda_1 + \alpha \lambda_2 + 2\alpha\beta \lambda_3 - \lambda_8) + \gamma[x_i(\lambda_1 + 2\alpha \lambda_3) \\
+ y_i(\lambda_2 + 2\beta \lambda_3) + \lambda_3 \gamma] = 0
\end{aligned}
\tag{12.4}
$$

and for (12.3)

$$
\begin{aligned}
x_i^2(\alpha \lambda_4 + \alpha^2 \lambda_6) + y_i^2(\beta \lambda_5 + \beta^2 \lambda_6 - \lambda_8) \\
+ x_i y_i(\beta \lambda_4 + \alpha \lambda_5 + 2\alpha\beta \lambda_6 - \lambda_7) \\
+ \gamma[x_i(\lambda_4 + 2\alpha \lambda_6) + y_i(\lambda_5 + 2\beta \lambda_6) + \lambda_6 \gamma]
\end{aligned}
\tag{12.5}
$$

Assume that $y \neq 0$ for the moment. A reasoning similar to the one employed in the proof of proposition 3.1 shows that $\lambda_i = 0, i = 1, \ldots, 8$. If $y = 0$, i.e., if the plane containing the N points goes through the optical center of the camera, we cannot conclude that all the λ_i are zero. In fact, in that case the images of the N points all lie on a straight line and the rank of matrix $\mathbf{A}$ is strictly less than 8.

7. As expected, 3-D lines work just as well as points. Think of a 3-D line as defined by two points M_1 and M_2. The images of those points are on the measured image line l represented by the nonzero vector $\mathbf{u}$. This yields two linear homogeneous equations in the coefficients of the perspective projection matrix $\tilde{\mathbf{P}}$ as follows:

$$\mathbf{u}^T \tilde{\mathbf{P}} \tilde{\mathbf{M}}_i = 0 \qquad i = 1, 2$$

If we take $\tilde{\mathbf{M}}_1 = \tilde{\mathbf{L}} = [\mathbf{L}^T, 0]^T$, the point at infinity of L, we have

$$\mathbf{u}^T \mathbf{P} \mathbf{L} = 0 \tag{12.6}$$

and for the other point M we have

$$\mathbf{u}^T (\mathbf{PM} + \mathbf{p}) = 0 \tag{12.7}$$

This is the equivalent of the linear approach for points. For the nonlinear approach, we write that that the euclidean distances of the image points to the line are zero and obtain the same equations as (12.6) and (12.7), in which we assume that $\mathbf{u} = [u_1, u_2, u_3]^T$ is normalized so as to satisfy $u_1^2 + u_2^2 = 1$. Indeed, in that case, those equations indicate that the distances are zero.

8. a. Let M, N, and Q be the points at infinity defining the three orthogonal directions. By definition, m, n, and q are the images of those three points. Therefore, the lines $\langle C, m \rangle, \langle C, n \rangle$, and $\langle C, q \rangle$ go through M, N, and Q, respectively. $\langle C, m \rangle$ is thus parallel to the first direction of lines, $\langle C, n \rangle$ to the second, and $\langle C, q \rangle$ to the third, from which the conclusion follows.

   b. Let q' be the point of $\langle m, n \rangle$ such that $\langle q, q' \rangle$ is perpendicular to $\langle m, n \rangle$ (see figure 12.6). Because $\langle C, q \rangle$ is perpendicular to the plane $(\langle C, m \rangle, \langle C, n \rangle)$, $\langle C, q' \rangle$ is perpendicular to $\langle m, n \rangle$. But since $\langle m, n \rangle$ is orthogonal to two lines of the plane (C, q, q') it is per-

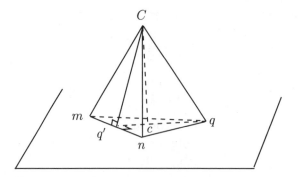

Figure 12.6   See problem 8.

pendicular to that plane and, in particular, to the line $\langle C, c \rangle$ of that plane. Similarly, we can show that $\langle C, c \rangle$ is orthogonal to $\langle n, q \rangle$ and $\langle q, m \rangle$, and thus to the plane (m, n, q). $\langle C, c \rangle$ is therefore the optical axis. This method allows us to recover the pixel coordinates u_0 and v_0 of the intersection of the optical axis with the image plane from the vanishing points of three orthogonal directions.

c. Assuming that we know α_u and α_v, we can use the new image coordinates u' and v' defined by equations (3.15). This is equivalent to multiplying matrix $\tilde{\mathbf{P}}$ of equation (3.21) on the left by matrix $\tilde{\mathbf{H}}$ defined by (3.14) and yields for $\tilde{\mathbf{P}}$ the desired form. In particular, note that $\mathbf{P} = \mathbf{R}$.

Let us assume that we know the three orthogonal directions $\mathbf{M}, \mathbf{N}$, and $\mathbf{Q}$, for example, and that they are the directions of the axes of our world coordinate system. Then we obtain

$$\tilde{\mathbf{P}} \begin{bmatrix} \mathbf{M} \\ 0 \end{bmatrix} = \mathbf{R}\mathbf{M} = \tilde{\mathbf{m}} \qquad \mathbf{R}\mathbf{N} = \tilde{\mathbf{n}} \qquad \mathbf{R}\mathbf{Q} = \tilde{\mathbf{q}}$$

Knowing $\mathbf{M}$ and $\tilde{\mathbf{m}}$, $\mathbf{N}$ and $\tilde{\mathbf{n}}$, $\mathbf{Q}$ and $\tilde{\mathbf{q}}$ yields $\mathbf{R}$.

Let us be slightly more precise. Let $\mathbf{m}', \mathbf{n}', \mathbf{q}'$ be the new pixel coordinates of the vanishing points. Define

$$\tilde{\mathbf{m}}' = \frac{1}{\sqrt{1 + \|\mathbf{m}'\|^2}} \begin{bmatrix} \mathbf{m}' \\ 1 \end{bmatrix}$$

and also define $\tilde{\mathbf{n}}'$ and $\tilde{\mathbf{q}}'$. Assume that $\mathbf{M}, \mathbf{N}$, and $\mathbf{Q}$ are normalized to unit norm. We want to find the rotation matrix $\mathbf{R}$ that minimizes

$$\|\mathbf{RM} - \tilde{\mathbf{m}}'\|^2 + \|\mathbf{RN} - \tilde{\mathbf{n}}'\|^2 + \|\mathbf{RQ} - \tilde{\mathbf{q}}'\|^2$$

A method for doing this using quaternions is discussed in section 11.4.3.1.

12.3   Answers to problems of chapter 4

1. a. Clear, since C is a sum of convex functions.

    b. It is sufficient to notice that

    $$(f_k - S(x_k))^2 = \int (S(x) - f(x))^2 \delta(x - x_k) dx$$

    Take $\Phi(x, S(x), S''(x)) = \lambda S''(x)^2 + (S(x) - f(x))^2 \sum_k \delta(x - x_k)$, apply equation (4.6), and note that

    $$f(x) \sum \delta(x - x_k) = \sum_k f_k \delta(x - x_k)$$

    c. If we substitute $R \otimes f(x)$ in the Euler-Lagrange equation, we obtain

    $$\lambda \sum_k f_k R^{(4)}(x - x_k) + \sum_k \sum_l f_l R(x_k - x_l) \delta(x - x_k)$$

    $$- \sum_k f_k \delta(x - x_k) = 0$$

    d. Perform the change of variable $x = x_k + u$; the coefficient of f_k now becomes

    $$\lambda R^{(4)}(u) + \sum_l R(x_l - x_k) \delta(u + x_k - x_l) - \delta(u)$$

    The functions $R^{(3)}(x)$ obtained by integrating this differential equation for different values of k are different if the x_k are not evenly spaced. If $x_k = kT$, we have $x_l - x_k = (l - k)T = x_{l-k}$, from which the result follows.

e. The three equations are obtained by writing

$$R_{k-1}(x_k) = R_k(x_k)\alpha_{k-1}x_k^3 + \beta_{k-1}x_k^2 + \gamma_{k-1}x_k + \delta_{k-1} = \alpha_k x_k^3 + \beta_k x_k^2$$
$$+ \gamma_k x_k + \delta_k$$

$$R'_{k-1}(x_k) = R'_k(x_k)3\alpha_{k-1}x_k^2 + 2\beta_{k-1}x_k + \gamma_{k-1} = 3\alpha_k x_k^2 + 2\beta_k x_k + \gamma_k$$

$$R''_{k-1}(x_k) = R''_k(x_k)6\alpha_{k-1}x_k + 2\beta_{k-1} = 6\alpha_k x_k + 2\beta_k$$

f. From the relation $R_k^{(3)}(x_k) - R_{k-1}^{(3)}(x_k) = -\frac{R(x_k)}{\lambda}$ we deduce $\alpha_k = \alpha_{k-1} - \frac{R(x_k)}{6\lambda}$

g.

$$\beta_k = \beta_{k-1} + \frac{x_k R(x_k)}{2\lambda}$$

$$\gamma_k = \gamma_{k-1} - \frac{x_k^2 R(x_k)}{2\lambda}$$

$$\delta_k = \delta_{k-1} + \frac{x_k^3 R(x_k)}{6\lambda}$$

2. The criterion C we minimize is given by

$$C = \sum_{(x,y)\in R} (f(x,y) - \sum_{k=1}^{n} a_k P_k(x,y))^2$$

Taking partial derivatives we obtain

$$\frac{\partial C}{\partial a_k} = -2 \sum_{(x,y)\in R} P_k(x,y)(f(x,y) - \sum_{k=1}^{n} a_k P_k(x,y))$$

We rewrite this expression as

$$-2 \sum_{(x,y)\in R} P_k(x,y)f(x,y) + 2\sum_{l} a_l (\sum_{(x,y)\in R} P_k(x,y)P_l(x,y))$$

and using the orthogonal property we obtain the result

$$a_k = \frac{\sum_{(x,y)\in R} P_k(x,y)f(x,y)}{\sum_{(x,y)\in R} P_k^2(x,y)}$$

3. By definition $\Lambda_m(\tau) = E(m(x)m(x+\tau))$, which is equal to

$$E[\int n(x-y)h(y)dy \int n(x+\tau-z)h(z)dz] =$$
$$\int\int E(n(x-y)n(x+\tau-z))h(y)h(z)dydz =$$
$$\int\int \Lambda_n(\tau-z+y)h(y)h(z)dydz =$$
$$\int[\int \Lambda_n(\tau-z+y)h(z)dz]h(y)dy =$$
$$\int \Lambda_n \otimes h(\tau+y)h(y)dy =$$
$$\int \Lambda_n \otimes h(u)h(u-\tau)du =$$
$$\int \Lambda_n \otimes h(u)h_-(\tau-u)du =$$
$$(\Lambda_n \otimes h) \otimes h_-(\tau) = \Lambda_n \otimes (h \otimes h_-)(\tau)$$

4. a. Consider the function $g(x) = H(n_f(x))$. Then the function
    $g'(x)H(n'_f(x)) = n'_f(x)\delta(n_f(x))H(n'_f(x))$ qualifies.

    b. Remember that

    $$\delta(x) = \int e^{2\pi i p x}dp$$
    $$H(x) = -\int \frac{i}{2\pi q}e^{2\pi i q x}dq$$
    $$xu(x) = \frac{1}{2\pi i}\int \mathcal{F}u(q)\frac{\partial e^{2i\pi q x}}{\partial q}dq$$

    where u is a C^1 function and $\mathcal{F}u$ is its Fourier transform. This allows us to write

    $$E(s) = \frac{1}{4\pi^2}\int\int \frac{1}{q}\frac{\partial E(e^{2i\pi(pn_f+qn'_f)})}{\partial q}dpdq$$

    c. Immediate through simple algebraic manipulations.

    d. Note that

    $$\int e^{-\frac{1}{2}\int(n(t)-k[pf(x-t)+qf'(x-t)])^2dt}dn = 0$$

    and use the definitions of $R_f(0)$ and $R''_f(0)$ at the end of section 4.3.1.4.

    e. Use the fact that

    $$\int e^{-2\pi^2 x^2}dx = \frac{1}{2}\sqrt{\frac{2}{\pi}}$$

5. Follow the hint.

6. Follow the hint.

7.
   a. We have seen in section 4.2.4 that the Euler-Lagrange equation for the problem of continuous approximation is

$$\lambda S^{(4)}(x) + S(x) = f(x)$$

The solution to this equation is given by

$$S(x) = \int R(x-y)f(y)dy$$

where the Green function $R(x,y)$ satisfies

$$\lambda \frac{d^4 R}{dx^4}(x) + R(x) = \delta(x)$$

For each value of λ we have a different Green function $R(x,\lambda)$ and $R(x,0) = \delta(x)$. If we take the Fourier transform of both sides of the previous equation, we obtain

$$\mathcal{F}R(\omega,\lambda) = \frac{1}{1 + \lambda\omega^4}$$

so we can write

$$R(x,\lambda) = \frac{1}{2\pi} \int \frac{1}{1 + \lambda\omega^4} e^{-i\omega x} d\omega$$

At $\lambda = 0$, the Green function goes to a delta function.
    If we define μ by $\lambda\mu^4 = 1$, we have for $x > 0$

$$R(x,\mu) = \frac{\mu}{2\sqrt{2}} e^{-\frac{|x|\mu}{\sqrt{2}}} \left(\cos \tfrac{|x|\mu}{\sqrt{2}} + \sin \tfrac{|x|\mu}{\sqrt{2}}\right)$$
$$\lambda\mu^4 = 1$$

   b. A simple computation shows that the primitive $g(x)$ of $h(x) = ae^{-\alpha|x|}\sin x\omega$ is equal to

$$-\frac{a}{\alpha^2 + \omega^2} e^{-\alpha|x|}(\omega \cos \omega |x| + \alpha \sin \omega |x|)$$

from which the conclusion follows.

   c. Some simple algebraic manipulations show that

$$g(n) = \frac{a}{2(\alpha^2 + \omega^2)} [(\omega - i\alpha)e^{-(\alpha-i\omega)|n|} + (\omega + i\alpha)e^{-(\alpha+i\omega)|n|}]$$

We then write

$$g_+(n) = \begin{cases} \frac{a}{2(\alpha^2+\omega^2)}[(\omega - i\alpha)e^{-(\alpha-i\omega)n} + (\omega + i\alpha)e^{-(\alpha+i\omega)n}] & n \geq 0 \\ 0 & n < 0 \end{cases}$$

and

$$g_-(n) = \begin{cases} 0 & n > 0 \\ \frac{a}{2(\alpha^2+\omega^2)}[(\omega - i\alpha)e^{(\alpha-i\omega)n} + (\omega + i\alpha)e^{(\alpha+i\omega)n}] & n \leq 0 \end{cases}$$

Let $u = \omega - i\alpha$ and $v = e^{-(\alpha-i\omega)}$. The z-transform $G_+(z)$ of $g_+(n)$ is found to be equal to

$$G_+(z) = \frac{u}{1 - vz^{-1}} + \frac{\overline{u}}{1 - \overline{v}z^{-1}} = \frac{u + \overline{u} - (u\overline{v} - \overline{u}v)z^{-1}}{1 - (v + \overline{v})z^{-1} + v\overline{v}z^{-2}}$$

This corresponds to a causal system with two conjugate poles, one of them being $v = e^{-\alpha}e^{i\omega}$. It is therefore stable. The corresponding recursive filter is

$$\frac{1}{2}o_+(n) = \omega i(n) - e^{-\alpha}(\omega \cos \omega + \alpha \sin \omega)i(n - 1)$$

$$+ e^{-\alpha}o_+(n - 1)\cos \omega - \frac{1}{2}e^{-2\alpha}o_+(n - 2)$$

8. a. The direction is the direction of the intersection of the plane defined by $\mathbf{k}$ and $\mathbf{G}$ with T_M, and this is precisely parallel to $\mathbf{G} \wedge (\mathbf{G} \wedge \mathbf{k})$.

b. Obvious from $\mathbf{G} \wedge (\mathbf{G} \wedge \mathbf{k}) = -[f_x, f_y, f_x^2 + f_y^2]^T$ and $\cos \alpha = \frac{\mathbf{k} \cdot \mathbf{p}}{\|\mathbf{p}\|}$.

c. The basis $\frac{\partial}{\partial x}, \frac{\partial}{\partial y}$ of T_M is

$$\frac{\partial}{\partial x} = [1, 0, f_x]^T \quad \frac{\partial}{\partial y} = [0, 1, f_y]^T$$

and thus $\mathbf{p} = -f_x\frac{\partial}{\partial x} - f_y\frac{\partial}{\partial y}$ and $L_{\mathbf{p}}r = -(f_x\frac{\partial r}{\partial x} + f_y\frac{\partial r}{\partial y})$. Moreover,

$$\frac{\partial r}{\partial x} = h'(\|\mathbf{g}\|)\frac{\partial\|\mathbf{g}\|}{\partial x} \quad \frac{\partial r}{\partial y} = h'(\|\mathbf{g}\|)\frac{\partial\|\mathbf{g}\|}{\partial y}$$

where $h(u) = -\frac{u}{\sqrt{1+u^2}}$. We know that $\frac{\partial\|\mathbf{g}\|}{\partial x} = \frac{f_x^2 f_x + f_{xy}f_y}{\|\mathbf{g}\|} = \frac{(Hg)_x}{\|\mathbf{g}\|}$ with a similar formula for $\frac{\partial\|\mathbf{g}\|}{\partial y}$. Therefore

$$L_{\mathbf{p}}r = -\frac{h'(\|\mathbf{g}\|)}{\|\mathbf{g}\|}\mathbf{g}^T H\mathbf{g}$$

12.4   Answers to problems of chapter 5

1. Choose $\varphi_1(x) = \theta_1$ and $U_1 = S^1 \div 0$, $\varphi_2(x) = \theta_2$ and $U_2 = S^1 \div \pi$. θ_1 and θ_2 are the angles defining the point x: $0 < \theta_1 < 2\pi$ and $-\pi < \theta_2 < \pi$. We then have

    $$\varphi_2 \circ \varphi_1^{-1}(\theta_1) = \pi - \theta_1, \quad \theta_1 \in U_1$$

    $$\varphi_1 \circ \varphi_2^{-1}(\theta_2) = \pi + \theta_2, \quad \theta_2 \in U_2$$

2. Let P be a point not on the axis of rotation going through O, i.e., a point such that $\text{Rot}(\mathbf{OP}) \neq \mathbf{OP}$. We can write equation (5.12) as

    $$\mathbf{OM}' = \text{Rot}(\mathbf{PM}) + \mathbf{T} + \text{Rot}(\mathbf{OP})$$

    which shows that changing the axis of rotation simply changes the translation vector.

3. a. As we saw in section 5.5.1, a rotation matrix is orthogonal:

    $$\mathbf{RR}^T = \mathbf{I} \tag{12.8}$$

    Deriving equation (12.8) with respect to α_i, we obtain

    $$\frac{\partial \mathbf{R}}{\partial \alpha_i}\mathbf{R}^T + \mathbf{R}\frac{\partial \mathbf{R}^T}{\partial \alpha_i} = 0 \tag{12.9}$$

    Equation (12.9) shows that matrix $\mathbf{B}_i = \frac{\partial \mathbf{R}}{\partial \alpha_i}\mathbf{R}^T$ is antisymmetric:

    $$\mathbf{B}_i + \mathbf{B}_i^T = \mathbf{0}$$

    Since clearly $\frac{\partial \mathbf{R}}{\partial \alpha_i} = \mathbf{B}_i\mathbf{R}$, we can write

    $$\frac{\partial \mathbf{RM}}{\partial \alpha_i} = \mathbf{b}_i \wedge \mathbf{RM}$$

    Computing $\frac{d\mathbf{RM}}{d\alpha}$, we obtain

    $$\frac{d\mathbf{RM}}{d\alpha} = [\frac{\partial \mathbf{RM}}{\partial \alpha_1} \frac{\partial \mathbf{RM}}{\partial \alpha_2} \frac{\partial \mathbf{RM}}{\partial \alpha_3}]$$

    $$= [\mathbf{b}_1 \wedge \mathbf{RM} \ \mathbf{b}_2 \wedge \mathbf{RM} \ \mathbf{b}_3 \wedge \mathbf{RM}]$$

Therefore

$$\frac{d\mathbf{RM}}{d\alpha}\mathbf{v} = (\sum_{i=1}^{3} v_i \mathbf{b}_i) \wedge \mathbf{RM} \tag{12.10}$$

b. i. We use the representation $\mathbf{R} = e^{\mathbf{H}}$ where $\mathbf{H}$ is antisymmetric.

$$\mathbf{H} = \begin{bmatrix} 0 & -c & b \\ c & 0 & -a \\ -b & a & 0 \end{bmatrix}$$

The vector $\mathbf{r} = [a, b, c]^T$ is parallel to the axis of rotation, and $\|\mathbf{r}\|^2 = \theta^2$, with θ the angle of rotation. We also have

$$\tilde{\mathbf{e}}_1 = \begin{bmatrix} 0 & 0 & 0 \\ 0 & 0 & -1 \\ 0 & 1 & 0 \end{bmatrix}$$

The three relations are then immediate.

ii. Verifying that $\mathbf{RR}^T = \mathbf{I}$ in this formula yields a useful relationship between f and g:

$$\mathbf{R}^T = \mathbf{I} - f(\theta)\mathbf{H} + g(\theta)\mathbf{H}^2$$

Therefore, using the fact than $\mathbf{H}^3 = -\theta^2\mathbf{H}$,

$$\mathbf{RR}^T = \mathbf{I} + (2g(\theta) - f^2(\theta) - \theta^2 g^2(\theta))\mathbf{H}^2$$

This yields

$$2g(\theta) - f^2(\theta) - \theta^2 g^2(\theta) = 0$$

iii. Using equation (5.46) we obtain

$$\frac{\partial \mathbf{R}}{\partial a} = a\frac{f'(\theta)}{\theta}\mathbf{H} + a\frac{g'(\theta)}{\theta}\mathbf{H}^2 + f(\theta)\tilde{\mathbf{e}}_1 + g(\theta)(\mathbf{H}\tilde{\mathbf{e}}_1 + \tilde{\mathbf{e}}_1\mathbf{H})$$

We notice that $\mathbf{H}^2$ and $\mathbf{H}\tilde{\mathbf{e}}_1 + \tilde{\mathbf{e}}_1\mathbf{H}$ are symmetric matrices, and write

$$\frac{\partial \mathbf{R}^T}{\partial a} = -a\frac{f'(\theta)}{\theta}\mathbf{H} - f(\theta)\tilde{\mathbf{e}}_1 + a\frac{g'(\theta)}{\theta}\mathbf{H}^2 + g(\theta)(\mathbf{H}\tilde{\mathbf{e}}_1 + \tilde{\mathbf{e}}_1\mathbf{H})$$

from this, we compute

$$\mathbf{R}\frac{\partial\mathbf{R}^T}{\partial a} = -\theta a(\frac{f'(\theta)}{\theta a} + g'(\theta)f(\theta) - g(\theta)f'(\theta))\mathbf{H}$$

$$- f(\theta)\tilde{\mathbf{e}}_1 + f(\theta)g(\theta)\mathbf{H}\tilde{\mathbf{e}}_1\mathbf{H}$$

$$+ \frac{a}{\theta}(g'(\theta) - f(\theta)f'(\theta) - \theta^2 g'(\theta)g(\theta))\mathbf{H}^2 \qquad (12.11)$$

$$+ g(\theta)(\mathbf{H}\tilde{\mathbf{e}}_1 + \tilde{\mathbf{e}}_1\mathbf{H})$$

$$- f^2(\theta)\mathbf{H}\tilde{\mathbf{e}}_1 + g^2(\theta)\mathbf{H}^2(\mathbf{H}\tilde{\mathbf{e}}_1 + \tilde{\mathbf{e}}_1\mathbf{H})$$

Using the fact that $\mathbf{H}^2\tilde{\mathbf{e}}_1\mathbf{H} = -a\mathbf{H}^2$, we can rewrite the previous equation as

$$\mathbf{R}\frac{\partial\mathbf{R}^T}{\partial a} = -\theta a(\frac{f'(\theta)}{\theta^2} + g'(\theta)f(\theta) - g(\theta)f'(\theta))\mathbf{H}$$

$$- f(\theta)\tilde{\mathbf{e}}_1 + f(\theta)g(\theta)\mathbf{H}\tilde{\mathbf{e}}_1\mathbf{H} + \frac{a}{\theta}(g'(\theta)$$

$$- f(\theta)f'(\theta) - \theta^2 g'(\theta)g(\theta) - \theta g^2(\theta))\mathbf{H}^2 \qquad (12.12)$$

$$+ g(\theta)(\mathbf{H}\tilde{\mathbf{e}}_1 + \tilde{\mathbf{e}}_1\mathbf{H}) - (f^2(\theta) + \theta^2 g^2(\theta))\mathbf{H}\tilde{\mathbf{e}}_1$$

Rewriting $\mathbf{H}\tilde{\mathbf{e}}_1$ as the sum of an odd and even component

$$\mathbf{H}\tilde{\mathbf{e}}_1 = \frac{\mathbf{H}\tilde{\mathbf{e}}_1 + \tilde{\mathbf{e}}_1\mathbf{H}}{2} + \frac{\mathbf{H}\tilde{\mathbf{e}}_1 - \tilde{\mathbf{e}}_1\mathbf{H}}{2}$$

the coefficient of $\mathbf{H}\tilde{\mathbf{e}}_1 + \tilde{\mathbf{e}}_1\mathbf{H}$ in equation (12.12) is

$$g(\theta) - \frac{f^2(\theta)}{2} - \frac{\theta^2 g^2(\theta)}{2}$$

which is equal to zero, thanks to equation (5.47). If we derive this equation with respect to θ, we obtain

$$g'(\theta) - f(\theta)f'(\theta) - \theta^2 g(\theta)g'(\theta) - \theta g^2(\theta) = 0$$

which shows that the coefficient of $\mathbf{H}^2$ in 12.12 is zero.

We are therefore left with the sum of three odd terms in $\mathbf{H}, \tilde{\mathbf{e}}_1$, and $\mathbf{H}\tilde{\mathbf{e}}_1 - \tilde{\mathbf{e}}_1\mathbf{H}$:

$$\mathbf{R}\frac{\partial \mathbf{R}^T}{\partial a} = -\theta a\left(\frac{f'(\theta)}{\theta^2} + g'(\theta)f(\theta) - g(\theta)f'(\theta) + \frac{f(\theta)g(\theta)}{\theta}\right)\mathbf{H}$$

$$- f(\theta)\tilde{\mathbf{e}}_1$$

$$\frac{1}{2}(f^2(\theta) + \theta^2 g^2(\theta))(\mathbf{H}\tilde{\mathbf{e}}_1 - \tilde{\mathbf{e}}_1\mathbf{H})$$

Using equation (5.47), the coefficient of $\mathbf{H}\tilde{\mathbf{e}}_1 - \tilde{\mathbf{e}}_1\mathbf{H}$ is $g(\theta)$. Using the expressions for f and g, the coefficient of $\mathbf{H}$ is

$$a\frac{\sin\theta - \theta}{\theta^3}$$

Finally

$$\mathbf{R}\frac{\partial \mathbf{R}^T}{\partial a} = a\frac{\sin\theta - \theta}{\theta^3}\mathbf{H} - f(\theta)\tilde{\mathbf{e}}_1 + g(\theta)(\mathbf{H}\tilde{\mathbf{e}}_1 - \tilde{\mathbf{e}}_1\mathbf{H})$$

Matrix $\mathbf{H}\tilde{\mathbf{e}}_1 - \tilde{\mathbf{e}}_1\mathbf{H}$ is given by

$$\mathbf{H}\tilde{\mathbf{e}}_1 - \tilde{\mathbf{e}}_1\mathbf{H} = \begin{bmatrix} 0 & b & c \\ -b & 0 & 0 \\ -c & 0 & 0 \end{bmatrix}$$

iv. If we compute the partials with respect to b and c, we get

$$\mathbf{R}\frac{\partial \mathbf{R}^T}{\partial b} = b\frac{\sin\theta - \theta}{\theta^3}\mathbf{H} - f(\theta)\tilde{\mathbf{e}}_2 + g(\theta)(\mathbf{H}\tilde{\mathbf{e}}_2 - \tilde{\mathbf{e}}_2\mathbf{H})$$

where

$$\mathbf{H}\tilde{\mathbf{e}}_2 - \tilde{\mathbf{e}}_2\mathbf{H} = \begin{bmatrix} 0 & -a & 0 \\ a & 0 & c \\ 0 & -c & 0 \end{bmatrix}$$

and also

$$\mathbf{R}\frac{\partial \mathbf{R}^T}{\partial c} = c\frac{\sin\theta - \theta}{\theta^3}\mathbf{H} - f(\theta)\tilde{\mathbf{e}}_3 + g(\theta)(\mathbf{H}\tilde{\mathbf{e}}_3 - \tilde{\mathbf{e}}_3\mathbf{H})$$

where

$$\mathbf{H}\tilde{\mathbf{e}}_3 - \tilde{\mathbf{e}}_3\mathbf{H} = \begin{bmatrix} 0 & 0 & -a \\ 0 & 0 & -b \\ a & b & 0 \end{bmatrix}$$

Plugging all this into formula (12.10), we obtain

$$\frac{d\mathbf{RM}}{d\alpha}\mathbf{v} = -(\mathbf{v}.\mathbf{r}\frac{\sin\theta - \theta}{\theta^3}\mathbf{H} - f(\theta)\tilde{\mathbf{v}} + g(\theta)\widetilde{\mathbf{v} \wedge \mathbf{r}})\mathbf{RM}$$

$$= \mathbf{b} \wedge \mathbf{RM}$$

with

$$\mathbf{b} = \frac{1 - f(\theta)}{\theta^2}(\mathbf{r}.\mathbf{v})\mathbf{r} + f(\theta)\mathbf{v} + g(\theta)\mathbf{r} \wedge \mathbf{v}$$

4.   Let us write the equation of the line

$$\alpha u + \beta v - \rho = 0$$

with the constraint that $\alpha^2 + \beta^2 = 1$.
   We want to minimize the following criterion:

$$C(\alpha, \beta, \rho) = \frac{1}{2}\sum_{i=1}^{p}(\alpha u_i + \beta v_i - \rho)^2$$

subject to the constraint $\alpha^2 + \beta^2 = 1$. We consider

$$C'(\alpha, \beta, \rho) = \frac{1}{2}\sum_{i=1}^{p}(\alpha u_i + \beta v_i - \rho)^2 + \frac{p\lambda}{2}(1 - \alpha^2 - \beta^2)$$

Taking the partial derivatives with respect to α, β, and ρ yields

$$\frac{\partial C'}{\partial \alpha} = p(\alpha S_{u^2} + \beta S_{uv} - \rho\overline{u} - \lambda\alpha)$$

$$\frac{\partial C'}{\partial \beta} = p(\alpha S_{uv} + \beta S_{v^2} - \rho\overline{v} - \lambda\beta)$$

$$\frac{\partial C'}{\partial \rho} = p(\rho - \alpha\overline{u} - \beta\overline{v})$$

Equating the last equation to 0 yields

$$\rho = \alpha\overline{u} + \beta\overline{v}$$

which proves in particular that the best approximating line goes through the center of gravity of the set of pixels. Replacing ρ with this value in the other two partial derivatives and equating them to 0 yields

$$\alpha(S_{u^2} - \overline{u}^2) + \beta(S_{uv} - \overline{uv}) - \lambda\alpha = 0$$

$$\alpha(S_{uv} - \overline{uv}) + \beta(S_{v^2} - \overline{v}^2) - \lambda\beta = 0$$

Answers to Problems

or, in matrix form:

$$\begin{bmatrix} \sigma_u^2 & \sigma_{uv} \\ \sigma_{uv} & \sigma_v^2 \end{bmatrix} \begin{bmatrix} \alpha \\ \beta \end{bmatrix} = \lambda \begin{bmatrix} \alpha \\ \beta \end{bmatrix} \qquad (12.13)$$

This equation shows that the vector $[\alpha, \beta]^T$ is an eigenvector of the covariance matrix of the set of pixels.

Let us compute the value of the criterion C:

$$C = \frac{p}{2}(\alpha^2 S_{u^2} + \beta^2 S_{v^2} + 2\alpha\beta S_{uv} - 2\rho(\alpha\overline{u} + \beta\overline{v}) + \rho^2)$$

Replace ρ by its value in the previous equation

$$C = \frac{p}{2}(\alpha^2 \sigma_u^2 + \beta^2 \sigma_v^2 + 2\alpha\beta\sigma_{uv})$$

which is equal to $\frac{p\lambda}{2}(\alpha^2 + \beta^2)$ according to equation (12.13). Thus $C = \frac{p\lambda}{2}$, which shows that we have to choose the eigenvector corresponding to the smallest eigenvalue of the covariance matrix (note that they are both greater than or equal to 0).

In order to have a more precise description of the solution, we can compute the eigenvectors of the covariance matrix or minimize with respect to ρ and θ the following criterion:

$$D(\theta, \rho) = \frac{1}{2}\sum_{i=1}^{p}(u_i \cos\theta + v_i \sin\theta - \rho)^2$$

We compute the two partial derivatives:

$$\frac{\partial D}{\partial \rho} = p(\rho - \overline{u}\cos\theta - \overline{v}\sin t)$$

$$\frac{\partial D}{\partial \theta} = p[(S_{v^2} - S_{u^2})\frac{\sin 2\theta}{2} + S_{uv}\cos 2\theta + \rho(\overline{u}\sin\theta - \overline{v}\cos\theta)]$$

Equating the first equation to 0, we find that $\rho = \overline{u}\cos\theta + \overline{v}\sin\theta$. Replacing ρ by this value in the second equation and equating it to 0 yields

$$(\sigma_v^2 - \sigma_u^2)\frac{\sin 2\theta}{2} + \sigma_{uv}\cos 2\theta = 0$$

Therefore

$$\tan 2\theta = \frac{2\sigma_{uv}}{\sigma_v^2 - \sigma_u^2}$$

This yields two values of θ modulo π differing by $\frac{\pi}{2}$. These two values define the directions of the two eigenvectors of the covariance matrix of the set of pixels.

5. According to equation (5.43), we need to compute the three quantities $\frac{\partial \sigma_u^2}{\partial \mathbf{m}_i}, \frac{\partial \sigma_v^2}{\partial \mathbf{m}_i}$, and $\frac{\partial \sigma_{uv}}{\partial \mathbf{m}_i}$. Using the definitions, we obtain

$$\frac{\partial \sigma_u^2}{\partial \mathbf{m}_i} = \frac{\partial S_{u^2}}{\partial \mathbf{m}_i} - \frac{\partial \overline{u}^2}{\partial \mathbf{m}_i} = \frac{2}{n}[u_i - \overline{u}, 0]$$

$$\frac{\partial \sigma_v^2}{\partial \mathbf{m}_i} = \frac{\partial S_{v^2}}{\partial \mathbf{m}_i} - \frac{\partial \overline{v}^2}{\partial \mathbf{m}_i} = \frac{2}{n}[0, v_i - \overline{v}]$$

$$\frac{\partial \sigma_{uv}}{\partial \mathbf{m}_i} = \frac{\partial S_{uv}}{\partial \mathbf{m}_i} - \frac{\partial \overline{uv}}{\partial \mathbf{m}_i} = \frac{1}{n}[v_i - \overline{v}, u_i - \overline{u}]$$

6. Let us compute the coordinates of the perpendicular projection A of m_1 on the line of equation $u + av + b = 0$. We write that the vector $\mathbf{m}_1 \mathbf{A}$ of coordinates $[u_A - u_1, v_A - v_1]^T$ is parallel to a vector normal to the line, for example $[1, a]^T$. This yields a first equation:

$$au_A - v_A - au_1 + v_1 = 0,$$

A second equation is obtained from the fact that A is on the line:

$$u_A + av_A + b = 0,$$

From this we obtain the coordinates of A:

$$\begin{cases} u_A = \frac{1}{1+a^2}[a(au_1 - v_1) - b] \\ \quad v_A = \frac{au_1 - v_1 + a^2 b}{1+a^2} \end{cases}$$

Similarly, we obtain for B

$$\begin{cases} u_B = \frac{1}{1+a^2}[a(au_p - v_p) - b] \\ \quad v_B = \frac{au_p - v_p + a^2 b}{1+a^2} \end{cases}$$

These equations define the coordinates of A and B as functions of the coordinates of the pixels m_i from which the uncertainty can be computed.

7. a. Consider the unit circle S^1. The problem is to find the points of S^1 that define the orientation of the line supporting $\mathbf{x}$.

    b. Obvious from the previous question.

c.
$$\frac{\partial \mathbf{y}}{\partial \mathbf{x}} = \pm \frac{1}{\|\mathbf{x}\|}(\mathbf{I} - \frac{\mathbf{x}\mathbf{x}^T}{\|\mathbf{x}\|^2})$$

d. We define the criterion C':

$$C'(\mathbf{x}, \mathbf{z}) = -(\mathbf{x}^T\mathbf{z})^2 + \lambda(\mathbf{z}^T\mathbf{z} - 1)$$

Taking the partial derivative with respect to $\mathbf{z}$, we obtain

$$\frac{1}{2}(\frac{\partial C'}{\partial \mathbf{z}})^T = -(\mathbf{x}^T\mathbf{z})\mathbf{x} + \lambda\mathbf{z}$$

Equating the first component to 0 allows us to compute $\lambda(\mathbf{x}, \mathbf{z})$:

$$\lambda = \frac{a}{u}(\mathbf{x}^T\mathbf{z})$$

e. We write that the second component of $(\frac{\partial C'}{\partial \mathbf{z}})^T$ must also equal 0, then replace λ in it with the previous value:

$$\frac{\mathbf{x}^T\mathbf{z}}{u}(av - bu) = 0$$

Thus, at the optimum, we have either $\mathbf{x}^T\mathbf{z} = 0$ or $av - bu = 0$. It is easy to show that the first case corresponds to a maximum of the criterion, and therefore we choose

$$\psi(\mathbf{x}, \mathbf{z}) = av - bu$$

$\psi = 0$ implies that the vectors $\mathbf{x}$ and $\mathbf{z}$ have the same direction, and therefore $\mathbf{z} = \pm\frac{\mathbf{x}}{\|\mathbf{x}\|}$.

f. From the definitions, we have

$$\frac{\partial \mathbf{\Phi}}{\partial \mathbf{z}} = \begin{bmatrix} \frac{\partial \psi}{\partial \mathbf{z}} \\ \mathbf{z}^T \end{bmatrix} \qquad \frac{\partial \mathbf{\Phi}}{\partial \mathbf{x}} = \begin{bmatrix} \frac{\partial \psi}{\partial \mathbf{x}} \\ \mathbf{0} \end{bmatrix}$$

Some simple algebra yields

$$\frac{\partial \mathbf{\Phi}}{\partial \mathbf{z}} = \begin{bmatrix} -b & a \\ u & v \end{bmatrix}$$

and

$$\frac{\partial \mathbf{\Phi}}{\partial \mathbf{x}} = \begin{bmatrix} v & -u \\ 0 & 0 \end{bmatrix}$$

This immediately yields

$$\mathbf{Df} = -\frac{1}{\mathbf{x}^T\mathbf{z}} \begin{bmatrix} v^2 & -uv \\ -uv & u^2 \end{bmatrix}$$

Using the constraint $\mathbf{z}^T\mathbf{z} = 1$, we can rewrite it as

$$\mathbf{Df} = -\frac{1}{\mathbf{x}^T\mathbf{z}}[\mathbf{I} - \mathbf{z}\mathbf{z}^T]$$

Because we know that $\mathbf{z} = \pm\frac{\mathbf{x}}{\|\mathbf{x}\|}$ at the optimum, we find that

$$\mathbf{Df} = \pm\frac{1}{\|\mathbf{x}\|}[\mathbf{I} - \frac{\mathbf{x}\mathbf{x}^T}{\|\mathbf{x}\|^2}]$$

as expected. We find that the rank of $\mathbf{Df}$ is in general 1, which is not surprising since we know from the theory developed in section 5.6.3 that it is less than or equal to the smallest of $m - p = 1$ and $n = 2$.

8. Do it yourself!

9. Do it yourself!

12.5 Answers to problems of chapter 6

1. According to equation (6.4), we have $z = d_{12}f/d$, and according to equation (6.5) we have $x = d_{12}w/d$. Therefore, if $z = h(x)$ we have $dh(d_{12}w/d) = d_{12}f$, which implicitly defines d as a function of w.

2. Expand h up to first order:

$$h(x_2) = h(x_1) + (x_2 - x_1)h'(x_1)$$

Replace in the expression of $DG = \frac{d_{12}|z_1 - z_2|}{|z_2x_1 - z_1x_2|}$.

$$DG = d_{12}\frac{|h'(x_1)|}{|h(x_1) - x_1h'(x_1)|}$$

Rewrite as

$$d_{12}\frac{|(h'(x_1) + h(x_1)) - h(x_1)|}{x_1(h'(x_1) + h(x_1)) - h(x_1)(1 + x_1)}$$

This is the expression $d_{12}\frac{|z_2-z_1|}{x_1 z_2 - x_2 z_1|}$ for the points of coordinates $(x_1, h(x_1))$ and $(x_2 = x_1 + 1, h'(x_1) + h(x_1))$. The first is on the object, the second on the tangent to the object at that point.

3. Let v_i be the retinal coordinates of $m_i, i = 1, 2, 3$. The disparity d_1 for the match (m_1, m_2) is equal to $v_1 - v_2$. The cyclopean coordinate of the corresponding point is $w_1 = \frac{v_1 + v_2}{2}$. Similarly, for the match (m_1, m_3) the disparity d_2 is $v_1 - v_3$ and the cyclopean coordinate is $w_2 = \frac{v_1 + v_3}{2}$. Thus the disparity gradient is $DG = |\frac{d_1 - d_2}{w_1 - w_2}| = 2$. As a consequence, if we impose $DG < 2$, we cannot have multiple matches and therefore the uniqueness constraint is satisfied.

4. From the analysis done in section 6.2.6, we have

$$\mathbf{T} = \frac{\mathbf{X}}{\|\mathbf{X}\|} \quad \mathbf{X} = \mathbf{U}_{t_1} \wedge \mathbf{U}_{t_2}$$

Therefore

$$\frac{d\mathbf{T}}{dS} = \kappa \mathbf{N} = \frac{d\mathbf{X}}{dS}\frac{\|\mathbf{X}\|^2 - 1}{\|\mathbf{X}\|^3}$$

The curvature κ of (C) is the norm of $\frac{d\mathbf{T}}{dS}$. The problem is to compute $\frac{d\mathbf{X}}{dS}$:

$$\frac{d\mathbf{X}}{dS} = \frac{d\mathbf{U}_{t_1}}{ds_1} \wedge \mathbf{U}_{t_2}\frac{ds_1}{dS} + \mathbf{U}_{t_1} \wedge \frac{d\mathbf{U}_{t_2}}{ds_2}\frac{ds_2}{dS}$$

s_1 and s_2 are the arclengths along (c_1) and (c_2). We know from equation (6.8) that

$$\frac{d\mathbf{U}_{t_i}}{ds_i} = \kappa_i(\mathbf{P}_i^{-1}\tilde{\mathbf{m}}_i) \wedge (\mathbf{P}_i^{-1}\begin{bmatrix} \mathbf{n}_i \\ 0 \end{bmatrix}) \qquad i = 1, 2$$

We must compute $\frac{ds_i}{dS}$ $i = 1, 2$. Let us again consider the perspective equation

$$\tilde{\mathbf{m}} = \tilde{\mathbf{P}}\tilde{\mathbf{M}} \tag{12.14}$$

In this equation, we assume that $\tilde{\mathbf{m}} = [U, V, W]^T$ and that $\tilde{\mathbf{M}} = [x, y, z, 1]^T$. The pixel coordinates u and v of m are given by

$$u = \frac{U}{W} \quad v = \frac{V}{W}$$

and we note that $\mathbf{m} = [u, v]^T$. Take the differential of both sides of equation (12.14)

$$\begin{bmatrix} \frac{dU}{ds} \\ \frac{dV}{ds} \\ \frac{dW}{ds} \end{bmatrix} ds = \tilde{\mathbf{P}} \begin{bmatrix} \mathbf{T} \\ 0 \end{bmatrix} dS = \mathbf{PT} dS$$

But we also have

$$\frac{du}{ds} = \frac{\frac{dU}{ds} W - U \frac{dW}{ds}}{W^2} \qquad \frac{dv}{ds} = \frac{\frac{dV}{ds} W - V \frac{dW}{ds}}{W^2}$$

and the unit tangent vector $\mathbf{t}$ to (c) is given by

$$\mathbf{t} = \begin{bmatrix} \frac{du}{ds} \\ \frac{dv}{ds} \end{bmatrix}$$

This yields

$$\begin{bmatrix} \frac{dU}{ds} \\ \frac{dV}{ds} \\ \frac{dW}{ds} \end{bmatrix} = W \begin{bmatrix} \mathbf{t} \\ 0 \end{bmatrix} + \frac{dW}{ds} \begin{bmatrix} \mathbf{m} \\ 1 \end{bmatrix}$$

We thus have

$$\left(W \begin{bmatrix} \mathbf{t} \\ 0 \end{bmatrix} + \frac{dW}{ds} \begin{bmatrix} \mathbf{m} \\ 1 \end{bmatrix} \right) ds = \mathbf{PT} dS$$

Let us denote by $\tilde{\mathbf{r}}$ the vector $[-u, v, 0]^T$. We notice that $\tilde{\mathbf{r}}^T \tilde{\mathbf{m}} = 0$. If we take the inner product of both sides of the previous equation with $\tilde{\mathbf{r}}$, we obtain

$$\frac{ds}{dS} = \frac{\tilde{\mathbf{r}}^T \mathbf{PT}}{W \mathbf{r}^T \mathbf{t}} \tag{12.15}$$

where $\mathbf{r} = [-u, v]^T$.

A final word is that, apparently, we do not know the $W_i, i = 1, 2, 3$. But in fact we know them through equation (12.14): M is reconstructed from $m_i, i = 1, 2, 3$. Its coordinates x, y, and z are then known, and so are the matrixes $\tilde{\mathbf{P}}_i$; therefore we can compute the W_i.

We have shown that

$$\frac{ds_i}{dS} = \frac{\tilde{\mathbf{r}}_i^T \mathbf{P}_i \mathbf{T}}{W_i \mathbf{r}_i^T \mathbf{t}_i} \qquad i = 1, 2$$

This means that we can compute $\frac{d\mathbf{X}}{dS}$. $\mathbf{N}$ is the unit vector parallel to $\frac{d\mathbf{X}}{dS} \frac{\|\mathbf{X}\|^2 - 1}{\|\mathbf{X}\|^3}$. The binormal $\mathbf{B}$ is equal to $\mathbf{T} \wedge \mathbf{N}$ by definition.

In order to recover the torsion ρ, we can use the Frenet formula $\frac{d\mathbf{B}}{dS} = \rho \mathbf{N}$. We know from the previous analysis that $\mathbf{N} = \varepsilon \frac{\mathbf{Y}}{\|\mathbf{Y}\|}$ with $\varepsilon = \text{sign}(\|\mathbf{X}\|^2 - 1)$ and $\mathbf{Y} = \frac{d\mathbf{X}}{dS}$. Thus

$$\frac{d\mathbf{B}}{dS} = \frac{\varepsilon}{\|\mathbf{X}\| \|\mathbf{Y}\|} \mathbf{X} \wedge \frac{d^2\mathbf{X}}{dS^2} + \frac{d(\frac{\varepsilon}{\|\mathbf{X}\| \|\mathbf{Y}\|})}{dS} \mathbf{X} \wedge \frac{d\mathbf{X}}{dS}$$

Since $\rho = \frac{d\mathbf{B}}{dS} \cdot \mathbf{N}$, we find that

$$\rho = -\frac{1}{\|\mathbf{X}\| \|\mathbf{Y}\|^2} (\mathbf{X}, \frac{d\mathbf{X}}{dS}, \frac{d^2\mathbf{X}}{dS^2})$$

The problem is thus to compute $\frac{d^2\mathbf{X}}{dS^2}$, which can be done, in principle.

5. a. We have $\mathbf{M} = \mathbf{R}\mathbf{M}' + \mathbf{t}$. The plane equation $\mathbf{n}^T\mathbf{M} - 1 = 0$ becomes $\mathbf{n}^T\mathbf{R}\mathbf{M}' + \mathbf{n}^T\mathbf{t} - 1 = 0$ which, because $\mathbf{n}^T\mathbf{t} = 0$, is equal to $(\mathbf{R}^T\mathbf{n})^T\mathbf{M}' - 1 = 0$.

    b. Since $\mathbf{n}^T\mathbf{M} = 1$, we have

    $$\lambda = \frac{1}{\mathbf{m}^T\mathbf{n}}$$

    c. From the previous question

    $$\mathbf{AB} = \frac{\mathbf{b}}{\beta} - \frac{\mathbf{a}}{\alpha}$$

    and thus $\mathbf{p} = \frac{\alpha\mathbf{b} - \beta\mathbf{a}}{\sqrt{\beta^2\|\mathbf{a}\|^2 + \alpha^2\|\mathbf{b}\|^2 - 2\alpha\beta\mathbf{a}^T\mathbf{b}}}$

    d. α, β, γ, and δ are linear homogeneous functions of the coordinates of $\mathbf{n}$. Therefore, $\mathbf{p}$ is homogeneous and of degree 0 in those coordinates, meaning that we can divide the numerator and denominator by $\cos\theta$ (if $\cos\theta \neq 0$). This makes $\mathbf{p}$ a function of $\tan\theta$ and ϕ only.

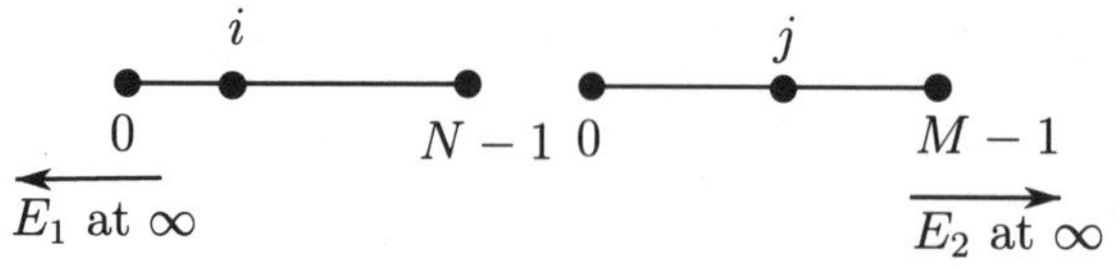

Figure 12.7   See problem 6.

e. Because $\mathbf{n}^T\mathbf{t} = 0$, $\tan\theta$ is given by the expression

$$\tan\theta = -\frac{t_z}{t_x\cos\phi + t_y\sin\phi}$$

f. $(\mathbf{p}^T\mathbf{q})^2 + (\mathbf{q}^T\mathbf{r})^2 + (\mathbf{r}^T\mathbf{s})^2 + (\mathbf{s}^T\mathbf{p})^2$

and it is a function of ϕ only.

g. Replace $\mathbf{n}$ by $\mathbf{R}^T\mathbf{n}$.

6. Consider the two scanlines of figure 12.7.

   The epipole E_1 in the left image is at infinity to the left of 0, while the epipole E_2 in the right image is at infinity to the right of $M-1$ (figure 12.7 is obtained as the limit of figure 6.9 when the two retinal planes rotate to become parallel to $\langle C_1, C_2 \rangle$). Thus, given a match (i,j) between a left pixel and a right pixel, and given a left pixel i' such that $i < i'$, the ordering constraint is satisfied for all right pixels j' such that the order (E_1, i, i') is different from the order (E_2, j, j'), that is, for those pixels j' such that $j' \geq j$.

7. The matrix $\mathbf{A}_i$ and the vector $\mathbf{b}_i$ can be written as

$$\mathbf{A}_i = \begin{bmatrix} \mathbf{q}_{i1}^T - u_i\mathbf{q}_{i3}^T \\ \mathbf{q}_{i2}^T - v_i\mathbf{q}_{i3}^T \end{bmatrix} \qquad \mathbf{b}_i = \begin{bmatrix} q_{i14} - u_iq_{i34} \\ q_{i24} - v_iq_{34} \end{bmatrix}$$

We conclude from this that $\frac{\partial \mathbf{A}_i}{\partial u_j} = \frac{\partial \mathbf{A}_i}{\partial v_j} = \mathbf{0}$ and that $\frac{\partial \mathbf{b}_i}{\partial u_j} = \frac{\partial \mathbf{b}_i}{\partial v_j} = \mathbf{0}$ if $i \neq j$. We also have

$$\frac{\partial \mathbf{A}_i}{\partial u_i} = \begin{bmatrix} -\mathbf{q}_{i3}^T \\ \mathbf{0} \end{bmatrix} \quad \frac{\partial \mathbf{A}_i}{\partial v_i} = \begin{bmatrix} \mathbf{0} \\ -\mathbf{q}_{i3}^T \end{bmatrix} \quad \frac{\partial \mathbf{b}_i}{\partial u_i} = \begin{bmatrix} -q_{i34} \\ 0 \end{bmatrix} \quad \frac{\partial \mathbf{b}_i}{\partial v_i} = \begin{bmatrix} 0 \\ -q_{i34} \end{bmatrix}$$

8. According to chapter 2, four point correspondences yield matrix $\mathbf{A}$ up to a scale factor. Thus we know that

$$\mathbf{A} = \frac{1}{\lambda}(\mathbf{R} + \frac{\mathbf{t}\mathbf{n}^T}{d})$$

Let (m_1, m_2) be one of the four correspondences. We can reconstruct the 3-D point M whose images are m_1 and m_2 using one of the techniques described in section 6.10.2. Let $\tilde{\mathbf{m}}_2 = [x, y, z]^T$ be its coordinates in the normalized coordinate system of the second camera. These coordinates are $\tilde{\mathbf{m}}_1 = \mathbf{R}\tilde{\mathbf{m}}_2 + \mathbf{t}$ in the normalized coordinate system of the first camera, and we can compute λ so that we have

$$\tilde{\mathbf{m}}_1 = \lambda \mathbf{A} \tilde{\mathbf{m}}_2$$

We now have $\mathbf{A} = \mathbf{R} + \frac{\mathbf{t}\mathbf{n}^T}{d}$, and we can recover $\mathbf{n}$ and d as follows:

$$\frac{\mathbf{n}}{d} = (\mathbf{A} - \mathbf{R})^T \frac{\mathbf{t}}{\|\mathbf{t}\|^2}$$

9. It is a simple matter to apply proposition 5.7. Criterion (6.20) is of the form $C(\mathbf{x}, \mathbf{z})$ where the measurement $\mathbf{x}$ is in R^{2n} and $\mathbf{z} = \mathbf{M}$ is in R^3. Let $\mathbf{y}_0 \equiv \mathbf{M}_0$ be a vector that minimizes the criterion (the point M_0 can be obtained by using a standard minimization program). We have

$$\mathbf{x}_0 = [\hat{\mathbf{m}}_1^T, \ldots, \hat{\mathbf{m}}_n^T]^T$$

Furthermore, the vectors $\mathbf{m}_i \equiv \mathbf{f}_i(\mathbf{M})$ are given by

$$\mathbf{f}_i(\mathbf{M}) = \begin{bmatrix} \frac{\mathbf{q}_{i1}^T \mathbf{M} + q_{i14}}{\mathbf{q}_{i3}^T \mathbf{M} + q_{i34}} \\ \frac{\mathbf{q}_{i2}^T \mathbf{M} + q_{i24}}{\mathbf{q}_{i3}^T \mathbf{M} + q_{i34}} \end{bmatrix}$$

Therefore it is easy to compute the Hessian $\mathbf{H}$ of C with respect to $\mathbf{z}$ at the point $(\mathbf{x}_0, \mathbf{y}_0)$: It is a 3×3 matrix.

We can also compute $\mathbf{K} = \frac{\partial(\frac{\partial C}{\partial \mathbf{z}})^T}{\partial \mathbf{x}})(\mathbf{x}_0, \mathbf{y}_0)$, which is a $3 \times 2n$ matrix. We model the pixels m_i as independent random points with covariance matrixes Λ_i and means $\hat{\mathbf{m}}_i$. The reconstructed point M is then modelled, up to the first order, by a random vector with mean $\mathbf{M}_0$ and with covariance matrix

$$\Lambda_M = \mathbf{H}^{-1}\mathbf{K}\Lambda\mathbf{K}^T\mathbf{H}^{-1T}$$

where $\Lambda = \text{diag}(\Lambda_1, \ldots, \Lambda_n)$.

12.6   Answers to problems of chapter 7

1.   From section 3.2.2 we know that $\mathbf{Cm}$ is parallel to $\mathbf{P}_0^{-1}\tilde{\mathbf{m}}$. Moreover, the perspective matrix of the camera in its second position is, according to section 3.3.2, equal to

$$\tilde{\mathbf{P}}_1 = \tilde{\mathbf{P}}_0 \begin{bmatrix} \mathbf{R}^T & -\mathbf{R}^T\mathbf{t} \\ \mathbf{0} & 1 \end{bmatrix} = [\mathbf{P}_0\mathbf{R}^T - \mathbf{P}_0\mathbf{R}^T\mathbf{t} + \mathbf{p}_0]$$

if we write $\tilde{\mathbf{P}}_0 = [\mathbf{P}_0\ \mathbf{p}_0]$. Thus, $\mathbf{C'm'}$ is parallel to

$$\mathbf{P}_1^{-1}\tilde{\mathbf{m}}' = \mathbf{R}\mathbf{P}_0^{-1}\tilde{\mathbf{m}}'$$

from which the result follows.

2.   If the displacement is a pure rotation, the unit vectors parallel to $\mathbf{Cm}$ and $\mathbf{Cm}'$ correspond to each other by the rotation $\mathbf{R}$. This means that

$$\frac{\mathbf{Cm}}{\|\mathbf{Cm}\|} = \mathbf{R}\frac{\mathbf{Cm}'}{\|\mathbf{Cm}'\|}$$

3.   We generalize the problem slightly as follows. Let

$$\tau_\nu = \sum_{i=1}^{n} x_i^\nu \qquad \nu = 1, 2, \ldots$$

and $\varphi_1, \ldots, \varphi_n$ be the elementary symmetric functions of $x_1, \ldots, x_n$ (we have $\tau_1 = \varphi_1$). We now derive a recursive formula for τ_ν. This is taken from the book by Hermann Weyl [Wey39].
   The polynomial

$$\psi(\lambda) = \Pi_{i=1}^{n}(1 - \lambda x_i) = 1 - \varphi_1\lambda + \varphi_2\lambda^2 - \cdots \pm \varphi_n\lambda^n$$

has the logarithmic derivative

$$-\frac{\psi'(\lambda)}{\psi(\lambda)} = \sum_{i=1}^{n} \frac{x_i}{1 - \lambda x_i} = \tau_1 + \tau_2\lambda^2 + \cdots$$

The Taylor expansion on the right side is to be understood in the formal sense. We then obtain

$$-\psi'(\lambda) = \psi(\lambda) \sum_{\nu=1}^{N} \tau_\nu\lambda^{\nu-1}$$

From this follow the recursive formulas

$$\varphi_1 = \tau_1$$

$$-2\varphi_2 = -\varphi_1\tau_1 + \tau_2$$

$$3\varphi_3 = \varphi_2\tau_1 - \varphi_1\tau_2 + \tau_3$$

$$\vdots$$

From the last two equations, we obtain

$$\tau_3 = -\frac{1}{2}\varphi_1^3 + \frac{3}{2}\varphi_1\tau_2 + 3\varphi_3$$

Equation (7.15) is then obvious if we take for the x_i the eigenvalues of the symmetric matrix $\mathbf{B}$.

4. a. Obvious from propositions 2.3 and 2.4.

 b. By definition of the cross-ratio

$$\{\langle \mathbf{x}, \mathbf{q}\rangle, \langle \mathbf{x}, \mathbf{p}_3\rangle; \langle \mathbf{x}, \mathbf{p}_1\rangle, \langle \mathbf{x}, \mathbf{p}_2\rangle\} = \frac{\theta_p - \theta_{p_1}}{\theta_p - \theta_{p_2}} : \frac{\theta_{p_3} - \theta_{p_1}}{\theta_{p_3} - \theta_{p_2}} = \frac{\theta_{p_3}}{\theta_p}$$

 c. $\dfrac{(\mathbf{p}_2, \mathbf{x}, \mathbf{p}_i)(\mathbf{p}_1, \mathbf{x}, \mathbf{p}_3)}{(\mathbf{p}_1, \mathbf{x}, \mathbf{p}_i)(\mathbf{p}_2, \mathbf{x}, \mathbf{p}_3)} = \dfrac{(\mathbf{p}_2', \mathbf{x}', \mathbf{p}_i')(\mathbf{p}_1', \mathbf{x}', \mathbf{p}_3')}{(\mathbf{p}_1', \mathbf{x}', \mathbf{p}_i')(\mathbf{p}_2', \mathbf{x}', \mathbf{p}_3')}$ $i = 4, 5, 6$

 d. Straightforward.

 e. Straightforward.

 f. $\mathbf{a}_i(\mathbf{u}) = [(p_3^{(i)}u_3 - p_2^{(i)}u_2)p_1^{(i)'}, (p_1^{(i)}u_1 - p_3^{(i)}u_3)p_2^{(i)'},$

$$(p_2^{(i)}u_2 - p_1^{(i)}u_1)p_3^{(i)'}]^T \qquad i = 4, 5, 6$$

 The equation of the cubic is

$$f(\mathbf{u}) = (\mathbf{a}_4(\mathbf{u}), \mathbf{a}_5(\mathbf{u}), \mathbf{a}_6(\mathbf{u})) = 0$$

 g. Replacing $\mathbf{u}$ with its value as a function of $\mathbf{x}$, one finds

$$f(\mathbf{u}) = (x_1 x_2 x_3)g(\mathbf{x})$$

 where $g(\mathbf{x})$ is of degree 3.

h. $i = 1, 2, 3$, by inspection of g, and $i = 4, 5, 6$, because $\mathbf{a}_i(\Phi\mathbf{p}_i) = \mathbf{0}, i = 4, 5, 6$

i. Apply the same method to the points $\mathbf{p}_1, \ldots, \mathbf{p}_5, \mathbf{p}_7$. The second cubic goes through $\mathbf{p}_1, \ldots, \mathbf{p}_5$ and $\mathbf{b}_1$, whose definition depends only upon $\mathbf{p}_4$ and $\mathbf{p}_5$.

j. Two cubics intersect in nine points in general. Since there are six of these points that do not correspond to solutions of the problem, there remain three.

5. Let us do it for $\mathbf{P}'$. The equation of the plane (C', l') in the coordinate system attached to the second position of the camera is $\mathbf{n}' \cdot \mathbf{M}' = 0$. Since $\mathbf{M} = \mathbf{R}\mathbf{M}' + \mathbf{t}$ represents the same point in the coordinate system attached to the first position of the camera, the equation of this plane becomes, in that coordinate system

$$\mathbf{n}' \cdot \mathbf{R}^T(\mathbf{M} - \mathbf{t}) = 0$$

for which the result for $\mathbf{P}'$ follows.

6. Using, as suggested, a system for algebraic computation, we find

$$\lambda_0 = e_1 e_2 e_3\, e_1' e_2' e_3'\, \frac{e_1(e_3' - e_2') + e_2(e_1' - e_3') + e_3(e_2' - e_1')}{\frac{1}{e_1}\left(\frac{1}{e_3'} - \frac{1}{e_2'}\right) + \frac{1}{e_2}\left(\frac{1}{e_1'} - \frac{1}{e_3'}\right) + \frac{1}{e_3}\left(\frac{1}{e_2'} - \frac{1}{e_1'}\right)}$$

A corresponding vector in the null space is

$$\mathbf{p}_0 = \begin{bmatrix} \frac{e_3' e_2 - e_2' e_3}{e_2' - e_3'} \\ \frac{e_1' e_3 - e_3' e_1}{e_3' - e_1'} \\ \frac{e_2' e_1 - e_1' e_2}{e_1' - e_2'} \end{bmatrix}$$

7. The idea of the proof is to define $\mathbf{B}$ as the matrix whose column vectors are the coordinates of the three singular points of Σ, which have been computed in section 7.3.2.6 and in problem 6. If we substitute $\mathbf{B}\mathbf{u}$ for $\mathbf{u}$ in the definition of $\Sigma\mathbf{u}$ we find that it does not depend upon the square terms u_1^2, u_2^2, and u_3^2, and therefore it can be written as $\mathbf{A}\Sigma_0$ for some 3×3 matrix $\mathbf{A}$.

8. a. A good candidate is $\mathbf{q} = \lambda_1\mathbf{q}_1 + \lambda_2\mathbf{q}_2 + \lambda_3\mathbf{q}_3$. We have to verify that it satisfies equation (2.11). It is easy to do using the fact that $\mathbf{q}_1, \mathbf{q}_2$,

and $\mathbf{q}_3$ satisfy equation (2.11) and, taken in pairs, equation (2.12) of section 2.5.1, since they all intersect at C.

b. Using the notations of section 2.5.1, since L intersects r, r', and r'', we can write the three equations

$$S(\mathbf{p}, \lambda_1 \mathbf{q}_1 + \lambda_2 \mathbf{q}_2 + \lambda_3 \mathbf{q}_3) = \sum_{i=1}^{3} \lambda_i S(\mathbf{p}, \mathbf{q}_i) = 0$$

$$S(\mathbf{p}, \lambda_1 \mathbf{q}_1' + \lambda_2 \mathbf{q}_2' + \lambda_3 \mathbf{q}_3') = \sum_{i=1}^{3} \lambda_i S(\mathbf{p}, \mathbf{q}_i') = 0$$

$$S(\mathbf{p}, \lambda_1 \mathbf{q}_1'' + \lambda_2 \mathbf{q}_2'' + \lambda_3 \mathbf{q}_3'') = \sum_{i=1}^{3} \lambda_i S(\mathbf{p}, \mathbf{q}_i'') = 0$$

c. In order for the previous system of linear equations in λ_1, λ_2, and λ_3 to have a nonzero solution, the following determinant must be equal to 0:

$$\begin{vmatrix} S(\mathbf{p}, \mathbf{q}_1) & S(\mathbf{p}, \mathbf{q}_2) & S(\mathbf{p}, \mathbf{q}_3) \\ S(\mathbf{p}, \mathbf{q}_1') & S(\mathbf{p}, \mathbf{q}_2') & S(\mathbf{p}, \mathbf{q}_3') \\ S(\mathbf{p}, \mathbf{q}_1'') & S(\mathbf{p}, \mathbf{q}_2'') & S(\mathbf{p}, \mathbf{q}_3'') \end{vmatrix}$$

This determinant is a homogeneous polynomial of degree 3 in $\mathbf{p}$.

9. a. Let $\tilde{\mathbf{m}}_1$ and $\tilde{\mathbf{m}}_2$ be two projective representations of m_1 and m_2. Since $m_1 \leftrightarrow m_2$, we have

$$\tilde{\mathbf{m}}_1 = \lambda \mathbf{A} \tilde{\mathbf{m}}_2 \tag{12.16}$$

where λ is a nonzero scalar. Let $\mathbf{a}_1^T, \mathbf{a}_2^T, \mathbf{a}_3^T$ be the three row vectors of $\mathbf{A}$, and let us choose $\tilde{\mathbf{m}}_i = [u_i, v_i, 1]^T, i = 1, 2$. This assumes that the pixels are not at infinity, i.e., that they are indeed points and not just directions. Equation (12.16) yields two equations that are linear in the coefficients of $\mathbf{A}$:

$$\begin{aligned} \mathbf{a}_1^T \tilde{\mathbf{m}}_2 - u_1 \mathbf{a}_3^T \tilde{\mathbf{m}}_2 &= 0 \\ \mathbf{a}_2^T \tilde{\mathbf{m}}_2 - v_1 \mathbf{a}_3^T \tilde{\mathbf{m}}_2 &= 0 \end{aligned} \tag{12.17}$$

b. Let $\tilde{\mathbf{l}}_1$ and $\tilde{\mathbf{l}}_2$ be two projective representations of l_1 and l_2. The point equation of l_1 is

$$\tilde{\mathbf{l}}_1^T \tilde{\mathbf{m}}_1 = 0$$

We know from equation (12.16) that $\tilde{\mathbf{m}}_1 = \lambda \mathbf{A}\tilde{\mathbf{m}}_2$, and therefore

$$\tilde{\mathbf{l}}_1^T \mathbf{A}\tilde{\mathbf{m}}_2 = 0$$

which proves that

$$\tilde{\mathbf{l}}_2 = \mu \mathbf{A}^T \tilde{\mathbf{l}}_1 \tag{12.18}$$

where μ is a nonzero scalar. In analogy with the case of points, let us write $\tilde{\mathbf{l}}_i = [r_i, s_i, 1]^T, i = 1, 2$. This assumes that the lines do not go through the origin of coordinates. This is the dual of the condition of the previous question. Let $\mathbf{b}_1, \mathbf{b}_2$, and $\mathbf{b}_3$ be the three column vectors of $\mathbf{A}$. Equation (12.18) yields two equations that are linear in the coefficients of $\mathbf{A}$:

$$\begin{aligned} \mathbf{b}_1^T\tilde{\mathbf{l}}_1 - r_2\mathbf{b}_3^T\tilde{\mathbf{l}}_1 = 0 \\ \mathbf{b}_2^T\tilde{\mathbf{l}}_1 - s_2\mathbf{b}_3^T\tilde{\mathbf{l}}_1 = 0 \end{aligned} \tag{12.19}$$

c. $\mathbf{A}$ is a collineation of $\mathcal{P}^2$ and is therefore determined by four or more point and line matches (see chapter 2). This is confirmed by the fact that each such match provides us with two linear equations in the coefficients of $\mathbf{A}$. Since $\mathbf{A}$ depends upon eight parameters, the conclusion follows. Let us now normalize $\mathbf{A}$ so that $a_{33} = 1$, and let $\mathbf{a} = [a_{11}, a_{12}, a_{13}, a_{21}, a_{22}, a_{23}, a_{31}, a_{32}]^T$, an 8×1 vector. Equations (12.17) can be written as

$$\mathbf{c}^T\mathbf{a} \equiv \begin{bmatrix} u_2 & v_2 & 1 & 0 & 0 & 0 & -u_1u_2 & -u_1v_2 \end{bmatrix}\mathbf{a} = u_1$$

$$\mathbf{d}^T\mathbf{a} \equiv \begin{bmatrix} 0 & 0 & 0 & u_2 & v_2 & 1 & -v_1u_2 & -v_1v_2 \end{bmatrix}\mathbf{a} = v_1$$

and equations (12.19) can be written as

$$\mathbf{e}^T\mathbf{a} \equiv \begin{bmatrix} r_1 & 0 & -r_1r_2 & s_1 & 0 & -r_2s_1 & 1 & 0 \end{bmatrix}\mathbf{a} = r_2$$

$$\mathbf{f}^T\mathbf{a} \equiv \begin{bmatrix} 0 & r_1 & -r_1s_2 & 0 & s_1 & -s_2s_1 & 0 & 1 \end{bmatrix}\mathbf{a} = s_2$$

If we have n point or line matches, we can write $2n$ linear equations in $\mathbf{a}$:

$$\mathbf{Xa} = \mathbf{b}$$

where $\mathbf{X}$ is a $2n \times 8$ matrix and $\mathbf{b}$ a $2n \times 1$ vector. If the rank of $\mathbf{X}$ is 8, the solution is

$$\mathbf{a} = (\mathbf{X}^T\mathbf{X})^{-1}\mathbf{X}^T\mathbf{b}$$

12.7   Answers to problems of chapter 8

1. Straightforward.

2. Straightforward.

$$\frac{\Lambda_1 + \Lambda_2}{4}$$

3. $\frac{1}{L^2}\mathbf{M}_1\mathbf{M}_2^T(\Lambda_1 + \Lambda_2)\mathbf{M}_1\mathbf{M}_2$

4. The principle of the method is the following. Integrating by parts, we can write

$$L_i = \frac{1}{\|\Omega\|}[s^i\cos((t-s)\|\Omega\|)]_{s=t_0}^{s=t} - \frac{i}{\|\Omega\|}M_{i-1}$$

$$M_i = -\frac{1}{\|\Omega\|}[s^i\sin((t-s)\|\Omega\|)]_{s=t_0}^{s=t} + \frac{i}{\|\Omega\|}L_{i-1}$$

which can be written in matrix form as

$$\begin{bmatrix} L_i \\ M_i \end{bmatrix} = \frac{i}{\|\Omega\|}\begin{bmatrix} 1 & 0 \\ 0 & -1 \end{bmatrix}\begin{bmatrix} L_{i-1} \\ M_{i-1} \end{bmatrix} + \mathbf{b}_i$$

with

$$\mathbf{b}_i = \frac{1}{\|\Omega\|}\begin{bmatrix} [s^i\cos((t-s)\|\Omega\|)]_{s=t_0}^{s=t} \\ -[s^i\sin((t-s)\|\Omega\|)]_{s=t_0}^{s=t} \end{bmatrix}$$

This recursive formula allows us to compute L_i and M_i for any value of $i > 0$ from the easily computed values of L_0 and M_0.

5. The measurement vector is $\mathbf{x} = [\mathbf{r}_1^T, \mathbf{r}_2^T]^T$ where the vector $\mathbf{r} = [a, b, M^T, l]^T$ (see section 8.4.2). The state is the kinematic screw, which we assume is constant, with $\mathbf{a} = [\Omega^T, \mathbf{V}^T]^T$. The measurement equation $\mathbf{f}_0$ is equal to $[\mathbf{g}_0, \mathbf{h}_0]^T$, with

$$\mathbf{g}_0 = \mathbf{U}_0\begin{bmatrix} a_1 \\ b_1 \\ 1 \end{bmatrix} \wedge \begin{bmatrix} a_2 \\ b_2 \\ 1 \end{bmatrix},$$

$$\mathbf{h}_0 = \mathbf{U}_0\mathbf{M}_1 + \mathbf{U}_1\mathbf{V} - \mathbf{M}_2$$

and

$$\mathbf{U}_0 = e^{(t-t_0)\hat{\Omega}}$$

We then have to derive all this carefully. We have

$$\frac{\partial \mathbf{g}_0}{\partial \mathbf{a}} = [\frac{\partial \mathbf{g}_0}{\partial \mathbf{V}}, \frac{\partial \mathbf{g}_0}{\partial \Omega}]$$

which is a 6×6 matrix. Clearly we have $\frac{\partial \mathbf{g}_0}{\partial \mathbf{V}} = \mathbf{0}$ and $\frac{\partial \mathbf{g}_0}{\partial \Omega}$ is a 3×3 matrix, which can be computed using the results of problem 3 of chapter 5. $\frac{\partial \mathbf{g}_0}{\partial \mathbf{x}} = [\frac{\partial \mathbf{g}_0}{\partial \mathbf{r}_1} \quad \frac{\partial \mathbf{g}_0}{\partial \mathbf{r}_2}]$ is a 3×12 matrix, assuming that we keep the three coordinates of the cross-product. Therefore we can write

$$\frac{\partial \mathbf{g}_0}{\partial \mathbf{r}_1} = [\mathbf{U}_0 \begin{bmatrix} 1 \\ 0 \\ 0 \end{bmatrix} \wedge \begin{bmatrix} a_2 \\ b_2 \\ 1 \end{bmatrix}, \ \mathbf{U}_0 \begin{bmatrix} 0 \\ 1 \\ 0 \end{bmatrix} \wedge \begin{bmatrix} a_2 \\ b_2 \\ 1 \end{bmatrix}, \ \mathbf{0}]$$

The last submatrix $\mathbf{0}$ is 3×4. We have similar results for matrix $\frac{\partial \mathbf{g}_0}{\partial \mathbf{r}_2}$.

Let us now look at $\mathbf{h}_0$. We have $\frac{\partial \mathbf{h}_0}{\partial \mathbf{x}} = [\frac{\partial \mathbf{h}_0}{\partial \mathbf{r}_1} \quad \frac{\partial \mathbf{h}_0}{\partial \mathbf{r}_2}]$, which is a 3×12 matrix, and $\frac{\partial \mathbf{h}_0}{\partial \mathbf{r}_1} = [\frac{\partial \mathbf{h}_0}{\partial a_1} \quad \frac{\partial \mathbf{h}_0}{\partial b_1} \quad \frac{\partial \mathbf{h}_0}{\partial \mathbf{M}_1} \quad \frac{\partial \mathbf{h}_0}{\partial l}] = [\mathbf{0} \ \mathbf{0} \ \mathbf{U}_0 \ \mathbf{0}]$, which is a 3×6 matrix. Similarly

$$\frac{\partial \mathbf{h}_0}{\partial \mathbf{r}_2} = [\mathbf{0} \ \mathbf{0} \ -\mathbf{I} \ \mathbf{0}]$$

We then have $\frac{\partial \mathbf{h}_0}{\partial \mathbf{a}} = [\frac{\partial \mathbf{h}_0}{\partial \Omega} \quad \frac{\partial \mathbf{h}_0}{\partial \mathbf{V}}]$. Clearly $\frac{\partial \mathbf{h}_0}{\partial \mathbf{V}} = \mathbf{U}_1$, and

$$\frac{\partial \mathbf{h}_0}{\partial \Omega} = \frac{\partial \mathbf{U}_0 \mathbf{M}_1}{\partial \Omega} + \frac{\partial \mathbf{U}_1 \mathbf{V}}{\partial \Omega}$$

$\frac{\partial \mathbf{U}_0 \mathbf{M}_1}{\partial \Omega}$ is obtained as a consequence of problem 3 of chapter 5 and $\frac{\partial \mathbf{U}_1 \mathbf{V}}{\partial \Omega}$ as follows. We notice that

$$\mathbf{U}_1(t) = \int_{t_0}^{t} \mathbf{U}_0(s) ds$$

Therefore

$$\frac{\partial \mathbf{U}_1(t) \mathbf{V}}{\partial \Omega} = \int_{t_0}^{t} \frac{\partial \mathbf{U}_0(t) \mathbf{V}}{\partial \Omega} ds$$

and we know how to compute $\frac{\partial \mathbf{U}_0(t) \mathbf{V}}{\partial \Omega}$

6. a. $\mathbf{Q} = \mathbf{P} + \lambda\mathbf{u}$ represents a point of L for $-\infty < \lambda < \infty$. The condition that $\mathbf{QM}_i$ be perpendicular to L can be written $\lambda = \mathbf{PM}_i \cdot \mathbf{u}$. Thus the distance d_i of M_i to L is equal to $\|\mathbf{PM}_i - (\mathbf{PM}_i \cdot \mathbf{u})\mathbf{u}\|$, and the conclusion follows from the fact that $C(\mathbf{P},\mathbf{u}) = \sum_{i=1}^{p} d_i^2$.

    b. Compute

$$\frac{1}{2}\left(\frac{\partial C}{\partial \mathbf{P}}\right)^T = \sum_{i=1}^{p}(-\mathbf{PM}_i + (\mathbf{PM}_i \cdot \mathbf{u})\mathbf{u} = \sum_{i=1}^{p}\mathbf{u} \wedge (\mathbf{M}_i\mathbf{P} \wedge \mathbf{u}) = p\mathbf{u} \wedge (\overline{\mathbf{M}}\mathbf{P} \wedge \mathbf{u})$$

    where $\overline{M}$ is the center of gravity of the points M_i. Setting this partial derivative equal to 0, we conclude that $\overline{\mathbf{M}}\mathbf{P}$ is parallel to $\mathbf{u}$ and therefore that L goes through $\overline{M}$.

    c. Since $\|\mathbf{u}\| = 1$, we consider the criterion

$$C' = C + \lambda(\|\mathbf{u}\|^2 - 1)$$

    Compute

$$\frac{1}{2}\left(\frac{\partial C'}{\partial \mathbf{u}}\right)^T = -\sum_{i=1}^{p}(\mathbf{PM}_i \cdot \mathbf{u})\mathbf{PM}_i + \lambda\mathbf{u} = -p\Lambda\mathbf{u} + \lambda\mathbf{u}$$

    where Λ is the covariance matrix of the points M_i (we chose $P = \overline{M}$). Setting this derivative equal to 0 shows that $\mathbf{u}$ is an eigenvector of Λ. Let us compute the corresponding value of C:

$$C = \sum_{i=1}^{p}(\mathbf{PM}_i \cdot \mathbf{PM}_i - \mathbf{u}^T\mathbf{PM}_i\mathbf{PM}_i^T\mathbf{u}) = \sum_{i=1}^{p}(\mathbf{PM}_i \cdot \mathbf{PM}_i) - p\mathbf{u}^T\Lambda\mathbf{u}$$

$$= \left(\sum_{i=1}^{p}\mathbf{PM}_i \cdot \mathbf{PM}_i\right) - \mu p$$

    where μ is an eigenvalue of Λ. In order to minimize C, we have to maximize this eigenvalue.

    d. The line representation $\mathbf{z}_0 = [\overline{\mathbf{M}}^T, \mathbf{u}_0^T]^T$ minimizes the criterion

$$C(\mathbf{x}, \mathbf{z}) = \sum_{i=1}^{p}[\|\mathbf{PM}_i\|^2 - (\mathbf{PM}_i \cdot \mathbf{u})^2]$$

    subject to the constraint $\|\mathbf{u}\|^2 - 1 = 0$. $\mathbf{u}_0$ is the eigenvector of matrix Λ corresponding to the largest eigenvalue, $\mathbf{x} = [\mathbf{M}_1^T, \ldots, \mathbf{M}_p^T]^T$, and $\mathbf{z} = [\mathbf{P}^T, \mathbf{u}^T]^T$. Therefore we can directly apply the results of section 5.6.3 to compute the uncertainty of z_0 from the uncertainty of x:

$$\frac{1}{2}(\frac{\partial C'}{\partial \mathbf{z}})^T = \frac{1}{2}(\frac{\partial C}{\partial \mathbf{z}})^T + \lambda \begin{bmatrix} 0 \\ \mathbf{u} \end{bmatrix}$$

We also have

$$\frac{1}{2}(\frac{\partial C}{\partial \mathbf{z}})^T = \begin{bmatrix} \frac{1}{2}(\frac{\partial C}{\partial \mathbf{P}})^T \\ \frac{1}{2}(\frac{\partial C}{\partial \mathbf{u}})^T \end{bmatrix} = p \begin{bmatrix} \mathbf{u} \wedge (\overline{\mathbf{M}}\mathbf{P} \wedge \mathbf{u}) \\ -\mathbf{P}\overline{\mathbf{M}}\mathbf{P}\overline{\mathbf{M}}^T\mathbf{u} - \Lambda\mathbf{u} \end{bmatrix}$$

Thus

$$\frac{1}{2}(\frac{\partial C'}{\partial \mathbf{z}})^T = p \begin{bmatrix} \mathbf{u} \wedge (\overline{\mathbf{M}}\mathbf{P} \wedge \mathbf{u}) \\ -\mathbf{P}\overline{\mathbf{M}}\mathbf{P}\overline{\mathbf{M}}^T\mathbf{u} - \Lambda\mathbf{u} + \frac{\lambda}{p}\mathbf{u} \end{bmatrix}$$

which is a 6×1 vector. Since $\frac{\partial C'}{\partial \mathbf{z}} = \mathbf{0}$, we can compute λ from, for example, the last coordinate of $\frac{\partial C'}{\partial \mathbf{z}} = \mathbf{0}$, replace it with this value in the fourth and the fifth (let us call them φ_1 and φ_2), and define

$$\Phi(\mathbf{x}, \mathbf{z}) = \begin{bmatrix} p\mathbf{u} \wedge (\overline{\mathbf{M}}\mathbf{P} \wedge \mathbf{u}) \\ \varphi_1(\mathbf{x}, \mathbf{z}) \\ \varphi_2(\mathbf{x}, \mathbf{z}) \\ \|\mathbf{u}\|^2 - 1 \end{bmatrix}$$

The mapping $\mathbf{f}: \mathbf{x} \rightarrow \mathbf{z}$ that was discussed in section 5.6 has its derivative equal to $-(\frac{\partial \Phi}{\partial \mathbf{z}})^{-1}\frac{\partial \Phi}{\partial \mathbf{x}}$, which can in principle be computed.

12.8   Answers to problems of chapter 9

1. Let us compute $\mathbf{v}_m(s + 1) \cdot \mathbf{t}(s + 1)$. According to equation (9.83), we have

$$\mathbf{v}_m(s + 1) \cdot \mathbf{t}(s + 1) =$$

$$\mathbf{v}_m(s) \cdot \mathbf{t}(s) + \mathbf{v}_m(s) \cdot (\mathbf{t}(s + 1) - \mathbf{t}(s)) +$$

$$\gamma\mathbf{n}(s) \cdot \mathbf{t}(s)(\mathbf{v}_m(s) \cdot \mathbf{n}(s) - \hat{\beta}(s)) +$$

$$\gamma\mathbf{n}(s) \cdot (\mathbf{t}(s + 1) - \mathbf{t}(s))(\mathbf{v}_m(s) \cdot \mathbf{n}(s) - \hat{\beta}(s))$$

$\mathbf{v}_m \cdot \mathbf{t}$ is the computed tangential field t, and since $\mathbf{n}(s) \cdot \mathbf{t}(s) = 0$ we have

$$t(s + 1) = t(s) + \mathbf{v}_m(s) \cdot \Delta\mathbf{t} + y\mathbf{n}(s) \cdot \Delta\mathbf{t}(\beta(s) - \hat{\beta}(s))$$

Using the approximation $\Delta\mathbf{t} = \kappa\mathbf{n}$ we obtain

$$\frac{\partial t}{\partial s} \sim \kappa\beta + y\kappa(\beta - \hat{\beta})$$

In practice, $y << 1$ and, if the local measurements are good, $\beta \sim \hat{\beta}$. Therefore we find that the reconstructed tangential field satisfies the following condition:

$$\frac{\partial t}{\partial s} \sim \kappa\beta$$

This equation should be compared with equation (9.25).

2. a. Straightforward.

   b. Straightforward.

   c. We have $\mathbf{U}_t \wedge \mathbf{U}_n = \varepsilon\mathbf{m}$. From equation (9.50) we have

   $$\mathbf{U}_n \cdot \mathbf{W} = (\mathbf{U}_n, \mathbf{U}_t, \dot{\mathbf{U}}_t + \mathbf{U}_t \wedge \mathbf{\Omega}) = -(\dot{\mathbf{U}}_t + \mathbf{U}_t \wedge \mathbf{\Omega}, \mathbf{U}_t, \mathbf{U}_n)$$

   Using equation (9.52), we have

   $$\mathbf{U}_n \cdot \mathbf{W} = \varepsilon((\kappa w + \frac{\partial\beta}{\partial s})\mathbf{U}_n - \beta\varepsilon\mathbf{k} + \mathbf{U}_t \wedge \mathbf{\Omega}) \cdot \mathbf{m}$$

   The result follows from $\mathbf{U}_n \cdot \mathbf{m} = 0$, $\mathbf{t} \wedge \mathbf{n} = \varepsilon\mathbf{k}$, and $\mathbf{m} \cdot \mathbf{k} = 1$.

   d. From section 9.5.3

   $$\Gamma = \frac{|u|}{\|\mathbf{W}\|^3} \|\mathbf{W} \wedge (\frac{\partial\mathbf{W}}{\partial s} \wedge \mathbf{W})\|$$

   and from equation (9.85)

   $$u = -\frac{\mathbf{U}_n \cdot \mathbf{W}}{z\|\mathbf{W}\|}$$

   e. Take the derivative of both sides with respect to S

   $$\frac{\partial x}{\partial S}\mathbf{B} + x\rho\mathbf{N} = \varepsilon u(\mathbf{W} \wedge \frac{\partial^2\mathbf{W}}{\partial s^2})$$

   Take the inner product of both sides with $\mathbf{N}$ to obtain ρx.

Now we have

$$\mathbf{N} = \mathbf{B} \wedge \mathbf{T} = \frac{\varepsilon}{x\|\mathbf{W}\|}(\mathbf{W} \wedge \frac{\partial \mathbf{W}}{\partial s}) \wedge \mathbf{W}$$

Thus

$$\rho x = \frac{\varepsilon}{x\|\mathbf{W}\|}((\mathbf{W} \wedge \frac{\partial \mathbf{W}}{\partial s}) \wedge \mathbf{W}, \mathbf{W}, \frac{\partial^2 \mathbf{W}}{\partial s^2})$$

Expand the determinant to find the answer.

3. We know that $w = v + \alpha$, and therefore $w = \alpha$ is equivalent to $v = 0$, i.e., $\frac{\partial s}{\partial \tau} = 0$. Since the motion of the curve is in a frontoparallel plane, the depth z is constant and equal to d. Therefore we have a very simple relationship between the differentials of the arclengths s and S:

$$ds = \frac{1}{d}\, dS$$

So we have $\frac{\partial s}{\partial \tau} = \frac{1}{d}\frac{\partial S}{\partial \tau}$, and the second term is equal to 0 for isometric motions.

4. a. $\mathbf{t}_0 = \frac{1}{u}\mathbf{P}'_S$

   $\mathbf{n}_\beta = -\frac{w}{u}\mathbf{P}'_S + \mathbf{P}'_\tau$

   b. Let us do the first one as follows: $[\mathbf{n}_\beta, \mathbf{t}_0]^1 = -\frac{w}{u}\frac{\partial(\frac{1}{u})}{\partial S} + \frac{1}{u}\frac{\partial(\frac{w}{u})}{\partial S} + \frac{\partial(\frac{1}{u})}{\partial \tau}$.
   From that we obtain

   $$[\mathbf{n}_\beta, \mathbf{t}_0]^1 = \frac{1}{u^2}(w_S - u_\tau)$$

   Similarly

   $$[\mathbf{n}_\beta, \mathbf{t}_0]^2 = 0$$

   c. Clearly we have $w_S - u_\tau = u\frac{\partial \alpha}{\partial s}$, and thus $[\mathbf{n}_\beta, \mathbf{t}_0]^1 = \frac{1}{u}\frac{\partial \alpha}{\partial s}$. Therefore

   $$L_{[\mathbf{n}_\beta, \mathbf{t}_0]} = \frac{\partial \alpha}{\partial s}L_{\mathbf{t}_0}$$

In particular

$$L_{[\mathbf{n}_\beta, \mathbf{t}_0]}\beta = \frac{\partial \alpha}{\partial s}\frac{\partial \beta}{\partial s}$$

5. a. Indeed, the reasoning that leads to equation (9.41) can be followed step by step for $\mathbf{W_B}$.

    b. We have

    $$\dot{\mathbf{W}}_\mathbf{B} = \dot{\mathbf{W}} \wedge \mathbf{Y} + \mathbf{W} \wedge \dot{\mathbf{Y}}$$

    and, because $\mathbf{W}_\mathbf{B}^T\mathbf{Y} = \mathbf{W}_\mathbf{B}^T\mathbf{W} = 0$, we have

    $$\mathbf{W_B} \wedge \dot{\mathbf{W}}_\mathbf{B} = -(\mathbf{W}_\mathbf{B}^T\dot{\mathbf{W}})\mathbf{Y} + (\mathbf{W}_\mathbf{B}^T\dot{\mathbf{Y}})\mathbf{W}$$

    Using $\mathbf{W_B} \wedge \Omega = (\mathbf{W}^T\Omega)\mathbf{Y} - (\mathbf{Y}^T\Omega)\mathbf{W}$, we can now compute

    $$\mathbf{W_B} \wedge (\dot{\mathbf{W}}_\mathbf{B} + \mathbf{W_B} \wedge \Omega) = -(\mathbf{W}_\mathbf{B}^T\dot{\mathbf{W}})\mathbf{Y} + (\mathbf{W}_\mathbf{B}^T\dot{\mathbf{Y}})\mathbf{W} + (\mathbf{W}^T\Omega)(\mathbf{W} \wedge \mathbf{Y}) \wedge \mathbf{Y}$$
    $$+ (\mathbf{Y}^T\Omega)\mathbf{W} \wedge (\mathbf{W} \wedge \mathbf{Y})$$

    Expand the triple products and group the terms:

    $$(-(\mathbf{W}_\mathbf{B}^T\dot{\mathbf{W}}) + (\mathbf{W}^T\Omega)(\mathbf{W}^T\mathbf{Y}) - (\mathbf{Y}^T\Omega)(\mathbf{W}^T\mathbf{W}))\mathbf{Y} +$$
    $$((\mathbf{W}_\mathbf{B}^T\dot{\mathbf{Y}}) - (\mathbf{W}^T\Omega)(\mathbf{Y}^T\mathbf{Y}) + (\mathbf{Y}^T\Omega)(\mathbf{W}^T\mathbf{Y}))\mathbf{W}$$

    Use some standard properties of determinants to obtain

    $$(\mathbf{Y}^T(\mathbf{W} \wedge (\dot{\mathbf{W}} + \mathbf{W} \wedge \Omega)))\mathbf{Y} + (\mathbf{W}^T(\mathbf{Y} \wedge (\dot{\mathbf{Y}} + \mathbf{Y} \wedge \Omega)))\mathbf{W} \qquad (12.20)$$

    c. By definition (see appendix C):

    $$L_{[\mathbf{v}_r, \mathbf{t}_0]} = L_{\mathbf{v}_r}L_{\mathbf{t}_0} - L_{\mathbf{t}_0}L_{\mathbf{v}_r} = wL_{\mathbf{t}_0}L_{\mathbf{t}_0} + L_{\mathbf{n}_\beta}L_{\mathbf{t}_0} - L_{\mathbf{t}_0}(wL_{\mathbf{t}_0}) - L_{\mathbf{t}_0}L_{\mathbf{n}_\beta}$$

    But

    $$L_{\mathbf{t}_0}(wL_{\mathbf{t}_0}) = \frac{\partial w}{\partial s}L_{\mathbf{t}_0} + wL_{\mathbf{t}_0}L_{\mathbf{t}_0}$$

    Thus

    $$L_{[\mathbf{v}_r, \mathbf{t}_0]} = L_{[\mathbf{n}_\beta, \mathbf{t}_0]} - \frac{\partial w}{\partial s}L_{\mathbf{t}_0}$$

    Because of equation (9.25)

    $$L_{[\mathbf{v}_r, \mathbf{t}_0]} = (\frac{\partial \alpha}{\partial s} - \frac{\partial w}{\partial s})L_{\mathbf{t}_0} = (\kappa\beta - \frac{\partial w}{\partial s})L_{\mathbf{t}_0} \qquad (12.21)$$

This implies that

$$\dot{\mathbf{Y}} = \frac{d(\frac{\partial \mathbf{W}}{\partial s})}{d\tau} = \frac{\partial \dot{\mathbf{W}}}{\partial s} + (\kappa\beta - \frac{\partial w}{\partial s})\frac{\partial \mathbf{W}}{\partial s}$$

d. As a consequence

$$\dot{\mathbf{Y}} + \mathbf{Y} \wedge \Omega = \frac{\partial(\dot{\mathbf{W}} + \mathbf{W} \wedge \Omega)}{\partial s} + (\kappa\beta - \frac{\partial w}{\partial s})\frac{\partial \mathbf{W}}{\partial s}$$

Because of the standard properties of determinants, $(\mathbf{W}^T(\mathbf{Y} \wedge (\dot{\mathbf{Y}} + \mathbf{Y} \wedge \Omega)))) = -(\mathbf{Y}^T(\mathbf{W} \wedge (\dot{\mathbf{Y}} + \mathbf{Y} \wedge \Omega))))$, and the previous equation yields

$$\mathbf{W} \wedge (\dot{\mathbf{Y}} + \mathbf{Y} \wedge \Omega) = \mathbf{W} \wedge \frac{\partial(\dot{\mathbf{W}} + \mathbf{W} \wedge \Omega)}{\partial s} + (\kappa\beta - \frac{\partial w}{\partial s})\mathbf{W} \wedge \frac{\partial \mathbf{W}}{\partial s}$$

Since $\mathbf{W} \wedge (\dot{\mathbf{W}} + \mathbf{W} \wedge \Omega) = \mathbf{0}$, the first term is equal to $-\frac{\partial \mathbf{W}}{\partial s} \wedge (\dot{\mathbf{W}} + \mathbf{W} \wedge \Omega)$, and finally

$$\mathbf{W} \wedge (\dot{\mathbf{Y}} + \mathbf{Y} \wedge \Omega) = -\mathbf{Y} \wedge (\dot{\mathbf{W}} + \mathbf{W} \wedge \Omega + (\kappa\beta - \frac{\partial w}{\partial s})\mathbf{W})$$

The inner product of this quantity with $\mathbf{Y}$ is identically 0, and therefore the second term of equation (12.20) is also. Since the first term is also zero if equation (9.54) is satisfied, the conclusion follows.

e. Let $\mathbf{W_N}$ be the direction of the normal to the 3-D curve (C). It can be defined as $\mathbf{W_N} = \mathbf{W} \wedge \mathbf{W_B}$. Since it is also rigidly attached to the moving object, it also satisfies equation (9.42):

$$\mathbf{W_N} \wedge (\dot{\mathbf{W}}_N + \mathbf{W_N} \wedge \Omega) = \mathbf{0}$$

Does this give us a new equation? The answer is no, because if we substitute $\mathbf{W} \wedge \mathbf{W_B}$ for $\mathbf{W_N}$ in this equation we obtain, after some algebra

$$(\mathbf{W_B} \cdot [\mathbf{W} \wedge (\dot{\mathbf{W}} + \mathbf{W} \wedge \Omega)])\mathbf{W_B} + (\mathbf{W} \cdot [\mathbf{W_B} \wedge (\dot{\mathbf{W}}_B + \mathbf{W_B} \wedge \Omega)])\mathbf{W}$$

which is identically zero as soon as equation (9.42) is satisfied by $\mathbf{W}$.

12.9 Answers to problems of chapter 10

1. a. Let ε be such that $\{K_1 \subset K_2 \oplus B_\varepsilon, \text{and} K_2 \subset K_1 \oplus B_\varepsilon\}$. This means that, for every $x \in K_1$, there exists $y \in K_2$ such that x is in the ball of center y and radius ε, and therefore $d(x,y) \le \varepsilon$. Similarly, for all $y \in K_2$, there exists $x \in K_1$ such that $d(x,y) \le \varepsilon$. The first case implies that $\rho(K_1, K_2) \le \varepsilon$, the second that $\rho(K_2, K_1) \le \varepsilon$. Thus $h(K_1, K_2) \le \inf_\varepsilon \{\varepsilon : K_1 \subset K_2 \oplus B_\varepsilon, \text{and} K_2 \subset K_1 \oplus B_\varepsilon\}$. Inversely, let us choose $\varepsilon = h(K_1, K_2)$ and assume that either $K_1 \not\subset K_2 \oplus B_\varepsilon$ or that $K_2 \not\subset K_1 \oplus B_\varepsilon$. In the first case there exists $x \in K_1$ and $x \notin K_2 \oplus B_\varepsilon$. Therefore there exists $y \in K_2$ such that $d(x,y) > h(K_1, K_2)$, a contradiction. Thus $\inf_\varepsilon \{\varepsilon : K_1 \subset K_2 \oplus B_\varepsilon, \text{and } K_2 \subset K_1 \oplus B_\varepsilon\} \le h(K_1, K_2)$.

   b. From the definition of h, we have $h(K_1, K_2) = 0 \iff \rho(K_1, K_2) = \rho(K_2, K_1) = 0$. Then $\rho(K_1, K_2) = 0 \iff d(x, K_2) = 0 \; \forall x \in K_1 \iff \forall x \in K_1, \; \exists y \in K_2, \; d(x,y) = 0$ because K_1 is compact, and this is equivalent to $K_1 \subseteq K_2$. Similarly we show that $\rho(K_2, K_1) = 0 \iff K_2 \subseteq K_1$, and thus we have shown that $h(K_1, K_2) = 0 \iff K_1 = K_2$.

   The symmetry is obvious: $h(K_1, K_2) = h(K_2, K_1)$.

   Consider the triangle inequality. We start with the usual triangle inequality

   $$d(x, y) \le d(x, z) + d(z, y) \quad \forall x \in K_1, y \in K_2, z \in K_3$$

   Take the minimum with respect to y:

   $$\min_{y \in K_2} d(x, y) \le d(x, z) + \min_{y \in K_2} d(z, y)$$

   This is the same as

   $$d(x, K_2) \le d(x, z) + d(z, K_2)$$

   Now take the minimum with respect to z:

   $$d(x, K_2) \le \min_{z \in K_3} d(x, z) + \min_{z \in K_3} d(z, K_2) \le d(x, K_3) + \rho(K_3, K_2)$$

   Finish by taking the maximum with respect to x:

   $$\rho(K_1, K_2) \le \rho(K_1, K_3) + \rho(K_3, K_2)$$

   One can similarly show that $\rho(K_2, K_1) \le \rho(K_2, K_3) + \rho(K_3, K_1)$, from which $h(K_1, K_2) \le h(K_1, K_3) + h(K_3, K_2)$ follows.

2. Let e_{min} be the smallest number of edges of a face in the graph $e_{min} \geq 3$. Each edge is adjacent to two regions, and therefore $2e$ is larger than $e_{min}f$ and we have

$$2e \geq 3f$$

Use the Euler formula $v - e + f = 2$ and this inequality to obtain the other two:

$$3f = 3e - 3v + 6 \leq 2e$$

implies

$$e \leq 3v - 6$$

and

$$2e = 2v + 2f - 4 \geq 3f$$

implies

$$f \leq 2v - 4$$

3. Figure 12.8 shows the Voronoi diagram of the points of the set S in a plane defined by a point of S_1 and the z-axis. It has $\theta(n)$ Voronoi edges. The Voronoi diagram of the whole set S is then obtained by "rotating" the one of figure 12.8, thus creating $\theta(n^2)$ Voronoi edges. These edges induce $\theta(n^2)$ Delaunay edges.

4. We give the proof in two dimensions. Assume for simplicity, but without loss of generality, that the inserted point M falls within only one Delaunay circle of the existing triangulation that is circumscribed to the triangle ABC. Let us show that the circle defined by the points M, A, and B does not contain any other data point. Suppose that it contains a point D. Then the triangle DAB has to be the second Delaunay triangle adjacent to the edge AB, and this is impossible because the circle circumscribed to the Delaunay triangle DAB contains M and we have assumed that M fell within only one Delaunay circle.

5. We prove it in two dimensions by making the following observation. Let $MP_1P_2, MP_2P_3, \ldots, MP_{n-1}P_n, MP_nP_1$ be the Delaunay triangles adjacent to M, and consider the union U of the circles circumscribed

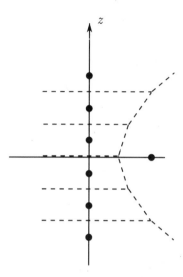

Figure 12.8 The Voronoi diagram of the intersection of the set S with a plane going through a point of S_1.

to these triangles. After computing the Delaunay triangulation of the points $P_1, P_2, \ldots, P_n$, the union of the Delaunay circles is included in U and therefore does not contain any other data point. Thus the local Delaunay triangulation yields a global one.

6. a. Obvious from proposition 10.5.

    b. If $M_i M_j$ does not cross its dual Voronoi edge, its midpoint P_{ij} is in the Voronoi cell of a point M_k ($k \neq i$ and $k \neq j$); thus $d(P_{ij}, M_k) < d(M_k, M_i)$ and $d(M_k, M_j)$, and M_k belongs to the interior of the disk of diameter $M_i M_j$.

7. a. Because of the symmetry, we have $K_a = \check{K}_a$. It is easy to verify that $V(X' \oplus K_a) = a(a + l(|\cos \theta| + |\sin \theta|))$ if the segment X' has length l and orientation θ. Since we have assumed that l and θ were independent, taking the expected value is easy, and since $\overline{|\cos \theta|} = \overline{|\sin \theta|} = \frac{1}{\pi} \int_{-\pi/2}^{\pi/2} \cos \theta \, d\theta = \frac{2}{\pi}$, we end up with

    $$\overline{ns} = \rho a (4\bar{l}/\pi + a)$$

    b. Obvious from the definition.

    c. Using the associativity of the Minkowsky addition, we write:

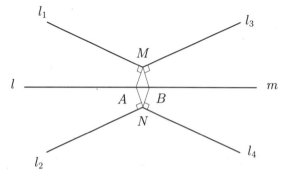

Figure 12.9   Redrawing figure 10.10.

$$X' \oplus K_a = (X' \oplus S_x) \oplus S_y$$

Because X' is convex, the area A_x of $X' \oplus S_x$ is given by

$$A_x = V(X' \oplus S_x) = V(X') + ay$$

where y is the length of the projection of X' on the y-axis. This is easy to check when X' is a convex polygon, and it remains true when the number of sides of the polygon grows arbitrarily large. Similarly, the area A of $(X' \oplus S_x) \oplus S_y$ is given by

$$A = V(X') + ay + a(x + a) = V(X') + a(x + y) + a^2$$

where x is the length of the projection of X' on the x-axis. Taking the expected value of both sides yields the proposed formula.

    d. We can apply the results of the previous question to the case where X' is a random segment. Therefore $\overline{A} = 0$.

8. a. Let us redraw figure 10.10 as follows. Because of the symmetry of the figure, the line $\langle A, B \rangle$ is the bisector of the two lines l_1 and l_2, the bisector of the two lines l_3 and l_4, and the bisector of the segment MN. The skeleton of X is made of three parts: the infinite half-line $\langle A, l \rangle$, which is part of the bisector of the two lines l_1 and l_2; the line segment AB, which is part of the bisector of the segment MN; and the infinite half-line $\langle B, m \rangle$, which is part of the bisector of the two lines l_3 and l_4. A and B are obtained as the intersection of the two lines perpendicular to l_1 and l_2 (l_3 and l_4, respectively) at M and N, respectively.

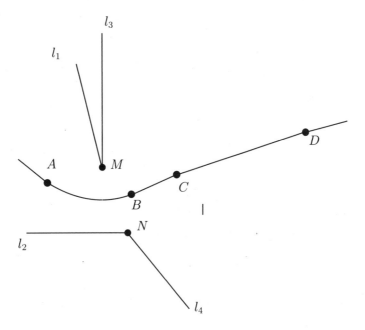

Figure 12.10 Redrawing figure 12.9.

    b. Let us redraw figure 12.9 as shown in figure 12.10. We can now describe the skeleton of X as the bisector of the two lines l_1 and l_2, a piece of the parabola with focal point M and directrix l_2, the bisector of the line segment MN, a piece of the parabola with focal point N and directrix l_3, and the bisector of the two lines l_3 and l_4. The reader who is interested in an algorithm for computing the skeleton of polygons is referred to the work by Lee [Lee82].

9. a. The vector $\mathbf{p}$ satisfies the two equations

$$\|\boldsymbol{\gamma}(s_i)\|^2 - 2\mathbf{p} \cdot \boldsymbol{\gamma}(s_i) = 0 \quad i = 1, 2$$

This is a system of two linear equations in two unknowns whose solution is

$$\mathbf{p} = \frac{1}{2(\boldsymbol{\gamma}(s_1) \wedge \boldsymbol{\gamma}(s_2))} \begin{bmatrix} \boldsymbol{\gamma}(s_2) \cdot \mathbf{n} & -\boldsymbol{\gamma}(s_1) \cdot \mathbf{n} \\ -\boldsymbol{\gamma}(s_2) \cdot \mathbf{t} & \boldsymbol{\gamma}(s_1) \cdot \mathbf{t} \end{bmatrix} \begin{bmatrix} \|\boldsymbol{\gamma}(s_1)\|^2 \\ \|\boldsymbol{\gamma}(s_2)\|^2 \end{bmatrix}$$

    b. Note that we have, in the vicinity of m

$$\boldsymbol{y}(s) = s\mathbf{t} + \frac{s^2}{2}\kappa\mathbf{n} + \mathbf{o}(s^2)$$

Using this expression to approximate the coordinates of p allows to prove the result.

c. Let r be a point of (c) in the vicinity of m, s its arclength, and q the point of the osculating circle to (c) at m of abscissa $\boldsymbol{y}(s) \cdot \mathbf{t}$ (we assume that $|\boldsymbol{y}(s) \cdot \mathbf{t}| \le R = \frac{1}{\kappa}$). The segment qr is parallel to the y-axis, and its algebraic value is equal to

$$\boldsymbol{y}(s) \cdot \mathbf{n} - R + \sqrt{R^2 - (\boldsymbol{y}(s) \cdot \mathbf{t})^2} = \boldsymbol{y}(s) \cdot \mathbf{n} - R + R\sqrt{1 - (\frac{\boldsymbol{y}(s) \cdot \mathbf{t}}{R})^2}$$

In order to answer the question, we need to expand $\boldsymbol{y}(s)$ up to the third order:

$$\boldsymbol{y}(s) = s\mathbf{t} + \frac{s^2}{2R}\mathbf{n} + \frac{s^3}{6}\boldsymbol{y}''(0) + \mathbf{o}(s^3)$$

From this we find that the algebraic value of qr is given by

$$\frac{s^3}{6}\boldsymbol{y}''(0) \cdot \mathbf{n} + o(s^3)$$

which changes sign when s changes sign if $\boldsymbol{y}''(0) \cdot \mathbf{n} \ne 0$: (c) crosses its osculating circle at m. If $\boldsymbol{y}''(0) \cdot \mathbf{n} = 0$, the next term in the expansion will be proportional to s^4 and the algebraic value will not change sign at the origin. The curve does not cross its osculating circle, but it is a special case.

d. Let $R' = 1/\kappa'$ be the radius of a circle centered on the normal to (c) at m and going through m. Using the same technique as in the previous question, we compute up to the second order the algebraic value of the segment qr, with q a point of the circle and r the corresponding point of (c). First we show the case in which the circle is centered on the same side of the normal as the osculating circle:

$$\frac{s^2}{2}(\frac{1}{R} - \frac{1}{R'}) + o(s^2)$$

Clearly, if $R' > R$ the curve is above the circle; for $R = R'$ we have the osculating circle, which crosses the curve in general; and if

$R' < R$ the curve is below the circle. In the case where the circle is centered on the other part of the normal, the previous expression becomes

$$\frac{s^2}{2}(\frac{1}{R} + \frac{1}{R'}) + o(s^2)$$

and the curve is always above the circle.

10. Let us consider an osculating sphere of radius R. It is centered on the normal to (S) at M, goes through M, and the abscissa of its center varies between $R_1 = 1/\kappa_1$ and $R_2 = 1/\kappa_2$. Let $R = 1/\kappa, \kappa \geq 0$. Let Q be a point of (S) in the vicinity of M of coordinates $[x, y, f(x, y)]^T$. We assume that $x^2 + y^2 < R^2$, and we consider the algebraic distance d between the surface and the osculating sphere in the direction of the z-axis.

Let us consider two cases:

a. $0 \leq \kappa_2 < \kappa_1$:

$$d = f(x, y) - R + R\sqrt{1 - \frac{x^2 + y^2}{R^2}} = \frac{\kappa_1}{2}x^2 + \frac{\kappa_2}{2}y^2 - \frac{\kappa}{2}(x^2 + y^2)$$
$$+ o(x^2 + y^2)$$

Rewrite this as

$$\frac{\kappa_1 - \kappa}{2}x^2 + \frac{\kappa_2 - \kappa}{2}y^2 + o(x^2 + y^2)$$

If $\kappa_2 < \kappa < \kappa_1$, then the algebraic distance is negative if $x^2 < \frac{\kappa - \kappa_2}{\kappa_1 - \kappa}y^2$ and positive otherwise. Thus the osculating sphere crosses the surface at M. If $\kappa = \kappa_1$ or if $\kappa = \kappa_2$, the algebraic distance is negative or positive, respectively, and thus the osculating sphere does not cross the surface at M. As shown in figure 12.11, the surface (S) lies between the two spheres of radii $1/\kappa_1$ and $1/\kappa_2$ and crosses all spheres centered on the normal to (S) of radii R such that $1/\kappa_1 < R < 1/\kappa_2$. Note that, according to the way we have oriented the normal (pointing toward X), it is the sphere of radius $1/\kappa_1$ that is included in X.

b. $\kappa_2 < 0 < \kappa_1$:

We must again distinguish two cases.

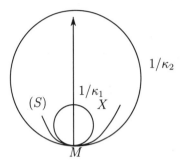

Figure 12.11 $0 \le \kappa_2 < \kappa_1$.

i. $|\kappa_2| \le \kappa_1$:

This case is similar to the previous one. If $0 \le \kappa < \kappa_1$, then the algebraic distance is negative if $x^2 < \frac{\kappa - \kappa_2}{\kappa_1 - \kappa} y^2$ and positive otherwise. Thus the osculating sphere crosses the surface at M. When the center of the osculating sphere crosses (S), we have

$$d = f(x,y) + R - R\sqrt{1 - \frac{x^2 + y^2}{R^2}} = \frac{\kappa_1}{2}x^2 + \frac{\kappa_2}{2}y^2 + \frac{\kappa}{2}(x^2 + y^2)$$
$$+ o(x^2 + y^2)$$

We can rewrite this as

$$d = \frac{\kappa_1 + \kappa}{2}x^2 + \frac{\kappa_2 + \kappa}{2}y^2 + o(x^2 + y^2)$$

Thus d is negative if $x^2 < -\frac{\kappa_2 + \kappa}{\kappa_1 + \kappa}y^2$ and positive otherwise, and the osculating sphere crosses the surface at M. If $\kappa = \kappa_1$ or $\kappa = -\kappa_2$, the algebraic distance is negative or positive, respectively, and thus the osculating sphere does not cross the surface at M. Just as in the previous case, the surface (S) lies between the two spheres centered on the normal to (S) of radii $1/\kappa_2$ (centered at the point of negative abscissa $1/\kappa_2$ and radius $1/|\kappa_2|$) and $1/\kappa_1$ (see figure 12.12).

ii. $|\kappa_2| > \kappa_1$:

The osculating sphere does not cross the surface for $\kappa = \kappa_1$, and so it crosses it when it is centered at the points of ab-

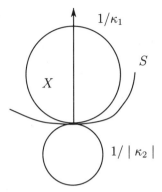

Figure 12.12 $\kappa_2 < 0 < \kappa_1$ and $|\kappa_2| \le \kappa_1$.

scissa strictly between $-\kappa_1$ and κ_1 and does not cross it when it is centered at the points of abscissa between κ_2 and $-\kappa_1$.

11. a. $\mathbf{NM} \wedge (\mathbf{AM} + \mathbf{v}) = \mathbf{0}$

    b. The points are at the intersection of the three quadrics that contains at most eight real points, in general.

12. If we write the equation of the conic

$$\frac{1}{2}\mathbf{m}^T\mathbf{Am} + \mathbf{m}^T\mathbf{v} + c = 0$$

we obtain the condition

$$\mathbf{nm} \times (\mathbf{Am} + \mathbf{v}) = 0$$

which is the equation of a conic. The (points) m solutions are at the intersection of this conic and the original conic. Therefore there are at most four real solutions.

13. a. $E = p(\mathbf{n}^T \Lambda \mathbf{n} + (\mathbf{n}^T\mathbf{M} + d)^2)$

    b. $\dfrac{\partial E}{\partial d} = 2p(\mathbf{n}^T\mathbf{M} + d)$

    At the minimum we must have $\frac{\partial E}{\partial d} = 0$, which shows that the optimal plane goes through M.

c. In order to introduce the constraint $\|\mathbf{n}\|^2 = 1$ we use the technique of the Lagrange multipliers and minimize the criterion $F = E + \lambda(1 - \|\mathbf{n}\|^2)$. Using the previous result, we have

$$(\frac{\partial F}{\partial \mathbf{n}})^T = 2(p\Lambda\mathbf{n} - \lambda\mathbf{n})$$

At the minimum we must have $(\frac{\partial F}{\partial \mathbf{n}})^T = \mathbf{0}$, and this shows that the normal $\mathbf{n}$ is an eigenvector of Λ. Assume that this is true ($\Lambda\mathbf{n} = \mu\mathbf{n}$) and compute E:

$$E = p\mu$$

In order to minimize E we have to choose μ as small as possible ($\mu \geq 0$ since Λ is a positive matrix).

14. a. This is just a matter of replacing N with P in $f(N)$ and using the definition of the center of the quadric.

   b. The ratio $\frac{d(C,M)^2}{d(C,m)^2}$ is equal to $\frac{1}{\lambda^2}$.

   c. It is clearly different from the sum of the squared distances of the points to the quadric.

15. Let us see how the equation of the quadric changes if $\mathbf{M} \rightarrow \mathbf{RM}' + \mathbf{t}$ where $\mathbf{R}$ is orthogonal, i.e., satisfies $\mathbf{RR}^T = \mathbf{I}$. It is easy to see that the matrix $\mathbf{A}$ that appears in the equation of the quadrics becomes $\mathbf{R}^T\mathbf{AR}$, and therefore $\mathbf{AA}^T \rightarrow \mathbf{R}^T\mathbf{AA}^T\mathbf{R}$ also. Now, for any matrix $\mathbf{B}$, its eigenvalues are the same as those of $\mathbf{P}^{-1}\mathbf{BP}$ for any invertible matrix $\mathbf{P}$; indeed, let $\mathbf{x}$ be an eigenvector of $\mathbf{B}$ with eigenvalue λ:

$$\mathbf{Bx} = \lambda\mathbf{x}$$

Letting $\mathbf{x} = \mathbf{Px}'$, we have $\mathbf{P}^{-1}\mathbf{BPx}' = \mathbf{P}^{-1}\mathbf{BPx} = \lambda\mathbf{P}^{-1}\mathbf{x} = \lambda\mathbf{x}'$, where $\mathbf{x}'$ is an eigenvalue of $\mathbf{P}^{-1}\mathbf{BP}$ with eigenvalue λ. This shows that the eigenvalues of $\mathbf{R}^T\mathbf{AA}^T\mathbf{R} = \mathbf{R}^{-1}\mathbf{AA}^T\mathbf{R}$ are the same as those of $\mathbf{AA}^T$, and therefore the trace is preserved.

16. With constraint 2 the equation of the quadric can be written as

$$\frac{1}{2}\mathbf{M}^T\mathbf{AM} + \mathbf{M}^T\mathbf{v} + 1 = 0$$

Now, suppose that $\mathbf{M} \rightarrow \mathbf{RM}' + \mathbf{t}$. The equation becomes

$$\frac{1}{2}\mathbf{M}'^T\mathbf{R}^T\mathbf{A}\mathbf{R}\mathbf{M}' + \mathbf{M}'^T(\mathbf{R}^T\mathbf{A}\mathbf{t} + \mathbf{R}^T\mathbf{v}) + \frac{1}{2}\mathbf{t}^T\mathbf{A}\mathbf{t} + \mathbf{t}^T\mathbf{v} + 1 = 0$$

If we were to solve the approximation problem in the new coordinate system, we would write the equation as

$$\frac{1}{2}\mathbf{M}'^T\mathbf{A}\mathbf{M}' + \mathbf{M}'^T\mathbf{v}' + 1 = 0$$

Identify the terms and obtain

$$\mathbf{A}' = \mathbf{R}^T\mathbf{A}\mathbf{R}$$

$$\mathbf{v}' = \mathbf{R}^T(\mathbf{A}\mathbf{t} + \mathbf{v})$$

$$1 = \frac{1}{2}\mathbf{t}^T\mathbf{A}\mathbf{t} + \mathbf{t}^T\mathbf{v} + 1$$

The last equation implies that $1/2\mathbf{t}^T(\mathbf{A}\mathbf{t} + \mathbf{v}) = 0$, which is not satisfied in general (note that it is satisfied if $\mathbf{t} = \mathbf{0}$, i.e., if the change of coordinate system is a pure rotation). Thus, if we impose constraint 2, the quadrics found by solving the minimization problem in two coordinate systems related by a rigid displacement are not in general related by the same rigid displacement.

17. Using the notations of appendix A.3, we have $\mathbf{x} = \mathbf{p}$. $\mathbf{z}$ is the vector whose coordinates are the first six coordinates of $\mathbf{x}$, and $\mathbf{y}$ is the vector whose coordinates are the last four coordinates of $\mathbf{x}$. Matrix $\mathbf{A}$ is the 10×10 matrix $\mathbf{P}$, and matrix $\mathbf{C}$ (matrix $\mathbf{D}$, respectively) is the 10×4 (10×6) submatrix of $\mathbf{A}$ obtained by selecting the last four (first six) columns. $\mathbf{z}$ is the eigenvector of the 6×6 symmetric positive matrix $\mathbf{E} = \mathbf{D}^T(\mathbf{I} - \mathbf{C}(\mathbf{C}^T\mathbf{C})^{-1}\mathbf{C}^T)$, and $\mathbf{y}$ is obtained from $\mathbf{z}$ by equation (A.3).

12.10   Answers to problems of chapter 11

1. Replace z_j and Z_j with $z + z_j'$ and $Z + Z_j'$, respectively, in $C(\theta, t)$. Expand and use the fact that $\sum_{j=1}^n z_j' = \sum_{j=1}^n Z_j' = 0$:

$$C(\theta, t) = n \mid ze^{i\theta} + t - Z \mid^2 + \sum_{j=1}^n \mid z_j'e^{i\theta} - Z_j' \mid^2$$

Since $\sum_{j=1}^{n} |z_j'e^{i\theta} - Z_j'|^2 = \sum_{j=1}^{n}(|z_j'|^2 + |Z_j'|^2) - 2Re(e^{i\theta}\sum_{j=1}^{n} z_j'\overline{Z_j'})$, the conclusion follows.

2. a. In order to compute $\mathbf{b}^{(1)}$ and $\mathbf{b}^{(2)}$, we use equations (11.3)-(11.6). Equation (11.3) yields $k^{(1)} = k^{(2)} = l'/l$. Then equation (11.5) yields

$$\tan\theta = \frac{a - a'}{1 + aa'}$$

But, if we denote by φ (φ', respectively) the angle of the supporting line of the first segment (second) with the horizontal axis, we have $a = -\tan\varphi$ ($a' = -\tan\varphi'$). This shows that

$$\tan\theta = \tan(\varphi' - \varphi)$$

and thus

$$\theta^{(1)} = \varphi' - \varphi \qquad \theta^{(2)} = \varphi' - \varphi + \pi$$

Equations (11.4) and (11.6) then yield the coordinates of $\mathbf{t}$. We have to compute $\cos\theta^{(1)}$, $\cos\theta^{(2)}$, $\sin\theta^{(1)}$, and $\sin\theta^{(2)}$. We use the relation $\cos\theta = \pm\frac{1}{\sqrt{1+\tan^2\theta}}$. We can always assume that $\varphi' - \varphi$ is between $-\pi/2$ and $\pi/2$ and therefore

$$\cos\theta^{(1)} = \frac{|1 + aa'|}{\sqrt{1 + a^2 + a'^2 + a^2a'^2}}$$

$$\sin\theta^{(1)} = \varepsilon\frac{a - a'}{\sqrt{1 + a^2 + a'^2 + a^2a'^2}}$$

$$\cos\theta^{(2)} = -\cos\theta^{(1)}$$

$$\sin\theta^{(1)} = -\sin\theta^{(1)}$$

where $\varepsilon = \pm 1 = \text{sign}(1 + aa')$.

b. According to equation (5.28) the covariance (weight) matrix of $\mathbf{b}^{(i)}$, $i = 1, 2$ is given by

$$\Lambda_{\mathbf{b}(i)} = [\frac{\partial\mathbf{b}^{(i)}}{\partial\mathbf{s}}, \frac{\partial\mathbf{b}^{(i)}}{\partial\mathbf{s}'}]\begin{bmatrix} \mathbf{R} & \mathbf{0} \\ \mathbf{0} & \mathbf{R}' \end{bmatrix}[\frac{\partial\mathbf{b}^{(i)}}{\partial\mathbf{s}}, \frac{\partial\mathbf{b}^{(i)}}{\partial\mathbf{s}'}]^T \quad i = 1, 2$$

All the partial derivatives can be computed from the results of the previous question (and the help of a system for algebraic computation).

3. There are four measurement equations; $\mathbf{a}$ is of dimension four and $\mathbf{x}$ is of dimension 8, and thus $\frac{\partial f}{\partial a}$ is a 4×4 matrix, whereas $\frac{\partial f}{\partial x}$ is a 4×8 matrix equal to $[\frac{\partial f}{\partial s}, \frac{\partial f}{\partial s'}]$. Writing

$$\mathbf{f}(\mathbf{x},\mathbf{a}) = \begin{bmatrix} l' - kl \\ x' - k(x \cos\theta + (ax+b)\sin\theta) + t_1 \\ a' - \frac{a - \tan\theta}{a\tan\theta + 1} \\ b' - \frac{t_1(\sin\theta - a\cos\theta) - t_2(\cos\theta + a\sin\theta) + bk}{a\sin\theta + \cos\theta} \end{bmatrix},$$

we can easily compute the required derivatives.

4. We rewrite criterion $C(\mathbf{R},\mathbf{t})$ as

$$C(\mathbf{R},\mathbf{t}) = \sum_{i=1}^{n} \|\mathbf{q}'_i - \mathbf{R}\mathbf{p}'_i + \mathbf{q} - \mathbf{R}\mathbf{p} - \mathbf{t}\|^2$$

Expand each term and notice that $\sum \mathbf{q}'_i = \sum \mathbf{p}'_i = \mathbf{0}$. This leaves us with:

$$C(\mathbf{R},\mathbf{t}) = n\|\mathbf{q} - \mathbf{R}\mathbf{p} - \mathbf{t}\|^2 + \sum_{i=1}^{n} \|\mathbf{q}'_i - \mathbf{R}\mathbf{p}'_i\|^2$$

Observe that, for any rotation matrix, the first term in the criterion, $\|\mathbf{q} - \mathbf{R}\mathbf{p} - \mathbf{t}\|^2$, can be made equal to zero by choosing $\mathbf{t} = \mathbf{q} - \mathbf{R}\mathbf{p}$. Therefore criterion C is minimized by finding the rotation that minimizes the second term, which then determines the translation. The best rotation $\hat{\mathbf{R}}$ minimizing $\sum_{i=1}^{n} \|\mathbf{q}'_i - \mathbf{R}\mathbf{p}'_i\|^2$ can be computed by exactly the same method as the one presented in section 11.4.3.1 using the representation of $\mathbf{R}$ by a quaternion.

5. a. Apply the definition of section 5.5.2 of the quaternion product to evaluate $\mathbf{n}'_i \times \mathbf{q} - \mathbf{q} \times \mathbf{n}_i$. We have, for example

$$\mathbf{n}'_i \times \mathbf{q} = (0, \mathbf{n}'_i) \times (s, \mathbf{v}) = (-\mathbf{n}'_i \cdot \mathbf{v}, s\mathbf{n}'_i + \mathbf{n}'_i \wedge \mathbf{v})$$

Thus we readily obtain

$$\mathbf{n}'_i \times \mathbf{q} - \mathbf{q} \times \mathbf{n}_i = ((\mathbf{n}_i - \mathbf{n}'_i) \cdot \mathbf{v}, -s(\mathbf{n}_i - \mathbf{n}'_i) + (\mathbf{n}_i + \mathbf{n}'_i) \wedge \mathbf{v})$$

and therefore we find the suggested form for $\mathbf{A}_i$.

b. Obvious from the previous question.

c. We drop the index i for convenience. We notice that $\mathbf{B} = \tilde{\mathbf{b}}'$ and that $\mathbf{b}^T\mathbf{b}' = 0$. Therefore, the three vectors $\mathbf{b}, \mathbf{b}'$, and $\mathbf{b} \wedge \mathbf{b}'$ are orthogonal. Let $[x, \mathbf{y}^T]^T$ be an eigenvector, and let λ be the corresponding eigenvalue. We obtain the following two equations:

$$x\mathbf{b}^T\mathbf{b} - \mathbf{b}^T\mathbf{B}\mathbf{y} = \lambda x \qquad (12.22)$$

$$-x\mathbf{B}^T\mathbf{b} + (\mathbf{b}^T\mathbf{y})\mathbf{b} - \mathbf{B}^2\mathbf{y} = \lambda\mathbf{y} \qquad (12.23)$$

The first equation yields $x(\mathbf{b}^T\mathbf{b} - \lambda) = \mathbf{b}^T\mathbf{B}\mathbf{y}$. To exploit the second, we note that, unless $x = 0$, it implies that $\mathbf{y}$ is in the plane $(\mathbf{b}, \mathbf{b} \wedge \mathbf{b}')$. Let us therefore write

$$\mathbf{y} = \alpha\mathbf{b} + \beta\mathbf{b} \wedge \mathbf{b}'$$

Replacing $\mathbf{y}$ by this value in equation (12.23), we obtain

$$x + \beta(\mathbf{b}'^T\mathbf{b}' - \lambda) = 0 \qquad (12.24)$$

$$\alpha(\mathbf{b}^T\mathbf{b} + \mathbf{b}'^T\mathbf{b}' - \lambda) = 0 \qquad (12.25)$$

Similarly, equation (12.22) yields

$$x(\mathbf{b}^T\mathbf{b} - \lambda) + \beta(\mathbf{b}'^T\mathbf{b}')(\mathbf{b}^T\mathbf{b}) = 0 \qquad (12.26)$$

We then consider the following three cases:

i. $\lambda = \mathbf{b}^T\mathbf{b} + \mathbf{b}'^T\mathbf{b}'$:
      Equations (12.24) and (12.26) yield $x = \beta\mathbf{b}^T\mathbf{b}$. The eigenspace is the set of four-dimensional vectors:

$$\begin{bmatrix} \beta\mathbf{b}^T\mathbf{b} \\ \alpha\mathbf{b} + \beta\mathbf{b}' \wedge \mathbf{b} \end{bmatrix}$$

   It is a vector space of dimension 2.

ii. $x \neq 0$, $\lambda = 0$:
      Equations (12.24) and (12.26) yield $x = -\beta\mathbf{b}'^T\mathbf{b}'$. Equation (12.25) yields $\alpha = 0$, and therefore the eigenspace is of dimension 1, generated by the vector $[-\mathbf{b}'^T\mathbf{b}', (\mathbf{b}' \wedge \mathbf{b})^T]^T$.

iii. $x = 0$, $\lambda = 0$:
      We find that $\mathbf{y} = \alpha\mathbf{b}'$. The eigenspace is of dimension 1, generated by the vector $[0, \mathbf{b}'^T]^T$.

6. Using the notations of that section, we have $\mathbf{x} = [\mathbf{p}^T, \mathbf{p}'^T]^T$, $\mathbf{p} = [a, b, c]^T$, $\mathbf{p}' = [a', b', c']^T$, and $\mathbf{m} = [a, b, 1]^T$. The measurement equation is

$$\mathbf{f}'(\mathbf{x}, \mathbf{r}) = \begin{bmatrix} a' - \frac{\mathbf{r}_2^T \mathbf{m}}{\mathbf{r}_1^T \mathbf{m}} \\ b' - \frac{\mathbf{r}_3^T \mathbf{m}}{\mathbf{r}_1^T \mathbf{m}} \end{bmatrix}$$

If we assume that the vector $\mathbf{r}$ representing the rotation is the one described in section 5.5.3, the relationship between the rotation matrix $\mathbf{R}$ and its representation $\mathbf{r} = [X_2, X_3, X_4]^T$ is given by equation (5.20). Otherwise, if we assume that the vector $\mathbf{r}$ representing the rotation is the one described in section 5.5.4, this relation is Rodrigues' equation (5.26). In both cases, $\frac{\partial \mathbf{f}'}{\partial \mathbf{x}}$ is a 2×6 matrix given by

$$\frac{\partial \mathbf{f}'}{\partial \mathbf{x}} = [\frac{\partial \mathbf{f}'}{\partial \mathbf{p}}, \frac{\partial \mathbf{f}'}{\partial \mathbf{p}'}] = [\frac{\partial \mathbf{f}'}{\partial a}, \frac{\partial \mathbf{f}'}{\partial b}, \mathbf{0}, \frac{\partial \mathbf{f}'}{\partial a'}, \frac{\partial \mathbf{f}'}{\partial b'}, \mathbf{0}]$$

$\frac{\partial \mathbf{f}'}{\partial \mathbf{r}}$ is a 2×3 matrix that is readily obtained if we can compute the 3×3 matrixes $\frac{\partial \mathbf{r}_i}{\partial \mathbf{r}}$, $i = 1, 2, 3$ (the $\mathbf{r}_i$ are the column vectors of the rotation matrix $\mathbf{R}$). This can be easily done using equations (5.20) or (5.26).

7. This problem is a good example of the application of many of the ideas presented in chapter 5. First the initial rotations are obtained, as explained in section 11.4.3.1, by using the representation of the rotations by quaternions as the solutions of four constrained minimization problems of the form

$$\min_{\mathbf{q}} \mathbf{q}^T \mathbf{A} \mathbf{q} \text{ subject to } \|\mathbf{q}\|^2 = 1$$

where the matrix $\mathbf{A}$ is a known function of $\mathbf{p}_1, \mathbf{p}'_1, \mathbf{p}_2,$ and $\mathbf{p}'_2$ (see problem 5). Let $\mathbf{q}_0$ be a quaternion solution of the previous minimization problem. Using the notations of section 5.6.3, we have $\mathbf{y} = \mathbf{q}_0$, $\mathbf{x} = [\mathbf{p}_1^T, \mathbf{p}_1'^T, \mathbf{p}_2^T, \mathbf{p}_2'^T]^T$, $\mathbf{z} = \mathbf{q}$, $C(\mathbf{x}, \mathbf{z}) = \mathbf{z}^T \mathbf{A} \mathbf{z}$, and $h(\mathbf{z}) = 1 - \|\mathbf{z}\|^2$. This section provides us with a first-order approximation $\Lambda_{\mathbf{q}_0}$ of the covariance (weight) matrix of $\mathbf{q}_0$ as a function of $\Lambda_{\mathbf{x}} = \mathrm{diag}(\mathbf{Q}_1, \mathbf{Q}'_1, \mathbf{Q}_2, \mathbf{Q}'_2)$.

From there on, we can compute $\mathbf{t}_0^{(k)}$ by solving the system of linear equations

$$c_1' = \frac{-\mathbf{t}^T \mathbf{R}_0 \mathbf{m}_1 + c_1}{\mathbf{r}_{01}^T \mathbf{m}_1}$$

$$c_2' = \frac{-\mathbf{t}^T \mathbf{R}_0 \mathbf{m}_2 + c_2}{\mathbf{r}_{01}^T \mathbf{m}_2}$$

$$c_k' = \frac{-\mathbf{t}^T \mathbf{R}_0 \mathbf{m}_3 + c_3}{\mathbf{r}_{01}^T \mathbf{m}_3}$$

where the rotation matrix $\mathbf{R}_0$ is obtained from the quaternion $\mathbf{q}_0$ using equation (5.19). We write the solution as $\mathbf{t}_0^{(k)} = \mathbf{g}_2(\mathbf{q}_0, \mathbf{p}_1, \mathbf{p}_1', \mathbf{p}_2, \mathbf{p}_2', \mathbf{p}_3, \mathbf{p}_k')$.

Finally, since we use a three-dimensional representation of $\mathbf{R}_0$ in what follows, we have to compute $\mathbf{r}_0$ as a function of $\mathbf{q}_0$. Indeed, we know from section 5.5.2 that $\mathbf{q}_0 = (\cos\theta_0/2, \mathbf{u}_0 \sin\theta_0/2)$ where θ_0 is the angle of rotation and $\mathbf{u}_0$ a unit vector parallel to the axis of rotation. Therefore we can write $\mathbf{r}_0 = \theta_0 \mathbf{u}_0 = \mathbf{g}_1(\mathbf{q}_0)$. We thus have

$$\begin{bmatrix} \mathbf{r}_0 \\ \mathbf{t}_0^{(k)} \end{bmatrix} = \mathbf{g}(\mathbf{q}_0, \mathbf{p}_1, \mathbf{p}_1', \mathbf{p}_2, \mathbf{p}_2', \mathbf{p}_3, \mathbf{p}_k') = \begin{bmatrix} \mathbf{g}_1(\mathbf{q}_0) \\ \mathbf{g}_2(\mathbf{q}_0, \mathbf{p}_1, \mathbf{p}_1', \mathbf{p}_2, \mathbf{p}_2', \mathbf{p}_3, \mathbf{p}_k') \end{bmatrix}$$

Equation (5.28) gives us the expression for the first-order approximation of the covariance (weight) matrix[1] of $\mathbf{b}_0^{(k)'} = [\mathbf{r}_0^T, \mathbf{t}_0^{(k)T}]^T$:

$$\Lambda_{\mathbf{b}_0^{(k)'}} = \mathbf{H}\,\mathrm{diag}(\Lambda_{\mathbf{q}_0}, \Lambda_{\mathbf{x}})\mathbf{H}^T$$

where we have taken $\mathbf{x} = [\mathbf{p}_1^T, \mathbf{p}_1'^T, \mathbf{p}_2^T, \mathbf{p}_2'^T, \mathbf{p}_3^T, \mathbf{p}_k'^T]^T$, $\Lambda_{\mathbf{x}} = \mathrm{diag}(\mathbf{Q}_1, \mathbf{Q}_1', \mathbf{Q}_2, \mathbf{Q}_2', \mathbf{Q}_3, \mathbf{Q}_k')$, and

$$\mathbf{H} = \begin{bmatrix} \frac{\partial \mathbf{g}_1}{\partial \mathbf{q}_0} & 0 & 0 & 0 & 0 & 0 & 0 \\ \frac{\partial \mathbf{g}_2}{\partial \mathbf{q}_0} & \frac{\partial \mathbf{g}_2}{\partial \mathbf{p}_1} & \frac{\partial \mathbf{g}_2}{\partial \mathbf{p}_1'} & \frac{\partial \mathbf{g}_2}{\partial \mathbf{p}_2} & \frac{\partial \mathbf{g}_2}{\partial \mathbf{p}_2'} & \frac{\partial \mathbf{g}_2}{\partial \mathbf{p}_3} & \frac{\partial \mathbf{g}_2}{\partial \mathbf{p}_k'} \end{bmatrix}$$

The required partial derivatives can be computed using the analytical expression of $\mathbf{g}_1$ and $\mathbf{g}_2$.

---

1. Note that we have $\mathbf{b}_0^{(k)'} \neq \mathbf{b}_0^{(k)}$ since we have assumed for simplicity that we have not updated $\mathbf{r}_0$ with the third correspondence.

8. The segment M is represented by the six-dimensional vector $\mathbf{s} = [a, b, \mathbf{M}^T, l]^T$ (see section 11.5.1). $\hat{T}(M)$ is represented by $\mathbf{s}' = [a', b', \mathbf{M}'^T, l']^T$. The displacement $\hat{T}$ is given by the rotation matrix $\hat{\mathbf{R}}$, which is represented by the three-dimensional vector $\hat{\mathbf{r}}$ (see section 5.5.3 or 5.5.4) and by the translation vector $\hat{\mathbf{t}}$, and we have $\mathbf{s}' = \mathbf{f}(\mathbf{s}, \hat{\mathbf{r}}, \hat{\mathbf{t}})$ where the function $\mathbf{f}$ is obtained from equations (11.13)–(11.16):

$$
\mathbf{f}(\mathbf{s}, \hat{\mathbf{r}}, \hat{\mathbf{t}}) =
\begin{bmatrix}
a' - \frac{\hat{\mathbf{r}}_1^T \mathbf{m}}{\hat{\mathbf{r}}_3^T \mathbf{m}} \\
b' - \frac{\hat{\mathbf{r}}_2^T \mathbf{m}}{\hat{\mathbf{r}}_3^T \mathbf{m}} \\
\mathbf{M}' - \hat{\mathbf{R}}\mathbf{M} + \hat{\mathbf{t}} \\
l' - l
\end{bmatrix}
\tag{12.27}
$$

We assume that M and $\hat{T}$ are independent and that the 12×12 covariance (weight) matrix Λ of $(\mathbf{s}, \hat{\mathbf{r}}, \hat{\mathbf{t}})$ is

$$
\Lambda =
\begin{bmatrix}
\mathbf{R} & \mathbf{0} \\
\mathbf{0} & \mathbf{P}
\end{bmatrix}
$$

Note that $\mathbf{R}$ is not a rotation matrix, but is rather the 6×6 covariance (weight) matrix of $\mathbf{s}$; $\mathbf{P}$ is the 6×6 covariance (weight) matrix of $\hat{T}$. Using the results of chapter 5 and in particular equation (5.28), we can write, up to the first order

$$
\Lambda_{\hat{T}(M)} = [\frac{\partial \mathbf{f}}{\partial \mathbf{s}}, \frac{\partial \mathbf{f}}{\partial \hat{\mathbf{r}}}, \frac{\partial \mathbf{f}}{\partial \hat{\mathbf{t}}}] \Lambda [\frac{\partial \mathbf{f}}{\partial \mathbf{s}}, \frac{\partial \mathbf{f}}{\partial \hat{\mathbf{r}}}, \frac{\partial \mathbf{f}}{\partial \hat{\mathbf{t}}}]^T
$$

Each of the required partial derivatives can be computed from equation (12.27).

A   Constrained Optimization

In this appendix we will show how to solve a constrained optimization problem that we find in chapters 3, 6, 7, 10, and 11. The problem is, given an $N \times M$ matrix $\mathbf{A}$, find an $M \times 1$ vector $\mathbf{x}$ that minimizes $\|\mathbf{Ax}\|$ subject to the constraints that $\|\mathbf{Bx}\|^2 = 1$, where $\mathbf{B}$ is a $P \times M$ matrix with $P < M$ that "selects" some coordinates of $\mathbf{x}$. Denoting by $\mathbf{z}$ the vector $\mathbf{Bx}$ and by $\mathbf{y}$ the $(M - P) \times 1$ vector made up of the other coordinates of vector $\mathbf{x}$, we have

$$\mathbf{Ax} = C\mathbf{y} + D\mathbf{z}$$

where matrices $\mathbf{C}$ and $\mathbf{D}$ are easily computed $N \times (M - P)$ and $N \times P$ matrices. The original optimization problem is now

$$\text{find} \quad \min_{\mathbf{y},\mathbf{z}} \|\mathbf{Cy} + \mathbf{Dz}\|^2 \tag{A.1}$$

subject to the constraint $\|\mathbf{z}\|^2 = 1$.

    Applying the technique of Lagrange multipliers, this problem is equivalent to

$$\text{find} \quad \min_{\mathbf{y},\mathbf{z}} R = \|\mathbf{Cy} + \mathbf{Dz}\|^2 + \lambda(1 - \|\mathbf{z}\|^2) \tag{A.2}$$

Computing the partial derivatives of criterion R with respect to the unknown vectors $\mathbf{y}$ and $\mathbf{z}$, we obtain

$$\frac{\partial R}{\partial \mathbf{y}} = 2(\mathbf{C}^T\mathbf{Cy} + \mathbf{C}^T\mathbf{Dz})$$

$$\frac{\partial R}{\partial \mathbf{z}} = 2(\mathbf{D}^T\mathbf{Dz} + \mathbf{D}^T\mathbf{Cy} - \lambda\mathbf{z})$$

Setting those partials equal to **0** yields

$$\mathbf{y} = -(\mathbf{C}^T\mathbf{C})^{-1}\mathbf{C}^T\mathbf{D}\mathbf{z} \tag{A.3}$$

$$(\mathbf{D}^T\mathbf{D} - \mathbf{D}^T\mathbf{C}(\mathbf{C}^T\mathbf{C})^{-1}\mathbf{C}^T\mathbf{D})\mathbf{z} = \lambda\mathbf{z} \tag{A.4}$$

Equation (A.4) expresses the fact that **z** is an eigenvector of the matrix $\mathbf{E} = \mathbf{D}^T\mathbf{D} - \mathbf{D}^T\mathbf{C}(\mathbf{C}^T\mathbf{C})^{-1}\mathbf{C}^T\mathbf{D}$. It can be slightly rewritten as

$$\mathbf{D}^T(\mathbf{I} - \mathbf{C}(\mathbf{C}^T\mathbf{C})^{-1}\mathbf{C}^T)\mathbf{D}\mathbf{z} = \lambda\mathbf{z} \tag{A.5}$$

Replacing **y** in criterion (A.1) by the value given by equation (A.3), we obtain:

$$\|(\mathbf{I} - \mathbf{C}(\mathbf{C}^T\mathbf{C})^{-1}\mathbf{C}^T)\mathbf{D}\mathbf{z}\|^2$$

Developing this expression yields

$$\mathbf{z}^T\mathbf{D}^T(\mathbf{I} - \mathbf{C}(\mathbf{C}^T\mathbf{C})^{-1}\mathbf{C}^T)(\mathbf{I} - \mathbf{C}(\mathbf{C}^T\mathbf{C})^{-1}\mathbf{C}^T)\mathbf{D}\mathbf{z} = \mathbf{z}^T\mathbf{D}^T(\mathbf{I} - \mathbf{C}(\mathbf{C}^T\mathbf{C})^{-1}\mathbf{C}^T)\mathbf{D}\mathbf{z}$$

$$= \lambda\|\mathbf{z}\|^2 = \lambda$$

The minimum error is therefore equal to the smallest eigenvalue of matrix **E**. Since the criterion is positive, we have to show that the eigenvalues of **E** are positive. Showing that **E** is a positive matrix is equivalent to showing that matrix $\mathbf{F} = \mathbf{I} - \mathbf{C}(\mathbf{C}^T\mathbf{C})^{-1}\mathbf{C}^T$ is positive. Let **x** be a nonzero eigenvector of **F**:

$$(\mathbf{I} - \mathbf{C}(\mathbf{C}^T\mathbf{C})^{-1}\mathbf{C}^T)\mathbf{x} = \lambda\mathbf{x} \tag{A.6}$$

Multiplying both sides by $\mathbf{C}^T$ yields

$$\lambda\mathbf{C}^T\mathbf{x} = 0$$

therefore we have two cases $\lambda = 0$ or $\mathbf{C}^T\mathbf{x} = \mathbf{0}$. If $\mathbf{C}^T\mathbf{x} = \mathbf{0}$, going back to equation (A.6)

$$\mathbf{x} = \lambda\mathbf{x}$$

and since we have assumed $\mathbf{x} \neq \mathbf{0}$, $\lambda = 1$. The eigenvalues of matrix **F** are either 0 or 1. Therefore **F** is positive and so is **E**.

B   Some Results from Algebraic Geometry

We will summarize some of the concepts from algebraic geometry that are required in chapter 7. For further information the reader may consult the book by Semple and Kneebone [SK52] or that by Semple and Roth [SR49].

B.1   Plane curves

A *plane curve* is given by the zeros of a homogeneous polynomial equation in three variables. Let $f(\mathbf{x})$ be a polynomial describing a plane curve. Then $f(\mathbf{x})$ has a Taylor expansion

$$f(\mathbf{a} + \mathbf{h}) = f(\mathbf{a}) + \mathbf{h}.\nabla f(\mathbf{a}) + \cdots$$

at each point $\mathbf{a}$. If the terms of the Taylor expansion vanish up to and including the rth term, then $f(\mathbf{x})$ is said to have order r at $\mathbf{a}$. Thus $\mathbf{a}$ is a point of $f(\mathbf{x})$ if and only if $r \geq 1$. If $r \geq 2$, then $f(\mathbf{x})$ is said to have a singularity of order r at $\mathbf{a}$.

   Bezout's theorem states that, if $f(\mathbf{x})$, $g(\mathbf{x})$ are plane curves of degrees m and n, respectively, such that neither is contained in the other, then $f(\mathbf{x})$ and $g(\mathbf{x})$ intersect at exactly mn points. It is important to count the number of intersections correctly. For example, if $f(\mathbf{x})$ and $g(\mathbf{x})$ are tangent at a point, then this counts as two towards the total of mn intersections. If $f(\mathbf{x})$ has a singularity of order h at a point, and $g(\mathbf{x})$ has a singularity of order k at the same point, then this counts as hk towards the total of intersections. Figure B.1 shows the intersection of two curves

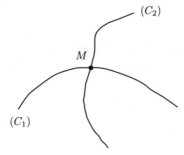

Figure B.1 Intersection of two curves at a regular point.

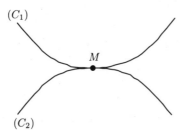

Figure B.2 Two curves tangent at regular points.

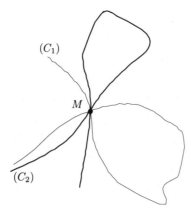

Figure B.3 Intersection of two curves at points of order 2.

at a regular point, figure B.2 shows the intersection of two curves tangent at a regular point, and figure B.3 shows the intersection of two curves at a point of order 2 on each curve.

B.2   The degree of an algebraic manifold

An algebraic manifold $\mathcal{N}$ in projective space $\mathcal{P}^m$ is the set of common zeros of a family of polynomials defined on $\mathcal{P}^m$. The dimension n of $\mathcal{N}$ is the dimension of the tangent space to $\mathcal{N}$ at a general point. Intuitively, the dimension of $\mathcal{N}$ is equal to the minimal number of parameters required to define $\mathcal{N}$. A plane curve is an example of an algebraic manifold of dimension 1, and the manifold $\mathcal{M}$ of essential matrixes defined in chapter 7 is an algebraic manifold of dimension 5, since the rotations contribute three parameters and the translations, which are only defined up to scale, contribute two parameters.

The degree of a plane curve is equal to the degree of the polynomial defining the curve. The degree also has a geometric interpretation as the number of intersections of a general line with the curve. The geometrical definition of degree extends to algebraic manifolds. Let $\mathcal{N}$ be an algebraic manifold in $\mathcal{P}^m$. A general linear subspace in $\mathcal{P}^m$ of dimension $m - n$ intersects $\mathcal{N}$ at a finite number d of points. This number d is defined as the degree of $\mathcal{N}$.

B.3   Resultants

The resultant of two polynomials arises naturally in connection with the problem of eliminating a common variable. Let $f(x)$ and $g(x)$ be two arbitrary polynomials of degrees m and n, respectively, and let

$$f(x) \equiv a_0 x^n + a_1 x^{n-1} + \cdots + a_n$$

$$g(x) \equiv b_0 x^m + b_1 x^{m-1} + \cdots + b_m \tag{B.1}$$

The resultant $R(f, g)$ of f and g is the determinant of order $m + n$:

$$R(f,g) = \det \begin{bmatrix} a_0 & a_1 & \ldots & a_n & 0 & \ldots & 0 \\ 0 & a_0 & \ldots & a_{n-1} & a_n & \ldots & 0 \\ \vdots & & & & & & \\ 0 & 0 & \ldots & & & & a_n \\ b_0 & b_1 & \ldots & b_m & 0 & \ldots & 0 \\ 0 & b_0 & \ldots & b_{m-1} & b_m & \ldots & 0 \\ \vdots & & & & & & \\ 0 & 0 & \ldots & & & & b_m \end{bmatrix} \left.\begin{matrix} \\ \\ \\ \\ \end{matrix}\right\} m \\ \left.\begin{matrix} \\ \\ \\ \\ \end{matrix}\right\} n$$

The fundamental property of $R(f,g)$ is that it is equal to 0 if and only if $a_0 = b_0 = 0$ or $f(x)$ and $g(x)$ have a nonconstant common factor.

Now suppose that $f(\mathbf{x})$, $g(\mathbf{x})$ are homogeneous polynomials of degrees m and n, respectively, in $\mathbf{x} = [x_1, x_2, x_3]^T$, and let $x = x_3$. Then the coefficients a_i, b_i of (B.1) are polynomials in x_1, x_2, and $R(f,g)$ is a homogeneous polynomial in x_1, x_2 of degree mn. The roots of $R(f,g) = 0$ correspond to the intersections of $f(\mathbf{x}), g(\mathbf{x})$.

C   Differential Geometry

In this appendix we will summarize the basic results that are needed in chapters 6 and 9.

C.1   Plane curves

A *planar curve* (c) is defined as a C^2 mapping $u \to \mathbf{m}(u)$ from an interval of R into R^2. We will assume that the parameter u is the arclength s of (c). We then have the well-known two-dimensional *Frenet formulas:*

$$\frac{d\mathbf{m}}{ds} = \mathbf{t} \quad \frac{d\mathbf{t}}{ds} = \kappa\mathbf{n} \quad \frac{d\mathbf{n}}{ds} = -\kappa\mathbf{t} \tag{C.1}$$

where $\mathbf{t}$ and $\mathbf{n}$ are the tangent and normal unit vectors to (c) at the point under consideration. They form the Frenet frame attached to the curve at m. κ is the curvature of (c), the inverse of the radius of curvature r.

C.2   Space curves

A space curve (C) is defined as a C^2 mapping $u \to \mathbf{M}(u)$ from an interval of R into R^3. We will assume that the parameter u is the arclength S of (C). We then have the well-known three-dimensional Frenet formulas:

$$\frac{d\mathbf{M}}{dS} = \mathbf{T} \quad \frac{d\mathbf{T}}{dS} = \kappa\mathbf{N} \quad \frac{d\mathbf{N}}{dS} = -\kappa\mathbf{T} - \rho\mathbf{B}$$
$$\frac{d\mathbf{B}}{dS} = \rho\mathbf{N} \tag{C.2}$$

where $\mathbf{T}$ is the tangent, $\mathbf{N}$ the normal, and $\mathbf{B}$ the binormal unit vectors to (C) at the point under consideration, κ the curvature, and ρ the torsion.

C.3   Surface patches

A surface patch (S) is defined as a C^2 mapping $(u, v) \rightarrow \mathbf{P}(u, v)$ from an open set of R^2 into R^3. Such a patch is intrinsically characterized, up to a rigid motion, by two quadratic forms, called the *two fundamental forms*, which are defined at every point of the patch (see section C.3.3 for a more precise statement).

The first quadratic form Φ_1 defines the length of a vector in the tangent plane T_P. More precisely, the two vectors $\mathbf{P}_u = \frac{\partial \mathbf{P}}{\partial u}$ and $\mathbf{P}_v = \frac{\partial \mathbf{P}}{\partial v}$ are parallel to this plane and define therein a system of coordinates. Each vector in the tangent plane can be defined as a linear combination $\lambda \mathbf{P}_u + \mu \mathbf{P}_v$. Its squared length is given by the value of the first fundamental form Φ_1:

$$\Phi_1(\lambda \mathbf{P}_u + \mu \mathbf{P}_v) = \lambda^2 E + 2\lambda\mu F + \mu^2 G$$

with the following definitions for E, F, and G:

$$E = \|\mathbf{P}_u\|^2 \quad F = \mathbf{P}_u \cdot \mathbf{P}_v \quad G = \|\mathbf{P}_v\|^2 \tag{C.3}$$

Moreover, the normal $\mathbf{N}_P$ to (S) is parallel to the cross-product $\mathbf{P}_u \wedge \mathbf{P}_v$ whose length is the quantity $H = \sqrt{EG - F^2}$.

The second fundamental quadratic form Φ_2 is related to curvature. For a vector $\mathbf{x} = \lambda \mathbf{P}_u + \mu \mathbf{P}_v$ in the tangent plane, we can consider all curves drawn on (S) tangent to $\mathbf{x}$ at P. All of these curves have all the same normal curvature, the ratio $\frac{\Phi_2(\mathbf{x})}{\Phi_1(\mathbf{x})}$, with the following definitions:

$$\Phi_2(\lambda \mathbf{P}_u + \mu \mathbf{P}_v) = \lambda^2 L + 2\lambda\mu M + \mu^2 N$$

and

$$L = \frac{\partial^2 \mathbf{P}}{\partial u^2} \cdot \frac{\mathbf{N}_P}{\|\mathbf{N}_P\|} \quad M = \frac{\partial^2 \mathbf{P}}{\partial u \partial v} \cdot \frac{\mathbf{N}_P}{\|\mathbf{N}_P\|} \quad N = \frac{\partial^2 \mathbf{P}}{\partial v^2} \cdot \frac{\mathbf{N}_P}{\|\mathbf{N}_P\|} \tag{C.4}$$

It is important to study the invariants of Φ_2, i.e., quantities which do not depend upon the parameterization (u, v) of (S). Φ_2 defines a linear mapping $T_P \rightarrow T_P$ by $\Phi_2(\mathbf{x}) = \psi(\mathbf{x}) \cdot \mathbf{x}$. The invariants of Φ_2 are those of ψ.

C.3.1   Principal directions

The *principal directions* are the eigenvectors of ψ. Their coordinates (λ, μ) in the coordinate system $(\mathbf{P}_u, \mathbf{P}_v)$ are solutions of the following equation:

$$(FL - EM)\lambda^2 + (GL - EN)\lambda\mu + (GM - FN)\mu^2 = 0$$

This yields the following possible values for λ and μ (they are defined up to a scale factor):

$$\lambda = EN - GL + \epsilon\sqrt{\Delta} \qquad\qquad (C.5)$$

$$\mu = 2(FL - EM) \qquad\qquad (C.6)$$

where $\epsilon = \pm 1$ and $\Delta = (GL - EN)^2 - 4(FL - EM)(GM - FN)$.

C.3.2 Principal curvatures

The *principal curvatures* are the eigenvalues of ψ. They are solutions of the following quadratic equation:

$$(EG - F^2)\rho^2 - \rho(LG + EN - 2FM) + LN - M^2 = 0 \qquad\qquad (C.7)$$

In particular, their product K and their half-sum H are the gaussian and mean curvatures of (S):

$$K = \frac{LN - M^2}{EG - F^2}$$

$$H = \frac{1}{2}\frac{LG + EN - 2FM}{EG - F^2}$$

All other invariants of Φ_2 are functions of these.

C.3.3 The Gauss and Codazzi-Mainardi equations and the Bonnet theorem

We stated earlier that a surface patch is characterized, up to a rigid motion, by its first and second fundamental forms. Things are, in fact, a bit more subtle in the following sense. The coefficients E, F, G, L, M, and N must satisfy three equations, the Gauss and Codazzi-Mainardi equations, which we will give next. Inversely, we have the Bonnet theorem:

Theorem C.1
[Bonnet] Given six differentiable functions E, F, G, L, M, and N that are defined on an open set V of R^2 and satisfy the conditions $E > 0$, $G > 0$, and $EG - F^2 > 0$, the Gauss and Codazzi-Mainardi equations, then for every $(u, v) \in V$ there exists a diffeomorphism from a neighborhood $U \subset V$

of (u, v) in R^3 such that the corresponding regular patch has $E, F, G, L, M,$ and N as coefficients of its first and second fundamental forms. Furthermore, if U is connected, for every other such diffeomorphism the two patches are related by a rigid transformation of R^3.

The proof can be found in the book by DoCarmo [DoC76], for example. This theorem is very important for our purpose since it shows that all the information about the spatiotemporal surface (S) is contained in nine coefficients (the six coefficients of the first and second fundamental form and the three Gauss and Codazzi-Mainardi equations).

These equations are obtained by expressing the derivatives of the three vectors $\mathbf{P}_u$, $\mathbf{P}_v$, and $\mathbf{N}_P$ in the basis they form and writing conditions of integrability. They can be written [DoC76] as:

$$(\Gamma_{12}^1)_u - (\Gamma_{11}^1)_v + \Gamma_{12}^2\Gamma_{12}^1 - \Gamma_{11}^2\Gamma_{22}^1 = FK \tag{C.8}$$

$$L_v - M_u = L\Gamma_{12}^1 + M(\Gamma_{12}^2 - \Gamma_{11}^1) - N\Gamma_{11}^2 \tag{C.9}$$

$$M_v - N_u = L\Gamma_{22}^1 + M(\Gamma_{22}^2 - \Gamma_{12}^1) - N\Gamma_{12}^2 \tag{C.10}$$

where K is the Gaussian curvature. The first equation is referred to as *Gauss's equation.*

The coefficients $\Gamma_{ij}^k, i, j, k = 1, 2$ are called the *Christoffel symbols of the second type.* They can be easily computed from the first fundamental form as follows. If we denote by $\mathbf{g}$ the symmetric matrix of Φ_1, the Christoffel symbols of the first kind are given by Cartan and Spivak [Car88, Spi79]:

$$\Gamma_{ikj} = \frac{1}{2}\left(\frac{\partial g_{ik}}{\partial u^j} + \frac{\partial g_{jk}}{\partial u^i} - \frac{\partial g_{ij}}{\partial u^k}\right) \qquad i, j, k = 1, 2 \tag{C.11}$$

They are symmetric with respect to the first and third index.

Now, following the standard tensor notation, we denote by g^{ij} the coefficients of the inverse $\mathbf{g}^{-1}$ of $\mathbf{g}$. The Christoffel symbols of the second type are then obtained as

$$\Gamma_{ij}^k = g^{kh}\Gamma_{ihj} \tag{C.12}$$

Equations (C.8)–(C.12) allow us to compute the Gauss and Codazzi-Mainardi equations from the first and second fundamental forms Φ_1 and Φ_2.

C.3.4   Lie derivatives

Let **V** be a function defined on (Σ) such that **V**(P) is a vector of T_P. **V** is called a *tangential vector field.* It is very convenient to consider the vectors of T_P as *differential operators* acting on the functions defined on (Σ). For example, $\mathbf{P}_u$ is the partial derivative with respect to u. We represent this action by $\mathbf{P}_u f = \frac{\partial f}{\partial u}$, and it becomes even more clear if we use the notation $\mathbf{P}_u = \frac{\partial}{\partial u}$. Each vector **V** of T_P is a linear combination of $\mathbf{P}_u$ and $\mathbf{P}_v$, which we write

$$\mathbf{V} = \alpha \frac{\partial}{\partial u} + \beta \frac{\partial}{\partial v}$$

α and β are the coordinates of **V** in the basis $(\mathbf{P}_u, \mathbf{P}_v)$ of T_P. From this it is clear that the action of **V** upon a function f which we note $L_{\mathbf{V}} f$ is defined by

$$L_{\mathbf{V}} f = \alpha \frac{\partial f}{\partial u} + \beta \frac{\partial f}{\partial v}$$

$L_{\mathbf{V}} f$ is the *Lie derivative* of f in the direction **V** of T_P. From this definition immediatly follows the following relation:

$$L_{\alpha_1 \mathbf{V}_1 + \alpha_2 \mathbf{V}_2} f = \alpha_1 L_{\mathbf{V}_1} f + \alpha_2 L_{\mathbf{V}_2} f$$

C.3.5   Lie brackets

Given two vector fields **V** and **W** on (Σ), we can consider the operator $L_{\mathbf{V}} L_{\mathbf{W}}$. It is a linear operator defined for functions f on (Σ), but unfortunately it is not a derivation, because it does not satisfy Leibniz' rule. On the other hand, it is easy to show that the *commutator* $L_{\mathbf{V}} L_{\mathbf{W}} - L_{\mathbf{W}} L_{\mathbf{V}}$ is a derivation and therefore a vector field, which is denoted $[\mathbf{V}, \mathbf{W}]$ and called the *Lie bracket* of **V** and **W**. By definition, we have:

$$L_{[\mathbf{V}, \mathbf{W}]} f = L_{\mathbf{V}} L_{\mathbf{W}} f - L_{\mathbf{W}} L_{\mathbf{V}} f$$

This allows us to compute the coordinates of $[\mathbf{V}, \mathbf{W}]$ in the basis $(\mathbf{P}_u, \mathbf{P}_v)$ of T_P, from those of **V** and **W**:

$$[\mathbf{V}, \mathbf{W}]^i = \sum_{j=1}^{2} V^j \frac{\partial W^i}{\partial u^j} - W^j \frac{\partial V^i}{\partial u^j} \qquad i = 1, 2 \tag{C.13}$$

where we use the same definition as in section C.3.3 for $u^i, i = 1, 2$ and V^i (resp. W^i) indicates the component of $\mathbf{V}$ (resp. $\mathbf{W}$) along the ith basis vector of T_P ($\mathbf{P}_u$ if $i = 1$, $\mathbf{P}_v$ if $i = 2$).

Bibliography

[AAK71] Y. I. Adbel-Aziz and H. M. Karara. Direct linear transformation into object space coordinates in close-range photogrammetry. In *Proceedings of the Symposium on Close-Range Photogrammetry*, University of Illinois, pages 1–18, January 1971.

[Abd78] Ikram Escandar Abdou. *Quantitative methods of edge detection.* Technical Report 830, University of Southern California Image Processing Institute, July 1978.

[AEI*85] T. Asano, M. Edahiro, H. Imai, M. Iri, and K. Murota. Bucketing techniques in computer geometry. In G. Toussaint, editor, *Computer Geometry*, North-Holland, 1985.

[AF86] N. Ayache and O. D. Faugeras. HYPER: A new approach for the recognition and positioning of two-dimensional objects. *IEEE Transactions on Pattern Analysis and Machine Intelligence*, 8(1):44–54, January 1986.

[AF87] N. Ayache and B. Faverjon. Efficient registration of stereo images by matching graph descriptions of edge segments. *The International Journal of Computer Vision*, 1(2): 107–132, April 1987.

[Agi72] G. J. Agin. *Representation and Description of Curved Objects.* Ph.D. thesis, Stanford University, October 1972.

[AH77] H. C. Andrews and B. R. Hunt. *Digital Image Restoration.* Prentice-Hall, 1977.

[AHU74] Alfred V. Aho, John E. Hopcroft, and Jeffrey D. Ullman. *The Design and Analysis of Computer Algorithms. Computer Science and Information Processing*, Addison-Wesley, 1974.

[AL87] N. Ayache and F. Lustman. Fast and reliable passive trinocular stereovision. In *Proceedings ICCV '87*, pages 422–427, IEEE, June 1987.

[Alt89] Simon A. Altmann. Hamilton, Rodrigues, and the quaternion scandal. *Mathematics Magazine*, 62(3):291–308, December 1989.

[ABB*73] A. P. Ambler, H. G. Barrow, C. M. Brown, R. M. Burstall, and R. J. Popplestone. A versatile computer-controlled assembly system. In *IJCAI*, pages 298–307, 1973.

[Ana89] P. Anandan. A computational framework and an algorithm for the measurement of visual motion. *The International Journal of Computer Vision*, 2(3):283–310, January 1989.

[Aya83] Nicholas Ayache. *Un Système de Vision Bidimensionnelle en Robotique Industrielle*. Ph.D. thesis, Université de Paris-Sud, Centre d'Orsay, June 1983.

[Aya88] Nicholas Ayache. *Construction et Fusion de Représentations Visuelles 3D: Applications à la Robotique Mobile*. Ph.D. thesis, Université de Paris-Sud, Centre d'Orsay, May 1988.

[Aya89] Nicholas Ayache. *Artificial Vision for Mobile Robots*. MIT Press, 1989.

[BA84] Michael Brady and Haruo Asada. Smoothed local symmetries and their implementation. In Michael Brady and Richard Paul, editors, *Robotics Research: The First International Symposium*, pages 331–354. MIT Press, 1984.

[Bak81] H. H. Baker. *Depth from Edge- and Intensity-Based Stereo*. Ph.D. thesis, University of Illinois, 1981.

[Bal81] D. H. Ballard. Generalizing the Hough transform to detect arbitrary shapes. *Pattern Recognition*, 13(2):111–122, 1981.

[Bar82] Stephen T. Barnard and Martin A. Fischler. Computational Stereo. *Computing Surveys*, 14(4):553–572, December 1982.

[Bas81] M. Basseville. Edge detection using sequential methods for change in level. *IEEE Transactions on Acoustic, Speech and Signal Processing*, ASSP 29(1):32–50, February 1981.

[BB81] H. H. Baker and T. O. Binford. Depth from edge- and intensity-based stereo. In *Proceedings 7th Joint Conference on Artificial Intelligence*, pages 631–636, August 1981.

[BB83] B. F. Buxton and H. Buxton. Monocular depth perception from optical flow by space-time signal processing. *Proceedings of the Royal Society London*, B 218:22–47, 1983.

[BB89] H. Harlyn Baker and Robert C. Bolles. Generalizing epipolar-plane image analysis on the spatiotemporal surface. *The International Journal of Computer Vision*, 3(1):33–49, 1989.

[BC82] R. C. Bolles and R. A. Cain. Recognizing and locating partially visible objects: The local-feature-focus method. *International Journal of Robotics Research*, 1(3):57–82, 1982.

[BC85] Paul J. Besl and R. C. Cain. Three dimensional object recognition. *ACM Computing Surveys*, 17(1):75–145, 1985.

[BC86] T. J. Broida and R. Chellappa. Kinematics and structure of a rigid object from a sequence of noisy images: a batch approach. In *Proc. International Conference on Computer Vision and Pattern Recognition*, pages 176–182. IEEE, June 1986.

[BC89] T. J. Broida and R. Chellappa. Experiments and uniqueness results on object structure and kinematics from a sequence of monocular images. In *Proceedings of the IEEE Workshop on Visual Motion*, pages 21–30. IEEE, March 1989.

[BC91] Fredrik Bergholm and Stefan Carlsson. A theory of optical flow. *CVGIP: Graphics Models and Image Processing*, 53(2):171–188, March 1991.

[BCC90] T. J. Broida, S. Chandrashekhar, and R. Chellappa. Recursive 3-D motion estimation from a monocular image sequence. *IEEE Transactions AES*, 26(4):639–656, July 1990.

[BEG81] M. Basseville, B. Espiau, and J. Gasnier. Edge detection using sequential methods for change in level. *IEEE Transactions on Acoustic, Speech and Signal Processing*, ASSP-29(1):24–31, February 1981.

[Ber89a] Fredrik Bergholm. Motion from flow along contours: A note on robustness and ambiguous cases. *The International Journal of Computer Vision*, 2(4):395–415, April 1989.

[Ber89b] Fredrik Bergholm. *On the Content of Information in Edges and Optical Flow*. Ph.D. thesis, Royal Institute of Technology, Department of Numerical Analysis and Computing Science, Stockholm, Sweden, May 1989.

[Bes88] Paul J. Besl. Geometric modelling and computer vision. *Proceedings of the IEEE*, 76(8):936–958, August 1988.

[Bes90] Paul J. Besl. The free-form surface matching problem. In H. Freeman, editor, *Machine Vision for Three Dimensional Scenes*, pages 25–71, Academic Press, 1990.

[BF84] Bir Bhanu and Olivier D. Faugeras. Shape matching of two-dimensional objects. *IEEE Transactions on Pattern Analysis and Machine Intelligence*, 6(2):137–156, 1984.

[BF88] Y. Bar-Shalom and T.E. Fortmann. *Tracking and Data Association*. Academic, New York, 1988.

[BH86] R. C. Bolles and Radu Horaud. 3DPO: A three-dimensional part orientation system. *International Journal of Robotics Research*, 5(3):3–26, 1986.

[Bin84] Thomas O. Binford. Stereo vision: Complexity and constraints. In Michael Brady and Richard Paul, editors, *Robotics Research*, pages 475–487, MIT Press, 1984.

[Blu78] Harry Blum and Roger Nagel. Shape description using weighted symmetric axis features. *Pattern Recognition*, 10:167–180, 1978.

[BM92] Paul J. Besl and Neil D. McKay. A method for registration of 3-D shapes. *IEEE Transactions on Pattern Analysis and Machine Intelligence*, 14(2):239–256, February 1992.

[Boi84] Jean Daniel Boissonnat. Geometric structures for three-dimensional shape representation. *ACM Transactions on Graphics*, 3(4):266–286, 1984.

[Bou86] Patrick Bouthemy. A method of integrating motion information along contours including segmentation. In *Proceedings of the eighth International Conference on Pattern Recognition*, pages 651–653, IEEE Computer Society Press, October 1986.

[Bou89] Patrick Bouthemy. A maximum likelihood framework for determining moving edges. *IEEE Transactions on Pattern Analysis and Machine Intelligence*, 11(5):499–511, May 1989.

[Bow81] A Bowyer. Computing Dirichlet tesselations. *The Computer Journal*, 162–166, 1981.

[BB78] N. Badler and R. Bajcsy. Three-dimensional representations for computer graphics and computer vision. *ACM Computer Graphics*, 3:153–160, August 1978.

[BPY*85] Michael Brady, Jean Ponce, Alan Yuille, and H. Asada. Describing surfaces. *Computer Vision, Graphics, and Image Processing*, 32:1–28, 1985.

[Bro71] Duane C. Brown. close-range camera calibration. *Photogrammetric Engineering*, 37(8):855–866, 1971.

[Bro81] Christopher M. Brown. Some mathematical and representational aspects of solid modelling. *IEEE Transactions on Pattern Analysis and Machine Intelligence*, 3(4):444–543, July 1981.

[Bro82] R. A. Brooks. Symbolic reasoning among 3D models and 2D images. *Artificial Intelligence Journal*, 17:285–348, 1982.

[Bro91] Rodney A. Brooks. Intelligence without representation. *Artificial Intelligence Journal*, 47:139–160, 1991.

[BS87] R. Bajcsy and F. Solina. Three-dimensional object representation revisited. In *Proceedings of the 1st International Conference on Computer Vision*, June 1987.

[BSF88] Y. Bar-Shalom and T. E. Fortmann. *Tracking and Data Association*. Academic Press, 1988.

[Buc88] T. Buchanan. The twisted cubic and camera calibration. *Computer Vision, Graphics, and Image Processing*, 42:130-132, 1988.

[Buc92] Thomas Buchanan. Critical sets for 3D reconstruction using lines. In *Proceedings of the 2nd European Conference on Computer Vision*, pages 730–738, May 1992.

[BZ87] Andrew Blake and Andrew Zisserman. *Visual Reconstruction*. MIT Press, 1987.

[Can83] J. F. Canny. *Finding edges and lines in images*. Technical Report AI-TR-720, Massachusets Institute of Technology Artificial Intelligence Laboratory, June 1983.

[Can86] J. F. Canny. A computational approach to edge detection. *IEEE Transactions on Pattern Analysis and Machine Intelligence*, 8:769-798, November 1986.

[Car88] Elie Cartan. *Leçons sur la géométrie des espaces de Riemann*. Jacques Gabay, 1988. Original edition, Gauthiers-Villars, 1946.

[Cha55] M. Chasles. Question no. 296. *Nouv. Ann. Math.*, 14:50, 1855.

[CLR90] Thomas H. Cormen, Charles E. Leiserson, and Ronald L. Rivest. *Introduction to Algorithms*. MIT Press, 1990.

[CP86] M. Crampin and F. A. E. Pirani. *Applicable differential geometry*. Volume 59 of *London Mathematical Society Lecture Note Series*, Cambridge University Press, 1986.

[CT90] Bruno Caprile and Vincent Torre. Using vanishing points for camera calibration. *The International Journal of Computer Vision*, 4(2):127-140, March 1990.

[DA89] Umesh R. Dhond and J. K. Aggarwal. Structure from stereo: A review. *IEEE Transactions on Pattern Analysis and Machine Intelligence*, 19(6):1489-1510, November-December 1989.

[Dav82] Larry S. Davis. Hierarchical generalized Hough transforms and line-segment based generalized Hough transforms. *Pattern Recognition*, 15:277, 1982.

[Dem88] Michel Demazure. *Sur Deux Problèmes de Reconstruction*. Technical Report 882, INRIA, July 1988.

[Der87] Rachid Deriche. Using Canny's criteria to derive an optimal edge detector recursively implemented. *The International Journal of Computer Vision*, 2:167-187, April 1987.

[DF90] Rachid Deriche and Olivier D. Faugeras. Tracking line segments. *Image and Vision Computing*, 8(4):261-270, November 1990. A shorter version appeared in the *Proceedings of the 1st ECCV*.

[DG88a] E. D. Dickmanns and V. Graefe. Applications of dynamic monocular machine vision. *Machine Vision and Applications*, 1:241–261, 1988.

[DG88b] E. D. Dickmanns and V. Graefe. Dynamic monocular machine vision. *Machine Vision and Applications*, 1:223–240, 1988.

[DH73] Richard O. Duda and Peter E. Hart. *Pattern Classification and Scene Analysis.* John Wiley & Sons, Inc., 1973.

[DHa86] Johan D'Hayer. Determining motion of image curves from local pattern changes. *Computer Vision, Graphics, and Image Processing*, 34:166–188, 1986.

[Dic87] E. D. Dickmanns. 4d-dynamic scene analysis with integral spatio-temporal models. In *Proceedings of ISSR '87*, pages 73–80, 1987.

[DK87] M. Dhome and T. Kasvand. Polyhedra recognition by hypothesis accumulation. *IEEE Transactions on Pattern Analysis and Machine Intelligence*, 9(3):429–438, 1987.

[DM92] Ernst D. Dickmanns and Birger D. Mysliwetz. Recursive 3-D road and relative ego-state recognition. *IEEE Transactions on Pattern Analysis and Machine Intelligence*, 14(2):199–213, February 1992.

[DMT90] Olivier Devillers, Stefan Meiser, and Monique Teillaud. *Fully dynamic Delaunay triangulation in logarithmic expected time per operation.* Technical Report 1349, INRIA, December 1990.

[DoC76] M. P. DoCarmo. *Differential Geometry of Curves and Surfaces.* Prentice-Hall, 1976.

[DRLR89] M. Dhome, M. Richetin, J.-T. Lapresté, and G. Rives. Determination of the attitude of 3-D objects from a single perspective view. *IEEE Transactions on Pattern Analysis and Machine Intelligence*, 11(12):1265–1278, 1989.

[DRR86] M. Dhome, M. Richetin, and G. Rives. Model-based recognition and location of local patterns in polygonal contours via hypothesis accumulation. In E. S. Gelsema and L. N. Kanal, editors, *Pattern Recognition in Practice II*, North-Holland, 1986.

[Dud72] R. D. Duda and P. E. Hart. Use of the Hough transformation to detect lines and curves in pictures. *Communications of the ACM*, 15:11–15, January 1972.

[Dur87] H. F. Durrant-Whyte. Consistent integration and propagation of disparate sensor observations. *International Journal of Robotics Research*, 6:3–24, 1987.

[DY80] Larry S. Davis and Simon Yam. *A generalized Hough-like transformation for shape recognition.* Technical Report TR-134, University of Texas at Austin Department of Computer Science, February 1980.

[ER87] B. Espiau and P. Rives. Closed-loop recursive estimation of 3D features for a mobile vision system. In *Proceedings of the IEEE International Conference on Robotics and Automation*, pages 1436–1443, 1987.

[Fai75] W. Faig. Calibration of close-range photogrammetry systems: Mathematical formulation. *Photogrammetric Engineering and Remote Sensing*, 41(12):1479–1486, 1975.

[Fau92] Olivier D. Faugeras. What can be seen in three dimensions with an uncalibrated stereo rig. In Giulio Sandini, editor, *Proceedings of the 2nd European Conference on Computer Vision*, pages 563–578, Springer-Verlag, 1992.

[FB81a] Olivier D. Faugeras and Marc Berthod. Improving consistency and reducing ambiguity in stochastic labelling: An optimization approach. *IEEE Transactions on Pattern Analysis and Machine Intelligence*, 3:412–424, July 1981.

[FB81b] M. A. Fischler and R. C. Bolles. Random sample consensus: A paradigm for model fitting with applications to image analysis and automated cartography. *Communications of the ACM*, 24:381–385, 1981.

[FDN89] Olivier D. Faugeras, Nourr-Eddine Deriche, and Nassir Navab. From optical flow of lines to 3D motion and structure. In *Proceedings of IEEERSJ International Workshop on Intelligent Robots and Systems '89*, pages 646–649, 1989.

[FH86] Olivier D. Faugeras and Martial Hébert. The representation, recognition, and locating of 3D shapes from range data. *International Journal of Robotics Research*, 5(3):27–52, 1986.

[Fin97] S. Finsterwalder. Die geometrischen Grundlagen der Photogrammetrie. *Jahresber. der Deutschen Math. Vereinigung*, 6(2):1–41, 1897.

[FJ92] Patrick J. Flynn and Anil K. Jain. 3D object recognition using invariant feature indexing of interpretation tables. *CVGIP: Image Understanding*, 55(2):119–129, March 1992.

[FL88] O. D. Faugeras and F. Lustman. Motion and structure from motion in a piecewise planar environment. *International Journal of Pattern Recognition and Artificial Intelligence*, 2(3):485–508, 1988.

[FLM92] Olivier D. Faugeras, Tuan Luong, and Steven Maybank. Camera self-calibration: Theory and experiments. In Giulio Sandini, editor, *Proceedings of the 2nd European Conference on Computer Vision*, pages 321–334, Springer-Verlag, 1992.

[FLB90] Olivier D. Faugeras, Elizabeth Lebras-Mehlman, and Jean-Daniel Boissonnat. Representing stereo data with the Delaunay triangulation. *Artificial Intelligence Journal*, 44(1-2): 41–87, July 1990. Also published as INRIA Tech. Report 788.

[FLT87] Olivier D. Faugeras, Francis Lustman, and Giorgio Toscani. Motion and structure from point and line matches. In *Proceedings of the First International Conference on Computer Vision*, pages 25–34, June 1987.

[FM90] Olivier D. Faugeras and Steven Maybank. Motion from point matches: Multiplicity of solutions. *The International Journal of Computer Vision*, 4(3): 225–246, June 1990. Also published as INRIA Tech. Report 1157.

[FM91] Olivier D. Faugeras and Steven Maybank. Mouvement à partir de points: nombre de solutions. *Comptes rendus de l'Académie des Sciences de Paris*, 177–183, 1991.

[FMZ*91] David Forsyth, Joseph L. Mundy, Andrew Zisserman, Chris Coello, Aaron Heller, and Charles Rothwell. Invariant descriptors for 3-D object recognition and pose. *IEEE Transactions on Pattern Analysis and Machine Intelligence*, 13(10):971–991, October 1991.

[FP86] W. Forstner and A. Pertl. Photogrammetric standard methods and digital image matching techniques for high precision surface measurements. In E. S. Gelsema and L. N. Kanal, editors, *Pattern Recognition in Practice II*, pages 57–72, Elsevier Science Publishers, 1986.

[FT86] Olivier D. Faugeras and Giorgio Toscani. The calibration problem for stereo. In *Proceedings CVPR '86*, pages 15–20, IEEE, June 1986.

[Fua91] Pascal Fua. Combining stereo and monocular information to compute dense depth maps that preserve depth discontinuities. In *Proceedings of the 12th International Joint Conference on Artificial Intelligence*, pages 1292–1298, August 1991.

[Gen77] D. B. Gennery. A stereovision system for an autonomous vehicle. In *Proceedings of the International Joint Conference on Artificial Intelligence*, pages 576–582, 1977.

[Gen80] D. B. Gennery. *Modelling the Environment of an Exploring Vehicle by means of Stereo Vision*. Ph.D. thesis, Stanford University, June 1980.

[GVL83] Gene H. Golub and Charles F. Van Loan. *Matrix computations*. John Hopkins University Press, 1983.

[GG84] Stuart Geman and Donald Geman. Stochastic relaxation, Gibbs distributions, and the Bayesian restoration of images. *IEEE Transactions on Pattern Analysis and Machine Intelligence*, 6(6):721–741, 1984.

[GH81] Marvin J. Greenberg and John R. Harper. *Algebraic Topology, A First Course*. Addison-Wesley, 1981.

[Gib50] J. J. Gibson. *The Perception of the Visual World*. Houghton Mifflin, 1950.

[GL84] W. Eric L. Grimson and T. Lozano-Pérez. Model-based recognition and localization from sparse range or tactile data. *International Journal of Robotics Research*, 3(3):3–35, 1984.

[GL87] W. Eric L. Grimson and T. Lozano-Pérez. Localizing overlapping parts by searching the interpretation tree. *IEEE Transactions on Pattern Analysis and Machine Intelligence*, 9(4):469–482, 1987.

[Gon89] S. Gong. Curve motion constraint equation and its applications. In *Proceedings Workshop on Visual Motion*, pages 73–80, 1989.

[GR78] B. Gold and L. R. Rabiner. *Theory and Application of Digital Signal Processing*. Prentice-Hall, 1978.

[Gri81a] W. E. L. Grimson. A computer implementation of a theory of human stereo vision. *Philosophical Transactions of the Royal Society of London*, B 292(1058):217–253, 1981.

[Gri81b] W. E. L. Grimson. *From Images to Surfaces*. MIT Press, 1981.

[Gri85] W. E. L. Grimson. Computational experiments with a feature based stereo algorithm. *IEEE Transactions on Pattern Analysis and Machine Intelligence*, 7(1):17–34, 1985.

[Gri89a] W. Eric L. Grimson. On the recognition of curved objects in two dimensions. *IEEE Transactions on Pattern Analysis and Machine Intelligence*, 11(6):632–644, 1989.

[Gri89b] W. Eric L. Grimson. On the recognition of parameterized 2D objects. *The International Journal of Computer Vision*, 2(4):353–372, April 1989.

[Gri90] W. Eric L. Grimson, *Object Recognition by Computer: The Role of Geometric Constraints*. MIT Press, 1990.

[GS69] K. R. Gabriel and R. R. Sokal. A new statistical approach to geographic variation analysis. *Systematic Zoology*, 18:259–278, 1969.

[GV91] Per-Olof Gutman and Mordekhai Velger. Tracking targets using adaptive Kalman filtering. *IEEE Transactions on Aerospace and Electronic Systems*, 26(5):691–698, September 1991.

[HA89] William Hoff and Narendra Ahuja. Surfaces from stereo: Integrating feature matching, disparity estimation, and contour detection. *IEEE Transactions on Pattern Analysis and Machine Intelligence*, 11(2):121–136, February 1989.

[Had23] Jacques Hadamard. *Lectures on the Cauchy Problem in Linear Partial Differential Equations*. Yale University Press, 1923.

[HS79] Robert M. Haralick and Linda G. Shapiro, The consistent labeling problem: Part 1. *IEEE Transactions on Pattern Analysis and Machine Intelligence*, 1(2):173–184, 1979.

[HE80] Robert M. Haralick and G. L. Elliot. Increasing tree search efficiency for constraint satisfaction problems. *Artificial Intelligence Journal*, 14:263–313, 1980.

[Har84] Robert Haralick. Digital step edges from zero crossing of second directional derivatives. *IEEE Transactions on Pattern Analysis and Machine Intelligence*, 6(1):58–68, January 1984.

[Har87] C. G. Harris. Determination of ego-motion from matched points. In *Proceedings of the 3rd Alvey Conference*, pages 189–192, September 1987.

[HB80] A. Herskovitz and T. O. Binford. *On boundary detection.* Technical Report AI Memo 183, Massachusets Institute of Technology Artificial Intelligence Laboratory, 1980.

[HC52] David Hilbert and S. Cohn-Vossen. *Geometry and the Imagination.* Chelsea, 1952.

[Heb83] Martial Hebert. *Reconnaissance de formes tridimensionnelles.* Ph.D. thesis, Université de Paris-Sud, Centre d'Orsay, September 1983.

[Hee88] David J. Heeger. Optical flow using spatiotemporal filters. *The International Journal of Computer Vision*, 1(4):279–302, January 1988.

[Hes63] O. Hesse. Die cubische Gleichung, von welcher die Lösung des Problems der Homographie von M. Chasles abhängt. *J. Reine Angew. Math.*, 62:188–192, 1863.

[HF89] Thomas S. Huang and Olivier D. Faugeras. Some properties of the E matrix in two-view motion estimation. *IEEE Transactions on Pattern Analysis and Machine Intelligence*, 11(12):1310–1312, December 1989.

[Hil84] Ellen C. Hildreth. *The Measurement of Visual Motion.* MIT Press, 1984.

[HJ92] David J. Heeger and Allan D. Jepson. Subspace methods for recovering rigid motion I: Algorithm and implementation. *The International Journal of Computer Vision*, 7(2):95–117, January 1992.

[HL83] R. M. Haralick and J. S. Lee. The facet approach to optic flow. In L. S. Bauman, editor, *Proceedings of the Image Understanding Workshop*, pages 84–93, 1983.

[HN91] Robert J. Holt and Arun N. Netravali. Camera calibration problem: Some new results. *CVGIP: Image Understanding*, 54(3):368–383, November 1991.

[Hof50] Walther Hofmann. *Das Problem der "Gefährlichen Flächen" in Theorie und Praxis.* Ph.D. thesis, Fakultät für Bauwesen der Technischen Hochschule München, December 1950.

[Hor86] Berthold Klaus Paul Horn. *Robot Vision.* MIT Press, 1986.

[Hor87] Berthold K. P. Horn. Motion fields are hardly ever ambiguous. *The International Journal of Computer Vision*, 1(3):263-278, 1987.

[Hor90] Berthold K. P. Horn. Relative orientation. *The International Journal of Computer Vision*, 4(1):59-78, January 1990.

[Hou62] P. V. C. Hough. Methods and Means for Recognizing Complex Patterns. U.S. Patent 3069654, December 1962.

[HS79] G. M. Hunter and K. Steiglitz. Operations on images using quadtrees. *IEEE Transactions on Pattern Analysis and Machine Intelligence*, 1:145-153, 1979.

[HS81] Berthold K. P. Horn and Brian G. Schunk. Determining optical flow. *Artificial Intelligence*, 17:185-203, 1981.

[HU87] Daniel P. Huttenlocher and Shimon Ullman. Object recognition using alignment. In *Proceedings of the First International Conference on Computer Vision*, pages 102-111, 1987.

[HU90] Daniel P. Huttenlocher and Shimon Ullman. Recognizing solid objects by alignment with an image. *The International Journal of Computer Vision*, 5(2):195-212, November 1990.

[Hue71] M. H. Hueckel, An operator which locates edges in digitized pictures. *Journal of the ACM*, 18(1):113-125, January 1971.

[HW88] B. K. P. Horn and E. J. Weldon. Direct methods for recovering motion. *The International Journal of Computer Vision*, 2(1):51-76, June 1988.

[Hwa89] Vincent S. S. Hwang. Tracking feature points in time-varying images using an opportunistic approach. *Pattern Recognition*, 22(3):247-256, 1989.

[HZ83] R. A. Hummel and S. W. Zucker. On the foundations of relaxation labeling processes. *IEEE Transactions on Pattern Analysis and Machine Intelligence*, 5:267-287, 1983.

[IE91] Sitharama S. Iyengar and Alberto Elfes, editors. *Autonomous Mobile Robots*. IEEE Computer Society Press, 1991.

[Jai89] Anil K. Jain. *Fundamentals of Digital Image Processing*. Prentice-Hall International Editions, 1989.

[Jar83] R. A. Jarvis. A perspective on range finding techniques for computer vision. *IEEE Transactions on Pattern Analysis and Machine Intelligence*, 5:122-139, March 1983.

[Jaz70] A. M. Jazwinsky. *Stochastic Processes and Filtering Theory*. Academic Press, 1970.

[Jul71] Bela Julesz. *Foundations of cyclopean perception*. University of Chicago Press, 1971.

[JW76] Francis A. Jenkins and Harvey E. White. *Fundamental of Optics*, 4th edition. McGraw-Hill, 1976.

[Kan87] Takeo Kanade, editor. *Three-Dimensional Machine Vision*. Kluwer Academic Publishers, 1987.

[Kan91] Kenichi Kanatani. Computational projective geometry. *CVGIP: Image Understanding*, 54(3):333–348, November 1991.

[Kas83] Michael Kass. A computational framework for the visual correspondence problem. In *Proceedings of the Eighth International Joint Conference on Artificial Intelligence*, pages 1043–1045, August 1983.

[Kas88] Michael Kass. Linear image features in stereopsis. *The International Journal of Computer Vision*, 1(4):357–368, January 1988.

[KBS75] Carolyn Kimme, Dana Ballard, and Jack Sklansky. Finding circles by an array of accumulators. *Communications of the ACM*, 18(2), February 1975.

[KMM77] R. E. Kelly, P. R. H. McConnell, and S. J. Mildenberger. The gestalt photomapper. *Photogrammetric Engineering and Remote Sensing*, 43:1407–1417, 1977.

[Knu68] Donald E. Knuth. *The Art of Computer Programming*, Addison-Wesley, 1968.

[Koe86] Jan J. Koenderink. Optic flow. *Vision Research*, 26(1):161–180, 1986.

[Koe90] Jan J. Koenderink. *Solid Shape*. MIT Press, 1990.

[Kra40] Josef Krames. Zur Ermittlung eines Objektes aus zwei Perspektiven. *Monatshefte für Mathematik und Physik*, 49:327–354, 1940.

[Kru13] E. Kruppa. Zur Ermittlung eines Objektes aus zwei Perspektiven mit innerer Orientierung. *Sitz.-Ber. Akad. Wiss., Wien, Math. Naturw. Kl., Abt. IIa.*, 122:1939–1948, 1913.

[KvD75] Jan J. Koenderink and A. J. van Doorn. Invariant properties of the motion parallax field due to the movement of rigid bodies relative to an observer. *Optica Acta*, 22:717–723, 1975.

[KvD76] J. J. Koenderink and A. J. van Doorn. Geometry of binocular vision and a model for stereopsis. *Biological Cybernetics*, 21:29–35, 1976.

[KvD78] Jan J. Koenderink and A. J. van Doorn. How an ambulant observer can construct a model of the environment from the geometrical structure of the visual inflow. In G. Hauske and E. Butenandt, editors, *Kybernetik 1978*, Oldenburg, München, 1978.

[KWT88] M. Kass, A. Witkin, and D. Terzopoulos. SNAKES: Active contour models. *The International Journal of Computer Vision*, 1:321–332, January 1988.

[KY90] Yoshifumi Kitamura and Masahiko Yachida. Three-dimensional data acquisition by trinocular vision. *Advanced Robotics*, 4(1):29-42, 1990.

[Lee82] D. T. Lee. Medial axis transformation of a planar shape. *IEEE Transactions on Pattern Analysis and Machine Intelligence*, 4(4):363-369, July 1982.

[Lev85] Martin D. Levine. *Vision in man and machine*. McGraw-Hill, 1985.

[LH86a] Y. Liu and T. S. Huang. Estimation of rigid body motion using straight line correspondences. In *Proceedings Workshop on Motion: Representation and Analysis*, pages 47-51. IEEE, May 1986.

[LH86b] Y. Liu and T. S. Huang. Estimation of rigid body motion using straight line correspondences: further results. In *Proceedings 8th ICPR*, pages 306-307. IEEE, October 1986.

[LH88a] Yuncai Liu and Thomas S. Huang. A linear algorithm for motion estimation using straight line Correspondences. *Computer Vision, Graphics, and Image Processing*, 44:35-57, 1988.

[LH88b] Yuncai Liu and Thomas S. Huang. Estimation of rigid body motion using straight line Correspondences. *Computer Vision, Graphics, and Image Processing*, 43:37-52, 1988.

[LH88c] H. C. Longuet-Higgins. Multiple interpretations of a pair of images of a surface. *Proceedings of the Royal Society of London*, A 418:1-15, 1988.

[LHD90] Yuncai Liu, Thomas S. Huang, and Olivier D. Faugeras. Determination of camera location from 2-D to 3-D line and point correspondences. *IEEE Transactions on Pattern Analysis and Machine Intelligence*, 12(1):28-37, January 1990.

[Li90] Stan Z. Li. Invariant surface segmentation through energy minimization with discontinuities. *The International Journal of Computer Vision*, 5(2):161-194, November 1990.

[Lon81] H.C. Longuet-Higgins. A Computer Algorithm for Reconstructing a Scene from Two Projections. *Nature*, 293:133-135, 1981.

[Lon88] H.C. Longuet-Higgins. Multiple interpretations of a pair of images of a surface. *Proc. Roy. Soc. Lond. A.*, 418:1-15, 1988.

[Low85] David Lowe. *Perceptual Organization and Visual Recognition*. Kluwer Academic Publishers, 1985.

[Low87] David Lowe. The viewpoint consistency constraint. *The International Journal of Computer Vision*, 1(1):57-72, 1987.

[LP61] H. J. Landau and H. O. Pollack. Prolate sphericalwave functions, Fourier analysis and uncertainty: II. *Bell System Technical Journal*, 40:65-84, 1961.

[LP80] H. C. Longuet-Higgins and K. Prazdny. The interpretation of moving retinal images. *Proceedings of the Royal Society of London*, B 208:385–387, 1980.

[LW88] Y. Lamdan and H. J. Wolfson. Geometric hashing: A general and efficient model-based recognition scheme. In *Proceedings of the 2nd International Conference on Computer Vision*, pages 238–249, December 1988.

[LY82] George R. Legters Jr. and Tzay Y. Young. A mathematical model for computer image tracking. *IEEE Transactions on Pattern Analysis and Machine Intelligence*, 4(6):583–594, November 1982.

[MA90] R. Mohr and E. Arbogast. It can be done without camera calibration. *Pattern Recognition Letters*, 12:39–43, 1990.

[Mal87] Jitendra Malik. Interpreting Line Drawings of Curved Objects. *International Journal of Computer Vision*, 1(1):73–103, 1987.

[Mar72] Alberto Martelli. Edge detection using heuristic search methods. *Computer Graphics and Image Processing*, 1:169–182, 1972.

[Mar82] D. Marr. *Vision*. W. H. Freeman and Co., 1982.

[Mat75] G. Matheron. *Random Sets and Integral Geometry*. John Wiley & Sons, 1975.

[May79] P. S. Maybeck. *Stochastic Models, Estimation and Control*. Academic Press, 1979.

[May87] S. J. Maybank. *A theoretical study of optical flow*. Ph.D. thesis, Birbeck College, University of London, 1987.

[May90a] S. J. Maybank. The projective geometry of ambiguous surfaces. *Proceedings of the Royal Society of London*, A 332:1–47, 1990.

[May90b] S. J. Maybank. Properties of essential matrices. *International Journal of Imaging Systems and technology*, 2:380–384, 1990.

[May90c] S. J. Maybank. Rigid velocities compatible with five image velocity vectors. *Image and Vision Computing*, 1(1):18–23, February 1990.

[May92] S. J. Maybank. *Theory of reconstruction from image motion*. Springer-Verlag, 1992.

[MB90] D. W. Murray and B. F. Buxton. *Experiments in the Machine Interpretation of Visual Motion*. MIT Press, 1990.

[MCB89] David W. Murray, David A. Castelow, and Bernard F. Buxton. From image sequences to recognized moving polyhedral objects. *The International Journal of Computer Vision*, 3(3):181–208, September 1989.

[MDR91] O. D. Monga, R. Deriche, and J. M. Rocchisani. 3-D edge detection using recursive filtering: Application to scanner images. *CVGIP: Image Understanding*, 53(1):76-87, January 1991.

[MF91] John E. W. Mayhew and John P. Frisby, editors. *3D Model Recognition from Stereoscopic Cues*. MIT Press, 1991.

[MH80] D. Marr and E. Hildreth. Theory of edge detection. *Proceedings of the Royal Society of London*, B 207:187-217, 1980.

[MK78] David Marr and H. K. Nishihara. Representation and recognition of the spatial organization of three-dimensional shapes. *Proceedings of the Royal Society of London*, B 200:269-274, 1978.

[MN85] Gérard Medioni and Ram Nevatia. Segment-based stereo matching. *Computer Vision, Graphics, and Image Processing*, 31:2-18, 1985.

[MF77] J. W. Modestino and R. W. Fries. Edge detection in noisy images using recursive digital filtering. *Computer Graphics and Image Processing*, 6:409-433, 1977.

[Moh92] Roger Mohr. Projective geometry and computer vision. In C. H. Chen, L. F. Pau, and P. S. P. Wang, editors, *Handbook of Pattern Recognition and Computer Vision*, World Scientific Publishing Company, 1992.

[Mon71] Ugo Montanari. On the optimal detection of curves in noisy pictures. *Communications of the ACM*, 14(5):335-345, May 1971.

[Mor77] H. P. Moravec. Towards automatic visual obstacle avoidance. In *Proceedings of the International Joint Conference on Artificial Intelligence*, page 584, 1977.

[Mor80] H. P. Moravec. *Obstacle Avoidance and Navigation in the Real World by a Seeing Robot Rover*. Ph.D. thesis, Stanford Artificial Intelligence Laboratory, 1980. Also published as Stanford Artificial Intelligence Memo 340.

[MP76] D. Marr and T. Poggio. Cooperative computation of stereo disparity. *Science*, 194:283-287, 1976.

[MP79] D. Marr and T. Poggio. A computational theory of human stereo vision. *Proceedings of the Royal Society of London*, B 204:301-328, 1979.

[MS80] D. W. Matula and R. R. Sokal. Properties of Gabriel graphs relevant to geographic variation research and the clustering of points in the plane. *Geographical Analysis*, 12:205-22, July 1980.

[MS87] L. Matthies and S. A. Shafer. Error modeling in stereo navigation. *IEEE Transactions on Robotics and Automation*, 3:239-248, 1987.

[MSK88] Larry Matthies, Richard Szeliski, and Takeo Kanade. Kalman filter-based algorithms for estimating depth from image sequences. *The International Journal of Computer Vision*, 3(3), September 1988.

[Mum87] David Mumford. The problem of robust shape descriptors. In *Proceedings of the First International Conference on Computer Vision*, pages 602–606, 1987.

[MW89] Peter Meer and Isaac Weiss. *Smoothed differential filters for images*. Technical Report CAR-TR-424, University of Maryland Computer Vision Laboratory, Center for Automation Research, February 1989.

[Nac82] Lee R. Nackman. Curvature relations in three-dimensional symmetric axes. *Computer Graphics and Image Processing*, 20:43–57, 1982.

[Nag83] H-H. Nagel. Displacement vectors derived from second order intensity variations in image sequences. *Computer Vision, Graphics, and Image Processing*, 21:85–117, 1983.

[Nag85a] H-H. Nagel. Analyse und Interpretation von Bildfolgen: Teil I. *Informatik-Spektrum*, 8:178–200, 1985.

[Nag85b] H-H. Nagel. Analyse und interpretation von bildfolgen: Teil II. *Informatik-Spektrum*, 8:312–327, 1985.

[Nag86] H-H. Nagel. Image sequences: Ten (octal) years from phenomenology towards a theoretical foundation. In *Proceedings 8th ICPR*, pages 1174–1185, IEEE, October 1986.

[Nag87] H-H. Nagel. On the estimation of optical flow: Relations between different approaches and some new results. *Artificial Intelligence Journal*, 33:299–324, 1987.

[NB86] Vishvjit Nalwa and Thomas O. Binford, On detecting edges. *IEEE Transactions on Pattern Analysis and Machine Intelligence*, PAMI-8(6):699–714, 1986.

[Nal88] Vishvjit S. Nalwa. Line-drawing interpretation: A mathematical framework. *The International Journal of Computer Vision*, 2(2):103–124, September 1988.

[Nal89] Vishvjit S. Nalwa. Representing oriented piecewise C^2 surfaces. *The International Journal of Computer Vision*, 3(2):131–153, 1989.

[NB77] Ramakant Nevatia and Thomas O. Binford. Description and recognition of curved objects. *Artificial Intelligence Journal*, 8:77–98, 1977.

[Neg89] S. Negahdaripour. Critical surface pairs and triplets. *The International Journal of Computer Vision*, 3(4):293–312, November 1989.

[Nev82] R. Nevatia. *Machine perception*. Prentice-Hall, 1982.

[Nis84] H. K. Nishihara. *PRISM, a practical real-time imaging stereo matcher*. Technical Report A.I. Memo 780, MIT, 1984.

[NP82] H. K. Nishihara and T. Poggio. Hidden cues in random line stereograms. *Nature*, 300:347–349, 1982.

[NP84] H. Keith Nishihara and Tomaso Poggio. Stereo vision for robotics. In Michael Brady and Richard Paul, editors, *Robotics Research*, pages 489–505, MIT Press, 1984.

[OK85] Y. Ohta and T. Kanade. Stereo by intra- and inter-scanline search. *IEEE Transactions on Pattern Analysis and Machine Intelligence*, 7, No 2:139–154, 1985.

[Oka81] A. Okamoto. Orientation and construction of models, part I: The orientation problem in close-range photogrammetry. *Photogrammetric Engineering and Remote Sensing*, 47(10):1437–1454, 81.

[Oka84] A. Okamoto. The model construction problem using the collinearity condition. *Photogrammetric Engineering and Remote Sensing*, L(6):705–711, 84.

[OS75] A. V. Oppenheim and R. Schafer. *Digital Signal Processing*. Prentice-Hall, 1975.

[OS79] M. Oshima and Y. Shirai. A scene description method using three-dimensional information. *Pattern Recognition*, 11:9–17, 1979.

[OS83] M. Oshima and Y. Shirai. Object recognition using three-dimensional information. *IEEE Transactions on Pattern Analysis and Machine Intelligence*, 5(4):353–361, July 1983.

[Pap65] A. Papoulis. *Probability, Random Variables and Stochastic Processes*. McGraw-Hill, 1965.

[Pav77] Theo Pavlidis. *Structural Pattern Recognition*. Springer-Verlag, 1977.

[Pav82] Theo Pavlidis. *Algorithms for Graphics and Image Processing*. Computer Science Press, 1982.

[PC87] J. Ponce and D. Chelberg. Finding the limbs and cusps of generalized cylinders. *The International Journal of Computer Vision*, 1(3):195–210, October 1987.

[Pen90] A. Pentland. Automatic extraction of deformable part models. *The International Journal of Computer Vision*, 4(2): 107–126, 1990.

[PHK92] Jean Ponce, Anthony Hoogs, and David J. Kriegman. On using CAD models to compute the pose of curved 3D objects. *CVGIP: Image Understanding*, 55(2):184–197, March 1992.

[PS85] F. Preparata and M. Shamos. *Computational Geometry*. Springer-Verlag, 1985.

[PM90] Pietro Perona and Jitendra Malik. *Detecting and localizing edges composed of steps, peaks and roofs.* Technical Report UCB/CSD 90/590, University of California at Berkeley Computer Science Division, November 1990.

[PMF85] S. B. Pollard, J. E. W. Mayhew, and J. P. Frisby. PMF: A stereo correspondence algorithm using a disparity gradient constraint. *Perception*, 14:449–470, 1985.

[Pon90] J. Ponce. Straight homogeneous generalized cylinders: Differential geometry and uniqueness results. *The International Journal of Computer Vision*, 4(1):79–100, January 1990.

[PPMF87] S. B. Pollard, J. Porrill, J. E. W. Mayhew, and J. P. Frisby. Matching geometrical descriptions in three-space. *Image and Vision Computing*, 5(2):73–78, 1987.

[PPP*89] S. B. Pollard, T. P. Pridmore, J. Porrill, J. E. W. Mayhew, and J. P. Frisby. Geometric modeling from multiple stereo views. *International Journal of Robotics Research*, 8(4):1–32, 1989.

[Pra78] W. K. Pratt. *Digital Image Processing.* John Wiley & Sons, 1978.

[Pra83] K. Prazdny. On the information in optical flows. *Computer Vision, Graphics, and Image Processing*, 22:239–259, 1983.

[Pre70] J. M. S. Prewitt. Object enhancement and extraction. In B. S. Lipkin and A. Rosenfeld, editors, *Picture Processing and Psychopictorics*, pages 75–149, Academic Press, 1970.

[PS88] F. Prêteux and Michel Schmitt. Boolean texture analysis and synthesis. In J. Serra, editor, *Image Analysis and Mathematical Morphology: Theoretical Advances*, chapter 18, Academic Press, 1988.

[PVY85] T. Poggio, H. Voorhees, and A. Yuille. *A regularized solution to edge detection.* A.I. Memo 833, Massachusetts Institute of Technology Artificial Intelligence Laboratory, May 1985.

[Req80] Aristides G. Requicha. Representations for rigid solids: Theory, methods, and systems. *Computing Surveys*, 12(4):437–464, December 1980.

[RF91] Luc Robert and Olivier D. Faugeras. Curve-based stereo: Figural continuity and curvature. In *CVPR91*, pages 57–62, IEEE, June 1991.

[RHZ76] Azriel Rosenfeld, Robert Hummel, and Steven Zucker. Scene labeling by relaxation operators. *IEEE Transactions on Systems, Man, and Cybernetics*, 6:420–433, 1976.

[Ric45] S. O. Rice. Mathematical Analysis of Random Noise. *Bell Systems Technical Journal*, 24:46–156, 1945.

[Riv90] P. Rives. Dynamic vision: Theoretical capabilities and practical problems. In G. E. Taylor, editor, *Kinematic and Dynamic Issues in Sensor Based Control*, Springer-Verlag, 1990.

[RK82] A. Rosenfeld and A. C. Kak. *Digital Picture Processing*, Second edition. Academic Press, 1982.

[RN88] K. Rao and R. Nevatia. Computing volume descriptions from sparse 3-D data. *The International Journal of Computer Vision*, 2(1), June 1988.

[Rob65] L. G. Roberts. Machine perception of three-dimensional solids. In J. Tippett, D. Berkowitz, L. Clapp, C. Koester and A. Vanderburgh, editors, *Optical and Electrooptical Information Processing*, pages 159-197, MIT Press, 1965.

[Rod40] O. Rodrigues. Des lois géométriques qui régissent les déplacements d'un système solide dans l'espace, et de la variation des coordonnées provenant de ces déplacements considérés indépendamment des causes qui peuvent les produire. *Journal de Mathématiques Pures et Appliquées*, 5:380-440, 1840.

[SA90] Minas E. Spetsakis and John Aloimonos. Structure from motion using line correspondences. *The International Journal of Computer Vision*, 4:171-183, 1990.

[Sam80] H. Samet. Region representation: Quadtrees from binary arrays. *Computer Graphics and Image Processing*, 13:88-93, 1980.

[Sam89] H. Samet. *Design and Analysis of Spatial Data Structures: Quadtrees, Octrees, and Other Hierarchical Methods*. Addison-Wesley, 1989.

[San76] Luis A. Santalo. *Integral Geometry and Geometric Probability*. Addison-Wesley, 1976.

[San89] Peter Sander. Generic curvature features from 3-D images. *IEEE Transactions on Systems, Man, and Cybernetics*, 19(6):1623-1635, 1989.

[SC92] Jun Shen and Serge Castan. An optimal linear operator for step edge detection. *CVGIP: Graphics Models and Image Processing*, 54(2):112-133, March 1992.

[Sch81] Larry L. Schumaker. *Spline Functions: Basic Theory*. John Wiley & Sons, Inc., 1981.

[Sch89] M. Schmitt. Some examples of algorithms analysis in computational geometry by means of mathematical morphological techniques. In J.-D. Boissonnat and J.-P. Laumond, editors, *Geometry and Robotics*, pages 225-246, Springer-Verlag, 1989.

[SDG79] K. S. Shanmugam, F. M. Dickey, and J. A. Green. An optimal frequency domain filter for edge detection in digital images. *IEEE Transactions on Pattern Analysis and Machine Intelligence*, PAMI-1:37–49, January 1979.

[Ser82] Jean Serra. *Image Analysis and Mathematical Morphology*. Academic Press, 1982.

[SJ87] Ishwar K. Sethi and Ramesh Jain. Finding trajectories of feature points in a monocular image sequence. *IEEE Transactions on Pattern Analysis and Machine Intelligence*, 9(1):56–73, January 1987.

[SK52] J. G. Semple and G. T. Kneebone. *Algebraic Projective Geometry*. Clarendon Press, Oxford, 1952. Reprinted 1979.

[SKB82] G. Stockman, S. Kopstein, and S. Benett. Matching images to models for registration and object detection via clustering. *IEEE Transactions on Pattern Analysis and Machine Intelligence*, 3(3):229–241, 1982.

[SM82] Robert J. Schalkoff and Eugene S. McVey. A model and tracking algorithm for a class of video targets. *IEEE Transactions on Pattern Analysis and Machine Intelligence*, 4(1):2–10, January 1982.

[SM92] F. Stein and G. Medioni. Structural indexing: Efficient 3-D object recognition. *IEEE Transactions on Pattern Analysis and Machine Intelligence*, 14(2):125–145, February 1992.

[Sob74] Irwin Sobel. On calibrating computer controlled cameras for perceiving 3-D scenes. *Artificial Intelligence Journal*, 5:184–198, 1974.

[Sob78] I. Sobel. Neighbourhood coding of binary images for fast contour following and general array binary processing. *Computer Graphics and Image Processing*, 8:127–135, 1978.

[Sor] H. W. Sorenson. *Comparison of Kalman, Bayesian and Maximum Likelyhood Estimation Techniques*, chapter 6.

[SP90] H. Shariat and K. E. Price. Motion estimation with more than two frames. *IEEE Transactions on Pattern Analysis and Machine Intelligence*, 12(5):417–434, May 1990.

[Spa85] Libor A. Spacek. *The Detection of Contours and their Visual Motion*. Ph.D. thesis, University of Essex at Cochester, December 1985.

[Spa91] Gunnar Sparr. An algebraic-analytic method for reconstruction from image correspondences. In *Proceedings 7th Scandinavian Conference on Image Analysis*, pages 274–281, 1991.

[Spi79] Michael Spivak. *A Comprehensive Introduction to Differential Geometry*, volumes 1–3, Second edition. Publish or Perish, Inc., 1979.

[SR49] J. G. Semple and L. Roth. *Introduction to Algebraic Geometry*. Clarendon Press, Oxford, 1949. Reprinted 1987.

[SS87] J. T. Schwartz and M. Sharir. Identification of partially obscured objects in two dimensions by matching of noisy "characteristic curves." *International Journal of Robotics Research*, 6(2):29-44, 1987.

[Stu69] Rudolf Sturm. Das Problem der Projektivität und seine Anwendung auf die Flächen zweiten Grades. *Math. Ann.*, 1:533-574, 1869.

[Sub88] Muralidhara Subbarao. Interpretation of image flow: Rigid curved surfaces in motion. *The International Journal of Computer Vision*, 2(1):77-96, June 1988.

[SZ90] Peter Sander and Steven W. Zucker. Inferring surface trace and differential structure from 3-D images. *IEEE Transactions on Pattern Analysis and Machine Intelligence*, PAMI-12(9):833-854, September 1990.

[Sze90] Richard Szeliski. Bayesian modeling of uncertainty in low-level vision. *The International Journal of Computer Vision*, 5(3):271-301, December 1990.

[TA77] A. N. Tikhonov and V. Y. Arsenin. *Solutions of Ill-posed Problems*. Winston and Sons, 1977.

[Ter86] Demetri Terzopoulos. Regularization of inverse visual problems involving discontinuities. *IEEE Transactions on Pattern Analysis and Machine Intelligence*, 8:413-424, 1986.

[TH82] Roger Tsai and Thomas S. Huang. Estimating Three-dimensional motion parameters of a rigid planar patch, II: Singular value decomposition. *IEEE Transactions on Acoustic, Speech and Signal Processing*, 30, 1982.

[TM87] D. W. Thomson and J. L. Mundy. Three-dimensional model matching from an unconstrained viewpoint. In *Proceedings of the International Conference on Robotics and Automation*, pages 208-220, 1987.

[TMV85] J. L. Turney, T. N. Mudge, and R. A. Volz. Recognizing partially occluded parts. *IEEE Transactions on Pattern Analysis and Machine Intelligence*, 7(4):410-421, 1985.

[TP86] V. Torre and T. Poggio. On edge detection. *IEEE Transactions on Pattern Analysis and Machine Intelligence*, 8(2):147-163, 1986.

[Tsa86] Roger Tsai. An efficient and accurate camera calibration technique for 3D machine vision. In *Proceedings CVPR '86*, pages 364-374, IEEE, June 1986.

[Tsa87] Roger Tsai. A versatile camera calibration technique for high-accuracy 3D machine vision metrology using off-the-shelf TV cameras and lenses. *IEEE Journal of Robotics and Automation*, 3(4):323-344, August 1987.

[Tsa89] Roger Tsai. Synopsis of recent progress on camera calibration for 3D machine vision. In Oussama Khatib, John J. Craig, and Tomás Lozano-Pérez, editors, *The Robotics Review*, pages 147–159, MIT Press, 1989.

[TVDF89] Giorgio Toscani, Régis Vaillant, Rachid Deriche, and Olivier D. Faugeras. Stereo camera calibration using the environment. In *Proceedings of the 6th Scandinavian Conference on Image Analysis, SCIA89*, pages 953–960, 1989.

[UGVT88] S. Uras, F. Girosi, A. Verri, and V. Torre. A computational approach to motion perception. *Biological Cybernetics*, 60:79–87, 1988.

[Ull79] Shimon Ullman. *The Interpretation of Visual Motion*. MIT Press, 1979.

[VGT89] Alessandro Verri, F. Girosi, and Vincente Torre. Mathematical properties of the 2D motion field: from singular points to motion parameters. *Journal of the Optical Society of America A*, 6:698–712, 1989.

[VGT90] Alessandro Verri, F. Girosi, and Vincente Torre. Differential techniques for optical flow. *Journal of the Optical Society of America A*, 7:912–922, 1990.

[VP89] Alessandro Verri and Tomaso Poggio. Motion field and optical flow: Qualitative properties. *IEEE Transactions on Pattern Analysis and Machine Intelligence*, 11(5):490–498, 1989.

[Wat81] D. F. Watson. Computing the n-dimensional Delaunay tesselation with application to Voronoi polytopes. *The Computer Journal*, 167–172, 1981.

[WBS89] A. D. Worrall, K. D. Baker, and G. D. Sullivan. Model based perspective inversion. *Image and Vision Computing*, 7(1):17–23, 1989.

[Wei91] Isaac Weiss. *High order differentiation filters that work*. Technical Report CAR-TR-545, University of Maryland Computer Vision Laboratory, Center for Automation Research, March 1991.

[Wey39] Hermann Weyl. *The Classical Groups*. Princeton University Press, 1939. Second edition, with supplement, eighth printing 1973.

[WHA87] J. Weng, T. S. Huang, and N. Ahuja. 3-D motion estimation, understanding, and prediction from noisy image sequences. *IEEE Transactions on Pattern Analysis and Machine Intelligence*, 9(3):370–389, 1987.

[Wil91] Richard P. Wildes. Direct recovery of three-dimensional scene geometry from binocular stereo disparity. *IEEE Transactions on Pattern Analysis and Machine Intelligence*, 13(8):761–774, August 1991.

[WKS87] Allen M. Waxman, Behrooz Kamgar-Parsi, and Muralidhara Subbarao. Closed-form solutions to image flow equations for 3D structure and motion. *The International Journal of Computer Vision*, 1:239–258, 1987.

[Wol83] P. R. Wolf. *Elements of Photogrammetry*. 2nd ed. McGraw-Hill, 1983.

[Wol90] H. Wolfson. Model based object recognition by "geometric hashing." In O. D. Faugeras, editor, *Computer Vision-ECCV90*, pages 526–536, Springer-Verlag, 1990.

[Won75] K. W. Wong. Mathematical formulation and digital analysis in close-range photogrammetry. *Photogrammetric Engineering and Remote Sensing*, 41(11):1355–1373, 75.

[WS91] Michael L. Walker and Lejun Shao. Estimating 3-D location parameters using dual number quaternions. *CVGIP: Image Understanding*, 54(3):358–367, November 1991.

[Wun41] Walter Wunderlich. Zur Eindeutigkeitsfrage der Hauptaufgabe der Photogrammetrie. *Monatshefte für Mathematik und Physik*, 50:151–164, 1941.

[Yac86] M. Yachida. 3D data acquisition by multiple views. In O. D. Faugeras and G. Giralt, editors, *Robotics Research: the Third International Symposium*, pages 11–18, MIT Press, 1986.

[YC90] G. S. Young and R. Chellappa. 3-D motion estimation using a sequence of noisy stereo images: Models, estimation, and uniqueness results. *IEEE Transactions on Pattern Analysis and Machine Intelligence*, 12(8):735–759, August 1990.

[Zel52] M. Zeller. *Textbook of Photogrammetry*. H. K. Lewis & Company, 1952.

[ZF92a] Z. Zhang and O. D. Faugeras. Three-dimensional motion computation and object segmentation in a long sequence of stereo frames. *The International Journal of Computer Vision*, 7(3):211–241, 1992. To appear.

[ZF92b] Zhang Zhengyou and Olivier D. Faugeras. *3D Dynamic Scene Analysis: A Stereo Based Approach*. Springer-Verlag, 1992.

[Zha90] Zhengyou Zhang. *Motion Analysis from a Sequence of Stereo Frames and Its Applications*. Ph.D. thesis, Université de Paris-Sud, Centre d'Orsay, 1990.

Index

Machine Interpretation of Line Drawings, Kokichi Sugihara, 1986

ACTORS: A Model of Concurrent Computation in Distributed Systems, Gul A. Agha, 1986

Knowledge-Based Tutoring: The GUIDON Program, William Clancey, 1987

AI in the 1980s and Beyond: An MIT Survey, edited by W. Eric L. Grimson and Ramesh S. Patil, 1987

Visual Reconstruction, Andrew Blake and Andrew Zisserman, 1987

Reasoning about Change: Time and Causation from the Standpoint of Artificial Intelligence, Yoav Shoham, 1988

Model-Based Control of a Robot Manipulator, Chae H. An, Christopher G. Atkeson, and John M. Hollerbach, 1988

A Robot Ping-Pong Player: Experiment in Real-Time Intelligent Control, Russell L. Andersson, 1988

Robotics Research: The Fourth International Symposium, edited by Robert C. Bolles and Bernard Roth, 1988

The Paralation Model: Architecture-Independent Parallel Programming, Gary Sabot, 1988

Concurrent System for Knowledge Processing: An Actor Perspective, edited by Carl Hewitt and Gul Agha, 1989

Automated Deduction in Nonclassical Logics: Efficient Matrix Proof Methods for Modal and Intuitionistic Logics, Lincoln Wallen, 1989

Shape from Shading, edited by Berthold K. P. Horn and Michael J. Brooks, 1989

Ontic: A Knowledge Representation System for Mathematics, David A. McAllester, 1989

Solid Shape, Jan J. Koenderink, 1990

Expert Systems: Human Issues, edited by Dianne Berry and Anna Hart, 1990

Artificial Intelligence: Concepts and Applications, edited by A. R. Mirzai, 1990

Robotics Research: The Fifth International Symposium, edited by Hirofumi Miura and Suguru Arimoto, 1990

Theories of Comparative Analysis, Daniel S. Weld, 1990

Artificial Intelligence at MIT: Expanding Frontiers, edited by Patrick Henry Winston and Sarah Alexandra Shellard, 1990

Vector Models for Data-Parallel Computing, Guy E. Blelloch, 1990